MODERNISM:
AN ANTHOLOGY OF
SOURCES AND DOCUMENTS

MODERNISM:
AN ANTHOLOGY OF
SOURCES AND DOCUMENTS

Edited by

Vassiliki Kolocotroni, Jane Goldman, and Olga Taxidou

The University of Chicago Press

We dedicate this book to
Randall Stevenson,
friend, colleague, fellow Modernist

The University of Chicago Press, Chicago 60637
Edinburgh University Press, UK
© Selection and editorial material
Vassiliki Kolocotroni, Jane Goldman, and
Olga Taxidou, 1998
All rights reserved. Published 1998
Printed in Great Britain

07 06 05 04 03 02 01   2 3 4 5 6

ISBN: 0-226-45073-2 (cloth)

ISBN: 0-226-45074-0 (ppbk)

Library of Congress Cataloging-in-Publication Data

Modernism : an anthology of sources and documents / edited by
    Vassiliki Kolocotroni, Jane Goldman, and Olga Taxidou.
        p.   cm.
    Includes index.
    ISBN 0-226-45073-2 (alk. paper). -- ISBN 0-226-45074-0 (pbk. :
alk. paper)
    1. Literature--Philosophy.   2. Aesthetics.   3. History-
-Philosophy.   I. Kolocotroni, Vassiliki.   II. Goldman, Jane, 1960-
. III. Taxidou, Olga.
PN49.M478   1998
801'.93--dc21   98-7889
                                                       CIP

CONTENTS

Introduction

Modernism is not a movement. It is a term that masks conflict and upheaval and any number of contradictory positions. This anthology preserves the term and respects its drawing power as the convenient demarcation of a period and a set of concerns, while seeking to amplify its familiar usage. The selection of material is driven by the need to provide interpretative tools and strategies for the understanding of literary Modernism, as well as by a revisionary impetus which extends beyond the question of periodisation. More than an alternative chronology or genealogy of Modernism, this sets out to be a rethinking of limits (of clear-cut beginnings and ends, of influences and developments); that is, an exploration of Modernism which is not based on an evolutionary model of literary history. In other words, the 'Modernism' which this anthology attempts to frame and illuminate does not follow from 'Romanticism' or 'Symbolism', nor does it precede 'Post-modernism' as literary category. Its '-ism', in fact, is partly on trial here. More so than other (and similarly problematic) critical constructs, Modernism comprises numerous, diverse and contesting, theories and practices which first flourished in a period that knew little of the term as it has now come to be understood.

The homogenisation of these diverse practices into Modernism as a movement and critical category occurred in the 1950s, by virtue of what Raymond Williams calls 'the post-war settlement and its accompanying, complicit academic endorsements'. The assumptions underlying this construction were firstly that the initial impetus of Modernism was over, and in its selective canonised form was thereafter to be known as 'High Modernism', and secondly that the essence of the Modernist impulse was the spirit of formal experimentation. This second assumption, in fact, was also the key emphasis in Clement Greenberg's influential definition of Modernism in art. According to Greenberg, it was the critical, self-reflexive, Kantian spirit that drove Modernist experimentation – the organic development and culmination of which was embodied by American Abstract Expressionism. These ideas came to dominate formulations concerning literary Modernism. This anthology, in its exploration of a wide range of material, much of which sits uneasily with such narrow formulaic approaches, seeks to unsettle and rethink rather than neatly define the term Modernism.

Rather than proffering the maps, the limits, the origins or the essences of Modernism, then, we have set out to sample its discursive formations. Our repositioning of Modernism may be considered Brechtian in approach in that we are concerned with opening up the contradictions and diversities within Modernism, with expanding its geographical limitations, with stressing its historical and ideological dimensions. But this is not to dilute the term with the sort of neutralising pluralism and relativism we have come to associate with Post-modernism. Like any Brechtian gesture, this anthology attempts to recover in Modernism its avant-garde modes of critique and to read its formations as vehicles for historical change. This is reflected in our use of the term, 'The Avant-Garde', as a central sectional heading in the anthology. Modernism, we understand, is not synonymous with the avant-garde, but we do recognise its being charged with the avant-garde's combative energies. Our selection emphasises the avant-garde's significance, not only as a historical moment when certain practitioners sought to liquidate the boundaries between art and life (indeed, art and politics), but also as a transformative power affecting all other aesthetic practices and theories (in terms of their necessary self-conscious positioning in relation to its challenges). The well-documented failure of historic avant-garde projects, and the internment of their corpses in our cosmopolitan museums of the modern, does not altogether neutralise or extinguish the power of the avant-garde moment, although it does, perhaps, account for Adorno's melancholy observation that 'Modernism is not a positive slogan'. *Modernism: An Anthology of Sources and Documents* is no such museum or mausoleum, we hope, but a storehouse for continuing engagements with the modern.

In the following pages readers may see for themselves the term Modernism emerging in contradictory formulations through the documents and debates of the period. Our selection and presentation of texts reveals a (previously unavailable) broad literary perspective. At the same time, however, the very concept of literature seems to fade in and out of other disciplines such as the visual arts, philosophy, and social and political theory. In placing these diverse documents side-by-side we do not simply intend to contextualise literature, but to stress its intertextuality. From this basic editing procedure transpires the realisation of the need to read literature in conjunction with other texts. This contributes, we hope, to the anthology's usefulness as a pedagogical tool for teachers and researchers alike. In offering, for the first time, an extensive range of sources for literary Modernism, it is our hope that this anthology will help generate more research and encourage fresh and insightful pedagogical explorations of the field.

The chronological range of documents runs from the mid-nineteenth century to about the mid-twentieth century (the early 1940s). This is to go both further backwards and further forwards in time than orthodox parameters (1910–30). Our inclusion of documents from the decade after 1930, traditionally a closing date for Modernism, not only emphasises their integral relation to Modernism rather than departure from it, but also invites reappraisal of the preceding years, traditionally designated a period of apolitical 'High Modernism'. Our selection, which does not extend beyond chronology into Post-modernism as recent critical collections have done (at the expense of theoretical clarity), closes in the 1940s, not to invite the belief that the concerns of Modernism, aesthetic, ideological, political or otherwise, have ended, but to allow for and encourage the intense explorations which the complexities of the period demand.

We hope our organisation of the anthology's material into three broad sections is both helpful and largely self-explanatory. We do not intend to persuade readers how to use our anthology (we hope it generates diversity), nor how to interpret its contents, but we do offer the following as a brief outline of contents and rationale.

Section I, THE EMERGENCE OF THE MODERN, presents cultural, political and scientific documents alongside aesthetic formulations on the modern. Although weighted to the mid- and late-nineteenth century, this section shows the modern currency of earlier texts in dialogue with later ones. In this sense, Marx, author of our first entry, is not the origin, but a touchstone, of emergent inflexions of the new. Visions of the modern in this period may characterise it variously as new, revolutionary, apocalyptic, degenerative or simply transitional. At the same time, new categories, discourses and disciplines emerge and interpret new social and cultural phenomena.

Our central, and pivotal, Section II, THE AVANT-GARDE, documents the rise of self-conscious formulations, declarations and manifestos from a spectrum of aesthetic, cultural and political positions, categories whose distinctions are sometimes dissolved, sometimes reinforced. What dominates here, however, is the sense of the modern as intervening and transformative in an international and revolutionary climate shaped by cataclysmic war and massive political and social upheaval. The sense of self-conscious, militant and collective positioning is reflected in the proliferation of '-isms' and '-ists'. Here the manifesto develops a status of its own, embodying rather than explicating the aesthetic gesture of the new – even while exploding the very category of the aesthetic.

Section III, MODERNISTS ON THE MODERN, documents the making of Modernist traditions in the 1910s and 1920s through the writing of key experimenters, impresarios and acolytes, and Modernist revisions and regroupings in the 1930s and after. This concluding subsection presents crises, mutations, and geographical relocations of the avant-garde as well as its political realignments in the context of the rise of Fascism, the spectre of war, and the revisionary impact of Socialist Realism. At the same time, we document key examples of new projects taking on the task of interpreting and countering the rising tide of totalitarianism. The closing extracts, from 'The Leaning Tower', Virginia Woolf's late polemical essay on class and writing, and from Richard Wright's admonitions on writing and racial violence, and his meditations on Edgar Allan Poe, signal the continuing power, range and diversity of Modernist positions in the 1940s. From two such disparate points on the cultural horizon comes, nevertheless, a recognisable convergence of Modernist critique and hope.

This anthology, like much of its contents, is the product of collective effort. We are greatly indebted to our many fellow researchers, students and colleagues in Modernism for the impetus to embark on this project (and the enthusiastic encouragement to keep going), and in several cases for specific suggestions and requests for entries. For assistance with contents and production, we would like to thank the following people especially:

Spilios Argiropoulos, Stephen Baker, Anne Coxall, John Coyle, Cairns Craig, Pat Devlin, Peter Faulkner, Douglas Gifford, Philip Hobsbaum, Andrew Hook, Sara Jillings, Stephen Johnson, Jackie Jones, Paddy Lyons, Graeme Macdonald, Donald Mackenzie, Gus McLean, Peter Manson, Anne Mason, Drew Milne, David Pascoe, Robin Purves, Marek Pytel, David Robb, Andrew Roberts, Stan Smith, Randall Stevenson, Stephen Thomson, Keith Williams and Duncan Wu. Particular thanks are due to Adrian Hunter for his editorial and research assistance and to Rachel Evans for compiling the index.

Vassiliki Kolocotroni
Jane Goldman
Olga Taxidou
July 1996

A note on presentation

Our aim in this anthology is to present as wide-ranging and diverse a selection of texts as possible. We have therefore decided on short extracts from lengthy originals. The Modernist predilection for brief manifesto or self-consciously fragmentary statement ensures, of course, the reproduction of many original texts in their volatile entirety. For reasons of space, and to encourage reader freedom, we have tried to keep cross-referencing to a minimum. Directions are given to interesting connections between entries, and to entries by the same author, where they occur in different sections. These directions appear in square brackets identifying section and entry number.

I

THE EMERGENCE OF THE MODERN

Ia

**The modern in cultural, political
and scientific thought**

1
Karl Marx (1818–83)
From Letter to Ruge, September 1843

Political theorist, economist and sociologist. After studies in Bonn and Berlin, Marx became editor of the Rheinische Zeitung *in Cologne in 1842. With the paper's suppression in 1843 he emigrated to Paris where he met Friedrich Engels and became involved with eminent French socialists. Moving to Brussels in 1847 Marx began to expound his ideas, firstly in* Poverty of Philosophy *(1847) which presents an economic interpretation of history, then with Engels in* The Communist Manifesto *(1848) which sets out the basis of Marx's social philosophy. After his expulsion from Cologne in 1849, he settled in London where he completed* Das Kapital *(1867). The following extract is from a letter to Arnold Ruge, at the time of their collaboration for the publication of the* Franco-German Yearbooks. *Here Marx stresses the importance of the task of critical philosophy and its relationship with political practice.*

[. . .]

We do not anticipate the world with our dogmas but instead attempt to discover the new world through the critique of the old. Hitherto philosophers have left the keys to all riddles lying in their desks, and the stupid, uninitiated world had only to wait around for the roasted pigeons of absolute science to fly into its open mouth. Philosophy has now become secularized and the most striking proof of this can be seen in the way that philosophical consciousness has joined battle not only outwardly, but inwardly too. If we have no business with the construction of the future or with organizing it for all time there can still be no doubt about the task confronting us at present: the *ruthless criticism of the existing order,* ruthless in that it will shrink neither from its own discoveries nor from conflict with the powers that be.

[. . .]

Reason has always existed, but not always in a rational form. Hence the critic can take his cue from every existing form of theoretical and practical consciousness and from this ideal and final goal implicit in the *actual* forms of existing reality he can deduce a true reality. Now as far as real life is concerned, it is precisely the *political* state which contains the postulates of reason in all its *modern* forms, even where it has not been the conscious repository of socialist requirements. But it does not stop there. It consistently assumes that reason has been realized and just as consistently it becomes embroiled at every point in a conflict between its ideal vocation and its actually existing premises.

[. . .]

Nothing prevents us, therefore, from lining our criticism with a criticism of politics, from taking sides in politics, i.e. from entering into real struggles and identifying ourselves with them. This does not mean that we shall confront the world with new doctrinaire principles and proclaim: Here is the truth, on your knees before it! It means that we shall develop for the world new principles from the existing principles of the world. We shall not say: Abandon your struggles, they are mere folly; let us provide you with the true campaign-slogans. Instead we shall simply show the world why it is struggling, and consciousness of this is a thing it *must* acquire whether it wishes or not.

The reform of consciousness consists *entirely* in making the world aware of its own consciousness, in arousing it from its dream of itself, in *explaining* its own actions to it. Like Feuerbach's critique of religion, our whole aim can only be to translate religious and political problems into their self-conscious human form.

Our programme must be: the reform of consciousness not through dogmas but by analysing mystical consciousness obscure to itself, whether it appears in religious or political form. It will then become plain that the world has long since dreamed of something of which it needs only to become conscious for it to possess it in reality. It will then become plain that our task is not to draw a sharp mental line between past and future but to *complete* the thought of the past. Lastly, it will become plain that mankind will not begin any *new* work, but will consciously bring about the completion of its old work.

We are therefore in a position to sum up the credo of our journal in a *single word*: the self-clarification (critical philosophy) of the struggles and wishes of the age. This is a task for the world and for us. It can succeed only as the product of united efforts. What is needed above all is a *confession*, and nothing more than that. To obtain forgiveness for its sins mankind needs only to declare them for what they are.

2
KARL MARX (1818–83) AND FRIEDRICH ENGELS (1820–95)
FROM *THE COMMUNIST MANIFESTO* 1848

The following extract is from the first section of the manifesto ('Bourgeois and Proletarians'), in Samuel Moore's 1888 translation from the original German text of 1848.

The modern bourgeois society that has sprouted from the ruins of feudal society has not done away with class antagonisms. It has but established new classes, new conditions of oppression, new forms of struggle in place of the old ones.

Our epoch, the ·epoch· of the bourgeoisie, possesses, however, this distinctive feature: it has simplified the class antagonisms. Society as a whole is more and more splitting up into two great hostile camps, into two great classes directly facing each other: Bourgeoisie and Proletariat.

[. . .]

The bourgeoisie, historically, has played a most revolutionary part.

The bourgeoisie, wherever it has got the upper hand, has put an end to all feudal, patriarchal, idyllic relations. It has pitilessly torn asunder the motley feudal ties that bound man to his 'natural superiors', and has left remaining no other nexus between man and man than naked self-interest, than callous 'cash payment'. It has drowned the most heavenly ecstasies of religious fervour, of chivalrous enthusiasm, of philistine sentimentalism, in the icy water of egotistical calculation. It has resolved personal worth into exchange value, and in place of the numberless indefeasible chartered freedoms, has set up that single, unconscionable freedom – Free Trade. In one word, for exploitation, veiled by religious and political illusions, it has substituted naked, shameless, direct, brutal exploitation.

The bourgeoisie has stripped of its halo every occupation hitherto honoured and looked up to with reverent awe. It has converted the physician, the lawyer, the priest, the poet, the man of science, into its paid wage-labourers.

The bourgeoisie has torn away from the family its sentimental veil, and has reduced the family relation to a mere money relation.

The bourgeoisie has disclosed how it came to pass that the brutal display of vigour in the Middle Ages, which Reactionists so much admire, found its fitting complement in the most slothful indolence. It has been the first to show what man's activity can bring about. It has accomplished wonders far surpassing Egyptian pyramids, Roman aqueducts, and Gothic cathedrals; it has conducted expeditions that put in the shade all former Exoduses of nations and crusades.

The bourgeoisie cannot exist without constantly revolutionizing the instruments of production, and thereby the relations of production, and with them the whole relations of society. Conservation of the old modes of production in unaltered form, was, on the contrary, the first condition of existence for all earlier industrial classes. Constant revolutionizing of production, uninterrupted disturbance of all social conditions, ever-lasting uncertainty and agitation distinguish the bourgeois epoch from all earlier ones. All fixed, fast-frozen relations, with their train of ancient and venerable prejudices and opinions are swept away, all new-formed ones become antiquated before they can ossify. All that is solid melts into air, all that is holy is profaned, and man is at last compelled to face with sober senses, his real conditions of life, and his relations with his kind.

The need of a constantly expanding market for its products chases the bourgeoisie over the whole surface of the globe. It must nestle everywhere, settle everywhere, establish connexions everywhere.

The bourgeoisie has through its exploitation of the world market given a cosmopolitan character to production and consumption in every country.

[. . .]

And as in material, so also in intellectual production. The intellectual creations of individual nations become common property. National one-sidedness and narrow-mindedness become more and more impossible, and from the numerous national and local literatures, there arises a world literature.

The bourgeoisie, by the rapid improvement of all instruments of production, by the immensely facilitated means of communication, draws all, even the most barbarian, nations into civilization. The cheap prices of its commodities are the heavy artillery with which it batters down all Chinese walls, with which it forces the barbarians' intensely obstinate hatred of foreigners to capitulate. It compels all nations, on pain of extinction, to adopt the bourgeois mode of production; it compels them to introduce what it calls civilization into their midst, i.e., to become bourgeois themselves. In one word, it creates a world after its own image.

The bourgeoisie has subjected the country to the rule of the towns. It has created enormous cities, has greatly increased the urban population as compared with the rural, and has thus rescued a considerable part of the population from the idiocy of rural life. Just as it has made the country dependent on the towns, so it has made barbarian and semi-barbarian countries dependent on the civilized ones, nations of peasants on nations of bourgeois, the East on the West.

[. . .]

Of all the classes that stand face to face with the bourgeoisie today, the proletariat alone is a really revolutionary class. The other classes decay and finally disappear in the face of modern industry; the proletariat is its special and essential product.

[. . .]

What the bourgeoisie, therefore, produces, above all, is its own grave-diggers. Its fall and the victory of the proletariat are equally inevitable.

[. . .]

3
RICHARD WILHELM WAGNER (1813–83)
FROM 'ART AND REVOLUTION' 1849

German composer and writer. Even in his early operas, Rienzi *(1842) and* The Flying Dutchman *(1843), Wagner was experimenting with the integration of music and drama. Much of his subsequent reputation is based on his innovations in this field. His major works,* The Ring of the Nibelung *(completed in 1876) and* Tristan and Isolde *(1865), embody his ideal of a radically new art form based on the synthesis of dramatic, verbal and musical symbolism. In the following extract from 'Art and Revolution' (written in 1849 and translated by William Ashton Ellis for the 1892 publication of* Richard Wagner's Prose Works: Vol. I), *Wagner speaks of the need for the creation of 'the perfect Art-work' as the fulfilment of the revolutionary goal of social and cultural regeneration.*

[. . .]

The perfect Art-work, the great united utterance of a free and lovely public life, the *Drama, Tragedy,* – howsoever great the poets who have here and there indited tragedies – is not yet born again: for reason that it cannot be *re-born*, but must be *born anew*.

Only the great *Revolution of Mankind*, whose beginnings erstwhile shattered Grecian Tragedy, can win for us this Art-work. For only this Revolution can bring forth from its hidden depths, in the new beauty of a nobler. Universalism, *that* which it once tore from the conservative spirit of a time of beautiful but narrow-meted culture – and tearing it, engulphed.

But only *Revolution*, not slavish *Restoration*, can give us back that highest Art-work. The task we have before us is immeasurably greater than that already accomplished in days of old. If the Grecian Art-work embraced the spirit of a fair and noble nation, the Art-work of the Future must embrace the spirit of a free mankind, delivered from every shackle of hampering nationality; its racial imprint must be no more than an embellishment, the individual charm of manifold diversity, and not a cramping barrier. We have thus quite other work to do, than to tinker at the resuscitation of old Greece. Indeed, the foolish restoration of a sham Greek mode of art has been attempted already, – for what will our artists not attempt, to order? But nothing better than an inane patchwork could ever come of it – the offspring of the same juggling endeavour which we find evinced by the whole history of our official civilisation, seized as it is with a constant wish to avoid the only lawful endeavour, the striving after Nature.

No, we do not wish to revert to Greekdom; for what the Greeks knew not, and, knowing not, came by their downfall: that know *we*. It is their very fall, whose cause we now perceive after years of misery and deepest universal suffering, that shows us clearly what we should become; it shows us that we must love all men before we can rightly love ourselves, before we can regain true joy in our own personality. From the dishonouring slave-yoke of universal journeymanhood, with its sickly Money-soul, we wish to soar to the free manhood of Art, with the star-rays of its World-soul; from the weary overburdened daylabourers of Commerce, we desire to grow to fair strong men, to whom the world belongs as an eternal, inexhaustible source of the highest delights of Art.

To this end we need the mightiest force of Revolution; for only *that* revolutionary force can boot us which presses forward to the goal – to that goal whose attainment alone can justify its earliest exercise upon the disintegration of Greek Tragedy and the dissolution of the Athenian State.

But whence shall we derive this force, in our present state of utmost weakness? Whence the manly strength against the crushing pressure of a civilisation which disowns all manhood, against the arrogance of a culture which employs the human mind as naught but steampower for its machinery? Whence the light with which to illumine the gruesome ruling heresy, that this civilisation and this culture are of more value in themselves than the true living Man? – that Man has worth and value only as a tool of these despotic abstract powers, and not by virtue of his manhood?

When the learned physician is at the end of his resources, in despair we turn at last to – *Nature*. Nature, then, and only Nature, can unravel the skein of this great world fate. If Culture, starting from the Christian dogma of the worthlessness of human nature, disown humanity: she has created for herself a foe who one day must inevitably destroy her, in so far as she no longer has place for manhood; for this foe is the eternal, and only living Nature. Nature, Human Nature, will proclaim this law to the twin sisters Culture and Civilisation: 'So far as I am contained in you, shall ye live and flourish; so far as I am not in you, shall ye rot and die!'

In the man-destroying march of Culture, however, there looms before us this happy result: the heavy load with which she presses Nature down, will one day grow so ponderous that it lends at last to down-trod, never-dying Nature the necessary impetus to hurl the whole cramping burden from her, with one sole thrust; and this heaping up of Culture will thus have *taught* to Nature her own gigantic force. The releasing of this force is – *Revolution*.

In what way, then, does this revolutionary force exhibit itself in the present social crisis? Is it not in the mechanic's pride in the moral consciousness of his labour, as opposed to the criminal passivity or immoral activity of the rich? Does he not wish, as in revenge, to elevate the principle of labour to the rank of the one and orthodox religion of society? To force the rich like him to work, – like him, by the sweat of their brow to gain their daily bread? Must we not fear that the exercise of this compulsion, the recognition of this principle, would raise at last the man-degrading journeymanhood to an absolute and universal might, and – to keep to our chief theme – would straightway make of Art an impossibility for all time?

In truth, this is the fear of many an honest friend of Art and many an upright friend of men, whose only wish is to preserve the nobler core of our present civilisation. But they mistake the true nature of the great social agitation. They are led astray by the windy theories of our socialistic doctrinaires, who would fain patch up an impossible compact with the present conditions of society. They are deceived by the immediate utterance of the indignation of the most suffering portion of our social system, behind which lies a deeper, nobler, natural instinct: the instinct which demands a worthy taste of the joys of life, whose material sustenance shall no longer absorb man's whole life-forces in weary service, but in which he shall rejoice as Man. Viewed closer, it is thus the straining from journeymanhood to artistic manhood, to the free dignity of Man.

It is for Art therefore, and Art above all else, to teach this social impulse its noblest meaning, and guide it toward its true direction. Only on the shoulders of this great social movement can true Art lift itself from its present state of civilised barbarianism, and take its post of honour. Each has a common goal, and the twain can only reach it when they recognise it jointly. This goal is *the strong fair Man*, to whom *Revolution* shall give his *Strength*, and *Art* his *Beauty!*

[. . .]

4
CHARLES DARWIN (1809–82)
FROM *THE ORIGIN OF SPECIES BY MEANS OF NATURAL SELECTION* 1859

English naturalist. Studied medicine at Edinburgh and biology at Cambridge. As a naturalist aboard HMS Beagle, *Darwin took part in a six-year (1831–36) scientific survey of South American waters and published several works on the geological and zoological discoveries of that voyage. His great project was the investigation of the origin of species, on which he worked for several years, although his thesis was not published until 1859.* The Origin of Species by Means of Natural Selection *put forward a theory of evolution which was both controversial and highly influential throughout Europe. In later works, Darwin produced supplements to his original treatise, the most important (and again controversial) of which was* The Descent of Man and Selection in Relation to Sex *(1871).*

[. . .]

If under changing conditions of life organic beings present individual differences in almost every part of their structure, and this cannot be disputed; if there be, owing to their geometrical rate of increase, a severe struggle for life at some age, season, or year, and this certainly cannot be disputed; then, considering the infinite complexity of the relations of all organic beings to each other and to their conditions of life, causing an infinite diversity in structure, constitution, and habits, to be advantageous to them, it would be a most extraordinary fact if no variations had ever occurred useful to each being's own welfare, in the same manner as so many variations have occurred useful to man. But if variations useful to any organic being ever do occur, assuredly individuals thus characterised will have the best chance of being preserved in the struggle for life; and from the strong principle of inheritance, these will tend to produce offspring similarly characterised. This principle of preservation, or the survival of the fittest, I have called Natural Selection. It leads to the improvement of each creature in relation to its organic and inorganic conditions of life; and consequently, in most cases, to what must be regarded as an advance in organisation. Nevertheless, low and simple forms will long endure if well fitted for their simple conditions of life.

Natural selection, on the principle of qualities being inherited at corresponding ages, can modify the egg, seed, or young, as easily as the adult. Amongst many animals, sexual selection will have given its aid to ordinary selection, by assuring to the most vigorous and best adapted males the greatest number of offspring. Sexual selection will also give characters useful to the males alone, in their struggles or rivalry with other males; and these characters will be transmitted to one sex or to both sexes, according to the form of inheritance which prevails.

Whether natural selection has really thus acted in adapting the various forms of life to their several conditions and stations, must be judged by the general tenor and balance of evidence given in the following chapters. But we have already seen how it entails extinction; and how largely extinction has acted in the world's history, geology plainly declares. Natural selection, also, leads to divergence of character; for the more organic beings diverge in structure, habits, and constitution, by so much the more can a large number be supported on the area, – of which we see proof by looking to the inhabitants of any small spot, and to the productions naturalised in foreign lands. Therefore, during the modification of the descendants of any one species, and during the incessant struggle of all species to increase in numbers, the more diversified the descendants become, the better will be their chance of success in the battle for life. Thus the small differences distinguishing varieties of the same species, steadily tend to increase, till they equal the greater differences between species of the same genus, or even of distinct genera.

We have seen that it is the common, the widely-diffused and widely-ranging species, belonging to the larger genera within each class, which vary most; and these tend to transmit to their modified offspring that superiority which now makes them dominant in their own countries. Natural selection, as has just been remarked, leads to divergence of character and to much extinction of the less improved and intermediate forms of life. On these principles, the nature of the affinities, and the generally well-defined distinctions between the innumerable organic beings in each class throughout the world, may be explained. It is a truly wonderful fact – the wonder of which we are apt to overlook from familiarity – that all animals and all plants throughout all time and space should be related to each other in groups, subordinate to groups, in the manner which we everywhere behold – namely, varieties of the same species most closely related, species of the same genus less closely and unequally related, forming sections and sub-genera, species of distinct genera much less closely related, and genera related in different degrees, forming sub-families, families, orders, sub-classes and classes. The several subordinate groups in any class cannot be ranked in a single file, but seem clustered round points, and these round other points, and so on in almost endless cycles. If species had been independently created, no explanation would have been possible of this kind of classification; but it is explained through inheritance and the complex action of natural selection, entailing extinction and divergence of character, as we have seen illustrated in the diagram.

The affinities of all the beings of the same class have sometimes been represented by a great tree. I believe this simile largely speaks the truth. The green and budding twigs may represent existing species; and those produced during former years may represent the long succession of extinct species. At each period of growth all the growing twigs have tried to branch out on all sides, and to overtop and kill the surrounding twigs and branches, in the same manner as species and groups of species have at all times overmastered other species in the great battle for life. The limbs divided into great branches, and these into lesser and lesser branches, were themselves once, when the tree was young, budding twigs; and this connection of the former and present buds by ramifying branches may well represent the classification of all extinct and living species in groups subordinate to groups. Of the many twigs which flourished when the tree was a mere bush, only two or three, now grown into great branches, yet survive and bear the other branches; so with the species which lived during long-past geological periods, very few have left living and modified descendants. From the first growth of the tree, many a limb and branch has decayed and dropped off; and these fallen branches of various sizes may represent those whole orders, families, and genera which have now no living representatives, and which are known to us only in a fossil state. As we here and there see a thin straggling branch springing from a fork low down in a tree, and which by some chance has been favoured and is still alive on its summit, so we occasionally see an animal like the Ornithorhynchus or Lepidosiren, which in some small degree connects by its affinities two large branches of life, and which has apparently been saved from fatal competition by having inhabited a protected station. As buds give rise by growth to fresh buds, and these, if vigorous, branch out and overtop on all sides many a feebler branch, so by generation I believe it has been with the great Tree of Life, which fills with its dead and broken branches the crust of the earth and covers the surface with its ever-branching and beautiful ramifications.

5

JOHANN JACOB BACHOFEN (1815–87)
FROM *MOTHER RIGHT* 1861

Swiss anthropologist and jurist. During visits to Italy and Greece, Bachofen studied the symbolism of early tombs and assembled information on primitive man, his laws and religions. In Mother Right *(Das Mutterrecht, 1861) he used these findings to investigate how the family unit functions as a social institution, and to suggest that matriarchal organisation of the family preceded modern day patriarchal arrangements. The following extract is from Bachofen's introduction, translated by Ralph Manheim for the 1967 edition of* Myth, Religion, and Mother Right: Selected Writings of J. J. Bachofen.

The present work deals with a historical phenomenon which few have observed and no one has investigated in its full scope. Up until now archaeologists have had nothing to say of mother right. The term is new and the family situation it designates unknown. The subject is extremely attractive, but it also raises great difficulties. The most elementary spadework remains to be done, for the culture period to which mother right pertains has never been seriously studied. Thus we are entering upon virgin territory.

We find ourselves carried back to times antedating classical antiquity, to an older world of ideas totally different from those with which we are familiar. Leaving the nations we commonly associate with the glory of the ancient world, we find ourselves among peoples who never achieved the level of classical culture. An unknown world opens before our eyes, and the more we learn of it, the stranger it seems. Everything contrasts with the idea of a highly developed culture; everywhere we find older conceptions, an independent way of life that can only be judged according to its own fundamental law. The matriarchal organization of the family seems strange in the light not only of modern but also of classical ideas. And the more primitive way of life to which it pertains, from which it arose, and through which alone it can be explained, seems very strange beside the Hellenic. The main purpose of the following pages is to set forth the moving principle of the matriarchal age, and to give its proper place in relationship both to the lower stages of development and to the higher levels of culture. Thus the scope of this work is far broader than its title indicates. I propose to investigate all aspects of matriarchal culture, to disclose its diverse traits and the fundamental idea which unites them. In this way I hope to restore the picture of a cultural stage which was overlaid or totally destroyed by the later development of the ancient world. This is an ambitious undertaking. But it is only by broadening our horizon that we can achieve true understanding and carry scientific thinking to that clarity and completeness which are the very essence of knowledge.

[. . .]

Our question has been answered: the mythical tradition may be taken as a faithful reflection of the life of those times in which historical antiquity is rooted. It is a manifestation of primordial thinking, an immediate historical revelation, and consequently a highly reliable historical source.

[. . .]

Since the beginning of all development lies in myth, myth must form the starting point for any serious investigation of ancient history. Myth contains the origins, and myth alone can reveal them. It is the origins which determine the subsequent development, which define its character and direction. Without knowledge of the origins, the science of history can come to no conclusion. A distinction between myth and history may be justified where it refers merely to a difference in mode of expression, but it has neither meaning nor justification when it creates a hiatus in the continuity of human development. The success of our undertaking depends essentially on the abandonment of any such distinction. The forms of family organization prevailing in the times known to us are not original forms, but the consequences of earlier stages. Considered alone, they disclose only themselves, not their causality; they are isolated data, elements of knowledge at most, but not of understanding. The strictness of the Roman patriarchal system points to an earlier system that had to be combatted and suppressed. And the same applies to the paternal system of Athens, the city of Athene, motherless daughter of Zeus.

[. . .]

The matriarchal period is indeed the poetry of history by virtue of the sublimity, the heroic grandeur, even the beauty to which woman rose by inspiring bravery and chivalry in men, by virtue of the meaning she imparted to feminine love and the chastity and restraint that she exacted of young men. To the ancients all this appeared in very much the same light as the chivalric nobility of the Germanic world to our own eyes. Like us, the ancients asked: What has become of those women whose unblemished beauty, whose chastity and high-mindedness could awaken love even in the immortals? What has become of the heroines whose praises were sung by Hesiod, poet of the matriarchy? What has become of the feminine assemblies with which Dike herself liked to engage in familiar discussions? But where, too, are those heroes without fear and without reproach, who, like the Lycian Bellerophon, great for his chivalry and blameless life, combined bravery with voluntary recognition of the feminine power? All warlike peoples, Aristotle remarks, serve the woman, and the study of later epochs teaches the same lesson: to defy danger, to seek out adventure, and to serve beauty – these virtues betoken the fullness of a nation's youth. Present conditions make all this look like fiction. But the highest poetry, more vibrant and moving than any fantasy, is the reality of history. The human race has experienced greater adventures than our imagination can conceive. The matriarchal age, with its figures, deeds, upheavals, is beyond the poetry of cultivated but enfeebled times. Let us never forget that when the power to perform high deeds flags, the flight of the spirit falters also, and incipient rot permeates all spheres of life at once.

[. . .]

Here we are carried back to our starting point. We began by showing matriarchy to be a universal phenomenon, independent of any special dogma or legislation. Now we can go further in our characterization and establish its quality of natural truth. Like childbearing motherhood, which is its physical image, matriarchy is entirely subservient to matter and to the phenomena of natural life, from which it derives the laws of its inner and outward existence; more strongly than later generations, the matriarchal peoples feel the unity of all life, the harmony of the universe, which they have not yet outgrown; they are more keenly aware of the pain of death and the fragility of tellurian existence, lamented by woman and particularly the mother. They yearn more fervently for higher consolation, which they find in the phenomena of natural life, and they relate this consolation to the generative womb, to conceiving, sheltering, nurturing mother love. Obedient in all things to the laws of physical existence, they fasten their eyes upon the earth, setting the chthonian powers over the powers of uranian light. They identify the male principle chiefly with the tellurian waters and subordinate the generative moisture to the *gremium matris* (maternal womb), the ocean to the earth. In a wholly material sense they devote themselves to the embellishment of material existence, to the ηρακτικη αρετη (practical virtues). Both in agriculture, which was first fostered by women, and in the erection of walls, which the ancients identified with the chthonian cult, they achieved a perfection which astonished later generations. No era has attached so much importance to outward form, to the sanctity of the body, and so little to the inner spiritual factor; in juridical life no other era has so consistently advocated maternal dualism and the principle of actual possession; and none has been so given to lyrical enthusiasm, this eminently feminine sentiment, rooted in the feeling of nature. In a word, matriarchal existence is regulated naturalism, its thinking is material, its development predominantly physical. Mother right is just as essential to this cultural stage as it is alien and unintelligible to the era of patriarchy.

[. . .]

The progress from the maternal to the paternal conception of man forms the most important turning point in the history of the relations between the sexes. The Demetrian and the Aphroditeanhetaeric stages both hold to the primacy of generative motherhood, and it is only the greater or lesser purity of its interpretation that distinguishes the two forms of existence. But with the transition to the paternal system occurs a change in fundamental principle; the older conception is wholly surpassed. An entirely new attitude makes itself felt. The mother's connection with the child is based on a material relationship, it is accessible to sense perception and remains always a natural truth. But the father as begetter presents an entirely different aspect. Standing in no visible relation to the child, he can never, even in the marital relation, cast off a certain fictive character. Belonging to the offspring only through the mediation of the mother, he always appears as the remoter potency.

[. . .]

All these attributes of fatherhood lead to one conclusion: the triumph of paternity brings with it the liberation of the spirit from the manifestations of nature, a sublimation of human existence over the laws of material life. While the principle of motherhood is common to all spheres of tellurian life, man, by the preponderant position he accords to the begetting potency, emerges from this relationship and becomes conscious of his higher calling. Spiritual life rises over corporal existence, and the relation with the lower spheres of existence is restricted to the physical aspect. Maternity pertains to the physical side of man, the only thing he shares with the animals: the paternal-spiritual principle belongs to him alone. Here he breaks through the bonds of tellurism and lifts his eyes to the higher regions of the cosmos. Triumphant paternity partakes of the heavenly light, while childbearing motherhood is bound up with the earth that bears all things; the establishment of paternal right is universally represented as an act of the uranian solar hero, while the defense of mother right is the first duty of the chthonian mother goddesses.

[. . .]

A comparison between these two spheres of life shows us the lawful development of the human spirit with a high degree of objective certainty. Everywhere the same ascent from earth to heaven, from matter to immateriality, from the mother to the father, everywhere the Orphic principle, which in the trend from below to above sees a successive purification of existence, and herein discloses its fundamental contrast with Christian doctrine and its dictum: 'For the man is not of the woman, but the woman of the man.'

[. . .]

A historical investigation which must be the first to gather, verify, and collate all its material, must everywhere stress the particular and only gradually progress to comprehensive ideas. Success depends on the most complete investigation and unprejudiced, purely objective appraisal of the material. From this circumstance follow the two criteria which will determine the organization of our forthcoming inquiry. The entire material is arranged according to nations; these supply our supreme principle of classification. Each section opens with a consideration of the most significant records. The very nature of this method precludes a logical progression in our exposition of the ideas relating to matriarchy; instead, we shall have to follow the documents regarding each people, stressing sometimes this and sometimes another aspect. Moreover, we shall have to deal repeatedly with one and the same question.

In a field of research offering so much that is new and wholly unknown, such differentiation and repetition should not be condemned or regretted. Both are inseparable from a system which otherwise possesses important advantages. The life of peoples is rich and varied. Influenced by circumstances and specific developments, the basic ideas of an individual nation at a given cultural stage take a great many different forms. Subsequently, similarities tend to recede and particular traits to come to the fore; and we shall see that under the influence of manifold circumstances a given aspect of life will decline at an early stage in one place and thrive in another. It is obvious that only a separate examination of each people can do justice to this wealth of historical formations and keep our investigation from dogmatic onesidedness. Research which aims at extending the field of history and the scope of our historical knowledge cannot content itself with merely erecting a system; rather it must strive to understand life in all its movements and manifestations. An all-embracing point of view may have great merit, but it can only be demonstrated by reference to detail: only when the general is combined with the specific and the total character of a cultural period is illustrated by the traits of individual peoples does the twofold need of the mind for unity and variety find satisfaction. Each nation that enters the sphere of our investigation provides the over-all picture and history of gynocracy with new facets and sheds new light on aspects formerly neglected. Thus our understanding will grow in the course of investigation; gaps will be filled in; initial observations will be confirmed, modified, or amplified by others; our knowledge will gradually be rounded out and gain inner cohesion; higher and higher perspectives will result; and finally they will all be joined in the unity of one supreme idea. Greater than our pleasure at the result is the satisfaction that comes from contemplation of its gradual development.

[. . .]

6
FRIEDRICH NIETZSCHE (1844–1900)
FROM PREFACE TO *HUMAN, ALL TOO HUMAN* 1878

German philosopher, critic and classicist. With the exception of The Birth of Tragedy *(1872) and the first volume of* Human, All Too Human *(1878), Nietzsche's major work belongs to the decade after he resigned his professorship of classics at Basle, Switzerland, in 1879. In* Thus Spoke Zarathustra *(1883–84),* Beyond Good and Evil *(1886) and* On the Genealogy of Morals *(1887) he undertook the project of a wide-reaching and radical revaluation of epistemology, rationality, morality and religion. In the following extract from the Preface to* Human, All Too Human, *translated by R. J. Hollingdale, Nietzsche speaks of the predicament and task lying ahead for the 'free spirits' whom he has had to invent and to whom he dedicates 'this melancholy-valiant book'.*

audacity: fearlessness daring, ect.

1

I have been told often enough, and always with an expression of great surprise, that all my writings, from *The Birth of Tragedy* to the most recently published *Prelude to a Philosophy of the Future*, have something that distinguishes them and unites them together: they all of them, I have been given to understand, contain snares and nets for unwary birds and in effect a persistent invitation to the overturning of habitual evaluations and valued habits. What? *Everything* only – human, all too human? It is with this sigh that one emerges from my writings, not without a kind of reserve and mistrust even in regard to morality, not a little tempted and emboldened, indeed, for once to play the advocate of the worst things: as though they have perhaps been only the worst slandered? My writings have been called a schooling in suspicion, even more in contempt, but fortunately also in courage, indeed in audacity. And in fact I myself do not believe that anyone has ever before looked into the world with an equally profound degree of suspicion, and not merely as an occasional devil's advocate, but, to speak theologically, just as much as an enemy and indicter of God; and anyone who could divine something of the consequences that lie in that profound suspiciousness, something of the fears and frosts of the isolation to which that unconditional *disparity of view* condemns him who is infected with it, will also understand how often, in an effort to recover from myself, as it were to induce a temporary self-forgetting, I have sought shelter in this or that – in some piece of admiration or enmity or scientificality or frivolity or stupidity; and why, where I could not find what I *needed*, I had artificially to enforce, falsify and invent a suitable fiction for myself (– and what else have poets ever done? and to what end does art exist in the world at all?). What I again and again needed most for my cure and self-restoration, however, was the belief that I was *not* thus isolated, not alone in *seeing* as I did – an enchanted surmising of relatedness and identity in eye and desires, a reposing in a trust of friendship, a blindness in concert with another without suspicion or question-marks, a pleasure in foregrounds, surfaces, things close and closest, in everything possessing colour, skin and apparitionality. Perhaps in this regard I might be reproached with having employed a certain amount of 'art', a certain amount of false-coinage. *defines art as false coinage.*

[...]

Supposing, however, that all this were true and that I was reproached with it with good reason, what do *you* know, what *could* you know, of how much cunning in self-preservation, how much reason and higher safeguarding, is contained in such self-deception – or of how much falsity I shall *require* if I am to continue to permit myself the luxury of *my* truthfulness? . . . Enough, I am still living; and life is, after all, not a product of morality: it *wants* deception, it *lives* on deception . . . but there you are, I am already off again, am I not, and doing what I have always done, old immoralist and bird-catcher that I am – speaking unmorally, extra-morally, 'beyond good and evil'? –

2

Thus when I needed to I once also *invented* for myself the 'free spirits' to whom this melancholy-valiant book with the title *Human, All Too Human* is dedicated: 'free spirits' of this kind do not exist, did not exist – but, as I have said, I had need of them at that time if I was to keep in good spirits while surrounded by ills (sickness, solitude, unfamiliar places, *acedia,* inactivity): as brave companions and familiars with whom one can laugh and chatter when one feels like laughing and chattering, and whom one can send to the Devil when they become tedious – as compensation for the friends I lacked. That free spirits of this kind *could* one day exist, that our Europe *will* have such active and audacious fellows among its sons of tomorrow and the next day, physically present and palpable and not, as in my case, merely phantoms and hermit's phantasmagoria: *I* should wish to be the last to doubt it. I see them already *coming,* slowly, slowly; and perhaps I shall do something to speed their coming if I describe in advance under what vicissitudes, upon what paths, I *see* them coming? –

3

One may conjecture that a spirit in whom the type 'free spirit' will one day become ripe and sweet to the point of perfection has had its decisive experience in a *great liberation* and that previously it was all the more a fettered spirit and seemed to be chained for ever to its pillar and corner. What fetters the fastest? What bonds are all but unbreakable? In the case of men of a high and select kind they will be their duties: that reverence proper to youth, that reserve and delicacy before all that is honoured and revered from of old, that gratitude for the soil out of which they have grown, for the hand which led them, for the holy place where they learned to worship – their supreme moments themselves will fetter them the fastest, lay upon them the most enduring obligation. The great liberation comes for those who are thus fettered suddenly, like the shock of an earthquake: the youthful soul is all at once convulsed, torn loose, torn away – it itself does not know what is happening. A drive and impulse rules and masters it like a command; a will and desire awakens to go off, anywhere, at any cost; a vehement dangerous curiosity for an undiscovered world flames and flickers in all its senses. 'Better to die than to go on living *here*' – thus responds the imperious voice and temptation: and this 'here', this 'at home' is everything it had hitherto loved! A sudden terror and suspicion of what it loved, a lightning-bolt of contempt for what it called 'duty', a rebellious, arbitrary, volcanically erupting desire for travel, strange places, estrangements, coldness, soberness, frost, a hatred of love, perhaps a desecrating blow and glance *backwards* to where it formerly loved and worshipped, perhaps a hot blush of shame at what it has just done and at the same time an exultation *that* it has done it, a drunken, inwardly exultant shudder which betrays that a victory has been won – a victory? over what? over whom? an enigmatic, question-packed, questionable victory, but the *first* victory nonetheless: such bad and painful things are part of the history of the great liberation. It is at the same time a sickness that can destroy the man who has it, this first outbreak of strength and will to self-determination, to evaluating on one's own account, this will to *free* will; and how much sickness is expressed in the wild experiments and singularities through which the liberated prisoner now seeks to demonstrate his mastery over things! He prowls cruelly around with an unslaked lasciviousness; what he captures has to expiate the perilous tension of his pride; what excites him he tears apart. With a wicked laugh he turns round whatever he finds veiled and through some sense of shame or other spared and pampered: he puts to the test what these things look like *when* they are reversed. It is an act of willfulness, and pleasure in willfulness, if now he perhaps bestows his favour on that which has hitherto had a bad reputation – if, full of inquisitiveness and the desire to tempt and experiment, he creeps around the things most forbidden. Behind all his toiling and weaving – for he is restlessly and aimlessly on his way as if in a desert – stands the question-mark of a more and more perilous curiosity. 'Can *all* values not be turned round? and is good perhaps evil? and God only an invention and finesse of the Devil? Is everything perhaps in the last resort false? And if we are deceived, are we not for that very reason also deceivers? *must* we not be deceivers?'

lascivious: lustful

[. . .]

4

From this morbid isolation, from the desert of these years of temptation and experiment, it is still a long road to that tremendous overflowing certainty and health which may not dispense even with wickedness, as a means and fish-hook of knowledge, to that *mature* freedom of spirit which is equally self-mastery and discipline of the heart and permits access to many and contradictory modes of thought – to that inner spaciousness and indulgence of superabundance which excludes the danger that the spirit may even on its own road perhaps lose itself and become infatuated and remain seated intoxicated in some corner or other, to that superfluity of formative, curative, moulding and restorative forces which is precisely the sign of *great* health, that superfluity which grants to the free spirit the dangerous privilege of living *experimentally* and of being allowed to offer itself to adventure: the master's privilege of the free spirit! In between there may lie long years of convalescence, years full of variegated, painfully magical transformations ruled and led along by a tenacious *will to health* which often ventures to clothe and disguise itself as health already achieved. There is a midway condition which a man of such a destiny will not be able to recall without emotion: it is characterized by a pale, subtle happiness of light and sunshine, a feeling of bird-like freedom, bird-like altitude, bird-like exuberance, and a third thing in which curiosity is united with a tender contempt. A 'free-spirit' – this cool expression does one good in every condition, it is almost warming. One lives no longer in the fetters of love and hatred, without yes, without no, near or far as one wishes, preferably slipping away, evading, fluttering off, gone again, again flying aloft; one is spoiled, as everyone is who has at some time seen a tremendous number of things *beneath* him – and one becomes the opposite of those who concern themselves with things which have nothing to do with them. Indeed, the free spirit henceforth has to do only with things – and how many things! – with which he is no longer *concerned* . . .

5

A step further in convalescence: and the free spirit again draws near to life – slowly, to be sure, almost reluctantly, almost mistrustfully. It again grows warmer around him, yellower, as it were; feeling and feeling for others acquire depth, warm breezes of all kind blow across him. It seems to him as if his eyes are only now open to what is *close at hand*. He is astonished and sits silent: where *had* he been? These close and closest things: how changed they seem! what bloom and magic they have acquired! He looks back gratefully – grateful to his wandering, to his hardness and self-alienation, to his viewing of far distances and bird-like flights in cold heights. What a good thing he had not always stayed 'at home', stayed 'under his own roof' like a delicate apathetic loafer! He had been *beside* himself: no doubt of that. Only now does he see himself – and what surprises he experiences as he does so! What unprecedented shudders! What happiness even in the weariness, the old sickness, the relapses of the convalescent! How he loves to sit sadly still, to spin out patience, to lie in the sun! Who understands as he does the happiness that comes in winter, the spots of sunlight on the wall! They are the most grateful animals in the world, also the most modest, these convalescents and lizards again half turned towards life: – there are some among them who allow no day to pass without hanging a little song of praise on the hem of its departing robe. And, to speak seriously: to become sick in the manner of these free spirits, to remain sick for a long time and then, slowly, slowly, to become healthy, by which I mean 'healthier', is a fundamental *cure* for all pessimism (the cancerous sore and inveterate vice, as is well known, of old idealists and inveterate liars). There is wisdom, practical wisdom, in for a long time prescribing even health for oneself only in small doses. –

6

At that time it may finally happen that, under the sudden illumination of a still stressful, still changeable health, the free, ever freer spirit begins to unveil the riddle of that great liberation which had until then waited dark, questionable, almost untouchable in his memory. If he has for long hardly dared to ask himself: 'why so apart? so alone? renouncing everything I once reverenced? renouncing reverence itself? why this hardness, this suspiciousness, this hatred for your own virtues?' – now he dares to ask it aloud and hears in reply something like an answer. 'You shall become master over yourself, master also over your virtues. Formerly *they* were your masters; but they must be only your instruments beside other instruments. You shall get control over your For and Against and learn how to display first one and then the other in accordance with your higher goal. You shall learn to grasp the sense of perspective in every value judgement – the displacement, distortion and merely apparent teleology of horizons and whatever else pertains to perspectivism; also the quantum of stupidity that resides in antitheses of values and the whole intellectual loss which every For, every Against costs us. You shall learn to grasp the *necessary* injustice in every For and Against, injustice as inseparable from life, life itself as *conditioned* by the sense of perspective and its injustice. You shall above all see with your own eyes where injustice is always at its greatest: where life has developed at its smallest, narrowest, neediest, most incipient and yet cannot avoid taking *itself* as the goal and measure of things and for the sake of its own preservation secretly and meanly and ceaselessly crumbling away and calling into question the higher, greater, richer – you shall see with your own eyes the problem of *order of rank*, and how power and right and spaciousness of perspective grow into the heights together. You shall' – enough: from now on the free spirit *knows* what 'you shall' he has obeyed, and he also knows what he now *can*, what only now he – *may* do . . .

7

This is how the free spirit elucidates to himself that enigma of liberation, and inasmuch as he generalizes his own case ends by adjudicating on what he has experienced thus. 'What has happened to me', he says to himself, 'must happen to everyone in whom a *task* wants to become incarnate and "come into the world"'. The secret force and necessity of this task will rule among and in the individual facets of his destiny like an unconscious pregnancy – long before he has caught sight of this task itself or knows its name. Our vocation commands and disposes of us even when we do not yet know it; it is the future that regulates our today. Given it is *the problem of order of rank* of which we may say it is *our* problem, we free spirits: it is only now, at the midday of our life, that we understand what preparations, bypaths, experiments, temptations, disguises the problem had need of before it was *allowed* to rise up before us, and how we first had to experience the most manifold and contradictory states of joy and distress in soul and body, as adventurers and circumnavigators of that inner world called 'man', as surveyors and gaugers of that 'higher' and 'one upon the other' that is likewise called 'man' – penetrating everywhere, almost without fear, disdaining nothing, losing noth-ing, asking everything, cleansing everything of what is chance and accident in it and as it were thoroughly sifting it – until at last we had the right to say, we free spirits: 'Here – a *new* problem! Here a long ladder upon whose rungs we ourselves have sat and climbed

– which we ourselves have at some time *been*! Here a higher, a deeper, a beneath-us, a tremendous long ordering, an order of rank, which we *see*: here – *our* problem!' –

[. . .]

7
MAX NORDAU (1849–1923)
FROM *DEGENERATION* 1883

Hungarian physician, controversialist and Jewish nationalist. Nordau's most controversial and popular work, Degeneration *dates from 1883 and is an acerbic attack on what he perceived to be the intellectual, moral and spiritual corruption of late-nineteenth century European societies. In particular, Nordau is scathing about the artists and writers of his day, their 'confused' aesthetic theories and the 'disturbing and corrupting influence' of their work. The following extract is from Book V ('The Twentieth Century'). It is prefaced by a short passage from Nordau's dedication to Professor Cæsar Lombroso, one of the first to develop a scientific notion of degeneracy. [See Ib 23]*

Degenerates are not always criminals, prostitutes, anarchists, and pronounced lunatics; they are often authors and artists. These, however, manifest the same mental characteristics, and for the most part the same somatic features, as the members of the above-mentioned anthropological family, who satisfy their unhealthy impulses with the knife of the assassin or the bomb of the dynamiter, instead of with pen and pencil.

Some among these degenerates in literature, music, and painting have in recent years come into extraordinary prominence, and are revered by numerous admirers as creators of a new art, and heralds of the coming centuries.

[. . .]

We stand now in the midst of a severe mental epidemic; of a sort of black death of degeneration and hysteria, and it is natural that we should ask anxiously on all sides: 'What is to come next?'

This question of eventuality presents itself to the physician in every serious case, and however delicate and rash, above all, however little scientific any prediction may be, he cannot evade the necessity of establishing a prognosis. For that matter, this is not purely arbitrary, not a blind leap into the dark; the most attentive observation of all the symptoms, assisted by experience, permits a generally just conclusion on the ulterior evolution of the evil.

It is possible that the disease may not have yet attained its culminating point. If it should become more violent, gain yet more in breadth and depth, then certain phenomena which are perceived as exceptions or in an embryo condition would henceforth increase to a formidable extent and develop consistently; others, which at present are only observed among the inmates of lunatic asylums, would pass into the daily habitual condition of whole classes of the population. Life would then present somewhat the following picture:

Every city possesses its club of suicides. By the side of this exist clubs for mutual assassination by strangulation, hanging, or stabbing. In the place of the present taverns houses would be found devoted to the service of consumers of ether, chloral, naphtha, and hashish. The number of persons suffering from aberrations of taste and smell has become so considerable that it is a lucrative trade to open shops for them where they can swallow in rich vessels all sorts of dirt, and breathe amidst surroundings which do not offend their sense of beauty nor their habits of comfort the odour of decay and filth. A number of new professions are being formed – that of injectors of morphia and cocaine; of commissioners who, posted at the corners of the streets, offer their arms to persons attacked by agoraphobia, in order to enable them to cross the roads and squares; of companies of men who by vigorous affirmations are charged to tranquillize persons afflicted with the mania of doubt when taken by a fit of nervousness, etc.

The increase of nervous irritability, far beyond the present standard, has made it necessary to institute certain measures of protection. After it has frequently come to pass that over-excited persons, being unable to resist a sudden impulse, have killed from their windows with air-guns, or have even openly attacked, the street boys who have uttered shrill whistles or piercingly sharp screams without rhyme or reason; that they have forced their way into strange houses where beginners are practising the piano or singing, and there committed murder; that they have made attempts with dynamite against tramways where the conductor rings a bell (as in Berlin) or whistles – it has been forbidden by law to whistle and bawl in the street; special buildings, managed in such a way that no sound penetrates to the outside, have been established for the practice of the piano and singing exercises; public conveyances have no right to make a noise, and the severest penalty is at the same time attached to the possession of air-guns. The barking of dogs having driven many people in the neighbourhood to madness and suicide, these animals cannot be kept in a town until after they have been made mute by severing the 'recurrent' nerve. A new legislation on subjects connected with the press forbids journalists, under severe penalties, to give detailed accounts of violence or suicides under peculiar circumstances. Editors are responsible for all punishable actions committed in imitation of their reports.

Sexual psychopathy of every nature has become so general and so imperious that manners and laws have adapted themselves accordingly. They appear already in the fashions. Masochists or passivists, who form the majority of men, clothe themselves in a costume which recalls, by colour and cut, feminine apparel. Women who wish to please men of this kind wear men's dress, an eyeglass, boots with spurs and riding-whip, and only show themselves in the street with a large cigar in their mouths. The demand of persons with the 'contrary' sexual sentiment that persons of the same sex can conclude a legal marriage has obtained satisfaction, seeing they have been numerous enough to elect a majority of deputies having the same tendency. Sadists, 'bestials,' nosophiles, and necrophiles, etc., find legal opportunities to gratify their inclinations. Modesty and restraint are dead superstitions of the past, and appear only as atavism and among the inhabitants of remote villages. The lust of murder is confronted as a disease, and treated by surgical intervention, etc.

The capacity for attention and contemplation has diminished so greatly that instruction at school is at most but two hours a day, and no public amusements, such as theatres, concerts, lectures, etc., last more than half an hour. For that matter, in the curriculum of studies, mental education is almost wholly suppressed, and by far the greater part of the time is reserved for bodily exercises; on the stage only representations of unveiled eroticism and bloody homicides, and to this, flock voluntary victims from all the parts, who aspire to the voluptuousness of dying amid the plaudits of delirious spectators.

The old religions have not many adherents. On the other hand, there are a great number of spiritualist communities who, instead of priests, maintain soothsayers, evokers of the dead, sorcerers, astrologers, and chiromancers, etc.

Books such as those of the present day have not been in fashion for a very long time. Printing is now only on black, blue, or golden paper; on another colour are single incoherent words, often nothing but syllables, nay, even letters or numbers only, but which have a symbolical significance which is meant to be guessed by the colour and print of the paper and form of the book, the size and nature of the characters. Authors soliciting popularity make comprehension easy by adding to the text symbolical arabesques, and impregnating the paper with a definite perfume. But this is considered vulgar by the refined and connoisseurs, and is but little esteemed. Some poets who publish no more than isolated letters of the alphabet, or whose works are coloured pages on which is absolutely nothing, elicit the greatest admiration. There are societies whose object it is to interpret them, and their enthusiasm is so fanatical that they frequently have fights against each other ending in murder.

[. . .]

It would be easy to augment this picture still further, no feature of which is invented, every detail being borrowed from special literature on criminal law and psychiatria, and observations of the peculiarities of neurasthenics, hysterics, and mattoids. This will be, in the near future, the condition of civilized humanity, if fatigue, nervous exhaustion, and the diseases and degeneration conditioned by them, make much greater progress.

Will it come to this? Well, no; I think not. And this, for a reason which scarcely perhaps permits of an objection: because humanity has not yet reached the term of its evolution; because the over-exertion of two or three generations cannot yet have exhausted all its vital powers. Humanity is not senile. It is still young, and a moment of over-exertion is not fatal for youth; it can recover itself. Humanity resembles a vast torrent of lava, which rushes, broad and deep, from the crater of a volcano in constant activity. The outer crust cracks into cold, vitrified scoriæ, but under this dead shell the mass flows, rapidly and evenly, in living incandescence.

As long as the vital powers of an individual, as of a race, are not wholly consumed, the organism makes efforts actively or passively to adapt itself, by seeking to modify injurious conditions, or by adjusting itself in some way so that conditions impossible to modify should be as little noxious as possible. Degenerates, hysterics, and neurasthenics are not capable of adaptation. Therefore they are fated to disappear. That which inexorably destroys them is that they do not know how to come to terms with reality. They are lost, whether they are alone in the world, or whether there are people with them who are still sane, or more sane than they, or at least curable.

They are lost if they are alone: for anti-social, inattentive, without judgment or prevision, they are capable of no useful individual effort, and still less of a common labour which demands obedience, discipline, and the regular performance of duty. They fritter away their life in solitary, unprofitable, æsthetic debauch, and all that their organs, which are in full regression, are still good for is enervating enjoyment. Like bats in old towers, they are niched in the proud monument of civilization, which they have found ready-made, but they themselves can construct nothing more, nor prevent any deterioration. They live, like parasites, on labour which past generations have accumulated for them; and when the heritage is once consumed, they are condemned to die of hunger.

But they are still more surely and rapidly lost if, instead of being alone in the world, healthy beings yet live at their side. For in that case they have to fight in the struggle for existence, and there is no leisure for them to perish in a slow decay by their own incapacity for work. The normal man, with his clear mind, logical thought, sound judgment, and strong will, sees, where the degenerate only gropes; he plans and acts where the latter dozes and dreams; he drives him without effort from all the places where the life-springs of Nature bubble up, and, in possession of all the good things of this earth, he leaves to the impotent degenerate at most the shelter of the hospital, lunatic asylum, and prison, in contemptuous pity. Let us imagine the drivelling Zoroaster of Nietzsche, with his cardboard lions, eagles, and serpents, from a toyshop, or the noctambulist Des Esseintes of the Decadents, sniffing and licking his lips, or Ibsen's 'solitary powerful' Stockmann, and his Rosmer lusting for suicide   let us imagine these beings in competition with men who rise early, and are not weary before sunset, who have clear heads, solid stomachs and hard muscles: the comparison will provoke our laughter.

[...]

Humanity has, to-day as much as ever, the tendency to reject all that it cannot digest. If future generations come to find that the march of progress is too rapid for them, they will after a time composedly give it up. They will saunter along at their own pace or stop as they choose. They will suppress the distribution of letters, allow railways to disappear, banish telephones from dwelling-houses, preserving them only, perhaps, for the service of the State, will prefer weekly papers to daily journals, will quit cities to return to the country, will slacken the changes of fashion, will simplify the occupations of the day and year, and will grant the nerves some rest again. Thus, adaptation will be effected in any case, either by the increase of nervous power or by the renunciation of acquisitions which exact too much from the nervous system.

As to the future of art and literature, with which these inquiries are chiefly concerned, that can be predicted with tolerable clearness. I resist the temptation of looking into too remote a future. Otherwise I should perhaps prove, or at least show as very probable, that in the mental life of centuries far ahead of us art and poetry will occupy but a very insignificant place. Psychology teaches us that the course of development is from instinct to knowledge, from emotion to judgment, from rambling to regulated association of ideas. Attention replaces fugitive ideation; will, guided by reason, replaces caprice. Observation, then, triumphs ever more and more over imagination and artistic symbolism – i.e., the introduction of erroneous personal interpretations of the universe is more and more driven back by an understanding of the laws of Nature. On the other hand, the march followed hitherto by civilization gives us an idea of the fate which may be reserved for art and poetry in a very distant future. That which originally was the most important occupation of men of full mental development, of the maturest, best, and wisest members of society, becomes little by little a subordinate pastime, and finally a child's amusement. Dancing was formerly an extremely important affair. It was performed on certain grand occasions, as a State function of the first order, with solemn ceremonies, after sacrifices and invocations to the gods, by the leading warriors of the tribe. To-day it is no more than a fleeting pastime for women and youths, and later on its last atavistic survival will be the dancing of children. The fable and the fairy-tale were once the highest productions of the human mind. In them the most hidden wisdom of the tribe and its most precious traditions were expressed. To-day they represent a species of literature only cultivated for the nursery. The verse which by rhythm, figurative expression, and rhyme trebly betrays its origin in the stimulations of rhythmically functioning subordinate organs, in association of ideas working according to external similitudes, and in that working according to consonance, was originally the only form of literature. To-day it is only employed for purely emotional portrayal; for all other purposes it has been conquered by prose, and, indeed, has almost passed into the condition of an atavistic language. Under our very eyes the novel is being increasingly degraded, serious and highly cultivated men scarcely deeming it worthy of attention, and it appeals more and more exclusively to the young and to women. From all these examples, it is fair to conclude that after some centuries art and poetry will have become pure atavisms, and will no longer be cultivated except by the most emotional portion of humanity – by women, by the young, perhaps even by children.

But, as I have said, I merely venture on these passing hints as to their yet remote destinies, and will confine myself to the immediate future, which is far more certain.

In all countries æsthetic theorists and critics repeat the phrase that the forms hither-to employed by art are henceforth effete and useless, and that it is preparing something perfectly new, absolutely different from all that is yet known. Richard Wagner first spoke of 'the art-work of the future,' and hundreds of incapable imitators lisp the term after him. Some among them go so far as to try to impose upon themselves and the world that some inexpressive banality, or some pretentious inanity which they have patched up, is this art-work of the future. But all these talks about sunrise, the dawn, new land, etc., are only the twaddle of degenerates incapable of thought. The idea that to-morrow morning at half-past seven o'clock a monstrous, unsuspected event will suddenly take place; that on Thursday next a complete revolution will be accomplished at a single blow, that a revelation, a redemption, the advent of a new age, is imminent – this is frequently observed among the insane; it is a mystic delirium.

[. . .]

The art and poetry of to-morrow, in all essential points, will be the art and poetry of to-day and yesterday, and the spasmodic seeking for new forms is nothing more than hysterical vanity, the freaks of strolling players and charlatanism. Its sole result has hitherto been childish declamation, with coloured lights and changing perfumes as accompaniments, and atavistic games of shadows and pantomimes, nor will it produce anything more serious in the future.

New forms! Are not the ancient forms flexible and ductile enough to lend expression to every sentiment and every thought? Has a true poet ever found any difficulty in pouring into known and standard forms that which surged within him, and demanded an issue?

[. . .]

8
WILLIAM MORRIS (1834–96)
FROM 'USEFUL WORK *VERSUS* USELESS TOIL' 1884

English designer, writer and socialist. Morris's work as a pattern designer effected a change in Victorian decorative taste and was the generating force of the English Arts and Crafts Movement. Through his political activities and visionary writings he made a profound contribution to the development of British socialism. Morris combined his thinking with a lifelong interest in the medieval and Gothic arts, and early in his career he was convinced by John Ruskin's theories on the moral and social significance of architecture. Ruskin's influence is also evident in the argument put forward by Morris in the following lecture delivered in 1884. [See Ib 7]

The above title may strike some of my readers as strange. It is assumed by most people nowadays that all work is useful, and by most *well-to-do* people that all work is desirable. Most people, well-to-do or not, believe that, even when a man is doing work which appears to be useless, he is earning his livelihood by it – he is 'employed', as the phrase goes; and most of those who are well-to-do cheer on the happy worker with congratulations and praises, if he is only 'industrious' enough and deprives himself of all pleasure and holidays in the sacred cause of labour. In short, it has become an article of the creed of modern morality that all labour is good in itself – a convenient belief to those who live on the labour of others. But as to those on whom they live, I recommend them not to take it on trust, but to look into the matter a little deeper.

Let us grant, first, that the race of man must either labour or perish. Nature does not give us our livelihood gratis; we must win it by toil of some sort or degree. Let us see, then, if she does not give us some compensation for this compulsion to labour, since certainly in other matters she takes care to make the acts necessary to the continuance of life in the individual and the race not only endurable, but even pleasurable.

You may be sure that she does so, that it is of the nature of man, when he is not diseased, to take pleasure in his work under certain conditions. And, yet, we must say in the teeth of the hypocritical praise of all labour, whatsoever it may be, of which I have made mention, that there is some labour which is so far from being a blessing that it is a curse; that it would be better for the community and for the worker if the latter were to fold his hands and refuse to work, and either die or let us pack him off to the workhouse or prison – which you will.

Here, you see, are two kinds of work – one good, the other bad; one not far removed from a blessing, a lightening of life; the other a mere curse, a burden to life.

What is the difference between them, then? This: one has hope in it, the other has not. It is manly to do the one kind of work, and manly also to refuse to do the other.

What is the nature of the hope which, when it is present in work, makes it worth doing?

It is threefold, I think – hope of rest, hope of product, hope of pleasure in the work itself; and hope of these also in some abundance and of good quality; rest enough and good enough to be worth having; product worth having by one who is neither a fool nor an ascetic; pleasure enough for all for us to be conscious of it while we are at work; not a mere habit, the loss of which we shall feel as a fidgety man feels the loss of the bit of string he fidgets with.

I have put the hope of rest first because it is the simplest and most natural part of our hope. Whatever pleasure there is in some work, there is certainly some pain in all work, the beast-like pain of stirring up our slumbering energies to action, the beast-like dread of change when things are pretty well with us; and the compensation for this animal pain is animal rest. We must feel while we are working that the time will come when we shall not have to work. Also the rest, when it comes, must be long enough to allow us to enjoy it; it must be longer than is merely necessary for us to recover the strength we have expended in working, and it must be animal rest also in this, that it must not be disturbed by anxiety, else we shall not be able to enjoy it. If we have this amount and kind of rest we shall, so far, be no worse off than the beasts.

As to the hope of product, I have said that Nature compels us to work for that. It remains for *us* to look to it that we *do* really produce something, and not nothing, or at least nothing that we want or are allowed to use. If we look to this and use our wills we shall, so far, be better than machines.

[. . .]

Thus worthy work carries with it the hope of pleasure in rest, the hope of the pleasure in our using what it makes, and the hope of pleasure in our daily creative skill.

All other work but this is worthless; it is slaves' work – mere toiling to live, that we may live to toil.

Therefore, since we have, as it were, a pair of scales in which to weigh the work now done in the world, let us use them. Let us estimate the worthiness of the work we do, after so many thousand years of toil, so many promises of hope deferred, such boundless exultation over the progress of civilization and the gain of liberty.

Now, the first thing as to the work done in civilization and the easiest to notice is that it is portioned out very unequally amongst the different classes of society. First, there are people – not a few – who do no work, and make no pretence of doing any.

Next, there are people, and very many of them, who work fairly hard, though with abundant easements and holidays, claimed and allowed; and lastly, there are people who work so hard that they may be said to do nothing else than work, and are accordingly called 'the working classes', as distinguished from the middle classes and the rich, or aristocracy, whom I have mentioned above.

It is clear that this inequality presses heavily upon the 'working' class, and must visibly tend to destroy their hope of rest at least, and so, in that particular, make them worse off than mere beasts of the field; but that is not the sum and end of our folly of turning useful work into useless toil, but only the beginning of it.

[. . .]

Civilization therefore wastes its own resources, and will do so as long as the present system lasts. These are cold words with which to describe the tyranny under which we suffer; try then to consider what they mean.

There is a certain amount of natural material and of natural forces in the world, and a certain amount of labour-power inherent in the persons of the men that inhabit it. Men urged by their necessities and desires have laboured for many thousands of years at the task of subjugating the forces of Nature and of making the natural material useful to them. To our eyes, since we cannot see into the future, that struggle with Nature seems nearly over, and the victory of the human race over her nearly complete. And, looking backwards to the time when history first began, we note that the progress of that victory has been far swifter and more startling within the last two hundred years than ever before. Surely, therefore, we moderns ought to be in all ways vastly better off than any who have gone before us. Surely we ought, one and all of us, to be wealthy, to be well furnished with the good things which our victory over Nature has won for us.

But what is the real fact? Who will dare to deny that the great mass of civilized men are poor? So poor are they that it is mere childishness troubling ourselves to discuss whether perhaps they are in some ways a little better off than their forefathers. They are poor; nor can their poverty be measured by the poverty of a resourceless savage, for he knows of nothing else than his poverty; that he should be cold, hungry, houseless, dirty, ignorant, all that is to him as natural as that he should have a skin. But for us, for the most of us, civilization has bred desires which she forbids us to satisfy, and so is not merely a niggard but a torturer also.

Thus then have the fruits of our victory over Nature been stolen from us, thus has compulsion by Nature to labour in the hope of rest, gain, and pleasure been turned into compulsion by man to labour in hope – of living to labour!

What shall we do then, can we mend it?

Well, remember once more that it is not our remote ancestors who achieved the victory over Nature, but our fathers, nay, our very selves. For us to sit hopeless and helpless then would be a strange folly indeed: be sure that we can amend it. What, then, is the first thing to be done?

[. . .]

The first step to be taken then is to abolish a class of men privileged to shirk their duties as men, thus forcing others to do the work which they refuse to do. All must work according to their ability, and so produce what they consume – that is, each man should work as well as he can for his own livelihood, and his livelihood should be assured to him; that is to say, all the advantages which society would provide for each and all of its members.

Thus, at last, would true Society be founded. It would rest on equality of condition. No man would be tormented for the benefit of another – nay, no one man would be tormented for the benefit of Society. Nor, indeed, can that order be called Society which is not upheld for the benefit of every one of its members.

But since men live now, badly as they live, when so many people do not produce at all, and when so much work is wasted, it is clear that, under conditions where all produced and no work was wasted, not only would every one work with the certain hope of gaining a due share of wealth by his work, but also he could not miss his due share of rest. Here, then, are two out of the three kinds of hope mentioned above as an essential part of worthy work assured to the worker. When class-robbery is abolished, every man will reap the fruits of his labour, every man will have due rest – leisure, that is. Some Socialists might say we need not go any further than this; it is enough that the worker should get the full produce of his work, and that his rest should be abundant. But though the compulsion of man's tyranny is thus abolished, I yet demand compensation for the compulsion of Nature's necessity. As long as the work is repulsive it will still be a burden which must be taken up daily, and even so would mar our life, even though the hours of labour were short. What we want to do is to add to our wealth without diminishing our pleasure. Nature will not be finally conquered till our work becomes a part of the pleasure of our lives.

[. . .]

We must begin to build up the ornamental part of life – its pleasures, bodily and mental, scientific and artistic, social and individual – on the basis of work undertaken willingly and cheerfully, with the consciousness of benefiting ourselves and our neighbours by it. Such absolutely necessary work as we should have to do would in the first place take up but a small part of each day, and so far would not be burdensome; but it would be a task of daily recurrence, and therefore would spoil our day's pleasure unless it were made at least endurable while it lasted. In other words, all labour, even the commonest, must be made attractive.

[. . .]

Now we have seen that the semi-theological dogma that all labour, under any circumstances, is a blessing to the labourer, is hypocritical and false; that, on the other hand, labour is good when due hope of rest and pleasure accompanies it. We have weighed the work of civilization in the balance and found it wanting, since hope is mostly lacking to it, and therefore we see that civilization has bred dire curse for men. But we have seen also that the work of the world might be carried on in hope and with pleasure if it were not wasted by folly and tyranny, by the perpetual strife of opposing classes.

It is Peace, therefore, which we need in order that we may live and work in hope and with pleasure. Peace so much desired, if we may trust men's words, but which has been so continually and steadily rejected by them in deeds. But for us, let us set our hearts on it and win it at whatever cost.

[. . .]

9
H. P. B. (HELENA PETROVA BLAVATSKY) (1831–91)
FROM *THE SECRET DOCTRINE* 1888

Russian spiritualist. In 1875 Madame Blavatsky co-founded the Theosophical Society which drew many of its tenets from her own work, including Isis Unveiled *(1877), a critique of modern science and religion that commended mysticism as the route to deeper understanding. With co-founder H. S. Olcott she edited a journal,* The Theosophist, *from 1879–88. Despite being declared a fraud by the London Society for Psychical Research in 1885, Blavatsky went on to produce several highly influential works, among them* Voice of Silence *(1889) and* The Secret Doctrine *(1888) from which the following extract is taken.*

[. . .]

The author does not feel it necessary to ask the indulgence of her readers and critics for the many defects of literary style, and the imperfect English which may be found in these pages. She is a foreigner, and her knowledge of the language was acquired late in life. The English tongue is employed because it offers the most widely-diffused medium for conveying the truths which it had become her duty to place before the world.

These truths are in no sense put forward as a *revelation*; nor does the author claim the position of a revealer of mystic lore, now made public for the first time in the world's history. For what is contained in this work is to be found scattered throughout thousands of volumes embodying the scriptures of the great Asiatic and early European religions, hidden under glyph and symbol, and hitherto left unnoticed because of this veil. What is now attempted is to gather the oldest tenets together and to make of them one harmonious and unbroken whole. The sole advantage which the writer has over her predecessors, is that she need not resort to personal speculations and theories. For this work is a partial statement of what she herself has been taught by more advanced students, supplemented, in a few details only, by the results of her own study and observation. The publication of many of the facts herein stated has been rendered necessary by the wild and fanciful speculations in which many Theosophists and students of mysticism have indulged, during the last few years, in their endeavour to, as they imagined, work out a complete system of thought from the few facts previously communicated to them.

It is needless to explain that this book is not the Secret Doctrine in its entirety, but a select number of fragments of its fundamental tenets, special attention being paid to some facts which have been seized upon by various writers, and distorted out of all resemblance to the truth.

But it is perhaps desirable to state unequivocally that the teachings, however fragmentary and incomplete, contained in these volumes, belong neither to the Hindu, the Zoroastrian, the Chaldean, nor the Egyptian religion, neither to Buddhism, Islam, Judaism nor Christianity exclusively. The Secret Doctrine is the essence of all these. Sprung from it in their origins, the various religious schemes are now made to merge back into their original element, out of which every mystery and dogma has grown, developed, and become materialised.

It is more than probable that the book will be regarded by a large section of the public as a romance of the wildest kind; for who has ever even heard of the book of Dzyan?

The writer, therefore, is fully prepared to take all the responsibility for what is contained in this work, and even to face the charge of having invented the whole of it. That it has many shortcomings she is fully aware; all that she claims for it is that, romantic as it may seem to many, its logical coherence and consistency entitle this new Genesis to rank, at any rate, on a level with the 'working hypotheses' so freely accepted by modern science. Further, it claims consideration, not by reason of any appeal to dogmatic authority, but because it closely adheres to Nature, and follows the laws of uniformity and analogy.

The aim of this work may be thus stated: to show that Nature is not 'a fortuitous concurrence of atoms,' and to assign to man his rightful place in the scheme of the Universe; to rescue from degradation the archaic truths which are the basis of all religions; and to uncover, to some extent, the fundamental unity from which they all spring; finally, to show that the occult side of Nature has never been approached by the Science of modern civilization.

If this is in any degree accomplished, the writer is content. It is written in the service of humanity, and by humanity and the future generations it must be judged. Its author recognises no inferior court of appeal. Abuse she is accustomed to; calumny she is daily acquainted with; at slander she smiles in silent contempt.

[. . .]

But all is doubt, negation, iconoclasm and brutal indifference, in our age of the hundred 'isms' and no religion. Every idol is broken save the Golden Calf.

Unfortunately, no nation or nations can escape their Karmic fate any more than units and individuals do. History itself is dealt with by the so-called historians as unscrupulously as legendary lore.

[. . .]

While Materialists deny everything in the universe, save matter, Archæologists are trying to dwarf antiquity, and seek to destroy every claim to ancient Wisdom by tampering with Chronology. Our present-day Orientalists and Historical writers are to ancient History that which the white ants are to the buildings in India. More dangerous even than those Termites, the modern Archæologists – the 'authorities' of the future in the matter of Universal History – are preparing for the History of past nations the fate of certain edifices in tropical countries: 'History will tumble down and break into atoms in the lap of the twentieth century, devoured to its foundations by her annalists,' said Michelet. Very soon, indeed, under their combined efforts, it will share the fate of those ruined cities in both Americas, which lie deeply buried under impassable virgin forests. Historical facts will remain as concealed from view by the inextricable jungles of modern hypotheses, denials and scepticism. But very happily *actual* History repeats herself, for she proceeds, like everything else, in cycles; and dead facts and events deliberately drowned in the sea of modern scepticism will ascend once more and reappear on the surface.

10
JAMES GEORGE FRAZER (1854–1941)
FROM *THE GOLDEN BOUGH* 1890–1915

British anthropologist and classical scholar. Frazer's The Golden Bough: A Study in Magic and Religion *(published in twelve volumes, 1890–1915) is an encyclopedic account of primitive myth and ritual that posits a line of development in modes of thought from magic, through organised religion, to modern-day science. The influence of Frazer's work is famously acknowledged in T. S. Eliot's Notes to* The Waste Land. *The following extracts are from Chapters 3 ('Sympathetic Magic') and 69 ('Farewell to Nemi').*

The Principles of Magic. — If we analyse the principles of thought on which magic is based, they will probably be found to resolve themselves into two; first, that like produces like, or that an effect resembles its cause; and, second, that things which have once been in contact with each other continue to act on each other at a distance after the physical contact has been severed. The former principle may be called the Law of Similarity, the latter the Law of Contact or Contagion. From the first of these principles, namely the Law of Similarity, the magician infers that he can produce any effect he desires merely by imitating it: from the second he infers that whatever he does to a material object will affect equally the person with whom the object was once in contact, whether it formed part of his body or not. Charms based on the Law of Similarity may be called Homoeopathic or Imitative Magic. Charms based on the Law of Contact or Contagion may be called Contagious Magic. To denote the first of these branches of magic the term Homoeopathic is perhaps preferable, for the alternative term Imitative or Mimetic suggests, if it does not imply, a conscious agent who imitates, thereby limiting the scope of magic too narrowly. For the same principles which the magician applies in the practice of his art are implicitly believed by him to regulate the operations of inanimate nature; in other words, he tacitly assumes that the Laws of Similarity and Contact are of universal application and are not limited to human actions. In short, magic is a spurious system of natural law as well as a fallacious guide of conduct; it is a false science as well as an abortive art. Regarded as a system of natural law, that is, as a statement of the rules which determine the sequence of events throughout the world, it may be called Theoretical Magic: regarded as a set of precepts which human beings observe in order to compass their ends, it may be called Practical Magic. At the same time it is to be borne in mind that the primitive magician knows magic only on its practical side; he never analyses the mental processes on which his practice is based, never reflects on the abstract principles involved in his actions. With him, as with the vast majority of men, logic is implicit, not explicit: he reasons just as he digests his food in complete ignorance of the intellectual and physiological processes which are essential to the one operation and to the other. In short, to him magic is always an art, never a science; the very idea of science is lacking in his undeveloped mind. It is for the philosophic student to trace the train of thought which underlies the magician's practice; to draw out the few simple threads of which the tangled skein is composed; to disengage the abstract principles from their concrete applications; in short, to discern the spurious science behind the bastard art.

If my analysis of the magician's logic is correct, its two great principles turn out to be merely two different misapplications of the association of ideas. Homoeopathic magic is founded on the association of ideas by similarity: contagious magic is founded on the association of ideas by contiguity. Homoeopathic magic commits the mistake of assuming that things which resemble each other are the same: contagious magic commits the mistake of assuming that things which have once been in contact with each other are always in contact. But in practice the two branches are often combined; or, to be more exact, while homoeopathic or imitative magic may be practised by itself, contagious magic will generally be found to involve an application of the homoeopathic or imitative principle. Thus generally stated the two things may be a little difficult to grasp, but they will readily become intelligible when they are illustrated by particular examples. Both trains of thought are in fact extremely simple and elementary. It could hardly be otherwise, since they are familiar in the concrete, though certainly not in the abstract, to the crude intelligence not only of the savage, but of ignorant and dull-witted people everywhere. Both branches of magic, the homoeopathic and the contagious, may conveniently be comprehended under the general name of Sympathetic Magic, since both assume that things act on each other at a distance through a secret sympathy, the impulse being transmitted from one to the other by means of what we may conceive as a kind of invisible ether, not unlike that which is postulated by modern science for a precisely similar purpose, namely, to explain how things can physically affect each other through a space which appears to be empty.

[. . .]

We are at the end of our enquiry, but as often happens in the search after truth, if we have answered one question, we have raised many more; if we have followed one track home, we have had to pass by others that opened off it and led, or seemed to lead, to far other goals than the sacred grove at Nemi. Some of these paths we have followed a little way; others, if fortune should be kind, the writer and the reader may one day pursue together. For the present we have journeyed far enough together, and it is time to part. Yet before we do so, we may well ask ourselves whether there is not some more general conclusion, some lesson, if possible, of hope and encouragement, to be drawn from the melancholy record of human error and folly which has engaged our attention in this book.

If then we consider, on the one hand, the essential similarity of man's chief wants everywhere and at all times, and on the other hand, the wide difference between the means he has adopted to satisfy them in different ages, we shall perhaps be disposed to conclude that the movement of the higher thought, so far as we can trace it, has on the whole been from magic through religion to science. In magic man depends on his own strength to meet the difficulties and dangers that beset him on every side. He believes in a certain established order of nature on which he can surely count, and which he can manipulate for his own ends. When he discovers his mistake, when he recognises sadly that both the order of nature which he had assumed and the control which he had believed himself to exercise over it were purely imaginary, he ceases to rely on his own intelligence and his own unaided efforts, and throws himself humbly on the mercy of certain great invisible beings behind the veil of nature, to whom he now ascribes all those far-reaching powers which he once arrogated to himself. Thus in the acuter minds magic is gradually superseded by religion, which explains the succession of natural phenomena as regulated by the will, the passion, or the caprice of spiritual beings like man in kind, though vastly superior to him in power.

But as time goes on this explanation in its turn proves to be unsatisfactory. For it assumes that the succession of natural events is not determined by immutable laws, but is to some extent variable and irregular, and this assumption is not borne out by closer observation. On the contrary, the more we scrutinise that succession the more we are struck by the rigid uniformity, the punctual precision with which, wherever we can follow them, the operations of nature are carried on. Every great advance in knowledge has extended the sphere of order and correspondingly restricted the sphere of apparent disorder in the world, till now we are ready to anticipate that even in regions where chance and confusion appear still to reign, a fuller knowledge would everywhere reduce the seeming chaos to cosmos. Thus the keener minds, still pressing forward to a deeper solution of the mysteries of the universe, come to reject the religious theory of nature as inadequate and to revert in a measure to the older standpoint of magic by postulating explicitly, what in magic had only been implicitly assumed, to wit, an inflexible regularity in the order of natural events, which, if carefully observed, enables us to foresee their course with certainty and to act accordingly. In short, religion, regarded as an explanation of nature, is displaced by science.

But while science has this much in common with magic that both rest on a faith in order as the underlying principle of all things, readers of this work will hardly need to be reminded that the order presupposed by magic differs widely from that which forms the basis of science. The difference flows naturally from the different modes in which the two orders have been reached. For whereas the order on which magic reckons is merely an extension, by false analogy, of the order in which ideas present themselves to our minds, the order laid down by science is derived from patient and exact observation of the phenomena themselves. The abundance, the solidity, and the splendour of the results already achieved by science are well fitted to inspire us with a cheerful confidence in the soundness of its method. Here at last, after groping about in the dark for countless ages, man has hit upon a clue to the labyrinth, a golden key that opens many locks in the treasury of nature. It is probably not too much to say that the hope of progress – moral and intellectual as well as material – in the future is bound up with the fortunes of science, and that every obstacle placed in the way of scientific discovery is a wrong to humanity.

Yet the history of thought should warn us against concluding that because the scientific theory of the world is the best that has yet been formulated, it is necessarily complete and final. We must remember that at bottom the generalisations of science or, in common parlance, the laws of nature are merely hypotheses devised to explain that ever-shifting phantasmagoria of thought which we dignify with the high-sounding names of the world and the universe. In the last analysis magic, religion, and science are nothing but theories of thought; and as science has supplanted its predecessors, so it may hereafter be itself superseded by some more perfect hypothesis, perhaps by some totally different way of looking at the phenomena – of registering the shadows on the screen – of which we in this generation can form no idea. The advance of knowledge is an infinite progression towards a goal that for ever recedes.

[. . .]

11
GUSTAVE LE BON (1841–1931)
FROM *THE CROWD: A STUDY OF THE POPULAR MIND* 1895

French psychologist and sociologist. Initially interested in archaeology and anthropology, Le Bon turned his attention to social psychology in the 1890s. His Les lois psychologiques de l'évolution des peuples (Psychology of Peoples) *was published in 1894 and expressed a provocative view of social evolution as a development along lines of racial and national character. The following extracts are from Le Bon's most influential work,* La psychologie des foules, *translated in 1895 as* The Crowd: A Study of the Popular Mind, *which is an analysis of 'the rise of the masses' as a phenomenon characteristic of the modern age.*

[. . .]

The great upheavals which precede changes of civilisation, such as the fall of the Roman Empire and the foundation of the Arabian Empire, seem at first sight determined more especially by political transformations, foreign invasion, or the overthrow of dynasties. But a more attentive study of these events shows that behind their apparent causes the real cause is generally seen to be a profound modification in the ideas of the peoples. The true historical upheavals are not those which astonish us by their grandeur and violence. The only important changes whence the renewal of civilisations results, affect ideas, conceptions, and beliefs. The memorable events of history are the visible effects of the invisible changes of human thought. The reason these great events are so rare is that there is nothing so stable in a race as the inherited groundwork of its thoughts.

The present epoch is one of these critical moments in which the thought of mankind is undergoing a process of transformation.

Two fundamental factors are at the base of this transformation. The first is the destruction of those religious, political, and social beliefs in which all the elements of our civilisation are rooted. The second is the creation of entirely new conditions of existence and thought as the result of modern scientific and industrial discoveries.

The ideas of the past, although half destroyed, being still very powerful, and the ideas which are to replace them being still in process of formation, the modern age represents a period of transition and anarchy.

[. . .]

The entry of the popular classes into political life – that is to say, in reality, their progressive transformation into governing classes – is one of the most striking characteristics of our epoch of transition. The introduction of universal suffrage, which exercised for a long time but little influence, is not, as might be thought, the distinguishing feature of this transference of political power. The progressive growth of the power of the masses took place at first by the propagation of certain ideas, which have slowly implanted themselves in men's minds, and afterwards by the gradual association of individuals bent on bringing about the realisation of theoretical conceptions. It is by association that crowds have come to procure ideas with respect to their interests which are very clearly defined if not particularly just, and have arrived at a consciousness of their strength. The masses are founding syndicates before which the authorities capitulate one after the other; they are also founding labour unions, which in spite of all economic laws tend to regulate the conditions of labour and wages. They return to assemblies in which the Government is vested, representatives utterly lacking initiative and independence, and reduced most often to nothing else than the spokesmen of the committees that have chosen them.

To-day the claims of the masses are becoming more and more sharply defined, and amount to nothing less than a determination to utterly destroy society as it now exists, with a view to making it hark back to that primitive communism which was the normal condition of all human groups before the dawn of civilisation.

[. . .]

Little adapted to reasoning, crowds, on the contrary, are quick to act. As the result of their present organisation their strength has become immense. The dogmas whose birth we are witnessing will soon have the force of the old dogmas; that is to say, the tyrannical and sovereign force of being above discussion. The divine right of the masses is about to replace the divine right of kings.

The writers who enjoy the favour of our middle classes, those who best represent their rather narrow ideas, their somewhat prescribed views, their rather superficial scepticism, and their at times somewhat excessive egoism, display profound alarm at this new power which they see growing; and to combat the disorder in men's minds they are addressing despairing appeals to those moral forces of the Church for which they formerly professed so much disdain. They talk to us of the bankruptcy of science, go back in penitence to Rome, and remind us of the teachings of revealed truth. These new converts forget that it is too late. Had they been really touched by grace, a like operation could not have the same influence on minds less concerned with the preoccupations which beset these recent adherents to religion. The masses repudiate to-day the gods which their admonishers repudiated yesterday and helped to destroy. There is no power, Divine or human, that can oblige a stream to flow back to its source.

[. . .]

Up to now these thoroughgoing destructions of a worn-out civilisation have constituted the most obvious task of the masses. It is not indeed to-day merely that this can
be traced. History tells us, that from the moment when the moral forces on which a
civilisation rested have lost their strength, its final dissolution is brought about by those
unconscious and brutal crowds known, justifiably enough, as barbarians. Civilisations
as yet have only been created and directed by a small intellectual aristocracy, never by
crowds. Crowds are only powerful for destruction. Their rule is always tantamount
to a barbarian phase. A civilisation involves fixed rules, discipline, a passing from
the instinctive to the rational state, forethought for the future, an elevated degree of
culture – all of them conditions that crowds, left to themselves, have invariably shown
themselves incapable of realising. In consequence of the purely destructive nature of
their power, crowds act like those microbes which hasten the dissolution of enfeebled
or dead bodies. When the structure of a civilisation is rotten, it is always the masses
that bring about its downfall. It is at such a juncture that their chief mission is plainly
visible, and that for a while the philosophy of number seems the only philosophy
of history.

Is the same fate in store for our civilisation? There is ground to fear that this is the
case, but we are not as yet in a position to be certain of it.

[. . .]

It is only by obtaining some sort of insight into the psychology of crowds that it
can be understood how slight is the action upon them of laws and institutions, how
powerless they are to hold any opinions other than those which are imposed upon
them, and that it is not with rules based on theories of pure equity that they are to be
led, but by seeking what produces an impression on them, and what seduces them.

[. . .]

12
THORSTEIN VEBLEN (1857–1927)
FROM *THE THEORY OF THE LEISURE CLASS* 1899

*American economist and social critic, founder of institutional economics. Veblen was one of the first
commentators on emergent corporate systems of capitalism, and was responsible for introducing to the
language such terms as 'conspicuous consumption' and 'status emulation'. An intellectual ally of the
philosopher John Dewey, he held a number of posts, and was editor of* The Dial *(1918–19). His best
known works are* The Theory of the Leisure Class: An Economic Study of Institutions
(1899) and The Higher Learning in America: A Memorandum on the Conduct of
Universities by Business Men *(1918).*

In what has been said of the evolution of the vicarious leisure class and its differentiation from the general body of the working classes, reference has been made to a further
division of labor – that between different servant classes. One portion of the servant
class, chiefly those persons whose occupation is vicarious leisure, come to undertake
a new, subsidiary range of duties – the vicarious consumption of goods. The most
obvious form in which this consumption occurs is seen in the wearing of liveries and

the occupation of spacious servants' quarters. Another, scarcely less obtrusive or less effective form of vicarious consumption, and a much more widely prevalent one, is the consumption of food, clothing, dwelling, and furniture by the lady and the rest of the domestic establishment.

[. . .]

The consumption of luxuries, in the true sense, is a consumption directed to the comfort of the consumer himself, and is, therefore, a mark of the master. Any such consumption by others can take place only on a basis of sufferance. In communities where the popular habits of thought have been profoundly shaped by the patriarchal tradition we may accordingly look for survivals of the tabu on luxuries at least to the extent of a conventional deprecation of their use by the unfree and dependent class. This is more particularly true as regards certain luxuries, the use of which by the dependent class would detract sensibly from the comfort or pleasure of their masters, or which are held to be of doubtful legitimacy on other grounds. In the apprehension of the great conservative middle class of Western civilization the use of these various stimulants is obnoxious to at least one, if not both, of these objections; and it is a fact too significant to be passed over that it is precisely among these middle classes of the Germanic culture, with their strong surviving sense of the patriarchal proprieties, that the women are to the greatest extent subject to a qualified tabu on narcotics and alcoholic beverages. With many qualifications – with more qualifications as the patriarchal tradition has gradually weakened – the general rule is felt to be right and binding that women should consume only for the benefit of their masters.

[. . .]

With the disappearance of servitude, the number of vicarious consumers attached to any one gentleman tends, on the whole, to decrease. The like is of course true, and perhaps in a still higher degree, of the number of dependents who perform vicarious leisure for him. In a general way, though not wholly nor consistently, these two groups coincide. The dependent who was first delegated for these duties was the wife, or the chief wife; and, as would be expected, in the later development of the institution, when the number of persons by whom these duties are customarily performed gradually narrows, the wife remains the last. In the higher grades of society a large volume of both these kinds of service is required; and here the wife is of course still assisted in the work by a more or less numerous corps of menials. But as we descend the social scale, the point is presently reached where the duties of vicarious leisure and consumption devolve upon the wife alone. In the communities of the Western culture, this point is at present found among the lower middle class.

And here occurs a curious inversion. It is a fact of common observance that in this lower middle class there is no pretense of leisure on the part of the head of the household. Through force of circumstances it has fallen into disuse. But the middle-class wife still carries on the business of vicarious leisure, for the good name of the household and its master. In descending the social scale in any modern industrial community, the primary fact – the conspicuous leisure of the master of the household – disappears at a relatively high point. The head of the middle-class household has been reduced by economic circumstances to turn his hand to gaining a livelihood by occupations which often partake largely of the character of industry, as in the case of the ordinary business man of today. But the derivative fact – the vicarious leisure and consumption rendered by the wife, and the auxiliary vicarious performance of leisure by menials – remains in vogue as a conventionality which the demands of reputability will not suffer to be slighted. It is by no means an uncommon spectacle to find a man applying himself to work with the utmost assiduity, in order that his wife may in due form render for him that degree of vicarious leisure which the common sense of the time demands.

[. . .]

The requirement of vicarious consumption at the hands of the wife continues in force even at a lower point in the pecuniary scale than the requirement of vicarious leisure. At a point below which little if any pretense of wasted effort, in ceremonial cleanness and the like, is observable, and where there is assuredly no conscious attempt at ostensible leisure, decency still requires the wife to consume some goods conspicuously for the reputability of the household and its head. So that, as the latter-day outcome of this evolution of an archaic institution, the wife, who was at the outset the drudge and chattel of the man, both in fact and in theory – the producer of goods for him to consume – has become the ceremonial consumer of goods which he produces. But she still quite unmistakably remains his chattel in theory; for the habitual rendering of vicarious leisure and consumption is the abiding mark of the unfree servant.

[. . .]

This latter-day uneasy reaching-out for some form of purposeful activity that shall at the same time not be indecorously productive of either individual or collective gain marks a difference of attitude between the modern leisure class and that of the quasi-peaceable stage.

[. . .]

In the narrower sphere of vicarious leisure a similar change has gone forward. Instead of simply passing her time in visible idleness, as in the best days of the patriarchal regime, the housewife of the advanced peaceable stage applies herself assiduously to household cares. The salient features of this development of domestic service have already been indicated.

Throughout the entire evolution of conspicuous expenditure, whether of goods or of services or human life, runs the obvious implication that in order to effectually mend the consumer's good fame it must be an expenditure of superfluities. In order to be reputable it must be wasteful. No merit would accrue from the consumption of the bare necessaries of life, except by comparison with the abjectly poor who fall short even of the subsistence minimum; and no standard of expenditure could result from such a comparison, except the most prosaic and unattractive level of decency. A standard of life would still be possible which should admit of invidious comparison in other respects than that of opulence; as, for instance, a comparison in various directions in the manifestation of moral, physical, intellectual, or æsthetic force. Comparison in all these directions is in vogue today; and the comparison made in these respects is commonly so inextricably bound up with the pecuniary comparison as to be scarcely distinguishable from the latter. This is especially true as regards the current rating of expressions of intellectual and æsthetic force or proficiency; so that we frequently interpret as æsthetic or intellectual a difference which in substance is pecuniary only.

[. . .]

13
HENRY ADAMS (1838–1918)
FROM *THE EDUCATION OF HENRY ADAMS* 1907

American historian and author. It was while visiting the Paris Exhibition of 1910 that Adams saw the huge dynamo that was to become for him the symbol of twentieth-century mechanisation and multiplicity. In contrast to this he placed his vision of the medieval world as the high point of cultural and ideological unity, symbolised by the Virgin, 'the ideal of human perfection'. Adams first expressed this idea in a scholarly historical work, Mont-Saint-Michel and Chartres *(1904), expanding it later in his autobiography,* The Education of Henry Adams *(1907). The following extract is from Chapter 25, 'The Dynamo and the Virgin', of that work, written in 1900.*

Until the Great Exposition of 1900 closed its doors in November, Adams haunted it, aching to absorb knowledge, and helpless to find it. He would have liked to know how much of it could have been grasped by the best-informed man in the world. While he was thus meditating chaos Langley came by, and showed it to him. At Langley's behest, the Exhibition dropped its superfluous rags and stripped itself to the skin, for Langley knew what to study, and why, and how; while Adams might as well have stood outside in the night, staring at the Milky Way. Yet Langley said nothing new, and taught nothing that one might not have learned from Lord Bacon, three hundred years before; but though one should have known the 'Advancement of Science' as well as one knew the 'Comedy of Errors,' the literary knowledge counted for nothing until some teacher should show how to apply it. Bacon took a vast deal of trouble in teaching King James I and his subjects, American or other, towards the year 1620, that true science was the development or economy of forces; yet an elderly American in 1900 knew neither the formula nor the forces; or even so much as to say to himself that his historical business in the Exposition concerned only the economics or developments of force since 1893, when he began to study at Chicago.

Nothing in education is so astonishing as the amount of ignorance it accumulates in the form of inert facts. Adams had looked at most of the accumulates in the form of inert facts. Adams had looked at most of the accumulations of art in the storehouses called Art Museums; yet he did not know how to look at the art exhibits of 1900. He had studied Karl Marx and his doctrines of history with profound attention, yet he could not apply them at Paris. Langley, with the ease of a great master of experiment, threw out of the field every exhibit that did not reveal a new application of force, and naturally threw out, to begin with, almost the whole art exhibit. Equally, he ignored almost the whole industrial exhibit. He led his pupil directly to the forces. His chief interest was in new motors to make his airship feasible, and he taught Adams the astonishing complexities of the new Daimler motor, and of the automobile, which, since 1893, had become a nightmare at a hundred kilometers an hour, almost as destructive as the electric tram which was only ten years older, and threatening to become as terrible as the locomotive steam-engine itself, which was almost exactly Adams's own age.

Then he showed his scholar the great hall of dynamos; and explained how little he knew about electricity or force of any kind, even of his own special sun, which spouted heat in inconceivable volume, but which, as far as he knew, might spout less or more, at any time, for all the certainty he felt in it. To him, the dynamo itself was but an ingenious channel for conveying somewhere the heat latent in a few tons of poor coal hidden in a dirty engine-house carefully kept out of sight; but to Adams the dynamo became a symbol of infinity. As he grew accustomed to the great gallery of machines, he began to feel the forty-foot dynamos as a moral force, much as the early Christians felt the Cross. The planet itself seemed less impressive, in its old-fashioned, deliberate, annual or daily revolution, than this huge wheel, revolving within arm's-length at some vertiginous speed, and barely murmuring – scarcely humming an audible warning to stand a hair's-breadth further for respect of power – while it would not wake the baby lying close against its frame. Before the end, one began to pray to it; inherited instinct taught the national expression of man before silent and infinite force. Among the thousand symbols of ultimate energy, the dynamo was not so human as some, but it was the most expressive.

Yet the dynamo, next to the steam-engine, was the most familiar of exhibits. For Adams's object its value lay chiefly in its occult mechanism. Between the dynamo in the gallery of machines and the engine-house outside, the break of continuity amounted to abysmal fracture for a historian's objects. No more relation could he discover between the steam and the electric current than between the Cross and the cathedral. The forces were interchangeable if not reversible, but he could see only an absolute *fiat* in electricity as in faith. Langley could not help him. Indeed, Langley seemed to be worried by the same trouble, for he constantly repeated that the new forces were anarchical, and especially that he was not responsible for the new rays, that were little short of parricidal in their wicked spirit towards science. His own rays, with which he had doubled the solar spectrum, were altogether harmless and beneficent; but Radium denied its God – or, what was to Langley the same thing, denied the truths of his Science. The force was wholly new.

A historian who asked only to learn enough to be as futile as Langley or Kelvin, made rapid progress under this teaching, and mixed himself up in the tangle of ideas until he achieved a sort of Paradise of ignorance vastly consoling to his fatigued senses. He wrapped himself in vibrations and rays which were new, and he would have hugged Marconi and Branly had he met them, as he hugged the dynamo; while he lost his arithmetic in trying to figure out the equation between the discoveries and the economies of force. The economies, like the discoveries, were absolute, supersensual, occult; incapable of expression in horse-power. What mathematical equivalent could he suggest as the value of a Branly coherer? Frozen air, or the electric furnace, had some scale of measurement, no doubt, if somebody could invent a thermometer adequate to the purpose; but X-rays had played no part whatever in man's consciousness, and the atom itself had figured only as a fiction of thought. In these seven years man had translated himself into a new universe which had no common scale of measurement with the old. He had entered a supersensual world, in which he could measure nothing except by chance collisions of movements imperceptible to each other, and so to some known ray at the end of the scale. Langley seemed prepared for anything, even for an indeterminable number of universes interfused – physics stark mad in metaphysics.

Historians undertake to arrange sequences, – called stories, or histories – assuming in silence a relation of cause and effect. These assumptions, hidden in the depths of dusty libraries, have been astounding, but commonly unconscious and childlike; so much so, that if any captious critic were to drag them to light, historians would probably reply, with one voice, that they had never supposed themselves required to know what they were talking about. Adams, for one, had toiled in vain to find out what he meant. He had even published a dozen volumes of American history for no other purpose than to satisfy himself whether, by the severest process of stating, with the least possible comment, such facts as seemed sure, in such order as seemed rigorously consequent, he could fix for a familiar moment a necessary sequence of human movement. The result had satisfied him as little as at Harvard College. Where he saw sequence, other men saw something quite different, and no one saw the same unit of measure. He cared little about his experiments and less about his statesmen, who seemed to him quite as ignorant as himself and, as a rule, no more honest; but he insisted on a relation of sequence, and if he could not reach it by one method, he would try as many methods as science knew. Satisfied that the sequence of men led to nothing and that the sequence of their society could lead no further, while the mere sequence of time was artificial, and the sequence of thought was chaos, he turned at last to the sequence of force; and thus it happened that, after ten years' pursuit, he found himself lying in the Gallery of Machines at the Great Exposition of 1900, with his historical neck broken by the sudden irruption of forces totally new.

Since no one else showed much concern, an elderly person without other cares had no need to betray alarm. The year 1900 was not the first to upset schoolmasters Copernicus and Galileo had broken many professorial necks about 1600; Columbus had stood the world on its head towards 1500; but the nearest approach to the revolution of 1900 was that of 310, when Constantine set up the Cross. The rays that Langley disowned, as well as those which he fathered, were occult, supersensual, irrational; they were a revelation of mysterious energy like that of the Cross; they were what, in terms of mediaeval science, were called immediate modes of the devine substance.

The historian was thus reduced to his last resources. Clearly if he was bound to reduce all these forces to a common value, this common value could have no measure but that of their attraction on his own mind. He must treat them as they had been felt; as convertible, reversible, interchangeable attractions on thought. He made up his mind to venture it; he would risk translating rays into faith. Such a reversible process would vastly amuse a chemist, but the chemist could not deny that he, or some of his fellow physicists, could feel the force of both. When Adams was a boy in Boston, the best chemist in the place had probably never heard of Venus except by way of scandal, or of the Virgin except as idolatry; neither had he heard of dynamos or automobiles or radium; yet his mind was ready to feel the force of all, though the rays were unborn and the women were dead.

Here opened another totally new education, which promised to be by far the most hazardous of all. The knife-edge along which he must crawl, like Sir Lancelot in the twelfth century, divided two kingdoms of force which had nothing in common but attraction. They were as different as a magnet is from gravitation, supposing one knew what a magnet was, or gravitation, or love. The force of the Virgin was still felt at Lourdes, and seemed to be as potent as X-rays; but in America neither Venus nor Virgin ever had value as force – at most as sentiment. No American had ever been truly afraid of either.

This problem in dynamics gravely perplexed an American historian. The Woman had once been supreme; in France she still seemed potent, not merely as a sentiment, but as a force. Why was she unknown in America? For evidently America was ashamed of her, and she was ashamed of herself, otherwise they would not have strewn fig-leaves so profusely all over her. When she was a true force, she was ignorant of fig-leaves, but the monthly-magazine-made American female had not a feature that would have been recognized by Adam. The trait was notorious, and often humorous, but anyone brought up among Puritans knew that sex was sin. In any previous age, sex was strength. Neither art nor beauty was needed. Everyone, even among Puritans, knew that neither Diana of the Ephesians nor any of the Oriental goddesses was worshipped for her beauty. She was goddess because of her force; she was the animated dynamo; she was reproduction – the greatest and most mysterious of all energies; all she needed was to be fecund.

[. . .]

All this was to American thought as though it had never existed. The true American knew something of the facts, but nothing of the feelings; he read the letter, but he never felt the law. Before this historical chasm, a mind like that of Adams felt itself helpless; he turned from the Virgin to the Dynamo as though he were a Branly coherer. On one side, at the Louvre and at Chartres, as he knew by the record of work actually done and still before his eyes, was the highest energy ever known to man, the creator of four-fifths of his noblest art, exercising vastly more attraction over the human mind than all the steam-engines and dynamos ever dreamed of; and yet this energy was unknown to the American mind. An American Virgin would never dare command; an American Venus would never dare exist.

The question, which to any plain American of the nineteenth century seemed as remote as it did to Adams, drew him almost violently to study, once it was posed; and on this point Langleys were as useless as though they were Herbert Spencers or dynamos. The idea survived only as art. There one turned as naturally as though the artist were himself a woman. Adams began to ponder, asking himself whether he knew of any American artist who had ever insisted on the power of sex, as every classic had always done; but he could think only of Walt Whitman; Bret Harte, as far as the magazines would let him venture; and one or two painters for the flesh-tones. All the rest had used sex for sentiment, never for force; to them, Eve was a tender flower, and Herodias an unfeminine horror. American art, like the American language and American education, was as far as possible sexless. Society regarded this victory over sex as its greatest triumph, and the historian readily admitted it, since the moral issue, for the moment, did not concern one who was studying the relations of unmoral force. He cared nothing for the sex of the dynamo until he could measure its energy.

Vaguely seeking a clue, he wandered through the art exhibit, and, in his stroll, stopped almost every day before St. Gaudens's General Sherman, which had been given the central post of honor. St. Gaudens himself was in Paris, putting on the work his usual interminable last touches, and listening to the usual contradictory suggestions of brother sculptors. Of all the American artists who gave to American art whatever life it breathed in the seventies, St. Gaudens was perhaps the most sympathetic, but certainly the most inarticulate. General Grant or Don Cameron had scarcely less instinct of rhetoric than he. All the others – the Hunts, Richardson, John La Farge, Standford White – were exuberant; only St. Gaudens could never discuss or dilate on an emotion, or suggest artistic arguments for giving to his work the forms that he felt. He never laid down the law, or affected the despot, or became brutalized like Whistler by the brutalities of his world. He required no incense; he was no egoist; his simplicity of thought was excessive; he could not imitate, or give any form but his own to the creations of his hand. No one felt more strongly than he the strength of other men, but the idea that they could affect him never stirred an image in his mind.

This summer his health was poor and his spirits were low. For such a temper, Adams was not the best companion, since his own gaiety was not *folle*; but he risked going now and then to the studio on Mont Parnasse to draw him out for a stroll in the Bois de Boulogne, or dinner as pleased his moods, and in return St. Gaudens sometimes let Adams go about in his company.

Once St. Gaudens took him down to Amiens, with a party of Frenchmen, to see the cathedral. Not until they found themselves actually studying the sculpture of the western portal, did it dawn on Adams's mind that, for his purposes, St. Gaudens on the spot had more interest to him than the cathedral itself. Great men before great monuments express great truths, provided they are not taken too solemnly. Adams never tired of quoting the supreme phrase of his idol Gibbon, before the Gothic cathedrals: 'I darted a contemptuous look on the stately monuments of superstition.' Even in the footnotes of his history, Gibbon had never inserted a bit of humor more human than this, and one would have paid largely for a photograph of the fat little historian, on the background of Notre Dame of Amiens, trying to persuade his readers – perhaps himself – that he was darting a contemptuous look on the stately monument, for which he felt in fact the respect which every man of his vast study and active mind always feels before objects worthy of it; but besides the humor, one felt also the relation. Gibbon ignored the Virgin, because in 1789 religious monuments were out of fashion. In 1900 his remark sounded fresh and simple as the green fields to ears that had heard a hundred years of other remarks, mostly no more fresh and certainly less simple. Without malice, one might find it more instructive than a whole lecture of Ruskin. One sees what one brings, and at that moment Gibbon brought the French Revolution. Ruskin brought reaction against the Revolution. St. Gaudens had passed beyond all. He liked the Stately monuments much more than he liked Gibbon or Ruskin; he loved their dignity; their unity; their scale; their lines; their lights and shadows; their decorative sculpture; but he was even less conscious than they of the force that created it all – the Virgin, the Woman – by whose genius 'the stately monuments of superstition' were built, through which she was expressed. He would have seen more meaning in Isis with the cow's horns, at Edfoo, who expressed the same thought. The art remained, but the energy was lost even upon the artist.

Yet in mind and person St. Gaudens was a survival of the 1500's; he bore the stamp of the Renaissance, and should have carried an image of the Virgin round his neck, or stuck in his hat, like Louis XI. In mere time he was a lost soul that had strayed by chance into the twentieth century, and forgotten where it came from. He writhed and cursed at his ignorance, much as Adams did at his own, but in the opposite sense. St. Gaudens was a child of Benvenuto Cellini, smothered in an American cradle. Adams was a quintessence of Boston, devoured by curiosity to think like Benvenuto. St. Gauden's art was starved from birth, and Adams's instinct was blighted from babyhood. Each had but half of a nature, and when they came together before the Virgin of Amiens they ought both to have felt in her the force that made them one; but it was not so. To Adams she became more than ever a channel of force; to St. Gaudens she remained as before a channel of taste.

For a symbol of power St. Gaudens instinctively preferred the horse, as was plain in his horse and Victory of the Sherman monument. Doubtless Sherman also felt it so. The attitude was so American that, for at least forty years, Adams had never realized that any other could be in sound taste. How many years had he taken to admit a notion of what Michael Angelo and Rubens were driving at? He could not say; but he knew that only since 1895 had he begun to feel the Virgin or Venus as force, and not everywhere even so. At Chartres – perhaps at Lourdes – possibly at Cnidos if one could still find there the divinely naked Aphrodite of Praxiteles – but otherwise one must look for force to the goddesses of Indian mythology. The idea died out long ago in the German and English stock. St. Gaudens at Amiens was hardly less sensitive to the force of the female energy than Matthew Arnold at the Grande Chartreuse. Neither of them felt goddesses as power – only as reflected emotion, human expression, beauty, purity, taste, scarcely even as sympathy. They felt a railway train as power; yet they, and all other artists, constantly complained that the power embodied in a railway train could never be embodied in art. All the steam in the world could not, like the Virgin, build Chartres.

Yet in mechanics, whatever the mechanicians might think, both energies acted as interchangeable forces on man, and by action on man all known force may be measured. Indeed, few men of science measured force in any other way. After once admitting that a straight line was the shortest distance between two points, no serious mathematician cared to deny anything that suited his convenience, and rejected no symbol, unproved or unproveable, that helped him to accomplish work. The symbol was force, as a compass-needle or a triangle was force, as the mechanist might prove by losing it, and nothing could be gained by ignoring their value. Symbol or energy, the Virgin had acted as the greatest force the Western world ever felt, and had drawn man's activities to herself more strongly than any other power, natural or super-natural, had ever done; the historian's business was to follow the track of the energy; to find where it came from and where it went to; its complex source and shifting channels; its values, equivalents, conversions. It could scarcely be more complex than radium; it could hardly be deflected, diverted, polarized, absorbed more perplexingly than other radiant matter. Adams knew nothing about any of them, but as a mathematical problem of influence on human progress, though all were occult, all reacted on his mind, and he rather inclined to think the Virgin easiest to handle.

The pursuit turned out to be long and tortuous, leading at last into the vast forests of scholastic science. From Zeno to Descartes, hand in hand with Thomas Aquinas, Montaigne, and Pascal, one stumbled as stupidly as though one were still a German student of 1860. Only with the instinct of despair could one force one's self into this old thicket of ignorance after having been repulsed at a score of entrances more promising and more popular. Thus far, no path had led anywhere, unless perhaps to an exceedingly modest living. Forty five years of study had proved to be quite futile for the pursuit of power; one controlled no more force in 1900 than in 1850, although the amount of force controlled by society had enormously increased. The secret of education still hid itself somewhere behind ignorance, and one fumbled over it as feebly as ever. In such labyrinths, the staff is a force almost more necessary than the legs; the pen becomes a sort of blind-man's dog, to keep him from falling into the gutters. The pen works for itself, and acts like a hand, modelling the plastic material over and over again to the form that suits it best. The form is never arbitrary, but is a sort of growth like crystallization, as any artist knows too well; for often the pencil or pen runs into side-paths and shapelessness, loses its relations, stops or is bogged. Then it has to return on its trail, and recover, if it can, its line of force. The result of a year's work depends more on what is struck out than on what is left in; on the sequence of the main lines of thought, than on their play or variety. Compelled once more to lean heavily on this support, Adams covered more thousands of pages with figures as formal as though they were algebra, laboriously striking out, altering, burning, experimenting, until the year had expired, the Exposition had long been closed, and winter drawing to its end, before he sailed from Cherbourg, on January 19 1901, for home.

14
SIGMUND FREUD (1856–1939)
FROM *THE INTERPRETATION OF DREAMS* 1900

Austrian neurologist and founder of psychoanalysis. Having studied medicine in Vienna, Freud joined the staff of the Vienna General Hospital in 1882. In collaboration with fellow neurologist Joseph Breuer he specialised in the treatment of hysteria by hypnosis, before moving to Paris in 1885 where he studied under Jean Martin Charcot and focused on experiments in psychopathology.

From that period onwards, and after his return to Vienna, Freud continued to experiment with and refine his conversational technique of 'free association' as an alternative to hypnosis, leading eventually to his formulation of the psychoanalytical method. After a break with Breuer over his theories of infantile sexuality, Freud pursued his own thinking on the significance of repression of sexual desires and produced the revolutionary study The Interpretation of Dreams (Die Traumdeutung) *in 1900. As 'Extraordinary Professor' of Neuropathology at the University of Vienna from 1902, he held weekly seminars in his home and produced a set of controversial but crucial studies including* The Psychopathology of Everyday Life *(1904) and* Three Essays on the Theory of Sexuality *(1905). In 1908 the weekly seminars at his house became the Vienna Psychoanalytical Society and, in 1910, the International Psychoanalytical Association, with Carl Jung as its first president. Despite a break with Jung and Alfred Adler, one of his earlier collaborators, Freud continued to produce groundbreaking work on psychoanalysis, developing and reworking his theories of the unconscious and of sexuality; and his studies of religion, war and civilisation as well as of the status of psychoanalysis as science. Important works from that period include* Totem and Taboo *(1913),* Beyond the Pleasure Principle *(1919–20),* Ego and Id *(1923) and* The Future of an Illusion *(1927). Freud's lifelong concern with human rationality, the future of civilisation and the nature of conflict led to the publication in 1933 of* Why War?, *in collaboration with Albert Einstein. Psychoanalysis was banned under the Nazi regime and Freud, of Jewish parentage, left Vienna in 1938 and spent his last year in London. The following extracts are taken from Chapters 3 ('A Dream is the Fulfilment of a Wish') and 6 ('The Dream-Work') of* The Interpretation of Dreams, *in James Strachey's translation for* The Standard Edition of the Complete Psychological Works of Sigmund Freud *(1953–74).*
[See IIIb 5]

[. . .]

When, after passing through a narrow defile, we suddenly emerge upon a piece of high ground, where the path divides and the finest prospects open up on every side, we may pause for a moment and consider in which direction we shall first turn our steps. Such is the case with us, now that we have surmounted the first interpretation of a dream. We find ourselves in the full daylight of a sudden discovery. Dreams are not to be likened to the unregulated sounds that rise from a musical instrument struck by the blow of some external force instead of by a player's hand [. . .] they are not meaningless, they are not absurd; they do not imply that one portion of our store of ideas is asleep while another portion is beginning to wake. On the contrary, they are psychical phenomena of complete validity – fulfilments of wishes; they can be inserted into the chain of intelligible waking mental acts; they are constructed by a highly complicated activity of the mind.

But no sooner have we begun to rejoice at this discovery than we are assailed by a flood of questions. If, as we are told by dream-interpretation, a dream represents a fulfilled wish, what is the origin of the remarkable and puzzling form in which the wish-fulfilment is expressed? What alteration have the dream-thoughts undergone before being changed into the manifest dream which we remember when we wake up? How does that alteration take place? What is the source of the material that has been modified into the dream? What is the source of the many peculiarities that are to be observed in the dream-thoughts – such, for instance, as the fact that they may be mutually contradictory? [. . .] Can a dream tell us anything new about our internal psychical processes? Can its content correct opinions we have held during the day?

[. . .]

Every attempt that has hitherto been made to solve the problem of dreams has dealt directly with their *manifest* content as it is presented in our memory. All such attempts have endeavoured to arrive at an interpretation of dreams from their manifest content or (if no interpretation was attempted) to form a judgement as to their nature on the basis of that same manifest content. We are alone in taking something else into account. We have introduced a new class of psychical material between the manifest content of dreams and the conclusions of our enquiry: namely, their *latent* content, or (as we say) the 'dream-thoughts', arrived at by means of our procedure. It is from these dream-thoughts and not from a dream's manifest content that we disentangle its meaning. We are thus presented with a new task which had no previous existence: the task, that is, of investigating the relations between the manifest content of dreams and the latent dream-thoughts, and of tracing out the processes by which the latter have been changed into the former.

The dream-thoughts and the dream-content are presented to us like two versions of the same subject-matter in two different languages. Or, more properly, the dream-content seems like a transcript of the dream-thoughts into another mode of expression, whose characters and syntactic laws it is our business to discover by comparing the original and the translation. The dream-thoughts are immediately comprehensible, as soon as we have learnt them. The dream-content, on the other hand, is expressed as it were in a pictographic script, the characters of which have to be transposed individually into the language of the dream-thoughts. If we attempted to read these characters according to their pictorial value instead of according to their symbolic relation, we should clearly be led into error. Suppose I have a picture-puzzle, a rebus, in front of me. It depicts a house with a boat on its roof, a single letter of the alphabet, the figure of a running man whose head has been conjured away, and so on. Now I might be misled into raising objections and declaring that the picture as a whole and its component parts are nonsensical. A boat has no business to be on the roof of a house, and a headless man cannot run. Moreover, the man is bigger than the house; and if the whole picture is intended to represent a landscape, letters of the alphabet are out of place in it since such objects do not occur in nature. But obviously we can only form a proper judgement of the rebus if we put aside criticisms such as these of the whole composition and its parts and if, instead, we try to replace each separate element by a syllable or word that can be represented by that element in some way or other. The words which are put together in this way are no longer nonsensical but may form a poetical phrase of the greatest beauty and significance. A dream is a picture-puzzle of this sort and our predecessors in the field of dream-interpretation have made the mistake of treating the rebus as a pictorial composition: and as such it has seemed to them nonsensical and worthless.

[. . .]

The first thing that becomes clear to anyone who compares the dream-content with the dream-thoughts is that a work of *condensation* on a large scale has been carried out. *Dreams are brief, meagre and laconic in comparison with the range and wealth of the dream-thoughts.* If a dream is written out it may perhaps fill half a page. The analysis setting out the dream-thoughts underlying it may occupy six, eight or a dozen times as much space. This relation varies with different dreams; but so far as my experience goes its direction never varies. As a rule one underestimates the amount of compression that has taken place, since one is inclined to regard the dream-thoughts that have been brought to light as the complete material, whereas if the work of interpretation is carried further it may reveal still more thoughts concealed behind the dream.

[. . .]

In making our collection of instances of condensation in dreams, the existence of another relation, probably of no less importance, had already become evident. It could be seen that the elements which stand out as the principal components of the manifest content of the dream are far from playing the same part in the dream-thoughts. And, as a corollary, the converse of this assertion can be affirmed: what is clearly the essence of the dream-thoughts need not be represented in the dream at all. The dream is, as it were, differently centred from the dream-thoughts – its content has different elements as its central point. [. . .] If we are considering a psychical process in normal life and find that one out of its several component ideas has been picked out and has acquired a special degree of vividness in consciousness, we usually regard this effect as evidence that a specially high amount of psychical value – some particular degree of interest – attaches to this predominant idea. But we now discover that, in the case of the different elements of the dream-thoughts, a value of this kind does not persist or is disregarded in the process of dream-formation. There is never any doubt as to which of the elements of the dream-thoughts have the highest psychical value; we learn that by direct judgement. In the course of the formation of a dream these essential elements, charged, as they are, with intense interest, may be treated as though they were of small value, and their place may be taken in the dream by other elements, of whose small value in the dream-thoughts there can be no question. At first sight it looks as though no attention whatever is paid to the psychical intensity of the various ideas in making the choice among them for the dream, and as though the only thing considered is the greater or less degree of multiplicity of their determination. What appears in dreams, we might suppose, is not what is *important* in the dream-thoughts but what occurs in them several times over. [. . .] We shall be led to conclude that the multiple determination which decides what shall be included in a dream is not always a primary factor in dream-construction but is often the secondary product of a psychical force which is still unknown to us. Nevertheless multiple determination must be of importance in choosing what particular elements shall enter a dream, since we can see that a considerable expenditure of effort is used to bring it about in cases where it does not arise from the dream-material unassisted.

It thus seems plausible to suppose that in the dream-work a psychical force is operating which on the one hand strips the elements which have a high psychical value of their intensity, and on the other hand, *by means of overdetermination,* creates from elements of low psychical value new values, which afterwards find their way into the dream-content. *If that is so, a transference and displacement of psychical intensities occurs in the process of dream-formation, and it is as a result of these that the difference between the text of the dream-content and that of the dream-thoughts comes about.* The process which we are here presuming is nothing less than the essential portion of the dream-work; and it deserves to be described as 'dream-displacement.' *Dream-displacement and dream-condensation are the two governing factors to whose activity we may in essence ascribe the form assumed by dreams.*

Nor do I think we shall have any difficulty in recognizing the psychical force which manifests itself in the facts of dream-displacement. *The consequence of the displacement is that the dream-content no longer resembles the core of the dream-thoughts and that the dream gives no more than a distortion of the dream-wish which exists in the unconscious.* But we are already familiar with dream-distortion. We traced it back to the censorship which is exercised by one psychical agency in the mind over another [. . .] Dream-displacement is one of the chief methods by which that distortion is achieved.

[. . .]

The question of the interplay of these factors – of displacement, condensation and overdetermination – in the construction of dreams, and the question which is a dominant factor and which a subordinate one – all of this we shall leave aside for later investigation.

[. . .]

But we can state provisionally a second condition which must be satisfied by those elements of the dream-thoughts which make their way into the dream: *they must escape the censorship imposed by resistance.*

[. . .]

15
GEORG SIMMEL (1858–1918)
FROM 'THE METROPOLIS AND MENTAL LIFE' 1903

German sociologist and philosopher. Simmel is mostly noted for his pioneering work in sociological methodology. He was particularly interested in how general patterns of social interaction might be identified through the study of individual subjects and their economic and political activities. The plight of individuals in the mass monied economy, and the threat to their integrity and independence posed by metropolitan living, are recurrent themes in his work. 'The Metropolis and Mental Life' was first published in 1903 and appears here in Edward A. Shils's translation.

The deepest problems of modern life flow from the attempt of the individual to maintain the independence and individuality of his existence against the sovereign powers of society, against the weight of the historical heritage and the external culture and technique of life. This antagonism represents the most modern form of the conflict which primitive man must carry on with nature for his own bodily existence. The eighteenth century may have called for liberation from all the ties which grew up historically in politics, in religion, in morality and in economics in order to permit the original natural virtue of man, which is equal in everyone, to develop without inhibition; the nineteenth century may have sought to promote, in addition to man's freedom, his individuality (which is connected with the division of labor) and his achievements which make him unique and indispensable but which at the same time make him so much the more dependent on the complementary activity of others; Nietzsche may have seen the relentless struggle of the individual as the prerequisite for his full development, while Socialism found the same thing in the suppression of all competition – but in each of these the same fundamental motive was at work, namely the resistance of the individual to being levelled, swallowed up in the social-technological mechanism.

When one inquires about the products of the specifically modern aspects of contemporary life with reference to their inner meaning – when, so to speak, one examines the body of culture with reference to the soul, as I am to do concerning the metropolis today – the answer will require the investigation of the relationship which such a social structure promotes between the individual aspects of life and those which transcend the existence of single individuals. It will require the investigation of the adaptations made by the personality in its adjustment to the forces that lie outside of it.

The psychological foundation, upon which the metropolitan individuality is erected, is the intensification of emotional life due to the swift and continuous shift of external and internal stimuli. Man is a creature whose existence is dependent on differences, i.e., his mind is stimulated by the difference between present impressions and those which have preceded. Lasting impressions, the slightness in their differences, the habituated regularity of their course and contrasts between them, consume, so to speak, less mental energy than the rapid telescoping of changing images, pronounced differences within what is grasped at a single glance, and the unexpectedness of violent stimuli. To the extent that the metropolis creates these psychological conditions – with every crossing of the street, with the tempo and multiplicity of economic, occupational and social life – it creates in the sensory foundations of mental life, and in the degree of awareness necessitated by our organization as creatures dependent on differences, a deep contrast with the slower, more habitual, more smoothly flowing rhythm of the sensory-mental phase of small town and rural existence. Thereby the essentially intellectualistic character of the mental life of the metropolis becomes intelligible as over against that of the small town which rests more on feelings and emotional relationships. These latter are rooted in the unconscious levels of the mind and develop most readily in the steady equilibrium of unbroken customs. The locus of reason, on the other hand, is in the lucid, conscious upper strata of the mind and it is the most adaptable of our inner forces. In order to adjust itself to the shifts and contradictions in events, it does not require the disturbances and inner upheavals which are the only means whereby more conservative personalities are able to adapt themselves to the same rhythm of events. Thus the metropolitan type – which naturally takes on a thousand individual modifications – creates a protective organ for itself against the profound disruption with which the fluctuations and discontinuities of the external milieu threaten it. Instead of reacting emotionally, the metropolitan type reacts primarily in a rational manner, thus creating a mental predominance through the intensification of consciousness, which in turn is caused by it. Thus the reaction of the metropolitan person to those events is moved to a sphere of mental activity which is least sensitive and which is furthest removed from the depths of the personality.

This intellectualistic quality which is thus recognized as a protection of the inner life against the domination of the metropolis, becomes ramified into numerous specific phenomena. The metropolis has always been the seat of money economy because the many-sidedness and concentration of commercial activity have given the medium of exchange an importance which it could not have acquired in the commercial aspects of rural life. But money economy and the domination of the intellect stand in the closest relationship to one another. They have in common a purely matter-of-fact attitude in the treatment of persons and things in which a formal justice is often combined with an unrelenting hardness. The purely intellectualistic person is indifferent to all things personal because, out of them, relationships and reactions develop which are not to be completely understood by purely rational methods – just as the unique element in events never enters into the principle of money. Money is concerned only with what is common to all, i.e., with the exchange value which reduces all quality and individuality to a purely quantitative level. All emotional relationships between persons rest on their individuality, whereas intellectual relationships deal with persons as with numbers, that is, as with elements which, in themselves, are indifferent, but which are of interest only insofar as they offer something objectively perceivable. It is in this very manner that the inhabitant of the metropolis reckons with his merchant, his customer, and with his servant, and frequently with the persons with whom he is thrown into obligatory association. These relationships stand in distinct contrast with the nature of the smaller circle in which the inevitable knowledge of individual characteristics produces, with an equal inevitability, an emotional tone in conduct, a sphere which is beyond the mere objective weighting of tasks performed and payments made. What is essential here as regards the economic-psychological aspect of the problem is that in less advanced cultures production was for the customer who ordered the product so that the producer and the purchaser knew one another. The modern city, however, is supplied almost exclusively by production for the market, that is, for entirely unknown purchasers who never appear in the actual field of vision of the producers themselves. Thereby, the interests of each party acquire a relentless matter of factness, and its rationally calculated economic egoism need not fear any divergence from its set path because of the imponderability of personal relationships. [. . .] The modern mind has become more and more a calculating one. The calculating exactness of practical life which has resulted from a money economy corresponds to the ideal of natural science, namely that of transforming the world into an arithmetical problem and of fixing every one of its parts in a mathematical formula. It has been money economy which has thus filled the daily life of so many people with weighing, calculating, enumerating and the reduction of qualitative values to quantitative terms. Because of the character of calculability which money has there has come into the relationships of the elements of life a precision and a degree of certainty in the definition of the equalities and inequalities and an unambiguousness in agreements and arrangements, just as externally this precision has been brought about through the general diffusion of pocket watches. It is, however, the conditions of the metropolis which are cause as well as effect for this essential characteristic. The relationships and concerns of the typical metropolitan resident are so manifold and complex that, especially as a result of the agglomeration of so many persons with such differentiated interests, their relationships and activities intertwine with one another into a many-membered organism. In view of this fact, the lack of the most exact punctuality in promises and performances would cause the whole to break down into an inextricable chaos. [. . .] For this reason the technique of metropolitan life in general is not conceivable without all of its activities and reciprocal relationships being organized and coordinated in the most punctual way into a firmly fixed framework of time which transcends all subjective elements. But here too there emerge those conclusions which are in general the whole task of this discussion, namely, that every event, however restricted to this superficial level it may appear, comes immediately into contact with the depths of the soul, and that the most banal externalities are, in the last analysis, bound up with the final decisions concerning the meaning and the style of life. Punctuality, calculability, and exactness, which are required by the complications and extensiveness of metropolitan life are not only most intimately connected with its capitalistic and intellectualistic character but also color the content of life and are conducive to the exclusion of those irrational, instinctive, sovereign human traits and impulses which originally seek to determine the form of life from within instead of receiving it from the outside in a general, schematically precise form. Even though those lives which are autonomous and characterized by these vital impulses are not entirely impossible in the city, they are, none the less, opposed to it *in abstracto*. It is in the light of this that we can explain the passionate hatred of personalities like Ruskin and Nietzsche for the metropolis – personalities who found the value of life only in unschematized individual expressions which cannot be reduced to exact equivalents and in whom, on that account, there flowed from the same source as did that hatred, the hatred of the money economy and of the intellectualism of existence.

The same factors which, in the exactness and the minute precision of the form of life, have coalesced into a structure of the highest impersonality, have, on the other hand, an influence in a highly personal direction. There is perhaps no psychic phenomenon which is so unconditionally reserved to the city as the blasé outlook. It is at first the consequence of those rapidly shifting stimulations of the nerves which are thrown together in all their contrasts and from which it seems to us the intensification of metropolitan intellectuality seems to be derived. On that account it is not likely that stupid persons who have been hitherto intellectually dead will be blasé because it stimulates the nerves to their utmost reactivity until they finally can no longer produce any reaction at all, so, less harmful stimuli, through the rapidity and the contradictoriness of their shifts, force the nerves to make such violent responses, tear them about so brutally that they exhaust their last reserves of strength and, remaining in the same milieu, do not have time for new reserves to form. This incapacity to react to new stimulations with the required amount of energy constitutes in fact that blasé attitude which every child of a large city evinces when compared with the products of the more peaceful and more stable milieu.

Combined with this physiological source of the blasé metropolitan attitude there is another which derives from a money economy. The essence of the blasé attitude is an indifference toward the distinctions between things. Not in the sense that they are not perceived, as is the case of mental dullness, but rather that the meaning and the value of the distinctions between things, and therewith of the things themselves, are experienced as meaningless. They appear to the blasé person in a homogeneous, flat and gray color with no one of them worthy of being preferred to another. This psychic mood is the correct subjective reflection of a complete money economy to the extent that money takes the place of all the manifoldness of things and expresses all qualitative distinctions between them in the distinction of 'how much'. To the extent that money, with its colorlessness and its indifferent quality, can become a common denominator of all values it becomes the frightful leveler – it hollows out the core of things, their peculiarities, their specific values and their uniqueness and incomparability in a way which is beyond repair. [. . .] We see that the self-preservation of certain types of personalities is obtained at the cost of devaluing the entire objective world, ending inevitably in dragging the personality downward into a feeling of its own valuelessness.

Whereas the subject of this form of existence must come to terms with it for himself, his self-preservation in the face of the great city requires of him a no less negative type of social conduct. The mental attitude of the people of the metropolis to one another may be designated formally as one of reserve. If the unceasing external contact of numbers of persons in the city should be met by the same number of inner reactions as in the small town, in which one knows almost every person he meets and to each of whom he has a positive relationship, one would be completely atomized internally and would fall into an unthinkable mental condition. Partly this psychological circumstance and partly the privilege of suspicion which we have in the face of the elements of metropolitan life (which are constantly touching one another in fleeting contact) necessitates in us that reserve, in consequence of which we do not know by sight neighbors of years standing and which permits us to appear to small-town folk so often as cold and uncongenial. Indeed, if I am not mistaken, the inner side of this external reserve is not only indifference but more frequently than we believe, it is a slight aversion, a mutual strangeness and repulsion which, in a close contact which has arisen any way whatever, can break out into hatred and conflict. The entire inner organization of such a type of extended commercial life rests on an extremely varied structure of sympathies, indifferences and aversions of the briefest as well as of the most enduring sort. This sphere of indifference is, for this reason, not as great as it seems superficially. Our minds respond, with some definite feeling, to almost every impression emanating from another person. The unconsciousness, the transitoriness and the shift of these feelings seem to raise them only into indifference. Actually this latter would be as unnatural to us as immersion into a chaos of unwished-for suggestions would be unbearable. From these two typical dangers of metropolitan life we are saved by antipathy which is the latent adumbration of actual antagonism since it brings about the sort of distanciation and deflection without which this type of life could not be carried on at all. Its extent and its mixture, the rhythm of its emergence and disappearance, the forms in which it is adequate – these constitute, with the simplified motives (in the narrower sense) an inseparable totality of the form of metropolitan life. What appears here directly as dissociation is in reality only one of the elementary forms of socialization.

This reserve with its overtone of concealed aversion appears once more, however, as the form or the wrappings of a much more general psychic trait of the metropolis. It assures the individual of a type and degree of personal freedom to which there is no analogy in other circumstances. It has its roots in one of the great developmental tendencies of social life as a whole; in one of the few for which an approximately exhaustive formula can be discovered. The most elementary stage of social organization which is to be found historically, as well as in the present, is this: a relatively small circle almost entirely closed against neighboring foreign or otherwise antagonistic groups but which has however within itself such a narrow cohesion that the individual member has only a very slight area for the development of his own qualities and for free activity for which he himself is responsible. Political and familial groups begin in this way as do political and religious communities; the self-preservation of very young associations requires a rigorous setting of boundaries and a centripetal unity and for that reason it cannot give room to freedom and the peculiarities of inner and external development of the individual. From this stage social evolution proceeds simultaneously in two divergent but none the less corresponding directions. In the measure that the group grows numerically, spatially, and in the meaningful content of life, its immediate inner unity and the definiteness of its original demarcation against others are weakened and rendered mild by reciprocal interactions and interconnections. And at the same time the individual gains a freedom of movement far beyond the first jealous delimitation, and gains also a peculiarity and individuality to which the division of labor in groups, which have become larger, gives both occasion and necessity. However much the particular conditions and forces of the individual situation might modify the general scheme, the state and Christianity, guilds and political parties and innumerable other groups have developed in accord with this formula. This tendency seems to me, however, to be quite clearly recognizable also in the development of individuality within the framework of city life. Small town life in antiquity as well as in the Middle Ages imposed such limits upon the movements of the individual in his relationships with the outside world and on his inner independence and differentiation that the modern person could not even breathe under such conditions. Even today the city dweller who is placed in a small town feels a type of narrowness which is very similar. The smaller the circle which forms our environment and the more limited the relationships which have the possibility of transcending the boundaries, the more anxiously the narrow community watches over the deeds, the conduct of life and the attitudes of the individual and the more will a quantitative and qualitative individuality tend to pass beyond the boundaries of such a community.

[. . .]

For the correlation, the factual as well as the historical validity of which we are here maintaining, is that the broadest and the most general contents and forms of life are intimately bound up with the most individual ones. Both have a common prehistory and also common enemies in the narrow formations and groupings, whose striving for self-preservation set them in conflict with the broad and general on the outside, as well as the freely mobile and individual on the inside. Just as in feudal times the 'free' man was he who stood under the law of the land, that is, under the law of the largest social unit, but he was unfree who derived his legal rights only from the narrow circle of a feudal community – so today in an intellectualized and refined sense the citizen of the metropolis is 'free' in contrast with the trivialities and prejudices which bind the small town person. The mutual reserve and indifference, and the intellectual conditions of life in large social units are never more sharply appreciated in their significance for the independence of the individual than in the dense crowds of the metropolis because the bodily closeness and lack of space make intellectual distance really perceivable for the first time. It is obviously only the obverse of this freedom that, under certain circumstances, one never feels as lonely and as deserted as in this metropolitan crush of persons. For here, as elsewhere, it is by no means necessary that the freedom of man reflect itself in his emotional life only as a pleasant experience.

It is not only the immediate size of the area and population which, on the basis of world-historical correlation between the increase in the size of the social unit and the degree of personal inner and outer freedom, makes the metropolis the locus of this condition. It is rather in transcending this purely tangible extensiveness that the metropolis also becomes the seat of cosmopolitanism. Comparable with the form of the development of wealth – (beyond a certain point property increases in ever more rapid progression as out of its own inner being) – the individual's horizon is enlarged. In the same way, economic, personal and intellectual relations in the city (which are its ideal reflection), grow in a geometrical progression as soon as, for the first time, a certain limit has been passed. Every dynamic extension becomes a preparation not only for a similar extension but rather for a larger one and from every thread which is spun out of it there continue, growing as out of themselves, an endless number of others.

[. . .]

The most significant aspect of the metropolis lies in this functional magnitude beyond its actual physical boundaries and this effectiveness reacts upon the latter and gives to it life, weight, importance and responsibility. A person does not end with limits of his physical body or with the area to which his physical activity is immediately confined but embraces, rather, the totality of meaningful effects which emanates from him temporally and spatially. In the same way the city exists only in the totality of the effects which transcend their immediate sphere. These really are the actual extent in which their existence is expressed. This is already expressed in the fact that individual freedom, which is the logical historical complement of such extension, is not only to be understood in the negative sense as mere freedom of movement and emancipation from prejudices and philistinism. Its essential characteristic is rather to be found in the fact that the particularity and incomparability which ultimately every person possesses in some way is actually expressed, giving form to life. That we follow the laws of our inner nature – and this is what freedom is – becomes perceptible and convincing to us and to others only when the expressions of this nature distinguish themselves from others; it is our irreplaceability by others which shows that our mode of existence is not imposed upon us from the outside.

Cities are above all the seat of the most advanced economic division of labor. [. . .] Exactly in the measure of its extension the city offers to an increasing degree the determining conditions for the division of labor. It is a unit which, because of its large size, is receptive to a highly diversified plurality of achievements while at the same time the agglomeration of individuals and their struggle for the customer forces the individual to a type of specialized accomplishment in which he cannot be so easily exterminated by the other. The decisive fact here is that in the life of a city, struggle with nature for the means of life is transformed into a conflict with human beings and the gain which is fought for is granted, not by nature, but by man. For here we find not only the previously mentioned source of specialization but rather the deeper one in which the seller must seek to produce in the person to whom he wishes to sell ever new and unique needs. The necessity to specialize one's product in order to find a source of income which is not yet exhausted and also to specialize a function which cannot be easily supplanted is conductive to differentiation, refinement and enrichment of the needs of the public which obviously must lead to increasing personal variation within this public.

All this leads to the narrower type of intellectual individuation of mental qualities to which the city gives rise in proportion to its size. There is a whole series of causes for this. First of all there is the difficulty of giving one's own personality a certain status within the framework of metropolitan life. Where quantitative increase of value and energy has reached its limits, one seizes on qualitative distinctions, so that, through taking advantage of the existing sensitivity to differences, the attention of the social world can, in some way, be won for oneself. This leads ultimately to the strangest eccentricities, to specifically metropolitan extravagances of self-distanciation, of caprice, of fastidiousness, the meaning of which is no longer to be found in the content of such activity itself but rather in its being a form of 'being different' – of making oneself noticeable. For many types of persons these are still the only means of saving for oneself, through the attention gained from others, some sort of self-esteem and the sense of filling a position. In the same sense there operates an apparently insignificant factor which in its effects, however, is perceptibly cumulative, namely, the brevity and rarity of meetings which are allotted to each individual as compared with social intercourse in a small city. For here we find the attempt to appear to-the-point, clear-cut and individual with extraordinarily greater frequency than where frequent and long association assures to each person an unambiguous conception of the other's personality.

This appears to me to be the most profound cause of the fact that the metropolis places emphasis on striving for the most individual forms of personal existence – regardless of whether it is always correct or always successful. The development of modern culture is characterised by the predominance of what one can call the objective spirit over the subjective; that is, in language as well as in law, in the technique of production as well as in art, in science as well as in the objects of domestic environment, there is embodied a sort of spirit [*Geist*], the daily growth of which is followed only imperfectly and with an even greater lag by the intellectual development of the individual. [. . .] This discrepancy is in essence the result of the success of the growing division of labor. For it is this which requires from the individual an ever more one-sided type of achievement which, at its highest point, often permits his personality as a whole to fall into neglect. In any case this overgrowth of objective culture has been less and less satisfactory for the individual. Perhaps less conscious than in practical activity and in the obscure complex of feelings which flow from him, he is reduced to a negligible quantity. He becomes a single cog as over against the vast overwhelming organization of things and forces which gradually take out of his hands everything connected with progress, spirituality and value. The operation of these forces results in the transformation of the latter from a subjective form into one of purely objective existence. It need only be pointed out that the metropolis is the proper arena for this type of culture which has outgrown every personal element. Here in buildings and in educational institutions, in the wonders and comforts of space-conquering technique, in the formations of social life and in the concrete institutions of the State is to be found such a tremendous richness of crystallizing, depersonalized cultural accomplishments that the personality can, so to speak, scarcely maintain itself in the face of it. From one angle life is made infinitely more easy in the sense that stimulations, interests, and the taking up of time and attention, present themselves from all sides and carry it in a stream which scarcely requires any individual efforts for its ongoing. But from another angle, life is composed more and more of these impersonal cultural elements and existing goods and values which seek to suppress peculiar personal interests and incomparabilities. As a result, in order that this most personal element be saved, extremities and peculiarities and individualizations must be produced and they must be over-exaggerated merely to be brought into the awareness even of the individual himself. The atrophy of individual culture through the hypertrophy of objective culture lies at the root of the bitter hatred which the preachers of the most extreme individualism, in the footsteps of Nietzsche, directed against the metropolis. But it is also the explanation of why indeed they are so passionately loved in the metropolis and indeed appear to its residents as the saviors of their unsatisfied yearnings.

When both of these forms of individualism which are nourished by the quantitative relationships of the metropolis, i.e., individual independence and the elaboration of personal peculiarities, are examined with reference to their historical position, the metropolis attains an entirely new value and meaning in the world history of the spirit. The eighteenth century found the individual in the grip of powerful bonds which had become meaningless – bonds of a political, agrarian, guild and religious nature – delimitations which imposed upon the human being at the same time an unnatural form and for a long time an unjust inequality. In this situation arose the cry for freedom and equality – the belief in the full freedom of movement of the individual in all his social and intellectual relationships which would then permit the same noble essence to emerge equally from all individuals as Nature had placed it in them and as it had been distorted by social life and historical development. Alongside of this liberalistic ideal there grew up in the nineteenth century from Goethe and the

Romantics, on the one hand, and from the economic division of labor on the other, the further tendency, namely, that individuals who had been liberated from their historical bonds sought now to distinguish themselves from one another. No longer was it the 'general human quality' in every individual but rather his qualitative uniqueness and irreplaceability that now became the criteria of his value. In the conflict and shifting interpretations of these two ways of defining the position of the individual within the totality is to be found the external as well as the internal history of our time. It is the function of the metropolis to make a place for the conflict and for the attempts at unification of both of these in the sense that its own peculiar conditions have been revealed to us as the occasion and the stimulus for the development of both. Thereby they attain a quite unique place, fruitful with an inexhaustible richness of meaning in the development of the mental life. They reveal themselves as one of those great historical structures in which conflicting life-embracing currents find themselves with equal legitimacy. Because of this, however, regardless of whether we are sympathetic or antipathetic with their individual expressions, they transcend the sphere in which a judge-like attitude on our part is appropriate. To the extent that such forces have been integrated, with the fleeting existence of a single-cell, into the root as well as the crown of the totality of historical life to which we belong – it is our task not to complain or to condone but only to understand.

16
AUGUST BEBEL (1840–1913)
FROM *WOMAN UNDER SOCIALISM* 1904

German socialist. For some forty years Bebel was one of the most prominent figures in European socialism, helping to found the German Social Democratic Party. His early career was taken up with his resistance to the policies of the Prussian Chancellor Bismarck and his wars to unify Germany in the 1860s and 1870s. From the 1880s he produced several seminal works on socialism, including Woman Under Socialism *in which he harnessed a detailed – and prophetic – consideration of the so-called 'woman question' to a critique of the existing capitalist order. The following extracts are from the 1904 English translation by Daniel de Leon of the 33rd German edition and are taken from Bebel's introduction and from Parts Three ('Woman in the Future') and Four ('Internationality'). [See IIa 20]*

We live in the age of a great social Revolution, that every day makes further progress. A growingly powerful intellectual stir and unrest is noticeable in all the layers of society; and the movement pushes towards deep-reaching changes. All feel that the ground they stand on shakes. A number of questions have risen; they occupy the attention of ever widening circles; and discussion runs high on their solution. One of the most important of these, one that pushes itself ever more to the fore, is the so-called 'Woman Question.'

The question concerns the position that woman should occupy in our social organism; how she may unfold her powers and faculties in all directions, to the end that she become a complete and useful member of human society, enjoying equal rights with all. From our view-point, this question coincides with that other: – what shape and organization human society must assume to the end that, in the place of oppression, exploitation, want and misery in manifold forms, there shall be physical and social health on the part of the individual and of society. To us, accordingly, the Woman Question is only one of the aspects of the general Social Question, which is now filling all heads, which is setting all minds in motion and which, consequently, can find its final solution only in the abolition of the existing social contradictions, and of the evils which flow from them.

[. . .]

The mass of the female sex suffers in two respects: On the one side woman suffers from economic and social dependence upon man. True enough, this dependence may be alleviated by formally placing her upon an equality before the law, and in point of rights; but the dependence is not removed. On the other side, woman suffers from the economic dependence that woman in general, the working woman in particular, finds herself in, along with the working-man.

Evidently, all women, without difference of social standing, have an interest – as the sex that in the course of social development has been oppressed, and ruled, and defiled by man – in removing such a state of things, and must exert themselves to change it, in so far as it can be changed by changes in the laws and institutions within the framework of the present social order. But the enormous majority of women are furthermore interested in the most lively manner in that the existing State and social order be radically transformed, to the end that both wage-slavery, under which the working-women deeply pine, and sex slavery, which is intimately connected with our property and industrial systems, be wiped out.

The larger portion by far of the women in society, engaged in the movement for the emancipation of woman, do not see the necessity for such a radical change. Influenced by their privileged social standing, they see in the more far-reaching working-women's movement dangers, not infrequently abhorrent aims, which they feel constrained to ignore, eventually even to resist. The class-antagonism, that in the general social movement rages between the capitalist and the working class, and which, with the ripening of conditions, grows sharper and more pronounced, turns up likewise on the surface of the Woman's Movement; and it finds its corresponding expression in the aims and tactics of those engaged in it.

All the same, the hostile sisters have, to a far greater extent than the male population – split up as the latter is in the class struggle – a number of points of contact, on which they can, although marching separately, strike jointly. This happens on all the fields, on which the question is the equality of woman with man, within modern society. This embraces the participation of woman in all the fields of human activity, for which her strength and faculties are fit; and also her full civil and political equality with man. These are very important, and as will be shown further on, very extensive fields. Besides all this the working woman has also a special interest in doing battle hand in hand with the male portion of the working class, for all the means and institutions that may protect the working woman from physical and moral degeneration, and which promise to secure to her the vitality and fitness necessary for motherhood and for the education of children. Furthermore, as already indicated, it is the part of the working-woman to make common cause with the male members of her class and of her lot in the struggle for a radical transformation of society, looking to the establishment of such conditions as may make possible the real economic and spiritual independence of both sexes, by means of social institutions that afford to all a full share in the enjoyment of all the conquests of civilization made by mankind.

The goal, accordingly, is not merely the realization of the equal rights of woman with man within present society, as is aimed at by the bourgeois woman emancipationists. It lies beyond, – the removal of all impediments that make man dependent upon man; and, consequently, one sex upon the other. Accordingly, this solution of the Woman Question coincides completely with the solution of the Social Question. It follows that he who aims at the solution of the Woman Question to its full extent, is necessarily bound to go hand in hand with those who have inscribed upon their banner the solution of the Social Question as a question of civilization for the whole human race. These are the Socialists, that is, the Social Democracy.

Of all existing parties in Germany, the Social Democratic Party is the only one which has placed in its programme the full equality of woman, her emancipation from all dependence and oppression. And the party has done so, not for agitational reasons, but out of necessity, out of principle. *There can be no emancipation of humanity without the social independence and equality of the sexes.*

[. . .]

The woman of future society is socially and economically independent; she is no longer subject to even a vestige of dominion and exploitation; she is free, the peer of man, mistress of her lot. Her education is the same as that of man, with such exceptions as the difference of sex and sexual functions demand. Living under natural conditions, she is able to unfold and exercise her mental powers and faculties. She chooses her occupation on such field as corresponds with her wishes, inclinations and natural abilities, and she works under conditions identical with man's. Even if engaged as a practical working-woman on some field or other, at other times of the day she may be educator, teacher or nurse, at yet others she may exercise herself in art, or cultivate some branch of science, and at yet others may be filling some administrative function. She joins in studies, enjoyments or social intercourse with either her sisters or with men, – as she may please or occasion may serve.

In the choice of love, she is, like man, free and unhampered. She woos or is wooed, and closes the bond from no considerations other than her own inclinations. This bond is a private contract, celebrated without the intervention of any functionary – just as marriage was a private contract until deep in the Middle Ages. Socialism creates in this nothing new: it merely restores, at a higher level of civilization and under new social forms, that which prevailed at a more primitive social stage, and before private property began to rule society.

Under the proviso that he inflict injury upon none, the individual shall himself oversee the satisfaction of his own instincts. *The satisfaction of the sexual instinct is as much a private concern as the satisfaction of any other natural instinct.* None is therefor accountable to others, and no unsolicited judge may interfere. How I shall eat, how I shall drink, how

I shall sleep, how I shall clothe myself, is my private affair, – exactly so my intercourse with a person of the opposite sex. Intelligence and culture, perfect individual freedom – qualities that become normal through the education and the conditions of future society – will guard everyone against the commission of acts that will redound to his injury.

[. . .]

Bourgeois marriage – we have proved the point beyond cavil – is the result of bourgeois property relations. This marriage, which is intimately related with private property and the right of inheritance – demands 'legitimate' children as heirs: it is entered into for the purpose of acquiring these: under the pressure of social conditions, it is forced even upon those who have nothing to bequeath: it becomes a social law, the violation of which the State punishes by imprisoning for a term of years the men or women who live in adultery and have been divorced.

In future society there is nothing to bequeath, unless the domestic equipment and personal inventory be regarded as inheritance: the modern form of marriage is thus devoid of foundation and collapses. The question of inheritance is thereby solved, and Socialism need not concern itself about abolishing the same. No right of inheritance can arise where there is no private property.

Woman is, accordingly, free, and her children, where she has any, do not impair her freedom: they can only fill all the fuller the cup of her enjoyments and her pleasure in life. Nurses, teachers, female friends, the rising female generations – all these are ready at hand to help the mother when she needs help.

[. . .]

That day is approaching with giant strides. Human society has traversed, in the course of thousands of years, all the various phases of development, to arrive in the end where it started from, – communistic property and complete equality and fraternity, but no longer among congeners alone, but among the whole human race. In that does the great progress consist. What bourgeois society has vainly striven for, and at which it suffers and is bound to suffer shipwreck – the restoration of freedom, equality and fraternity among men – Socialism will accomplish. Bourgeois society could only set up the theory; here, as in so many other respects, their practice was at odds with their theories. It is for Socialism to harmonize the theory with the practice.

Nevertheless, while man returns to the starting point in his development, the return is effected upon an infinitely higher social plane than that from which he started. Primitive society held property in common in the gens and clan, but only in the rawest and most undeveloped stage. The process of development that took place since, reduced, it is true, the common property to a small and insignificant vestige, broke up the gentes, and finally atomized the whole of society; but, simultaneously, it raised mightily the productivity of that society in its various phases and the manifoldness of social necessities, and it created out of the gentes and tribes nations and great States, although again it produced a condition of things that stood in violent contradiction with social requirements. The task of the future is to end the contradiction by the re-transformation upon the broadest basis, of property and productive powers into collective property.

Society re-takes what once was its own, but, in accord with the newly created conditions of production, it places its whole mode of life upon the highest stage of culture, which enables all to enjoy what under more primitive circumstances was the privilege of individuals or of individual classes only.

Now woman again fills the active *role* that once was hers in primitive society. She does not become the mistress, she is the equal of man.

'The end of social development resembles the beginning of human existence. The original equality returns. The mother-web of existence starts and rounds up the cycle of human affairs' – thus writes Bachofen, in his frequently quoted work 'Das Mutterrecht', forecasting coming events. [. . .] The complete emancipation of woman, and her equality with man is the final goal of our social development, whose realization no power on earth can prevent; – and this realization is possible only by a social change that shall abolish the rule of man over man – hence also of capitalists over workingmen. Only then will the human race reach its highest development. The 'Golden Age' that man has been dreaming of for thousands of years, and after which he has been longing, will have come at last. Class rule will have reached its end for all time, and, along with it, the rule of man over woman.

[. . .]

The battle is then on between New and Old Society. Masses of people step upon the stage; an abundance of intelligence is enlisted, such as the world never before saw engaged in any contest, and never again will see gathered for such a purpose. *It is the last social struggle of all.* Standing at the elevation of this century, the sight is obvious of the steady coming to a head of the forces for the struggle in which the New Ideas will triumph.

The new social system will then rear itself upon an international basis. The peoples will fraternize; they will reach one another the hand, and they will endeavor to gradually extend the new conditions over all the races of the earth. No people any longer approaches another as an enemy, bent upon oppression and exploitation; or as the representative of a strange creed that it seeks to impose upon others; – they will meet one another as friends, who seek to raise all human beings to the height of civilization. The labors of the new social order in its work of colonization and civilization will differ as essentially in both purpose and method from the present, as the two social orders are essentially different from each other. Neither powder nor lead, neither 'firewater' (liquor) nor Bible will be used. The task of civilization is entered upon with the instruments of peace, which will present the civilizers to the savages, not as enemies, but as benefactors. Intelligent travelers and investigators have long learned to know how successful is that path.

When the civilized peoples shall have reached the point of joining in a large federation, the time will have come when for evermore the storms of war shall have been lain. Perpetual peace is no dream, as the gentlemen who strut about in uniforms seek to make people believe. That day shall have come the moment the peoples shall have understood their true interests: these are not promoted by war and dissension, by armaments that bear down whole nations; they are promoted by peaceful, mutual understandings, and jointly laboring in the path of civilization.

[. . .]

17
W. E. B. (WILLIAM EDWARD BURGHARDT) DU BOIS (1868–1963)
FROM *THE SOULS OF BLACK FOLK* 1903

African-American activist-intellectual, historian, sociologist, journalist, poet, novelist, editor and spokesman. Du Bois, an opponent of Booker T. Washington and Marcus Garvey, rose from poverty to a glittering academic career. He graduated from Harvard with a PhD in sociology in 1896; and from 1894–1910 was a professor and researcher at Wilberforce, Pennsylvania, and Atlanta Universities. His impressive sociological study, The Philadelphia Negro, *completed in 1897, led to his appointment as Director of the Atlanta University Studies of the Negro Problem. His most famous publication is* The Souls of Black Folk *(1903) from which the extract below is taken. In opposition to the conservatism of Washington, Du Bois founded the Niagara movement (1905–09), which became the National Association for the Advancement of Colored People. Du Bois was Director of Publicity and Research for the NAACP from 1910–34 and edited its magazine,* The Crisis, *which was an important forum for emergent black writers. He organised the Pan-African Congresses of 1919, 1921, 1923, and 1927; and founded a Black theatre group in Harlem, Krigwa Players, in 1927. He resigned from the NAACP and* The Crisis *in 1934, having decided on a strategy for Blacks of 'purposeful segregation for economic defense'. He occupied the chair of sociology at Atlanta University from 1934–44 and was founding editor of the magazine,* Phylon. *In 1961 Du Bois joined the American Communist Party and became a citizen of Ghana in 1963.* The Autobiography of W. E. B. Du Bois *was published in 1968. [See IIIa 25, 26]*

[. . .]

After the Egyptian and Indian, the Greek and Roman, the Teuton and Mongolian, the Negro is a sort of seventh son, born with a veil, and gifted with second-sight in this American world, – a world which yields him no true self-consciousness, but only lets him see himself through the revelation of the other world. It is a peculiar sensation, this double-consciousness, this sense of always looking at one's self through the eyes of others, of measuring one's soul by the tape of a world that looks on in amused contempt and pity. One ever feels his two-ness, – an American, a Negro; two souls, two thoughts, two unreconciled strivings; two warring ideals in one dark body, whose dogged strength alone keeps it from being torn asunder.

The history of the American Negro is the history of this strife, – this longing to attain self-conscious manhood, to merge his double self into a better and truer self. In this merging he wishes neither of the older selves to be lost. [. . .] He simply wishes to make it possible for a man to be both a Negro and an American, without being cursed and spit upon by his fellows, without having the doors of Opportunity closed roughly in his face.

This, then, is the end of his striving: to be a co-worker in the kingdom of culture, to escape both death and isolation, to husband and use his best powers and his latent genius. These powers of body and mind have in the past been strangely wasted, dispersed, or forgotten. The shadow of a mighty Negro past flits through the tale of Ethiopia the Shadowy and of Egypt the Sphinx. Throughout history, the powers of single black men flash here and there like falling stars, and die sometimes before the world has rightly gauged their brightness. Here in America, in the few days since Emancipation, the black man's turning hither and thither in hesitant and doubtful striving has often made his very strength to lose effectiveness, to seem like absence of power, like weakness. And yet it is not weakness, – it is the contradiction of double aims. The double-aimed struggle of the black artisan – on the one hand to escape white contempt for a nation of mere hewers of wood and drawers of water, and on the other hand to plough and nail and dig for a poverty-stricken horde – could only result in making him a poor craftsman, for he had but half a heart in either cause. By the poverty and ignorance of his people, the Negro minister or doctor was tempted toward quackery and demagogy; and by the criticism of the other world, toward ideals that made him ashamed of his lowly tasks. The would-be black *savant* was confronted by the paradox that the knowledge his people needed was a twice-told tale to his white neighbors, while the knowledge which would teach the white world was Greek to his own flesh and blood. The innate love of harmony and beauty that set the ruder souls of his people a-dancing and a-singing raised but confusion and doubt in the soul of the black artist; for the beauty revealed to him was the soul-beauty of a race which his larger audience despised, and he could not articulate the message of another people. This waste of double aims, this seeking to satisfy two unreconciled ideals, has wrought sad havoc with the courage and faith and deeds of ten thousand people, – has sent them often wooing false gods and invoking false means of salvation, and at times has even seemed about to make them ashamed of themselves.

Away back in the days of bondage they thought to see in one divine event the end of all doubt and disappointment; few men ever worshipped Freedom with half such unquestioning faith as did the American Negro for two centuries. To him, so far as he thought and dreamed, slavery was indeed the sum of all villainies, the cause of all sorrow, the root of all prejudice; Emancipation was the key to a promised land of sweeter beauty than ever stretched before the eyes of wearied Israelites. In song and exhortation swelled one refrain – Liberty; in his tears and curses the God he implored had Freedom in his right hand. At last it came, – suddenly, fearfully, like a dream. With one wild carnival of blood and passion came the message in his own plaintive cadences: –

> 'Shout, O children!
> Shout, you're free!
> For God has bought your liberty!'

Years have passed away since then, – ten, twenty, forty; forty years of national customed seat at the Nation's feast. In vain do we cry to this our vastest social problem: –

> 'Take any shape but that, and my firm nerves
> Shall never tremble!'

The Nation has not yet found peace from its sins; the freedman has not yet found freedom his promised land. Whatever of good may have come in these years change, the shadow of a deep disappointment rests upon the Negro people, – a disappointment all the more bitter because the unattained ideal was unbounded save the simple ignorance of a lowly people.

[. . .]

But the facing of so vast a prejudice could not but bring the inevitable self-questioning, self-disparagement, and lowering of ideals which ever accompany repression and breed in an atmosphere of contempt and hate. Whisperings and portents came borne upon the four winds: Lo! we are diseased and dying, cried the dark hosts; we cannot write, our voting is vain; what need of education, since we must always cook and serve? And the Nation echoed and enforced this self-criticism, saying: Be content to be servants, and nothing more; what need of higher culture for half-men? Away with the black man's ballot, by force or fraud, – and behold the suicide of a race! Nevertheless, out of the evil came something of good, – the more careful adjustment of education to real life, the clearer perception of the Negroes' social responsibilities, and the sobering realization of the meaning of progress.

So dawned the time of *Sturm und Drang*: storm and stress to-day rocks our little boat on the mad waters of the world-sea; there is within and without the sound of conflict, the burning of body and rending of soul; inspiration strives with doubt, and faith with vain questionings. The bright ideals of the past, – physical freedom, political power, the training of brains and the training of hands, – all these in turn have waxed and waned, until even the last grows dim and overcast. Are they all wrong, – all false? No, not that, but each alone was over-simple and incomplete, – the dreams of a credulous race-childhood, or the fond imaginings of the other world which does not know and does not want to know our power. To be really true, all these ideals must be melted and welded into one. The training of the schools we need to-day more than ever, – the training of deft hands, quick eyes and ears, and above all the broader, deeper, higher culture of gifted minds and pure hearts. The power of the ballot we need in sheer self-defence, – else what shall save us from a second slavery? Freedom, too, the long-sought, we still seek, – the freedom of life and limb, the freedom to work and think, the freedom to love and aspire. Work, culture, liberty, – all these we need, not singly but together, not successively but together, each growing and aiding each, and all striving toward that vaster ideal that swims before the Negro people, the ideal of human brotherhood, gained through the unifying ideal of Race; the ideal of fostering and developing the traits and talents of the Negro, not in opposition to or contempt for other races, but rather in large conformity to the greater ideals of the American Republic, in order that some day on American soil two world-races may give to each those characteristics both so sadly lack. We the darker ones come even now not altogether empty-handed: there are to-day no truer exponents of the pure human spirit of the Declaration of Independence than the American Negroes; there is no true American music but the wild sweet melodies of the Negro slave; the American fairy tales and folk-lore are Indian and African; and, all in all, we black men seem the sole oasis of simple faith and reverence in a dusty desert of dollars and smartness. Will America be poorer if she replace her brutal dyspeptic blundering with light-hearted but determined Negro humility? or her coarse and cruel wit with loving jovial good-humor? or her vulgar music with the soul of the Sorrow Songs?

Merely a concrete test of the underlying principles of the great republic is the Negro Problem, and the spiritual striving of the freedmen's sons is the travail of souls whose burden is almost beyond the measure of their strength, but who bear it in the name of an historic race, in the name of this the land of their fathers' fathers, and in the name of human opportunity.

[. . .]

18
HENRI BERGSON (1859–1941)
FROM *CREATIVE EVOLUTION* 1907

French philosopher. Following on from his pioneering work on the concept of time and how we experience it, Bergson's 1907 central text, L'Évolution créatrice, *asserted that evolution was a creative rather than a mechanistic process. He claimed that an enduring creative urge (an 'élan vital') as opposed to natural selection was responsible for the evolution of species. Bergson's vitalist philosophical model was both highly influential and immensely popular and helped shape an understanding of the inner dynamic of time, memory and experience which inspired much Modernist writing. The following extract is taken from the opening chapter of* Creative Evolution, *in Arthur Mitchell's 1911 translation.*

The existence of which we are most assured and which we know best is unquestionably our own, for of every other object we have notions which may be considered external and superficial, whereas, of ourselves, our perception is internal and profound. What, then, do we find? In this privileged case, what is the precise meaning of the word 'exist'? Let us recall here briefly the conclusions of an earlier work.

I find, first of all, that I pass from state to state. I am warm or cold, I am merry or sad, I work or I do nothing, I look at what is around me or I think of something else. Sensations, feelings, volitions, ideas – such are the changes into which my existence is divided and which colour it in turns. I change, then, without ceasing. But this is not saying enough. Change is far more radical than we are at first inclined to suppose.

For I speak of each of my states as if it formed a block and were a separate whole. I say indeed that I change, but the change seems to me to reside in the passage from one state to the next: of each state, taken separately, I am apt to think that it remains the same during all the time that it prevails. Nevertheless, a slight effort of attention would reveal to me that there is no feeling, no idea, no volition which is not undergoing change every moment: if a mental state ceased to vary, its duration would cease to flow. Let us take the most stable of internal states, the visual perception of a motionless external object. The object may remain the same, I may look at it from the same side, at the same angle, in the same light; nevertheless the vision I now have of it differs from that which I have just had, even if only because the one is an instant older than the other. My memory is there, which conveys something of the past into the present. My mental state, as it advances on the road of time, is continually swelling with the duration which it accumulates: it goes on increasing – rolling upon itself, as a snowball on the snow. Still more is this the case with states more deeply internal, such as sensations, feelings, desires, etc., which do not correspond, like a simple visual perception, to an unvarying external object. But it is expedient to disregard this uninterrupted change, and to notice it only when it becomes sufficient to impress a new attitude on the body, a new direction on the attention. Then, and then only, we find that our state has changed. The truth is that we change without ceasing, and that the state itself is nothing but change.

This amounts to saying that there is no essential difference between passing from one state to another and persisting in the same state. If the state which 'remains the same' is more varied than we think, on the other hand the passing from one state to another resembles, more than we imagine, a single state being prolonged; the transition is continuous. But, just because we close our eyes to the unceasing variation of every psychical state, we are obliged, when the change has become so considerable as to force itself on our attention, to speak as if a new state were placed alongside the previous one. Of this new state we assume that it remains unvarying in its turn, and so on endlessly. The apparent discontinuity of the psychical life is then due to our attention being fixed on it by a series of separate acts: actually there is only a gentle slope, but in following the broken line of our acts of attention, we think we perceive separate steps. True, our psychic life is full of the unforeseen. A thousand incidents arise, which seem to be cut off from those which precede them, and to be disconnected from those which follow. Discontinuous though they appear, however, in point of fact they stand out against the continuity of a background on which they are designed, and to which indeed they owe the intervals that separate them; they are the beats of the drum which break forth here and there in the symphony. Our attention fixes on them because they interest it more, but each of them is borne by the fluid mass of our whole psychical existence. Each is only the best illuminated point of a moving zone which comprises all that we feel or think or will – all, in short, that we are at any given moment. It is this entire zone which in reality makes up our state. Now, states thus defined cannot be regarded as distinct elements. They continue each other in an endless flow.

But, as our attention has distinguished and separated them artificially, it is obliged next to reunite them by an artificial bond. It imagines, therefore, a formless *ego*, indifferent and unchangeable, on which it threads the psychic states which it has set up as independent entities. Instead of a flux of fleeting shades merging into each other, it perceives distinct and, so to speak, *solid* colours, set side by side like the beads of a necklace; it must perforce then suppose a thread, also itself solid, to hold the beads together. But if this colourless substratum is perpetually coloured by that which covers it, it is for us, in its indeterminateness, as if it did not exist, since we only perceive what is coloured, or, in other words, psychic states. As a matter of fact, this substratum has no reality; it is merely a symbol intended to recall unceasingly to our consciousness the artificial character of the process by which the attention places clean-cut states side by side, where actually there is a continuity which unfolds. If our existence were composed of separate states with an impassive ego to unite them, for us there would be no duration. For an ego which does not change does not *endure*, and a psychic state which remains the same so long as it is not replaced by the following state does not *endure* either. Vain, therefore, is the attempt to range such states beside each other on the ego supposed to sustain them: never can these solids strung upon a solid make up that duration which flows. What we actually obtain in this way is an artificial imitation of the internal life, a static equivalent which will lend itself better to the requirements of logic and language, just because we have eliminated from it the element of real time. But, as regards the psychical life unfolding beneath the symbols which conceal it, we readily perceive that time is just the stuff it is made of.

There is, moreover, no stuff more resistant nor more substantial. For our duration is not merely one instant replacing another; if it were, there would never be anything but the present – no prolonging of the past into the actual, no evolution, no concrete duration. Duration is the continuous progress of the past which gnaws into the future and which swells as it advances. And as the past grows without ceasing, so also there is no limit to its preservation. Memory, as we have tried to prove, is not a faculty of putting away recollections in a drawer, or of inscribing them in a register. There is no register, no drawer; there is not even, properly speaking, a faculty, for a faculty works intermittently, when it will or when it can, whilst the piling up of the past upon the past goes on without relaxation. In reality, the past is preserved by itself, automatically. In its entirety, probably, it follows us at every instant; all that we have felt, thought and willed from our earliest infancy is there, leaning over the present which is about to join it, pressing against the portals of consciousness that would fain leave it outside. The cerebral mechanism is arranged just so as to drive back into the unconscious almost the whole of this past, and to admit beyond the threshold only that which can cast light on the present situation or further the action now being prepared – in short, only that which can give *useful* work. At the most, a few superfluous recollections may succeed in smuggling themselves through the half-open door. These memories, messengers from the unconscious, remind us of what we are dragging behind us unawares. But, even though we may have no distinct idea of it, we feel vaguely that our past remains present to us. What are we, in fact, what is our *character*, if not the condensation of the history that we have lived from our birth – nay, even before our birth, since we bring with us prenatal dispositions? Doubtless we think with only a small part of our past, but it is with our entire past, including the original bent of our soul, that we desire, will and act. Our past, then, as a whole, is made manifest to us in its impulse; it is felt in the form of tendency, although a small part of it only is known in the form of idea.

From this survival of the past it follows that consciousness cannot go through the same state twice. The circumstances may still be the same, but they will act no longer on the same person, since they find him at a new moment of his history. Our personality, which is being built up each instant with its accumulated experience, changes without ceasing. By changing, it prevents any state, although superficially identical with another, from ever repeating it in its very depth. That is why our duration is irreversible. We could not live over again a single moment, for we should have to begin by effacing the memory of all that had followed. Even could we erase this memory from our intellect, we could not from our will.

Thus our personality shoots, grows and ripens without ceasing. Each of its moments is something new added to what was before. We may go further: it is not only something new, but something unforeseeable. Doubtless, my present state is explained by what was in me and by what was acting on me a moment ago. In analysing it I should find no other elements. But even a superhuman intelligence would not have been able to foresee the simple indivisible form which gives to these purely abstract elements their concrete organization. For to foresee consists of projecting into the future what has been perceived in the past, or of imagining for a later time a new grouping, in a new order, of elements already perceived. But that which has never been perceived, and which is at the same time simple, is necessarily unforeseeable. Now such is the case with each of our states, regarded as a moment in a history that is gradually unfolding: it is simple, and it cannot have been already perceived, since it concentrates in its indivisibility all that has been perceived and what the present is adding to it besides. It is an original moment of a no less original history.

The finished portrait is explained by the features of the model, by the nature of the artist, by the colours spread out on the palette; but, even with the knowledge of what explains it, no one, not even the artist, could have foreseen exactly what the portrait would be, for to predict it would have been to produce it before it was produced – an absurd hypothesis which is its own refutation. Even so with regard to the moments of our life, of which we are the artisans. Each of them is a kind of creation. And just as the talent of the painter is formed or deformed – in any case, is modified – under the very influence of the works he produces, so each of our states, at the moment of its issue, modifies our personality, being indeed the new form that we are just assuming. It is then right to say that what we do depends on what we are; but it is necessary to add also that we are, to a certain extent, what we do, and that we are creating ourselves continually. This creation of self by self is the more complete, the more one reasons on what one does. For reason does not proceed in such matters as in geometry, where impersonal premises are given once for all, and an impersonal conclusion must perforce be drawn. Here, on the contrary, the same reasons may dictate to different persons, or to the same person at different moments, acts profoundly different, although equally reasonable. The truth is that they are not quite the same reasons, since they are not those of the same person, nor of the same moment. That is why we cannot deal with them in the abstract, from outside, as in geometry, nor solve for another the problems by which he is faced in life. Each must solve them from within, on his own account. But we need not go more deeply into this. We are seeking only the precise meaning that our consciousness gives to this word 'exist,' and we find that, for a conscious being, to exist is to change, to change is to mature, to mature is to go on creating oneself endlessly.

[. . .]

19
WILHELM WORRINGER (1881–1965)
FROM *ABSTRACTION AND EMPATHY* 1908

German art theorist. Worringer's study was originally written as a doctoral thesis in 1906 and was published in Munich in 1908. In his foreword to the 1948 impression, Worringer describes how the book 'influenced many personal lives and the spiritual life of a whole era . . . It became an "Open Sesame" for the formulation of a whole range of questions important to the epoch'. He also acknowledges the intellectual and spiritual influence of Georg Simmel ('perhaps the secret and unconscious midwife at the birth of my inspiration'). Simmel was among the first appreciative readers of Worringer's thesis. Subtitled 'A Contribution to the Psychology of Style', the study provided the theoretical impetus for many Modernists' interest in primitive art and for the validation of abstract forms. Reproduced here are extracts from Chapter One, in Michael Bullock's translation of the third edition of 1910.

[. . .]

Our investigations proceed from the presupposition that the work of art, as an autonomous organism, stands beside nature on equal terms and, in its deepest and innermost essence, devoid of any connection with it, in so far as by nature is understood the visible surface of things. Natural beauty is on no account to be regarded as a condition of the work of art, despite the fact that in the course of evolution it seems to have become a valuable element in the work of art, and to some extent indeed positively identical with it.

This presupposition includes within it the inference that the specific laws of art have, in principle, nothing to do with the aesthetics of natural beauty. It is therefore not a matter of, for example, analysing the conditions under which a landscape appears beautiful, but of an analysis of the conditions under which the representation of this landscape becomes a work of art.

Modern aesthetics, which has taken the decisive step from aesthetic objectivism to aesthetic subjectivism, i.e. which no longer takes the aesthetic as the starting-point of its investigations, but proceeds from the behaviour of the contemplating subject, culminates in a doctrine that may be characterised by the broad general name of the theory of empathy.

[. . .]

For the basic purpose of my essay is to show that this modern aesthetics, which proceeds from the concept of empathy, is inapplicable to wide tracts of art history. Its Archimedian point is situated at *one* pole of human artistic feeling alone. It will only assume the shape of a comprehensive aesthetic system when it has united with the lines that lead from the opposite pole.

We regard as this counter-pole an aesthetics which proceeds not from man's urge to empathy, but from his urge to abstraction. Just as the urge to empathy as a preassumption of aesthetic experience finds its gratification in the beauty of the organic, so the urge to abstraction finds its beauty in the life-denying inorganic, in the crystalline or, in general terms, in all abstract law and necessity.

We shall endeavour to cast light upon the antithetic relation of empathy and abstraction, by first characterising the concept of empathy in a few broad strokes.

The simplest formula that expresses this kind of aesthetic experience runs: Aesthetic enjoyment is objectified self-enjoyment. To enjoy aesthetically means to enjoy myself in a sensuous object diverse from myself, to empathise myself into it. 'What I empathise into it is quite generally life. And life is energy, inner working, striving and accomplishing. In a word, life is activity. But activity is that in which I experience an expenditure of energy. By its nature, this activity is an activity of the will. It is endeavour or volition in motion.'

[. . .]

The crucial factor is, therefore, rather the sensation itself, i.e. the inner motion, the inner life, the inner self-activation.

The presupposition of the act of empathy is the general apperceptive activity. 'Every sensuous object, in so far as it exists for me, is always the product of two components, of that which is sensuously given and of my apperceptive activity.'

[. . .]

Apperceptive activity becomes aesthetic enjoyment in the case of positive empathy, in the case of the unison of my natural tendencies to self-activation with the activity demanded of me by the sensuous object. In relation to the work of art also, it is this positive empathy alone which comes into question. This is the basis of the theory of empathy, in so far as it finds practical application to the work of art.

[. . .]

The aim of the ensuing treatise is to demonstrate that the assumption that this process of empathy has at all times and at all places been the presupposition of artistic creation, cannot be upheld. On the contrary, this theory of empathy leaves us helpless in the face of the artistic creations of many ages and peoples. It is of no assistance to us, for instance, in the understanding of that vast complex of works of art that pass beyond the narrow framework of Graeco-Roman and modern Occidental art. Here we are forced to recognise that quite a different psychic process is involved, which explains the peculiar, and in our assessment purely negative, quality of that style.

[. . .]

The value of a work of art, what we call its beauty, lies, generally speaking, in its power to bestow happiness. The values of this power naturally stand in a causal relation to the psychic needs which they satisfy. Thus the 'absolute artistic volition' is the gauge for the quality of these psychic needs.

No psychology of the need for art – in the terms of our modern standpoint: of the need for style – has yet been written. It would be a history of the feeling about the world and, as such, would stand alongside the history of religion as its equal. By the feeling about the world I mean the psychic state in which, at any given time, mankind found itself in relation to the cosmos, in relation to the phenomena of the external world. This psychic state is disclosed in the quality of psychic needs, i.e. in the constitution of the absolute artistic volition, and bears outward fruit in the work of art, to be exact in the style of the latter, the specific nature of which is simply the specific nature of the psychic needs. Thus the various gradations of the feeling about the world can be gauged from the stylistic evolution of art, as well as from the theogony of the peoples.

Every style represented the maximum bestowal of happiness for the humanity that created it. This must become the supreme dogma of all objective consideration of the history of art. What appears from our standpoint the greatest distortion must have been at the time, for its creator, the highest beauty and the fulfilment of his artistic volition. Thus all valuations made from our standpoint, from the point of view of our modern aesthetics, which passes judgement exclusively in the sense of the Antique or the Renaissance, are from a higher standpoint absurdities and platitudes.

[. . .]

The need for empathy can be looked upon as a presupposition of artistic volition only where this artistic volition inclines toward the truths of organic life, that is toward naturalism in the higher sense. The sensation of happiness that is released in us by the reproduction of organically beautiful vitality, what modern man designates beauty, is a gratification of that inner need for self-activation in which Lipps sees the presupposition of the process of empathy. In the forms of the work of art we enjoy ourselves. Aesthetic enjoyment is objectified self-enjoyment. The value of a line, of a form, consists for us in the value of the life that it holds for us. It holds its beauty only through our own vital feeling, which, in some mysterious manner, we project into it.

Recollection of the lifeless form of a pyramid or of the suppression of life that is manifested, for instance, in Byzantine mosaics tells us at once that here the need for empathy, which for obvious reasons always tends toward the organic, cannot possibly have determined artistic volition. Indeed, the idea forces itself upon us that here we have an impulse directly opposed to the empathy impulse, which seeks to suppress precisely that in which the need for empathy finds its satisfaction.

This counter-pole to the need for empathy appears to us to be the urge to abstraction. My primary concern in this essay is to analyse this urge and to substantiate the importance it assumes within the evolution of art.

The extent to which the urge to abstraction has determined artistic volition we can gather from actual works of art, on the basis of the arguments put forward in the ensuing pages. We shall then find that the artistic volition of savage peoples, in so far as they possess any at all, then the artistic volition of all primitive epochs of art and, finally, the artistic volition of certain culturally developed Oriental peoples, exhibit this abstract tendency. Thus the urge to abstraction stands at the beginning of every art and in the case of certain peoples at a high level of culture remains the dominant tendency, whereas with the Greeks and other Occidental peoples, for example, it slowly recedes, making way for the urge to empathy. This provisional statement is substantiated in the practical section of the essay.

Now what are the psychic presuppositions for the urge to abstraction? We must seek them in these peoples' feeling about the world, in their psychic attitude toward the cosmos. Whereas the precondition for the urge to empathy is a happy pantheistic relationship of confidence between man and the phenomena of the external world, the urge to abstraction is the outcome of a great inner unrest inspired in man by the phenomena of the outside world; in a religious respect it corresponds to a strongly transcendental tinge to all notions. We might describe this state as an immense spiritual dread of space.

[. . .]

The situation is similar as regards the spiritual dread of space in relation to the extended, disconnected, bewildering world of phenomena. The rationalistic development of mankind pressed back this instinctive fear conditioned by man's feeling of being lost in the universe. The civilised peoples of the East, whose more profound world-instinct opposed development in a rationalistic direction and who saw in the world nothing but the shimmering veil of Maya, they alone remained conscious of the unfathomable entanglement of all the phenomena of life, and all the intellectual mastery of the world-picture could not deceive them as to this. Their spiritual dread of space, their instinct for the relativity of all that is, did not stand, as with primitive peoples, *before* cognition, but *above* cognition.

Tormented by the entangled inter-relationship and flux of the phenomena of the outer world, such peoples were dominated by an immense need for tranquillity. The happiness they sought from art did not consist in the possibility of projecting themselves into the things of the outer world, of enjoying themselves in them, but in the possibility of taking the individual thing of the external world out of its arbitrariness and seeming fortuitousness, of eternalising it by approximation to abstract forms and, in this manner, of finding a point of tranquillity and a refuge from appearances. Their most powerful urge was, so to speak, to wrest the object of the external world out of its natural context, out of the unending flux of being, to purify it of all its dependence upon life, i.e. of everything about it that was arbitrary, to render it necessary and irrefragable, to approximate it to its *absolute* value. Where they were successful in this, they experienced that happiness and satisfaction which the beauty of organic-vital form affords *us*; indeed, they knew no other beauty, and therefore we may term it their beauty.

[. . .]

The style most perfect in its regularity, the style of the highest abstraction, most strict in its exclusion of life, is peculiar to the peoples at their most primitive cultural level. A causal connection must therefore exist between primitive culture and the highest, purest regular art-form. And the further proposition may be stated: The less mankind has succeeded, by virtue of its spiritual cognition, in entering into a relation of friendly confidence with the appearance of the outer world, the more forceful is the dynamic that leads to the striving after this highest abstract beauty.

Not that primitive man sought more urgently for regularity in nature, or experienced regularity in it more intensely; just the reverse: it is because he stands so lost and spiritually helpless amidst the things of the external world, because he experiences only obscurity and caprice in the inter-connection and flux of the phenomena of the external world, that the urge is so strong in him to divest the things of the external world of their caprice and obscurity in the world-picture and to impart to them a value of necessity and a value of regularity. To employ an audacious comparison: it is as though the instinct for the 'thing in itself' were most powerful in primitive man.

Increasing spiritual mastery of the outside world and habituation to it mean a blunting and dimming of this instinct. Only after the human spirit has passed, in thousands of years of its evolution, along the whole course of rationalistic cognition, does the feeling for the 'thing in itself' re-awaken in it as the final resignation of knowledge. That which was previously instinct is now the ultimate product of cognition. Having slipped down from the pride of knowledge, man is now just as lost and helpless *vis-à-vis* the world-picture as primitive man, once he has recognised that 'this visible world in which we are is the work of Maya, brought forth by magic, a transitory and in itself unsubstantial semblance, comparable to the optical illusion and the dream, of which it is equally false and equally true to say that it is, as that it is not' (Schopenhauer, *Kritik der Kantischen Philosophie*).

This recognition was fruitless, however, because man had become an individual and broken away from the mass. The dynamic force resting in an undifferentiated mass pressed together by a common instinct had alone been able to create from out of itself those forms of the highest abstract beauty. The individual on his own was too weak for such abstraction.

It would be a misconstruction of the psychological preconditions for the genesis of this abstract art form, to say that a craving for regularity led men to reach out for geometric regularity, for that would presuppose a spiritual-intellectual penetration of abstract form, would make it appear the product of reflection and calculation. We have more justification for assuming that what we see here is a purely instinctive creation, that the urge to abstraction created this form for itself with elemental necessity and without the intervention of the intellect. Precisely because intellect had not yet dimmed instinct, the disposition to regularity, which after all is already present in the germ-cell, was able to find the appropriate abstract expression.

[. . .]

If we now repeat the formula which we found to be the basis of the aesthetic experience resulting from the urge to empathy: 'Aesthetic enjoyment is objectified self-enjoyment', we at once become conscious of the polar antithesis between these two forms of aesthetic enjoyment. On the one hand the ego as a clouding of the greatness of the work of art, as a curtailment of its capacity for bestowing happiness, on the other the most intimate union between ego and work of art, which receives all its life from the ego alone.

This dualism of aesthetic experience, as characterised by the aforementioned two poles, is – a remark which will serve to conclude this chapter – not a final one. These two poles are only gradations of a common need, which is revealed to us as the deepest and ultimate essence of all aesthetic experience: this is the need for self-alienation.

In the urge to abstraction the intensity of the self-alienative impulse is incomparably greater and more consistent. Here it is not characterised, as in the need for empathy, by an urge to alienate oneself from individual being, but as an urge to seek deliverance from the fortuitousness of humanity as a whole, from the seeming arbitrariness of organic existence in general, in the contemplation of something necessary and irrefragable. Life as such is felt to be a disturbance of aesthetic enjoyment.

[. . .]

20
ADOLF LOOS (1870–1933)
FROM 'ORNAMENT AND CRIME' 1908

Austrian architect. From as early as 1898, Loos was expressing his contempt for the ornamental fussiness of European Art Nouveau and American neo-classicist architecture. In 1910, his theories took form in the stark geometrical simplicity of the Steiner House in Vienna, considered by many historians of architecture to be the first Modernist residence. His most famous structure, the Goldman and Salatsch Building, with its extensive plane surfaces of polished marble, was completed the same year, also in Vienna. Both these works considerably influenced Modernist architecture after the First World War. The essay from which the following extracts are taken dates from 1908 and appears in Harold Meek's translation for Ludwig Münz and Gustav Künstler's Adolf Loos: Pioneer of Modern Architecture *(1966). [See IIIb 1]*

The human embryo goes through all the phases of animal life while still inside the womb. When man is born, his instincts are those of a new-born dog. His childhood runs through all the changes corresponding to the history of mankind. At the age of two he looks like a Papuan, at four like one of an ancient Germanic tribe, at six like Socrates, at eight like Voltaire. When he is eight years old, he becomes conscious of violet, the colour discovered by the eighteenth century, for until then violets were blue and purple-fish were red. The physicist today points out colours in the spectrum of the sun that have already been named, but whose comprehension has been reserved for future generations.

The child is amoral. So is the Papuan, to us. The Papuan kills his enemies and eats them. He is no criminal. But if a modern man kills someone and eats him, he is a criminal or a degenerate.

The Papuan tattoos his skin, his boat, his rudder, his oars; in short, everything he can get his hands on. He is no criminal. The modern man who tattoos himself is a criminal or a degenerate. There are prisons in which eighty per cent of the prisoners are tattooed. Tattooed men who are not behind bars are either latent criminals or degenerate aristocrats. If someone who is tattooed dies in freedom, then he does so a few years before he would have committed murder.

The urge to decorate one's face and everything in reach is the origin of the graphic arts. It is the babbling of painting. All art is erotic.

The first ornament invented, the cross, was of erotic origin. The first work of art, the first artistic act, which the first artist scrawled on the wall to give his exuberance vent. A horizontal line: the woman. A vertical line: the man penetrating her. The man who created this felt the same creative urge as Beethoven, he was in the same state of exultation in which Beethoven created the Ninth.

But the man of our own times who covers the walls with erotic images from an inner compulsion is a criminal or a degenerate. Of course, this urge affects people with such symptoms of degeneracy most strongly in the lavatory. It is possible to estimate a country's culture by the amount of scrawling on lavatory walls. In children this is a natural phenomenon: their first artistic expression is scribbling erotic symbols on walls. But what is natural for a Papuan and a child, is degenerate for modern man. I have discovered the following truth and present it to the world: *cultural evolution is equivalent to the removal of ornament from articles in daily use*. I thought I was giving the world a new source of pleasure with this; it did not thank me for it. People were sad and despondent. What oppressed them was the realization that no new ornament could be created. What every Negro can do, what all nations and ages have been able to do, why should that be denied to us, men of the nineteenth century? What humanity had achieved in earlier millennia without decoration has been carelessly tossed aside and consigned to destruction. We no longer possess carpenters' benches from the Carolingian period, but any trash that exhibited the merest trace of decoration was collected and cleaned up, and splendid palaces built to house it. People walked sadly around the showcases, ashamed of their own impotence. Shall every age have a style of its own and our age alone be denied one? By style they meant decoration. But I said: Don't weep! Don't you see that the greatness of our age lies in its inability to produce a new form of decoration? We have conquered ornament, we have won through to lack of ornamentation. Look, the time is nigh, fulfilment awaits us. Soon the streets of the town will glisten like white walls. Like Zion, the holy city, the metropolis of heaven. Then we shall have fulfilment.

But there are some pessimists who will not permit this. Humanity must be kept down in the slavery of decoration. People progressed far enough for ornament to give them pleasure no longer, indeed so far that a tattooed face no longer heightened their aesthetic sensibility, as it did with the Papuans, but diminished it. They were sophisticated enough to feel pleasure at the sight of a smooth cigarette case while they passed over a decorated one, even at the same price. They were happy with their clothes and glad that they did not have to walk about in red velvet pants with gold braid like monkeys at a fair. And I said: Look, Goethe's death chamber is more magnificent than all the Renaissance grandeur and a smooth piece of furniture more beautiful than all the inlaid and carved museum pieces. Goethe's language is finer than all the florid similes of the Pegnitz Shepherds.

The pessimist heard this with displeasure and the State, whose task it is to retard the cultural progress of the people, took up the fight for the development and revival of ornament. Woe to the State whose revolutions are made by Privy Councillors! A sideboard was soon on show in the Vienna Museum of Arts and Crafts called 'The Rich Haul of Fish', soon there were cupboards called 'The Enchanted Princess' or something similar, relating to the ornament that covered these unfortunate pieces. The Austrian government takes its task so seriously that it makes sure that puttees do not disappear from the borders of the Austro-Hungarian Monarchy. It forces every civilized twenty-year-old man to wear puttees instead of knitted hose for three years. For every government still labours under the supposition that a nation on a low standard is easier to govern.

All right, then, the plague of ornament is recognized by the State and subsidized by State funds. But I look on this as retrogression. I do not allow the objection that ornament heightens a cultivated man's joy in life; I do not allow the objection: 'but what if the ornament is beautiful . . .' As far as I am concerned, and this goes for all cultivated people, ornament does not give zest to life. If I want to eat some gingerbread, I choose a piece that is quite plain, and not in the shape of a heart or a baby or a horseman, and gilded all over. The man from the fifteenth century will not understand me. But all modern people will. The advocate of ornament believes that my urge for simplicity is equivalent to a mortification of the flesh. No, my dear art school professor, I'm not mortifying myself. I prefer it that way. The spectacular menus of past centuries, which all include decorations to make peacocks, pheasants and lobsters appear even tastier, produce the opposite effect on me. I walk though a culinary display with revulsion at the thought that I am supposed to eat these stuffed animal corpses. I eat roast beef.

The immense damage and devastation wrought on aesthetic development by the revival of decoration could easily be overcome, for no one, not even governments, can arrest the evolution of mankind. It can only be retarded. We can wait. But it is a crime against the national economy that human labour, money and material should thereby be ruined. This kind of damage cannot be put right by time.

The tempo of cultural progress suffers through stragglers. I may be living in 1908, yet my neighbour still lives in 1900 and that one over there in 1880. It is a misfortune for a country if the cultural development of its people is spread over such a long period.

[. . .]

Stragglers slow down the cultural progress of nations and humanity; for ornament is not only produced by criminals; it itself commits a crime, by damaging men's health, the national economy and cultural development. Where two people live side by side with the same needs, the same demands on life and the same income, and yet belong to different cultures, the following process may be observed from the economic point of view: the man from the twentieth century becomes ever richer, the one from the eighteenth ever poorer. I am supposing that each lives according to his inclinations. The twentieth century man can pay for his needs with much less capital and can therefore save. The vegetables he likes are simply boiled in water and then served with a little melted butter. The other man doesn't enjoy them until honey and nuts have been added and someone has been busy cooking them for hours. Decorated plates are very dear, while the plain white china that the modern man likes is cheap. One man accumulates savings, the other one debts. So it is with whole nations. Woe to the country that lags behind in cultural development! The English become richer and we poorer.

[. . .]

Even greater is the damage ornament inflicts on the workers. As ornament is no longer a natural product of our civilization, it accordingly represents backwardness or degeneration, and the labour of the man who makes it is not adequately remunerated.

Conditions in the woodcarving and turning trades, the criminally low prices paid to embroiderers and lacemakers, are well known. The producers of ornament must work twenty hours to earn the wages a modern worker gets in eight. Decoration adds to the price of an object as a rule, and yet it can happen that a decorated object, with the same outlay in materials and demonstrably three times as much work, is offered for sale at half the price of a plain object. The lack of ornament means shorter working hours and consequently higher wages. Chinese carvers work sixteen hours, American workers eight. If I pay as much for a smooth box as for a decorated one, the difference in labour time belongs to the worker. And if there were no ornament at all – a circumstance that will perhaps come true in a few millennia – a man would have to work only four hours instead of eight, for half the work done at present is still for ornamentation.

Ornament is wasted labour and hence wasted health. That's how it has always been. Today, however, it is also wasted material, and both together add up to wasted capital.

As ornament is no longer organically linked with our culture, it is also no longer an expression of our culture. Ornament as created today has no connection with us, has no human connections at all, no connection with the world as it is constituted. It cannot be developed. What has happened to the decorations of Otto Eckmann and those of Van de Velde? The artist always used to stand at the forefront of humanity, full of health and vigour. But the modern ornamentalist is a straggler, or a pathological case. He rejects even his own products within three years. To cultivated people they are unbearable immediately, others are aware of their unbearableness only after some years. Where are the works of Otto Eckmann today? Where will Olbrich's work be in ten years' time? Modern ornament has no forbears and no descendants, no past and no future. It is joyfully welcomed by uncultivated people, to whom the true greatness of our time is a closed book, and after a short period is rejected.

Mankind today is healthier than ever, only a few people are sick. But these few tyrannize over the worker who is so healthy that he cannot invent ornament. They force him to make the ornaments they have invented in the greatest variety of materials.

[. . .]

Modern men who revere ornament as a sign of the artistic expression of earlier generations, will immediately recognize the painfully laboured and sickly ornament of today. No-one can create ornament now who lives on our level of culture.

It is different for people and nations who have not yet attained this level.

I am preaching to the aristocrats; I mean, to the people in the forefront of humanity who still fully appreciate the needs and strivings of those beneath them. They understand the native weaving ornaments into textiles to a certain rhythm, which can be seen only when torn apart, the Persian knotting his carpet, the Slovak peasant woman embroidering her lace, the old lady crocheting wonderful objects in beads and silk. The aristocrat lets them be, for he knows they work in moments of revelation. The revolutionary would go there and say 'This is all nonsense'. Just as he would pull the old woman away from the roadside shrine with the words: 'There is no God'. But among the aristocrats the atheist raises his hat on passing a church.

I am preaching to the aristocrats. I tolerate ornaments on my own body if they afford my fellow-men pleasure. Then they are a pleasure to me, too. I put up with the ornaments of the natives, the Persians, the Slovak peasant woman and my shoemaker's ornaments, for these workers have no other means of reaching the heights of their existence. We have art, which has replaced ornament. We go to Beethoven or *Tristan* after the cares of the day. My shoemaker can't. I must not take away his joy as I have nothing to replace it with. But whoever goes to the Ninth Symphony and then sits down to design a wallpaper pattern is either a rogue or a degenerate.

Lack of ornament has pushed the other arts to unimagined heights. Beethoven's symphonies would never have been written by a man who was obliged to go about in silk, velvet and lace. Those who run around in velvet nowadays are not artists but buffoons or house painters. We have become more refined, more subtle. The herd must distinguish themselves by the use of various colours, modern man uses his clothes like a mask. His individuality is so strong that he does not need to express it any longer by his clothing. Lack of ornament is a sign of spiritual strength. Modern man uses the ornaments of earlier and foreign cultures as he thinks fit. He concentrates his own powers of invention on other things.

21
KARL KRAUS (1874–1936)
'THE GOOD CONDUCT MEDAL' 1909

Austrian writer. Renowned for his pointed satiric vision and innovative use of language, Kraus founded and edited the literary and political review Die Fackel *('The Torch', 1899–1936). In his essays and aphoristic writings he targeted what he saw as the complacencies of the Austrian bourgeoisie and the reckless liberalism of the press. In the following piece from 1909, Kraus focuses on the sexual hypocrisy of a male-dominated society. This translation is from Harry Zohn (ed.),* In These Great Times: A Karl Kraus Reader, *1984. [See IIa 11]*

In Austria there is a climax of culpability for young girls who embrace vice. A distinction is made between girls who are guilty of the unauthorized practice of prostitution; girls who falsely state that they are under the supervision of the morals division of the police; and finally, girls who are licensed to practice prostitution but not to wear a good conduct medal. At first glance this classification is confusing, but it is thoroughly in keeping with the actual situation. A girl who seemed suspicious to a detective (nothing seems more suspicious to a detective than a girl!) stated that she was under the supervision of the morals division of the police. She had only been kidding, but the matter was investigated. Since her statement proved to be false, the police launched an investigation for unauthorized practice of prostitution. But since this suspicion also proved to be unjustified and it turned out that the girl was not practicing prostitution at all, the public prosecutor brought action for making false statements. The girl was charged with 'having arrogated to herself a social position that she was not entitled to.' Since she was practicing neither licensed nor unlicensed prostitution, she was a swindler; and she escaped being sentenced only because during the hearing she answered the judge's question as to what had been in her mind by saying, 'Nothing.' To recapitulate, then: The girl had claimed that she was under the supervision of the morals division of the police. Because this was an untruth, an investigation was launched on suspicion of immoral conduct. She was able to prove that she was not immoral enough to engage in immoral conduct, but she could not prove that she was moral enough to be under the supervision of the morals division of the police. So the only thing to do was to accuse her of making false statements – which in Austria, after all, is the basis for sentencing even murderers if it cannot be proved that they have committed a murder.

Let us now go a step further. If a girl is licensed to practice prostitution, it could happen that she suppresses that fact and fraudulently states that she is not licensed to practice prostitution. She would then be arrogating to herself an immoral conduct in which she engaged not because she is authorized to do so but though she is not authorized to do so, whereas in reality she is authorized only to engage in the immoral conduct that she is authorized to engage in. Such cases rarely occur in practice, and the judgments of the Superior Court fluctuate. But the most difficult case recently occurred in Wiener-Neustadt. In a local brothel there is a girl who is licensed to practice prostitution and who has not previously run into trouble. She never arrogated to herself any immoral conduct that she does not engage in, and she has not even been shown to have falsely stated that she does not practice a prostitution which she is licensed to practice. But the devil was riding this girl of the clean record, and one evening she walked around the parlor of the house wearing a good conduct medal on her chest. 'By so doing she aroused in the customers . . .' Well, what do you suppose she aroused in the customers? Not what you might think, but the opposite: annoyance. And when a *fille de joie* arouses annoyance in the customers of a bawdyhouse, it is presumably high time for the public prosecutor's office to take action. In point of fact, the girl was charged with an arousal for which she was not licensed. The lower-court judge acquitted her, saying that a good conduct medal was not a military decoration and the annoyance was merely of the kind that should be dealt with by the police. This, to be sure, was an admission on the part of the judge that the girl would have been guilty if she had worn, say, the Takowa medal. It is obvious that the unauthorized wearing of a medal might have made a journalist culpable, but not a prostitute. But in Wiener-Neustadt the women's movement seems to have progressed to the point where both sexes are deemed equally capable of medal-hunting. In any case, the lower-court judge did say that a good conduct medal was not a military decoration. The public prosecutor was of a different opinion, however: he appealed the verdict, and the Superior Court imposed on the defendant a fine of twenty crowns. The Superior Court said that a good conduct medal was a badge of honor equivalent to any military decoration. And the Court regarded 'the wearing of the medal in a brothel' as a particularly aggravating circumstance. When the defendant was asked what she could have been thinking of, she answered, 'Nothing.' But this time that answer did her not one bit of good, for it is better that a respectable girl presume to be a prostitute than that a prostitute presume to wear a good conduct medal. What was her excuse? She said that a civilian had given it to her; he was a generous man and gave her the medal as her 'wages of shame'. But then she should have stuck it in her stocking. Only customers are entitled to wear a badge of honor in a bawdyhouse, and if this should arouse the annoyance of the girls, the girls would be guilty of a culpable action. But if a customer gives a girl a good conduct medal instead of twenty crowns, she is not allowed to wear the medal, or else she has to give the twenty crowns to the court. For justice is a whore that won't let herself be stiffed, and collects the wages of shame even from the poor!

22
MILLICENT GARRETT FAWCETT (1847–1929)
FROM 'WOMEN'S SUFFRAGE' 1911

English suffragette and educational reformer. Fawcett opposed the militancy of the Pankhursts but campaigned for women's suffrage and access to higher education. She was a founder of Newnham College, Cambridge (1871) and President of the National Union of Women's Suffrage Societies between 1897 and 1919. Her books include Political Economy for Beginners *(1870) and* The Women's Victory – and After *(1920). The following extract is taken from the article 'Women's Suffrage', published in* The Englishwoman, *No. 30, June 1911. [See IIa 20]*

The Political Situation

Without a doubt we are higher up on the ladder of success than we have ever been before. There has been something which can only be called a collapse in the opposition to women's suffrage. The personnel of the Parliament of December 1910 is very much the same as that of January 1910; but the anti-suffrage vote in the House of Commons has fallen since last July from 189 to 88. There is a rout all along the line.

The second reading of our Bill in the House of Commons on May 5th was carried by 167, the second time within three years that the House has voted for Women's Suffrage by nearly three to one. On May 10th, the question of women's suffrage for graduates of the University was raised at the ordinary general meeting of Convocation of the University of London. The attendance was unusually large. The anti-suffragists were represented by a most accomplished speaker and member of the Executive Committee of Anti-Suffrage League, Dr. Heber Hart, and after a long discussion, the vote was given in favour of women's suffrage by 247 to 28, or nearly nine to one, whereupon, amid cheers and laughter (see *Times*, May 10th), it was resolved to ask the Prime Minister to receive a deputation on the subject.

The motto from the *Purgatorio*, which has cheered our hearts many a time, was never more appropriate than at the present moment:

'Non aver tema, disse il mio Signore:
Fatti sicur, chè noi siamo a buen punto:
Non stringer, ma rallarga ogni vigore.

We are in a stronger position than we have ever been in before, but that is not a reason for relaxing: it is a reason for straining every effort not only to make good our foothold, but to gain ground and push on to a higher point still.

Now is the time for a supreme effort, and all the real suffragists in the country are fully realising this and are making it. The National Union through its splendid organization, covering the country from Shetland to Land's End, will leave no stone unturned to press the Government for facilities for the Bill this session. The militant societies are working as hard as the constitutional societies, and are now acting on lines in which the constitutional societies can cordially co-operate. On May 12th the annual council of the British Women's Temperance Association, representing 145,000 women, passed, with only one dissentient, a strongly-worded resolution urging the Government to pass the Bill into law this session.

[. . .]

There is no time to lose. If the Women's Suffrage Bill is not passed in the House of Commons through all its stages this session, it will probably be too late for the Bill to get the advantage of the provisions of the Parliament Bill before the next Dissolution. Mr. Scott, as a practical politician, was most emphatic on this point.

> Unless (he said) you are alive to the danger which lies ahead, and unless you press upon the Government, with an insistence for greater than you have used as yet, the necessity of passing this Bill this Session or next, you may find that after all you are left out in the cold.

The Parliament Bill, it must be remembered, provides that a Bill which passes unaltered through the House of Commons in three successive Sessions shall become law even should it be rejected by the House of Lords. But the Parliament Bill also shortens the duration of Parliaments from seven years to five, and therefore it is all important to get our Bill through its stages in the Commons at the earliest possible time after the election of a new Parliament.

[. . .]

The question is how long will Parliament go on giving enormous and ever-increasing majorities in favour of the principle of Women's Suffrage without going on to embody it in practical legislation? Women are becoming more and more impatient with all the shuffling and delay with which this great question is treated by successive Governments. Even the Liberal women are saying there is a point where 'patience becomes slavishness'. How long are we to endure that a large and ever-increasing body of women all over the country have to give up all other pursuits and occupations and to give every shilling they can spare to work for Women's Suffrage, at a time too when the Prime Minister is for ever declaring that the aim of this Government is 'the establishment in all its fullness of representative Government?' What kind of representation is it from which half the people are left out? If Women's Suffrage were carried a large body of able and patriotic women would be set free to work for other things. At least 80,000*l.* a year would also be set free, as Miss Ashton pointed out last month at the National Union Women's Suffrage Convention. Women are spending quite as much each year for suffrage, that is to gain the simplest and most elementary of the rights of free citizenship. If we were not in our own judgment compelled to spend it for this great object, this sum would be free to be devoted to other purposes. Lord Haldane said he hoped Women's Suffrage would be carried soon, 'so that we may have the energy, the great capacity, and the organizing power of women' applied to the particular job which he has in hand. There will be no difficulty in finding a large field of choice for our energies and cheques. But it is becoming every day more and more plain that it is wicked waste to tie us to the eternal round of asking Governments to consider the meaning of their own professions and act upon them, of keeping up an output of about 1,000 meetings a month, of perpetually organizing processions and other demonstrations in order to prove that we really believe that the business of representation is to represent.

The case for Women's Suffrage, strong as it was before, has been made stronger by the proposal of the Government to provide 400*l.* a year for every Member of Parliament. It furnishes a new example of the well-known fact that the word 'man' in an Act of Parliament includes 'woman' when there is anything to pay or any penalty to be inflicted, but does not include 'woman' when reference is made to privileges granted by the State. Women are to pay their share of the salaries of Members of Parliament, but have no constitutional means whatever of influencing them or of controlling them. A decision to provide salaries for Members, unaccompanied by any declaration on the part of the Government that they are prepared to extend the advantages of representation to women, will give a great impulse to the tax-resistance movement among women. To many naturally quiet and law-abiding women it will be the last straw, the one insult too much, to bear which quietly and without protest would indeed be 'patience carried to the point of slavishness', as the Liberal ladies graphically put it. As I have said thus much about one of the Chancellor's measures, may I to a certain extent walk in a white sheet about another? Last year I said in a letter to the *Times:* 'The political genius of the Celt is for destruction; he can destroy but he can seldom create.' The Insurance Bill makes me wish to take this back and to be sorry I ever said it. The Insurance Bill is a great measure of constructive statesmanship. It will do much to lift the whole industrial population of the country to a higher level of material well-being. It will relieve them of the most cruel of anxieties. Women are not left out. They are to have a share in the privileges granted by the State. I am not actuary enough to say whether the benefits proposed for women are in exact proportion to the contributions made by them and on their behalf; and some of the criticisms about the maternity benefit and the cessation of benefit, so far as women are concerned, upon marriage appear to me to be well founded. These are points which will need careful consideration in Committee and upon which women themselves ought to have a voice. But it is something, nay, it is much, that for the first time the national service which a woman renders when she endures months of impaired health and puts her own life in jeopardy to give her country another citizen is recognised in legislation.

23
LOU ANDREAS-SALOMÉ (1861–1937)
FROM *THE FREUD JOURNAL OF LOU ANDREAS-SALOMÉ* 1912, 1913

Russian-born German writer, feminist and psychoanalyst. Andreas-Salomé's long and adventurous life brought her in contact with some of the most influential and diverse personalities of the early part of the twentieth century. Intellectual, novelist and 'new woman', Andreas-Salomé was passionately admired and pursued by Nietzsche his close friend the philosopher Paul Rée, the poet Rainer Maria Rilke and the Orientalist Professor F. C. Andreas. The most significant encounter in Andreas-Salomé's career, however, was with Sigmund Freud and psychoanalysis. Andreas-Salomé met Freud in 1912 and became involved with the Vienna Circle of psychoanalysts, including Adler. This last association was a frequent source of concern to Freud. From 1914 onwards, Andreas-Salomé practised psychoanalysis and wrote prolifically on the subject. One of Ibsen's earliest admirers, she produced a celebratory study of his work. Similar studies include, Friedrich Nietzsche in His Works *(1894),* Rainer Maria Rilke *(1928) and* My Thanks to Freud *(1931). She also wrote essays on love, women, sex and religion. The following extracts are taken from the 1965 edition of her 'Freud Journal', in Stanley A. Leavy's translation.*

[. . .]

Precisely as dreams in accord with their latent content are rationalized into manifest forms which we are able to recall, so our waking also proceeds. Only, from our waking point of view, we ignore and devaluate still more thoroughly the latent contribution – if indeed we take thought of it at all during the daytime. But in reality no one quite grasps the feeling that his life is lived as if behind a curtain, behind all the conscious events of waking existence. If we are inclined to doubt the truthfulness of journals and memoirs, it is not just on account of their conscious or half-conscious omissions. Above all it is because the construction of memoirs, like narrated dreams, amounts to a rationalization of experience, *eo ipso* a falsification of its latent essence. If a person thinks back over the entire course of his life, he is struck by the discontinuity and poor selectivity of the points that stand out clearly in his memory. Transitions and bridges of logical reflection must do their best to provide the connections. Many 'unforgettable' events are strikingly banal, indifferent, or meaningless, while incidents which have claimed our deepest interest have to our sorrow become unintelligible in their precious details. Here too, by means of the associative process, significant latent content may very likely evolve out of the fragments, exactly as with the dream; the picture which emerges in all these lines, broken at the surface but pressing vertically into the depths, is a picture quite different from the horizontal structure of our waking memory.

So, too, a *literary* technique could be imagined (that old dream of mine!) which would be true to that very unity of formation. It would concentrate its poetic creativity on just this, instead of on spatiotemporal representation – which we all feel ought to be *non*-literary, i.e., it ought to be simple and true like factual information. On such grounds the latter approach to writing keeps any mature person away from epic productions of otherwise greater literary quality and turns him instead to the intensively detailed psychological analysis of the modern novel, in the correct expectation that the picture can be validly completed only psychologically. The analysis, however, deals abstractly and unpoetically with the colorful living form and loses the *unity* of the images through their isolation. Instead, it should restrict itself to that which can be really suggested only through the agency of poetry, namely that unity which psychoanalysis constructs piecemeal; of it Freud remarked once that to bring about the construction of the completed analysis in reverse from the end to the beginning would require an artist. The supremely individual stays back by itself away from the typical, in which, in its special form, everything is once more recognized and so the great elemental themes recur, which children love and legends created. Yes, the fairy tale itself, the descendant of the legend, would become genuine and possible again, not 'imitation.' (marginal note: Poetry is something between the dream and its interpretation.)

Awakening from dreams, one often retains, quite independently of the present content of the dream, the feeling as of a merry dance. Then one feels more clearly that the essential unity of the state of mind lies far behind the dream fragments. The dream is split up and made manifold to oblige the rationalizing process. Conversely with waking, or the waking state in the logical sense: *its* very reality lies in the *cleavage* between the ego and that which confronts the ego. The faculty of having an inner experience tends toward *unification*. When we are awake we hold to be unreal whatever is purely subjective and is found to be unrelated to the external world; for the external world is of its substance and can be separated only by artifice. The unreal in the dream therefore is just what emerges from subjectivity into all the manifold dream realities. In this way the dream tends to reach out of the fundamental reality of the unconscious which unites both subject and object.

Just because the dream does have this tendency, it possesses a touch of the pathological element that is characteristic of neurosis and even psychosis. As far as the waking state, on the contrary, tends toward reunification, *its* reality is also rooted in unconscious reality; *en route*, however, in every moment of life, waking life is split and hence in principle it, too, resembles illness, except for the fact that it more successfully approaches its aim. From the first stirrings of the dream all the way to full consciousness we are only *en route*.

[. . .]

The way in which one beholds a person in psychoanalysis is something that goes beyond all affect toward him; somewhere in the depths both aversion and love become only differences of degree.

A relationship is achieved beyond one's own fidelity or infidelity.

Approximately this way: if hitherto one had so swiftly and so forcefully penetrated the partner that he too soon and to one's own disappointment was left behind, one now would turn quietly, strangely, and see him following and be close to him. And yet not close to him, but to all. Close anew to all, and in it, to oneself. And all the vanished persons of the past arise anew, whom one has sinned against by letting them go; they are there as from all eternity, marked by eternity – peaceful, monumental, and one with being itself, as the rock figures of Abu Simbel are one with the Egyptian rock and yet, in the form of men, sit enthroned over the water and the landscape.

24
OSWALD SPENGLER (1880–1936)
FROM *THE DECLINE OF THE WEST* 1918–22

German social theorist and philosopher. Spengler's reputation rests on his two-volume study of the philosophy of history, The Decline of the West *(written between 1918 and 1922). In this work, he claims that the philosophical historian is uniquely placed not just to retail the past but to predict the forms and developments of the future. Spengler offers the thesis that civilisations have a functional life-cycle. As he saw it, the West had already had its period of creative culture and was now ensconced in a materialist and contemplative inertia. The future, he predicted, would be a matter of unrelenting decline. The following extracts are from Volume I (subtitled* Form and Actuality*), in Charles Francis Atkinson's 1926 translation.*

To-day we think in continents, and it is only our philosophers and historians who have not realized that we do so. Of what significance to us, then, are conceptions and purviews that they put before us as universally valid, when in truth their furthest horizon does not extend beyond the intellectual atmosphere of Western Man?

Examine, from this point of view, our best books. When Plato speaks of humanity, he means the Hellenes in contrast to the barbarians, which is entirely consonant with the ahistoric mode of the Classical life and thought, and his premises take him to conclusions that *for Greeks* were complete and significant. When, however, Kant philosophizes, say on ethical ideas, he maintains the validity of his theses for men of all times and places. He does not say this in so many words, for, for himself and his readers, it is something that goes without saying. In his æsthetics he formulates the principles, not of Phidias's art, or Rembrandt's art, but of Art generally. But what he poses as necessary forms of thought are in reality only necessary forms of Western thought, though a glance at Aristotle and his essentially different conclusions should have sufficed to show that Aristotle's intellect, not less penetrating than his own, was of different structure from it. The categories of the Westerner are just as alien to Russian thought as those of the Chinaman or the ancient Greek are to him. For us, the effective and complete comprehension of Classical root-words is just as impossible as that of Russian and Indian, and for the modern Chinese or Arab, with their utterly different intellectual constitutions, 'philosophy from Bacon to Kant' has only a curiosity-value.

It is *this* that is lacking to the Western thinker, the very thinker in whom we might have expected to find it – insight into the *historically relative* character of his data, which are expressions of *one specific existence and one only*; knowledge of the necessary limits of their validity; the conviction that his 'unshakable' truths and 'eternal' views are simply true for him and eternal for his world-view; the duty of looking beyond them to find out what the men of other Cultures have with equal certainty evolved out of themselves. That and nothing else will impart completeness to the philosophy of the future, and only through an understanding of the living world shall we understand the symbolism of history. Here there is nothing constant, nothing universal. We must cease to speak of the forms of 'Thought', the principles of 'Tragedy', the mission of 'The State'. Universal validity involves always the fallacy of arguing from particular to particular.

[. . .]

In this book is attempted for the first time the venture of predetermining history, of following the still untravelled stages in the destiny of a Culture, and specifically of the

only Culture of our time and on our planet which is actually in the phase of fulfilment
– the West-European-American.

Hitherto the possibility of solving a problem so far-reaching has evidently never
been envisaged, and even if it had been so, the means of dealing with it were either
altogether unsuspected or, at best, inadequately used.

Is there a logic of history? Is there, beyond all the casual and incalculable elements
of the separate events, something that we may call a metaphysical structure of historic
humanity, something that is essentially independent of the outward forms – social,
spiritual and political – which we see so clearly? Are not these actualities indeed
secondary or derived from that something? Does world-history present to the seeing
eye certain grand traits, again and again, with sufficient constancy to justify certain
conclusions? And if so, what are the limits to which reasoning from such premisses
may be pushed?

Is it possible to find in life itself – for human history is the sum of mighty life
courses which already have had to be endowed with ego and personality, in customary
thought and expression, by predicating entities of a higher order like 'the Classical'
or 'the Chinese Culture', 'Modern Civilization' – a series of stages which must
be traversed, and traversed moreover in an ordered and obligatory sequence? For
everything organic the notions of birth, death, youth, age, lifetime are fundamentals
– may not these notions, in this sphere also, possess a rigorous meaning which no
one has as yet extracted? In short, is all history founded upon general biographic
archetypes?

The decline of the West, which at first sight may appear, like the corresponding
decline of the Classical Culture, a phenomenon limited in time and space, we now
perceive to be a philosophical problem that, when comprehended in all its gravity,
includes within itself every great question of Being.

If therefore we are to discover in what form the destiny of the Western Culture will
be accomplished, we must first be clear as to what culture *is*, what its relations are to
visible history, to life, to soul, to nature, to intellect, what the forms of its manifestation
are and how far these forms – peoples, tongues and epochs, battles and ideas, states
and gods, arts and craft-works, sciences, laws, economic types and world-ideas, great
men and great events – may be accepted and pointed to as symbols.

The means whereby to identify dead forms is Mathematical Law. The means
whereby to understand living forms is Analogy. By these means we are enabled to
distinguish polarity and periodicity in the world.

[. . .]

Thus our theme, which originally comprised only the limited problem of present-
day civilization, broadens itself into a new philosophy – *the* philosophy of the future,
so far as the metaphysically-exhausted soil of the West can bear such, and in any case
the only philosophy which is within the *possibilities* of the West-European mind in its
next stages. It expands into the conception of *a morphology of world history*, of the world-
as-history in contrast to the morphology of the world-as-nature that hitherto has been
almost the only theme of philosophy.

[. . .]

This, then, is our task. We men of the Western Culture are, with our historical sense, an exception and not a rule. World-history is *our* world picture and not all mankind's. Indian and Classical man formed no image of a world in progress, and perhaps when in due course the civilization of the West is extinguished, there will never again be a Culture and a human type in which 'world-history' is so potent a form of the waking consciousness.

[. . .]

Ib

Modern aesthetics

1

EDGAR ALLAN POE (1809–49)
FROM REVIEW OF NATHANIEL HAWTHORNE'S *TWICE-TOLD TALES* 1842

American short-story writer, poet and critic. In all his poetry and fiction, Poe exemplified the theories set out in his critical writings. Most important among these was his concept of poetic unity which stated that a poem must be of one mood or prevailing emotion. For his theory of the short story he added the dicta of a complete action performed in a single location on a single day to the unities of mood and effect. Poe's significance was quickly acknowledged abroad, especially in France, where Baudelaire and Mallarmé translated his work. His 'Philosophy of Composition' (1846) provided the theoretical basis for the French Symbolist movement. Its central assertions are found in a condensed form in his review of Hawthorne's Twice-Told Tales *written in 1842, extracts from which are reproduced below.*

[. . .]

The tale proper, in our opinion, affords unquestionably the fairest field for the exercise of the loftiest talent, which can be afforded by the wide domains of mere prose. Were we bidden to say how the highest genius could be most advantageously employed for the best display of its own powers, we should answer, without hesitation – in the composition of a rhymed poem, not to exceed in length what might be perused in an hour. Within this limit alone can the highest order of true poetry exist. We need only here say, upon this topic, that, in almost all classes of composition, the unity of effect or impression is a point of the greatest importance. It is clear, moreover, that this unity cannot be thoroughly preserved in productions whose perusal cannot be completed at one sitting. We may continue the reading of a prose composition, from the very nature of prose itself, much longer than we can persevere, to any good purpose, in the perusal of a poem. This latter, if truly fulfilling the demands of the poetic sentiment, induces an exaltation of the soul which cannot be long sustained. All high excitements are necessarily transient. Thus a long poem is a paradox. And, without unity of impression, the deepest effects cannot be brought about. Epics were the offspring of an imperfect sense of Art, and their reign is no more. A poem *too* brief may produce a vivid, but never an intense or enduring impression. Without a certain continuity of effort – without a certain duration or repetition of purpose – the soul is never deeply moved. There must be the dropping of the water upon the rock.

[. . .]

Were we called upon however to designate that class of composition which, next to such a poem as we have suggested, should best fulfil the demands of high genius – should offer it the most advantageous field of exertion – we should unhesitatingly speak of the prose tale, as Mr. Hawthorne has here exemplified it. We allude to the short prose narrative, requiring from a half-hour to one or two hours in its perusal. The ordinary novel is objectionable, from its length, for reasons already stated in substance. As it cannot be read at one sitting, it deprives itself, of course, of the immense force derivable from *totality*. Worldly interests intervening during the pauses of persual, modify, annul, or counteract, in a greater or less degree, the impressions of the book. But simple cessation in reading would, of itself, be sufficient to destroy the true unity. In the brief tale, however, the author is enabled to carry out the fulness of his intention, be it what it may. During the hour of persual the soul of the reader is at the writer's control. There are no external or extrinsic influences – resulting from weariness or interruption.

A skilful literary artist has constructed a tale. If wise, he has not fashioned thoughts to accommodate his incidents; but having conceived, with deliberate care, a certain unique or single *effect* to be wrought out, he then invents such incidents – he then combines such events as may best aid him in establishing this preconceived effect. If his very initial sentence tend not to the outbringing of this effect, then he has failed in his first step. In the whole composition there should be no word written, of which the tendency, direct or indirect, is not to the one pre-established design. And by such means, with such care and skill, a picture is at length painted which leaves the mind of him who contemplates it with a kindred art, a sense of the fullest satisfaction. The idea of the tale has been presented unblemished, because undisturbed; and this is an end unattainable by the novel. Undue brevity is just as exceptionable here as in the poem; but undue length is yet more to be avoided.

We have said that the tale has a point of superiority even over the poem. In fact, while the *rhythm* of this latter is an essential aid in the development of the poem's highest idea – the idea of the Beautiful – the artificialities of this rhythm are an inseparable bar to the development of all points of thought or expression which have their basis in *Truth*. But Truth is often, and in very great degree, the aim of the tale. Some of the finest tales are tales of ratiocination. Thus the field of this species of composition, if not in so elevated a region on the mountain of Mind, is a table-land of far vaster extent than the domain of the mere poem. Its products are never so rich, but infinitely more numerous, and more appreciable by the mass of mankind. The writer of the prose tale, in short, may bring to his theme a vast variety of modes or inflections of thought and expression – (the ratiocinative, for example, the sarcastic or the humorous) which are not only antagonistical to the nature of the poem, but absolutely forbidden by one of its most peculiar and indispensable adjuncts: we allude of course, to rhythm. It may be added, here, *par parenthèse*, that the author who aims at the purely beautiful in a prose tale is laboring at great disadvantage. For Beauty can be better treated in the poem. Not so with terror, or passion, or horror, or a multitude of such other points.

[. . .]

2
WALT WHITMAN (1819–92)
FROM PREFACE TO *LEAVES OF GRASS* 1855

American poet and essayist. Whitman saw the first edition of his 'wonderful and ponderous book' Leaves of Grass *through the presses in 1855. It was the first of nine editions that he would publish in his lifetime. In the preface to the first edition, Whitman set out his vision of the status of the ideal poet in relation to the USA, nature, the universe. Integrating a diverse set of philosophies — from Carlyle to the pseudosciences — he declared his belief in the greatness of the freedom that mankind could achieve within the limits of his being. The poems in* Leaves of Grass *were remarkable for their formal and rhetorical eclecticism, and Whitman is generally regarded as the pioneer of free-verse form.*

[. . .]

The American poets are to enclose old and new for America is the race of races. Of them a bard is to be commensurate with a people. To him the other continents arrive as contributions . . . he gives them reception for their sake and his own sake. His spirit responds to his country's spirit . . . he incarnates its geography and natural life and rivers and lakes. [. . .] Of all mankind the great poet is the equable man. Not in him but off from him things are grotesque or eccentric or fail of their sanity. Nothing out of its place is good and nothing in its place is bad. He bestows on every object or quality its fit proportions neither more nor less. He is the arbiter of the diverse and he is the key. He is the equalizer of his age and land.

[. . .]

The greatest poet hardly knows pettiness or triviality. If he breathes into anything that was before thought small it dilates with the grandeur and life of the universe. He is a seer . . . he is individual . . . he is complete in himself . . . the others are as good as he, only he sees it and they do not. He is not one of the chorus . . . he does not stop for any regulation . . . he is the president of regulation. What the eyesight does to the rest he does to the rest. Who knows the curious mystery of the eyesight? The other senses corroborate themselves, but this is removed from any proof but its own and foreruns the identities of the spiritual world. A single glance of it mocks all the investigations of man and all the instruments and books of the earth and all reasoning. What is marvellous? what is unlikely? what is impossible or baseless or vague? after you have once just opened the space of a peachpit and given audience to far and near and to the sunset and had all things enter with electric swiftness softly and duly without confusion or jostling or jam.

[. . .]

The rhyme and uniformity of perfect poems show the free growth of metrical laws and bud from them as unerringly and loosely as lilacs or roses on a bush, and take shapes as compact as the shapes of chestnuts and oranges and melons and pears, and shed the perfume impalpable to form. The fluency and ornaments of the finest poems or music or orations or recitations are not independent but dependent. All beauty comes from beautiful blood and a beautiful brain. If the greatnesses are in conjunction in a man or woman it is enough . . . the fact will prevail through the universe . . . but the gaggery and gilt of a million years will not prevail. Who troubles himself about his ornaments or fluency is lost. This is what you shall do: Love the earth and sun and the animals, despise riches, give alms to every one that asks, stand up for the stupid and crazy, devote your income and labor to others, hate tyrants, argue not concerning God, have patience and indulgence toward the people, take off your hat to nothing known or unknown or to any man or number of men, go freely with powerful uneducated persons and with the young and with the mothers of families, read these leaves in the open air every season of every year of your life, re-examine all you have been told at school or church or in any book, dismiss whatever insults your own soul, and your very flesh shall be a great poem and have the richest fluency not only in its words but in the silent lines of its lips and face and between the lashes of your eyes and in every motion and joint of your body.

[. . .]

The known universe has one complete lover and that is the greatest poet. [. . .] The greatest poet has less a marked style and is more the channel of thoughts and things without increase or diminution, and is the free channel of himself. He swears to his art, I will not be meddlesome, I will not have in my writing any elegance or effect or originality to hang in the way between me and the rest like curtains. I will have nothing hang in the way, not the richest curtains.

[. . .]

The direct trial of him who would be the greatest poet is today. If he does not flood himself with the immediate age as with vast oceanic tides . . . and if he does not attract his own land body and soul to himself and hang on its neck with incomparable love and plunge his semitic muscle into its merits and demerits . . . and if he be not himself the age transfigured . . . and if to him is not opened the eternity which gives similitude to all periods and locations and processes and animate and inanimate forms, and which is the bond of time, and rises up from its inconceivable vagueness and infiniteness in the swimming shape of today, and is held by the ductile anchors of life, and makes the present spot the passage from what was to what shall be, and commits itself to the representation of this wave of an hour and this one of the sixty beautiful children of the wave – let him merge in the general run and wait his development . . . [. . .]

There will soon be no more priests. Their work is done. They may wait awhile . . . perhaps a generation or two . . . dropping off by degrees. A superior breed shall take their place . . . the gangs of kosmos and prophets en masse shall take their place. A new order shall arise and they shall be the priests of man, and every man shall be his own priest. The churches built under their umbrage shall be the churches of men and women. Through the divinity of themselves shall the kosmos and the new breed of poets be interpreters of men and women and of all events and things. They shall find their inspiration in real objects today, symptoms of the past and future. . . . They shall not deign to defend immortality or God or the perfection of things or liberty or the exquisite beauty and reality of the soul. They shall arise in America and be responded to from the remainder of the earth.

The English language befriends the grand American expression . . . it is brawny enough and limber and full enough. On the tough stock of a race who through all change of circumstance was never without the idea of political liberty, which is the animus of all liberty, it has attracted the terms of daintier and gayer and subtler and more elegant tongues. It is the powerful language of resistance . . . it is the dialect of common sense. It is the speech of the proud and melancholy races and of all who aspire. It is the chosen tongue to express growth faith self-esteem freedom justice equality friendliness amplitude prudence decision and courage. It is the medium that shall well nigh express the inexpressible.

[. . .]

3
GUSTAVE FLAUBERT (1821–80)
FROM LETTER TO MLLE LEROYER DE CHANTEPIE, 18 MARCH 1857

French novelist and short-story writer. Flaubert's Madame Bovary *(1857) has been called the first modern novel and its influence on modern and Modernist writers is cited on many a preface with novelists paying homage to Flaubert's style. In the letter from which we extract below, translated by Francis Steegmuller, Flaubert is concerned with the question of impersonality in art – a central feature of his style, as well as a delicate and poignant issue for him at a time when he was being prosecuted for the 'immorality' of his work. [See IIIa 2]*

the absence of human character

I hasten to thank you; I have received everything you sent. Thank you for the letter, the books, and above all for the portrait. I am touched by this delicate attention.

I am going to read your three volumes slowly and attentively – that is (I am sure in advance), as they deserve.

But I am prevented from doing so for the moment, since before returning to the country I have to do some archaeological work in one of the least-known periods of antiquity – a task which is preparation for another task. I am going to write a novel whose action will take place three centuries before Christ. I feel the need of taking leave of the modern world· my pen has been steeped in it too long, and I am as weary of portraying it as I am disgusted by the sight of it.

With a reader such as you, Madame, one who is so understanding, frankness is a duty. I therefore answer your questions: *Madame Bovary* is based on no actual occurrence. It is a *totally fictitious* story; it contains none of my feelings and no details from my own life. The illusion of truth (if there is one) comes, on the contrary, from the book's impersonality It is one of my principles that a writer should not be his own theme. An artist must be in his work like God in creation, invisible and all-powerful; he should be everywhere felt, but nowhere seen.

Va Woolf

Meryl Streep

Furthermore, Art must rise above personal emotions and nervous susceptibilities. It is time to endow it with pitiless method, with the exactness of the physical sciences. Still, for me the capital difficulty remains style, form, that indefinable Beauty implicit in the conception and representing, as Plato said, the splendor of Truth.

For a long time, Madame, I led a life like yours. I too spent several years completely alone in the country, hearing in winter no sound but the rustle of the wind in the trees and the cracking of the drift-ice on the Seine under my window. If I have arrived at some understanding of life, it is because I have lived little in the ordinary sense of the word; I have eaten meagerly, but ruminated much; I have seen all kinds of people, and visited various countries. I have traveled on foot and on camel-back. I am acquainted with Parisian speculators and Damascus Jews, with Italian ruffians and

Negro mountebanks. I made a pilgrimage to the Holy Land and was lost in the snows of Parnassus – which may be taken symbolically.

Do not complain; I have been here and there in the world and have a thorough knowledge of that Paris you dream of; there is nothing to equal a good book at your fireside, the reading of *Hamlet* or *Faust* on a day when your responses are keen. My own dream is to buy a little palace in Venice, on the Grand Canal.

So there, Madame – part of your curiosity is gratified. To complete my portrait and biography, add only this: I am thirty-five, five feet eight, with the shoulders of a stevedore and the nervous irritability of a young lady of fashion. I am a bachelor and a recluse.

[. . .]

If all you needed to be a poet were to have sensitive nerves, I should be greater than Shakespeare – or Homer either, for I imagine he was without nerves. But this is blasphemy . . .

You often find children who are upset by music. They show great talent and remember tunes at a single hearing. When they play the piano they grow excited and their hearts beat faster. They get thin and pale, and fall ill; and like dogs they feel their nerves shrivel with pain at the very sound of music. It is not they that are the future Mozarts. Their *vocation* has been displaced; the spirit has passed into the flesh where it remains sterile, and the flesh decays; the result is neither genius nor good health.

It is the same with art. Feeling does not make poetry; and the more personal you are, the poorer you will be. That has always been my sin; I have always put myself into everything I have done. There I am, for instance, in Saint Anthony's place; the *Temptation* was mine and not the reader's. *The less one feels a thing, the more fit one is to express it in its true nature* (as it always is, in itself, in its generic being and divorced from all ephemeral conditions). But one must have the faculty for *making oneself feel.* This faculty is neither more nor less than genius; *which is*, to have the object posed in front of one.

4
MATTHEW ARNOLD (1822–88)
FROM 'ON THE MODERN ELEMENT IN LITERATURE' 1857

English poet and critic. Arnold's career as a poet began in 1849 with the publication of The Strayed Reveller *and ended with the publication of* New Poems *in 1867. The first in his series of critical writings,* Essays in Criticism, *appeared in 1865 (a second edition appeared posthumously in 1888) and included 'The Function of Criticism at the Present Time' in which he sought to expand the range and significance of criticism, claiming for it an application beyond the merely literary. In* Culture and Anarchy *(1869) he dealt more explicitly with the dilemmas of his age, commending the study of culture – 'the pursuit of total perfection' – as antedote to the standardless 'anarchy' of Victorian society. The following extracts are from Arnold's inaugural lecture as Professor of Poetry at Oxford, delivered in 1857.*

[. . .]

An intellectual deliverance is the peculiar demand of those ages which are called modern; and those nations are said to be imbued with the modern spirit most eminently in which the demand for such a deliverance has been made with most zeal, and satisfied with most completeness. Such a deliverance is emphatically, whether we will or no, the demand of the age in which we ourselves live. All intellectual pursuits our age judges according to their power of helping to satisfy this demand; of all studies it asks, above all, the question, how far they can contribute to this deliverance.

I propose, on this my first occasion of speaking here, to attempt such a general survey of ancient classical literature and history as may afford us the conviction – in presence of the doubts so often expressed of the profitableness, in the present day, of our study of this literature – that, even admitting to their fullest extent the legitimate demands of our age, the literature of ancient Greece is, even for modern times, a mighty agent of intellectual deliverance; even for modern times, therefore, an object of indestructible interest.

But first let us ask ourselves why the demand for an intellectual deliverance arises in such an age as the present, and in what the deliverance itself consists? The demand arises, because our present age has around it a copious and complex present, and behind it a copious and complex past; it arises, because the present age exhibits to the individual man who contemplates it the spectacle of a vast multitude of facts awaiting and inviting his comprehension. The deliverance consists in man's comprehension of this present and past. It begins when our mind begins to enter into possession of the general ideas which are the law of this vast multitude of facts. It is perfect when we have acquired that harmonious acquiescence of mind which we feel in contemplating a grand spectacle that is intelligible to us; when we have lost that impatient irritation of mind which we feel in the presence of an immense, moving, confused spectacle which, while it perpetually excites our curiosity, perpetually baffles our comprehension.

This, then, is what distinguishes certain epochs in the history of the human race, and our own amongst the number; – on the one hand, the presence of a significant spectacle to contemplate; on the other hand, the desire to find the true point of view from which to contemplate this spectacle. He who has found that point of view, he who adequately comprehends this spectacle, has risen to the comprehension of his age: he who communicates that point of view to his age, he who interprets to it that spectacle, is one of his age's intellectual deliverers.

The spectacle, the facts, presented for the comprehension of the present age, are indeed immense. The facts consist of the events, the institutions, the sciences, the arts, the literatures, in which human life has manifested itself up to the present time: the spectacle is the collective life of humanity. And everywhere there is connexion, everywhere there is illustration: no single event, no single literature, is adequately comprehended except in its relation to other events, to other literatures. The literature of ancient Greece, the literature of the Christian Middle Age, so long as they are regarded as two isolated literatures, two isolated growths of the human spirit, are not adequately comprehended; and it is adequate comprehension which is the demand of the present age.

[. . .]

But all facts, all the elements of the spectacle before us, have not an equal value – do not merit a like attention: and it is well that they do not, for no man would be adequate to the task of thoroughly mastering them all.

[. . .]

What facts, then, let us ask ourselves, what elements of the spectacle before us, will naturally be most interesting to a highly developed age like our own, to an age making the demand which we have described for an intellectual deliverance by means of the complete intelligence of its own situation? Evidently, the other ages similarly developed, and making the same demand. And what past literature will naturally be most interesting to such an age as our own? Evidently, the literatures which have most successfully solved for *their* ages the problem which occupies ours: the literatures which in their day and for their own nation have adequately comprehended, have adequately represented, the spectacle before them. A significant, a highly-developed, a culminating epoch, on the one hand, – a comprehensive, a commensurate, an adequate literature, on the other, – these will naturally be the objects of deepest interest to our modern age. Such an epoch and such a literature are, in fact, *modern*, in the same sense in which our own age and literature are modern; they are founded upon a rich past and upon an instructive fulness of experience.

[. . .]

And I shall not, I hope, be thought to magnify too much my office if I add, that it is to the poetical literature of an age that we must, in general, look for the most perfect, the most adequate interpretation of that age, – for the performance of a work which demands the most energetic and harmonious activity of all the powers of the human mind. Because that activity of the whole mind, that genius, as Johnson nobly describes it, 'without which judgment is cold and knowledge is inert; that energy which collects, combines, amplifies, and animates,' is in poetry at its highest stretch and in its most energetic exertion.

What we seek, therefore, what will most enlighten us, most contribute to our intellectual deliverance, is the union of two things; it is the coexistence, the simultaneous appearance, of a great epoch and a great literature.

Now the culminating age in the life of ancient Greece I call, beyond question, a great epoch; the life of Athens in the fifth century before our era I call one of the highly developed, one of the marking, one of the modern periods in the life of the whole human race.

[. . .]

There was the utmost energy of life there, public and private; the most entire freedom, the most unprejudiced and intelligent observation of human affairs. Let us rapidly examine some of the characteristics which distinguish modern epochs; [. . .] To begin with what is exterior. One of the most characteristic outward features of a *modern* age, of an age of advanced civilization, is the banishment of the ensigns of war and bloodshed from the intercourse of civil life. Crime still exists, and wars are still carried on; but within the limits of civil life a circle has been formed within which man can move securely, and develop the arts of peace uninterruptedly.

[. . .]

An important inward characteristic, again, is the growth of a tolerant spirit; that spirit which is the offspring of an enlarged knowledge; a spirit patient of the diversities of habits and opinions. Other characteristics are the multiplication of the conveniences of life, the formation of taste, the capacity for refined pursuits. And this leads us to the supreme characteristic of all: the intellectual maturity of man himself; the tendency to observe facts with a critical spirit; to search for their law, not to wander among them at random; to judge by the rule of reason, not by the impulse of prejudice or caprice.

[. . .]

In the flowering period of the life of Greece, therefore, we have a culminating age, one of the flowering periods of the life of the human race: in the poetry of that age we have a literature commensurate with its epoch. It is most perfectly commensurate in the poetry of Pindar, Aeschylus, Sophocles, Aristophanes; these, therefore, will be the supremely interesting objects in this literature; but the stages in literature which led up to this point of perfection, the stages in literature which led downward from it, will be deeply interesting also.

[. . .]

Homer himself is eternally interesting; he is a greater poetical power than even Sophocles or Aeschylus; but his age is less interesting than himself. Aeschylus and Sophocles represent an age as interesting as themselves; the names, indeed, in their dramas are the names of the old heroic world, from which they were far separated; but these names are taken, because the use of them permits to the poet that free and ideal treatment of his characters which the highest tragedy demands; and into these figures of the old world is poured all the fulness of life and of thought which the new world had accumulated. This new world in its maturity of reason resembles our own; and the advantage over Homer in their great significance for *us*, which Aeschylus and Sophocles gain by belonging to this new world, more than compensates for their poetical inferiority to him.

[   ]

In the Roman world, then, we have found a highly modern, a deeply significant, an interesting period – a period more significant and more interesting, because fuller, than the great period of Greece; but we have not a commensurate literature. In Greece we have seen a highly modern, a most significant and interesting period, although on a scale of less magnitude and importance than the great period of Rome; but then, co-existing with the great epoch of Greece there is what is wanting to that of Rome, a commensurate, an interesting literature.

The intellectual history of our race cannot be clearly understood without applying to other ages, nations, and literatures the same method of inquiry which we have been here imperfectly applying to what is called classical antiquity. But enough has at least been said, perhaps, to establish the absolute, the enduring interest of Greek literature, and, above all, of Greek poetry.

5
CHARLES BAUDELAIRE (1821–67)
FROM 'THE PAINTER OF MODERN LIFE' 1859–60

French poet and critic. Baudelaire's entire œuvre may be seen as one of the key formulations of the modern in literature and art. As a Symbolist poet, he helps to connect late Romanticism with early Modernism, and in his art criticism, he responds to the concerns of his time (the relationship between art and revolutionary politics, the challenge of Realism and the new technologies of art, the phenomenon of fashion and life in the metropolis) with analyses which look forward to the next century. His fame (or notoriety) as a poet rests mainly with the collection Les Fleurs du mal *(1857), for which he was prosecuted on charges of impropriety in 1864. Later works include* Les Paradis artificiels *(1860) and* Petits Poèmes en prose *(1869). The following extracts are taken from an article written between 1859–60 and published in 1863, appearing here in P. E. Charvet's translation for the 1972 edition of* Baudelaire: Selected Writings on Art and Artists. *In this discussion of the painter Constantin Guys, Baudelaire articulates his famous definition of modernity as 'the transient, the fleeting, the contingent', as well as providing a number of sketches of fragments of 'modern life'.*

I.   Beauty, fashion and happiness

[. . .]

The past is interesting, not only because of the beauty that the artists for whom it was the present were able to extract from it, but also as past, for its historical value. The same applies to the present. The pleasure we derive from the representation of the present is due, not only to the beauty it can be clothed in, but also to its essential quality of being the present.

I have here in front of me a series of fashion plates, the earliest dating from the Revolution, the most recent from the Consulate or thereabouts. These costumes, which many thoughtless people, the sort of people who are grave without true gravity, find highly amusing, have a double kind of charm, artistic and historical. They are very often beautiful and wittily drawn, but what to me is at least as important, and what I am glad to find in all or nearly all of them, *is the moral attitude and the aesthetic value of the time.* The idea of beauty that man creates for himself affects his whole attire, ruffles or stiffens his coat, gives curves or straight lines to his gestures and even, in process of time, subtly penetrates the very features of his face. Man comes in the end to look like his ideal image of himself. These engravings can be translated into beauty or ugliness: in ugliness they become caricatures; in beauty, antique statues.

The women who wore these dresses looked more or less like one or the other, according to the degree of poetry or vulgarity evident in their faces. The living substance gave suppleness to what appears too stiff to us. The viewer's imagination can even today see a marching man in this tunic or the shrug of a woman's shoulder beneath that shawl. One of these days perhaps some theatre or other will put on a play where we shall see a revival of the fashions in which our fathers thought themselves just as captivating as we ourselves think we are, in our modest garments (which also have their attractiveness, to be sure, but rather of a moral and spiritual kind); and, if

[handwritten top margin: beauty denotes something eternal — taps a sense of awe. but we ascribe this 'Beauty' is through our subjective passion — towards that awe]

they are worn and given life to by intelligent actors and actresses, we shall be surprised at our having laughed at them so thoughtlessly. The past, whilst retaining its ghostly piquancy, will recapture the light and movement of life, and become present.

[handwritten margin: Faulkner — "The past is never dead. It's not even past"]

[. . .]

Here we have indeed a golden opportunity *to establish a rational and historical theory of beauty, in contrast to the theory of a unique and absolute beauty, and to show that beauty is always and inevitably compounded of two elements*, although the impression it conveys is one; for the difficulty we may experience in distinguishing the variable elements that go to make beauty's unity of impression does not in any way invalidate the need of variety in its composition. Beauty is made up, on the one hand, of an element that *is eternal and invariable*, though to determine how much of it there is is extremely difficult, and, on the other, of *a relative circumstantial element*, which we may like to call, successively or at one and the same time, *contemporaneity, fashion, morality, passion*. Without this second element, which is like the amusing, teasing, appetite-whetting coating of the divine cake, the first element would be indigestible, tasteless, unadapted and inappropriate to human nature. I challenge anyone to find any sample whatsoever of beauty that does not contain these two elements.

[handwritten margin: contingent of / we are all beauty subjective / artistic]

Let me take as an example the two extreme stages of history. In hieratic art duality is evident at the first glance; the eternal element of beauty reveals itself only by permission and under the control of the religion the artist belongs to. In the most frivolous work of a sophisticated artist, belonging to one of those ages we vaingloriously call civilized, the duality is equally apparent; the eternal part of beauty will be both veiled and expressed, if not through fashion, then at least through the individual temperament of the artist. *The duality of art is an inevitable consequence of the duality of man. If you like it that way, you may identify the eternally subsisting portion as the soul of art, and the variable element as its body.* That is why Stendhal, that impertinent, teasing, even repugnant mind (whose impertinences are, nevertheless, usefully thought-provoking), came close to the truth, much closer than many other people, when he said: '*The beautiful is neither more nor less than the promise of happiness.*' No doubt this definition oversteps the mark; it subordinates beauty much too much to the infinitely variable ideal of happiness; it divests beauty too lightly of its aristocratic character, but it has the great merit of getting away from the mistake of the academicians.

[. . .]

III. An artist, man of the world, man of crowds, and child

Today I want to talk to my readers about a singular man, whose originality is so powerful and clear-cut that it is self-sufficing, and does not bother to look for approval. None of his drawings is signed, if by signature we mean the few letters, which can be so easily forged, that compose a name, and that so many other artists grandly inscribe at the bottom of their most carefree sketches. But all his works are signed with his dazzling soul, and art-lovers who have seen and liked them will recognize them easily from the description I propose to give of them. M. C. G. *loves mixing with the crowds, loves* being incognito, and carries his originality to the point of modesty.

For ten whole years I wanted to make the acquaintance of M.G., who is by nature a great traveller and very cosmopolitan. I knew that he had for a long time been working for an English illustrated paper and that in it had appeared engravings from his travel sketches (Spain, Turkey, the Crimea). Since then I have seen a considerable mass of these on-the-spot drawings from life, and I have thus been able to 'read' a detailed and daily account, infinitely preferable to any other, of the Crimean campaign. The same paper had also published (without signature, as before) a large quantity of compositions by this artist from the new ballets and operas. When at last I ran him to ground I saw at once that I was not dealing exactly with an artist *but rather with a man of the world*. In this context, pray interpret the word 'artist' in a very narrow sense, and the expression 'man of the world' in a very broad one. *By 'man of the world', I mean a man of the whole world, a man who understands the world and the mysterious and legitimate reasons behind all its customs; by 'artist', I mean a specialist, a man tied to his palette like a serf to the soil.* M.G. does not like being called an artist. Is he not justified to a small extent? He takes an interest in everything the world over, he wants to know, understand, assess everything that happens on the surface of our spheroid. *The artist moves little, or even not at all, in intellectual and political circles.* If he lives in the Bréda quarter he knows nothing of what goes on in the Faubourg Saint-Germain. With two or three exceptions, which it is unnecessary to name, the majority of artists are, let us face it, very skilled brutes, mere manual labourers, village pub-talkers with the minds of country bumpkins. Their talk, inevitably enclosed within very narrow limits, quickly becomes a bore to the *man of the world*, to *the spiritual citizen of the universe*.

Thus to begin to understand M.G., the first thing to note is this: that curiosity may be considered the starting point of his genius.

Do you remember a picture (for indeed it is a picture!) written by the most powerful pen of this age and entitled *The Man of the Crowd*? Sitting in a café, and looking through the shop window, a convalescent is enjoying the sight of the passing crowd, and identifying himself in thought with all the thoughts that are moving around him. He has only recently come back from the shades of death and breathes in with delight all the spores and odours of life; as he has been on the point of forgetting everything, he remembers and passionately wants to remember everything. In the end he rushes out into the crowd in search of a man unknown to him whose face, which he had caught sight of, had in a flash fascinated him. Curiosity had become a compelling, irresistible passion.

Now imagine an artist perpetually in the spiritual condition of the convalescent, and you will have the key to the character of M.G.

But convalescence is like a return to childhood. The convalescent, like the child, enjoys to the highest degree the faculty of taking a lively interest in things, even the most trivial in appearance. Let us hark back, if we can, by a retrospective effort of our imaginations, to our youngest, our morning impressions, and we shall recognize that they were remarkably akin to the vividly coloured impressions that we received later on after a physical illness, provided that illness left our spiritual faculties pure and unimpaired. *The child sees everything as a novelty; the child is always 'drunk'. Nothing is more like what we call inspiration than the joy the child feels in drinking in shape and colour.* I will venture to go even further and declare that inspiration has some connection with congestion, that every sublime thought is accompanied by a more or less vigorous nervous impulse that reverberates in the cerebral cortex. *The man of genius has strong nerves; those of the child are weak.* In the one, reason has assumed an important role; in the other, sensibility occupies almost the whole being. *But genius is no more than childhood recaptured at will, childhood equipped now with man's physical means to express itself, and with the analytical mind that enables it to bring order into the sum of experience, involuntarily amassed.*

[. . .]

The crowd is his domain, just as the air is the bird's, and water that of the fish. His passion and his profession is to merge with the crowd. For the perfect idler, for the passionate observer it becomes an immense source of enjoyment to establish his dwelling in the throng, in the ebb and flow, the bustle, the fleeting and the infinite. To be away from home and yet to feel at home anywhere; to see the world, to be at the very centre of the world, and yet to be unseen of the world, such are some of the minor pleasures of those independent, intense and impartial spirits, who do not lend themselves easily to linguistic definitions. *The observer is a prince enjoying his incognito wherever he goes.* The lover of life makes the whole world into his family, just as the lover of the fair sex creates his from all the lovely women he has found, from those that could be found, and those who are impossible to find, just as the picture lover lives in an enchanted world of dreams painted on canvas. *Thus the lover of universal life moves into the crowd as though into an enormous reservoir of electricity. He, the lover of life, may also be compared to a mirror as vast as this crowd; to a kaleidoscope endowed with consciousness, which with every one of its movements presents a pattern of life, in all its multiplicity, and the flowing grace of all the elements that go to compose life.* It is an ego athirst for the non-ego, and reflecting it at every moment in energies more vivid than life itself, always inconstant and fleeting. 'Any man', M.G. once said, in one of those talks he rendered memorable by the intensity of his gaze, and by his eloquence of gesture,' any man who is not weighed down with a sorrow so searching as to touch all his faculties, and who is bored in the midst of the crowd, is a fool! A fool! and I despise him!'

When, as he wakes up, M.G. opens his eyes and sees the sun beating vibrantly at his window-panes, he says to himself with remorse and regret: 'What an imperative command! What a fanfare of light! Light everywhere for several hours past! Light I have lost in sleep! and endless numbers of things bathed in light that I could have seen and have failed to!' And off he goes! And he watches the flow of life move by, majestic and dazzling. He admires the eternal beauty and the astonishing harmony of life in the capital cities, a harmony so providentially maintained in the tumult of human liberty. He gazes at the landscape of the great city, landscapes of stone, now swathed in the mist, now struck in full face by the sun. He enjoys handsome equipages, proud horses, the spit and polish of the grooms, the skilful handling by the page boys, the smooth rhythmical gait of the women, the beauty of the children, full of the joy of life and proud as peacocks of their pretty clothes; in short, life universal. If in a shift of fashion, the cut of a dress has been slightly modified, if clusters of ribbons and curls have been dethroned by rosettes, if bonnets have widened and chignons have come down a little on the nape of the neck, if waist-lines have been raised and skirts become fuller, you may be sure that from a long way off his eagle's eye will have detected it. A regiment marches by, maybe on its way to the ends of the earth, filling the air of the boulevard with its martial airs, as light and lively as hope; and sure enough M.G. has already seen, inspected and analysed the weapons and the bearing of this whole body of troops. *Harness, highlights, bands, determined mien, heavy and grim mustachios, all these details flood chaotically into him; and within a few minutes the poem that comes with it all is virtually composed.* And then his soul will vibrate with the soul of the regiment, marching as though it were one living creature, proud image of joy and discipline!

But evening comes. The witching hour, the uncertain light, when the sky draws its curtains and the city lights go on. The gaslight stands out on the purple background of the setting sun. Honest men or crooked customers, wise or irresponsible, all are saying to themselves: 'The day is done at last!' Good men and bad turn their thoughts to pleasure, and each hurries to his favourite haunt to drink the cup of oblivion. M.G. will be the last to leave any place where the departing glories of daylight linger, where poetry echoes, life pulsates, music sounds; any place where a human passion offers a subject to his eye where natural man and conventional man reveal themselves in strange beauty, where the rays of the dying sun play on the fleeting pleasure of the 'depraved animal!' 'Well, there, to be sure, is a day well filled,' murmurs to himself a type of reader well-known to all of us; 'each one of us has surely enough genius to fill it in the same way.' No! few men have the gift of seeing; fewer still have the power to express themselves. And now, whilst others are sleeping, this man is leaning over his table, his steady gaze on a sheet of paper, exactly the same gaze as he directed just now at the things about him, brandishing his pencil, his pen, his brush, splashing water from the glass up to the ceiling, wiping his pen on his shirt, hurried, vigorous, active, as though he was afraid the images might escape him, quarrelsome though alone, and driving himself relentlessly on. And things seen are born again on the paper, natural and more than natural, beautiful and better than beautiful, strange and endowed with an enthusiastic life, like the soul of their creator. The weird pageant has been distilled from nature. *All the materials, stored higgledy-piggledy by memory, are classified, ordered, harmonized, and undergo that deliberate idealization, which is the product of a childlike perceptiveness, in other words a perceptiveness that is acute and magical by its very ingenuousness.*

IV.　Modernity

And so, walking or quickening his pace, he goes his way, for ever in search. In search of what? We may rest assured that this man, such as I have described him, *this solitary mortal endowed with an active imagination, always roaming the great desert of men, has a nobler aim than that of the pure idler, a more general aim, other than the fleeting pleasure of circumstance. He is looking for that indefinable something we may be allowed to call 'modernity',* for want of a better term to express the idea in question. *The aim for him is to extract from fashion the poetry that resides in its historical envelope, to distil the eternal from the transitory.* If we cast our eye over our exhibitions of modern pictures, we shall be struck by the general tendency of our artists to clothe all manner of subjects in the dress of the past. Almost all of them use the fashions and the furnishings of the Renaissance, as David used Roman fashions and furnishings, but there is this difference, that David, having chosen subjects peculiarly Greek or Roman, could not do otherwise than present them in the style of antiquity, whereas the painters of today, choosing, as they do, subjects of a general nature, applicable to all ages, will insist on dressing them up in the fashion of the Middle Ages, of the Renaissance, or of the East. This is evidently sheer laziness; for it is much more convenient to state roundly that everything is hopelessly ugly in the dress of a period than to apply oneself to the task of extracting the mysterious beauty that may be hidden there, however small or light it may be. *Modernity is the transient, the fleeting, the contingent; it is one half of art, the other being the eternal and the immovable. There was a form of modernity for every painter of the past;* the majority of the fine portraits that remain to us from former times are clothed in the dress of their own day. They are perfectly harmonious works because the dress, the hairstyle, and even the gesture, the expression and the smile (each age has its carriage, its expression and its smile) form a whole, full of vitality. *You have no right to despise this transitory fleeting element, the metamorphoses of which are so frequent, nor to dispense with it. If you do, you inevitably fall into the emptiness of an abstract and indefinable beauty, like that of the one and only woman of the time before the Fall.* If for the dress of the day, which is necessarily right, you substitute another, you are guilty of a piece of nonsense that only a fancy-dress ball imposed by fashion can excuse. Thus the goddesses, the nymphs, and sultanas of the eighteenth century are portraits in the spirit of their day.

[. . .]

Woe betide the man who goes to antiquity for the study of anything other than ideal art, logic and general method! By immersing himself too deeply in it, he will no longer have the present in his mind's eye; he throws away the value and the privileges afforded by circumstance; *for nearly all our originality comes from the stamp that time impresses upon our sensibility.*

IX. The dandy

Dandyism, which is an institution outside the law, has a rigorous code of laws that all its subjects are strictly bound by, however ardent and independent their individual characters may be.

[. . .]

These beings have no other status but that of cultivating the idea of beauty in their own persons, of satisfying their passions, of feeling and thinking. Thus they possess, to their hearts' content, and to a vast degree, both time and money, without which fantasy, reduced to the state of ephemeral reverie, can scarcely be translated into action. It is unfortunately very true that, without leisure and money, love can be no more than an orgy of the common man, or the accomplishment of a conjugal duty. Instead of being a sudden impulse full of ardour and reverie, it becomes a distastefully utilitarian affair.

If I speak of love in the context of dandyism, the reason is that love is the natural occupation of men of leisure. But the dandy does not consider love as a special aim in life. If I have mentioned money, the reason is that money is indispensable to those who make an exclusive cult of their passions, but the dandy does not aspire to wealth as an object in itself; an open bank credit could suit him just as well; he leaves that squalid passion to vulgar mortals. Contrary to what a lot of thoughtless people seem to believe, dandyism is not even an excessive delight in clothes and material elegance. *For the perfect dandy, these things are no more than the symbol of the aristocratic superiority of his mind.* Thus, in his eyes, enamoured as he is above all of distinction, perfection in dress consists in absolute simplicity, which is, indeed, the best way of being distinguished. What then can this passion be, which has crystallized into a doctrine, and has formed a number of outstanding devotees, this unwritten code that has moulded so proud a brotherhood? *It is, above all, the burning desire to create a personal form of originality, within the external limits of social conventions. It is a kind of cult of the ego which can still survive the pursuit of that form of happiness to be found in others, in woman for example, which can even survive what are called illusions. It is the pleasure of causing surprise in others, and the proud satisfaction of never showing any oneself.* A dandy may be blase, he may even suffer pain, but in the latter case he will keep smiling, like the Spartan under the bite of the fox.

Clearly, then, dandyism in certain respects comes close to spirituality and to stoicism, but a dandy can never be a vulgar man. If he were to commit a crime, he might perhaps be socially damned, but if the crime came from some trivial cause, the disgrace would be irreparable. Let the reader not be shocked by *this mixture of the grave and the gay;* let him rather reflect that there is a sort of grandeur in all follies, a driving power in every sort of excess. A strange form of spirituality indeed! For those who are its high priests and its victims at one and the same time, all the complicated material conditions they subject themselves to, from the most flawless dress at any time of day or night to the most risky sporting feats, are no more than a series of gymnastic exercises suitable to strengthen the will and school the soul.

[. . .]

Fastidious, unbelievables, beaux, lions or dandies: whichever label these men claim for themselves, one and all stem *from the same origin, all share the same characteristic of opposition and revolt; all are representatives of what is best in human pride, of that need, which is too rare in the modern generation, to combat and destroy triviality. That is the source, in your dandy, of that haughty, patrician attitude, aggressive even in its coldness.* Dandyism appears especially in those periods of transition when democracy has not yet become all-powerful, and when aristocracy is only partially weakened and discredited. In the confusion of such times, a certain number of men, disenchanted and leisured 'outsiders', but all of them richly endowed with native energy, *may conceive the idea of establishing a new kind of aristocracy,* all the more difficult to break down because established on the most precious, the most indestructible faculties, on the divine gifts that neither work nor money can give. *Dandyism is the last flicker of heroism in decadent ages;* and the sort of dandy discovered by the traveller in Northern America in no sense invalidates this idea; for there is no valid reason why we should not believe that the tribes we call savage are not the remnants of great civilizations of the past. *Dandyism is a setting sun; like the declining star, it is magnificent, without heat and full of melancholy. But alas! the rising tide of democracy, which spreads everywhere and reduces everything to the same level, is daily carrying away these last champions of human pride, and submerging, in the waters of oblivion, the last traces of these remarkable myrmidons.*

[. . .]

6
ARTHUR RIMBAUD (1854–91)
FROM LETTER TO PAUL DEMENY, 15 MAY 1871

French poet. Returning home in 1870 after wanderings in northern France, Rimbaud began writing the technically innovative poems that captured the attention of Paul Verlaine, who paid for him to come to Paris. 'Le Bateau ivre' ('The Drunken Boat'), a masterpiece of verbal virtuosity and outrageous imagery, was composed in 1871. Rimbaud and Verlaine embarked on a scandalous and violent affair that resulted in Verlaine's imprisonment. Une Saison en enfer (A Season in Hell, *1873*) *is partly Rimbaud's account of their relationship. It was around this time that he began composing his influential prose poems, later published as* Les Illuminations (1886). *The following extract is from a letter to his friend Paul Demeny, in Wallace Fowlie's translation for the 1966 edition of* Rimbaud: Complete Works, Selected Letters.

Charleville, 15 May 1871

I have decided to give you an hour of new literature. I begin at once with a song of today:

Parisian War Song
Spring is evident, for . . .

. . .

A. Rimbaud

– Here is some prose on the future of poetry: –

All ancient poetry ended in Greek poetry, harmonious life. – From Greece to the romantic movement – Middle Ages – there are writers and versifiers. From Ennius to Theroldus, from Theroldus to Casimir Delavigne, it is all rhymed prose, a game, degradation and glory of countless idiotic generations. Racine is pure, strong and great. – If his rhymes had been blown out and his hemistichs mixed up, the Divine Fool would today be as unknown as any old author of *Origins*. – After Racine, the game gets moldy. It has lasted two thousand years!

Neither joke, nor paradox. Reason inspires me with more enthusiasm on the subject than a Young France would have with rage. Moreover, *newcomers* are free to condemn the ancestors. We are at home and we have the time.

Romanticism has never been carefully judged. Who would have judged it? The critics! The Romantics? who prove so obviously that a song is so seldom a work, that is to say, a thought sung and understood by the singer.

For *I* is someone else. If brass wakes up a trumpet, it is not its fault. This is obvious to me: I am present at this birth of my thought: I watch it and listen to it: I draw a stroke of the bow: the symphony makes its stir in the depths, or comes on to the stage in a leap.

If old imbeciles had not discovered only the false meaning of the Ego, we would not have to sweep away those millions of skeletons which, for time immemorial, have accumulated the results of their one-eyed intellects by claiming to be the authors!

In Greece, as I have said, verses and lyres give rhythm to Action. After that, music and rhymes are games and pastimes. The study of this past delights the curious: several rejoice in reviving those antiquities – it is for them. Universal intelligence has always thrown out its ideas naturally; men picked up a part of these fruits of the mind: people acted through them and wrote books about them. Things continued thus: man not working on himself, not yet being awake, or not yet in the fulness of the great dream. Civil servants, writers: author, creator, poet, that man never existed!

The first study of the man who wants to be a poet is the knowledge of himself, complete. He looks for his soul, inspects it, tests it, learns it. As soon as he knows it, he must cultivate it! It seems simple: in every mind a natural development takes place; so many *egoists* call themselves authors, there are many others who attribute their intellectual progress to themselves! – But the soul must be made monstrous.

[. . .]

Imagine a man implanting and cultivating warts on his face.
I say one must be a *seer*, make oneself a *seer*.

The Poet makes himself a *seer* by a long, gigantic and rational *derangement* of *all the senses*. All forms of love, suffering, and madness. He searches himself. He exhausts all poisons in himself and keeps only their quintessences. Unspeakable torture where he needs all his faith, all his superhuman strength, where he becomes among all men the great patient, the great criminal, the one accursed – and the supreme Scholar! – Because he reaches the *unknown*! Since he cultivated his soul, rich already, more than any man! He reaches the unknown, and when, bewildered, he ends by losing the intelligence of his visions, he has seen them. Let him die as he leaps through unheard of and unnamable things: other horrible workers will come; they will begin from the horizons where the other one collapsed!

[. . .]

Therefore the poet is truly the thief of fire.

He is responsible for humanity, even for the *animals*; he will have to have his inventions smelt, felt, and heard; if what he brings back from *down there* has form, he gives form; if it is formless, he gives formlessness. A language must be found. Moreover, every word being an idea, the time of a universal language will come! One has to be an academician – deader than a fossil – to complete a dictionary in any language whatsoever. Weak people would begin *to think* about the first letter of the alphabet, and they would soon rush into madness!

This language will be of the soul for the soul, containing everything, smells, sounds, colors, thought holding on to thought and pulling. The poet would define the amount of the unknown awakening in his time in the universal soul: he would give more – than the formulation of his thought, than the annotation *of his march toward Progress*! Enormity becoming normal, absorbed by all, he would really be a *multiplier of progress*!

This future will be materialistic, as you see. – Always filled with *Number* and *Harmony*, these poems will be made to endure. – Fundamentally, it would be Greek poetry again in a way.

Eternal art would have its functions, since poets are citizens. Poetry will not lend its rhythm to action, it *will be in advance*.

These poets will exist. When the endless servitude of woman is broken, when she lives for and by herself, man – heretofore abominable – having given her her release, she too will be a poet! Woman will find some of the unknown! will her world of ideas differ from ours? – She will find strange, unfathomable, repulsive, delicious things; we will take them, we will understand them.

Meanwhile, let us ask the *poet* for the *new* – ideas and forms.

[. . .]

7
JOHN RUSKIN (1819–1900)
FROM *LECTURES ON ART* 1870; FROM *ARATRA PENTELICI* 1872

English author and art critic. One of the most influential critics of his day, Ruskin inspired many a shift in the aesthetic sensibility of the late-Victorian period. His writings on medieval art, as well as his impassioned attacks on nineteenth-century free-market economic practices and their attendant social evils influenced a generation of artists (amongst them William Morris who published and prefaced 'The Nature of the Gothic' – a chapter from Ruskin's Stones of Venice *– in 1892. Ruskin's style was celebrated by Marcel Proust, who produced a number of translations or homages to his work. Reproduced below are short extracts from 'A Caution to Realists' (*Lectures on Art, *1870) and on 'The Theory of Resemblance' (*Aratra Pentelici, *1872).*

[. . .]

A Caution to Realists

[. . .] Much that I have endeavoured to teach on this subject has been gravely misunderstood, by both young painters and sculptors, especially by the latter. Because I am always urging them to imitate organic forms, they think, if they carve quantities of flowers and leaves, and copy them from the life, they have done all that is needed. But the difficulty is not to carve quantities of leaves. Anybody can do that. The difficulty is, never anywhere to have an *unnecessary* leaf.

From the Elgin marbles, down to the lightest tendril that curls round a capital in the thirteenth century, every piece of stone that has been touched by the hand of a master, becomes soft with under-life, not resembling nature merely in skin-texture, nor in fibres of leaf, or veins of flesh; but in the broad, tender, unspeakably subtle undulation of its organic form.

[. . .]

The Theory of Resemblance

[. . .] All second-rate artists – (and remember, the second-rate ones are a loquacious multitude, while the great come only one or two in a century; and then, silently) all second-rate artists will tell you that the object of fine art is not resemblance, but some kind of abstraction more refined than reality. Put that out of your heads at once. The object of the great Resemblant Arts is, and always has been, to resemble; and to resemble as closely as possible. It is the function of a good portrait to set the man before you in habit as he lived, and I would we had a few more that did so. It is the function of a good landscape to set the scene before you in its reality; to make you, if it may be, think the clouds are flying, and the streams foaming. It is the function of the best sculptor – the true Dædalus – to make stillness look like breathing, and marble look like flesh.

And in all great times of art, this purpose is as naïvely expressed as it is steadily held. All the talk about abstraction belongs to periods of decadence. In living times, people see something living that pleases them; and they try to make it live for ever, or to make something as like it as possible, that will last for ever. They paint their statues, and inlay the eyes with jewels, and set real crowns on the heads; they finish, in their pictures, every thread of embroidery, and would fain, if they could, draw every leaf upon the trees. And their only verbal expression of conscious success is that they have made their work 'look real.'

[. . .]

8
WALTER PATER (1839–94)
CONCLUSION TO *THE RENAISSANCE* [1873] 1893

English essayist and critic. Throughout his writings Pater sought to counter the prevailing Victorian view that art should be evaluated in terms of its utilitarian, educational and moral qualities. His reviews of the work of major Renaissance artists were first collected in Studies in the History of the Renaissance *(1873, later retitled* The Renaissance: Studies in Art and Poetry*). The concluding essay to this collection was withdrawn from the second edition (1877) after charges of hedonism and moral corruption were levelled against it and was reinstated in a revised form in the third edition of the collection (1888). (Extracts from the fourth, and last, edition, which Pater revised in 1893, are reproduced below.) In it he makes his famous and influential statement that art exists for its own sake. His views brought him into association with the Pre-Raphaelite Brotherhood in his own day and later influenced Oscar Wilde, Lionel Johnson and others in the Aesthetic Movement of the 1890s. The emphasis in his writings on the transitory, the untimely and the evanescent, crystallised in the recurrent motif of 'the moment', connect his vision of aesthetic experience with those of Charles Baudelaire, James Joyce and Virginia Woolf.*

To regard all things and principles of things as inconstant modes of fashions has more and more become the tendency of modern thought. Let us begin with that which is without – our physical life. Fix upon it in one of its more exquisite intervals, the moment, for instance, of delicious recoil from the flood of water in summer heat. What is the whole physical life in that moment but a combination of natural elements to which science gives their names? But those elements, phosphorus and lime and delicate fibres, are present not in the human body alone: we detect them in places most remote from it. Our physical life is a perpetual motion of them – the passage of the blood, the waste and repairing of the lenses of the eye, the modification of the tissues of the brain under every ray of light and sound – processes which science reduces to simpler and more elementary forces. Like the elements of which we are composed, the action of these forces extends beyond us: it rusts iron and ripens corn. Far out on every side of us those elements are broadcast, driven in many currents; and birth and gesture and death and the springing of violets from the grave are but a few out of ten thousand resultant combinations. That clear, perpetual outline of face and limb is but an image of ours, under which we group them – a design in a web, the actual threads of which pass out beyond it. This at least of flame-like our life has, that it is but the concurrence, renewed from moment to moment, of forces parting sooner or later on their ways.

Or if we begin with the inward world of thought and feeling, the whirlpool is still more rapid, the flame more eager and devouring. There it is no longer the gradual darkening of the eye, the gradual fading of colour from the wall – movements of the shore-side, where the water flows down indeed, though in apparent rest – but the race of the mid-stream, a drift of momentary acts of sight and passion and thought. At first sight experience seems to bury us under a flood of external objects, pressing upon us with a sharp and importunate reality, calling us out of ourselves in a thousand forms of action. But when reflexion begins to play upon those objects they are dissipated under its influence; the cohesive force seems suspended like some trick of magic; each object is loosed into a group of impressions – colour, odour, texture – in the mind of the observer. And if we continue to dwell in thought on this world, not of objects in the solidity with which language invests them, but of impressions, unstable, flickering, inconsistent, which burn and are extinguished with our consciousness of them, it contracts still further: the whole scope of observation is dwarfed into the narrow chamber of the individual mind. Experience, already reduced to a group of impressions, is ringed round for each one of us by that thick wall of personality through which no real voice has ever pierced on its way to us, or from us to that which we can only conjecture to be without. Every one of those impressions is the impression of the individual in his isolation, each mind keeping as a solitary prisoner its own dream of a world. Analysis goes a step further still, and assures us that those impressions of the individual mind to which, for each one of us, experience dwindles down, are in perpetual flight; that each of them is limited by time, and that as time is infinitely divisible, each of them is infinitely divisible also; all that is actual in it being a single moment, gone while we try to apprehend it, of which it may ever be more truly said that it has ceased to be than that it is. To such a tremulous wisp constantly re-forming itself on the stream, to a single sharp impression, with a sense in it, a relic more or less fleeting, of such moments gone by, what is real in our life fines itself down. It is with this movement, with the passage and dissolution of impressions, images, sensations, that analysis leaves off – that continual vanishing away, that strange, perpetual, weaving and unweaving of ourselves.

Philosophiren, says Novalis, *ist dephlegmatisiren, vivificiren*. The service of philosophy, of speculative culture, towards the human spirit, is to rouse, to startle it to a life of constant and eager observation. Every moment some form grows perfect in hand or face; some tone on the hills or the sea is choicer than the rest; some mood of passion or insight or intellectual excitement is irresistibly real and attractive to us, – for that moment only. *Not the fruit of experience, but experience itself, is the end. A counted number of pulses only is given to us of a variegated, dramatic life.* How may we see in them all that is to be seen in them by the finest senses? How shall we pass most swiftly from point to point, and be present always at the focus where the greatest number of vital forces unite in their purest energy?

To burn always with this hard, gem-like flame, to maintain this ecstasy, is success in life. In a sense it might even be said that our failure is to form habits: for, after all, habit is relative to a stereotyped world, and meantime it is only the roughness of the eye that makes any two persons, things, situations, seem alike. *While all melts under our feet, we may well grasp at any exquisite passion, or any contribution to knowledge that seems by a lifted horizon to set the spirit free for a moment, or any stirring of the senses, strange dyes, strange colours, and curious odours, or work of the artist's hands, or the face of one's friend.* Not to discriminate every moment some passionate attitude in those about us, and in the very brilliancy of their gifts some tragic dividing of forces on their ways, is, on this short day of frost and sun, to sleep before evening. With this sense of the splendour of our experience and of its awful brevity, gathering all we are into one desperate effort to see and touch, we shall hardly have time to make theories about the things we see and touch. What we have to do is to be for ever curiously testing new opinions and courting new impressions, never acquiescing in a facile orthodoxy, of Comte, or of Hegel, or of our own. Philosophical theories or ideas, as points of view, instruments of criticism, may help us to gather up what might otherwise pass unregarded by us. 'Philosophy is the microscope of thought'. The theory or idea or system which requires of us the sacrifice of any part of this experience, in consideration of some interest into which we cannot enter, or some abstract theory we have not identified with ourselves, or of what is only conventional, has no real claim upon us.

One of the most beautiful passages of Rousseau is that in the sixth book of the *Confessions*, where he describes the *awakening in him of the literary sense. An undefinable taint of death had* clung always about him, and now in early manhood he believed himself smitten by mortal disease. He asked himself how he might make as much as possible of the interval that remained; and he was not biassed by anything in his previous life when he decided that it must be by intellectual excitement, which he found just then in the clear, fresh writings of Voltaire. Well! we are all *condamnés*, as Victor Hugo says: we are all under sentence of death but with a sort of indefinite reprieve – *les hommes sont tous condamnés à mort avec des sursis indéfinis*: we have an interval, and then our place knows us no more. Some spend this interval in listlessness, some in high passions, the wisest, at least among 'the children of this world', in art and song. *For our one chance lies in expanding that interval, in getting as many pulsations as possible into the given time. Great passions may give us this quickened sense of life, ecstasy and sorrow of love, the various forms of enthusiastic activity, disinterested or otherwise, which come naturally to many of us. Only be sure it is passion – that it does yield you this fruit of a quickened, multiplied consciousness.* Of such wisdom, the poetic passion, the desire of beauty, the love of art for its own sake, has most. For art comes to you proposing frankly to give nothing but the highest quality to your moments as they pass, and simply for those moments' sake.

9
AUGUST STRINDBERG (1849–1912)
FROM PREFACE TO *MISS JULIE* 1888

Swedish playwright, novelist, painter and autobiographer. Strindberg is chiefly known for his 'gender plays' The Father *(1887) and* Miss Julie *(1888), which have more recently been read as charting a crisis in masculinity, especially when considered as a response to the emergent feminist movement at the turn of the century. These works may also be seen to be in dialogue with Ibsen's* A Doll's House *(1879),* Ghosts *(1881) and* Hedda Gabler *(1890). Strindberg very quickly abandoned Naturalism for a more symbolic type of theatre which was later to influence Expressionism and Surrealism. His later plays,* To Damascus *(1901),* A Dream Play *(1901) and* The Ghost Sonata *(1907) express religious and metaphysical concerns. In 1899, influenced by the French director Antoine's 'Théâtre Libre', Strindberg founded 'The Scandinavian Experimental Theatre', where* Miss Julie *was first performed. The following extract from Strindberg's Preface to the play appears in Michael Meyer's translation.*

The theatre, and indeed art in general, has long seemed to me a *Biblia pauperum*, a Bible in pictures for the benefit of the illiterate; with the dramatist as a lay preacher hawking contemporary ideas in a popular form, popular enough for the middle classes, who comprise the bulk of playgoers, to be able to grasp without too much effort what the minority is arguing about. The theatre has always been a primary school for the young, the semi-educated, and women, all of whom retain the humble faculty of being able to deceive themselves and let themselves be deceived – in other words, to accept the illusion, and react to the suggestion, of the author. Nowadays the primitive process of intuition is giving way to reflection, investigation and analysis, and I feel that the theatre, like religion, is on the way to being discarded as a dying form which we lack the necessary conditions to enjoy. This hypothesis is evidenced by the theatrical crisis now dominating the whole of Europe; and, not least, by the fact that in those cultural strongholds which have nurtured the greatest thinkers of our age, namely England and Germany, the art of writing plays is, like most of the other fine arts, dead.

[. . .]

I have suggested many possible motivations for Miss Julie's unhappy fate. The passionate character of her mother; the upbringing misguidedly inflicted on her by her father; her own character; and the suggestive effect of her fiancé upon her weak and degenerate brain. Also, more immediately, the festive atmosphere of Midsummer Night; her father's absence; her menstruation; her association with animals; the intoxicating effect of the dance; the midsummer twilight; the powerfully aphrodisiac influence of the flowers; and, finally, the chance that drove these two people together into a private room – plus of course the passion of the sexually inflamed man.

I have therefore not suggested that the motivation was purely physiological, nor that it was exclusively psychological. I have not attributed her fate solely to her heritage, nor thrown the entire blame on to her menstruation, or her lack of morals. I have not set out to preach morality. This, in the absence of a priest, I have left to a cook.

This multiplicity of motives is, I like to think, typical of our times. And if others have done this before me, then I congratulate myself in not being alone in my belief in these 'paradoxes' (the word always used to describe new discoveries).

[. . .]

Since they are modern characters, living in an age of transition more urgently hysterical at any rate than the age which preceded it, I have drawn my people as split and vacillating, a mixture of the old and the new. And I think it not improbable that modern ideas may, through the media of newspapers and conversation, have seeped down into the social stratum which exists below stairs.

My souls (or characters) are agglomerations of past and present cultures, scraps from books and newspapers, fragments of humanity, torn shreds of once-fine clothing that has become rags, in just the way that a human soul is patched together. I have also provided a little documentation of character development, by making the weaker repeat words stolen from the stronger, and permitting the characters to borrow 'ideas', or, as the modern phrase is, accept suggestions from each other.

Miss Julie is a modern character – not that the half-woman, the man-hater, has not existed in every age, but because, now that she has been discovered, she has stepped forward into the limelight and begun to make a noise. The half-woman is a type that pushes herself to the front, nowadays selling herself for power, honours, decorations and diplomas, as formerly she used to for money. She is synonymous with corruption. They are a poor species, for they do not last, but unfortunately they propagate their like by the wretchedness they cause; and degenerate men seem unconsciously to choose their mates from among them, so that their number is increased. They engender an indeterminate sex to whom life is a torture, but fortunately they go under, either because they cannot adapt themselves to reality, or because their repressed instinct breaks out uncontrollably, or because their hopes of attaining equality with men are shattered. It is a tragic type, providing the spectacle of a desperate battle against Nature – and tragic also as a Romantic heritage now being dissipated by Naturalism, which thinks that the only good lies in happiness – and happiness is something that only a strong and hardy species can achieve.

[. . .]

The monologue is nowadays abominated by our realists as being contrary to reality, but if I motivate it I make it realistic, and can thus use it to advantage. It is after all realistic that a speaker should walk up and down alone in his room reading his speech aloud, that an actor should rehearse his part aloud, a servant-girl talk to her cat, a mother prattle to her child, an old maid jabber at her parrot, a sleeper talk in his sleep. And, to give the actor the chance for once to create for himself, and get off the author's leash, it is better that monologues should be implied rather than specified. For, since it matters little what one says in one's sleep, or to one's parrot or cat (for it does not influence the action), so a talented actor, attuned to the atmosphere and situation, may be able to improvise better than the author, who cannot calculate in advance how much needs to be said, or for how long the audience will accept the illusion.

As is known, the Italian theatre has, in certain instances, returned to improvisation and thereby created actors who themselves create, on the author's blueprint. This may well be a step forward, or even a new species of art, of which we shall be able to say that it is an art that engenders art.

Where a monologue would seem unrealistic, I have resorted to mime, which leaves the player even more freedom to create and so gain independent recognition. But in order not to make too great a demand upon the audience, I have allowed music, well motivated by the midsummer dance, to exercise its illusory power during the dumb play. Here I would ask the musical director to take care when choosing his pieces not to evoke an alien atmosphere by echoes from popular operettas or dance tunes, or folk melodies with specific associations.

The ballet which I have introduced must not be smudged into a so-called 'crowd scene', because crowd scenes are always badly acted, and a mob of buffoons would seize the chance to be clever and so destroy the illusion. Since simple people do not improvise when they wish to be spiteful, but use ready-to-hand material, I have not written new words for them but have borrowed a little-known song which I discovered myself in the country-side near Stockholm. The words are circumlocutory rather than direct, but that is as it should be, for the cunning (weakness) of servile people is not of the type that engages in direct assault. So there must be no chattering or clowning in what is, after all, a serious piece of action, no coarse sniggering in a situation which drives the nails into the coffin of a noble house.

As regards the décor, I have borrowed from the impressionist painters asymmetry and suggestion (i.e., the part rather than the whole), believing that I have thereby helped to further my illusion. The fact that one does not see the whole room and all the furniture leaves room for surmise – in other words, the audience's imagination is set in motion and completes its own picture. I have also profited by eliminating those tiresome exits through doors; for stage doors are made of canvas and flap at the slightest touch; they will not even allow an angry father to express his fury by stumping out after a bad dinner and slamming the door 'so that the whole house shakes'. (In the theatre, the door simply waves.) I have likewise confined myself to a single set, both to enable the characters to accustom themselves to their *milieu*, and to get away from the tradition of scenic luxury. But when one has only one set, one is entitled to demand that it be realistic – though nothing is more difficult than to make a room which looks like a room, however skilful the artist may be at creating fire-spouting volcanoes and waterfalls. Even if the walls have to be of canvas, it is surely time to stop painting them with shelves and kitchen utensils. We have so many other stage conventions in which we are expected to believe that we may as well avoid overstraining our imagination by asking it to believe in painted saucepans.

I have placed the rear wall and the table at an angle so that the actors shall be able to face each other and be seen in demi-profile when they sit opposite each other at the table. In a performance of the opera *Aida* I once saw a backcloth at an angle which led one's eyes off into an unknown perspective: nor did it look as though it had been arranged thus simply out of a spirit of reaction against the boredom of straight lines.

Another perhaps not unnecessary innovation would be the removal of the footlights. This illumination from below is said to serve the purpose of making actors fatter in the face; but I would like to ask: 'Why should all actors be fat in the face?' Does not this under-lighting annihilate all subtle expressions in the lower half of the face, particularly around the mouth? Does it not falsify the shape of the nose, and throw shadows up over the eyes? Even if this were not so, one thing is certain: that pain is caused to the actors' eyes, so that any realistic expression is lost. For the footlights strike the retina on parts of it which are normally protected (except among sailors, who see the sun reflected from the water), so that one seldom sees any attempt at ocular expression other than fierce glares either to the side or up towards the gallery, when the whites of the eyes become visible. Perhaps this is also the cause of that tiresome habit, especially among actresses, of fluttering eyelashes. And when anyone on the stage wishes to speak with his eyes, he has no alternative but to look straight at the audience, thereby entering into direct contact with them outside the framework of the play – a bad habit which rightly or wrongly, is known as 'greeting one's friends'.

Would not side-lights of sufficient power (with reflectors, or some such device) endow the actor with this new resource, enabling him to reinforce his mime with his principal weapon of expression, the movement of his eyes?'

I have few illusions of being able to persuade the actor to play *to* the audience and not with them, though this would be desirable. I do not dream that I shall ever see the full back of an actor throughout the whole of an important scene, but I do fervently wish that vital scenes should not be played opposite the prompter's box as though they were duets milking applause. I would have them played at whatever spot the situation might demand. So no revolutions, but simply small modifications; for to turn the stage into a room with the fourth wall missing, so that some of the furniture would have its back to the audience, would, I suppose, at this juncture, simply serve as a distraction.

A word about make-up; which I dare not hope will be listened to by the ladies, who prefer beauty to truth. But the actor might well ponder whether it is to his advantage to paint an abstract character upon his face which will remain sitting there like a mask. Imagine a gentleman dipping his finger into soot and drawing a line of bad temper between his eyes, and suppose that, wearing this permanently fierce expression, he were called upon to deliver a line smiling? How dreadful would be the result! And how is this false forehead, smooth as a billiard ball, to wrinkle when the old man gets really angry?

In a modern psychological drama, where the subtler reactions should be mirrored in the face rather than in gesture and sound, it would surely be best to experiment with strong side-lights on a small stage and with the actor wearing no make-up, or at best a minimum.

If we could then dispense with the visible orchestra, with their distracting lampshades and faces turned towards the audience; if we could have the stalls raised so that the spectator's sightline would be above the actors' knees; if we could get rid of the side-boxes (my particular *bête noire*), with their tittering diners and ladies nibbling at cold collations, and have complete darkness in the auditorium during the performance, and, first and foremost, a *small* stage and a *small* auditorium – then perhaps a new drama might emerge, and the theatre might once again become a place for educated people.

While we await such a theatre, one must write to create a stock of plays in readiness for the repertoire that will, some day, be needed.

I have made an attempt! If it has failed, there will, I hope, be time enough to make another!

10
OSCAR WILDE (1854–1900)
PREFACE TO *THE PICTURE OF DORIAN GRAY* 1890

Irish dramatist, essayist, poet and wit. At Oxford Wilde was influenced by the aesthetic theories of John Ruskin and Walter Pater, calling the latter's Renaissance *his 'golden book'. In the London of the 1890s he was a leading figure in the Aesthetic movement, with its slogan (derived from Pater) of 'art for art's sake'. His major work appeared in the last decade of his life: the society comedies* Lady Windermere's Fan *(1892) and* The Importance of Being Earnest *(1895) which are merciless exposés of Victorian hypocrisy, and the sensational novel,* The Picture of Dorian Gray, *influenced by the French Decadents. This originally appeared in* Lippincott's Magazine *in 1890 and was published in book form the following year. Wilde's* Salome *was originally written in French and was translated by Lord Alfred Douglas (1894), whose father Wilde unsuccessfully sued for libel for addressing him as a 'sodomite'. Subsequently imprisoned for his homosexuality, Wilde wrote* De Profundis *(published 1905) in his cell. On his release in 1897 he went to France.* The Ballad of Reading Gaol *was published in 1898. Reprinted below is the Preface to* The Picture of Dorian Gray, *containing in condensed and typically aphoristic form Wilde's aesthetic credo. More elaborate versions include the essays 'The Decay of Lying' (1889) and 'The Critic as Artist' (1890).*

The artist is the creator of beautiful things.

To reveal art and conceal the artist is art's aim.

The critic is he who can translate into another manner or a new material his impression of beautiful things.

The highest, as the lowest, form of criticism is a mode of autobiography.

Those who find ugly meanings in beautiful things are corrupt without being charming. This is a fault.

Those who find beautiful meanings in beautiful things are the cultivated. For these there is hope. They are the elect to whom beautiful things mean only Beauty.

There is no such thing as a moral or an immoral book.

Books are well written, or badly written. That is all.

The nineteenth-century dislike of Realism is the rage of Caliban seeing his own face in a glass.

The nineteenth-century dislike of Romanticism is the rage of Caliban not seeing his own face in a glass.

The moral life of man forms part of the subject-matter of the artist, but the morality of art consists in the perfect use of an imperfect medium. No artist desires to prove anything. Even things that are true can be proved.

No artist has ethical sympathies. An ethical sympathy in an artist is an unpardonable mannerism of style.

No artist is ever morbid. The artist can express everything.

Thought and language are to the artist instruments of an art.

Vice and virtue are to the artist materials for an art. From the point of view of form, the type of all the arts is the art of the musician. From the point of view of feeling, the actor's craft is the type.

All art is at once surface and symbol.

Those who go beneath the surface do so at their peril.

Those who read the symbol do so at their peril.

It is the spectator, and not life, that art really mirrors.

Diversity of opinion about a work of art shows that the work is new, complex, and vital.

When critics disagree the artist is in accord with himself.

We can forgive a man for making a useful thing as long as he does not admire it. The only excuse for making a useless thing is that one admires it intensely.

All art is quite useless.

11
THOMAS HARDY (1840–1928)
'THE SCIENCE OF FICTION' 1891

English poet and novelist. The essay reprinted below was composed towards the end of Hardy's major creative period as a novelist (1878–95). Though not a literary theorist, Hardy did hold strong opinions on the controversies of his day. 'The Science of Fiction' is a succinct intervention in the debate about literary realism and can be read usefully alongside the more substantial theses of Henry James and Edgar Allan Poe. The essay was Hardy's contribution to a symposium in the New Review *in April 1891.*

Since Art is science with an addition, since some science underlies all Art, there is seemingly no paradox in the use of such a phrase as 'the Science of Fiction'. One concludes it to mean that comprehensive and accurate knowledge of realities which must be sought for, or intuitively possessed, to some extent, before anything deserving the name of an artistic performance in narrative can be produced.

The particulars of this science are the generals of almost all others. The materials of Fiction being human nature and circumstances, the science thereof may be dignified by calling it the codified law of things as they really are. No single pen can treat exhaustively of this. The Science of Fiction is contained in that large work, the cyclopaedia of life.

In no proper sense can the term 'science' be applied to other than this fundamental matter. It can have no part or share in the construction of a story, however recent speculations may have favoured such an application. We may assume with certainty that directly the constructive stage is entered upon, Art – high or low – begins to exist.

The most devoted apostle of realism, the sheerest naturalist, cannot escape, any more than the withered old gossip over her fire, the exercise of Art in his labour or pleasure of telling a tale. Not until he becomes an automatic reproducer of all impressions whatsoever can he be called purely scientific, or even a manufacturer on scientific principles. If in the exercise of his reason he select or omit, with an eye to being more truthful than truth (the just aim of Art), he transforms himself into a technicist at a move.

As this theory of the need for the exercise of the Dædalian faculty for selection and cunning manipulation has been disputed, it may be worth while to examine the contrary proposition. That it should ever have been maintained by such a romancer as M. Zola, in his work on the *Roman Expérimental*, seems to reveal an obtuseness to the disproof conveyed in his own novels which, in a French writer, is singular indeed. To be sure that author – whose powers in story-telling, rightfully and wrongfully exercised, may be partly owing to the fact that he is not a critic – does in a measure concede something in the qualified counsel that the novel should keep as close to reality *as it can*; a remark which may be interpreted with infinite latitude, and would no doubt have been cheerfully accepted by Dumas *père* or Mrs. Radcliffe. It implies discriminative choice; and if we grant that we grant all. But to maintain in theory what he abandons in practice, to subscribe to rules and to work by instinct, is a proceeding not confined to the author of *Germinal* and *La Faute de l'Abbé Mouret*.

The reasons that make against such conformation of storywriting to scientific processes have been set forth so many times in examining the theories of the realist, that it is not necessary to recapitulate them here. Admitting the desirability, the impossibility of reproducing in its entirety the phantasmagoria of experience with infinite and atomic truth, without shadow, relevancy, or subordination, is not the least of them. The fallacy appears to owe its origin to the just perception that with our widened knowledge of the universe and its forces, and man's position therein, narrative, to be artistically convincing, must adjust itself to the new alignment, as would also artistic works in form and colour, if further spectacles in their sphere could be presented. Nothing but the illusion of truth can permanently please, and when the old illusions begin to be penetrated, a more natural magic has to be supplied.

Creativeness in its full and ancient sense – the making a thing or situation out of nothing that ever was before – is apparently ceasing to satisfy a world which no longer believes in the abnormal – ceasing at least to satisfy the van-couriers of taste; and creative fancy has accordingly to give more and more place to realism, that is, to an artificiality distilled from the fruits of closest observation.

This is the meaning deducible from the work of the realists, however stringently they themselves may define realism in terms. Realism is an unfortunate, an ambiguous word, which has been taken up by literary society like a view-halloo, and has been assumed in some places to mean copyism, and in others pruriency, and has led to two classes of delineators being included in one condemnation.

Just as bad a word is one used to express a consequence of this development, namely 'brutality', a term which, first applied by French critics, has since spread over the English school like the other. It aptly hits off the immediate impression of the thing meant; but it has the disadvantage of defining impartiality as a passion, and a plan as a caprice. It certainly is very far from truly expressing the aims and methods of conscientious and well-intentioned authors who, notwithstanding their excesses, errors, and rickety theories, attempt to narrate the *vérité vraie*.

To return for a moment to the theories of the scientific realists. Every friend to the novel should and must be in sympathy with their error, even while distinctly perceiving it. Though not true, it is well founded. To advance realism as complete copyism, to call the idle trade of story-telling a science, is the hyperbolic flight of an admirable enthusiasm, the exaggerated cry of an honest reaction from the false, in which the truth has been impetuously approached and overleapt in fault of lighted on.

Possibly, if we only wait, the third something, akin to perfection, will exhibit itself on its due pedestal. How that third something may be induced to hasten its presence, who shall say? Hardly the English critic.

But this appertains to the Art of novel-writing, and is outside the immediate subject. To return to the 'science'. . . . Yet what is the use? Its very comprehensiveness renders the attempt to dwell upon it a futility. Being an observative responsiveness to everything within the cycle of the suns that has to do with actual life, it is easier to say what it is not than to categorise its *summa genera*. It is not, for example, the paying of a great regard to adventitious externals to the neglect of vital qualities, not a precision about the outside of the platter and an obtuseness to the contents. An accomplished lady once confessed to the writer that she could never be in a room two minutes without knowing every article of furniture it contained and every detail in the attire of the inmates, and, when she left, remembering every remark. Here was a person, one might feel for the moment, who could prime herself to an unlimited extent and at the briefest notice in the scientific data of fiction; one who, assuming her to have some slight artistic power, was a born novelist. To explain why such a keen eye to the superficial does not imply a sensitiveness to the intrinsic is a psychological matter beyond the scope of these notes; but that a blindness to material particulars often accompanies a quick perception of the more ethereal characteristics of humanity, experience continually shows.

A sight for the finer qualities of existence, an ear for the 'still sad music of humanity', are not to be acquired by the outer senses alone, close as their powers in photography may be. What cannot be discerned by eye and ear, what may be apprehended only by the mental tactility that comes from a sympathetic appreciativeness of life in all of its manifestations, this is the gift which renders its possessor a more accurate delineator of human nature than many another with twice his powers and means of external observation, but without that sympathy. To see in half and quarter views the whole picture, to catch from a few bars the whole tune, is the intuitive power that supplies the would-be storywriter with the scientific bases for his pursuit. He may not count the dishes at a feast, or accurately estimate the value of the jewels in a lady's diadem; but through the smoke of those dishes, and the rays from these jewels, he sees written on the wall: —

> We are such stuff
> As dreams are made of, and our little life
> Is rounded with a sleep.

Thus, as aforesaid, an attempt to set forth the Science of Fiction in calculable pages is futility; it is to write a whole library of human philosophy, with instructions how to feel.

Once in a crowd a listener heard a needy and illiterate woman saying of another poor and haggard woman who had lost her little son years before: 'You can see the ghost of that child in her face even now.'

That speaker was one who, though she could probably neither read nor write, had the true means towards the 'Science' of Fiction innate within her; a power of observation informed by a living heart. Had she been trained in the technicalities, she might have fashioned her view of mortality with good effect; a reflection which leads to a conjecture that, perhaps, true novelists, like poets, are born, not made.

12
STÉPHANE MALLARMÉ (1842–98)
FROM 'CRISIS IN POETRY' 1886–95

French poet. Mallarmé's early career is marked by his fascination with the work of Baudelaire, whose interest in the relationship between reality and an imagined world influenced two of Mallarmé's major works, Hérodiade *(1864) and* L'Après-midi d'un faune *(1865). Along with Paul Verlaine, he originated and led the Symbolist movement in poetry, developing theories about the nature of language. He published several highly inventive and evocative elegies to such figures as Baudelaire, Wagner and Poe. In 'Le tombeau d'Edgar Poe' appears the famous phrase 'Donner un sens plus pur aux mots de la tribu' which in T. S. Eliot's later rendition becomes 'To purify the dialect of the tribe', a self-contained statement of almost programmatic significance for Modernist poetry. The following extracts from 'Crisis in Poetry' (1886–95) are reprinted here from the 1956 edition of Mallarmé's* Selected Prose, Poems, Essays, and Letters, *translated by Bradford Cook.*

A fundamental and fascinating crisis in literature is now at hand.

Such is the plain and present truth in the eyes of all those for whom literature is of primary importance. What we are witnessing as the finale of our own century is not upheaval (as was the case a hundred years ago), but rather a fluttering in the temple's veil – meaningful folds and even a little tearing.

[. . .]

It will be agreed that because of the priority on magic power which is given to rhyme, French poetry has been intermittent ever since its evolution. It shines for a moment, dies out, and waits. There is extinction – or rather wear and tear which reveal the weft; there is repetition. After an almost century-long period of poetic orgy and excess which can be compared only to the Renaissance, the latest poetic urge (counteracting a number of different circumstances) is being fulfilled not by a darkening or cooling off process, but, on the contrary, by a variation in continuing brilliance. The retempering

of verse, ordinarily a secret affair, is now being done openly: poets are <u>resorting</u> to
<u>delightful approximations.</u>

The kind of treatment that has been given to the hieratic canon of verse can, I think,
be divided into three graduated parts.

Official prosody has cut and dried rules; there lies its obstinacy. It gives its official
approval to such 'wise' procedures as the observance of the hemistich, and pronounces
judgment on the slightest effort to simulate versification. It is like the law which states,
for example, that abstinence from theft is the essence of honesty. But this is precisely
what we need least to learn; for if we have not understood it by ourselves from the
first, it is useless to obey it.

Those who are still faithful to the alexandrine, i.e., to the modern hexameter, have
gone inside it and loosened this rigid, childish metrical mechanism; and so, now that
such artificial metronomes have been abolished, there is joy for our ears alone in
perceiving all possible combinations and interrelationships of twelve tones.

[. . .]

But the truly remarkable fact is this: <u>for the first time in the literary history of any
nation, along with the general and traditional great organ of orthodox verse which
finds its ecstasy on an ever-ready keyboard,</u> any poet with an individual technique and
ear can build his own instrument, so long as his fluting, bowing, or drumming are
accomplished – play that instrument and dedicate it, along with others, to Language.

Thus we have won a great new freedom; and it is my firm belief that no beauty of
the past has been destroyed as a result. I am convinced that the solemn poetic tradition
which was mainly established by our classical genius will continue to be observed on
all important occasions. But whenever it shall seem unfitting to disturb the echoes of
that venerable past for sentimental or narrative purposes, we shall be careful to avoid
such disturbance. Each soul is a melody; its strands must be bound up. Each poet has
his flute or viol, with which to do so.

In my opinion, we have been late in finding the true condition and possibility not
only of poetic self-expression, but of free and individual modulation.

Languages are imperfect because multiple; <u>the supreme language is missing.</u>
Inasmuch as thought consists of writing without pen and paper, without whispering
even, without the sound of the immortal Word, the diversity of languages on earth
means that no one can utter words which would bear the miraculous stamp of Truth
Herself Incarnate. This is clearly nature's law – we stumble on it with a smile of
resignation – to the effect that we have no sufficient reason for equating ourselves
with God. But then, esthetically, I am disappointed when I consider how impossible
it is for language to express things by means of certain keys which would reproduce
their brilliance and aura – keys which do exist as a part of the instrument of the human
voice, or among languages, or sometimes even in one language.

[. . .]

We <u>dream of words brilliant</u> at once in meaning and sound, or darkening in meaning
and so in sound, luminously and elementally self-succeeding. But, let us remember that
<u>if our dream were fulfilled,</u> *verse would not exist* – verse which, in all its wisdom, atones
for the sins of languages, comes nobly to their aid.

Strange mystery – and so, equally mysterious and meaningful, prosody sprang forth in primitive times.

The ideal would be a reasonable number of words stretched beneath our mastering glance, arranged in enduring figures, and followed by silence.

[. . .]

But the crisis in poetry lies less in the very interesting interregnum or rest treatment undergone by versification, than in certain new states of our poetic mind.

We now *hear* undeniable rays of light, like arrows gilding and piercing the meanderings of song. I mean that, since Wagner appeared, Music and Verse have combined to form Poetry.

Either one of these two elements, of course, may profitably stand apart in triumph and integrity, in a quiet concert of its own if it chooses not to speak distinctly. Or else the poem can tell of their reassociation and restrengthening: the instrumentation is brightened to the point of perfect clarity beneath the orchestral veil, while verse flies down into the evening darkness of the sound. That modern meteor – the symphony – approaches thought with the consent or ignorance of the musician. And thought itself is no longer expressed merely in common language.

Thus Mystery bursts forth ineffably throughout the heavens of Its own impersonal magnificence, wherein it was ordained that the orchestra should complement our age-old effort to make the spoken word our only form of music.

Twin symbols interrelated.

The Decadent or Mystic Schools (as they call themselves or as they were hastily labeled by the public press) find their common meeting ground in an Idealism which (as in the case of fugues and sonatas) shuns the materials in nature, avoids any thought that might tend to arrange them too directly or precisely, and retains only the suggestiveness of things. The poet must establish a careful relationship between two images, from which a third element, clear and fusible, will be distilled and caught by our imagination. We renounce that erroneous esthetic (even though it has been responsible for certain masterpieces) which would have the poet fill the delicate pages of his book with the actual and palpable wood of trees, rather than with the forest's shuddering or the silent scattering of thunder through the foliage. A few well-chosen sounds blown heavenward on the trumpet of true majesty will suffice to conjure up the architecture of the ideal and only habitable palace – palace of no palpable stone, else the book could not be properly closed. . . .

It is not *description* which can unveil the efficacy and beauty of monuments, or the human face in all their maturity and native state, but rather evocation, *allusion, suggestion*. These somewhat arbitrary terms reveal what may well be a very decisive tendency in modern literature, a tendency which limits literature and yet sets it free. For what is the magic charm of art, if not this: that, beyond the confines of a fistful of dust or of all other reality, beyond the book itself, beyond the very text, it delivers up that volatile scattering which we call the Spirit, Who cares for nothing save universal musicality.

Speech is no more than a commercial approach to reality. In literature, allusion is sufficient: essences are distilled and then embodied in Idea.

Song, when it becomes impalpable joy, will rise to heaven.

This is the ideal I would call Transposition; Structure is something else.

If the poem is to be pure, the poet's voice must be stilled and the initiative taken by the words themselves, which will be set in motion as they meet unequally in collision. And in an exchange of gleams they will flame out like some glittering swath of fire sweeping over precious stones, and thus replace the audible breathing in lyric poetry of old – replace the poet's own personal and passionate control of verse.

The inner structures of a book of verse must be inborn; in this way, chance will be totally eliminated and the poet will be absent. From each theme, itself predestined, a given harmony will be born somewhere in the parts of the total poem and take its proper place within the volume, because, for every sound, there is an echo. Motifs of like pattern will move in balance from point to point. There will be none of the sublime incoherence found in the page-settings of the Romantics, none of the artificial unity that used to be based on the square measurements of the book. Everything will be hesitation, disposition of parts, their alternations and relationships – all this contributing to the rhythmic totality, which will be the very silence of the poem, in its blank spaces, as that silence is translated by each structural element in its own way. (Certain recent publications have heralded this sort of book; and if we may admit their ideals as complements to our own, it must then be granted that young poets have seen what an overwhelming and harmonious totality a poem must be, and have stammered out the magic concept of the Great Work.) Then again, the perfect symmetry of verses within the poem, of poems within the volume, will extend even beyond the volume itself; and this will be the creation of many poets who will inscribe, on spiritual space, the expanded signature of genius – as anonymous and perfect as a work of art.

Chimaera, yes! And yet the mere thought of it is proof (reflected from Her scales) that during the last twenty-five years poetry has been visited by some nameless and absolute flash of lightning – like the muddied, dripping gleams on my windowpane which are washed away and brightened by streaming showers of rain ⊣revealing that, in general, all books contain the amalgamation of a certain number of age-old truths; that actually there is only one book on earth, that it is the law of the earth, the earth's true Bible. The difference between individual works is simply the difference between individual interpretations of one true and established text, which are proposed in a mighty gathering of those ages we call civilized or literary.

Certainly, whenever I sit at concerts, amid the obscurity and ecstasy of sound I always perceive the nascent form of some one of those poems which have their origin and dwelling in human life – a poem more understandable because unheard, because the composer, in his desire to portray its majestic lines, was not even *tempted* to 'explain everything'. My feeling – or my doubtlessly ineradicable prejudice as a writer – is that nothing will endure if it remains unspoken; that our present task, precisely (now that the great literary rhythms I spoke of are being broken up and scattered in a series of distinct and almost orchestrated shiverings), is to find a way of transposing the symphony to the Book: in short, to regain our rightful due. For, undeniably, the true source of Music must not be the elemental sound of brasses, strings, or wood winds, but the intellectual and written word in all its glory – Music of perfect fullness and clarity, the totality of universal relationships.

One of the undeniable ideals of our time is to divide words into two different categories first, for vulgar or immediate, second, for essential purposes.

The first is for narrative, instruction, or description (even though an adequate exchange of human thoughts might well be achieved through the silent exchange of money). The elementary use of language involves that universal *journalistic style* which characterizes all kinds of contemporary writing, with the exception of literature.

Why should we perform the miracle by which a natural object is almost made to disappear beneath the magic waving wand of the written word, if not to divorce that object from the direct and the palpable, and so conjure up its *essence* in all purity?

When I say: 'a flower!' then from that forgetfulness to which my voice consigns all floral form, something different from the usual calyces arises, something all music, essence, and softness: the flower which is absent from all bouquets.

Language, in the hands of the mob, leads to the same facility and directness as does money. But, in the Poet's hands, it is turned, above all, to dream and song; and, by the constituent virtue and necessity of an art which lives on fiction, it achieves its full efficacy.

Out of a number of words, poetry fashions a single new word which is total in itself and foreign to the language – a kind of incantation. Thus the desired isolation of language is effected; and chance (which might still have governed these elements, despite their artful and alternating renewal through meaning and sound) is thereby instantly and thoroughly abolished. Then we realize, to our amazement, that we had never truly heard this or that ordinary poetic fragment; and, at the same time, our recollection of the object thus conjured up bathes in a totally new atmosphere.

13
PAUL VALÉRY (1871–1945)
FROM 'INTRODUCTION TO THE METHOD OF LEONARDO DA VINCI' 1895

French poet, critic and essayist. Valéry's infatuation with the work of Edgar Allan Poe and Stéphane Mallarmé led him to write and publish several Symbolist poems early in his career. Around 1894, however, a failed love affair prompted him to abandon poetry and to enter into a period of intellectual and meditative asceticism when he spent his time reflecting on the nature of consciousness, scientific reasoning and language. He developed his own conception of an ideal disembodied intellect which he called 'Monsieur Teste' and published essays on what he understood the role of the artist in the modern world to be. The following extract is from an 1895 essay, translated by Thomas McGreevy for the 1950 edition of Valéry's Selected Writings.

[. . .]

As the elusive art of music unites the liberties of sleep with the development and consistency of extreme attention and makes a synthesis of intimate things which last only a moment, so the fluctuations of the psychic equilibrium give one a glimpse of deviating modes of existence. We have in us forms of sensibility which, though they may be born, may not develop. They are instants snatched from the implacable criticism of the passage of time; they cannot survive if our being is to function fully: either we perish or they disperse. But they are monsters full of lessons for us, these monsters of the intelligence, these transitory stages, these spaces in which the continuity, the relation, the mobility we know, are altered; empires in which illumination is associated with sorrow; powerhouses where the orientation of fears and desires sends us on strange circuits; matter which consists of time; abysses literally of sorrow, or love, or quietude; regions curiously attached to themselves; non-Archimedean realms which defy movement; perpetuities in a flash of lightning; surfaces that shape themselves to our nausea, bend under our lightest decisions. [. . .] One cannot say that they are real; one cannot say that they are not real. Who has not experience of them does not know the value of natural intelligence and of even the most ordinary environment; he does not understand the true fragility of the world – which has no relation to so simple a thing as our alternative of being or not being. The wonder is not that things should be; ie it is that there should be such things and not such other things. *The image of this world is part of a family of images, an infinite group, all the elements of which we possess – but unconsciously – consciousness of possession is the secret of the inventors.*

I.

The consciousness as it emerges from these gaps, these personal deviations in which weakness and the presence of poisons in the nervous system, but also the power as well as the subtlety of the attention and a most exquisite logic, a cultivated mysticism, all, severally, direct it, the consciousness, then, comes to suspect all accustomed reality of being only one solution amongst many others of universal problems. It tells itself that things should be somewhat different from what they are without its being very different from itself. It dares to consider its body and its world as almost arbitrary restrictions imposed on the range of its functions. It sees itself as corresponding, or as responding, not to a world, but to some system of a higher order the elements of which may themselves be worlds. It is capable of more interior combinations than are necessary for living; it judges itself deeper than the abyss of physical life and death. And this attitude to its own position cannot react back on itself, so far is it withdrawn, placed beyond all things, so much has it applied itself to the task of *never figuring in anything that it might imagine or agree to.* It has become no more than a dark body which absorbs everything and gives out nothing.

Drawing from these exact observations and from these inevitable pretensions a dangerous boldness; strong in this type of independence and unchangingness that it has to admit it possesses, it postulates itself in the end as the direct heir and image of that being that has no form, no origin, on which devolves, to which is related, the whole effort of the cosmos. A little more and it will admit as necessary existences only two entities, both of them essentially unknown: itself and X; both of them abstracted from everything, implicated in everything, implicating everything; equal and consubstantial.

The man who has been led by a mind that works tirelessly to this contact with living shadows, to this point of pure being, sees himself naked and destitute, reduced to the supreme poverty of power without a purpose, victim, masterpiece, perfection of simplification and dialectic order; his state comparable to that reached by the richest mind when it has become assimilated to itself, when it has recognized itself and consummated itself in a little group of characters and symbols. The work which we devote to the object of our reflections he has expended on the subject which reflects.

He is no longer concerned to choose or to create, to maintain or to develop himself. Genius is now entirely consumed, cannot even be used to any further purpose. It was no more than a means to attain to the last simplicity. There is no act of genius which would not be *less* than the act of being. An imbecile is created and informed by a magnificent law; the most powerful mind finds nothing better than itself.

To sum up, being constrained to define itself by the sum of things and excess of knowledge over the sum of things, this perfected consciousness, which, to establish itself, has to begin by denying an infinite number of faiths, an infinite number of elements, and by exhausting the objects of its force without exhausting the force itself, this perfected consciousness differs as little as could be wished from nothingness. It reminds one absurdly of an audience invisible in the darkness of a theater which cannot see itself, which can see only the spectacle before it, and which, yet, all the time, invincibly feels itself the center of a breathlessly interesting evening. It is complete, impenetrable, absolute night; but filled with things, eager, secretly organized, made up of organisms which limit and compress themselves; a compact night, its shadows packed with organisms which live, breathe, warm themselves and which defend, each according to its nature, their places and functions. Before this intense, mysterious assembly, are all the things of sensibility, intelligibility, possibility, glittering and moving in an enclosed framework. Nothing can be born, die, or exist in any degree, or have time, place, form or meaning, except on this stage which the fates have circumscribed, and having separated which, from nobody knows what primordial confusion, as on the first day darkness was separated from light, they have opened and subordinated to the condition of *being seen*. [. . .]

14
ALFRED JARRY (1873–1907)
'PRELIMINARY ADDRESS AT THE FIRST PERFORMANCE OF *UBU ROI*,
10 DECEMBER 1896'

French dramatist, novelist, poet and pataphysician. Jarry's grotesque and bizarre drama, Ubu Roi *(King Ubu, 1896) is generally regarded as the founding work in the tradition of the Theatre of the Absurd, or the genre which sought to deconstruct conventional notions about the world and representation. Jarry's work foregrounds absurdity and incoherence in defiance of any authoritarian imposition of logic. He is also the originator and father of 'pataphysics', 'the science of imaginary solutions', later practitioners of which include many Dadaists and Surrealists. Jarry's address to the first performance of* Ubu Roi *is reprinted here, from Roger Shattuck's and Simon Watson Taylor's 1965 edition of the* Selected Works of Alfred Jarry. *[See IIb 13]*

Ladies and Gentlemen,

It should be quite unnecessary (apart from being slightly absurd for an author to talk about his own play) for me to come up here with a few words before the production of *Ubu Roi* after so many more distinguished people have spoken kindly of it: among whom I would especially like to thank Messieurs Silvestre, Mendès, Scholl, Lorrain and Bauer – in fact, my only excuse for speaking to you now is that I am afraid that their generosity found Ubu's belly far more swollen with satirical symbols than we have really been able to stuff it with for this evening's entertainment.

The Swedenborgian Doctor Mises has quite rightly compared rudimentary works with the most perfect achievements, and embryonic forms with the most evolved creatures, pointing out that the former categories lack any element of accident, protuberance or special characteristics, leaving them a practically spherical form like the ovule or Mister Ubu; and, equally, that the latter possess so many personal attributes that they too take on a spherical form, by virtue of the axiom that the smoothest body is the one presenting the greatest number of different facets. Which is why you are free to see in Mister Ubu as many allusions as you like, or, if you prefer, just a plain puppet, a schoolboy's caricature of one of his teachers who represented for him everything in the world that is grotesque.

This is the point of view that the Théâtre de l'Œuvre is going to give you this evening. A few actors have agreed to lose their own personalities during two consecutive evenings by performing with masks over their faces so that they can mirror the mind and soul of the man-sized marionettes that you are about to see. As the play has been put on in some haste and in a spirit of friendly improvisation, Ubu has not had time to obtain his own real mask, which would have been very awkward to wear in any case, and his confederates, too, will be decked out in only approximate disguise. It was very important that, if the actors were to be as much like marionettes as possible, we should have fairground music scored for brass and gongs and megaphones – which we simply did not have time to get together. But let us not be too hard on the Théâtre de l'Œuvre: our main intention is to bring Ubu to life through the versatile genius of Monsieur Gémier, and tonight and tomorrow are the only evenings when Monsieur Ginisty – and the current production of Villiers de l'Isle-Adam – is free to let us borrow him. We are going to make do with three complete acts, followed by two acts incorporating some cuts. I have made all the cuts the actors wanted (even sacrificing several passages essential to the understanding of the play), and for their benefit I have kept in scenes which I would have been only too happy to eliminate. For, however much we may have wanted to be marionettes, we have not quite hung each character from a string, which may not necessarily have been an absurd idea but would certainly have been rather awkward for us, and in any case we were not quite sure exactly how many people were going to be available for our crowd scenes, whereas with real marionettes a handful of pulleys and strings serves to control a whole army. So in order to fill our stage you will see leading characters such as Ubu and the Czar talking to each other while prancing around on their cardboard horses (which, incidentally, we have been up all night painting). At least the first three acts and the closing scenes will be played in full, just as they were written.

And we also have the ideal setting, for just as a play can be set in Eternity by, say, letting people fire revolvers in the year one thousand or thereabouts, so you will see doors opening onto snow-covered plains under blue skies, mantelpieces with clocks on them swinging open to turn into doorways, and palm trees flourishing at the foot of beds so that little elephants perching on bookshelves can graze on them.

As for our nonexistent orchestra, we shall have to conjure up in our imagination all its sound and fury, contenting ourselves meanwhile with a few drums and pianos executing Ubu's themes from the wings.

And the action, which is about to start, takes place in Poland, that is to say Nowhere.

15
JOSEPH CONRAD (1857–1924)
PREFACE TO *THE NIGGER OF THE 'NARCISSUS'* 1897

Polish-born English novelist and short-story writer. Conrad first went to sea for the French Merchant service in 1874, sailing to the West Indies and along the Venezuelan coast. His experience there would later form the basis of his novel Nostromo *(1904). In 1878 he came to England and served for sixteen years in the British Navy. Seafaring provided Conrad with material for most of his major fiction, including* The Nigger of the 'Narcissus' *(1897),* Youth *(1902),* Lord Jim *(1900),* The Shadow-Line *(1917). In 1894 he took command of a Congo river steamboat, an experience that deeply affected him and which is reworked in his* Heart of Darkness *(1899). Conrad's Preface to* The Nigger of the 'Narcissus' *which is reprinted below is an early formulation of his aesthetic credo. [See IIIa 2]*

A work that aspires, however humbly, to the condition of art should carry its justification in every line. And art itself may be defined as a single-minded attempt to render the highest kind of justice to the visible universe, by bringing to light the truth, manifold and one, underlying its every aspect. It is an attempt to find in its forms, in its colours, in its light, in its shadows, in the aspects of matter, and in the facts of life what of each is fundamental, what is enduring and essential – their one illuminating and convincing quality – the very truth of their existence. The artist, then, like the thinker or the scientist, seeks the truth and makes his appeal. Impressed by the aspect of the world the thinker plunges into ideas, the scientist into facts – whence, presently, emerging they make their appeal to those qualities of our being that fit us best for the hazardous enterprise of living. They speak authoritatively to our common sense, to our intelligence, to our desire of peace, or to our desire of unrest; not seldom to our prejudices, sometimes to our fears, often to our egoism – but always to our credulity. And their words are heard with reverence, for their concern is with weighty matters: with the cultivation of our minds and the proper care of our bodies, with the attainment of our ambitions, with the perfection of the means and the glorification of our precious aims.

It is otherwise with the artist.

Confronted by the same enigmatical spectacle the artist descends within himself, and in that lonely region of stress and strife, if he be deserving and fortunate, he finds the terms of his appeal. His appeal is made to our less obvious capacities: to that part of our nature which, because of the warlike conditions of existence, is necessarily kept out of sight within the more resisting and hard qualities – like the vulnerable body within a steel armour. His appeal is less loud, more profound, less distinct, more stirring – and sooner forgotten. Yet its effect endures for ever. The changing wisdom of successive generations discards ideas, questions facts, demolishes theories. But the artist appeals to that part of our being which is not dependent on wisdom; to that in us which is a gift and not an acquisition – and, therefore, more permanently enduring. He speaks to our capacity for delight and wonder, to the sense of mystery surrounding our lives; to our sense of pity, and beauty, and pain; to the latent feeling of fellowship with all creation – and to the subtle but invincible conviction of solidarity that knits together the loneliness of innumerable hearts, to the solidarity in dreams, in joy, in sorrow, in aspirations, in illusions, in hope, in fear, which binds men to each other, which binds together all humanity – the dead to the living and the living to the unborn.

It is only some such train of thought, or rather of feeling, that can in a measure explain the aim of the attempt, made in the tale which follows, to present an unrestful episode in the obscure lives of a few individuals out of all the disregarded multitude of the bewildered, the simple, and the voiceless. For, if any part of truth dwells in the belief confessed above, it becomes evident that there is not a place of splendour or a dark corner of the earth that does not deserve, if only a passing glance of wonder and pity. The motive, then, may be held to justify the matter of the work; but this preface, which is simply an avowal of endeavour, cannot end here – for the avowal is not yet complete.

Fiction – if it at all aspires to be art – appeals to temperament. And in truth it must be, like painting, like music, like all art, the appeal of one temperament to all the other innumerable temperaments whose subtle and resistless power endows passing events with their true meaning, and creates the moral, the emotional atmosphere of the place and time. Such an appeal to be effective must be an impression conveyed through the senses; and, in fact, it cannot be made in any other way, because temperament, whether individual or collective, is not amenable to persuasion. All art, therefore, appeals primarily to the senses, and the artistic aim when expressing itself in written words must also make its appeal through the senses, if its high desire is to reach the secret spring of responsive emotions. It must strenuously aspire to the plasticity of sculpture, to the colour of painting, and to the magic suggestiveness of music – which is the art of arts. And it is only through complete, unswerving devotion to the perfect blending of form and substance; it is only through an unremitting never-discouraged care for the shape and ring of sentences that an approach can be made to plasticity, to colour, and that the light of magic suggestiveness may be brought to play for an evanescent instant over the commonplace surface of words: of the old, old words, worn thin, defaced by ages of careless usage.

The sincere endeavour to accomplish that creative task, to go as far on that road as his strength will carry him, to go undeterred by faltering, weariness, or reproach, is the only valid justification for the worker in prose. And if his conscience is clear, his answer to those who, in the fullness of a wisdom which looks for immediate profit, demand specifically to be edified, consoled, amused; who demand to be promptly improved, or encouraged, or frightened, or shocked, or charmed, must run thus: My task which I am trying to achieve is, by the power of the written word to make you hear, to make you feel – it is, before all, to make you see. That – and no more, and it is everything. If I succeed, you shall find there according to your deserts: encouragement, consolation, fear, charm – all you demand – and, perhaps, also that glimpse of truth for which you have forgotten to ask.

To snatch in a moment of courage, from the remorseless rush of time, a passing phase of life, is only the beginning of the task. The task approached in tenderness and faith is to hold up unquestioningly, without choice and without fear, the rescued fragment before all eyes in the light of a sincere mood. It is to show its vibration, its colour, its form; and through its movement, its form, and its colour, reveal the substance of its truth – disclose its inspiring secret: the stress and passion within the core of each convincing moment. In a single-minded attempt of that kind, if one be deserving and fortunate, one may perchance attain to such clearness of sincerity that at last the presented vision of regret or pity, of terror or mirth, shall awaken in the hearts of the beholders that feeling of unavoidable solidarity; of the solidarity in mysterious origin, in toil, in joy, in hope, in uncertain fate, which binds men to each other and all mankind to the visible world.

It is evident that he who, rightly or wrongly, holds by the convictions expressed above cannot be faithful to any one of the temporary formulas of his craft. The enduring part of them – the truth which each only imperfectly veils – should abide with him as the most precious of his possessions, but they all: Realism, Romanticism, Naturalism, even the unofficial sentimentalism (which, like the poor, is exceedingly difficult to get rid of), all these gods must, after a short period of fellowship, abandon him – even on the very threshold of the temple – to the stammerings of his conscience and to the outspoken consciousness of the difficulties of his work. In that uneasy solitude the supreme cry of Art for Art itself, loses the exciting ring of its apparent immorality. It sounds far off. It has ceased to be a cry, and is heard only as a whisper, often incomprehensible, but at times and faintly encouraging.

Sometimes, stretched at ease in the shade of a roadside tree, we watch the motions of a labourer in a distant field, and after a time, begin to wonder languidly as to what the fellow may be at. We watch the movements of his body, the waving of his arms, we see him bend down, stand up, hesitate, begin again. It may add to the charm of an idle hour to be told the purpose of his exertions. If we know he is trying to lift a stone, to dig a ditch, to uproot a stump, we look with a more real interest at his efforts; we are disposed to condone the jar of his agitation upon the restfulness of the landscape; and even, if in a brotherly frame of mind, we may bring ourselves to forgive his failure. We understood his object, and, after all, the fellow has tried, and perhaps he had not the strength – and perhaps he had not the knowledge. We forgive, go on our way – and forget.

And so it is with the workman of art. Art is long and life is short, and success is very far off. And thus, doubtful of strength to travel so far, we talk a little about the aim – the aim of art, which, like life itself, is inspiring, difficult – obscured by mists. It is not in the clear logic of a triumphant conclusion; it is not in the unveiling of one of those heartless secrets which are called the Laws of Nature. It is not less great, but only more difficult.

To arrest, for the space of a breath, the hands busy about the work of the earth, and compel men entranced by the sight of distant goals to glance for a moment at the surrounding vision of form and colour, of sunshine and shadows; to make them pause for a look, for a sigh, for a smile – such is the aim, difficult and evanescent, and reserved only for a very few to achieve. But sometimes, by the deserving and the fortunate, even that task is accomplished. And when it is accomplished – behold! – all the truth of life is there: a moment of vision, a sigh, a smile – and the return to an eternal rest.

16
ARTHUR SYMONS (1865–1945)
FROM *THE SYMBOLIST MOVEMENT IN LITERATURE* 1899

English critic and poet. A frequenter of the Rhymer's Club in London in the 1890s, Symons was acquainted with, amongst others, Oscar Wilde, Ernest Dowson and W. B. Yeats. He became a prominent figure in the Decadent movement of the 1890s, contributing to The Yellow Book *and editing* The Savoy *from 1896. Symons is credited with introducing French Symbolism to English readers through this influential study, published in 1899 with a dedication to W. B. Yeats. The following extracts are taken from Symons's introduction.*

Without symbolism there can be no literature; indeed, not even language. What are words themselves but symbols, almost as arbitrary as the letters which compose them, mere sounds of the voice to which we have agreed to give certain significations, as we have agreed to translate these sounds by those combinations of letters? Symbolism began with the first words uttered by the first man, as he named every living thing; or before them, in heaven, when God named the world into being. And we see, in these beginnings, precisely what Symbolism in literature really is: a form of expression, at the best but approximate, essentially but arbitrary, until it has obtained the force of a convention, for an unseen reality apprehended by the consciousness. It is sometimes permitted to us to hope that our convention is indeed the reflection rather than merely the sign of that unseen reality. We have done much if we have found a recognisable sign.

'A symbol,' says Comte Goblet d'Alviella, in his book on *The Migration of Symbols*, 'might be defined as a representation which does not aim at being a reproduction'. Originally, as he points out, used by the Greeks to denote 'the two halves of the tablet they divided between themselves as a pledge of hospitality', it came to be used of every sign, formula, or rite by which those initiated in any mystery made themselves secretly known to one another. Gradually the word extended its meaning, until it came to denote every conventional representation of idea by form, of the unseen by the visible. 'In a Symbol,' says Carlyle, 'there is concealment and yet revelation: hence therefore, by Silence and by Speech acting together, comes a double significance.' And, in that fine chapter of *Sartor Resartus*, he goes further, vindicating for the word its full value: 'In the Symbol proper, what we can call a Symbol, there is ever, more or less distinctly and directly, some embodiment and revelation of the Infinite; the Infinite is made to blend itself with the Finite, to stand visible, and as it were, attainable there.'

It is in such a sense as this that the word Symbolism has been used to describe a movement which, during the last generation, has profoundly influenced the course of French literature. All such words, used of anything so living, variable, and irresponsible as literature, are, as symbols themselves must so often be, mere compromises, mere indications. Symbolism, as seen in the writers of our day, would have no value if it were not seen also, under one disguise or another, in every great imaginative writer. What distinguishes the Symbolism of our day from the Symbolism of the past is that it has now become conscious of itself, in a sense in which it was unconscious even in Gérard de Nerval, to whom I trace the particular origin of the literature which I call Symbolist. The forces which mould the thought of men change, or men's resistance to them slackens; with the change of men's thought comes a change of literature, alike in its inmost essence and in its outward form: after the world has starved its soul long enough in the contemplation and the re-arrangement of material things, comes the turn of the soul; and with it comes the literature of which I write in this volume, a literature in which the visible world is no longer a reality, and the unseen world no longer a dream.

[. . .]

There is such a thing as perfecting form that form may be annihilated. All the art of Verlaine is in bringing verse to a bird's song, the art of Mallarmé in bringing verse to the song of an orchestra. In Villiers de l'Isle-Adam drama becomes an embodiment of spiritual forces, in Maeterlinck not even their embodiment, but the remote sound of their voices. It is all an attempt to spiritualise literature, to evade the old bondage of rhetoric, the old bondage of exteriority. Description is banished that beautiful things may be evoked, magically; the regular beat of verse is broken in order that words may fly, upon subtler wings. Mystery is no longer feared, as the great mystery in whose midst we are islanded was feared by those to whom that unknown sea was only a great void. We are coming closer to nature, as we seem to shrink from it with something of horror, disdaining to catalogue the trees of the forest. And as we brush aside the accidents of daily life, in which men and women imagine that they are alone touching reality, we come closer to humanity, to everything in humanity that may have begun before the world and may outlast it.

Here, then, in this revolt against exteriority, against rhetoric, against a materialistic tradition; in this endeavour to disengage the ultimate essence, the soul, of whatever exists and can be realised by the consciousness; in this dutiful waiting upon every symbol by which the soul of things can be made visible; literature, bowed down by so many burdens, may at last attain liberty, and its authentic speech. In attaining this liberty, it accepts a heavier burden; for in speaking to us so intimately, so solemnly, as only religion had hitherto spoken to us, it becomes itself a kind of religion, with all the duties and responsibilities of the sacred ritual.

17
W. B. (WILLIAM BUTLER) YEATS (1865–1939)
FROM 'THE SYMBOLISM OF POETRY' 1900

Irish poet, dramatist, politician, awarded the Nobel Prize in 1923. Born in Dublin, Yeats was brought up there, and in London and Sligo. His early verse is characterised by a dreamy romanticism which is nevertheless disciplined by an interest in heroic Irish history and legendry, and in Theosophy, magic and mysticism. His meeting with the actress and nationalist Maud Gonne in 1889 prompted him to search for a more popular, colloquial style, expressive of his 'normal, reasoning self'. This discovery is reflected in the volumes In the Seven Woods *(1903) and* The Green Helmet and Other Poems *(1910). Yeats's relationship with Lady Gregory had convinced him of the virtues of the aristocrat-peasant relationship and of the Philistinism of the middle classes, an opinion strengthened by his involvement with the Irish National Theatre in the late 1890s. Having left Ireland for a time, he was inspired to return by the 1916 Easter Rising and became a senator in the Irish Free State in 1922. His change in commitment coincided with a change in poetic approach from* The Wild Swans at Coole *(1919) onwards. Yeats attempted to add a metaphysical element to his verse, forming a complex and idiosyncratic system of Symbolism combined with a cyclical theory of history. These ideas, worked out in* A Vision *(1925; 1937), formed the basis for the major volumes,* The Tower *(1928) and* The Winding Stair *(1933). The following extract is from the essay 'The Symbolism of Poetry', written in 1900. [See IIIa 6, IIIb 14]*

I.

Symbolism, as seen in the writers of our day, would have no value if it were not seen also, under one disguise or another, in every great imaginative writer,' writes Mr. Arthur Symons in *The Symbolist Movement in Literature*, a subtle book which I cannot praise as I would, because it has been dedicated to me; and he goes on to show how many profound writers have in the last few years sought for a philosophy of poetry in the doctrine of symbolism, and how even in countries where it is almost scandalous to seek for any philosophy of poetry, new writers are following them in their search.

[. . .]

Goethe has said, 'a poet needs all philosophy, but he must keep it out of his work,' though that is not always necessary; and almost certainly no great art, outside England, where journalists are more powerful and ideas less plentiful than elsewhere, has arisen without a great criticism, for its herald or its interpreter and protector, and it may be for this reason that great art, now that vulgarity has armed itself and multiplied itself, is perhaps dead in England.

All writers, all artists of any kind, in so far as they have had any philosophical or critical power, perhaps just in so far as they have been deliberate artists at all, have had some philosophy, some criticism of their art; and it has often been this philosophy, or this criticism, that has evoked their most startling inspiration, calling into outer life some portion of the divine life, or of the buried reality, which could alone extinguish in the emotions what their philosophy or their criticism would extinguish in the intellect. They have sought for no new thing, it may be, but only to understand and to copy the pure inspiration of early times, but because the divine life wars upon our outer life, and must needs change its weapons and its movements as we change ours, inspiration has come to them in beautiful startling shapes. The scientific movement brought with it a literature which was always tending to lose itself in externalities of all kinds, in opinion, in declamation, in picturesque writing, in word-painting, or in what Mr. Symons has called an attempt 'to build in brick and mortar inside the covers of a book'; and now writers have begun to dwell upon the element of evocation, of suggestion, upon what we call the symbolism in great writers.

inspired by Mallarmé

[...]

All sounds, all colours, all forms, either because of their preordained energies or because of long association evoke indefinable and yet precise emotions, or, as I prefer to think, call down among us certain disembodied powers, whose footsteps over our hearts we call emotions; and when sound, and colour, and form are in a musical relation, a beautiful relation to one another, they become, as it were, one sound, one colour, one form, and evoke an emotion that is made out of their distinct evocations and yet is one emotion. The same relation exists between all portions of every work of art, whether it be an epic or a song, and the more perfect it is, and the more various and numerous the elements that have flowed into its perfection, the more powerful will be the emotion, the power, the god it calls among us. Because an emotion does not exist, or does not become perceptible and active among us, till it has found its expression, in colour or in sound or in form, or in all of these, and because no two modulations or arrangements of these evoke the same emotion, poets and painters and musicians, and in a less degree because their effects are momentary, day and night and cloud and shadow, are continually making and unmaking mankind. It is indeed only those things which seem useless or very feeble that have any power, and all those things that seem useful or strong, armies, moving wheels, modes of architecture, modes of government, speculations of the reason, would have been a little different if some mind long ago had not given itself to some emotion, as a woman gives herself to her lover, and shaped sounds or colours or forms, or all of these, into a musical relation, that their emotion might live in other minds. A little lyric evokes an emotion, and this emotion gathers others about it and melts into their being in the making of some great epic; and at last, needing an always less delicate body, or symbol, as it grows more powerful, it flows out, with all it has gathered, among the blind instincts of daily life, where it moves a power within powers, as one sees ring within ring in the stem of an old tree. This is maybe what Arthur O'Shaughnessy meant when he made his poets say they had built Nineveh with their sighing; and I am certainly never sure, when I hear of some war, or of some religious excitement, or of some new manufacture, or of anything else that fills the ear of the world, that it has not all happened because of something that a boy piped in Thessaly. I remember once telling a seeress to ask one among the gods who, as she believed, were standing about her in their symbolic bodies, what would come of a charming but seeming trivial labour of a friend, and the form answering, 'the devastation of peoples and the overwhelming of cities'. I doubt indeed if the crude circumstance of the world, which seems to create all our emotions, does more than reflect, as in multiplying mirrors, the emotions that have come to solitary men in moments of poetical contemplation; or that love itself would be more than an animal hunger but for the poet and his shadow the priest, for unless we believe that outer things are the reality, we must believe that the gross is the shadow of the subtle, that things are wise before they become foolish, and secret before they cry out in the market-place.

[. . .]

III.

The purpose of rhythm, it has always seemed to me, is to prolong the moment of contemplation, the moment when we are both asleep and awake, which is the one moment of creation, by hushing us with an alluring monotony, while it holds us waking by variety, to keep us in that state of perhaps real trance, in which the mind liberated from the pressure of the will is unfolded in symbols. If certain sensitive persons listen persistently to the ticking of a watch, or gaze persistently on the monotonous flashing of a light, they fall into the hypnotic trance; and rhythm is but the ticking of a watch made softer, that one must needs listen, and various, that one may not be swept beyond memory or grow weary of listening; while the patterns of the artist are but the monotonous flash woven to take the eyes in a subtler enchantment. I have heard in meditation voices that were forgotten the moment they had spoken; and I have been swept, when in more profound meditation, beyond all memory but of those things that came from beyond the threshold of waking life. I was writing once at a very symbolical and abstract poem, when my pen fell on the ground; and as I stooped to pick it up, I remembered some fantastic adventure that yet did not seem fantastic, and then another like adventure, and when I asked myself when these things had happened, I found that I was remembering my dreams for many nights. I tried to remember what I had done the day before, and then what I had done that morning; but all my waking life had perished from me, and it was only after a struggle that I came to remember it again, and as I did so that more powerful and startling life perished in its turn. Had my pen not fallen on the ground and so made me turn from the images that I was weaving into verse, I would never have known that meditation had become trance, for I would have been like one who does not know that he is passing through a wood because his eyes are on the pathway. So I think that in the making and in the understanding of a work of art, and the more easily if it is full of patterns and symbols and music, we are lured to the threshold of sleep, and it may be far beyond it, without knowing that we have ever set our feet upon the steps of horn or of ivory.

IV.

Besides emotional symbols, symbols that evoke emotions alone, – and in this sense all alluring or hateful things are symbols, although their relations with one another are too subtle to delight us fully, away from rhythm and pattern, – there are intellectual symbols, symbols that evoke ideas alone, or ideas mingled with emotions; and outside the very definite traditions of mysticism and the less definite criticism of certain modern poets, these alone are called symbols. Most things belong to one or another kind, according to the way we speak of them and the companions we give them, for symbols, associated with ideas that are more than fragments of the shadows thrown upon the intellect by the emotions they evoke, are the playthings of the allegorist or the pedant, and soon pass away. If I say 'white' or 'purple' in an ordinary line of poetry, they evoke emotions so exclusively that I cannot say why they move me; but if I bring them into the same sentence with such obvious intellectual symbols as a cross or a crown of thorns, I think of purity and sovereignty. Furthermore, innumerable meanings, which are held to 'white' or to 'purple' by bonds of subtle suggestion, and alike in the emotions and in the intellect, move visibly through my mind, and move invisibly beyond the threshold of sleep, casting lights and shadows of an indefinable wisdom on what had seemed before, it may be, but sterility and noisy violence. It is the intellect that decides where the reader shall ponder over the procession of the symbols, and if the symbols are merely emotional, he gazes from amid the accidents and destinies of the world; but if the symbols are intellectual too, he becomes himself a part of pure intellect, and he is himself mingled with the procession. If I watch a rushy pool in the moonlight, my emotion at its beauty is mixed with memories of the man that I have seen ploughing by its margin, or of the lovers I saw there a night ago; but if I look at the moon herself and remember any of her ancient names and meanings, I move among divine people, and things that have shaken off our mortality, the tower of ivory, the queen of waters, the shining stag among enchanted woods, the white hare sitting upon the hilltop, the fool of Faery with his shining cup full of dreams, and it may be 'make a friend of one of these images of wonder,' and 'meet the Lord in the air.'

[. . .]

In an earlier time he would have been of that multitude whose souls austerity withdrew, even more perfectly than madness could withdraw his soul, from hope and memory, from desire and regret, that they might reveal those processions of symbols that men bow to before altars, and woo with incense and offerings. But being of our time, he has been like Maeterlinck, like Villiers de l'Isle-Adam in *Axël*, like all who are preoccupied with intellectual symbols in our time, a foreshadower of the new sacred book, of which all the arts, as somebody has said, are beginning to dream. How can the arts overcome the slow dying of men's hearts that we call the progress of the world, and lay their hands upon men's heart-strings again, without becoming the garment of religion as in old times?

V.

If people were to accept the theory that poetry moves us because of its symbolism, what change should one look for in the manner of our poetry? A return to the way of our fathers, a casting out of descriptions of nature for the sake of nature, of the moral law for the sake of the moral law, a casting out of all anecdotes and of that brooding over scientific opinion that so often extinguished the central flame in Tennyson, and of that vehemence that would make us do or not do certain things; or, in other words, we should come to understand that the beryl stone was enchanted by our fathers that it might unfold the pictures in its heart, and not to mirror our own excited faces, or the boughs waving outside the window. With this change of substance, this return to imagination, this understanding that the laws of art, which are the hidden laws of the world, can alone bind the imagination, would come a change of style, and we would cast out of serious poetry those energetic rhythms, as of a man running, which are the invention of the will with its eyes always on something to be done or undone; and we would seek out those wavering, meditative, organic rhythms, which are the embodiment of the imagination, that neither desires nor hates, because it has done with time, and only wishes to gaze upon some reality, some beauty; nor would it be any longer possible for anybody to deny the importance of form, in all its kinds, for although you can expound an opinion, or describe a thing, when your words are not quite well chosen, you cannot give a body to something that moves beyond the senses, unless your words are as subtle, as complex, as full of mysterious life, as the body of a flower or of a woman. The form of sincere poetry, unlike the form of the 'popular poetry,' may indeed be sometimes obscure, or ungrammatical as in some of the best of the *Songs of Innocence and Experience*, but it must have the perfections that escape analysis, the subtleties that have a new meaning every day, and it must have all this whether it be but a little song made out of a moment of dreamy indolence, or some great epic made out of the dreams of one poet and of a hundred generations whose hands were never weary of the sword.

18
MARCEL PROUST (1871–1922)
FROM 'DAYS OF READING: I' 1905

French novelist. A dandy until his thirty-fourth year, Proust mostly led an ascetic, hermetic existence triggered by the traumatic experience of his mother's death. Before undertaking the vast (and hugely influential for Modernism) À la recherche du temps perdu *(comprising thirteen volumes, seven of which were published between 1913–22, the final six posthumously) Proust spent six years studying and translating works of John Ruskin. In* À la recherche, *Proust famously put Henri Bergson's ideas into literary practice, most notably the concept of involuntary memory. The following extract from the preface to his translation of Ruskin's* Bible of Amiens *first appeared in 1905 in the magazine* La Renaissance latine *as 'Sur la lecture'. As* Journées de lecture, I (Journées de lecture, II *being the preface to his translation of Ruskin's* Sesame and Lilies) *it was subsequently published in the collection* Pastiches et mélanges *in 1919. The extract reproduced below is taken from* Marcel Proust: A Selection from His Miscellaneous Writings, *translated by Gerard Hopkins, 1948. [See Ia 18, IIIa 34]*

No days, perhaps, of all our childhood are ever so fully lived as those that we had regarded as not being lived at all: days spent wholly with a favourite book. Everything that seemed to fill them full for others we pushed aside, because it stood between us and the pleasures of the Gods: the game to which we might be summoned by a friend just as we had reached the most exciting part; the intrusive bee or the troublesome ray of sunlight that forced us to look up from the page or to change our seat; the 'snack' we had been made to bring, but had left untasted by us on the bench, while overhead the sun shone with diminished heat in the blue sky; dinner, which drew us back to the house, though our thoughts, while we ate, were wholly of the moment when, the meal at long last ended, we should be free to go upstairs, there to finish the interrupted chapter. All these things which figure in our memories only as having been obstacles to reading, have really sunk so deep and left so sweet a trace (much more precious, so we have come to think, than what we then were reading with such passion) that if now we should happen to turn the pages of those ancient books, they would be for us nothing but a calendar of days long past, in which we hope to see reflected the houses and the ponds that are no more.

[. . .]

And here, as I am about to approach *Of King's Treasuries*, I have thought it well, before attempting to show why, in my opinion, reading ought not to play the preponderant part in life which Ruskin ascribes to it in that little book, to exclude from my general criticism those delightful excursions into books which mark our childhood, the recollection of which must hover like a blessing over the memories of each one of us. Doubtless, by the length and the nature of the reflections here printed, I have shown, perhaps to excess, what was in my mind – that their peculiar heritage to us is the setting of times and places in which they were conducted. I have not been able to free myself from the spell they exercise. Meaning to speak of them, it is not of books that I have spoken, because it was not of books that they spoke to me. But perhaps the memories, that, one by one, they called up in my mind, have been awakened, too, in that of my reader, with the result that he may have been led, after loitering awhile in those flowery byways, to recreate in his own imagination the original psychological activity which goes by the name of 'reading', and with sufficient clarity to make it possible for him now to follow, as in the intimacy of his own thoughts, the few comments which I still have to make.

It is a matter of general knowledge that *Of Kings' Treasuries* is a lecture on the subject of reading which Ruskin delivered in the Town Hall of Rusholme, near Manchester, on the 6th December, 1864, with the object of supporting the creation of a library in the Rusholme Institute.

[. . .]

It is my intention here to discuss only the main thesis put forward by Ruskin, without bothering about its historical origins. It can be adequately summed up in these words of Descartes: 'The reading of all good books is like talking with those noble men of past centuries who were their authors.' Ruskin may, perhaps, have been ignorant of this rather dry comment by the French philosopher, but the thought that we find in his lecture is identical with it, though wrapped round in Apollonian gold into which have run the colours of the English fog, until the resultant tone resembles that which glows in the landscapes of his favourite painter.

[. . .]

I have attempted, in my notes to *Sesame and Lilies*, to show that reading can never be thus equated with conversation with any living man, no matter how wise; that what makes a book and a friend so different, one from another, has nothing whatever to do with the greater or less degree of their wisdom, but with the manner of our communication, reading, as opposed to conversation, consisting, for each one of us, in *receiving* another's thought, while all the time, ourselves, remaining alone, that is to say, continuing to enjoy that intellectual power which comes to us in solitude, and which conversation at once destroys – continuing in a state of mind which allows us to be inspired, to let the mind work fruitfully upon itself. Had Ruskin drawn the logical conclusion from certain other truths which he states somewhat further on, he would probably have found himself in agreement with me. But, quite clearly, he made no effort to strike to the heart even of the idea of the nature of reading. All he wanted to do was to make us realise the value of reading, to tell us a sort of beautiful Platonic myth, with that same simplicity with which the Greeks have demonstrated almost all the great truths, leaving to modern scruples the task of investigating them. But, if I hold that reading, in its prime essence – which consists in a miraculous and fruitful power of being able to remain in communication with others even when we are encased in our own spiritual solitude – is something more than, something different from, what Ruskin thought it – I still do not believe that it plays the overwhelmingly important part in our mental existence which he appears to maintain.

Its limitations are the direct consequences of its virtues; and, if we ask what, precisely, those virtues are, I find the answer to lie in the kind of reading that we enjoy in childhood. What that book was which, a few pages back, you watched me reading beside the dining room fire, or upstairs, in my bedroom, ensconced in an armchair with a crochet-work antimacassar, or, on fine afternoons, beneath the hazels and the hawthorns of the park, where breezes from the distant view played silently about me, bringing to my careless senses, with no word spoken, the smell of the clover and the hay on which, from time to time, I would rest my weary eyes – you do not know. Peer as closely as you may, you can never find the answer to that question across the gulf of twenty years, and must rely upon my memory – more suited to that species of vision – to tell you that it was Théophile Gautier's *Le Capitaine Fracasse*. Two or three passages in it I loved with an especial fervour, thinking them the most original, the loveliest, in the whole volume. It was impossible for me to believe that any other author had written anything comparable. But I had the feeling that their beauty corresponded to a reality of which Théophile Gautier gave me but a few fleeting glimpses. And, since I was convinced that he *must* know the whole of it, I longed to read others of his books, books containing passages no less beautiful, and designed to give me information on all the subjects on which I wanted to have his views.

[. . .]

Indeed, the great, the marvellous power possessed by good books (which makes us realise the part, at once essential yet limited, that reading can play in our mental lives) lies in this, that what the author may treat as 'Conclusions' can, for the reader, be 'Incitements'. We have a strong feeling that our own wisdom begins just where that of the author finishes, and we want him to give us answers when all that he can offer are desires. And these desires books can awake in us only by compelling us to contemplate the final beauty to which they provide a gate, by squeezing the last drop from the art of which they are the embodiment. As the result of a curious but providential law of our mental vision (a law, perhaps, which means that we can never receive the truth from anybody, but must always be creating it for ourselves), what is the end of their wisdom inevitably appears to us as the beginning of ours, so that it is at the precise moment when they have told us all they have to tell that they wake in us the feeling that, as yet, they have told us nothing at all.

But if we put to them questions that they cannot answer, we demand of them, too, replies that would be for us empty of all instruction. For one of the effects of the love which the poets wake in us, is that it makes us attach a literal significance to matters which, for them, are expressive only of emotions personal to themselves. In each picture that they show us, they seem to be doing no more than let us catch sight of some marvellous place, different from all other places in the world, deep into which we would have them guide us.

[. . .]

What makes them seem to us more beautiful than the rest of the world is that they give, like some vague reflection, the effect that they produced on genius. It would appear to us just as remarkable, just as despotic, no matter what insignificant and submissive corner of the world they might have happened to paint. The appearance with which they charm and hallucinate us, and into which we long to penetrate, is the very essence of that something – in a two-dimensional rendering – that mirage caught and fixed upon a piece of canvas – which is what we mean by 'vision'. The mist which our eager eyes would pierce is the last word of the painter's art. The supreme effort of the writer, as of the graphic artist, can do no more than lift for us a corner of the veil of ugliness and insignificance which leaves us incurious before the spectacle of the universe.

[. . .]

There are however, certain cases, certain pathological cases, if I may so describe them, of mental depression, for which reading can become a species of curative discipline, whose function it is, by repeated stimulus, to re-introduce the mind into the life of the spirit. Here, books play a part analogous to that of psychotherapy in particular types of neurasthenic ailments.

We know that there are diseases of the nervous system, as a result of which the patient, though he may have nothing organically wrong with him, becomes bogged in a sort of paralysis of the will, as in some deep rut, from which he cannot extricate himself unaided, and in which he will, at long last, perish utterly unless a strong and helping hand is stretched to him. His brain, his limbs, his lungs, his stomach, all are intact. There is no *physical* reason why he should not work, walk, endure cold, and eat as usual. But though he is perfectly capable of performing these actions, he lacks the will to do so. A state of organic decay sets in which will end by producing the equivalent of all the ailments from which, in reality, he does not suffer, and which are the incurable consequences of his lack of will-power, unless a stimulus which he cannot find in himself is provided from outside, provided, that is, by a doctor who can do his willing for him until such time as his own responses shall have been gradually re-educated. Now, there are minds of a certain type that it is possible to compare with cases of this kind, minds which a species of laziness or frivolity prevents from striking spontaneously into their own deepest regions where the real life of the spirit has its origins. Once they have been shown the way, they are perfectly capable of discovering for themselves, and of exploiting, the rich veins that lie there: but without this help from outside, they will continue to live on the surface in a state of perpetual unawareness, in a sort of passivity, which makes them the playthings of every passing pleasure, and reduces them to the stature of those who surround them, dissipating their energies so that, like the man of gentle birth who, because, since earliest childhood, he had shared the life of highway-robbers, forgot even his name because it was so many years since he had used it, they will end by erasing in themselves all feeling and all memory of spiritual greatness, unless some external stimulus inject a kind of mental strength, thus enabling them to re-discover the power to think for themselves and to become creative. Now, this stimulus which the lazy mind cannot find on its own account, and which must come from outside, cannot be effective unless it reaches down to the roots of that loneliness in the individual, shorn of which, as we have seen, the creative activity, which is precisely what has got to be revived, cannot come into operation. The lazy mind can get nothing from *pure* solitude, because it is incapable, unaided, of getting its creative activity to work. Nor will mere conversation, no matter how elevated in tone, nor the most urgent advice, have any effect, since these things can do nothing to produce such a highly individualised activity. What, then, is needed is some sort of intervention, which, though it may come from elsewhere, does stir the requisite consciousness in ourselves, an impulse having its origin outside ourselves, but received into the very centre of our personal loneliness. This, as I have explained, is the true definition of reading, and it fits no other activity. The only discipline that can exercise a beneficent influence on minds of the kind I have been describing, is that of reading – Q.E.D. as the geometricians say. But the important thing to realise is that reading can be only a stimulus, and can never become a substitute for the working of our own minds. It confines its operation to restoring to us the use of our own faculties, just as in the cases of nervous disease to which I have referred, the psychotherapist can do no more than re-educate in the patient the *will* to employ his stomach, his limbs and his brain, which have nothing organically the matter with them. Whether it is that every human mind suffers, to some extent, from this sort of laziness, this stagnation of the lower levels of consciousness, or whether the excitement that follows in the wake of certain kinds of reading, and, without being absolutely necessary, does exercise a beneficent influence on a man's work, the fact remains that a very large number of writers have always been in the habit of reading a passage from some good book before themselves settling down to work. Thus, Emerson scarcely ever began to write without first reading a few pages of Plato, nor is Dante the only poet whom Virgil piloted to the gates of Paradise.

So long as reading is treated as a guide holding the keys that open the door to buried regions of ourselves, into which, otherwise, we should never penetrate, the part it can play in our lives is salutary. On the contrary, it becomes dangerous when, instead of waking us to the reality of our own mental processes, it becomes a substitute for them: when truth appears to us, not as an ideal which we can realise only as a result of our own thinking and our own emotional efforts, but as a material *object* which exists between the pages of a book, like honey made by others, to be possessed merely by stretching out our hands to a bookshelf and passively digesting it in a mood of bodily and mental torpor.

19
WILLIAM ARCHER (1856–1924)
FROM 'HENRIK IBSEN: PHILOSOPHER OR POET' 1905

British theatre critic. After moving from Edinburgh to London in the late 1870s, Archer began writing theatre reviews for the London Figaro. *In 1884 he became drama critic for* The World *and his work for that journal was collected in five volumes entitled* Theatrical 'World' *(1893–97). Archer is credited with having introduced the work of Ibsen to British audiences through his translations and productions of the Norwegian's plays, beginning in 1880 with* Pillars of Society. *His edition of Ibsen's* Collected Plays *was published in twelve volumes between 1906 and 1912. The following extracts are from an essay of 1905.*

Ibsen is a great poet, a great creator of men and women, a great inventor and manipulator of those critical conjunctures in life which are the material of drama. He is also, no doubt, a moralist. He has a high ideal of human character, and he scourges unsparingly both the individual and the social turpitudes which prevent the realization of that ideal. But he has no definite, consistent, clearly thought-out moral or social system to inculcate. His primary concern is the projection of character, and its development by aid of an interesting, moving, absorbing action. As no serious action in life is devoid of moral significance, so there is no play of Ibsen's that does not raise a number of moral issues. It may even be for the sake of one or more of these moral issues that he chooses one action rather than another. But his characters always live a life of their own, independent of any ethical intention in the play. Only where the poet falls distinctly beneath himself do we feel that their speech or action is conditioned by his moral design; and, on the other hand, they often, as it were, take the bit between their teeth, and leave the moral design away in the dim distance. Moreover, the ethical intentions discernible in one play are often inconsistent, superficially at any rate, with those of the next. Being, as I say, a poet, and not a systematic thinker, Ibsen sees one side of a case intensely at one moment, and the other side at another moment, with no less intensity. In this multiplicity of his points of view we have the reason why so many different people are able to 'quintessentiate' their own doctrines out of Ibsen's work. The doctrines are there beyond dispute; but the process of quintessentiation consists in ignoring the contradictory doctrines which are there no less.

[. . .]

It is not in the least doubtful how Ibsen himself desires to be regarded. He has asserted again and again, in opposition to his expositors, that he is not primarily a thinker, but a dramatist. He did his best to impress this even on M. Lourié, who quotes from a private letter of his (dated 19th February, 1899) the following words: 'I would beg you to remember that the thoughts thrown out in my plays proceed from my dramatic personages who utter them, and are neither in matter nor in form to be attributed to me personally.' Still more explicit is one of the poet's declarations to Count Prozor, his French translator: 'If,' he says, 'in transporting to the stage certain men and women whom I have seen and known, certain facts which I have witnessed or which have been related to me – and if, in throwing an atmosphere of poetry over the whole – I succeed in stimulating the minds of my audiences, different ideas will germinate in different brains, and will no doubt have had my play for their point of departure. And of course I don't deny that, as I wrote, such and such ideas may have traversed my own mind too. But this is entirely a secondary matter. The main thing in a theatrical creation is, and must be, action, life.' It is abundantly manifest, then, that if M. Lourié and the other quintessentiators are right in regarding Ibsen's plays as primarily philosophic essays, in which the action is a more or less negligible quantity, Ibsen's life-work must be, from his own point of view, a gigantic failure. But they are not right: they are utterly and hopelessly wrong. In another paper I have tried to suggest certain reasons and excuses for their error. Here let me confine myself to showing, very briefly, in one typical instance, how impossible it is to extract from Ibsen's works a consistent body of social doctrine – impossible, that is to say, without arbitrarily ignoring whatever does not happen to tally with the case you want to make out.

As Ibsen's most famous play is *A Doll's House*, in which Nora Helmer somewhat vehemently asserts her right to a soul of her own, it is commonly assumed that Ibsen is above everything a champion of 'women's rights' – of 'female emancipation', in the sense which political agitators assign to the term. M. Lourié has not the slightest doubt on this point. 'Ibsen,' he says, 'has consecrated the puissance of his pen to the defense of Woman'; and he goes off into a demonstration that 'the modern woman has already proved that she possesses the same intellectual capacities as man, and that there is no branch of human activity in which she cannot replace, and often even surpass him.' Apparent exceptions to this rule are explained on the ground of inadequate education, insufficient opportunity, ingrained prejudice, and so forth. In short, M. Lourié gives us a treatise of several pages on the ordinary topics of latter-day feminism.

But there is not a word of all this in Ibsen. He nowhere seeks to show that woman 'possesses the same intellectual capacities' as man; he nowhere claims for her a right to take part with man in every 'branch of human activity'. He allows her a soul to be saved, and he makes one of his heroines seek her own salvation in breaking out of the cage of marriage. Beyond this, I defy any one to discover in Ibsen the smallest championship of 'woman's rights' in the sectarian sense of the word. Would he give women the suffrage? He does not say. Does he consider them fitted for the learned professions, for commerce, for engineering, for soldiering, for sailoring? If he does, he has kept the secret. He has drawn many noble women, true; but also many vulgar, base, and abom-inable women. If every poet who drew beautiful female characters were a champion of 'woman's rights', it would be the most gloriously championed cause in all history.

[. . .]

It may perhaps be thought that I am, personally, an opponent of female emancipa-tion, and am simply trying, like M. Lourié, to read my own views into Ibsen. This is not so. Though I do not quite believe with M. Lourié that woman can do everything that man can do, as well and probably better, I am in favor of removing all legal restrictions on her activities. I would always vote, for instance, in favor of female suffrage, though I am not quite inconsolable at the tardiness of its coming. This topic of female emancipation is only one out of many that I might equally well have chosen to illustrate my point – namely, that the poet whom the commentators are always striving to enlist in this or that party or sect, in reality stands entirely outside sects and parties, and simply uses them for his dramatic purposes. If you want a deliberate and consistent body of doctrine, you must go, not to Ibsen, but to Tolstoy. In his own person, in one of his lyric poems, Ibsen has said, 'My calling is to question, not to answer.' One of the very few characters – two or three at most – in which we are justified in recognizing some trace, some aspect, of the poet's own personality, says of himself, 'I am glad that it is my mission to be the thirteenth at table.' At all our banquets of sectarian self-gratulation Ibsen plays the part of this disquieting guest, as he did at that feminist festival in Christiania.

20
HENRY JAMES (1843–1916)
FROM 'THE ART OF FICTION' 1894; PREFACE TO *THE PRINCESS CASAMASSIMA* 1906

American novelist. As an expatriate in Paris from 1875–76, James made the acquaintance of the Russian novelist Ivan Turgenev and several prominent French writers – Émile Zola, Edmond de Goncourt, Guy de Maupassant – all of whom affirmed his notion (prompted by Flaubert's experiments in narrative) that plot could be subordinate to an interest in character. Moving to London, James produced his first major works, culminating in The Portrait of a Lady *(1881). In the 1880s and 1890s he wrote prolifically, producing several experimental novels and collections of short stories. In addition, he began to theorise on the nature of fiction and in 1894 produced the essay 'The Art of Fiction', extracts from which are reprinted here. Also reproduced below is an extract from his Preface to* The Princess Casamassima, *from 1906.*

Only a short time ago it might have been supposed that the English novel was not what the French call *discutable*. It had no air of having a theory, a conviction, a consciousness of itself behind it – of being the expression of an artistic faith, the result of choice and comparison. I do not say it was necessarily the worse for that: it would take much more courage than I possess to intimate that the form of the novel as Dickens and Thackeray (for instance) saw it had any taint of incompleteness. It was, however, *naïf* (if I may help myself out with another French word); and evidently if it be destined to suffer in any way for having lost its *naïveté* it has now an idea of making sure of the corresponding advantages. During the period I have alluded to there was a comfortable, good-humoured feeling abroad that a novel is a novel, as a pudding is a pudding, and that our only business with it could be to swallow it. But within a year or two, for some reason or other, there have been signs of returning animation – the era of discussion would appear to have been to a certain extent opened.

[...]

The only reason for the existence of a novel is that it does attempt to represent life. When it relinquishes this attempt, the same attempt that we see on the canvas of the painter, it will have arrived at a very strange pass. It is not expected of the picture that it will make itself humble in order to be forgiven; and the analogy between the art of the painter and the art of the novelist is, so far as I am able to see, complete. Their inspiration is the same, their process (allowing for the different quality of the vehicle), is the same, their success is the same. They may learn from each other, they may explain and sustain each other. Their cause is the same, and the honour of one is the honour of another. [. . .] That is the only general description (which does it justice) that we may give of the novel. But history also is allowed to represent life; it is not, any more than painting, expected to apologise. The subject-matter of fiction is stored up likewise in documents and records, and if it will not give itself away, as they say in California, it must speak with assurance, with the tone of the historian. Certain accomplished novelists have a habit of giving themselves away which must often bring tears to the eyes of people who take their fiction seriously. I was lately struck, in reading over many pages of Anthony Trollope, with his want of discretion in this particular. In a digression, a parenthesis or an aside, he concedes to the reader that he and this trusting friend are only 'making believe'. He admits that the events he narrates have not really happened, and that he can give his narrative any turn the reader may like best. Such a betrayal of a sacred office seems to me, I confess, a terrible crime; it is what I mean by the attitude of apology, and it shocks me every whit as much in Trollope as it would have shocked me in Gibbon or Macaulay. It implies that the novelist is less occupied in looking for the truth (the truth, of course I mean, that he assumes, the premises that we must grant him, whatever they may be), than the historian, and in doing so it deprives him at a stroke of all his standing-room. To represent and illustrate the past, the actions of men, is the task of either writer, and the only difference that I can see is, in proportion as he succeeds, to the honour of the novelist, consisting as it does in his having more difficulty in collecting his evidence, which is so far from being purely literary. It seems to me to give him a great character, the fact that he has at once so much in common with the philosopher and the painter; this double analogy is a magnificent heritage.

[. . .]

It goes without saying that you will not write a good novel unless you possess the sense of reality; but it will be difficult to give you a recipe for calling that sense into being. Humanity is immense, and reality has a myriad forms; the most one can affirm is that some of the flowers of fiction have the odour of it, and others have not; as for telling you in advance how your nosegay should be composed, that is another affair. It is equally excellent and inconclusive to say that one must write from experience; to our suppositions aspirant such a declaration might savour of mockery. What kind of experience is intended, and where does it begin and end? Experience is never limited, and it is never complete; it is an immense sensibility, a kind of huge spider-web of the finest silken threads suspended in the chamber of consciousness, and catching every air-borne particle in its tissue. It is the very atmosphere of the mind; and when the mind is imaginative – much more when it happens to be that of a man of genius – it takes to itself the faintest hints of life, it converts the very pulses of the air into revelations. The young lady living in a village has only to be a damsel upon whom nothing is lost to make it quite unfair (as it seems to me) to declare to her that she shall have nothing to say about the military. Greater miracles have been seen than that, imagination assisting, she should speak the truth about some of these gentlemen. I remember an English novelist, a woman of genius, telling me that she was much commended for the impression she had managed to give in one of her tales of the nature and way of life of the French Protestant youth. She had been asked where she learned so much about this recondite being, she had been congratulated on her peculiar opportunities. These opportunities consisted in her having once, in Paris, as she ascended a staircase, passed an open door where, in the household of a *pasteur*, some of the young Protestants were seated at table round a finished meal. The glimpse made a picture; it lasted only a moment, but that moment was experience. She had got her direct personal impression, and she turned out of her type. She knew what youth was, and what Protestantism; she also had the advantage of having seen what it was to be French, so that she converted these ideas into a concrete image and produced a reality. Above all, however, she was blessed with the faculty which when you give it an inch takes an ell, and which for the artist is a much greater source of strength than any accident of residence or of place in the social scale. The power to guess the unseen from the seen, to trace the implication of things, to judge the whole piece by the pattern, the condition of feeling life in general so completely that you are well on your way to knowing any particular corner of it – this cluster of gifts may almost be said to constitute experience, and they occur in country and in town, and in the most differing stages of education. If experience consists of impressions, it may be said that impressions *are* experience, just as (have we not seen it?) they are the very air we breathe. Therefore, if I should certainly say to a novice, 'Write from experience and experience only,' I should feel that this was rather a tantalising monition if I were not careful immediately to add, 'Try to be one of the people on whom nothing is lost!'

[. . .]

Preface to *The Princess Casamassima*

The simplest account of the origin of *The Princess Casamassima* is, I think, that this fiction proceeded quite directly, during the first year of a long residence in London, from the habit and the interest of walking the streets. I walked a great deal – for exercise, for amusement, for acquisition, and above all I always walked home at the evening's end, when the evening had been spent elsewhere, as happened more often than not; and as to do this was to receive many impressions, so the impressions worked and sought an issue, so the book after a time was born. It is a fact that, as I look back, the attentive exploration of London, the assault directly made by the great city upon an imagination quick to react, fully explains a large part of it. There is a minor element that refers itself to another source, of which I shall presently speak; but the prime idea was unmistakeably the ripe round fruit of perambulation. One walked of course with one's eyes greatly open, and I hasten to declare that such a practice, carried on for a long time and over a considerable space, positively provokes, all round, a mystic solicitation, the urgent appeal, on the part of everything, to be interpreted and, so far as may be, reproduced 'Subjects' and situations, character and history, the tragedy and comedy of life, are things of which the common air, in such conditions, seems pungently to taste; and to a mind curious, before the human scene, of meanings and revelations the great grey Babylon easily becomes, on its face, a garden bristling with an immense illustrative flora. Possible stories, presentable figures, rise from the thick jungle as the observer moves, fluttering up like startled game, and before he knows it indeed he has fairly to guard himself against the brush of importunate wings. He goes on as with his head in a cloud of humming presences – especially during the younger, the initiatory time, the fresh, the sharply-apprehensive months or years, more or less numerous. We use our material up, we use up even the thick tribute of the London streets – if perception and attention but sufficiently light our steps. But I think of them as lasting, for myself, quite sufficiently long; I think of them as even still – dreadfully changed for the worse in respect to any romantic idea as I find them – breaking out on occasion into eloquence, throwing out deep notes from their vast vague murmur.

[. . .]

21
EDWARD GORDON CRAIG (1872–1966)
FROM 'THE ACTOR AND THE *ÜBER-MARIONETTE*' 1907

English theatre practitioner and theoretician. Craig's main theatrical experiment was with 'total theatre', later to become a key Modernist concept. Combining the late-Romantic actor-manager role of Henry Irving, his first employer, with more avant-garde models of performance, Craig formulated radical and essentially anti-illusionist theories of stage production, mainly focusing on design and acting (proposing, for example, the replacement of the actor by the Über-marionette*). His theories parallel those of the Russian Constructivist Vsevolod Meyerhold, though still placed within an idealist, quasi-Romantic tradition (rather than a materialist or Formalist one). From 1897 onwards, Craig worked with some of the outstanding personalities of his time, including Beerbohm Tree, Otto Brahm, Max Reinhardt, Eleonora Duse and Stanislavsky. He moved to Italy in 1908 where he published the influential journal* The Mask *(1908–29). The journal along with his books,* The Art of the Theatre *(1905) and* On the Art of the Theatre *(1911), proved crucial for the development of theories of the modern stage and were translated into all the major European languages. The following extract is taken from a 1907 essay which was fisrt published in* The Mask *in 1909. [See IIa 23]*

[. . .]

'To save the theatre, the theatre must be destroyed, the actors and actresses must all die of the plague . . . They make art impossible.' (Eleanora Duse: *Studies in Seven Arts*, Arthur Symons.)

It has always been a matter for argument whether or no acting is an art, and therefore whether the actor is an artist, or something quite different. There is little to show us that this question disturbed the minds of the leaders of thought at any period, though there is much evidence to prove that had they chosen to approach this subject as one for their serious consideration, they would have applied to it the same method of inquiry as used when considering the arts of music and poetry, of architecture, sculpture and painting.

On the other hand there have been many warm arguments in certain circles on this topic. Those taking part in it have seldom been actors, very rarely men of the theatre at all, and all have displayed any amount of illogical heat and very little knowledge of the subject. The arguments against acting being an art, and against the actor being an artist, are generally so unreasonable and so personal in their detestation of the actor, that I think it is for this reason the actors have taken no trouble to go into the matter. So now regularly with each season comes the quarterly attack on the actor and on his jolly calling; the attack usually ending in the retirement of the enemy. As a rule it is the literary or private gentlemen who fill the enemy's rank. On the strength of having gone to see plays all their lives, or on the strength of never having gone to see a play in their lives, they attack for some reason best known to themselves. I have followed these regular attacks season by season, and they seem mostly to spring from irritability, personal enmity, or conceit. They are illogical from beginning to end. There can be no such attack made on the actor or his calling. My intention here is not to join in any such attempt; I would merely place before you what seem to me to be the logical facts of a curious case, and I believe that these admit of no dispute whatever.

Acting is not an art. It is therefore incorrect to speak of the actor as an artist. For accident is an enemy of the artist. Art is the exact antithesis of pandemonium, and pandemonium is created by the tumbling together of many accidents. Art arrives only by design. Therefore in order to make any work of art it is clear we may only work in those materials with which we can calculate. Man is not one of these materials.

The whole nature of man tends towards freedom; he therefore carries the proof in his own person that as *material* for the theatre he is useless. In the modern theatre, owing to the use of the bodies of men and women *as their material*, all which is presented there is of an accidental nature. The actions of the actor's body, the expression of his face, the sounds of his voice, all are at the mercy of the winds of his emotions: these winds, which must blow for ever round the artist, moving without unbalancing him. But with the actor, emotion *possesses* him; it seizes upon his limbs, moving them whither it will. He is at its beck and call, he moves as one in a frantic dream or as one distraught, swaying here and there; his head, his arms, his feet, if not utterly beyond control, are so weak to stand against the torrent of his passions, that they are ready to play him false at any moment. It is useless for him to attempt to reason with himself. Hamlet's calm directions (the dreamer's, not the logician's directions, by the way) are thrown to the winds. His limbs refuse, and refuse again to obey his mind the instant emotion warms, while the mind is all the time creating the heat which shall set these emotions afire. As with his movement, so is it with the expression of his face. The mind struggling and succeeding for a moment, in moving the eyes, or the muscles of the face whither it will; the mind bringing the face for a few moments into thorough subjection, is suddenly swept aside by the emotion which has grown hot through the action of the mind. Instantly, like lightning, and before the mind has time to cry out and protest, the hot passion has mastered the actor's expression. It shifts and changes, sways and turns, it is chased by emotion from the actor's forehead between his eyes and down to his mouth; now he is entirely at the mercy of emotion, and crying out to it: 'Do with me what you will!' His expression runs a mad riot hither and thither, and lo! 'Nothing is coming of nothing.' It is the same with his voice as it is with his movements. Emotion cracks the voice of the actor. It sways his voice to join in the conspiracy against his mind. Emotion works upon the voice of the actor, and he produces the impression of discordant emotion. It is of no avail to say that emotion is the spirit of the gods, and is precisely what the artist aims to produce; first of all this is not true, and even if it were quite true, every stray emotion, every casual feeling, cannot be of value. Therefore the mind of the actor, we see, is less powerful than his emotion, for emotion is able to win over the mind to assist in the destruction of that which the mind would produce; and as the mind becomes the slave of the emotion it follows that accident upon accident must be continually occurring. So then, we have arrived at this point: that emotion is the cause which first of all creates, and secondly destroys. Art, as we have said, can admit of no accidents. That, then, which the actor gives us, is not a work of art; it is a series of accidental confessions. In the beginning the human body was not used as material in the Art of the Theatre. In the beginning the emotions of men and women were not considered as a fit exhibition for the multitude. An elephant and a tiger in an arena suited the taste better, when the desire was to excite.

. . . the body of man . . . is *by nature* utterly useless as a material for an art. I am fully aware of the sweeping character of this statement; and as it concerns men and women who are alive, and who as a class are ever to be loved, more must be said lest I give unintentional offence. I know perfectly well that what I have said here is not yet going to create an exodus of all the actors from all the theatres in the world, driving them into sad monasteries where they will laugh out the rest of their lives, with the Art of the Theatre as the main topic for amusing conversation. As I have written elsewhere, the theatre will continue its growth and actors will continue for some years to hinder its development. But I see a loophole by which in time the actors can escape from the bondage they are in. They must create for themselves a new form of acting, consisting for the main part of symbolical gesture. Today they *impersonate* and interpret; tomorrow they must *represent* and interpret; and the third day they must create. By this means style may return. Today the actor impersonates a certain being. He cries to the audience: 'Watch me; I am now pretending to be so and so, and I am now pretending to do so and so;' and then he proceeds to *imitate* as exactly as possibly, that which he has announced he will *indicate*. For instance, he is Romeo. He tells the audience that he is in love, and he proceeds to show it, by kissing Juliet. This, it is claimed, is a work of art: it is claimed for this that it is an intelligent way of suggesting thought. Why – why, that is just as if a painter were to draw upon the wall a picture of an animal with long ears and then write under it 'This is a donkey'. The long ears made it plain enough, one would think, without the inscription, and any child of ten does as much. The difference between the child of ten and the artist is that the artist is he who by drawing certain signs and shapes creates the impression of a donkey: and the greater artist is he who creates the impression of the whole genus of donkey, the *spirit* of the thing.

The actor looks upon life as a photo-machine looks upon life; and he attempts to make a picture to rival a photograph. He never dreams of his art as being an art such for instance as music. He tries to reproduce Nature; he seldom thinks to invent with the aid of Nature, and he never dreams of *creating*. As I have said, the best he can do when he wants to catch and convey the poetry of a kiss, the heat of a fight, or the calm of death, is to copy slavishly, photographically – he kisses – he fights – he lies back and mimics death – and, when you think of it, is not all this dreadfully stupid? Is it not a poor art and a poor cleverness, which cannot convey the spirit and essence of an idea to an audience, but he can only show an artless copy, a facsimile of the thing itself? This is to be an imitator, not an artist. This is to claim kinship with the ventriloquist.

There is a stage expression of the actor 'getting under the skin of the part'. A better one would be getting '*out* of the skin of the part altogether'. 'What, then,' cries the red-blooded and flashing actor, 'is there to be no flesh and blood in this same art of the theatre of yours? No life?' It depends what you call life, signor, when you use the word in relation with the idea of art. The painter means something rather different to actuality when he speaks of life in his art, and the other artists generally mean something essentially spiritual; it is only the actor, the ventriloquist, or the animal-stuffer who, when they speak of putting life into their work, mean some actual and lifelike reproduction, something blatant in its appeal, that it is for this reason I say that it would be better if the actor should get out of the skin of the part altogether. If there is any actor who is reading this, is there not some way by which I can make him realise the preposterous absurdity of this delusion of his, this belief that he should aim to make an actual copy, a reproduction?

. . . I am not sure I do not wish that photography had been discovered before painting, so that we of this generation might have had the intense joy of advancing, showing that photography was pretty well in its way, but there was something better! 'Do you hold that our work is on a level with photography?' 'No, indeed, it is not half as exact. It is less of an art even than photography. . . .'

Eleanora Duse has said: 'To save the theatre, the theatre must be destroyed, the actors and actresses must all die of the plague. They poison the air, they make art impossible.'

We may believe her. . . . The actor must go, and in his place comes the inanimate figure – the Über-marionette we may call him, until he has won for himself a better name. Much has been written about the puppet, or marionette. There are some excellent volumes upon him, and he has also inspired several works of art. Today in his least happy period many people come to regard him as rather a superior doll – and to think he has developed from the doll. This is incorrect. He is a descendant of the stone images of the old temples – he is today a rather degenerate form of a god. Always the close friend of children, he still knows how to select and attract his devotees.

When any one designs a puppet on paper, he draws a stiff and comic-looking thing. Such a one has not even perceived what is contained in the idea which we now call the marionette. He mistakes gravity of face and calmness of body for blank stupidity and angular deformity. Yet even modern puppets are extraordinary things. The applause may thunder or dribble, their hearts beat no faster, no slower, their signals do not grow hurried or confused; and, though drenched in a torrent of bouquets and love, the face of the leading lady remains as solemn, as beautiful and as remote as ever. There is something more than a flash of genius in the marionette, and there is something in him more than the flashiness of displayed personality. The marionette appears to me to be the last echo of some noble and beautiful art of a past civilisation. But as with all art which has passed into fat or vulgar hands, the puppet has become a reproach. All puppets are now but low comedians.

They imitate the comedians of the larger and fuller blooded stage. They enter only to fall on their back. They drink only to reel, and make love only to raise a laugh. They have forgotten the counsel of their mother the Sphinx. Their bodies have lost grave grace, they have become stiff. Their eyes have lost that infinite subtlety of seeming to see; now they only stare. They display and jingle their wires and are cock-sure in their wooden wisdom. They have failed to remember that their art should carry on it the same stamp of reserve that we see at times on the work of other artists, and that the highest art is that which conceals the craft and forgets the craftsman. . . .

May we not look forward with hope to that day which shall bring back to us once more the figure, or symbolic creature, made also by the cunning of the artist, so that we can gain once more the 'noble artificiality' which the old writer speaks of? Then shall we no longer be under the cruel influence of the emotional confessions of weakness which are nightly witnessed by the people and which in their turn create in the beholders the very weaknesses which are exhibited. To that end we must study to remake these images – no longer content with a puppet, we must create an Über-marionette. The Über-marionette will not compete with life – rather will it go beyond it. Its ideal will not be the flesh and blood but rather the body in trance – it will aim to clothe itself with a death-like beauty while exhaling a living spirit. Several times in the course of this essay has a word or two about Death found its way on to the paper – called there by the incessant clamouring of 'Life! Life! Life!' which the realists keep up. And this might be easily mistaken for an affectation, especially by those who have no sympathy or delight in the power and the mysterious joyousness which is in all passionless works of art. . . .

To speak of a puppet with most men and women is to cause them to giggle. They think at once of the wires; they think of the stiff hands and the jerky movements; they tell me it is 'a funny little doll'. But let me tell them a few things about these puppets. Let me again repeat that they are the descendants of a great and noble family of images, images which were indeed made 'in the likeness of God'; and that many centuries ago these figures had a rhythmical movement and not a jerky one; had no need for wires to support them, nor did they speak through the nose of the hidden manipulator. . . . I pray earnestly for the return of the image – the Über-marionette to the theatre; and when he comes again and is but seen, he will be loved so well that once more will it be possible for the people to return to their ancient joy in ceremonies – once more will Creation be celebrated – homage rendered to existence – and divine and happy intercession made to Death.

22
ISADORA DUNCAN (1877–1927)
FROM *MY LIFE* 1927

American dancer. Duncan moved to London in 1899 and spent the rest of her life touring Europe, performing and propagating her ideas on dance education and art. Her organicist theory of dance derived from a renewed notion of classicism with quasi-Romantic and Orientalist elements. In the following extracts from her autobiography, published in 1927, the year of her tragic death, Duncan gives an account of the creation of her dance school for children, of her relationship with Edward Gordon Craig and, finally, of her mediation between Craig and Eleonora Duse during rehearsals for the ground-breaking (though short-lived) production of Ibsen's Rosmerholm *in Florence.*

[. . .]

I returned to Berlin with the determination to start my long-dreamed-of school – no longer to delay it, but to start at once. I confided these plans to my mother and sister, Elizabeth, who were equally enthusiastic. We immediately set out to find a house for the future school with such speediness as marked everything else we did. Within a week we found a villa, on Trauden Strasse in Grünewald, which was just passing from the workmen's hands, and we bought it.

We acted exactly as though we were people in *Grimm's Fairy Tales*. We went down to Wertheimer's and actually bought forty little beds, each covered with white muslin curtains, drawn back with blue ribbons. We set about to make of our villa a real children's Paradise. In the central hall we placed a copy of the heroic figure of the Amazon twice the size of life. In the large dancing-room, the bas-reliefs of Luca della Robbia and the dancing children of Donatello. In the bedroom, the blue and white babies and the Madonna and Child, also in blue and white, encrusted with garlands of fruit – the work of Luca della Robbia.

I placed these different ideal representations of the child form in the school, the bas-reliefs and sculptures of dancing children in their youngest years, in books and paintings too, because they showed the child form as it was dreamed of by the painters and sculptors of all ages; paintings of children dancing on Greek vases, tiny figures from Tanagra and Bœtia, the group of Donatello's dancing children because it is a radiant child melody, and the dancing children of Gainsborough.

All these figures have a certain fraternity in the naïve grace of their form and their movements, as if the children of all ages met each other and joined their hands across the centuries, and the real children of my school, moving and dancing in the midst of these forms, would surely grow to resemble them, to reflect unconsciously, in their movements and their faces, a little of the joy and the same childlike grace. It would be the first step toward their becoming beautiful, the first step toward the new art of the dance.

I also placed in my school the figures of young girls dancing, running, jumping – those young girls of Sparta who, in the gymnasiums, were trained in severe exercises so that they might become the mothers of heroic warriors; those fleet-footed runners who took the annual prizes, exquisite images in terra cotta, with flying veils and flowing garments; young girls dancing hand-in-hand, at the Panathens. They represented the future ideal to attain, and the pupils of my school, learning to feel an intimate love for these forms, would grow each day to resemble them, and would become each day a little more imbued with the secret of this harmony, for I enthusiastically believed that it was only upon awakening the will for beauty that one could obtain beauty.

Also, in order to attain to that harmony I desired, they must each day go through certain exercises chosen with the aim in view. But these exercises were conceived in a way to coincide with their own intimate will, so that they accomplished them with good humour and eagerness. Each one was not only to be a means toward an end, but an end in itself, and that end was to render each day of life complete and happy.

[. . .]

The nature of these daily exercises is to make of the body, in each state of its development, an instrument as perfect as possible, an instrument for the expression of that harmony which, evolving and changing through all things, is ready to flow into the being prepared for it.

[. . .]

Their studies and their observations were not to be limited to the forms in art, but were, above all, to spring from the movements in Nature. The movements of the clouds in the wind, the swaying trees, the flight of a bird, and the leaves which turn, all were to have a special significance for them. They were to learn to observe the quality peculiar to each movement. They were to feel in their souls a secret attachment, unknowable to others, to initiate them into Nature's secrets; for all the parts of their supple bodies, trained as they would be, would respond to the melody of Nature and sing with her.

To gather children for our school, we announced in the leading newspapers that the Isadora Duncan School was open for the adoption of talented children, with the purpose that they become disciples of that Art which I hoped to give to thousands of the children of the people. Certainly the sudden opening of this school, without the proper premeditation or capital or organisation, was the most rash undertaking imaginable; one that drove my manager to distraction. He was continually planning world tours for me, and I was continually insisting upon, first, spending a year in Greece, which he called wasted time, and now, stopping my career altogether for the adoption and training of what he considered absolutely useless children. But this was quite in keeping with all our other undertakings, most unpractical and untimely and impulsive.

[. . .]

At that time my popularity in Berlin was almost unbelievable. They called me the Göttliche Isadora. It was even bruited about that when sick people were brought into my theatre they became well. And every matinée one could see the strange sight of sick people being brought in on litters. I had never worn any other dress than the little white tunic, bare feet, and sandals. And my audience came to my performances with an absolutely religious ecstasy.

One night, as I was returning from a representation, the students took the horses out of my carriage and drew me through the famous Sieges Allee. In the middle of the Allee they called for a speech. I stood up in the victoria – in those days there were no automobiles – and I addressed the students thus:

'There is no greater art,' I said, 'than the art of the sculptor. But why do you, lovers of art, permit this horrible outrage in the middle of your city? Look at these statues! You are art students, but if you were really students of art you would take stones to-night and demolish them! Art? They, art? No! They are the visions of the Kaiser.'

The students were of my opinion and yelled their approbation, and if it had not been for the police who came along, we might have carried out my wish and destroyed those horrible statues in the city of Berlin.

[. . .]

Gordon Craig is one of the most extraordinary geniuses of our epoch – a creature like Shelley, made of fire and lightning. He was the inspirer of the whole trend of the modern theatre. True, he has never taken an active part in the practical life of the stage. He has stayed apart and dreamed, and his dreams have inspired all that is beautiful in the modern theatre to-day. Without him, we should never have had Reinhardt, Jacques Corpeau, Stanislavsky. Without him, we would still be back in the old realistic scenery, every leaf shimmering on the trees, all the houses with their doors opening and shutting.

Craig was a brilliant companion. He was one of the few people I have ever met who was in a state of exaltation from morning till night. Even with the first cup of coffee his imagination caught fire and was sparkling. An ordinary walk through the streets with him was like a promenade in Thebes of ancient Egypt with a superior High Priest.

Whether due to his extraordinary near-sightedness or not, he would suddenly stop, take out his pencil and paper-block, and, looking at a fearful specimen of modern German architecture, a *neuer kinst praktisch* apartment house, explain how beautiful it was. He would then commence a feverish sketch of it which, when completed, resembled the Temple of Denderah of Egypt.

He always entered in a state of wild excitement over a tree or a bird or a child he had seen on his way. One never spent a dull moment with him. No, he was always either in the throes of highest delight or the other extreme – in those moods which suddenly followed after, when the whole sky seemed to turn black, and a sudden apprehension filled all the air. One's breath was slowly pumped from the body, and nothing was left anywhere but the blackness of anguish.

Unfortunately, as time progressed, these dark moods became more and more frequent. Why? Well, principally because whenever he said, 'My work. My work!' as he often did, I replied gently, 'Oh, yes, your work. How wonderful. You are a genius but, you know, there is my school'; and his fist would come down on the table, 'Yes, but my work.' And I would answer, 'Certainly, very important. Your work is the setting, but the first is the living being, for from the soul radiates everything. First my school, the radiant human being moving in perfect beauty; then your work, the perfect setting for this being.'

These discussions often ended in thunderous and gloomy silences. Then the woman in me, alarmed, would awaken. 'Oh, darling, have I offended you?' And he, 'Offended? Oh, no! All women are damned nuisances, and you are a damned nuisance, interfering with my work. My work! My work!'

He would go out, slamming the door. Only the noise of the slammed door would awaken me to the terrible catastrophe. I would await his return and, when he didn't return, spend the night in stormy and tragic weeping. Such was the tragedy. These scenes, oft repeated, ended by making life quite inharmonious and impossible.

It was my fate to inspire the great love of this genius; and it was my fate to endeavour to reconcile the continuing of my own career with his love. Impossible combination!

After the first few weeks of wild, impassioned love-making, there began the waging of the fiercest battle that was ever known, between the genius of Gordon Craig and the inspirations of my Art.

'Why don't you stop this?' he used to say. 'Why do you want to go on the stage and wave your arms about? Why don't you stay at home and sharpen my lead pencils?'

And yet Gordon Craig appreciates my Art as no one else has ever appreciated it. But his *amour propre*, his jealousy as an artist, would not allow him to admit that any woman could really be an artist.

[. . .]

I presented Gordon Craig to Duse. She was at once charmed and interested in his views of the theatre. After a few meetings of mutual enthusiasm, she invited us to come to Florence, and wished Craig to arrange a representation. So it was decided that Gordon Craig was to create the scenes for Ibsen's *Rosmersholm*, for Eleanora Duse, in Florence.

[. . .]

In the first scene in *Rosmersholm* I believe Ibsen describes the sitting-room as 'comfortably furnished in old-fashioned style'. But Craig had been pleased to see the interior of a great Egyptian temple, with enormously high ceiling, extending upward to the skies, with walls receding into the distance. Only, unlike an Egyptian temple, at the far end there was a great, square window. In Ibsen's description, the window looks out into an avenue of old trees leading to a courtyard. Craig had been pleased to see this in dimensions of ten metres by twelve. It looked out upon a flaming landscape of yellows, reds, and greens, which might have been some scene in Morocco. It could not possibly have been an old-fashioned courtyard.

Eleanora, looking rather disconcerted, said, 'I see this as a small window. It cannot possibly be a large one.'

To which Craig thundered in English, 'Tell her I won't have any damned woman interfering with my work!'

Which I discreetly translated to Eleanora, 'He says he admires your opinions and will do everything to please you.'

Then, turning to Craig, I again diplomatically translated Duse's objections as, 'Eleonora Duse says, as you are a great genius, she will not make any suggestions on your sketches, but will pass them as they are.'

Then Craig immured himself in the theatre, where he began, with dozens of huge pots of paint before him, and a big brush, to paint the scene actually himself. For he could find no Italian workmen who understood just what he meant. He could not find the proper canvas, so he took sacking and had it sewed together. For days, a chorus of old Italian women sat upon the stage and stitched sacking. Young Italian painters rushed about the stage trying to carry out orders given by Craig, while Craig, with his long hair tossed about, shouted to them, dipped the brushes into the paint-boxes, mounted ladders in perilous positions; stayed in the theatre all day and almost all night.

[. . .]

One command he gave, 'Keep Duse out of the theatre. Do not let her come here. If she does, I will take the train and go away.'

Whereas Duse was filled with desire to see what was going on. It was my task, without offending her, to keep her from going to the theatre. I used to take her for long walks in the gardens, where the lovely statues and exquisite flowers calmed her nerves.

[. . .]

The *décors* for *Rosmersholm* were progressing. Each time I went to the theatre to take Craig his luncheon or his dinner, I found him in a state bordering between anger and frantic joy. One hour he believed it would be the greatest vision the artistic world would see. The next, he would cry that he could get nothing in this country – no paints, no good workmen; that he must do everything himself.

The hour approached when Eleanora should see the completed scene – I had especially kept her away by such manoeuvres as I could invent. When the day arrived, I called for her at the appointed hour and took her to the theatre. She was in a state of intense nervous excitement which, I feared, might at any moment break out, like a stormy day, into a violent tempest.

[. . .]

Finally, after what seemed hours of waiting, when I felt Eleanora's rising temper was ready to break out at any moment, the curtain slowly rose.

Oh, how can I describe what appeared before our astonished, enraptured eyes? Did I speak of an Egyptian temple? No Egyptian temple has ever revealed such beauty. No Gothic cathedral, no Athenian palace. Never have I seen such a vision of loveliness. Through vast blue spaces, celestial harmonies, mounting lines, colossal heights, one's soul was drawn toward the light of this great window which showed beyond, no little avenue but the infinite universe. Within these blue spaces was all the thought, the meditation, the earthly sorrow of man. Beyond the window was all the ecstasy, the joy, the miracle of his imagination. Was this the living-room of Rosmersholm? I do not know what Ibsen would have thought. Probably he would have been as we were – speechless, carried away.

Eleanora's hand grasped mine. I felt her arms around me. She had me in a strong embrace. I saw the tears were running down her beautiful face. For some time we sat, clutched in one another's arms, silent – Eleanora from her admiration and joy of art, and I from the great relief I found when she was pleased, after all my previous misgivings. So we remained. Then she took me by the hand and dragged me from the box, striding with her long steps through the dark corridor up to the stage. She stood upon the stage, and, in that voice which was Duse, called: 'Gordon Craig! Come here!'

Craig came from the side wing, looking as shy as a boy. Duse enveloped him in her arms and then, from her lips, came such a string of Italian words of adulation that I could not translate them fast enough for Craig. They flowed from her lips like water streaming from a fountain.

Craig did not weep from emotion as we did, but he remained for a long time silent, which, on his part, was a sign of great feeling.

Duse then called all the company to her. They had been waiting unconcernedly behind the stage. She made them an impassioned speech in this wise:

'It is my destiny to have found this great genius, Gordon Craig. I now intend to spend the rest of my career (*sempre, sempre*) devoting myself only to showing the world his great work.'

She then went on with renewed eloquence to denounce the whole modern trend of the theatre, all modern scenery, the modern conception of an actor's life and vocation.

Holding the hand of Craig all the time she spoke, and turning again and again to him, she told of his genius and of the new great resurrection of the theatre. 'Only through Gordon Craig,' she said over and over again, 'will we poor actors find release from this monstrosity, this charnel-house, which is the theatre of to-day!'

[. . .]

The first evening of *Rosmersholm* an immense, expectant public filled the theatre in Florence. When the curtain rose, there was one gasp of admiration. The result could not have been otherwise. That single performance of *Rosmersholm* is remembered in Florence to this day by connoisseurs of Art.

[. . .]

23
GEORGE BERNARD SHAW (1856–1950)
FROM *THE SANITY OF ART* 1908

Irish dramatist, critic, novelist and socialist. From his early socio-political novels, like An Unsocial Socialist *(1887), Shaw turned to drama in the 1890s, encouraged by his friend William Archer whose passion for Ibsen he shared. Along with Archer, Shaw became a key defender of Ibsen's work and produced some of his most important critical essays in the process. The essay from which an extract is reproduced below was originally commissioned by the American anarchist Benjamin Tucker in his capacity as editor of the magazine* Liberty *and was published in July 1895 under the title 'A Degenerate's View of Nordau'. The following version appeared as a small revised edition in 1908 (published by the New Age Press in London and by Tucker in New York) and was subtitled* An Exposure of Some Current Nonsense about Artists Being Degenerate. *[See Ia 7]*

My dear Tucker,

I have read Max Nordau's Degeneration at your request: two hundred and sixty thousand mortal words, saying the same thing over and over again. That is the proper way to drive a thing into the mind of the world, though Nordau considers it a symptom of insane 'obsession' on the part of writers who do not share his own opinions. His message to the world is that all our characteristically modern works of art are symptoms of disease in the artists, and that these diseased artists are themselves symptoms of the nervous exhaustion of the race by overwork.

To me, who am a professional critic of art, and have for many successive London seasons had to watch the grand march past of books, of pictures, of concerts and operas, and of stage plays, there is nothing new in Dr. Nordau's outburst. I have heard it all before. At every new wave of energy in art the same alarm has been raised; and as these alarms always had their public, like prophecies of the end of the world, there is nothing surprising in the fact that a book which might have been produced by playing the resurrection man in the old newspaper rooms of our public libraries, and collecting all the exploded bogey-criticisms of the last half-century into a huge volume, should have a considerable success.

[. . .]

Nordau's book

After this long preamble, you will have no difficulty in understanding the sort of book Nordau has written. Imagine a huge volume, stuffed with the most slashing of the criticisms which were hurled at the Impressionists, the Tone Poets, and the philosophers and dramatists of the Schopenhauerian revival, before these movements had reached the point at which it began to require some real courage to attack them. Imagine a rehash not only of the newspaper criticisms of this period, but of all its little parasitic paragraphs of small-talk and scandal, from the long-forgotten jibes against Oscar Wilde's momentary attempt to bring knee-breeches into fashion years ago, to the latest scurrilities about 'the New Woman'. Imagine the general staleness and occasional putrescence of this mess disguised by a dressing of the terminology invented by Krafft-Ebing, Lombroso, and all the latest specialists in madness and crime, to describe the artistic faculties and propensities as they operate in the insane. Imagine all this done by a man who is a vigorous and capable journalist, shrewd enough to see that there is a good opening for a big reactionary book as a relief to the Wagner and Ibsen booms, bold enough to let himself go without respect to persons or reputations, lucky enough to be a stronger, clearer-headed man than ninety-nine out of a hundred of his critics, besides having a keener interest in science: a born theorist, reasoner and busybody; therefore able, without insight, or even any very remarkable intensive industry (he is, like most Germans, extensively industrious to an appalling degree), to produce a book which has made a very considerable impression on the artistic ignorance of Europe and America. For he says a thing as if he meant it; he holds superficial ideas obstinately, and sees them clearly; and his mind works so impetuously that it is a pleasure to watch it – for a while. All the same, he is the dupe of a theory which would hardly impose even on the gamblers who have a system or martingale founded on a solid rock of algebra, by which they can infallibly break the bank at Monte Carlo. 'Psychiatry' takes the place of algebra in Nordau's martingale.

This theory of his is, at bottom, nothing but the familiar delusion of the used-up man that the world is going to the dogs. But Nordau is too clever to be driven back on ready-made mistakes – he makes them for himself in his own way. He appeals to the prodigious extension of the quantity of business a single man can transact through the modern machinery of social intercourse: the railway, the telegraph and telephone, the post and so forth. He gives appalling statistics of the increase of railway mileage and shipping, of the number of letters written per head of the population, of the newspapers which tell us things (mostly lies) of which we used to know nothing.

[. . .]

Then follow more statistics of 'the constant increase of crime, madness and suicide', of increases in the mortality from diseases of the nerves and heart, of increased consumption of stimulants, of new nervous diseases like 'railway spine and railway brain', with the general moral that we are all suffering from exhaustion, and that symptoms of degeneracy are visible in all directions, culminating at various points in Wagner's music, Ibsen's dramas, Manet's pictures, Tolstoy's novels, Whitman's poetry, Dr. Jaeger's woollen clothing, vegetarianism, scepticism as to vivisection and vaccination, Anarchism and Humanitarianism, and, in short, everything that Dr. Nordau does not happen to approve of.

[. . .]

Echolalia

Let me describe to you one or two of his artifices as a special pleader making the most of the eddies at the sides of the stream of progress. Take as a first specimen the old and effective trick of pointing out, as 'stigmata of degeneration' in the person he is abusing, features which are common to the whole human race.

[. . .]

Nordau turns the trick inside out by trusting to the fact that people are in the habit of assuming that uniformity and symmetry are laws of nature: for example, that every normal person's face is precisely symmetrical, that all persons have the same number of bones in their bodies, and so on. He takes advantage of this popular error to claim asymmetry as a stigma of degeneration. As a matter of fact, perfect symmetry or uniformity does not exist in nature.

[. . .]

Another unfailing trick is the common one of having two names for the same thing, one abusive, the other complimentary, for use according to circumstances. You know how it is done: 'We trust the Government will be firm' in one paper and 'We hope the obstinate elements in the Cabinet will take warning in time' in another. The powers of Empires armed to the teeth to impose their will by fire and sword on weaker communities are called simply Sanctions. Repudiations of national debts are called stabilizations of the currency. The following is a typical specimen of Nordau's use of this device. First, let me explain that when a man with a turn for rhyming goes mad, he repeats rhymes as if he were quoting a rhyming dictionary. You say 'Come' to him, and he starts away with 'Dumb, plum, sum, rum, numb, gum' and so on. This the doctors call echolalia.

[. . .]

People do not write such things for the sake of conveying information, but for the sake of amusing and pleasing, just as people do not eat strawberries and cream to nourish their bones and muscles, but to enjoy the taste of a toothsome dish. A lunatic may plead that he eats kitchen soap and tin tacks on the same ground; and as far as I can see the lunatic would completely shut up Nordau by this answer; for Nordau is absurd enough, in the case of rhyming, to claim that every rhyme made for its own sake, as proved by the fact that it does not convey an intelligible statement of fact of any kind, convicts the rhymer of echolalia. He can thus convict any poet whom he dislikes of being a degenerate by simply picking out a rhyme which exists for its own sake, or a pun, or what is called a burden in a ballad, and claiming them as symptoms of echolalia, supporting this diagnosis by carefully examining the poem for contradictions and inconsistencies as to time, place, description, or the like. It will occur to you probably that by this means he must bring out Shakespear as the champion instance of poetic degeneracy, since Shakespear was an incorrigible punster.

[. . .]

But no: Shakespear, not being a nineteenth-century poet, would have spoiled the case for modern degeneration by shewing that its symptoms existed before the telegraph and the railway were dreamt of; and besides, Nordau likes Shakespear, just as he likes Goethe, and holds him up as a model of sanity in contrast to the nineteenth-century poets. Thus Wagner is a degenerate because he made puns; and Shakespear, who made worse ones, is a great poet.

[. . .]

Nordau's trick of calling rhyme echolalia when he happens not to like the rhymer is reapplied in the case of authorship, which he calls graphomania when he happens not to like the author. He insists that Wagner, who was a voluminous author as well as a composer, was a graphomaniac; and his proof is that in his books we find 'the restless repetition of one and the same strain of thought . . . Opera and Drama, Judaism in Music, Religion and the State, Art and Religion, and the Vocation of Opera are nothing more than the amplification of single passages in The Art-Work of the Future'. This is a capital example of Nordau's limited power of attention. The moment that limited power is concentrated on his theory of degeneration, he loses sight of everything else, and drives his one borrowed horse into every obstacle on the road. To those of us who can attend to more than one thing at a time, there is no observation more familiar and more frequently confirmed than that this growth of pregnant single sentences into whole books which Nordau discovers in Wagner, balanced as it always is by the contraction of whole boyish chapters into single epigrams, is the process by which all great writers, speakers, artists and thinkers elaborate their life-work.

[. . .]

In a country where art was really known to the people, instead of being merely read about, it would not be necessary to spend three lines on such a work. But in England, where nothing but superstitious awe and self-mistrust prevents most men from thinking about art as Nordau boldly speaks about it; where to have a sense of art is to be one in a thousand, the other nine hundred and ninety-nine being either Philistine voluptuaries or Calvinistic anti-voluptuaries, it is useless to pretend that Nordau's errors will be self-evident. Already we have native writers, without half his cleverness or energy of expression, clumsily imitating his sham-scientific vivisection in their attacks on artists whose work they happen to dislike. Therefore, in riveting his book to the counter, I have used a nail long enough to go through a few pages by other people as well; and that must be my excuse for my disregard of the familiar editorial stigma of degeneracy which Nordau calls Agoraphobia, or Fear of Space.

[. . .]

II

THE AVANT-GARDE

IIa

Formulations and declarations

1
GUSTAVE COURBET (1819–77)
FROM *REALIST MANIFESTO* 1855

French painter. Although his self-portrait Courbet with Black Dog *was accepted by the Paris Salon in 1842, Courbet was in conflict with the art establishment throughout his career. As leader of the Realist movement, he departed radically from the prevalent ideas of Romantic and neo-classical painting, in choice of subject and form. Painting, according to Courbet, was 'an essentially concrete art', a 'physical language, the words of which consist of all visible objects'. Along with his fellow Realist, writer and philosopher, Pierre Joseph Proudhon, Courbet proclaimed that the duty of the artist was to focus on the present, on modernity, rather than to reinvent or mystify the past. The following statement was made in 1855, the year the Exposition Universelle refused his entry and Courbet mounted a defiant exhibition close by, entitled* Le Réalisme, G. Courbet.

The label of realist has been imposed on me just as the label of romantic was imposed on the men of 1830. Labels have never, in any age, given a very accurate idea of things; if it were otherwise, the works would be superfluous.

Without discussing the appropriateness, more or less justified, of a designation which nobody, it is to be hoped, has taken very seriously, I shall confine myself to a few words of explanation in order to prevent misunderstanding.

I have studied the art of the ancients and of the moderns without adherence to a system and without prejudice. It was not my wish to imitate the one or to copy the other; nor was it my idea to attain the idle goal of *art for art's sake*! No! I simply wished to draw from a knowledge of the whole tradition a reasoned and independent sense of my own individuality.

'To know in order to create, that was my idea. To be capable of depicting the manners, ideas, and appearance of my time as I see it, in short, to produce living art, that is my goal.

2
ÉMILE ZOLA (1840–1902)
FROM 'NATURALISM ON THE STAGE' 1880

French novelist, critic and journalist. Zola began by writing poetry, including two unpublished epics on the evolution of man. In 1864 he turned to prose and published a collection of stories, followed in 1867 by a novel, Thérèse Raquin, *in which he first experimented with the literary adaptation of (popular at the time) forms of scientific determinism. Zola's 'Naturalism' partly hinges on such notions as the importance of heredity and of cerebral infirmity, which, however, could be eradicated by education and medicine. With his major series of twenty novels,* Les Rougon-Macquart, *Zola attempted a Naturalist account of humanity, or, as he puts it in his 1871 preface to the first of the volumes* (La Fortune des Rougon), *'Taking into account of the two-fold question of temperaments and environments, I shall try to find and trace out the thread which leads mathematically from one man to another'. 'Naturalism on the Stage' is a key formulation of the features and of the artistic and social importance of Naturalism. It first appeared in Russian, in the St Petersburg newspaper* The Messenger of Europe *and was then published in the collection* Le Roman expérimental *in 1880. The following extract is taken from Belle M. Sherman's translation for the 1964 edition of* The Experimental Novel and Other Essays.

[. . .]

We shall enter upon a century in which man, grown more powerful will make use of nature and will utilize its laws to produce upon the earth the greatest possible amount of justice and freedom. There is no nobler, higher, grander end. Here is our rôle as intelligent beings to penetrate to the wherefore of things, to become superior to these things, and to reduce them to a condition of subservient machinery.

Well, this dream of the physiologist and the experimental doctor is also that of the novelist, who employs the experimental method in his study of man as a simple individual and as a social animal. Their object is ours; we also desire to master certain phenomena of an intellectual and personal order, to able to direct them. We are, in a word, experimental moralists, showing by experiment in what way a passion acts in a certain social condition. The day which we gain control of the mechanism of this passion we can treat it and reduce it, or at least make it inoffensive as possible. And in this consists the practical utility and high morality of our naturalistic works which experiment on man, and which dissect piece by piece this human machinery in order to set it going through the influence of the environment. When things have advanced further, when we are in possession of the different laws, it will only be necessary to work upon the individuals and the surroundings if we wish to find the best social condition. In this way we shall construct a practical sociology, and our work will be a help to political and economical sciences. I do not know, I repeat, of a more noble work, nor of a grander application. To be the master of good and evil, to regulate life, to regulate society, to solve in time all the problems of socialism, above all, to give justice a solid foundation by solving through experiment the questions of criminality – is not this being the most useful and the most moral workers in the human workshop?

[. . .]

In our rôle as experimental moralists we show mechanism of the useful and the useless, we disengage the determinism of the human and social phenomena so that, in their turn, the legislators can one day dominate and control these phenomena. In a word we are working with the whole country toward that great object, the conquest of nature and the increase of man's power a hundredfold. Compare with ours the work of the idealistic writers, who rely upon irrational and the supernatural, and whose every flight upward is followed by a deeper fall into metaphysical chaos. We are the ones who possess strength and morality.

My personal opinion is that naturalism dates from the first line ever written by man.

From that day truth was laid down as the necessary foundation of all art. If we look upon humanity as an army marching through the ages, bent upon the conquest of the true, in spite of every form of wretchedness and infirmity, we must place writers and savants in the van. It is from this point of view that we should write the history of a universal literature, and not from that of an absolute ideal or a common aesthetical measure, which is perfectly ridiculous. [. . .]

Naturalism, that is, a return to nature; it is this operation which the savants performed on the day when they decided to set out from the study of bodies and phenomena, to build on experiment, and to proceed by analysis. Naturalism in letters is equally the return to nature and to man, direct observation, exact anatomy, the acceptance and depicting of what is. The task was the same for the writer as for the savant. One and the other replaced abstractions by realities, empirical formulas by rigorous analysis. Thus, no more abstract characters in books, no more lying inventions, no more of the absolute; but real characters, the true history of each one, the story of daily life. It was a question of commencing all over again; of knowing man down to the sources of his being before coming to such conclusions as the idealists reached, who invented types of character out of the whole cloth; and writers had only to start the edifice at the foundation, bringing together the greatest number of human data arranged in their logical order. This is naturalism; starting in the first thinking brain, if you wish; but whose greatest evolution, the definite evolution, without doubt took place in the last century.

So great an evolution in the human mind could not take place without bringing on a social overthrow. The French Revolution was this overthrow, this tempest which was to wipe out the old world, to give place to the new. We are the beginning of this new world, we are the direct children of naturalism in all things, in politics as in philosophy, in science as in literature and in art. I extend the bounds of this word naturalism because in reality it includes the entire century, the movement of contemporaneous intelligence, the force which is sweeping us onward, and which is working toward the molding of future centuries.

[. . .]

It arises from the earth on which we walk; it grows every hour, penetrates and animates all things. It is the strength of our productions, the pivot upon which our society turns. It is found in the sciences, which continued on their tranquil way during the folly of romanticism; it is found in all the manifestations of human intelligence, disengaging itself more and more from the influences of romanticism which once for a moment seemed to have submerged it. It renews the arts, sculpture, and, above all, painting; it extends the field of criticism and history; it makes itself felt in the novel; and it is by means of the novel, by means of Balzac and Stendhal, that it lifts itself above romanticism, thus visibly relinking the chain with the eighteenth century. The novel is its domain, its field of battle and of victory. It seems to have chosen the novel in order to demonstrate the power of its method, the glory of the truth, the inexhaustible novelty of human data. To-day it takes possession of the stage, it has commenced to transform the theater, which is the last fortress of conventionality. When it shall triumph there its evolution will be complete; the classical formulas will find themselves definitely and solidly replaced by the naturalistic formula, which should be right be the formula of the new social condition.

[. . .]

I have said that the naturalistic novel is simply an inquiry into nature, beings, and things. It no longer interests itself in the ingenuity of a well-invented story, developed according to certain rules. Imagination has no longer place, plot matters little to the novelist, who bothers himself with neither development mystery, nor *dénouement*; I mean that he does not intervene to take away from or add to reality; he does not construct a framework out of the whole cloth according to the needs of a preconceived idea. You start from the point that nature is sufficient, that you must accept it as it is, without modification or pruning; it is grand enough, beautiful enough to supply its own beginning, its middle, and its end. Instead of imagining an adventure, of complicating it, of arranging stage effects, which scene by scene will lead to a final conclusion, you simply take the life study of a person or a group of persons, whose actions you faithfully depict. The work becomes a report, nothing more; it has but the merit of exact observation, of more or less profound penetration and analysis, of the logical connection of facts. Sometimes, even, it is not an entire life, with a commencement and an ending, of which you tell; it is only a scrap of an existence, a few years in the life of a man or a woman, a single page in a human history, which has attracted the novelist in the same way that the special study of a mineral can attract a chemist. The novel is no longer confined to one special sphere; it has invaded and taken possession of all spheres. Like science, it is the master of the world. It touches on all subjects: writes history; treats of physiology and psychology; rises to the highest flights of poetry; studies the most diverse subjects – politics, social economy, religion, and manners. Entire nature is its domain. It adopts the form which pleases it, taking the tone which seems best, feeling no longer bounded by any limit. In this we are far distant from the novel that our fathers were acquainted with. It was a purely imaginative work, whose sole end was to charm and distract its readers. In ancient rhetorics the novel is placed at the bottom, between the fables and light poetry. Serious men disdained novels, abandoned them to women, as a frivolous and compromising recreation. This opinion is still held in the country and certain academical centers. The truth is that the masterpieces of modern fiction say more on the subject of man and nature than do the graver works of philosophy, history, and criticism. In them lies the modern tool.

I pass to another characteristic of the naturalistic novel. It is impersonal; I mean to say by that that the novelist is but a recorder who is forbidden to judge and to conclude. The strict rôle of a savant is to expose the facts, to go to the end of analysis without venturing into synthesis; the facts are thus: experiment tried in such and such conditions gives such and such results; and he stops there, for if he wishes to go beyond the phenomena he will enter into hypothesis; we shall have probabilities, not science. Well! the novelist should equally keep to known facts, to the scrupulous study of nature, if he does not wish to stray among lying conclusions. He himself disappears, he keeps his emotion well in hand, he simply shows what he has seen. Here is the truth; shiver or laugh before it, draw from it whatever lesson you please, the only task of the author has been to put before you true data. There is, besides, for this moral impersonality of the work a reason in art. The passionate or tender intervention of the writer weakens a novel, because it ruins the clearness of its lines, and introduces a strange element into the facts which destroys their scientific value. One cannot well imagine a chemist becoming incensed with azote, because this body is injurious to life, or sympathizing with oxygen for the contrary reason. In the same way, a novelist who feels the need of becoming indignant with vice, or applauding virtue, not only spoils the data he produces, for his intervention is as trying as it is useless, but the work loses its strength; it is no longer a marble page, hewn from the block of reality; it is matter worked up, kneaded by the emotions of the author, and such emotions are always subject to prejudices and errors. A true work will be eternal, while an impressionable work can at best tickle only the sentiment of a certain age. [. . .]

The naturalistic formula, however complete and defined in the novel, is very far from being so on the stage, and I conclude from that that it will be completed, that it will assume sooner or later there its scientific rigor, or else the stage will become flat, and more and more inferior. [. . .]

It is very evident that the naturalistic evolution will extend itself more and more, as it possesses the intelligence of the age. While the novelists are digging always further forward, producing newer and more exact data, the stage will flounder deeper every day in the midst of its romantic fictions, its worn-out plots, and its skillfulness of handicraft. The situation will be the more sad because the public will certainly acquire a taste for reality in reading novels. The movement is making itself forcibly felt even now. There will come a time when the public will shrug its shoulders and demand an innovation. Either the theater will be naturalistic or it will not be at all; such is the formal conclusion. [. . .]

The wonderful power of the stage must not be forgotten, and its immediate effect on the spectators. There is no better instrument for propagating anything. If the novel, then, is read by the fireside, in several instances, with a patience tolerating the longest details, the naturalistic drama should proclaim before all else that it has no connection with this isolated reader, but with a crowd who cry out for clearness and conciseness. I do not see that the naturalistic formula is antagonistic to this conciseness and this clearness. It is simply a question of changing the composition and the body of the work. The novel analyzes at great length and with a minuteness of detail which overlooks nothing; the stage can analyze as briefly as it wishes by actions and words. A word, a cry, in Balzac's works is often sufficient to present the entire character. This cry belongs essentially to the stage. As to the acts, they are consistent with analysis in action, which is the most striking form of action one can make. When we have gotten rid of the child's play of a plot, the infantile game of tying up complicated threads in order to have the pleasure of untying them again; when a play shall be nothing more than a real and logical story – we shall then enter into perfect analysis; we shall analyze necessarily the double influence of characters over facts, of facts over characters. [. . .]

I now come to the language. They pretend to say that there is a special style for the stage. They want it to be a style altogether different from the ordinary style of speaking, more sonorous, more nervous, written in a higher key, cut in facets, no doubt to make the chandelier jets sparkle. [. . .]

What I want to hear on the stage is the language as it is spoken every day; if we cannot produce on the stage a conversation with its repetitions, its length, and its useless words, at least the movement and the tone of the conversation could be kept; the particular turn of mind of each talker, the reality, in a word, reproduced to the necessary extent.

[. . .]

I yearn for life with its shiver, its breath, and its strength; I long for life as it is.

We shall yet have life on the stage as we already have it in the novel. This pretended logic of actual plays, this equality and symmetry obtained by processes of reasoning, which come from ancient metaphysics, will fall before the natural logic of facts and beings such as reality presents to us. Instead of a stage of fabrication we shall have a stage of observation. How will the evolution be brought about? Tomorrow will tell us. I have tried to foresee, but I leave to genius the realization. I have already given my conclusion: Our stage will be naturalistic, or it will cease to exist. [. . .]

3
DESMOND MACCARTHY (1877–1952)
'THE POST-IMPRESSIONISTS' 1910

British literary journalist, member of the Bloomsbury Group, educated at Eton and Trinity College, Cambridge, where he was elected an Apostle in 1896. An important critic of Bernard Shaw's early plays at the Royal Court, he was a contributor to The Spectator *and became editor of the New* Quarterly. *MacCarthy was a great Ibsen and Chekhov enthusiast. He contributed to (1913–19), and then edited (1920–27), the* New Statesman. *He became senior literary critic at* The Sunday Times *in 1928. In 1910 Roger Fry persuaded MacCarthy to act as secretary and agent to the first Post-Impressionist exhibition, and to perform the 'ticklish' task of writing the introduction to the exhibition catalogue, which is reproduced below.*

The pictures collected together in the present Exhibition are the work of a group of artists who cannot be defined by any single term. The term 'Synthesists', which has been applied to them by learned criticism, does indeed express a quality underlying their diversity; and it is the principal business of this introduction to expand the meaning of that word, which sounds too like the hiss of an angry gander to be a happy appellation. As a definition it has the drawback that this quality, common to all, is not always the one most impressive in each artist. In no school does individual temperament count for more. In fact, it is the boast of those who believe in this school, that its methods enable the individuality of the artist to find completer self-expression in his work than is possible to those who have committed themselves to representing objects more literally. This, indeed, is the first source of their quarrel with the Impressionists: the Post-Impressionists consider the Impressionists too naturalistic.

Yet their own connection with Impressionism is extremely close; Cézanne, Gauguin and Van Gogh all learnt in the Impressionist school. There are pictures on the walls by these three artists, painted in their earlier years, which at first strike the eye as being more Impressionist than anything else; but nevertheless, the connection of these artists with the Impressionists is accidental rather than intrinsic.

By the year 1880 the Impressionists had practically won their battle; nor is it likely any group of artists will ever have to fight so hard a one again. They have conquered for future originality, if not the right of a respectful hearing, at least of a dubious attention. By 1880 they had convinced practically everybody whose opinion counted, that their methods and ideas were at any rate those of artists, not those of cranks and charlatans. About this date the reaction against Impressionism, which this Exhibition represents, began to be distinctly felt. The two groups had one characteristic in common: the resolve of each artist to express his own temperament, and never to permit contemporary ideals to dictate to him what was beautiful, significant, and worthy to be painted. But the main current of Impressionism lay along the line of recording hitherto unrecognised aspects of objects; they were interested in analysing the play of light and shadow into a multiplicity of distinct colours; they refined upon what was already illusive in nature. In the pictures of Seurat, Cross, and Signac exhibited, this scientific interest in the representation of colour is still uppermost; what is new in these pictures is simply the method of representing the vibration of light by painting objects in dots and squares. The Post-Impressionists on the other hand were not concerned with recording impressions of colour or light. They were interested in the discoveries of the Impressionists only so far as these discoveries helped them to express emotions which the objects themselves evoked; their attitude towards nature was far more independent, not to say rebellious. It is true that from the earliest times artists have regarded nature as 'the mistress of the masters'; but it is only in the nineteenth century that the close imitation of nature, without any conscious modification by the artist, has been proclaimed as a dogma. The Impressionists were artists, and their imitations of appearances were modified, consciously and unconsciously, in the direction of unity and harmony; of course, as artists, they selected and arranged. But the receptive, passive attitude towards the appearances of things often hindered them from rendering their real significance. Impressionism encouraged an artist to paint a tree as it appeared to him at the moment under particular circumstances. It insisted so much upon the importance of his rendering his exact impression that his work often completely failed to express a tree at all; as transferred to canvas it was just so much shimmer and colour. The 'treeness' of the tree was not rendered at all; all the emotion and associations such as trees may be made to convey in poetry were omitted.

This is the fundamental cause of quarrel between the Impressionists and the group of painters whose pictures hang on these walls. They said in effect to the Impressionists: 'You have explored nature in every direction, and all honour to you; but your methods and principles have hindered artists from exploring and expressing that emotional significance which lies in things, and is the most important subject matter of art. There is much more of that significance in the work of earlier artists who had not a tenth part of your skill in representing appearance. We will aim at that; though by our simplification of nature we shock and disconcert our contemporaries, whose eyes are now accustomed to your revelation, as much as you originally disconcerted your contemporaries by your subtleties and complications.' And there is no denying that the work of the Post-Impressionists is sufficiently disconcerting. It may even appear ridiculous to those who do not recall the fact that a good rocking-horse often had more of the true horse about it than an instantaneous photograph of a Derby winner.

The artists who felt most the restraints which the Impressionist attitude towards nature imposed upon them, naturally looked to the mysterious and isolated figure of Cézanne as their deliverer. Cézanne himself had come in contact with Manet and his art is derived directly from him. Manet, it is true, is also regarded as the father of Impressionism. To him Impressionism owes nearly all its power, interest and importance. He was a revolutionary in the sense that he refused to accept the pictorial convention of his time. He went back to seventeenth-century Spain for his inspiration. Instead of accepting the convention of light and shade falling upon objects from the side, he chose what seemed an impossibly difficult method of painting, that of representing them with light falling full upon them. This led to a very great change in the method of modelling, and to simplification of planes in his pictures which resulted in something closely akin to simple linear designs. He adopted, too, hitherto unknown oppositions of colour. In fact he endeavoured to get rid of chiaroscuro.

Regarded as a hopeless revolutionary, he was naturally drawn to other young artists, who found themselves in the same predicament; and through his connection with them and with Monet he gradually changed his severe, closely constructed style for one in which the shifting, elusive aspects of nature were accentuated. In this way he became one of the Impressionists and in his turn influenced them. Cézanne, however, seized upon precisely that side of Manet and his followers, which Monet and the other Impressionists ignored. Cézanne, when rendering the novel aspects of nature to which Impressionism was drawing attention, aimed first at a design which should produce the coherent, architectural effect of the masterpieces of primitive art. Because Cézanne thus showed how it was possible to pass from the complexity of the appearance of things to the geometrical simplicity which design demands, his art has appealed enormously to later designers. They recognise in him a guide capable of leading them out of the *cul de sac* into which naturalism had led them. Cézanne himself did not use consciously his new-found method of expression to convey ideas and emotions. He appealed first and foremost to the eye, and to the eye alone. But the path he indicated was followed by two younger artists, Van Gogh and Gauguin, with surprising results. Van Gogh's morbid temperament forced him to express in paint his strongest emotions, and in the methods of Cézanne he found a means of conveying the wildest and strangest visions conceived by any artist of our time. Yet he, too, accepts in the main the general appearance of nature; only before every scene and every object he searches first for the quality which originally made it appear so strangely to him: *that* he is determined to record at any sacrifice.

Gauguin is more of a decorator. He felt that while modern art had opened up undiscovered aspects of nature, it had to a great extent neglected the fundamental laws of abstract form, and above all had failed to realise the power which abstract form and colour can exercise over the imagination of the spectator. He deliberately chose, therefore, to become a decorative painter, believing that this was the most direct way of impressing upon the imagination the emotion he wished to perpetuate. In his Tahitian pictures by extreme simplification he endeavoured to bring back into modern painting the significance of gesture and movement characteristic of primitive art.

The followers of these men are pushing their ideas further and further. In the work of Matisse, especially, this search for an abstract harmony of line, for rhythm, has been carried to lengths which often deprive the figure of all appearance of nature. The general effect of his pictures is that of a return to primitive, even perhaps of a return to barbaric, art. This is inevitably disconcerting; but before dismissing such pictures as violently absurd, it is fair to consider the nature of the problem which the artist who would use abstract design as his principle of expression, has to face. His relation to a modern public is peculiar. In the earliest ages of art the artist's public were able to share in each successive triumph of his skill, for every advance he made was also an advance towards a more obvious representation of things as they appeared to everybody. Primitive art, like the art of children, consists not so much in an attempt to represent what the eye perceives, as to put a line round a mental conception of the object. Like the work of the primitive artist, the pictures children draw are often extraordinarily expressive. But what delights them is to find they are acquiring more and more skill in producing a deceptive likeness of the object itself. Give them a year of drawing lessons and they will probably produce results which will give the greatest satisfaction to them and their relations; but to the critical eye the original expressiveness will have vanished completely from their work.

The development of primitive art (for here we are dealing with men and not children) is the gradual absorption of each newly observed detail into an already established system of design. Each new detail is hailed with delight by their public. But there comes a point when the accumulations of an increasing skill in mere representation begin to destroy the expressiveness of the design, and then, though a large section of the public continue to applaud, the artist grows uneasy. He begins to try to unload, to simplify the drawing and painting, by which natural objects are evoked, in order to recover the lost expressiveness and life. He aims at *synthesis* in design; that is to say, he is prepared to subordinate consciously his power of representing the parts of his picture as plausibly as possible, to the expressiveness of his whole design. But in this retrogressive movement he has the public, who have become accustomed to extremely plausible imitations of nature, against him at every step; and what is more, his own self-consciousness hampers him as well.

The movement in art represented in this exhibition is widely spread. Although, with the exception of the Dutchman, Van Gogh, all the artists exhibited are Frenchmen, the school has ceased to be specifically a French one. It has found disciples in Germany, Belgium, Russia, Holland, Sweden. There are Americans, Englishmen and Scotchmen in Paris who are working and experimenting along the same lines. But the works of the Post-Impressionists are hardly known in England, although so much discussed upon the Continent. The exhibition organised by Mr. Robert Dell at Brighton last year has been our only chance of seeing them. The promoters of this exhibition have therefore thought it would be interesting to provide an opportunity for a greater number to judge these artists. The ladies and gentlemen on the Honorary Committee, though they are not responsible for the choice of the pictures, by lending their names have been kind enough to give this project their general support.

4
T. E. (THOMAS ERNEST) HULME (1883–1917)
FROM 'ROMANTICISM AND CLASSICISM' 1911

British poet, essayist, translator and thinker, described by T. S. Eliot as 'classical, reactionary and revolutionary'. Hulme was killed in action in the First World War. His rejection of Romanticism in favour of the classical 'hard, dry image' was an important influence on Imagism. Five of the six of his poems published in his lifetime appeared as 'The Complete Works of T. E. Hulme' in Orage's New Age *in February 1912. The magazine also published his articles on Henri Bergson and on 'Romanticism and Classicism' (1911), extracts from which are reproduced below. He translated Bergson's* Introduction to Metaphysics *and Georges Sorel's* Reflections on Violence *in 1913. Herbert Read edited the contents of his notebooks in two volumes:* Speculations *(1924) and* Notes on Language and Style *(1929).*

I want to maintain that after a hundred years of romanticism, we are in for a classical revival, and that the particular weapon of this new classical spirit, when it works in verse, will be fancy. And in this I imply the superiority of fancy – not superior generally or absolutely, for that would be obvious nonsense, but superior in the sense that we use the word good in empirical ethics – good for something, superior for something. I shall have to prove then two things, first that a classical revival is coming, and, secondly, for its particular purposes, fancy will be superior to imagination.

So banal have the terms Imagination and Fancy become that we imagine they must have always been in the language. Their history as two differing terms in the vocabulary of criticism is comparatively short. Originally, of course, they both mean the same thing; they first began to be differentiated by the German writers on aesthetics in the eighteenth century.

I know that in using the words 'classic' and 'romantic' I am doing a dangerous thing. They represent five or six different kinds of antitheses, and while I may be using them in one sense you may be interpreting them in another. In this present connection I am using them in a perfectly precise and limited sense. I ought really to have coined a couple of new words, but I prefer to use the ones I have used, as I then conform to the practice of the group of polemical writers who make most use of them at the present day, and have almost succeeded in making them political catchwords.

[. . .]

The best way of gliding into a proper definition of my terms would be to start with a set of people who are prepared to fight about it – for in them you will have no vagueness. (Other people take the infamous attitude of the person with catholic tastes who says he likes both.)

About a year ago, a man whose name I think was Fauchois gave a lecture at the Odéon on Racine, in the course of which he made some disparaging remarks about his dullness, lack of invention and the rest of it. This caused an immediate riot: fights took place all over the house; several people were arrested and imprisoned, and the rest of the series of lectures took place with hundreds of gendarmes and detectives scattered all over the place. These people interrupted because the classical ideal is a living thing to them and Racine is the great classic. That is what I call a real vital interest in literature. They regard romanticism as an awful disease from which France had just recovered.

The thing is complicated in their case by the fact that it was romanticism that made the revolution. They hate the revolution, so they hate romanticism.

I make no apology for dragging in politics here; romanticism both in England and France is associated with certain political views, and it is in taking a concrete example of the working out of a principle in action that you can get its best definition.

What was the positive principle behind all the other principles of 1789? I am talking here of the revolution in as far as it was an idea; I leave out material causes – they only produce the forces. The barriers which could easily have resisted or guided these forces had been previously rotted away by ideas. This always seems to be the case in successful changes; the privileged class is beaten only when it has lost faith in itself, when it has itself been penetrated with the ideas which are working against it.

It was not the rights of man – that was a good solid practical war-cry. The thing which created enthusiasm, which made the revolution practically a new religion, was something more positive than that. People of all classes, people who stood to lose by it, were in a positive ferment about the idea of liberty. There must have been some idea which enabled them to think that something positive could come out of so essentially negative a thing. There was, and here I get my definition of romanticism. They had been taught by Rousseau that man was by nature good, that it was only bad laws and customs that had suppressed him. Remove all these and the infinite possibilities of man would have a chance. This is what made them think that something positive could come out of disorder, this is what created the religious enthusiasm. Here is the root of all romanticism: that man, the individual, is an infinite reservoir of possibilities; and if you can so rearrange society by the destruction of oppressive order then these possibilities will have a chance and you will get Progress.

One can define the classical quite clearly as the exact opposite to this. Man is an extraordinarily fixed and limited animal whose nature is absolutely constant. It is only by tradition and organization that anything decent can be got out of him.

This view was a little shaken at the time of Darwin. You remember his particular hypothesis, that new species came into existence by the cumulative effect of small variations – this seems to admit the possibility of future progress. But at the present day the contrary hypothesis makes headway in the shape of De Vries's mutation theory, that each new species comes into existence, not gradually by the accumulation of small steps, but suddenly in a jump, a kind of sport, and that once in existence it remains absolutely fixed. This enables me to keep the classical view with an appearance of scientific backing.

Put shortly, these are the two views, then. One, that man is intrinsically good, spoilt by circumstance; and the other that he is intrinsically limited, but disciplined by order and tradition to something fairly decent. To the one party man's nature is like a well, to the other like a bucket. The view which regards man as a well, a reservoir full of possibilities, I call the romantic; the one which regards him as a very finite and fixed creature, I call the classical.

[. . .]

It would be a mistake to identify the classical view with that of materialism. On the contrary it is absolutely identical with the normal religious attitude. I should put it in this way: That part of the fixed nature of man is the belief in the Deity. This should be as fixed and true for every man as belief in the existence of matter and in the objective world. It is parallel to appetite, the instinct of sex, and all the other fixed qualities. Now at certain times, by the use of either force or rhetoric, these instincts have been suppressed – in Florence under Savonarola, in Geneva under Calvin, and here under the Roundheads. The inevitable result of such a process is that the repressed instinct bursts out in some abnormal direction. So with religion. By the perverted rhetoric of Rationalism, your natural instincts are suppressed and you are converted into an agnostic. Just as in the case of the other instincts, Nature has her revenge. The instincts that find their right and proper outlet in religion must come out in some other way. You don't believe in a God, so you begin to believe that man is a god. You don't believe in Heaven, so you begin to believe in a heaven on earth. In other words, you get romanticism. The concepts that are right and proper in their own sphere are spread over, and so mess up, falsify and blur the clear outlines of human experience. It is like pouring a pot of treacle over the dinner table. Romanticism then, and this is the best definition I can give of it, is spilt religion.

I must now shirk the difficulty of saying exactly what I mean by romantic and classical in verse. I can only say that it means the result of these two attitudes towards the cosmos, towards man, in so far as it gets reflected in verse. The romantic, because he thinks man infinite, must always be talking about the infinite; and as there is always the bitter contrast between what you think you ought to be able to do and what man actually can, it always tends, in its later stages at any rate, to be gloomy. I really can't go any further than to say it is the reflection of these two temperaments, and point out examples of the different spirits. On the one hand I would take such diverse people as Horace, most of the Elizabethans and the writers of the Augustan age, and on the other side Lamartine, Hugo, parts of Keats, Coleridge, Byron, Shelley and Swinburne.

I know quite well that when people think of classical and romantic in verse, the contrast at once comes into their mind between, say, Racine and Shakespeare. I don't mean this; the dividing line that I intend is here misplaced a little from the true middle. That Racine is on the extreme classical side I agree, but if you call Shakespeare romantic, you are using a different definition to the one I give. You are thinking of the difference between classic and romantic as being merely one between restraint and exuberance. I should say with Nietzsche that there are two kinds of classicism, the static and the dynamic. Shakespeare is the classic of motion.

What I mean by classical in verse, then, is this. That even in the most imaginative flights there is always a holding back, a reservation. The classical poet never forgets this finiteness, this limit of man. He remembers always that he is mixed up with earth. He may jump, but he always returns back; he never flies away into the circumambient gas.

You might say if you wished that the whole of the romantic attitude seems to crystallize in verse round metaphors of flight. Hugo is always flying, flying over abysses, flying up into the eternal gases. The word infinite in every other line.

In the classical attitude you never seem to swing right along to the infinite nothing. If you say an extravagant thing which does exceed the limits inside which you know man to be fastened, yet there is always conveyed in some way at the end an impression of yourself standing outside it, and not quite believing it, or consciously putting it forward as a flourish. You never go blindly into an atmosphere more than the truth, an atmosphere too rarefied for man to breathe for long. You are always faithful to the conception of a limit. It is a question of pitch; in romantic verse you move at a certain pitch of rhetoric which you know, man being what he is, to be a little high-falutin. – pretentious

[. . .]

I want now to give the reasons which make me think that we are nearing the end of the romantic movement.

The first lies in the nature of any convention or tradition in art. A particular convention or attitude in art has a strict analogy to the phenomena of organic life. It grows old and decays. It has a definite period of life and must die. All the possible tunes get played on it and then it is exhausted; moreover its best period is its youngest.

[. . .]

This period of exhaustion seems to me to have been reached in romanticism. We shall not get any new efflorescence of verse until we get a new technique, a new convention, to turn ourselves loose in.

Objection might be taken to this. It might be said that a century as an organic unity doesn't exist, that I am being deluded by a wrong metaphor, that I am treating a collection of literary people as if they were an organism or state department. Whatever we may be in other things, an objector might urge, in literature in as far as we are anything at all – in as far as we are worth considering – we are individuals, we are persons, and as distinct persons we cannot be subordinated to any general treatment. At any period at any time, an individual poet may be a classic or a romantic just as he feels like it. You at any particular moment may think that you can stand outside a movement. You may think that as an individual you observe both the classic and the romantic spirit and decide from a purely detached point of view that one is superior to the other.

The answer to this is that no one, in a matter of judgment of beauty, can take a detached standpoint in this way. Just as physically you are not born that abstract entity, man, but the child of particular parents, so you are in matters of literary judgment. Your opinion is almost entirely of the literary history that came just before you, and you are governed by that whatever you may think.

[. . .]

The amount of freedom in man is much exaggerated. That we are free on certain rare occasions, both my religion and the views I get from metaphysics convince me. But many acts which we habitually label free are in reality automatic. [. . .]

I can put the same thing in slightly different form. Here is a question of a conflict of two attitudes, as it might be of two techniques. The critic, while he has to admit that changes from one to the other occur, persists in regarding them as mere variations to a certain fixed normal, just as a pendulum might swing. I admit the analogy of the pendulum as far as movement, but I deny the further consequence of the analogy, the existence of the point of rest, the normal point.

When I say that I dislike the romantics, I dissociate two things: the part of them in which they resemble all the great poets, and the part in which they differ and which gives them their character as romantics. It is this minor element which constitutes the particular note of a century, and which, while it excites contemporaries, annoys the next generation. It was precisely that quality in Pope which pleased his friends, which we detest. Now, anyone just before the romantics who felt that, could have predicted that a change was coming. It seems to me that we stand just in the same position now. I think that there is an increasing proportion of people who simply can't stand Swinburne.

When I say that there will be another classical revival I don't necessarily anticipate a return to Pope. I say merely that now is the time for such a revival. Given people of the necessary capacity, it may be a vital thing; without them we may get a formalism something like Pope. When it does come we may not even recognize it as classical. Although it will be classical it will be different because it has passed through a romantic period. To take a parallel example: I remember being very surprised, after seeing the Post-Impressionists, to find in Maurice Denis's account of the matter that they consider themselves classical in the sense that they were trying to impose the same order on the mere flux of new material provided by the impressionist movement, that existed in the more limited materials of the painting before.

There is something now to be cleared away before I get on with my argument, which is that while romanticism is dead in reality, yet the critical attitude appropriate to it still continues to exist.

[...]

So that if good classical verse were to be written tomorrow very few people would be able to stand it.

I object even to the best of the romantics. I object still more to the receptive attitude. I object to the sloppiness which doesn't consider that a poem is a poem unless it is moaning or whining about something or other. [...] The thing has got so bad now that a poem which is all dry and hard, a properly classical poem, would not be considered poetry at all. How many people now can lay their hands on their hearts and say they like either Horace or Pope? They feel a kind of chill when they read them.

The dry hardness which you get in the classics is absolutely repugnant to them. Poetry that isn't damp isn't poetry at all. They cannot see that accurate description is a legitimate object of verse. Verse to them always means a bringing in of some of the emotions that are grouped round the word infinite.

The essence of poetry to most people is that it must lead them to a beyond of some kind. Verse strictly confined to the earthly and the definite (Keats is full of it) might seem to them to be excellent writing, excellent craftsmanship, but not poetry. So much has romanticism debauched us, that, without some form of vagueness, we deny the highest.

In the classic it is always the light of ordinary day, never the light that never was on land or sea. It is always perfectly human and never exaggerated: man is always man and never a god.

But the awful result of romanticism is that, accustomed to this strange light, you can never live without it. Its effect on you is that of a drug.

There is a general tendency to think that verse means little else than the expression of unsatisfied emotion. People say: 'But how can you have verse without sentiment?' You see what it is: the prospect alarms them. A classical revival to them would mean the prospect of an arid desert and the death of poetry as they understand it, and could only come to fill the gap caused by that death. Exactly why this dry classical spirit should have a positive and legitimate necessity to express itself in poetry is utterly inconceivable to them.

[. . .]

It is an objection which ultimately I believe comes from a bad metaphysic of art. You are unable to admit the existence of beauty without the infinite being in some way or another dragged in.

[. . .]

Now it is quite obvious to anyone who holds this kind of theory that any poetry which confines itself to the finite can never be of the highest kind. It seems a contradiction in terms to them. And as in metaphysics you get the last refuge of a prejudice, so it is now necessary for me to refute this.

Here follows a tedious piece of dialectic, but it is necessary for my purpose. I must avoid two pitfalls in discussing the idea of beauty. On the one hand there is the old classical view which is supposed to define it as lying in conformity to certain standard fixed forms; and on the other hand there is the romantic view which drags in the infinite. I have got to find a metaphysic between these two which will enable me to hold consistently that a neoclassic verse of the type I have indicated involves no contradiction in terms. It is essential to prove that beauty may be in small, dry things.

The great aim is accurate, precise and definite description. The first thing is to recognize how extraordinarily difficult this is. It is no mere matter of carefulness, you have to use language, and language is by its very nature a communal thing; that is, it expresses never the exact thing but a compromise – that which is common to you, me and everybody. But each man sees a little differently, and to get out clearly and exactly what he does see, he must have a terrific struggle with language, whether it be with words or the technique of other arts. Language has its own special nature, its own conventions and communal ideas. It is only by a concentrated effort of the mind that you can hold it fixed to your own purpose. I always think that the fundamental process at the back of all the arts might be represented by the following metaphor. You know what I call architect's curves – flat pieces of wood with all different kinds of curvature. By a suitable selection from these you can draw approximately any curve you like. The artist I take to be the man who simply can't bear the idea of that 'approximately'. He will get the exact curve of what he sees whether it be an object or an idea in the mind. I shall here have to change my metaphor a little to get the process in his mind. Suppose that instead of your curved pieces of wood you have a springy piece of steel of the same types of curvature as the wood. Now the state of tension or concentration of mind, if he is doing anything really good in this struggle against the ingrained habit of the technique, may be represented by a man employing all his fingers to bend the steel out of its own curve and into the exact curve which you want. Something different to what it would assume naturally.

[. . .]

I have still to show that in the verse which is to come, fancy will be the necessary weapon of the classical school. The positive quality I have talked about can be manifested in ballad verse by extreme directness and simplicity, such as you get in 'On Fair Kirkconnel Lea'. But the particular verse we are going to get will be cheerful, dry and sophisticated, and here the necessary weapon of the positive quality must be fancy.

[. . .]

It isn't the scale or kind of emotion produced that decides, but this one fact: Is there any real zest in it? Did the poet have an actually realized visual object before him in which he delighted? It doesn't matter if it were a lady's shoe or the starry heavens.

[. . .]

When the analogy has not enough connection with the thing described to be quite parallel with it, where it overlays the thing it described and there is a certain excess, there you have the play of fancy – that I grant is inferior to imagination.

But where the analogy is every bit of it necessary for accurate description in the sense of the word accurate I have previously described, and your only objection to this kind of fancy is that it is not serious in the effect it produces, then I think the objection to be entirely invalid. If it is sincere in the accurate sense, when the whole of the analogy is necessary to get out the exact curve of the feeling or thing you want to express – there you seem to me to have the highest verse, even though the subject be trivial and the emotions of the infinite far away.

[. . .]

Now the characteristic of the intellect is that it can only represent complexities of the mechanical kind. It can only make diagrams, and diagrams are essentially things whose parts are separate one from another. The intellect always analyses – when there is a synthesis it is baffled. That is why the artist's work seems mysterious. The intellect can't represent it. This is a necessary consequence of the particular nature of the intellect and the purposes for which it is formed. It doesn't mean that your synthesis is ineffable, simply that it can't be definitely stated.

Now this is all worked out in Bergson, the central feature of his whole philosophy. It is all based on the clear conception of these vital complexities which he calls 'intensive' as opposed to the other kind which he calls 'extensive', and the recognition of the fact that the intellect can only deal with the extensive multiplicity. To deal with the intensive you must use intuition.

[. . .]

A powerfully imaginative mind seizes and combines at the same instant all the important ideas of its poem or picture, and while it works with one of them, it is at the same instant working with and modifying all in their relation to it and never losing sight of their bearings on each other – as the motion of a snake's body goes through all parts at once and its volition acts at the same instant in coils which go contrary ways.

A romantic movement must have an end of the very nature of the thing. It may be deplored, but it can't be helped – wonder must cease to be wonder.

I guard myself here from all the consequences of the analogy, but it expresses at any rate the inevitableness of the process. A literature of wonder must have an end as inevitably as a strange land loses its strangeness when one lives in it. Think of the lost ecstasy of the Elizabethans. 'Oh my America, my new found land' [John Donne, 'Elegy XIX: Going to Bed'], think of what it meant to them and of what it means to us. Wonder can only be the attitude of a man passing from one stage to another, it can never be a permanently fixed thing.

5
CHARLOTTE PERKINS GILMAN (1860–1935)
FROM *THE MAN-MADE WORLD OR OUR ANDROCENTRIC CULTURE* 1911

American feminist and writer. Educated at the Rhode Island School of Design, she moved to California where her first stories, including 'The Yellow Wall-Paper' and a collection of poetry, In This Our World, *were published in 1892 and 1893. Her active involvement with the feminist movement included lecturing on women's issues and their wider social ramifications. Her study* Women and Economics *was published in 1898, followed by the founding in 1909 of the journal* Forerunner, *which she edited until 1916. Later works include* The Man-Made World *(1911, from which the following extracts are taken) and* His Religion and Hers *(1923). [See IIa 20, IIIb 7]*

It is no easy matter to deny or reverse a universal assumption. The human mind has had a good many jolts since it began to think, but after each upheaval it settles down as peacefully as the vine-growers on Vesuvius, accepting the last lava crust as permanent ground.

What we see immediately around us, what we are born into and grow up with, be it mental furniture or physical, we assume to be the order of nature.

If a given idea has been held in the human mind for many generations, as almost all our common ideas have, it takes sincere and continued effort to remove it; and if it is one of the oldest we have in stock, one of the big, common, unquestioned world ideas, vast is the labor of those who seek to change it.

Nevertheless, if the matter is one of importance, if the previous idea was a palpable error, of large and evil effect, and if the new one is true and widely important, the effort is worth making.

The task here undertaken is of this sort. It seeks to show that what we have all this time called 'human nature' and deprecated, was in great part only male nature, and good enough in its place; that what we have called 'masculine' and admired as such, was in large part human, and should be applied to both sexes; that what we have called 'feminine' and condemned, was also largely human and applicable to both. Our androcentric culture is so shown to have been, and still to be, a masculine culture in excess, and therefore undesirable.

In the preliminary work of approaching these facts it will be well to explain how it can be that so 'wide and serious an error should have been made by practically all men?' The reason is simply that they were men. They were males, and saw women as females – and not otherwise.

So absolute is this conviction that the man who reads will say, 'Of course! How else are we to look at women except as females? They are females, aren't they?' Yes, they are, as men are males unquestionably; but there is possible the frame of mind of the old marquise who was asked by an English friend how she could bear to have the footman serve her breakfast in bed – to have a man in her bed-chamber – and replied sincerely, 'Call you that thing there a man?'

The world is full of men, but their principal occupation is human work of some sort; and women see in them the human distinction preponderantly. Occasionally some unhappy lady marries her coachman – long contemplation of broad shoulders having an effect, apparently; but in general women see the human creature most; the male creature only when they love.

To the man, the whole world was his world; his because he was male; and the whole world of woman was the home; because she was female. She had her prescribed sphere, strictly limited to her feminine occupations and interests; he had all the rest of life; and not only so, but, having it, insisted on calling it male.

This accounts for the general attitude of men toward the now rapid humanization of women. From her first faint struggles toward freedom and justice, to her present valiant efforts toward full economic and political equality, each step has been termed 'unfeminine', and resented as an intrusion upon man's place and power. Here shows the need of our new classification, of the three distinct fields of life – masculine, feminine and human.

As a matter of fact, there is a 'woman's sphere', sharply defined and quite different from his; there is also a 'man's sphere', as sharply defined and even more limited; but there remains a common sphere – that of humanity, which belongs to both alike.

In the earlier part of what is known as 'the woman's movement', it was sharply opposed on the ground that women would become 'unsexed'. Let us note in passing that they have become unsexed in one particular, most glaringly so, and that no one has noticed or objected to it.

As part of our androcentric culture, we may point to the peculiar reversal of sex characteristics which makes the human female carry the burden of ornament. She alone, of all human creatures, has adopted the essentially masculine attribute of special sex-decoration; she does not fight for her mate, as yet, but she blooms forth as the peacock and bird of paradise, in poignant reversal of nature's laws, even wearing masculine feathers to further her feminine ends.

Woman's natural work as a female is that of the mother; man's natural work as a male is that of the father; their mutual relation to this end being a source of joy and well-being when rightly held: but human work covers all our life outside of these specialities. Every handicraft, every profession, every science, every art, all normal amusements and recreations, all government, education, religion; the whole living world of human achievement: all this is human.

That one sex should have monopolized all human activities, called them 'man's work', and managed them as such, is what is meant by the phrase 'Androcentric Culture'.

Men and art

Among the many counts in which women have been proven inferior to men in human development is the oft-heard charge that there are no great women artists. Where one or two are proudly exhibited in evidence, they are either pooh-poohed as not very great, or held to be the trifling exceptions which do but prove the rule.

Defenders of women generally make the mistake of over-estimating their performances, instead of accepting, and explaining, the visible facts. What are the facts as to the relation of men and women to art? And what, in especial, has been the effect upon art of a solely masculine expression? [. . .]

As soon as the male of our species assumed the exclusive right to perform all social functions, he necessarily brought to that performance the advantages – and disadvantages – of maleness, of those dominant characteristics, desire, combat, self-expression.

Desire has overweighted art in many visible forms, it is prominent in painting and music, almost monopolizes fiction, and has pitifully degraded dancing.

Combat is not so easily expressed in art, where even competition is on a high plane; but the last element is the main evil, self-expression. This impulse is inherently and incradicably masculine. It rests on that most basic of distinctions between the sexes, the centripetal and centrifugal forces of the universe. In the very nature of the sperm-cell and the germ-cell we find this difference: the one attracts, gathers, draws in; the other repels, scatters, pushes out. That projective impulse is seen in the male nature everywhere, the constant urge toward expression, to all boasting and display. This spirit, like all things masculine, is perfectly right and admirable in its place.

It is the duty of the male, as a male, to vary; bursting forth in a thousand changing modifications – the female, selecting, may so incorporate beneficial changes in the race. It is his duty to thus express himself – an essentially masculine duty; but masculinity is one thing, and art is another. Neither the masculine nor the feminine has any place in art – Art is Human.

It is not in any faintest degree allied to the personal process of reproduction; but is a social process, a most distinctive social process, quite above the plane of sex. The true artist transcends his sex, or her sex. If this is not the case, the art suffers. [. . .]

But the main evils of a too masculine art lie in the emphasis laid on the self-expression. The artist, passionately conscious of how he feels, strives to make other people aware of these sensations. This is now so generally accepted by critics, so seriously advanced by painters, that what is called 'the art world' accepts it as established.

If a man paints the sea, it is not to make you see and feel as a sight of that same ocean would, but to make you see and feel how he, personally, was affected by it; a matter surely of the narrowest importance. The ultra-masculine artist, extremely sensitive, necessarily, and full of the natural urge to expression of the sex, uses the medium of art as ingenuously as the partridge-cock uses his wings in drumming on the log, or the bull moose stamps and bellows; not narrowly as a mate call, but as a form of expression of his personal sensations.

The higher the artist the more human he is, the broader his vision, the more he sees for humanity, and expresses for humanity, and the less personal, the less ultra-masculine, is his expression.

The art which gives humanity consciousness is the most vital art. Our greatest dramatists are lauded for their breadth of knowledge of 'human nature,' their range of emotion and understanding; our greatest poets are those who most deeply and widely experience and reveal the feelings of the human heart; and the power of fiction is that it can reach and express this great field of human life with no limits but those of the author.

When fiction began it was the legitimate child of oral tradition, a product of natural brain activity; the legend constructed instead of remembered. (This stage is with us yet as seen in the constant changes in repetition of popular jokes and stories.)

Fiction to-day has a much wider range; yet it is still restricted, heavily and most mischievously restricted. [. . .]

As it is, our great sea of fiction is steeped and dyed and flavored all one way. A young man faces life – the seventy year stretch, remember, and is given book upon book wherein one set of feelings is continually vocalized and overestimated. He reads forever of love, good love and bad love, natural and unnatural, legitimate and illegitimate; with the *unavoidable inference that there is nothing else going on.*

If he is a healthy young man he breaks loose from the whole thing, despises 'love stories' and takes up life as he finds it. But what impression he does receive from fiction is a false one, and he suffers without knowing it from lack of the truer, broader views of life it failed to give him.

A young woman faces life – the seventy year stretch remember; and is given the same books – with restrictions. Remember the remark of Rochefoucauld, 'There are thirty good stories in the world and twenty-nine cannot be told to women.' There is a certain broad field of literature so grossly androcentric that for very shame men have tried to keep it to themselves. But in a milder form, the spades all named teaspoons, or at the worst appearing as trowels – the young woman is given the same fiction. Love and love and love – from 'first sight' to marriage. There it stops – just the fluttering ribbon of announcement – 'and lived happily ever after.'

Is that kind of fiction any sort of picture of a woman's life? Fiction, under our androcentric culture, has not given any true picture of woman's life, very little of human life, and a disproportioned section of man's life.

As we daily grow more human, both of us, this noble art is changing for the better so fast that a short lifetime can mark the growth. New fields are opening and new laborers are working in them. But it is no swift and easy matter to disabuse the race mind from attitudes and habits inculcated for a thousand years. What we have been fed upon so long we are well used to, what we are used to we like, what we like we think is good and proper.

The widening demand for broader, truer fiction is disputed by the slow racial mind; and opposed by the marketers of literature on grounds of visible self-interest, as well as lethargic conservatism.

It is difficult for men, heretofore the sole producers and consumers of literature; and for women, new to the field, and following masculine canons because all the canons were masculine; to stretch their minds to a recognition of the change which is even now upon us. [. . .]

The art of fiction is being re-born in these days. Life is discovered to be longer, wider, deeper, richer, than these monotonous players of one tune would have us believe.

The humanizing of woman of itself opens five distinctly fresh fields of fiction: First, the position of the young woman who is called upon to give up her 'career' – her humanness – for marriage, and who objects to it. Second, the middle-aged woman who at last discovers that her discontent is social starvation – that it is not more love that she wants, but more business in life: Third, the inter-relation of women with women – a thing we could never write about before because we never had it before: except in harems and convents: Fourth, the interaction between mothers and children; this not the eternal 'mother and child', wherein the child is always a baby, but the long drama of personal relationship; the love and hope, the patience and power, the lasting joy and triumph, the slow eating disappointment which must never be owned to a living soul – here are grounds for novels that a million mothers and many million children would eagerly read: Fifth, the new attitude of the full-grown woman, who faces the demands of love with the high standards of conscious motherhood.

There are other fields, broad and brilliantly promising, but this chapter is meant merely to show that our one-sided culture has, in this art, most disproportionately overestimated the dominant instincts of the male – Love and War – an offence against art and truth, and an injury to life.

6
ROGER FRY (1866–1934)
'THE FRENCH GROUP' 1912

British artist, impresario and art critic, member of the Bloomsbury Group. He was responsible for the first major exhibition of modern European art (Van Gogh, Gauguin, Cézanne) in Britain, at the Grafton Galleries, London, 1910, and coined the term Post-Impressionism for the event. Fry studied in Italy and from 1905 to 1910 was director of the Metropolitan Museum in New York. With the assistance of Clive Bell, he followed up the scandalous 1910 exhibition with a second Post-Impressionist exhibition in 1912 which showed the work of British artists including Vanessa Bell (Clive Bell's wife and Fry's lover for a time), credited with some of the earliest examples of abstract painting in Europe. Fry was founder of the Omega Workshops in London (1913–21) which employed artists in the production of textiles, pottery and furniture. His highly influential Formalist theories of art are also important in the development of theories of literary Formalism. His most important publications are Vision and Design *(1920) and* Transformations

(1926). Virginia Woolf published his biography, Roger Fry, *in 1940. The following extract is Fry's introduction, 'The French Group', from the catalogue of the second Post-Impressionist exhibition, 1912.*

When the first Post-Impressionist Exhibition was held in these Galleries two years ago the English public became for the first time fully aware of the existence of a new movement in art, a movement which was the more disconcerting in that it was no mere variation upon accepted themes but implied a reconsideration of the very purpose and aim as well as the methods of pictorial and plastic art. It was not surprising therefore that a public which had come to admire above everything in a picture the skill with which the artist produced illusion should have resented an art in which such skill was completely subordinated to the direct expression of feeling. Accusations of clumsiness and incapacity were freely made, even against so singularly accomplished an artist as Cézanne. Such darts, however, fall wide of the mark, since it is not the object of these artists to exhibit their skill or proclaim their knowledge, but only to attempt to express by pictorial and plastic form certain spiritual experiences; and in conveying these, ostentation of skill is likely to be even more fatal than downright incapacity.

Indeed, one may fairly admit that the accusation of want of skill and knowledge, while ridiculous in the case of Cézanne is perfectly justified as regards one artist represented (for the first time in England) in the present Exhibition, namely, Rousseau. Rousseau was a custom-house officer who painted without any training in the art. His pretentions to paint made him the butt of a great deal of ironic wit, but scarcely any one now would deny the authentic quality of his inspiration or the certainty of his imaginative conviction. Here then is one case where want of skill and knowledge do not completely obscure, though they may mar expression. And this is true of all perfectly naïve and primitive art. But most of the art here seen is neither naïve nor primitive. It is the work of highly civilised and modern men trying to find a pictorial language appropriate to the sensibilities of the modern outlook.

Another charge that is frequently made against these artists is that they allow what is merely capricious, or even what is extravagant and eccentric, in their work – that it is not serious, but an attempt to impose on the good-natured tolerance of the public. This charge of insincerity and extravagance is invariably made against any new manifestation of creative art. It does not of course follow that it is always wrong. The desire to impose by such means certainly occurs, and is sometimes temporarily successful. But the feeling on the part of the public may, and I think in this case does, arise from a simple misunderstanding of what these artists set out to do. The difficulty springs from a deep-rooted conviction, due to long-established custom, that the aim of painting is the descriptive imitation of natural forms. Now, these artists do not seek to give what can, after all, be but a pale reflex of actual appearance, but to arouse the conviction of a new and definite reality. They do not seek to imitate form, but to create form; not to imitate life, but to find an equivalent for life. By that I mean that they wish to make images which by the clearness of their logical structure, and by their closely-knit unity of texture, shall appeal to our disinterested and contemplative imagination with something of the same vividness as the things of actual life appeal to our practical activities. In fact, they aim not at illusion but at reality.

The logical extreme of such a method would undoubtedly be the attempt to give up all resemblance to natural form, and to create a purely abstract language of form – a visual music; and the later works of Picasso show this clearly enough. They may or may not be successful in their attempt. It is too early to be dogmatic on the point, which can only be decided when our sensibilities to such abstract form have been more practised than they are at present. But I would suggest that there is nothing ridiculous in the attempt to do this. Such a picture as Picasso's *Head of a Man* would undoubtedly be ridiculous if, having set out to make a direct imitation of the actual model, he had been incapable of getting a better likeness. But Picasso did nothing of the sort. He has shown in his *Portrait of Mlle. L. B.* that he could do so at least as well as any one if he wished, but he is here attempting to do something quite different.

No such extreme abstraction marks the work of Matisse. The actual objects which stimulated his creative invention are recognisable enough. But here, too, it is an equivalence, not a likeness, of nature that is sought. In opposition to Picasso, who is preeminently plastic, Matisse aims at convincing us of the reality of his forms by the continuity and flow of his rhythmic line, by the logic of his space relations, and, above all, by an entirely new use of colour. In this, as in his markedly rythmic design, he approaches more than any other European to the ideals of Chinese art. His work has to an extraordinary degree that decorative unity of design which distinguishes all the artists of this school.

Between these two extremes we may find ranged almost all the remaining artists

[. . .]

But however various the directions in which different groups are exploring the newly found regions of expressive form they all alike derive in some measure from the great originator of the whole idea, Cézanne. And since one must always refer to him to understand the origin of these ideas, it has been thought well to include a few examples of his work in the present Exhibition, although this year it is mainly the moderns, and not the old masters that are represented.

[. . .]

Finally, I should like to call attention to a distinguishing characteristic of the French artists seen here, namely, the markedly Classic spirit of their work. This will be noted as distinguishing them to some extent from the English, even more perhaps from the Russians, and most of all from the great mass of modern painting in every country. I do not mean by Classic, dull, pedantic, traditional, reserved, or any of those similar things which the word is often made to imply. Still less do I mean by calling them Classic that they paint *Visits to Æsculapius* or *Nero at the Colosseum*. I mean that they do not rely for their effect upon associated ideas, as I believe Romantic and Realistic artists invariably do.

All art depends upon cutting off the practical responses to sensations of ordinary life, thereby setting free a pure and as it were disembodied functioning of the spirit; but in so far as the artist relies on the associated ideas of the objects which he represents, his work is not completely free and pure, since romantic associations imply at least an imagined practical activity. The disadvantage of such an art of associated ideas is that its effect really depends on what we bring with us: it adds no entirely new factor to our experience. Consequently, when the first shock of wonder or delight is exhausted the work produces an ever lessening reaction. Classic art, on the other hand, records a positive and disinterestedly passionate state of mind. It communicates a new and otherwise unattainable experience. Its effect, therefore, is likely to increase with familiarity. Such a classic spirit is common to the best French work of all periods from the twelfth century onwards, and though no one could find direct reminiscences of a Nicholas Poussin here, his spirit seems to revive in the work of artists like Derain. It is natural enough that the intensity and singleness of aim with which these artists yield themselves to certain experiences in the face of nature may make their work appear odd to those who have not the habit of contemplative vision, but it would be rash for us, who as a nation are in the habit of treating our emotions, especially our aesthetic emotions, with a certain levity, to accuse them of caprice or insincerity. It is because of this classic concentration of feeling (which by no means implies abandonment) that the French merit our serious attention. It is this that makes their art so difficult on a first approach but gives it its lasting hold on the imagination.

7
CLIVE BELL (1881–1964)
'THE ENGLISH GROUP' 1912

Art critic and member of the Bloomsbury Group. Educated at Trinity College, Cambridge, Bell also studied in Paris. In 1907 he married the artist Vanessa Bell (sister of Virginia Woolf). He coined the term Significant Form to describe the Post-Impressionist art he introduced in the second Post-Impressionist exhibition in 1912. Although closely linked with Roger Fry, their ideas on art should not be considered synonymous. Bell developed his theory of Significant Form to account for not only Post-Impressionism but all art in his influential book, Art *(1914). His other important publications are* Civilization *(1928) and* Proust *(1929). 'The English Group' (1912) introduces the work of British Post-Impressionists (including his wife) from the catalogue of the second Post-Impressionist exhibition.*

For the Second Post-Impressionist Exhibition I have been asked to choose a few English pictures, and to say something about them. Happily, there is no need to be defensive. The battle is won. We all agree, now, that any form in which an artist can express himself is legitimate, and the more sensitive perceive that there are things worth expressing that could never have been expressed in traditional forms. We have ceased to ask, 'What does this picture represent?' and ask instead, 'What does it make us feel?' We expect a work of plastic art to have more in common with a piece of music than with a coloured photograph.

The first thing to be considered is the relation of these English artists to the movement. That such a revolutionary movement was needed is proved, I think, by the fact that every one of them has something to say which could not have been said in any other form. New wine abounded and the old bottles were found wanting. These artists are of the movement because, in choice of subject, they recognise no authority but the truth that is in them; in choice of form, none but the need of expressing it. That is Post-Impressionism.

Their debt to the French is enormous. I believe it could be computed and stated with some precision. For instance, it could be shown that each owes something, directly or indirectly, to Cézanne. But detective-work of this sort would be as profitless here as elsewhere. I am concerned only to discover in the work of these English painters some vestige of those qualities that distinguish Post-Impressionists from the mass – qualities that can be seen to advantage in the work of the French masters here exhibited, and to perfection in those of their master, Cézanne. These qualities I will call simplification and plastic design.

What I mean by 'simplification' is obvious. A literary artist who wishes to express what he feels for a forest thinks himself under no obligation to give an account of its flora and fauna. The Post-Impressionist claims similar privileges: those facts that any one can observe for himself or discover in a text-book he leaves to the makers of Christmas-cards and diagrams. He simplifies, omits details, that is to say, to concentrate on something more important – on the significance of form.

We can regard an object solely as a means and feel emotion for it as such. It is possible to contemplate emotionally a coal-scuttle as the friend of man. We can consider it in relation to the toes of the family circle and the paws of the watch-dog. And, certainly, this emotion can be suggested in line and colour. But the artist who would do so can but describe the coal-scuttle and its patrons, trusting that his forms will remind the spectator of a moving situation. His description may interest, but, at best, it will move us far less than that of a capable writer. Yet most English painters have attempted nothing more serious. Their drawing and design have been merely descriptive; their art, at best, romantic.

How, then, does the Post-Impressionist regard a coal-scuttle? He regards it as an end in itself, as a significant form related on terms of equality with other significant forms. Thus have all great artists regarded objects. Forms and the relation of forms have been for them, not means of suggesting emotion but objects of emotion. It is this emotion they have expressed. Their drawing and design have been plastic and not descriptive. That is the supreme virtue of modern French art: of nothing does English stand in greater need.

If, bearing in mind the difference between the treatment of form as an object of emotion and the treatment of form as a means of description, we turn, now, to these pictures, an important distinction will become apparent. We shall notice that the art of Mr. Wyndham Lewis, whatever else may be said of it, is certainly not descriptive. Hardly at all does it depend for its effect on association or suggestion. There is no reason why a mind sensitive to form and colour, though it inhabit another solar system, and a body altogether unlike our own, should fail to appreciate it. On the other hand, fully to appreciate some pictures by Mr. Fry or Mr. Duncan Grant it is necessary to be a human being, perhaps, even, an educated European of the twentieth century. 'Fully', I say, because both Mr. Fry and Mr. Grant – and, for that matter, all the painters here represented – are true plastic artists; wherefore the most important qualities in their work are quite independent of place or time, or a particular civilisation or point of view. Theirs is an art that stands on its own feet instead of leaning upon life; and herein it differs from traditional English art, which, robbed of historical and literary interest, would cease to exist. It is just because these Englishmen have expelled or reduced to servitude those romantic and irrelevant qualities that for two centuries have made our art the laughing-stock of Europe, that they deserve as much respect and almost as much attention as superior French artists who have had no such traditional difficulties to surmount.

No one of understanding, I suppose, will deny the superiority of the Frenchmen. They, however, have no call to be ashamed of their allies. For the essential virtue is common to both. Looking at these pictures every visitor will be struck by the fact that they are neither pieces of handsome furniture, nor pretty knick-knacks, nor tasteful souvenirs, but passionate attempts to express profound emotions. All are manifestations of a spiritual revolution which proclaims art a religion, and forbids its degradation to the level of a trade. They are intended neither to please, to flatter, nor to shock, but to express great emotions and to provoke them.

8
ROBERT DELAUNAY (1885–1941)
'LIGHT' 1912;
'NOTES ON THE CONSTRUCTION OF THE REALITY OF PURE PAINTING' 1912

French artist. He studied with his uncle, Charles Damour, in Paris 1895–1900, and was an apprentice-student of the theatre designer Ronsin (1902) before becoming a painter in 1904. He undertook military service between 1907 and 1908, and married the Russian artist Sonia Terk (who became known as Sonia Delaunay) in 1910 when his work began to be influenced by Cézanne's painting and the Cubism of Picasso and Braque. While in Paris they became associated with the Blaue Reiter and Orphism groups, and Delaunay's name became synonymous with Simultanism. Delaunay was a close friend of the poets Guillaume Apollinaire and Blaise Cendrars. He lived in Spain and Portugal between 1914 and 1920, and was set-designer for Diaghilev's ballet Cleopatra *(1918). He returned to Paris in 1920. In the 1920s he was connected with literary Dadaism and Surrealism, and painted portraits of writers such as Tristan Tzara and Philippe Soupault, and he also worked with Sonia Delaunay on the decor of a number of films. The Delaunays, passionate advocates of public art, were commissioned to organise the decoration of the Railway Pavilion and the Pavilion of the Air at the 1937 Paris International Exhibition. Reproduced below are two short pieces, both written in 1912. 'Light' was first published in German in* Der Sturm *(1913) and appears here in a translation by Gustav Vriesen and Max Imdahl from* Robert Delaunay: Light and Colour *(1969). 'Notes on the Construction of the Reality of Pure Painting' (translated by Sherry A. Buckberrough, 1957) was first published as 'Reality, Pure Painting' in* Der Sturm *(1912).*

'Light'

Impressionism is the birth of *Light* in painting.

Light reaches us through our perception.

Without visual perception, no light, no movement.

Light in Nature creates movement of colors.

The movement is provided by the relationships *of uneven measures*, of color contrasts among themselves and [it] constitutes *Reality.*

This reality is endowed with *Depth* (we see as far as the stars), and thus becomes *rhythmic Simultaneity.*

Simultaneity in light is *the harmony, the rhythm of colors* which creates *Men's Sight.*

Human sight is endowed with the greatest Reality since it comes to us directly from contemplation of the Universe.

The Eye is our highest sense, the one that communicates most closely with our *brain, our consciousness*, the idea of the vital movement of the *world*, and *its movement is simultaneity.*

Our comprehension is correlative with our *perception. Let us try to see.*

Auditory perception does not suffice for our knowledge of the Universe; it has no *depth.*

Its movement is *successive*, it is a kind of mechanism; *its principle is the time of mechanical* clocks which, like them, has no relation to our perception *of visual movement in the Universe.*

This is the evenness of things in geometry.

Its character makes it resemble *the Object conceived geometrically.*

The *Object* is not endowed with *Life*, with movement.

When it has the *appearance of movement*, it becomes *successive, dynamic.*

Its greatest limitation is of a *practical order. Vehicles.*

The railroad is *the image* of this successiveness

which resembles *parallels: the evenness of Track.*

So with Architecture, Sculpture.

The mightiest object on Earth is subject to these same laws.

It will become the appearance of height:

The Eiffel Tower;

of breadth:

Cities;

length:

Tracks.

Art in *Nature is rhythmic and abhors constraint.*

If art is attached *to the Object*, it becomes *descriptive, divisive, literary.*

It lowers itself to imperfect *means of expression*, it condemns itself of its own accord, it is its own negation, *it does not break free of imitative Art.*

If likewise it represents *the visual relationships* of an object or *between objects* without *light playing the role of governing the representation.*

It is conventional, it does not achieve *plastic purity*; it is a *weakness*; it is the negation of life, of *the sublimity of the Art of painting.*

For Art to reach the limits of sublimity, it must approach our *harmonic Vision: clarity*.

Clarity will be color, proportions; these proportions are composed of various simultaneous measures within an action.

This action must be representative harmony, *the synchromatic movement (simultaneity) of light*, which is the *only reality*.

This synchromatic action will then be the Subject which is the representative harmony.

'Notes on the Construction of the Reality of Pure Painting'

Realism is the eternal quality in all the arts which necessarily determines beauty and its permanence, and which is sufficient for that.

Let us seek purity of means in painting, the clearest expression of beauty.

In impressionism – and I include in that term all the tendencies that reacted to it: neo-impressionism, precubism, neocubism, in other words, everything that represents technique and scientific procedure – we find ourselves face to face with nature, far from all the correctness of styles, whether Italian, Gothic, African, or any other.

From this point of view, impressionism is undeniably a victory, but an incomplete one. The first stammer of souls brimming over in the face of nature, and still somewhat stunned by this great reality. Their enthusiasm has done away with all the false ideas and archaic procedures of traditional painting (draftsmanship, geometry, perspective, etc . . . all the neo-classical, moribund, pseudo-intellectual academy . . .)

One can date the movement of liberation back to the impressionists with their precursors: El Greco, a few English painters, and our own revolutionary Delacroix. It was a great period of preparation in the search for the only reality: 'light', which finally brought all these experiments and reactions together.

One of the major problems of modern painting today is still the way in which the light that is necessary to all vital expressions of beauty functions. It was Seurat who discovered the 'contrast of complementaries' in light.

Seurat was one of the first theoreticians of light. Contrast became a means of expression. His premature death broke the continuity of his discoveries. Among the impressionists, he may be considered the one who attained the ultimate in means of expression.

His creation remains the discovery of the contrast of complementary colors. (Optical blending by means of dots, used by Seurat and his associates, was only a technique; it did not yet have the importance of contrasts used as a means of construction in order to arrive at pure expression.)

He used this first means to arrive at a specific representation of nature. His paintings are kinds of fleeting images.

Simultaneous contrast was not discovered, that is to say, achieved, by the most daring impressionists; yet it is the only basis of pure expression in painting today.

Means of expression must not be personal; on the contrary, they must be within the comprehension of every intuition of the beautiful, and an artist's *métier* must be of the same nature as his plastic representation.

The simultaneity of colors through simultaneous contrasts and through all the (uneven) quantities that emanate from the colors, in accordance with the way they are expressed in the movement represented – that is the only reality one can construct through painting.

We are no longer dealing here either with effects (impressionism and neo-impressionism, Claude Monet, Sisley, Renoir, Pissarro, etc ...), or with objects (impressionism, cubism, Derain, Picasso, Braque, Metzinger, etc ...) or with images (impressionism, neocubism, Gleizes, Fauconnier, Herbin, H. Rousseau, Seurat, Cézanne, P. Gauguin, Signac, H. Matisse, etc ...).

We are attaining a purely expressive art, one that excludes all the styles of the past, archaic, geometric, and is becoming a plastic art with only one purpose: to inspire human nature toward beauty (neither literature, nor technique, nor procedure).

Light is not a method, it slides toward us, it is communicated to us by our sensibility.

Without the perception of light (the eye) there can be no movement.

Our eyes are the windows between our nature and our soul. Our eyes are the receptacles of the present and, therefore, of our sensibility. We can't do anything without sensibility, without light. Consequently, our soul finds its most perfect sensation of life in harmony, and this harmony results only from the simultaneity with which the quantities and the conditions of light reach the soul (the supreme sense) by the intermediary of the eyes. And the soul judges the forms of the image of nature by comparison with the artifice of painting.

The creator takes note of everything that exists in the universe through entity, succession, imagination, and simultaneity.

Nature, therefore, engenders the science of painting.

The first paintings were simply a line encircling the shadow of a man made by the sun on the surface of the earth.

But how far removed we are, with our contemporary means, from these effigies – we who possess light (light colors, dark colors, their complementaries, their intervals, and their simultaneity) and all the quantities of colors emanating from the intellect to create harmony.

Harmony is sensibility ordered by the creator, who must try to render the greatest degree of realistic expression, or what might be called the subject.

The subject is harmonic proportion, and this proportion is composed of various simultaneous elements in a single action.

The subject is eternal in the work of art, and it must be apparent to the initiated in all its order, all its science.

Without the subject, there are no possibilities. This does not, however, mean a literary and, therefore, anecdotic subject; the subject of painting is exclusively plastic, and it results from vision. It must be the pure expression of human nature.

The eternal subject is to be found in nature itself: the inspiration and clear vision characteristic of the wise man, who discovers the most beautiful and powerful boundaries.

9
ERIK SATIE (1866–1925)
'THE MUSICIAN'S DAY' 1913;
'SOME NOTES ON MODERN MUSIC' 1919

French composer. Having abandoned his studies at the Paris Conservatoire, Satie worked for many years as a café pianist. His involvement with the Rosicrucian movement inspired several compositions, most notably Mass of the Poor *(1895). Satie's sparse, witty style represented a reaction against the dominant French Romanticism and Impressionism and is closely linked to the Surrealist and Dadaist movements in art. Much of his music abandons traditional tonal form and structure and is harmonically inventive. His manuscripts often lack key signatures or barlines and give eccentric, parodic directions to players. Satie's ballet* Parade *– scored in part for typewriters, ticker tape and a lottery wheel – was produced in 1917. It was in his programme notes to this work that Apollinaire first used the term 'Surrealism'. The short pieces which follow were written in 1913 and 1919 respectively and were translated by Nigel Wilkins for his 1980 edition of* The Writings of Eric Satie.

The Musician's Day

An artist must organize his life.

Here is the exact timetable of my daily activities:

Get up: 7.18 am; be inspired: 10.23 to 11.47 am. I take lunch at 12.11 pm and leave the table at 12.14 pm.

Healthy horse-riding, out in my grounds: 1.19 to 2.53 pm. More inspiration: 3.12 to 4.07 pm.

Various activities (fencing, reflection, immobility, visits, contemplation, swimming, etc. . . .): 4.21 to 6.47 pm.

Dinner is served at 7.16 and ends at 7.20 pm. Then come symphonic readings, out loud: 8.09 to 9.59 pm.

I go to bed regularly at 10.37 pm. Once a week (on Tuesdays) I wake up with a start at 3.19 am.

I eat only white foodstuffs: eggs, sugar, scraped bones; fat from dead animals; veal, salt, coconuts, chicken cooked in white water; mouldy fruit, rice, turnips; camphorated sausage, things like spaghetti, cheese (white), cotton salad and certain fish (minus their skins).

I boil my wine and drink it cold mixed with fuchsia juice. I have a good appetite, but never talk while eating, for fear of strangling myself.

I breathe carefully (a little at a time). I very rarely dance. When I walk, I hold my sides and look rigidly behind me.

Serious in appearance, if I laugh it is not on purpose. I always apologize about it nicely.

My sleep is deep, but I keep one eye open. My bed is round, with a hole cut out to let my head through. Once every hour a servant takes my temperature and gives me another.

I have long subscribed to a fashion magazine. I wear a white bonnet, white stockings and a white waistcoat.

My doctor has always told me to smoke. Part of his advice runs:

– Smoke away, my dear chap: if you don't, someone else will.

Some Notes on Modern Music

In order to combat 'advanced' ideas in Politics or in Art, all means are justified – especially underhand means. 'New' artists – those who 'change something' – have always suffered attacks from their enemies who wage war on the newness of trends – and visions – which they cannot understand.

In Art as in Politics: Jaurès was attacked in the same way as Manet, Berlioz, Wagner, Picasso, Verlaine and so many others. That is always 'starting up' again and it is always the same people who resist Progress in all its shapes and forms: the upholders of the 'status quo', the good folk who 'know what they like'.

In this newspaper I wish to speak up for some of my musical comrades who belong to 'advanced' circles. It seemed proper and useful to do it here, in a setting for which I have much sympathy and where I feel at home. Isn't it natural for an 'advanced' artist to be 'advanced' in Politics? Isn't yes the answer?

Well, my friends, that is rare – very rare I would say, if I dared, and more rare than you could possibly imagine. So, M. Saint-Saëns – that great patriot – had his moment of 'advancement'. It is true that this moment of 'advancement' was not yesterday, nor even the day before yesterday. We know what M. Saint-Saëns has done for all kinds of musicians. Ah! that splendid M. Saint-Saëns is no 'good chap'. How well he knows how to put into practice the saying: *All for me, nothing for the others*. What a charming man! And he does not like socialists. Still, it's better that way. Don't you think so?

Politically and socially, Debussy was far from having the same rugged approach that he had musically. This Revolutionary in Art was very bourgeois in daily life. He was not keen on 'eight-hour days' or other social changes, I can assure you. Raising salaries – except his own, of course – was not something which pleased him. He had his 'point of view'. A strange anomaly.

I must tell you – and it gives me much pleasure to do so – that the 'young' musicians share our opinions much more. They 'are coming along'. They are not frightened by what we seek. That is a step forward – don't you agree? They can see that artistic aspirations should match their social attitudes.

But who are these 'young' musicians deserving of your attention?

In the next edition of 'notes', I shall tell you about these 'youngsters'; I shall tell you what they have written; I shall tell you where you can hear their works; and I shall be happy if my efforts can encourage the development of musical culture in our great socialist family, a delightful family that I love wholeheartedly.

10
PERCY WYNDHAM LEWIS (1882–1957)
FROM 'THE CUBIST ROOM' 1914

English writer and artist. Born in Canada, Lewis moved to London in 1893 where he won a scholarship to the Slade School of Art. After some years in Paris he returned to London to begin writing stories and exhibit paintings. In 1914 he founded the avant-garde, Vorticist journal Blast. *He served as an artillery officer in the First World War and published his first novel,* Tarr, *in 1918. Lewis's Modernist* oeuvre *carries a strong critical, Nietzschean and satirical inflection, apparent in novels like* The Apes of God *(1930, a mockery of fashionable, art-conscious 1920s London), and* The Revenge for Love *(1937, a political satire in the context of the Spanish Civil War). His numerous political and critical writings appeared in volumes such as* The Art of Being Ruled *(1925),* Time and Western Man *(1927) and* Men Without Art *(1934). Lewis spent the years of the Second World War in the USA and Canada, and later worked as art critic for* The Listener. *The following piece appeared in* The Egoist, *January 1st, 1914. [See IIb 1a, 7]*

Futurism, one of the alternative terms for modern painting, was patented in Milan. It means the Present with the Past rigidly excluded, and flavoured strongly with H. G. Wells' dreams of the dance of monstrous and arrogant Machinery, to the frenzied clapping of men's hands. But Futurism will never mean anything else, in painting, than the art practised by the five or six Italian painters grouped beneath Marinetti's influence. Gino Severini, the foremost of them, has for subject matter the night resorts of Paris. This, as subject matter, is obviously not of the future. For we all foresee in a century or so everybody being put to bed at 7 o'clock in the evening by a State Nurse. Therefore the Pan Pan at the Monaco will be, for Ginos of the Future, an archaistic experience.

Cubism means, chiefly, the art, superbly severe and so far morose, of those who have taken the genius of Cézanne as a starting point, and organised the character of the works he threw up in his indiscriminate and grand labour. It is the reconstruction of a simpler earth, left as choked and muddy fragments by him. Cubism includes much more than this, but the 'cube' is implicit in that master's painting.

To be done with terms and tags, post impressionism is an insipid and pointless name invented by a journalist, which has been naturally ousted by the better word 'Futurism' in public debate on modern art.

This room is chiefly composed of works by a group of painters, consisting of Frederick Etchells, Cuthbert Hamilton, Edward Wadsworth, C. R. W. Nevinson, and the writer of this foreword. These painters are not accidentally associated here, but form a vertigineous but not exotic island, in the placid and respectable archipelago of English art. This formation is undeniably of volcanic matter, and even origin; for it appeared suddenly above the waves following certain seismic shakings beneath the surface. It is very closely-knit and admirably adapted to withstand the imperturbable Britannic breakers which roll pleasantly against its sides.

Beneath the Past and the Future the most sanguine would hardly expect a more different skeleton to exist than that respectively of ape and man. Man with an aeroplane is still merely a bad bird. But a man who passes his days amid the rigid lines of houses, a plague of cheap ornamentation, noisy street locomotion, the Bedlam of the press, will evidently possess a different habit of vision to a man living amongst the lines of a landscape. As to turning the back, most wise men, Egyptians, Chinese or what not, have remained where they found themselves, their appetite for life sufficient to reconcile them, and allow them to create significant things. Suicide is the obvious course for the dreamer, who is a man without an anchor of sufficient weight.

The work of this group of artists for the most part underlines such geometric bases and structure of life, and they would spend their energies rather in showing a different skeleton and abstraction than formerly could exist than a different degree of hairiness or dress. All revolutionary painting to-day has in common the rigid reflections of steel and stone in the spirit of the artist; that desire for stability as though a machine were being built to fly or kill with; an alienation from the traditional photographer's trade and realisation of the value of colour and form as such independently of what recognisable form it covers or encloses. People are invited, in short, to change entirely their idea of the painter's mission, and penetrate, deferentially, with him into a transposed universe as abstract as, though different from, the musicians.

[. . .]

11
KARL KRAUS (1874–1936)
FROM 'IN THESE GREAT TIMES' 1914

Reproduced below are extracts from one of Kraus's polemical, satirical pieces from Die Fackel, *1914. This translation is from Harry Zohn (ed.),* In These Great Times: A Karl Kraus Reader, *1984. [See Ia 21]*

In these great times which I knew when they were this small; which will become small again, provided they have time left for it; and which, because in the realm of organic growth no such transformation is possible, we had better call fat times and, truly, hard times as well; in these times in which things are happening that could not be imagined and in which what can no longer be *imagined* must *happen*, for if one could imagine it, it would not happen; in these serious times which have died laughing at the thought that they might become serious; which, surprised by their own tragedy, are reaching for diversion and, catching themselves redhanded, are groping for words; in these loud times which boom with the horrible symphony of actions which produce reports and of reports which cause actions: in these times you should not expect any words of my own from me – none but these words which barely manage to prevent silence from being misinterpreted. Respect for the immutability, the subordination of language before this misfortune is too deeply rooted in me. In the realm of poverty of imagination where people die of spiritual famine without feeling spiritual hunger, where pens are dipped in blood and swords in ink, that which is not thought must be done, but that which is only thought is unutterable. Expect no words of my own from me. Nor would I be able to say anything new, for in the room in which one writes there is such noise, and at this time one should not determine whether it comes from animals, from children, or merely from mortars. He who encourages deeds with words desecrates words and deeds and is doubly despicable. This occupation is not extinct. Those who now have nothing to say because actions are speaking continue to talk. Let him who has something to say come forward and be silent!

[. . .]

For me (the insatiable one who does not have sacrifices enough), the line commanded by fate has not been reached. For me it is war only if only those who are unfit are sent off to it. Otherwise my peace has no peace; I secretly prepare for the great times and think thoughts that I can tell only to the Good Lord and not to the good state which now does not permit me to tell it that it is too tolerant. For if the state does not now have the idea of choking off the so-called freedom of the press, which does not notice a few white spots, then it never will; and if I were to put this into its head, the state would do violence to the idea, and my text would be the only victim. So I shall have to wait, though I am the only Austrian who cannot wait but would like to see the end of the world replaced by a simple auto-da-fé. The idea which I should like to put into the heads of the actual holders of nominal power is only an *idée fixe* of mine. But an unstable state of ownership, that of a state and of a civilized world, is saved by such fixed ideas

[. . .]

I am of the opinion that, things being the way they are, it would be better if people did not come into the world at all, I am an eccentric. But if I maintain that under such circumstances no one will come into the world in the future and that at a later date boot-heels may come into the world but without the persons to go with them, because they were not able to keep pace with their own development and stayed behind as the last obstacle to their progress – if I maintain this sort of thing, I am a fool who deduces the whole condition from a symptom, the plague from a bubo. If I were not a fool but an educated man, I would draw such bold conclusions from a bacillus and not from a bubo, and people would believe me. How foolish to say that one should confiscate the bubo to rid oneself of the plague! But I am truly of the opinion that in this time, however we may call it or evaluate it, whether it is out of joint or already set right, whether it is accumulating murder and rottenness before the eyes of a Hamlet or is already becoming ripe for the arm of a Fortinbras – that in its condition the root lies at the surface. This sort of thing can be made clear by a great confusion, and what was once paradoxical is now confirmed by the great times. Since I am neither a politician nor his half-brother, an esthete, I would not dream of denying the necessity of anything that is happening or of complaining that mankind does not know how to die in beauty. I know full well that cathedrals are rightfully bombarded by people if they are rightfully used by people as military posts. 'No offence i' the world', says Hamlet. But the jaws of hell gape at this question: When will the greater period of the war begin, the war of cathedrals against people? I know very well that at times it is necessary to transform markets into battlefields so that these might turn into markets again. But one cloudy day people will see things more clearly and ask whether it is right to miss not a single step on the direct road away from God, and whether the eternal mystery from which man originates and the mystery into which he enters really encompass only a business secret that gives man superiority over man and even over man's maker. Someone who wants to expand ownership and someone who merely defends it – both live in a state of ownership, always below and never above ownership. One declares it, the other one explains it. Are we not afraid of something superior to ownership when unparalleled human victims have been seen and suffered, and when behind the language of spiritual uplift, after the intoxicating music has died away, this confession breaks through between earthly and heavenly hosts one grey morning: 'What the traveling salesmen must do now is keep putting out their feelers and feeling out their customers!' Mankind consists of customers. Behind flags and flames, heroes and helpers, behind all fatherlands an altar has been erected at which pious science wrings its hands: God created the consumer! Yet God did not create the consumer that he might prosper on earth but for something higher: that the dealer might prosper on earth, for the consumer was created naked and becomes a dealer only when he sells clothes. The necessity to eat in order to live cannot be disputed philosophically, though the public nature of this function evidences an ineradicable lack of modesty. Culture is the tacit agreement to let the means of subsistence disappear behind the purpose of existence. Civilization is the subordination of the latter to the former. This is the ideal that progress serves, and to this ideal it supplies its armaments. Progress lives to eat, and at times supplies proof that it can even die to eat. It endures hardship so that it may prosper.

It applies pathos to the premises. The utmost affirmation of progress has long since decreed that demand be governed by supply, that we eat so that another person might get his fill, and that a peddler interrupt even our thinking when he offers us what we do not happen to need. Progress, under whose feet the grass mourns and the forest turns into paper from which newspaper plants grow, has subordinated the purpose of life to the means of subsistence and turned us into the nuts and bolts for our tools. The tooth of time is hollow; for when it was sound, there came the hand that lives on fillings. Where all energy has been expended to make life frictionless, nothing remains that still needs such care. In such a region individuality can live, but can no longer be born. With its emotional desires it may be a guest where it will be surrounded by automata pushing past and forward in comfort and prosperity without face and greeting. As a referee between natural values it will make a different decision. It will certainly not opt for this country's supineness, which has saved its intellectual life for the promotion of its merchandise, has surrendered to a romanticization of foodstuffs, and has placed 'art in the service of the businessman'. The decision is between spiritual power and horsepower. After the hustle and bustle of business no breed will realize its full potential; at best it will be fit for pleasure. The tyranny of necessity grants its slaves three kinds of freedom; opinion free from intellect, entertainment free from art, and orgies free from love. Thank God there are still goods that get stuck when freight is supposed to be constantly rolling. For in the final analysis, civilization does live on culture. If the horrible voice which these days is allowed to outshout the commands urges traveling salesmen in the language of its obtrusive phantasm to put out their feelers and feel out their customers through the gunsmoke; if in the face of unheard-of things it brings itself to make the heroic decision to claim the battlefields for the hyenas, then it possesses some of that dreary sincerity with which the *Zeitgeist* grins at its martyrs. All right, we are sacrificing ourselves for ready-made goods; we are consumers and live in such a way that the means may consume the end. All right, if a torpedo is useful to us, let it be more permissible to curse God than to curse a torpedo! And necessities which a world gone astray in the labyrinth of economies has set for itself demand their martyrs; and the ghastly editorial writer of passions, the registering Jewish plutocrat, the man who sits at the cash register of world history collects victories and daily records the turnover in blood. The tenor of his couplings and headlines which shriek with greed for profit is such that he claims the number of dead and wounded and prisoners as assets; sometimes he confuses mine and thine with mines and times; but gently underlining his modesty and perhaps in keeping with impressions gleaned from circles in the know, and without abandoning his power of imagination, he permits himself to make a strategic distinction between 'laymen's questions and laymen's answers'. And if he then ventures to pronounce a blessing on the so very gratifying upsurge of heroic feelings, to send his greetings and best wishes to the army and to cheer up his 'good soldiers' in the jargon of efficiency as though it were the end of a satisfying day at the stock exchange, there is allegedly 'only one voice' which takes umbrage at it, truly only one that is uttering it today – but what good is it when there is just this one voice whose echo ought to be nothing less than a storm of the elements rebelling at the spectacle of a time which has the courage to call itself great and does not issue an ultimatum to such a champion!

The surface is at the root and sticks to it. The subjugation of mankind to the economy has left it only the freedom of hostility; and if progress sharpened its weapons, it created for mankind the most murderous weapon of all, one that relieved it, beyond its sacred necessity, of its last concern about its spiritual salvation: the press. Progress, which also has logic at its disposal, replies that the press is nothing but one of the professional associations that subsist on an existing need. But if this is as true as it is correct, and if the press is nothing other than an imprint of life, then I know what the score is, for I know what this life is like. And then it happens to occur to me, it becomes clear to me on a cloudy day, that life is only an imprint of the press. If I learned to underestimate life in the days of progress, I was bound to overestimate the press. What is it? Just a messenger? One who also bothers us with his opinion? Who torments us with his impressions? Who brings the mental image along with the fact? Who tortures us almost to death with his detailed reports about the atmosphere or with his perceptions of observations of minute details, and with his constant repetition of the whole? Who drags behind himself a train of informed, knowledgeable, sophisticated, outstanding personalities who are supposed to accredit him and agree with him – important parasites on the superfluous? Is the press a messenger? No, it is the event itself. A speech? No, life itself. It not only lays claim to the real events being its news *about* the events; it also creates this uncanny identity which always makes it seem that actions are reported before they are performed, often the mere possibility of an action, and in any case it produces a situation in which war correspondents are not permitted to observe, but warriors are turned into reporters. In this sense I do not mind if people say that all my life I have overestimated the press. It is not a messenger (how could a messenger demand and receive so much?); it is the event itself. Once again the instrument has got the better of us. We have raised the person whose job it is to announce a conflagration – and who probably ought to play the most subordinate role in the state – above the world, above the fire and above the house, above reality and above our imagination. But we, like Cleopatra, curious and disappointed, ought to beat the messenger for his message.

[...]

Through decades of practice he has produced in mankind that degree of unimaginativeness which enables it to wage a war of extermination against itself. Since the unlimited promptness of his machinery has made it unnecessary for mankind to have any ability to experience and to extend experience intellectually, the reporter can only just manage to instil into it that death-defying courage with which mankind is rushing into this war. He has the reflected glory of heroic qualities at his disposal, and his misused language beautifies a misused life – as though eternity had saved its apex for the age in which the reporter lives. But do people have any idea what life the newspaper expresses? A life that has long been an expression of *it!* Do people realize just what half a century owes to this loosed intelligence in the way of murdered intellect, plundered nobility, and desecrated holiness? Does anyone know what vital resources the Sunday belly of such a rotary beast has swallowed up before it can appear 250 pages thick? Do people stop to think how much had to be systematically spent on telegrams, telephones, and photographs to teach a society which was still open to inner possibilities that broad astonishment at the tiniest fact which finds its clichés in the horrid language of these messengers when 'groups formed' somewhere or the public began to 'mass'? Since all of modern life has been subsumed under a quantity which is no longer measured but has always been attained – a quantity that finally will have no other recourse but to swallow itself – since the self-evident record leaves no more room for doubt and the painful completeness makes any further calculation unnecessary, the consequence is that, exhausted by this multiplicity, we no longer have any use for the result. Accordingly, at a time when twice a day and in twenty repetitions we are served up impressions of the impressions of all externals, the great quantity breaks down into individual fates which only the individuals perceive, so that suddenly the unbegrudged hero's death, even in the vanguard, is declared a cruel fate. But some day people might find out what a trifling matter such a world war was as compared to the intellectual self-mutilation of mankind by means of its press and how at bottom it constituted only one of the press's emanations. A few decades ago, Bismarck, who also overestimated the press, was still able to recognize that 'what the sword has gained for us Germans is spoiled by the press' and impute to the press the blame for three wars. Today the connections between catastrophes and editorial offices are far more profound and hence less clear. For in the age of those who live through it, deeds are stronger than words, but the echo is stronger than the deed. We live on the echo, and in this topsy-turvy world the echo arouses the call.

[...]

Certainly, all of us are primarily dependent on the interests of this one business. If one reads a newspaper only for information, one does not learn the truth, not even the truth about the paper. The truth is that the newspaper is not a statement of contents but the contents themselves; and more than that, it is an instigator. If it prints lies about horrors, these turn into horrors. There is more injustice in the world because there is a press which fabricated it and deplores it! It is not nations that strike one another; rather, it is the international disgrace, the profession which rules the world not despite its irresponsibility but by virtue of it, that deals wounds, tortures prisoners, baits foreigners, and turns gentlemen into rowdies. Its only authority is its unprincipledness, which, in association with a rascally will, can change printer's ink directly into blood. O last, unholy wonder of the times! At first everything was a lie, and they always lied so that lies might be told only elsewhere; but now, thrown into the neurasthenia of hatred, everything is true. There are various nations, but there is only one press. The newspaper dispatch is an instrument of war like a grenade, which has no consideration for circumstances either. You believe, but they know better, and you have to pay dearly for your belief. The heroes of obtrusiveness, people with whom no soldier would lie down in the trenches, though he has to submit to being interviewed by them, break into recently abandoned royal castles so that they can report, 'We got there first!' It would be far less shameful to be paid for committing atrocities than for fabricating them. The bravoes of this sphere of activity sit at home, unless they have the good fortune to tell anecdotes in the correspondents' quarters or be pushy right up to the front, and they teach fear to the nations day after day until these have some justification really to feel fear. Of the quantity which is the substance of this time each of us gets a share that he processes emotionally, and the telegraph wires and the cinema screen make what we have in common so graphic to us that we go home contented.

But if the reporter has killed our imagination with his truth, he threatens our life with his lies. His imagination is the cruelest substitute for the imagination we once had. For if one side claims that the other side kills women and children, both sides believe it and do it. Don't people yet feel that the word of an undisciplined creature, usable in the days of military discipline, carries farther than a mortar and that the spiritual fortresses of these times are structures that will collapse in an emergency? If the states had the discernment to settle for universal conscription and do without wire dispatches, a world war, truly, would be milder. And if before the outbreak of such a war they had the courage to drive the representatives of the other trade together at an internationally agreed upon carrion-pit, who knows – the nations might be spared it. But before journalists and the diplomats they use disarm, human beings have to pay the price.

[. . .]

Never before has there been such a rush to join up with banality, and the sacrifice of the leading intellects is so rapid as to give rise to the suspicion that they had no self to sacrifice but acted on the heroic desire to save themselves where it is now safest: in clichéland. But the really sad thing is that literature does not feel its obtrusiveness nor the superiority of the common man who finds in clichés the experience that is his due. To seek rhymes, and bad ones, to express the enthusiasm of others, to welcome troops with whoops, confirm that a mob will rob, and condemn those who pillage a village is surely the paltriest achievement that society can expect of its intellects in hard times. The unarticulated sounds that have reached us from enemy poets at least evidence individual feelings of excitement which reduce an artist to a private person with national limitations. At least they were the poem that the uproar of actualities made of the poets. The reproach of barbarism in wartime was false information. But the barbarism in peacetime which is ready to rhyme when things get serious and which turns someone else's experience into an editorial is an inexpungible disgrace.

[. . .]

Perhaps even the smallest war has always been an action that cleansed the surface and had an effect on the inside. What effect does this great war have which is great by virtue of the forces against which the greatest war ought to be waged? Is it a redemption or only the end? Or is it only a continuation? May the consequences of this extensive affair be no worse than its concomitants which it did not have the strength to kick away! May it never happen that emptiness throws its weight around even more than before as it refers to the hardships it has endured; that idleness gains glory; that pettiness appeals to the world-historical background; and that the hand that reaches into our pocket first shows us its scars.

[. . .]

May the times grow great enough not to fall prey to a victor who places his heel on the intellect and the economy, great enough to overcome the nightmare of the opportunity to have a victory redound to the credit of those uninvolved in it, the opportunity for wrongheaded chasers after decorations in peacetime to divest themselves of what honor they have left, for utter stupidity to discard foreign words and names of dishes, and for slaves whose ultimate goal all their lives has been the 'mastery' of languages henceforth to desire to get around in the world with the ability *not* to master languages! What do you who are in the war know about the war?! You are fighting! You have not remained behind! Even those who have sacrificed their ideals to life will some day have the privilege of sacrificing life itself. May the times grow so great that they measure up to these sacrifices and never so great that they transcend their memory as they grow into life!

12
RICHARD HUELSENBECK
FROM 'ZURICH 1916, AS IT REALLY WAS' 1928

German writer, later a psychoanalyst in New York. Along with Hugo Ball, Hans Arp, Tristan Tzara and Marcel Janco, fellow pacifists and expatriate artists, Huelsenbeck was the co-founder of Cabaret Voltaire, the little café and meeting place of the Dada movement, in Zurich in 1916. The following year he brought Dada to Berlin where the movement assumed political and revolutionary features. In the following extract from a 1928 piece (originally published in Die Neue Bücherschau, *Vol. 6, 12), Huelsenbeck writes about the increasing politicisation of Dada and the growing distance between the Zurich and Berlin movements. The piece appears in J. M. Ritchie's translation, from* The Era of German Expressionism *(ed. Paul Raabe, 1974). [See IIb 6]*

I first met Hugo Ball in Munich in 1912. He was then dramaturg with the Kammerspiele. He immediately impressed me by his superior intelligence and his profound knowledge of things. We became friends. With the help of Hans Leybold and Klabund we founded the *Revolution*, which was our form of resistance to Imperial

Germany. Ball wrote a poem against the Virgin Mary which brought about the journal's downfall. Several law-suits were launched against us and we were scheduled for the same fate as Panizza. But they failed to realize that we were much younger, more resilient and aggressive. Invective, threats, bureaucratic unpleasantness poured off our backs. The measures taken against us could never be as bad as our worst imaginings. We knew the 'blimps' and bureaucratic antiques behind their desks and ink-wells before they even let fly at us with their decrees. No verdict against us could match the level of hatred we felt for them. It's still interesting that it was Ball who wrote against the Virgin Mary. Later, in Ticino, he would have considered it a deadly sin, but in Munich he would have nothing to do with religion.

Shortly before the outbreak of war we met in Berlin. If I'm not mistaken, Ball was editor of Reclam's *Universum* at the time. Or maybe it was some other illustrated journal. The life he led was miserable, but he was unremitting in his efforts to grasp the intellectual values and underlying spirit of the age. When war broke out our hatred for official Germany and everything associated with it changed into a kind of paroxysm of rage. We couldn't see a uniform without clenching our fists. We considered our most practical course. Revolutionary resistance to the well-oiled war machines would have been madness, Pfemfert's *Aktion* could offer some intellectual consolations, it is true, but no way to freedom. My reaction against the 'spirit' which I identified with Imperial German post-classical culture began. Side by side with the sabre-swinging officers strode the German University Professor, a volume of Goethe clutched to his heart like a charm. The Manifesto of the German Men of Letters seemed to me the height of hypocrisy. It is completely grotesque to reproach us and say we should have worked for the proletariat then, for there was no proletarian organization, legal or illegal. For the pure-minded pacifist there was only one solution: to leave a country whose actions and politics one could not accept. Was Germany guilty of starting the war? No? Then stay in your country and fight. Is she guilty? Yes? Then leave for Switzerland and try to deepen your knowledge of the situation from a neutral standpoint and take action when the time comes. To a certain extent we were misinformed because we thought Germany and its leaders at the time far more cunning than they really were. We thought it was all cold calculation, we saw the Emperor, the Victory Allee, the gleaming uniforms, the Krupp factories, we heard the demand to shoot at fathers and brothers and we sensed a deep-seated plot aimed at all the fundamental values of humanity. We saw the Generals as a kind of intellectual advance party of the Devil. We dragged men who were probably mindless idiots up to our own level and made them morally responsible.

On the other hand, we considered it morally right, valuable, and absolutely essential to turn our back on Germany because for one reason it was dangerous to do so. Anybody could let himself be called up and keep up a stream of critical comment. But they did nothing to stop the war machine. Our aim was to record our insight into the real causes of the war. Often we were unsure. Was it really Germany's fault? Is it possible for a country, such a great country and one that was our spiritual fatherland after all, to set the world alight? In Zurich a pamphlet appeared which claimed to have proved this beyond the shadow of a doubt. Not *Entente* propaganda. A German had sat down and written a confession of the things he knew. It shatters me to this day when I think how anguished we were over the truth. Bowed down and heavy with such ideas we arrived in a city in which the scum of international profiteering had begun to settle. I saw very little of the Swiss themselves during the war. We had the feeling they didn't like us, that they felt we might disturb their peace, and the really important things we had to say ran completely counter to what they thought. Among the whores, speculators and *petit bourgeois* (who gaped with red-rimmed eyes at the relaxed moral standards) moved the uniforms of captured French and German officers. When they became aware of each other they went as stiff as ramrods, but they still saluted each other. That made a deep impression on us.

And would it have been better for us to join a workers' organization instead of founding a cabaret? Anybody who argues in this way knows nothing of the conditions as they were then in Zurich and reveals a surprising lack of insight into the human psyche.

[. . .]

I have never been a politician and even today I don't see myself as one. I am simply not cut out to be one. My *métier* is writing; there will always be people like that. I'm in favour of everybody realizing what he is capable of and pursuing what he is best at. This seems to me a fundamental principle which cannot be qualified by any political or economic theory, it's more of a precept of human tolerance without which relationships between men are wicked, unbearable and morally perverted. I have no reason for holding back with my confession of faith. I shall never deny that I am a Socialist, but my socialism has a humane basis. I am what orthodox party members contemptuously call an 'emotional Communist'. I have an inherent watchful instinct that protects against anything brutal, mean and socially unjust.

[. . .]

In those days I associated with the Cabaret Voltaire and Dadaism because I realized that some form of cultural protest (and Dadaism was never anything more) was necessary and that this was where I could accomplish something. I devoted myself to Dadaism first in Zurich and later in Germany with such intensity that it undermined my health and my so-called literary career. That was no joke. In the term Dada we concentrated all the rage, contempt, superiority and human revolutionary protest we were capable of. Had I joined a political party, no matter which, I should have accomplished far less at the time. After all, several million people must have heard the word Dada resounding in their ears and a few tens of thousands must have realized that Dada was the ironic and contemptuous response to a culture which had shown itself worthy of flame-throwers and machine-guns.

Ball's case is much more difficult. While I grew more and more convinced that the world should and could be changed, Ball believed that no compromise could be found between the feeling for what was right and just and the force necessary to bring about social order.

[. . .]

That Ball should call his Cabaret 'Voltaire' indicated that he was obsessed by cultural criticism. He fought Germany and Protestantism because he considered these powers unethical, socially inferior and culturally corrupt. He detected a connection between Protestantism and Hegelianism and became suspicious of all exploiters of dialectics as a result. He dreamed his way into a spiritual sphere which, knowing neither 'yes' nor 'no', had room for the absolute.

[. . .]

The Cabaret Voltaire in which Dadaism was born was nothing like the usual run of crude comedy (this is the picture our latter-day critics seem to have of it); no, it was a cultural platform on which everybody could give free expression to his opinion. Germany has never seen anything like it. Even if only for the reason that no deals were made there.

[. . .]

Zurich 1916 as it really was? It was exactly like our ideas. There weren't any Swiss around in Zurich in those days. There were crooks, whores, international rabble and our spiritual hunger for truth. Were there any workers' organizations? Yes! A totally fossilized, scared Social Democrat Party, no Communists. A group of discontented Social Democrats who gathered round the 'rebel', Brupbacher, who in those days called himself an anarchist and who is now a Communist member of parliament. We had contacts with all of them, exchanged opinions. There was also one great man who was later to revolutionize one part of the world: Lenin. He lived in the street where we had our Cabaret, directly opposite.

Seeing the racketeers on the terraces of the Bar au Lac one had the feeling that decadent European culture stank to high heaven. People moved like puppets, like projections on a screen. Whoever said anything worth listening to? What was there to stir anyone's feelings? Where could one see any escape from the spiritual and physical pressures of war?

[. . .]

No, Swiss social conditions were no concern of ours. The cultural protest we put on was a beacon for all in Europe with eyes to see. Portrayal and reminder of the collapse of post-classical middle-class culture. Revelation of a new emotional primitive path. In this work we have given of our best, expended all our energies. It would be ridiculous if after the event we were to claim to be something different from what we were. The collapse was something we experienced collectively as a group of intellectuals who stayed at their posts and knew what they were doing. Afterwards Ball left for Ticino. I myself went back to Germany towards the end of 1916. Here conditions made action imperative. The people were starving, the soldiers were beginning to revolt. The Naval Mutiny had just been put down with draconic severity. This was it. There's nothing I said or did then I want to take back. The German Revolution did not fail because I appeared in a Cabaret. It did not fail because certain people who felt competent on cultural issues took part. It did not fail of a surfeit of romanticism, but of a lack of romanticism, a missing impetus, a pathological lack of revolutionary temperament. In my opinion it failed because of the small-minded, timid and therefore malicious spirit of the mediocre type of German who, incapable of any heroic gesture, is frequently found among party officials. If the German Revolution, German Social Democracy had known how to attract more men like us, it would not have failed. Every movement which despises the spiritual is bound to get bogged down. This has all been said before, but the Germans cannot be told often enough.

13
GUILLAUME APOLLINAIRE (1880–1918)
'ART AND THE WAR: CONCERNING AN ALLIED EXHIBITION' 1916;
PROGRAMME FOR *PARADE*, 18 MAY 1917

French poet. Apollinaire is one of the key figures of the European avant-garde. An active participant in the bohemian life of Paris from the age of twenty, he befriended the young Picasso and introduced him to African art and to the work of the naif *Henri ('Douanier') Rousseau. With Picasso, Apollinaire formulated the aesthetic principles of Cubism and his influential study* Cubist Painters *was published in 1913 (an extract from that work is reproduced in the following section). His poetry collections* Alcools *(1913) and* Calligrammes *(1918) are marked by audacious technical experimentation, most notably with typography. His* Les Mamelles de Tiresias *(1917) is a pioneering work of Surrealist drama. Reproduced below, in Susan Suleiman's translation for the 1972 edition of* Apollinaire on Art: Essays and Reviews 1902–1918, *are two short pieces from 1916 and 1917 respectively. In 'Art and the War', Apollinaire writes as the spokesman of the French avant-garde in typically provocative and declamatory style. The Programme for* Parade *is a document of one of the great (and typically explosive and short-lived) moments of the Paris avant-garde: a collaboration of Erik Satie (music), Léonide Massine (choreography) and Picasso (scenery and costumes) to create, in Jean Cocteau's words, 'a realistic ballet', or, as Apollinaire puts it, 'something totally new . . . so true, so lyrical, so human, and so joyful'. [See IIb 3]*

Art and the War: Concerning an Allied Exhibition

An association has just been founded 'for the defense and affirmation of modern works'. On this occasion, we asked M. Guillaume Apollinaire, the habitual spokesman for the most avant-garde artistic doctrines, to give us an article that we publish herewith purely for its documentary value. Of course, it goes without saying that the ideas expressed by M. Guillaume Apollinaire are solely his own and that the hospitality here accorded to his article does not imply that we are wholly in agreement with the convictions he expresses.

Having made these reservations, we are happy to present to our readers a defense that we believe may interest them by keeping them abreast of one of the most recent developments in ultramodern art.

A certain press has succeeded in making the French public believe that 'modern' is synonymous with 'boche'. And taking advantage of the *union sacrée* as well as of the fact that the majority of modern artists are of fighting age and serving in the Army, certain journalists are seizing every opportunity to fling the epithet 'boche' at their heads.

The trend, however, is beginning to be reversed. As M. Raoul Ponchon himself recently declared, not without a trace of ill-humor: 'Cubism is not boche'. Also, in response to some articles by my colleague Roger Allard, M. Louis Dimier, who can hardly be suspected of favoring anything even vaguely associated with the word 'boche', went so far as to write for *L'Action française* an article that treated cubism without antipathy.

In fact, the Germans have distinguished themselves very little in modern art; confining oneself simply to the field of painting and, within that, to its most avant-garde movement, cubism, one cannot cite a single German name worth mentioning. And yet before the war, there were a great many boche painters in Paris, but none of them succeeded in making even a minor name for himself in the modern school that was flourishing in France.

Actually, cubism and its sister movement, futurism, are so essentially the products of Latin civilization that the small number of artists who constitute these schools – or rather, this school – are all French, Spanish, or Italian.

The bilious censors who are so eager to label anything they do not like 'boche' might have seen that the modern school of painting had victoriously and with the most admirable courage fought against academicism. And academicism, which *is* of boche origin, will not recover from the battle.

If those in authority had been aware of this, we would not now have this regrettable Allied exhibition at the Luxembourg Museum. What we are being shown here are the most academically Winckelmannian works of Italy and England, gathered under one roof by people whose incompetence is at times overwhelmingly Ruskinian.

It is truly a pity to see how indifferent the authorities are to the art that constitutes the glory of France in the eyes of foreigners.

People are saying that we must organize good-will exhibitions in neutral countries; we ought to take this opportunity to modernize our unfortunate Luxembourg Museum, which never failed to astonish foreigners who came to Paris and were scandalized to find how little weight was accorded in France to French painting.

Today, any one who has strolled through the rooms of our national museum devoted to the works of living artists will easily understand why an association, Art and Liberty, was recently formed for the affirmation and defense of modern works of art.

Parade

Definitions of *Parade* are blossoming everywhere, like the lilac bushes of this tardy spring. . . .

It is a scenic poem transposed by the innovative musician Erik Satie into astonishingly expressive music, so clear and simple that it seems to reflect the marvelously lucid spirit of France.

The cubist painter Picasso and the most daring of today's choreographers, Léonide Massine, have here consummately achieved, for the first time, that alliance between painting and the dance, between the plastic and mimetic arts, that is the herald of a more comprehensive art to come.

There is nothing paradoxical about this. The Ancients, in whose lives music played such an important role, were totally unaware of harmony, which constitutes the very basis of modern music.

This new alliance – I say new, because until now scenery and costumes were linked only by factitious bonds – has given rise, in *Parade*, to a kind of surrealism, which I consider to be the point of departure for a whole series of manifestations of the New Spirit that is making itself felt today and that will certainly appeal to our best minds. We may expect it to bring about profound changes in our arts and manners through universal joyfulness, for it is only natural, after all, that they keep pace with scientific and industrial progress.

Having broken with the choreographic tradition cherished by those who used to be known, in Russia, under the strange name of 'balletomanes', Massine has been careful not to yield to the temptation of pantomime. He has produced something totally new – a marvelously appealing kind of dance, so true, so lyrical, so human, and so joyful that it would even be capable (if it were worth the trouble) of illuminating the terrible black sun of Dürer's *Melancholy*. Jean Cocteau has called this a realistic ballet. Picasso's cubist costumes and scenery bear witness to the realism of his art.

This realism – or this cubism, if you will – is the influence that has most stirred the arts over the past ten years.

The costumes and scenery in *Parade* show clearly that its chief aim has been to draw the greatest possible amount of aesthetic emotion from objects. Attempts have often been made to return painting to its barest elements. In most of the Dutch painters, in Chardin, in the impressionists, one finds hardly anything but painting.

Picasso goes further than any of them. This is clearly evident in *Parade*, a work in which one's initial astonishment is soon replaced by admiration. Here the aim is, above all, to express reality. However, the motif is not reproduced but represented – more precisely, it is not represented but rather suggested by means of an analytic synthesis that embraces all the visible elements of an object and, if possible, something else as well: an integral schematization that aims to reconcile contradictions by deliberately renouncing any attempt to render the immediate appearance of an object. Massine has adapted himself astonishingly well to the discipline of Picasso's art. He has identified himself with it, and his art has become enriched with delightful inventions, such as the realistic steps of the horse in *Parade*, formed by two dancers, one of whom does the steps of the forelegs and the other those of the hind legs.

The fantastic constructions representing the gigantic and surprising figures of The Managers, far from presenting an obstacle to Massine's imagination, have, one might say, served to give it a liberating impetus.

All in all, *Parade* will change the ideas of a great many spectators. They will be surprised, that is certain; but in a most agreeable way, and charmed as well; *Parade* will reveal to them all the gracefulness of the modern movements, a gracefulness they never suspected.

A magnificent vaudeville Chinaman will make their imaginations soar; the American Girl cranking up her imaginary car will express the magic of their daily lives, whose wordless rites are celebrated with exquisite and astonishing agility by the acrobat in blue and white tights.

14
ANTONIO GRAMSCI (1891–1937)
'MARINETTI THE REVOLUTIONARY' 1916; 'THEATRE AND CINEMA' 1921

Italian theorist and political activist, mainly known for his writings on cultural politics and aesthetics. Gramsci was leader of the Italian Communist Party and was a Communist deputy in the Italian parliament when he was arrested by fascists in Rome in 1926. He spent the rest of his life in prison and in hospital. His writings on culture form an important part of the Marxist debates on culture, commitment and Formalism. Gramsci's particular contribution to these debates revolves around his concern with avant-garde art and popular culture. His key concepts of hegemony, the relationship between centre and periphery, the role of the intellectual and the function of civil society are developed in Selections from Cultural Writings *and* Selections from the Prison Notebooks, *both published posthumously. 'Theatre and Cinema' was first published in* Avanti! *in 1916 and 'Marinetti the Revolutionary' in* L'Ordine Nuovo, *in 1921. They are translated by William Boelhower for* Selections from Cultural Writings *(David Forgacs and Geoffrey Nowell-Smith eds, London 1985). [See IIb 1a]*

Marinetti the Revolutionary

This incredible, enormous, colossal event has happened, which, if divulged, threatens completely to destroy all the prestige and reputation of the Communist International: during the Second Congress in Moscow, comrade Lunacharsky, in his speech to the Italian delegates (a speech given, mark you, in Italian, excellent Italian even; so that any suspicion of a dubious interpretation must *a priori* be rejected), said that in Italy there lives a revolutionary intellectual by the name of Filippo Tommaso Marinetti. The philistines of the workers' movement are extremely shocked. It is now certain that to the insults of being called 'Bergsonian voluntarists, pragmatists and spiritualists' will be added the more deadly one of 'Futurists! Marinettians!' Since such a fate awaits us, let us see if we can raise ourselves to a self-awareness of our new intellectual position.

Many groups of workers looked kindly towards Futurism (before the European war). It happened very often (before the war) that groups of workers would defend the Futurists from the attacks of cliques of professional 'artists' and 'littérateurs'. This point established, this historical observation made, the question automatically arises: 'In this attitude of the workers was there an intuition (here we are with the word intuition: Bergsonians, Bergsonians) of an unsatisfied need in the proletarian field?' We must answer: 'Yes. The revolutionary working class was and is aware that it must found a new state, that by its tenacious and patient labour it must elaborate a new economic structure and found a new civilization.' It is relatively easy to outline right from this moment the shape of the new state and the new economic structure. In this absolutely practical field, we are convinced that for a certain time the only possible thing to do will be to exercise an iron-like power over the existing organization, over that constructed by the bourgeoisie. From this conviction comes the stimulus to struggle for the conquest of power and from it comes the formula by which Lenin has characterized the workers' state: 'For a certain time the workers' state cannot be other than a bourgeois state without the bourgeoisie.'

vulgar economism
Hegemony
– like Mallarmé

The battlefield for the creation of a new civilization is, on the other hand, absolutely mysterious, absolutely characterized by the unforeseeable and the unexpected. Having passed from capitalist power to workers' power, the factory will continue to produce the same material things that it produces today. But in what way and under what forms will poetry, drama, the novel, music, painting and moral and linguistic works be born? It is not a material factory that produces these works. It cannot be reorganized by a workers' power according to a plan. One cannot establish its rate of production for the satisfaction of immediate needs, to be controlled and determined statistically. Nothing in this field is foreseeable except for this general hypothesis: there will be a proletarian culture (a civilization) totally different from the bourgeois one and in this field too class distinctions will be shattered. Bourgeois careerism will be shattered and there will be a poetry, a novel, a theatre, a moral code, a language, a painting and a music peculiar to proletarian civilization, the flowering and ornament of proletarian social organization. What remains to be done? Nothing other than to destroy the present form of civilization. In this field, 'to destroy' does not mean the same as in the economic field. It does not mean to deprive humanity of the material products that it needs to subsist and to develop. It means to destroy spiritual hierarchies, prejudices, idols and ossified traditions. It means not to be afraid of innovations and audacities, not to be afraid of monsters, not to believe that the world will collapse if a worker makes grammatical mistakes, if a poem limps, if a picture resembles a hoarding or if young men sneer at academic and feeble-minded senility. The Futurists have carried out this task in the field of bourgeois culture. They have destroyed, destroyed, destroyed, without worrying if the new creations produced by their activity were on the whole superior to those destroyed. They have had confidence in themselves, in the impetuosity of their youthful energies. *They have grasped sharply and clearly that our age, the age of big industry, of the large proletarian city and of intense and tumultuous life, was in need of new forms of art, philosophy, behaviour and language.* This sharply revolutionary and absolutely *Marxist* idea came to them when the Socialists were not even vaguely interested in such a question, when the Socialists certainly did not have as precise an idea in politics and economics, when the Socialists would have been frightened (as is evident from the current fear of many of them) by the thought that it was necessary to shatter the machine of bourgeois power in the state and the factory. In their field, the field of culture, the Futurists are revolutionaries. In this field it is likely to be a long time before the working classes will manage to do anything more creative than the Futurists have done. When they supported the Futurists, the workers' groups showed that they were not afraid of *destruction*, certain as they were of being able to create poetry, paintings and plays, like the Futurists; these workers were supporting historicity, the possibility of a proletarian culture created by the workers themselves.

Theatre and Cinema

They say that the cinema is killing the theatre. They say that in Turin the theatrical firms have kept their houses closed during the summer months because the public is deserting the theatre and thronging to the cinemas. The new film industry has sprung up and caught on in Turin. In Turin luxurious cinemas have been opened, with few equals in Europe, and are always crowded out.

There would seem to be some basis to the sad observation that the audience's taste has degenerated and that bad times are round the corner for the theatre.

We, however, are thoroughly convinced that these complaints are founded on a jaded aestheticism and can easily be shown to depend on a false assumption. The reason for the success of the cinema and its absorption of former theatre audiences is purely economic. The cinema offers exactly the same sensations as the popular theatre, but under better conditions, without the choreographic contrivances of a false intellectualism, without promising too much while delivering little. The usual stage presentations are nothing but cinema. The most commonly staged productions are nothing but fabrics of external facts, lacking any human content, in which talking puppets move about variously, without ever drawing out a psychological truth, without ever managing to impose on the listener's creative imagination a character or passions that are truly felt and adequately expressed. Psychological insincerity and lame artistic expression have reduced the theatre to the same level as the pantomime. The sole aim is to create in the audience the illusion of a life which is only outwardly different from everyone's normal life. Only the geographical horizon, the social environment, of the characters is changed, all the things which in life are subjects for the picture postcard, for visual curiosity, not for artistic curiosity or the curiosity of fantasy. And nobody can deny that in this respect the film is incontrovertibly superior to the stage. It is more complete and more varied. It is silent; in other words it reduces the role of the artists to movement alone, to being machines without souls, to what they really are in the theatre as well. It is ludicrous to take it out on the cinema. Talking about vulgarity, banality, etc., is feeble rhetoric. Those who really believe that the theatre has an artistic function should instead be happy with this competition. It serves to precipitate things, to bring the theatre back to its true character. There is no doubt that a large proportion of the public needs to be entertained (to relax by shifting its field of attention) with a pure visual distraction. By becoming an industry, the theatre has recently tried to satisfy this need alone. It has become quite simply a business, a shop dealing in cheap junk. It is only by accident that they put on productions that have an eternal universal value. The cinema, which can fulfil this function more easily and more cheaply, is more successful than the theatre and is tending to replace it. The theatrical firms and companies will eventually realize that they need to change tack if they want to stay in being. It is not true that the public is deserting the theatres. We have seen theatres that were empty for a large number of productions fill up, become suddenly crowded for a special evening when a masterpiece was exhumed or even more modestly, a typical work of a past style, but which had a particular quality of its own. What the theatre now offers as an exception must become the rule. Shakespeare, Goldoni, Beaumarchais may indeed require active effort to be properly staged but they are also beyond any banal competition. D'Annunzio, Bernstein, Bataille will always be more successful in the cinema. The grimace and the physical contortion find in the film material more appropriate to their expression. And the useless, boring and insincere rhetorical tirades will once again become literature, nothing but literature, dead and buried in books and libraries.

15
VICTOR SHKLOVSKY (1893–1984)
FROM 'ART AS TECHNIQUE' 1917

Russian literary critic. Shklovsky was a leading theorist and practitioner in the mode of linguistic criticism that has become known as Russian Formalism. The movement emerged from two groups, The Moscow Linguistic Circle (1915) and The Society for the Study of Poetic Language (1916), who sought to give the study of literature a scientific foundation by focusing on the formal and stylistic devices used in the language of literary texts. The extracts reprinted here come from Shklovsky's influential essay, 'Art as Technique' (1917) where he develops his key concept of ostranenie, *or defamiliarisation, which describes how literary language acts to disrupt or impede the automised, habituated perceptions we fall into as language users. The translation is from* Russian Formalist Criticism: Four Essays *(1965) by Lee T. Lemon and Marion J. Reis.*

'Art is thinking in images.' This maxim, which even high school students parrot, is nevertheless the starting point for the erudite philogist who is beginning to put together some kind of systematic literary theory.

[. . .]

Poetry is a special way of thinking; it is, precisely, a way of thinking in images, a way which permits what is generally called 'economy of mental effort', a way which makes for 'a sensation of the relative ease of the process'. Aesthetic feeling is the reaction to this economy.

'Without imagery there is no art' – 'Art is thinking in images.' These maxims have led to far-fetched interpretations of individual works of art. Attempts have been made to evaluate even music, architecture, and lyric poetry as imagistic thought.

[. . .]

Nevertheless, the definition *'Art is thinking in images'*, which means (I omit the usual middle terms of the argument) that art is the making of symbols, has survived the downfall of the theory which supported it. It survives chiefly in the wake of Symbolism, especially among the theorists of the Symbolist movement.

Many still believe, then, that thinking in images – thinking in specific scenes of 'roads and landscape' and 'furrows and boundaries' – is the chief characteristic of poetry. Consequently, they should have expected the history of 'imagistic art,' as they call it, to consist of a history of changes in imagery. But we find that images change little; from century to century, from nation to nation, from poet to poet, they flow on without changing. Images belong to no one: they are 'the Lord's'. The more you understand an age, the more convinced you become that the images a given poet used and which you thought his own were taken almost unchanged from another poet. The works of poets are classified or grouped according to the new techniques that poets discover and share, and according to their arrangement and development of the resources of language; poets are much more concerned with arranging images than with creating them. Images are given to poets; the ability to remember them is far more important than the ability to create them.

[. . .]

Poetic imagery is a means of creating the strongest possible impression. As a method it is, depending upon its purpose, neither more nor less effective than other poetic techniques; it is neither more nor less effective than ordinary or negative parallelism, comparison, repetition, balanced structure, hyperbole, the commonly accepted rhetorical figures, and all those methods which emphasize the emotional effect of an expression (including words or even articulated sounds). But poetic imagery only externally resembles either the stock imagery of fables and ballads or thinking in images.

[. . .]

Poetic imaginary is but one of the devices of poetic language. Prose imagery is a means of abstraction: a little watermelon instead of a lampshade, or a little watermelon instead of a head, is only the abstraction of one of the object's characteristics, that of roundness. It is no different from saying that the head and the melon are both round. This is what is meant, but it has nothing to do with poetry.

[. . .]

We must, then, speak about the laws of expenditure and economy in poetic language not on the basis of an analogy with prose, but on the basis of the laws of poetic language.

If we start to examine the general laws of perception, we see that as perception becomes habitual, it becomes automatic. Thus, for example, all of our habits retreat into the area of the unconsciously automatic; if one remembers the sensations of holding a pen or of speaking in a foreign language for the first time and compares that with his feeling at performing the action for the ten thousandth time, he will agree with us. Such habituation explains the principles by which, in ordinary speech, we leave phrases unfinished and words half expressed. In this process, ideally realized in algebra, things are replaced by symbols. Complete words are not expressed in rapid speech; their initial sounds are barely perceived.

[. . .]

This characteristic of thought not only suggests the method of algebra, but even prompts the choice of symbols (letters, especially initial letters). By this 'algebraic' method of thought we apprehend objects only as shapes with imprecise extensions; we do not see them in their entirety but rather recognize them by their main characteristics. We see the object as though it were enveloped in a sack. We know what it is by its configuration, but we see only its silhouette. The object, perceived thus in the manner of prose perception, fades and does not leave even a first impression; ultimately even the essence of what it was is forgotten. Such perception explains why we fail to hear the prose word in its entirely [. . .] and, hence, why (along with other slips of the tongue) we fail to pronounce it. The process of 'algebrization', the over-automatization of an object, permits the greatest economy of perceptive effort.

[...]

And so life is reckoned as nothing. Habitualization devours works, clothes, furniture, one's wife, and the fear of war [...] And art exists that one may recover the sensation of life; it exists to make one feel things, to make the stone *stony*. The purpose of art is to impart the sensation of things as they are perceived and not as they are known. The technique of art is to make objects 'unfamiliar', to make forms difficult, to increase the difficulty and length of perception because the process of perception is an aesthetic end in itself and must be prolonged. *Art is a way of experiencing the artfulness of an object; the object is not important.*

The range of poetic (artistic) work extends from the sensory to the cognitive, from poetry to prose, from the concrete to the abstract: from Cervantes' Don Quixote – scholastic and poor nobleman, half consciously bearing his humiliation in the court of the duke – to the broad but empty Don Quixote of Turgenev; from Charlemagne to the name 'king' [in Russian 'Charles' and 'king' obviously derive from the same root, *korol*]. The meaning of a work broadens to the extent that artfulness and artistry diminish; thus a fable symbolizes more than a poem, and a proverb more than a fable.

[...]

After we see an object several times, we begin to recognize it. The object is in front of us and we know about it, but we do not see it – hence we cannot say anything significant about it. Art removes objects from the automatism of perception in several ways. Here I want to illustrate a way used repeatedly by Leo Tolstoy, that writer who, for Merezhkovsky at least, seems to present things as if he himself saw them, saw them in their entirety, and did not alter them.

Tolstoy makes the familiar seem strange by not naming the familiar object. He describes an object as if he were seeing it for the first time, an event as if it were happening for the first time. In describing something he avoids the accepted names of its parts and instead names corresponding parts of other objects.

[...]

Tolstoy described the dogmas and rituals he attacked as if they were unfamiliar, substituting everyday meanings for the customarily religious meanings of the words common in church ritual. Many persons were painfully wounded; they considered it blasphemy to present as strange and monstrous what they accepted as sacred. Their reaction was due chiefly to the technique through which Tolstoy perceived and reported his environment. And after turning to what he had long avoided, Tolstoy found that his perceptions had unsettled his faith.

The technique of defamiliarization is not Tolstoy's alone. I cited Tolstoy because his work is generally known.

Now, having explained the nature of this technique, let us try to determine the approximate limits of its application. I personally feel that defamiliarization is found almost everywhere form is found.

[...]

Quite often in literature the sexual act itself is defamiliarized; for example, the *Decameron* refers to 'scraping out a barrel', 'catching nightingales', 'gay wool-beating work', (the last is not developed in the plot). Defamiliarization is often used in describing the sexual organs.

A whole series of plots is based on such a lack of recognition.

[. . .]

Such constructions as 'the pestle and the mortar', or 'Old Nick and the infernal regions' (*Decameron*), are also examples of the technique of defamiliarization. And in my article on plot construction I write about defamiliarization in psychological parallelism. Here, then, I repeat that the perception of disharmony in a harmonious context is important in parallelism. The purpose of parallelism, like the general purpose of imagery, is to transfer the usual perception of an object into the sphere of a new perception – that is, to make a unique semantic modification.

In studying poetic speech in its phonetic and lexical structure as well as in its characteristic distribution of words and in the characteristic thought structures compounded from the words, we find everywhere the artistic trademark – that is, we find material obviously created to remove the automatism of perception; the author's purpose is to create the vision which results from that deautomatized perception. A work is created 'artistically' so that its perception is impeded and the greatest possible effect is produced through the slowness of the perception. As a result of this lingering, the object is perceived not in its extension in space, but, so to speak, in its continuity. Thus 'poetic language' gives satisfaction. According to Aristotle, poetic language must appear strange and wonderful; and, in fact, it is often actually foreign: the Sumerian used by the Assyrians, the Latin of Europe during the Middle Ages, the Arabisms of the Persians, the Old Bulgarian of Russian literature, or the elevated, almost literary language of folk songs.

[. . .]

The language of poetry is, then, a difficult, roughened, impeded language. In a few special instances the language of poetry approximates the language of prose, but this does not violate the principle of 'roughened' form.

[. . .]

Just now a still more characteristic phenomenon is under way. Russian literary language, which was originally foreign to Russia, has so permeated the language of the people that it has blended with their conversation. On the other hand, literature has now begun to show a tendency towards the use of dialects.

[. . .]

And currently Maxim Gorky is changing his diction from the old literary language to the new literary colloquialism of Leskov. Ordinary speech and literary language have thereby changed places (see the work of Vyacheslav Ivanov and many others). And finally, a strong tendency, led by Khlebnikov, to create a new and properly poetic language has emerged. In the light of these developments we can define poetry as *attenuated, tortuous* speech. Poetic speech is *formed speech*. Prose is ordinary speech – economical, easy, proper, the goddess of prose [*dea prosae*] is a goddess of the accurate, facile type, of the 'direct' expression of a child.

[. . .]

Thus the rhythm of prose is an important automatizing element; the rhythm of poetry is not. There is 'order' in art, yet not a single column of a Greek temple stands exactly in its proper order; poetic rhythm is similarly disordered rhythm. Attempts to systematize the irregularities have been made, and such attempts are part of the current problem in the theory of rhythm. It is obvious that the systematization will not work, for in reality the problem is not one of complicating the rhythm but of disordering the rhythm – a disordering which cannot be predicted. Should the disordering of rhythm become a convention, it would be ineffective as a device for the roughening of language.

[. . .]

16
JOHN REED (1887–1920)
FROM *TEN DAYS THAT SHOOK THE WORLD* 1919

Prominent left-wing American journalist and war correspondent who became a supporter and friend of Lenin. He was married to the writer Louise Bryant. He reported on the revolution in Mexico and his book, Insurgent Mexico *(1914), was an important contribution to debate on American involvement there. Reed admired and was associated with the IWW (the Industrial Workers of the World – 'Wobblies'). Arrested in their Paterson silk workers strike of 1913, he was one of the main organisers (along with Mabel Dodge) of the Strike Pageant in Madison Square Gardens in which the strikers themselves were the principal performers. He is most famous for his eye-witness account of the Russian Revolution,* Ten Days That Shook the World *(1919). His reports first appeared in the November/December 1917 edition of* The Masses, *the radical paper that partially financed his trip to Russia. Reed, along with many of its contributors and editors, was indicted for obstructing the draft and because of his reputation as an extremist Bolshevik agitator, was the object of heavy surveillance, and frequently arrested. Lenin contributed a warm preface to the first edition of* Ten Days That Shook the World, *and there were twelve Soviet editions of the book before its publication was suspended in 1930. Many of the figures Reed portrayed were liquidated in Stalin's purges. The first edition of* Ten Days That Shook the World *took advantage of innovations in printing techniques to reproduce Russian placards and posters which contribute to its montage style. Reproduced here is a short piece from Reed's introduction.*

We who were left behind made for the Tsarskoye Selo station. Up the Nevsky, as we passed, Red Guards were marching, all armed, some with bayonets and some without. The early twilight of winter was falling. Heads up they tramped in the chill mud, irregular lines of four, without music, without drums. A red flag crudely lettered in gold, 'Peace! Land!' floated over them. They were very young. The expression on their faces was that of men who know they are going to die. . . . Half-fearful, half-contemptuous, the crowds on the sidewalk watched them pass, in hateful silence. . . .

At the railroad station nobody knew just where Kerensk was, or where the front lay. Trains went no further, however, than Tsarskoye. . . .

Исполнительный Комитет
Петроградскаго Сов.
Рабочихъ и Солдатскихъ
Депутатовъ
Военный Отдѣлъ

28 Октября 191 .

№ 1435

УДОСТОВѢРЕНІЕ.

Настоящее удостовѣреніе дано представителю Американской Соціалъ-демократіи Интернаціоналисту, товарищу ДЖОНУ РИДЪ въ томъ, Военно-Революціонный Комитетъ Петербургскаго Совѣта Рабочихъ и Солдатскихъ Депутатовъ предоставилъ имъ право его одного проѣзда по всему Сѣверному фронту въ цѣляхъ освѣдомленія нашихъ Американскихъ товарищей интернаціоналистовъ съ событіями въ Россіи.

Предсѣдатель:

Секретарь:

This pass was issued upon the recommendation of Trotzky three days after the Bolshevik Revolution. It gives me the right of free travel to the Northern front—and an added note on the back extends the permission to all fronts. It will be noticed that the text speaks of the "Petersburg," instead of the "Petrograd" Soviet; it was the fashion among thorough-going internationalists to abolish all names which smacked of "patriotism" but at the same time it would not do to restore the "Saint." . .

[Translation]

Executive Committee
Petrograd Soviet of
Workers' & Soldiers'
Deputies
Military Section
28th October, 1917
No. 1435

CERTIFICATE

The present certificate is given to the representative of the American Social Democracy, the internationalist comrade John Reed. The Military Revolutionary Committee of the Petersburg Soviet of Workers' and Soldiers' Deputies gives him the right of free travel through the entire Northern front, for the purpose of reporting to our American comrades-internationalists concerning events in Russia.

For the President
For the Secretary

Our car was full of commuters and country people going home, laden with bundles and evening papers. The talk was all of the Bolshevik rising. Outside of that, however, one would never have realised that civil war was rending mighty Russia in two, and that the train was headed into the zone of battle. Through the window we could see, in the swiftly-deepening darkness, masses of soldiers going along the muddy road toward the city, flinging out their arms in argument. A freight-train, swarming with troops and lit up by huge bonfires, was halted on a siding. That was all. Back along the flat horizon the glow of the city's lights faded down the night. A street-car crawled distantly along a far-flung suburb. . . .

Tsarskoye Selo station was quiet, but knots of soldiers stood here and there talking in low tones and looking uneasily down the empty track in the direction of Gatchina. I asked some of them which side they were on. 'Well,' said one, 'we don't exactly know the rights of the matter. . . . There is no doubt that Kerensky is a provocator, but we do not consider it right for Russian men to be shooting Russian men.'

In the station commandant's office was a big, jovial, bearded common soldier, wearing the red arm-band of a regimental committee. Our credentials from Smolny commanded immediate respect. He was plainly for the Soviets, but bewildered.

'The Red Guards were here two hours ago, but they went away again. A Commissar came this morning, but he returned to Petrograd when the Cossacks arrived.'

'The Cossacks are here then?'

He nodded, gloomily. 'There has been a battle. The Cossacks came early in the morning. They captured two or three hundred of our men, and killed about twenty-five.'

'Where are the Cossacks?'

'Well, they didn't get this far. I don't know just where they are. Off that way. . . .' He waved his arm vaguely westward.

17
'A MEMBER OF THE AUDIENCE: STORMING THE WINTER PALACE' 1920

Playwright, director, theatre theorist Nikolay Yevreinov (1879–1953) explored concepts of 'theatricalism' and the 'theatre instinct'. He directed 'The Storming of the Winter Palace' in Petrograd on the third anniversary of the October Revolution in 1920. This legendary mass spectacle involved eight thousand participants – equipped with motorcycles and armoured cars – and one hundred thousand spectators. It was considered by Yevreinov as a triumph of theatricality over reality – this storming was 'more real than the real one'. The 'eyewitness account' reproduced below is taken from Huntley Carter's 1929 book The Theatre and Cinema of Soviet Russia.

Two large stages, White and Red, had been erected in front of the Winter Palace, the immense semi-circle of which formed the background of the play. To the right was a white one; to the left a red one. In the center they were connected by a high arched bridge. At the start 1,500 people were the actors. They included some professional actors, pupils of the theater schools, members of the Club for Proletarian Culture, of the Theater Societies, of the Red Army, and the Baltic Fleet. But at the conclusion more than 100,000 people were participating, pouring out from the tribunes and from the houses. The spectacle began at ten at night. A searchlight attached to the top of the Alexander Column lit up as bright as day the white stage to the right, on which the Provisional Government of Kerensky was holding a meeting. From the other side, from the invisible Red stage, an indistinct murmur was proceeding; it was the low murmur of the multitude who had had enough of the war, but who had to submit to Kerensky's word of command, as the ministerial council under the presidency of the Tribune had just resolved to pursue the war to a victorious termination. The searchlight was turned on to the Red stage. There one saw workmen and women, children and cripples reeling home tired from the factories; maimed soldiers toiling up to the bridge because the order had been issued that new armies were to be formed. At the same time on the White stage capitalists pushed sacks of money with their bellies towards Kerensky's throne, and ministers jumped from the ministerial bench and collected all the valuables in a heap, whilst from the dark side the cry of 'Lenin' rose above the murmurs, at first indistinctly, then louder and louder. Next Kerensky was seen on his throne at the head of the ministerial bench gesticulating, waving his hands energetically and pointing to the money-bags. But the ministers remained undecided. They fidgetted about on their bench as from the invisible Red stage the tumultuous sounds became more rhythmic and more collective; one could now hear the notes of a song, which might or might not be the 'International'. Kerensky was still speaking and gesticulating to the ministerial bench, but the restlessness and indecision had become general. The whole row, clad in grey, were seen to bend over together to the right, then with a sudden jerk to the left. This was repeated several times with increasingly violent movements. Then came Kerensky's celebrated women's battalions. They mounted the stage with parodied movements, waved their rifles, and shouted to Kerensky, 'Miriturae te saluant'. As the White stage became wrapped in darkness, the Red one was illuminated. Workmen, women and children, soldiers with arms, and people of all kinds were seen crowding round a gigantic Red Flag. The factories, the prisons – large red scenic constructions with barred windows, their interiors lit up with glaring red light – opened their doors wide. Crowds increasingly emerged from them, and clustered round the Red Flag. From the collective surging crowd the 'International' rose as a powerful articulate chorus. The word 'Lenin' was hurled to the sky as by one mighty shout from a hundred thousand throats. In the meanwhile the battalions had drawn up in order round the flag, ready to march across that bridge which connected the two stages. The searchlight was switched on the White stage. The ministerial bench was rocking as if shaken by a storm. A volley came from the Red side. Kerensky's bodyguard rushed with waving rifles to the bridge. The ministerial bench fell with a crash. From a side street of Uritzky Square two motor cars rushed up to the White stage, sounding their horns furiously. With a desperate leap, Kerensky sprang from his throne over the fallen ministerial bench to the steps which led from the stage to the ground, where the motor cars received him and his ministers. They rushed madly across the square past the column to the Winter Palace, the gates of which opened with the rapidity of lightning and admitted them.

The Winter Palace now began to take a part in the play. All the first story windows were suddenly illuminated by a most brilliant light. At the same time fighting on the bridge continued. Accompanied by the rattle of machine guns and wild firing, an action developed, and hand to hand fighting took place between the Red Army and the Whites, who had remained behind. Dead and wounded fell down the steps, tumbling over the parapet of the bridge on to the pavement of the square below. In the meanwhile the lights in the Winter Palace were turned on, turned off, and again turned on. For several minutes the battle raged on the bridge, till at last a decision was reached. The whole fighting mass of the Red Army, united and conscious of its strength, this mass singing the 'International', pressed down the steps towards the Winter Palace. Regiments emerged from side streets of the Uritzky Square, and joined those coming from the stage in tens and tens of thousands.

Now from the direction of the Neva the sound of thunder was suddenly heard. It came from the 'Aurora', the historic battleship that bombarded the Winter Palace in November, 1917, which was firing its guns from the same position where it still lay anchored in the Neva, having been ordered to participate in the mystery play of the Revolution.

Again the Winter Palace came into action. A gate opened and cars rushed through with Kerensky and his adherents. They made for the Millionaya, and so away.

A hundred thousand were approaching the Winter Palace. The immense square was crowded with marching, running, singing, shouting people, all pressing towards the Winter Palace. Rifle shots, the rattle of machine guns, the terrible thunder from the 'Aurora' all this was awful, arresting, almost indescribable. Then came rockets to announce the end. The guns of the 'Aurora' became silent, the shouting died down, and the mass melted in the night.

No one who sees a mass spectacle of the kind can fail to be impressed by its magnitude, and the almost ecstatic spirit of the multitude. Of course, it bears various interpretations. The political minded will see in it a habit of counter-revolutionists to avail themselves of the opportunity afforded by a 'theatrical bombardment' to foment risings and to teach the method of carrying them out. The sociologist, the historian, the mystic, the moralist, the psychologist will each see it in his own way also. As for that rarity, the man of the theater possessing social ideals, to him it can appear only as a revelation, pregnant with suggestion towards that theater of the future which shall fully answer the need of spiritual social service.

18
GEORG LUKÁCS (1885–1971)
FROM *THE THEORY OF THE NOVEL* 1920

Hungarian Marxist philosopher and critic. Following the early study Soul and Form *(1910) and marking a shift in his thinking and methodology towards a Hegelian approach,* The Theory of the Novel: A Historico-Philosophical Essay on the Forms of Great Epic Literature *was Lukács's response to the outbreak of the First World War. The final version of the book was written in the winter of 1914–15 and was first published in book form in 1920. He later wrote*

of the 'mood of permanent despair over the state of the world' in which the book was produced. This
'outlook on a Dostoevskian world' was at the same time a formulation of the impact of contemporary
scientific and philosophical 'discoveries' on modern literary form. In 1918 he joined the Hungarian
Communist Party, but following the defeat of the 1919 uprising he moved to Vienna, and finally
Moscow, where he lived from 1930 until 1944. After the Second World War, he returned to Hungary
to take up an academic post and to join the short-lived revolutionary government in 1956 as Minister
of Culture. His major Marxist thesis, History and Class Consciousness *(1923) was heresy to*
the Russian Communist Party and was later repudiated by Lukács himself. The following extracts
from The Theory of the Novel *are from Anna Bostock's 1971 translation. [See IIIb 33]*

Happy are those ages when the starry sky is the map of all possible paths – ages whose
paths are illuminated by the light of the stars. Everything in such ages is new and yet
familiar, full of adventure and yet their own. The world is wide and yet it is like a
home, for the fire that burns in the soul is of the same essential nature as the stars; the
world and the self, the light and the fire, are sharply distinct, yet they never become
permanent strangers to one another, for fire is the soul of all light and all fire clothes
itself in light. Thus each action of the soul becomes meaningful and rounded in this
duality: complete in meaning – in *sense* – and complete for the senses; rounded because
the soul rests within itself even while it acts; rounded because its action separates
itself from it and, having become itself, finds a centre of its own and draws a closed
circumference round itself. 'Philosophy is really homesickness,' says Novalis: 'it is the
urge to be at home everywhere.'

   That is why philosophy, as a form of life or as that which determines the form and
supplies the content of literary creation, is always a symptom of the rift between 'inside'
and 'outside', a sign of the essential difference between the self and the world, the
incongruence of soul and deed. That is why the happy ages have no philosophy, or why
(it comes to the same thing) all men in such ages are philosophers, sharing the utopian
aim of every philosophy. For what is the task of true philosophy if not to draw that
archetypal map? What is the problem of the transcendental *locus* if not to determine
how every impulse which springs from the innermost depths is co-ordinated with a
form that it is ignorant of, but that has been assigned to it from eternity and that
must envelop it in liberating symbols? When this is so, passion is the way, pre-
determined by reason, towards complete self-being and from madness come enigmatic
yet decipherable messages of a transcendental power, otherwise condemned to silence.
There is not yet any interiority, for there is not yet any exterior, any 'otherness' for
the soul. The soul goes out to seek adventure; it lives through adventures, but it does
not know the real torment of seeking and the real danger of finding; such a soul never
stakes itself; it does not yet know that it can lose itself, it never thinks of having to
look for itself. Such an age is the age of the epic.

[. . .]

   The irony of the novel is the self-correction of the world's fragility: inadequate
relations can transform themselves into a fanciful yet well-ordered round of misunder-
standings and cross-purposes, within which everything is seen as many-sided, within
which things appear as isolated and yet connected, as full of value and yet totally

devoid of it, as abstract fragments and as concrete autonomous life, as flowering and as decaying, as the infliction of suffering and as suffering itself.

Thus a new perspective of life is reached on an entirely new basis – that of the indissoluble connection between the relative independence of the parts and their attachment to the whole. But the parts, despite this attachment, can never lose their inexorable, abstract self-dependence: and their relationship to the totality, although it approximates as closely as possible to an organic one, is nevertheless not a true-born organic relationship but a conceptual one which is abolished again and again.

The consequence of this, from the compositional point of view, is that, although the characters and their actions possess the infinity of authentic epic literature, their structure is essentially different from that of the epic. The structural difference in which this fundamentally conceptual pseudo-organic nature of the material of the novel finds expression is the difference between something that is homogeneously organic and stable and something that is heterogeneously contingent and discrete. Because of this contingent nature, the relatively independent parts are more independent, more self-contained than those of the epic and must therefore, if they are not to destroy the whole, be inserted into it by means which transcend their mere presence.

[. . .]

The inner form of the novel has been understood as the process of the problematic individual's journeying towards himself, the road from dull captivity within a merely present reality – a reality that is heterogeneous in itself and meaningless to the individual – towards clear self-recognition. After such self-recognition has been attained, the ideal thus formed irradiates the individual's life as its immanent meaning; but the conflict between what is and what should be has not been abolished and cannot be abolished in the sphere wherein these events take place – the life sphere of the novel; only a maximum conciliation – the profound and intensive irradiation of a man by his life's meaning – is attainable. The immanence of meaning which the form of the novel requires lies in the hero's finding out through experience that a mere glimpse of meaning is the highest that life has to offer, and that this glimpse is the only thing worth the commitment of an entire life, the only thing by which the struggle will have been justified.

[. . .]

The novel is the epic of a world that has been abandoned by God. The novel hero's psychology is demonic; the objectivity of the novel is the mature man's knowledge that meaning can never quite penetrate reality, but that, without meaning, reality would disintegrate into the nothingness of inessentiality. These are merely different ways of saying the same thing. They define the productive limits of the possibilities of the novel – limits which are drawn from within – and, at the same time, they define the historico-philosophical moment at which great novels become possible, at which they grow into a symbol of the essential thing that needs to be said. The mental attitude of the novel is virile maturity, and the characteristic structure of its matter is discreteness, the separation between interiority and adventure.

'I go to prove my soul,' says Browning's Paracelsus, and if the marvellous line is out of place it is only because it is spoken by a dramatic hero. The dramatic hero knows no adventure, for, through the force of his attained soul that is hallowed by destiny, the event which should have been his adventure becomes destiny upon the merest contact with that soul, becomes a simple occasion for him to prove himself, a simple excuse for disclosing what was prefigured in the act of his attaining the soul. The dramatic hero knows no interiority, for interiority is the product of the antagonistic duality of soul and world, the agonising distance between psyche and soul; and the tragic hero has attained his soul and therefore does not know any hostile reality; everything exterior is, for him, merely an expression of a pre-determined and adequate destiny. Therefore the dramatic hero does not set out to prove himself: he is a hero because his inner security is given *a priori*, beyond the reach of any test or proof; the destiny-forming event is, for him, only a symbolic objectivation, a profound and dignified ceremony.

(The essential inner stylelessness of modern drama, and of Ibsen in particular, derives from the fact that his major figures have to be tested, that they sense within themselves the distance between themselves and their soul, and, in their desperate desire to pass the tests with which events confront them, try to bridge that distance. The heroes of modern drama experience the preconditions of drama; the drama itself unfolds in the process of stylisation which the dramatist should have completed, as a phenomenological precondition of his work, before beginning to write it.)

[. . .]

For the novel, irony consists in this freedom of the writer in his relationship to God, the transcendental condition of the objectivity of form-giving. Irony, with intuitive double vision, can see where God is to be found in a world abandoned by God; irony sees the lost, utopian home of the idea that has become an ideal, and yet at the same time it understands that the ideal is subjectively and psychologically conditioned, because that is its only possible form of existence; irony, itself demonic, apprehends the demon that is within the subject as a metasubjective essentiality, and therefore, when it speaks of the adventures of errant souls in an inessential, empty reality, it intuitively speaks of past gods and gods that are to come; irony has to seek the only world that is adequate to it along the *via dolorosa* of interiority, but is doomed never to find it there; irony gives form to the malicious satisfaction of God the creator at the failure of man's weak rebellions against his mighty, yet worthless creation and, at the same time, to the inexpressible suffering of God the redeemer at his inability to re-enter that world. Irony, the self-surmounting of a subjectivity that has gone as far as it was possible to go, is the highest freedom that can be achieved in a world without God. That is why it is not only the sole possible *a priori* condition for a true, totality-creating objectivity but also why it makes that totality – the novel – the representative art-form of our age: because the structural categories of the novel constitutively coincide with the world as it is today.

The greatest discrepancy between idea and reality is time: the process of time as duration. The most profound and most humiliating impotence of subjectivity consists not so much in its hopeless struggle against the lack of idea in social forms and their human representatives, as in the fact that it cannot resist the sluggish, yet constant progress of time; that it must slip down, slowly yet inexorably, from the peaks it has laboriously scaled; that time – that ungraspable, invisibly moving substance – gradually robs subjectivity of all its possessions and imperceptibly forces alien contents into it. That is why only the novel, the literary form of the transcendent homelessness of the idea, includes real time – Bergson's *durée* – among its constitutive principles.

[. . .]

19
LEON TROTSKY (LEV DAVIDOVICH BRONSTEIN) (1879–1940)
FROM *LITERATURE AND REVOLUTION* 1923

Russian Jewish revolutionary, born in the Ukraine and educated in Odessa. In 1902 Trotsky escaped from Siberia, where he had been sent after his arrest as a member of a Marxist group and joined Lenin in London. He returned to Russia after the March 1917 Revolution, joined the Bolshevik Party and helped organise the November Revolution. Following the Revolution, he served as commissar for foreign affairs and war. After Lenin's death in 1924, Trotsky's influence declined and in 1927 he was exiled in Central Asia by Stalin. He became the leading figure in the Left opposition to Stalin, which culminated in the formation of the Fourth International in the 1930s. Trotsky's political writings focused on theories of uneven economic development and permanent revolution. His writings on culture form an important part of the Modernist debates about Formalism and 'committed' art. From 1917 onwards, he opposed the notion of 'proletarian culture' and sided with avant-garde movements, supporting the relative autonomy of art against vulgar and mechanistic Marxist views. His views on cultural and political hegemony parallel those of Gramsci, whose letter to Trotsky on Italian Futurism was printed in the Russian edition of Literature and Revolution *in 1923. [See IIIb 36]*

Our Marxist conception of the objective social dependence and social utility of art, when translated into the language of politics, does not at all mean a desire to dominate art by means of decrees and orders. It is not true that we regard only that art as new and revolutionary which speaks of the worker, and it is nonsense to say that we demand that the poets should describe inevitably a factory chimney, or the uprising against capital! Of course the new art cannot but place the struggle of the proletariat in the center of its attention. But the plow of the new art is not limited to numbered strips. On the contrary, it must plow the entire field in all directions. Personal lyrics of the very smallest scope have an absolute right to exist within the new art. Moreover, the new man cannot be formed without a new lyric poetry. But to create it, the poet himself must feel the world in a new way. If Christ alone or Sabaoth himself bends over the poet's embraces, then this only goes to prove how much behind the times his lyrics are and how socially and aesthetically inadequate they are for the new man. Even where such terminology is not a survival of experience so much as of words, it shows psychological inertia and therefore stands in contradiction to the consciousness of the new man. No one is going to prescribe themes to a poet or intends to prescribe them. Please write about anything you can think of! But allow the new class which considers itself, and with reason, called upon to build a new world, to say to you in any given case: It does not make new poets of you to translate the philosophy of life of the seventeenth century into the language of the Acméists. The form of art is, to a certain and very large degree, independent, but the artist who creates this form, and the spectator who is enjoying it, are not empty machines, one for creating form and the other for appreciating it. They are living people, with a crystallized psychology representing a certain unity, even if not entirely harmonious. This psychology is the result of social conditions. The creation and perception of art forms is one of the functions of this psychology. And no matter how wise the Formalists try to be, their whole conception is simply based upon the fact that they ignore the psychology unity of the social man, who creates and who consumes what has been created.

What are we to understand under the term realism? At various periods and by various methods, realism gave expression to the feelings and needs to different social groups. Each one of these realistic schools is subject to a separate and social literary definition, and a separate formal and literary estimation. What have they in common? A definite and important feeling for the world. It consists in a feeling for life as it is, in an artistic acceptance of reality, and not in a shrinking from it, in an active interest in the concrete stability and mobility of life. It is a striving either to picture life as it is or to idealize it, either to justify or to condemn it, either to photograph it or generalize and symbolize it. But it is always a preoccupation with our life of three dimensions as a sufficient and invaluable theme for art. In this large philosophic sense, and not in the narrow sense of a literary school, one may say with certainty that the new art will be realistic. The Revolution cannot live together with mysticism. Nor can the Revolution live together with romanticism, if that which Pilnyak, the Imagists, and others call romanticism is, as it may be feared, mysticism shyly trying to establish itself under a new name. This is not being doctrinaire, this is an insuperable psychological fact. Our age cannot have a shy and portable mysticism, something like a pet dog that is carried along 'with the rest'. Our age wields an ax. Our life, cruel, violent, and disturbed to its very bottom, says: 'I must have an artist of a single love. Whatever way you take hold of me, whatever tools and instruments created by the development of art you choose, I leave to you, to your temperament and to your genius. But you must understand me as I am, you must take me as I will become, and there must be no one else besides me.'

This means a realistic monism, in the sense of a philosophy of life, and not a 'realism' in the sense of the traditional arsenal of literary schools. On the contrary, the new artist will need all the methods and processes evolved in the past, as well as a few supplementary ones, in order to grasp the new life. And this is not going to be artistic eclecticism, because the unity of art is created by an active world-attitude and active life-attitude.

De Maupassant hated the Eiffel Tower, in which no one is forced to imitate him. But it is undoubtedly true that the Eiffel Tower makes a dual impression; one is attracted by the technical simplicity of its form, and, at the same time, repelled by its aimlessness. It is an extremely rational utilization of material for the purpose of making a high structure. But what is it for? It is not a building, but an exercise. At present, as everyone knows, the Eiffel Tower serves as a radio station. This gives it a meaning, and makes it aesthetically more unified. But if the tower had been built from the very beginning as a radio station, it probably would have attained a higher rationality of form, and so therefore a higher perfection of art.

[. . .]

Take the penknife as an example [of purposefulness]. The combination of art and technique can proceed along two fundamental lines; either art embellishes the knife and pictures an elephant, a prize beauty, or the Eiffel Tower on its handle or art helps technique to find an 'ideal' for the knife, that is, such a form which will correspond most adequately to the material of a knife and its purpose. To think that this task can be solved by purely technical means is incorrect, because purpose and material allow for innumerable . . . variations. To make an 'ideal' knife, one must have, besides the knowledge of the properties the material and the methods of its use, both imagination and taste. In accord with the entire tendency of industrial culture, we think that the artistic imagination in creating material objects will be directed towards working out the ideal form of a thing as a thing, and not towards the embellishment of the thing as an aesthetic premium to itself. If this is true for penknives, it will be truer still for wearing apparel, furniture, theatres, and cities. This does not mean the doing away with 'machine-made' art, not even in the most distant future. But it seems that the direct cooperation between art and all branches of technique will become of paramount importance.

Does this mean that industry will absorb art, or that art will lift industry up to itself on Olympus? This question can be answered either way, depending on whether the problem is approached from the side of industry, or from the side of art. But in the object attained, there is no difference between either answer. Both answers signify a gigantic expansion of the scope and artistic quality of industry and we understand here, under industry, the entire field without excepting the industrial activity of man; mechanical and electrified agriculture will also become part of industry.

The wall will fall not only between art and industry, but simultaneously between art and nature also. This is not meant in the sense of Jean-Jacques Rousseau that art will come nearer to a state of nature, but that nature will become more 'artificial'. The present distribution of mountains and rivers, of fields, of meadows, of steppes, of forests, and of seashores, cannot be considered final. Man has already made changes in the map of nature that are not few nor insignificant. But they are mere pupils' practice in comparison with what is coming. Faith merely promises to move mountains; but technology, which takes nothing 'on faith', is actually able to cut down mountains and move them. Up to now this was done for industrial purposes (mines) or for railways (tunnels); in the future this will be done on an immeasurably larger scale, according to a general industrial and artistic plan. Man will occupy himself with re-registering mountains and rivers, and will earnestly and repeatedly make improvements in nature. In the end, he will have rebuilt the earth, if not in his own image, at least according to his own taste. We have not the slightest fear that this taste will be bad. [. . .]

It is difficult to predict the extent of self-government which the man of the future may reach or the heights to which he may carry his technique. Social construction and psycho-physical self-education will become two aspects of one and the same process. And the arts – literature, drama, painting, music, and architecture – will lend this process beautiful form. More correctly, the shell in which the cultural construction and self-education of Communist man will be enclosed, will develop all the vital elements of contemporary art to the highest point. Man will become immeasurably stronger, wiser, and subtler; his body will become more harmonized, his movements more rhythmic, his voice more musical. The forms of life will become dynamically dramatic. The average human type will rise to the heights of an Aristotle, a Goethe, or a Marx. And above this ridge new peaks will rise.

20
ALEXANDRA KOLLONTAI (1872–1952)
FROM 'MAKE WAY FOR THE WINGED EROS' 1923

Russian revolutionary, feminist, writer and diplomat. Daughter of a Russian general, Kollontai abandoned a life of privilege to embark on a mission of spreading revolutionary awareness among women workers. In 1916 she toured the USA, *speaking out against American intervention in the First World War. Following the October Revolution, and as the only woman in the Lenin cabinet, Kollontai became commissar for public welfare. One of her projects in that capacity was the short-lived Ministry for Motherhood which was meant to provide communal spaces and state support for the upbringing of children. She wrote extensively on the role of women under Communism, advocating the relaxation of laws on marriage, divorce and illegitimate children to enhance the status of women. To that effect, Kollontai wrote novels as well as a number of essays and propaganda pieces, arguing always that relations between the sexes should be freed from the conditioning of the bourgeois ideology of property. She is credited with the feminist motto 'The personal is political'. The following extracts from one of Kollontai's 'Letters to the Toiling Youth' (published in the journal* Molodaia Gvardiia, 3, *1923) are taken from* Bolshevik Visions: First Phase of the Cultural Revolution in Soviet Russia, Part I, *edited by William G. Rosenberg, 1990. [See Ia 16]*

You ask me, my young comrade, what place does proletarian ideology give to love? It disturbs you that working class youth 'is now more occupied with love and other such questions' than with the large tasks which are before the working people's republic. If that is the case (and from afar it is difficult for me to judge this), then let us look for the explanation of this phenomenon, and then it will be easier to find an answer to the first question: what place does love occupy in the ideology of the working class?

[. . .]

Not long ago, in the years of acute civil war and struggle with devastation, this enigma was of little concern to anyone in Russia. Other feelings, other more real passions and emotions possessed humanity. Before the threatening face of the great insurgent-rebel, gentle-winged eros ('the god of love') had to disappear timidly from the surface of life. There was no time for love's 'joys and anguishes', no surplus of emotional energy. Such is the law of the preservation of the social-emotional energy of mankind. This energy, in sum, always directs itself toward the major, most immediate goal of the historical moment. The master of the situation for a time was the uncomplicated, natural call of nature – the biological instinct of reproduction, the attraction of two sexual individuals. Man and woman easily, much easier than formerly, much more simply than formerly, came together and separated. They came together without painful, heartfelt emotions and separated without tears and pain.

'Love was without joy.
Separation will have no sorrow.'

Prostitution, of course, disappeared, and similarly there increased a free contact of the sexes (without mutual obligations), whose driving force was the bare instinct of reproduction (unadorned by feelings of love). This fact frightened some people. But in those years the relations between the sexes could really not have been organized differently. Either marriage would continue to be held in the firm, tested, feeling of community, of friendship of many years duration, strengthened still further by the seriousness of the moment, or the marriage contact would arise in passing, in the midst of a pursuit of the cause, for the satisfaction of purely biological need, from which both sides hurried to untie themselves, so that it would not interfere with the fundamental, the major thing: the work for the revolution.

[. . .]

The new labor communist society is being built on the principle of comradeship, of solidarity. But what is solidarity? It is not only the awareness of a community of interests, but further a sincere emotional tie established among members of the working collective. A social structure built on solidarity and cooperation, however, demands that the given society possess a highly developed 'potential of love', that is a capacity of people to experience mutual sympathy. Without the presence of these sensations, there cannot be solidarity. That is why proletarian ideology strives to nurture and strengthen in each member of the working class the feeling of sympathy for the sufferings and needs of one's class compatriots, a sensitive understanding of the needs of the other, a profound, heartfelt consciousness of his or her tie with the other members of the collective. But all these sympathetic feelings – sensitivity, compassion, responsiveness flow from one common source, the capacity to love; to love not in the narrow sexual, but rather in the broad meaning of the word.

Love is a heartfelt emotion of a binding and consequently an organizing character. The bourgeoisie marvelously understood and took into account the fact that love is a great connecting force. Therefore, striving to solidify the family, bourgeois ideology turned 'conjugal love' into a moral virtue. To be a 'good family man' in the eyes of the bourgeoisie was a great and valued quality.

The proletariat cannot help but consider the psycho-social role which the feeling of love in the broad sense of the word and in the sphere of relations between the sexes, can and must play, not in the area of solidifying family-marital relations, but in the sphere of the development of collectivist solidarity.

What is the ideal of love of the working class? What feelings, what experiences will proletarian ideology build into the foundation of the relations between the sexes?

Each epoch has its own ideal of love; each class strives in its own interests to insert its own content into the moral conception of love. Each level of culture, bearing the ever richer spiritual and emotional experiences of mankind, paints the gentle tones of the wings of Eros with its own special color. The content making up the concept of love altered with successive levels of development of the economy and social life. The shades of emotions which were component parts of the feeling of love either were strengthened, or conversely, died off.

From an uncomplicated biological instinct – the striving for reproduction, inherent in all forms of animals from the highest to the lowest, divided into representatives of the opposite sexes – love has, with the passage of its thousands of years of existence, accumulated newer and newer spiritual-emotional experiences. From a biological phenomenon, love became a psycho-social factor.

[. . .]

The many-sidedness of love, under the hegemony of bourgeois ideology and bourgeois-capitalist life, created a series of severe and insoluble emotional dramas. Already from the end of the nineteenth century, the many-sidedness of love was made a favorite theme of writer-psychologists. 'Love for two' even 'love for three' occupied and confused thoughtful representatives of bourgeois culture with its mysteriousness. Already in the 1860s our Russian thinker-publicist A. Herzen (Iskander) tried to reveal this complexity of the soul, this bifurcation of feeling in his novel *Who Is Guilty?* And Chernyshevsky approached the resolution of this problem in his social narrative *What Is To Be Done?* The greatest writers of Scandinavia – (Gamsun, Ibsen, Bjernsen, Geierstam) have also touched on this duality of feeling, this splintering of love. The French fiction writers of the last century returned to it more than once; Romain Rolland, who is close to communism in spirit, writes about it, and Maeterlinck, who is far from us. Such poetic geniuses as Goethe and Byron, such bold pioneers in the area of the inter-relations of the sexes as George Sand, tried in living practice to resolve this complex problem, this 'mystery of love'. Herzen, the author of *Who Is Guilty?* as well as many other great thinkers, poets and social activists, knew it in his own experience. And now the shoulders of many 'not so great' people are burdened by the weight of 'this mystery of the duality of love', and these people are searching in vain for the key to its resolution within the boundaries of bourgeois thought. But meanwhile, the key is in the hands of the proletariat. Only the ideology and life of the new laboring humanity can unravel this complex problem of emotion.

We are here speaking of the duality of love, of the complexities of 'winged Eros', but one must not confuse such duality with sexual relations without Eros, between one man and many women or one woman and many men. Polygamy, in which emotion plays no part, can entail unpleasant harmful consequences (premature exhaustion of the organism, an increase in chances for venereal diseases in contemporary conditions, etc.), but such ties, no matter how intricate they might be, do not create 'emotional dramas'. The 'drama', the conflicts, begin when there is love in its many-faceted nuances and manifestations. The woman loves one man 'with the heights of her soul', with her thoughts, strivings, and wishes, in harmony with his. Another strongly attracts her by the force of physical affinity. In one woman, a man tests the feeling of thoughtful affection, of concerned pity, in another he finds support and understanding for the best strivings of his 'ego'. To which of the two must he devote the fullness of Eros? And why must he tear and maim his soul, if only the presence of both one and the other spiritual tie gives him a completeness of being?

Under the bourgeois system, such a bifurcation of spirit and emotion carries with it inevitable sufferings. Over thousands of years, the culture based on the institution of property nourished in people the conviction that the feeling of love also must have the principle of property as its base. Bourgeois ideology taught, rammed into the heads of people, that love, especially when reciprocal, allows for the mastery of the heart of the loved person entirely and indivisibly. Such an ideal, such an exclusiveness of love, flowed naturally from the established form of conjugal pair marriage and from the bourgeois ideal of the 'all-embracing love' of two spouses. But can such an ideal answer the interests of the working class? Is it not, on the contrary, important and desirable from the point of view of proletarian ideology, that the feelings of people become richer, many-chorded? Is not the many-chorded quality of the spirit and many-sidedness of the soul that very factor which facilitates the growth and nourishment of a complex, intermeshed net of spiritual-emotional ties, by which the social-labor collective is bound? The more these threads are extended from spirit to spirit, from heart to heart, from mind to mind, then the more firmly will be inculcated the spirit of solidarity and the more easily the ideal of the working class, association and unity, will be realized.

Exclusiveness of love, like 'all-embracing' love, cannot be the ideal of love conditioning the relations between the sexes from the point of view of proletarian ideology. On the contrary, the proletariat, taking into account the many-sidedness and many-chorded nature of 'winged Eros', is not thrown into indescribable horror and moral indignation by this discovery, like the hypocritical morality of the bourgeoisie. On the contrary, the proletariat rushes to direct this phenomenon (the result of complex social causes) into a course which will answer its class aims in the moment of struggle and in the moment of the construction of a communist society.

[. . .]

In this new society, communist in soul and emotions, against a background of joyful unity and comradely community of all members of the working, creative collective, Eros will occupy an honored place, as an emotion magnifying human happiness. What will this new reformed Eros be? The boldest fantasy is unable to capture its form. But one thing is clear. The more firmly bound the new humanity by strong chains of solidarity, the higher will be its spiritual and emotional ties in all spheres of life, creativity, and community, and the less place there will remain for love in the contemporary meaning of the word. Contemporary love is always at fault in that it preoccupies the thoughts and feelings of 'loving hearts', but at the same time isolates and separates the loving pair from the collective. Such a separation of the 'loving couple' and moral isolation from the collective, in which the interests, aims, and strivings of all the members are interwoven in a thick net, will become not only superfluous, but psychologically unrealizable. In this new world, the recognized, normal and desirable form of communion of the sexes probably will rest on a healthy, free, natural attraction (without perversions and excesses), on a 'transformed Eros'.

But until then we find ourselves at the crossroads of two cultures. And in this transitional period, accompanied by the fiery combat of two worlds on all fronts, including the ideological front, the proletariat is interested in that which by all measures will facilitate the most rapid accumulation of reserves of 'sympathetic feelings'. In this period the moral ideal conditioning the communion of the sexes is not the naked instinct of sex, but rather the many-sided loving-friendly emotions of both man and woman. These emotions, to answer the newly-formed demands of the new proletarian morality, must base themselves on three fundamental principles:

(1) equality in mutual relations (without male egocentrism and slavish dissolution of her own personality in love by the woman).

(2) mutual recognition of the rights of the other, without pretentions of indivisibly possessing the heart and spirit of the other (a feeling of property cultivated by bourgeois culture).

(3) comradely sensitivity, an ability to heed and understand the work of the spirit of a close and beloved person (bourgeois culture demanded this sensitivity in love on the part of the woman).

But proclaiming the rights of 'winged Eros' (of love), the ideology of the working class also subordinates the love of members of the laboring collective toward one another to a more powerful feeling – love and duty to the collective. However great the love connecting two sexes, however many tender and spiritual ties bind them together, such bonds with the entire collective must be still stronger and more numerous and more organic. Bourgeois morality demanded everything for the beloved person. The morality of the proletariat prescribes – everything for the collective.

But I hear your question. Let it be so. Let loving communion, on the soil of a strengthened spirit of comradeship, become the ideal of the working class. But does not this ideal, this 'moral criterion' of love again impose a heavy hand on romantic feelings? What if it crumples, cripples the gentle wings of 'easily frightened Eros'? Having freed love from the fetters of bourgeois morality, are we not binding it with new chains?

Yes, you are right. The ideology of the proletariat, discarding bourgeois 'morality' in the spheres of romantic-marital relations, nevertheless inevitably works out its own class morality, its own new rules of communion between the sexes, which more closely meet the demands of the working class, nurture the feelings of the members of the class in a given direction, and by so doing put certain chains on emotion. Insofar as the matter concerns love, cultivated by bourgeois culture, the proletariat must undoubtedly pluck many feathers from the wings of the Eros of bourgeois origin. But to complain that the laboring class is putting its stamp on the relations between the sexes in order to bring the emotion love into alignment with its tasks, means not to have the ability to look into the future. It is clear that in place of the former feathers in the wings of Eros, the ideology of the ascending class will succeed in cultivating new feathers of an heretofore unseen beauty, strength and brightness. Do not forget that love inevitably changes form and transforms itself together with change in the cultural-economic base of humanity.

If in loving relations blind, demanding, all embracing passion weakens; if the feeling of possession and the egoistical desire to forever fasten the beloved around oneself is washed away; if the self-satiety of the man and criminal renunciation of her own 'I' on the part of the woman disappears; then there will develop other valued aspects of love. Respect for the personality of the other and the ability to consider others' rights will grow stronger. A mutual sincere sympathy will develop. The striving to express love not only in kisses and embraces, but in togetherness of action, in unity of will, in joint creation, will grow.

The task of proletarian ideology is not to banish Eros from the social community, but only to rearm its quiver with the arrows of a new structure, to nurture the feeling of love between the sexes in the spirit of the greatest force, comradely solidarity.

21
DZIGA VERTOV (1896–1954)
FROM 'A KINO-EYE DISCUSSION' 1924

Russian film maker. Vertov worked as a newsreel cameraman during the Russian Revolution. In 1918 he was made director of the newsreel section of the new Soviet cinema. The following year he established the Kinoki (or Film-Eye) group of experimental documentarists. The group issued manifestos against theatricalism in cinema, proclaiming instead the supremacy of factual material. In 1922 the group instituted a weekly newsreel Kino-Pravda (Film Truth) which integrated documentary material with older news footage. Vertov experimented widely with camera techniques such as slow-motion, close-ups and crosscutting. His theories formed the basis of the resurgent cinéma vérité of the 1960s. The following extracts from Vertov's writings date from 1924. They were translated from the French by David Robinson for Cinema in Revolution: The Heroic Era of the Soviet Film *(Luda and Jean Schnitzer and Marcel Martin eds, 1973).*

From a Kino-Eye Discussion

If we want to understand clearly the effect of films on the audience, we have first to agree about two things:
1. What audience?
2. What effect upon the audience are we talking about?

On the movie-house *habitué*, the ordinary fiction film acts like a cigar or cigarette on a smoker. Intoxicated by the cine-nicotine, the spectator sucks from the screen the substance which soothes his nerves. A cine-object made with the materials of newsreel largely sobers him up, and gives him the impression of a disagreeable-tasting antidote to the poison.

Quite the opposite effect is produced in the case of the virgin spectator who has never seen cinema, and therefore has not been exposed to the fiction film. His education, his habit will start from the film which we shall show him. If, after a course of our *Kino-Pravda* we show him a fiction film, he will find it as bitter as a non-smoker would find his first strong cigarette.

We import quite enough of this tobacco from abroad. Amongst it, it should be said, there are a good many more fag-ends than cigarettes. The cine-cigarettes go to the best theatres, the fag-ends are destined for the provinces, the masses.

To intoxicate and suggest – the essential method of the fiction film approximates it to a religious influence, and makes it possible after a certain time to keep a man in a permanent state of over-excited unconsciousness. ... Musical shows, theatrical and cine-theatrical performances and so on above all act upon the subconscious of the spectator or listener, distorting his protesting consciousness in every possible way.

Consciousness or Subconsciousness

We rise against the collusion between the 'director-enchanter' and the public which is submitted to the enchantment.

The conscious alone can fight against magical suggestions of every kind.

The conscious alone can form a man of firm convictions and opinions.

We need conscious people, not an unconscious mass, ready to yield to any suggestion.

Long live the consciousness of the pure who can see and hear!

Down with the scented veil of kisses, murders, doves and conjuring tricks!

Long live the class vision!

Long live Kino-Eye!

Fragments From a Journal

Our movement is called Kino-Eye. Those of us who fight for the idea of Kino-Eye call ourselves Kino-Eyes. . . . We have many enemies. This is essential. Of course it hinders our bringing our ideas into life. But on the other hand it throws us into the struggle, and sharpens our thoughts.

We are carrying the battle against art cinema, and it is hurled back at us a hundredfold. With the fragments left over by the art cinema – and often without means of any kind – we build our cine-objects.

Kino-Pravda has been kept out of the theatres, but the opinion of the public and of the independent press could not be disguised. *Kino-Pravda* has been greeted unequivocally as a turning-point in Russian cinema

[. . .]

22
LUIS BUÑUEL (1900–83)
'SUBURBS' 1923

Spanish Surrealist film maker and director. Buñuel entered the University of Madrid in 1917 where he met the poet Federigo García Lorca, and the Surrealist painter Salvador Dalí with whom he collaborated on the outrageous Surrealist anti-clerical, anti-bourgeois films, Un Chien andalou *(1928:* An Andulusian Dog*) and* L'Age d'or *(1930:* The Golden Age*). His documentary film on Spanish poverty,* Las Hurdes *(1932), was banned in Spain. In 1947 he settled in Mexico. Buñuel's fascination with the relationship of dream to reality, the nature of obsession and the instability of social structure is reflected in the films made after his return to Spain in 1960. The following piece dates from 1923 and is taken from Francisco Aranda's* Luis Buñuel: A Critical Biography *(trans. David Robinson, 1975). [See IIb 13]*

Suburbs, outskirts, last houses of the city. This essay is about this crazy conglomeration of mud-walls, hillocks, dried up beetles, etc.

They are not the great suburbs of a London: rowdy, seedy, but full of feverish movement. They are those others of the little provincial capital, where poor and idle people live, 'things of shreds and tatters'.

These suburbs have the anodine and expressive complexity of the garret. They are like the junk-room of the city. There is all that is mothy or useless.

In that absurd aesthetic which so much characterizes the suburb, everything is askew, symbolized by the object which crosses our path: the empty tin can, the ravening dog, the burst-bellied mouse or the bent and dusty gas lamp.

All its psychological and material perspective – hostile and sad – remains in our final spiritual plane. The soul of the suburb strangles anything within it that can possess life and movement. In the watercolour which we paint at once with the palette of our senses, we use no more than one colour: grey.

All the racket and shrieking which emerges from the great mouth of the city here becomes obsessing and is united in the monotony which smears the atmosphere of the suburb. Happiness hangs like rags from the eaves, scarcely ever stirred by the breeze of children's voices; the voices of the children who are seen through the dungheaps and to whom no one tells stories.

Our gaze is wounded from time to time – our gaze which has for the suburb the egoist 'God forgive you, brother' of fallen things – by the sign 'TAVERN' in degenerate letters, sick to the core, and which here loses even the proud and vibrant quality which, like wine, this title has everywhere else.

Sheltering under the walls of some little yard, we see at times the earth hills cohabiting with these hundred vague and useless objects – because already one hundred hands have taken all their vitality – and which bury our imagination as in a grave. These little yards suffer nostalgia for bleating, and in the groin of their ochre walls are jewels of vervaine, filthy and forgotten.

In the subjective observation of the suburb the twilight is lit by the evening oil lamp, and then everything is made more rendingly inert. Our soul is lugubriously whipped by the rag hanged by the electric cable or the cries which drift through the air like bats. Far-off the weak lantern wings the eye of sunset, and the rag-dressed shadows take shelter, stretching out their silent and imploring hands.

The endless yawn of the suburb, its fringed and withered eyes, are always the huge maleficence of the city. Even when day dances gaily through the nearby rooftops, it is immediately seized by the snare of the endless sadness of the suburb, which is the black brush-stroke upon the riotous gaiety of the town. These lethargic quarters belong to the land of the incurable, the doomed. Their emotion is the emotion of dried trees. The inhabitants have become victims of the rabid bite which the soul of the suburb produces. This suburbophobia has no cure other than the premature injection of some sacks of gold.

Among the grace of the words figures that of the suburb, dressed in rags, stained with grease, and on its face the brand of the gulf which sleeps in the entries of the houses.

[. . .]

23
VSEVOLOD MEYERHOLD (1874–1940)
FROM 'THE RECONSTRUCTION OF THE THEATRE' 1929

Russian actor, director and film-maker. He was one of the first theatre makers to align his work with the Bolshevik revolution. His influences range from late Russian and European Symbolism to the Constructivists of the 1920s. He sought to make a revolutionary theatre which would incorporate the latest technological developments – hence his 'biomechanics'. Meyerhold's view of technology as emancipatory force is similar to that of Walter Benjamin, who visited him and watched his rehearsals at the Moscow State Higher Theatre Workshop of which he became director in 1921. Meyerhold's theories of acting can also be seen to parallel those of Edward Gordon Craig, whose writings he translated into Russian. In 1937 he was criticised in Pravda *and a year later the Meyerhold Theatre was closed down. In 1939 Meyerhold and his wife, Zinaida Raikh, were arrested and later both murdered. The following extract is taken from the essay – 'The Reconstruction of the Theatre', written in 1929 and translated by Edward Braun (from Richard Drain ed.,* Twentieth-Century Theatre: A Sourcebook, *1995). [See Ib 21, IIIb 3]*

Comrades – when we come to discuss the influence which the modern revolutionary theatre can exert upon the spectator at a time when its own organizers have still to agree on the precise form it should take, we must not overlook a single aspect of it, particularly in view of the need to take account of the demands both of our Party and of the new spectator. Once the theatre is regarded as a means of agitation, it follows that the first concern of all those concerned in the theatre is the clarity of the message conveyed from the stage; the spectator will want to know precisely why a play is being performed and what the director and actors are trying to say in it.

We can induce the spectator to join us in examining a wide range of topics presented as a debate, but employing dramatic situations and characters. We can persuade him to reason and to argue. This ability to start the spectator's brain working is just one of the theatre's properties. But it has another, quite different property: it can stimulate the spectator's feelings and steer him through a complex labyrinth of emotions. Since the theatre has the power to stimulate the emotions as well as the intellect, it follows that it is wrong for a play as a work of art to limit itself to sheer rhetoric, employing raisonneurs and indulging in dialogues borrowed from the so-called 'conversational theatre'. We reject such a theatre as a mere debating chamber. I could recite this lecture to piano or orchestral accompaniment, leaving pauses for the audience to listen to the music and digest my arguments; but it would not transform my lecture and you, the audience, into a dramatic performance.

Since a dramatic performance depends on laws peculiar to the theatre, it is not enough for it to appeal purely to the spectator's intellect. A play must do more than prompt some idea or depict events in such a way as to invite automatic conclusions. Actors do not perform simply to demonstrate the idea of the author, the director or themselves; their struggles, the whole dramatic conflict has a far higher aim than the mere exposition of thesis and antithesis. It is not for that that the public goes to the theatre.

My principal aim today is to try to resolve the confusion which to this day is troubling the theatrical front. In trying to do this, I shall refer to events abroad as well as in the Soviet Union; I must consider not only our world but the world at large. The masses, hungering for spectacle as well as bread, want entertainment which appeals to the heart as well as the intellect, which engages them totally. For this reason our theatre managers and directors must aim to make their productions sparkle with interest and variety. The aim of the theatrical powers that be is to provide as much variety as possible, and for this reason they must try whenever possible to employ every art form.

There was a time when Wagner's idea of a new theatre which would be a dramatic synthesis of words, music, lighting, rhythmical movement and all the magic of the plastic arts was regarded as purely utopian. Now we can see that this is exactly what a production should be: we should employ all the elements which the other arts have to offer and fuse them to produce a concerted effect on the audience.

The theatre which relies on the rhetoric of raisonneurs, which is purely agitatory and thus anti-artistic has long since been exposed as a harmful phenomenon. Other theatres have been successfully propagandist by actually silencing the actor at the play's climax, introducing music to heighten the tension (e.g. *Bubus, the Teacher* by my theatre and *Days in the Melting Pot* by the Leningrad Young Workers' Theatre). You must regard the dramatic theatre as a musical theatre as well. In taking advantage of every possible technical advance, the theatre cannot afford to ignore the cinematograph; the action of the actor on stage can be juxtaposed with his filmed image on a screen.

Alternatively, we might see the dramatic theatre transformed into a kind of revue in which the actor appears now as a dramatic artist, now as an opera singer, now as a dancer, now as an equilibrist, now as a gymnast, now as a clown. Thus, by employing elements of the other arts the theatre can make the performance more diverting and deepen the spectator's comprehension of it.

[. . .] We can see now that all those thundering broadsides of ours were just so many blank charges: all those speeches *à thèse*, those attempts at 'agitation', so often dull and sometimes just plain stupid, those schematized types, signalling their characters as though by semaphore: one signal for the virtuous 'reds', another for the evil 'whites'.

And what about all those scenes in so-called revolutionary plays depicting 'the decline of Europe'? Has it not struck you that the reason for their success is their blatant disregard for the directives of the Glavrepertkom? Dramatists and directors present a picture of 'decadence' in the hope of disgusting the audience. But far from being disgusted, the spectator falls into raptures over the 'delights' before him: he enjoys watching unclothed women dancing the foxtrot, he enjoys listening to jazz. And why does he enjoy it? Surely because the so-called 'positive' scenes are full of dreary raisonneurs; there's not one single character who radiates the fervour demanded by such objects as socialist reconstruction.

The theatre is faced with a new task. The theatre must work on the spectator in order to awaken and strengthen in him a militancy strong enough to help him conquer the oblomovism, manilovism, hypocrisy, erotomania and pessimism within herself. How can we acquaint the manual labourers of socialism with the full magnitude of the revolution? How can we imbue them with that 'life-giving force' (to quote

Comrade Stalin) which will carry the masses forward to a world of new revolutionary creative effort?

How indeed, if not through the theatre?

And once again the actor stands out as the main transmitter of the invigorating shock. But what must we do to make this shock effective, to help the actor transmit it to the audience? Above all, we must strengthen those elements of the production which strike directly at the spectator's emotions.

In the light of present conditions we must take down that old slogan which has been so violently distorted by the more diehard of our critics. I mean: 'Down with beauty in the theatre!' When we started to build stage-constructions in place of old-style sets we thundered: 'Down with beauty!' We meant that painted designs pandered to the snob with his own peculiar conception of the function of the theatre; to such spectators painted sets seemed indispensable.

The modern spectator, who developed his own sense of style during the struggles of the Revolution and has shown himself quite ready to accept the extremes of stylized production (he has become familiar with stylization through watching productions at the Meyerhold Theatre and theatres of that type, as well as club performances at which he can experience the impact of a theatre employing the most primitive means) the modern spectator finds constructions wholly convincing.

Now that the taste of the mass spectator has become far more sophisticated, we must think in terms of more complex musical spectacles. So surely it is time we reconsidered the slogan, 'Down with beauty'. By employing a good sound construction (as a convenient platform for acting) we do not free ourselves from the obligation to construct it beautifully. When Ford markets a good sound automobile he also tries to make it look beautiful, even if his conception of beauty is different from, say, that of the 'World of Art'. We must realize that the beauty of Ford's car is a direct outcome of its efficiency and reliability.

Today's aesthetic must take account of the new standards which have been created by new social conditions. The art of today is different from the art of feudal or bourgeois society. We must understand clearly what we mean by beauty and reject all beauty that is not utilitarian. We need beauty today as much as we ever did in order to counteract the effects of the 'oblomovism' whose roots are spreading rapidly through our society. And now that the kulaks are putting out even stronger roots in our villages, now that the Church is ensnaring our youth, it is time we all told the so-called 'Kulturträger' of the theatre to make still greater efforts to help our art flood the country with beauty.

24
ERWIN PISCATOR (1893–1966)
FROM 'BASIC PRINCIPLES OF SOCIOLOGICAL DRAMA' 1929

German actor, director and theatre theoretician. Piscator's first productions were for army theatre units during the First World War, where he was also wounded. Throughout his life he was concerned with creating and theorising a political theatre. He started in 1920 with agit-prop experimentations, while still a member of the German Communist Party. He utilised modern technologies of the stage, most famously, projections, in his production Flags *(1924) and popular styles, like revues and cabaret, in* The Red Revue *(1924). He fell out of favour with the Communist Party in 1927 and continued to work in political theatre with dwindling resources. The Bauhaus director Walter Gropius (see below, section IIb) designed a 'total theatre' for Piscator's productions, though this was never realised. When the Nazis came to power, he was working in the Soviet Union but soon moved to the United States, as many of his Soviet collaborators were being arrested. He taught in New York until the McCarthy purges drove him back to Berlin in 1951. During his final years Piscator ran the Free Volksbühne Theatre in the western sector of the city. The following extracts date from 1929 and are translated by Hugh Rorrison (from Richard Drain ed.,* Twentieth-Century Theatre: A Sourcebook, *1995).*

1   The function of man

The War finally buried bourgeois individualism under a hail of steel and a holocaust of fire. Man, the individual, existing as an isolated being, independent (at least seemingly) of social connections, revolving egocentrically around the concept of the self, in fact lies buried beneath a marble slab inscribed 'The Unknown Soldier'. Or, as Remarque formulated it, 'The generation of 1914 perished in the war, even if some did survive the shellfire.' What came back had nothing more in common with concepts like man, mankind, and humanity, which had symbolised the eternal nature of the God-given order in the parlours of prewar days. [. . .]

The epoch whose social and economic conditions have in fact perhaps deprived the individual of his right to be a man, without affording him the higher humanity of a new society, has raised itself on a pedestal as the new hero. It is no longer the private, personal fate of the individual, but the times and the fate of the masses that are the heroic factors in the new drama.

Does the individual lose the attributes of his personality in the process? Does he love, hate or suffer less than the heroes of former generations? Certainly not, but all his emotional complexes are seen from a new angle. It is no longer one man alone, insulated, a world in himself, who experiences his fate; that man is inseparably bound up with the great political and economic factors of the times, as Brecht once pointedly observed: 'Every Chinese coolie is forced to take part in world politics to earn his daily bread.' He is bound in all his utterances to the destiny of the age, regardless of what his station in life might be.

For us, man portrayed on the stage is significant as a social function. It is not his relationship to himself, nor his relationship to God, but his relationship to society which is central. Whenever he appears, his class or social stratum appears with him. His moral, spiritual or sexual conflicts are conflicts with society. The Ancients may have focused on his relationship to the Fates, the Middle Ages on his relationship to God, Relationalism on his relationship to nature, Romanticism on his relationship to the power of the emotions –: a time in which the relationship of individuals in the community to one another, the revision of human values, the realignment of social relationships is the order of the day cannot fail to see mankind in terms of society and the social problems of the times, i.e., as a political being.

The excessive stress on the political angle – and it is not our work, but the disharmony in current social conditions which makes every sign of life political – may in a sense lead to a distorted view of human ideals, but the distorted view at least has the advantage of corresponding to reality.

We, as revolutionary Marxists, cannot consider our task complete if we produce an uncritical copy of reality, conceiving the theatre as a mirror of the times. We can no more consider this our task than we can overcome this state of affairs by theatrical means alone, nor can we conceal the disharmony with a discreet veil, nor can we present man as a creature of sublime greatness in times which in fact socially distort him – in a word, it is not our business to produce an idealistic effect. The business of revolutionary theatre is to take reality as its point of departure and to magnify the social discrepancy, making it an element of our indictment, our revolt, our new order.

2   The significance of the technical side

It has probably become clear from what has already been stated that technical innovations were never an end in themselves for me. Any means I have used or am currently in the process of using were designed to elevate the events on the stage onto a historical plane and not just to enlarge the technical range of the stage machinery.

This elevation, which was inextricably bound up with the use of Marxist dialectics in the theatre, had not been achieved by the plays themselves. My technical devices had been developed to cover up the deficiencies of the dramatists' products. [. . .]

It is not mere chance that in an age whose technical achievements tower above its achievements in every other field the stage should become highly technical. And neither is it mere chance that this technical invasion should receive an impetus from a sector which is in conflict with the social order. Intellectual and social revolutions have always been closely bound up with technical upheavals. And a change in the function of the theatre was inconceivable without bringing the stage equipment technically up to date. In this regard it seems to me that we have just caught up with something which should have been done long ago. With the exception of the revolving stage and electric light the stage at the beginning of the twentieth century was still in the same position that Shakespeare had left it in: a square segment, a picture frame through which the spectator gets a 'forbidden look' at a strange world. The insurmountable gulf between stage and auditorium has decisively shaped international drama for three centuries. It was a drama of make-believe. The theatre existed for three hundred years on the fiction that there were no spectators in the house. Even works which were revolutionary in their day deferred to this assumption, were forced to defer to it. Why? Because the theatre as an institution, as a piece of apparatus, as a house had never until 1917 been in the hands of the oppressed class, and because that class had never been in a position to liberate the theatre structurally as well as intellectually. This task was taken in hand straight away and with the utmost energy by the stage directors of Revolutionary Russia. I had no choice but to follow the same path in my conquest of the theatre, but in our context that path led neither to the end of the theatre, nor, at least to date, to a change in theatre architecture, but only to radical changes in stage machinery, which, taken all in all, amounted to the destruction of the old box form.

From the Proletarisches Theater to *Storm over Gotland* I was sustained by various sources in my attempts to put an end to bourgeois forms and replace them with a form which would bring the spectator into the theatre not as a fictitious concept but as a living force. This tendency was, of course, in the beginning political, and all technical means were subordinate to it. And if these means were subordinate, still incomplete, strained, overemphatic, the reason is to be sought in the conflict with a house which was without provision for them.

IIb

Manifestos

velocity
+ technologies of
speed

1
FUTURISM

1a
FILIPPO TOMMASO MARINETTI (1876–1944)
'THE FOUNDING AND MANIFESTO OF FUTURISM 1909';
'THE VARIETY THEATRE' 1913

Italian poet, founder and editor of the journal Poesia. *Marinetti abandoned Symbolism in favour of the ultra-modern concepts of simultaneism, speed and dynamism which became the key principles of the Futurist movement. A militant nationalist, he soon became a follower of Mussolini's Fascism, as well as a tireless promoter of Italian art and his own version of avant-garde practice. To that end, he toured Europe extensively and his appearances and interventions were typically surrounded by an atmosphere of scandal and notoriety. The manifesto reproduced below was originally published in the Paris newspaper* Le Figaro, *in 1909. 'The Variety Theatre' was written in 1913. Both pieces appear in R. W. Flint's translation for the 1972 Farrar, Straus and Giroux edition of Marinetti's* Selected Works.

The Founding and Manifesto of Futurism 1909

We had stayed up all night, my friends and I, under hanging mosque lamps with domes of filigreed brass, domes starred like our spirits, shining like them with the prisoned radiance of electric hearts. For hours we had trampled our atavistic ennui into rich oriental rugs, arguing up to the last confines of logic and blackening many reams of paper with our frenzied scribbling.

An immense pride was buoying us up, because we felt ourselves alone at that hour, alone, awake, and on our feet, like proud beacons or forward sentries against an army of hostile stars glaring down at us from their celestial encampments. Alone with stokers feeding the hellish fires of great ships, alone with the black spectres who grope in the red-hot bellies of locomotives launched down their crazy courses, alone with drunkards reeling like wounded birds along the city walls.

Suddenly we jumped, hearing the mighty noise of the huge double-decker trams that rumbled by outside, ablaze with coloured lights, like villages on holiday suddenly struck and uprooted by the flooding Po and dragged over falls and through gorges to the sea.

Then the silence deepened. But, as we listened to the old canal muttering its feeble prayers and the creaking bones of sickly palaces above their damp green beards, under the windows we suddenly heard the famished roar of automobiles.

'Let's go!' I said. 'Friends, away! Let's go! Mythology and the Mystic Ideal are defeated at last. We're about to see the Centaur's birth and, soon after, the first flight of Angels! . . . We must shake the gates of life, test the bolts and hinges. Let's go! Look there, on the earth, the very first dawn! There's nothing to match the splendour of the sun's red sword, slashing for the first time through our millennial gloom!'

We went up to the three snorting beasts, to lay amorous hands on their torrid breasts. I stretched out on my car like a corpse on its bier, but revived at once under the steering wheel, a guillotine blade that threatened my stomach.

The raging broom of madness swept us out of ourselves and drove us through streets as rough and deep as the beds of torrents. Here and there, sick lamplight through window glass taught us to distrust the deceitful mathematics of our perishing eyes.

I cried, 'The scent, the scent alone is enough for our beasts.'

And like young lions we ran after Death, its dark pelt blotched with pale crosses as it escaped down the vast violet living and throbbing sky.

But we had no ideal Mistress raising her divine form to the clouds, nor any cruel Queen to whom to offer our bodies, twisted like Byzantine rings! There was nothing to make us wish for death, unless the wish to be free at last from the weight of our courage!

And on we raced, hurling watchdogs against doorsteps, curling them under our burning tyres like collars under a flatiron. Death, domesticated, met me at every turn, gracefully holding out a paw, or once in a while hunkering down, making velvety caressing eyes at me from every puddle.

'Let's break out of the horrible shell of wisdom and throw ourselves like pride-ripened fruit into the wide, contorted mouth of the wind!

Let's give ourselves utterly to the Unknown, not in desperation but only to replenish the deep wells of the Absurd!'

The words were scarcely out of my mouth when I spun my car around with the frenzy of a dog trying to bite its tail, and there, suddenly, were two cyclists coming towards me, shaking their fists, wobbling like two equally convincing but nevertheless contradictory arguments. Their stupid dilemma was blocking my way – Damn! Ouch! . . . I stopped short and to my disgust rolled over into a ditch with my wheels in the air. . . .

O maternal ditch, almost full of muddy water! Fair factory drain! I gulped down your nourishing sludge; and I remembered the blessed black breast of my Sudanese nurse. . . . When I came up – torn, filthy, and stinking – from under the capsized car, I felt the white-hot iron of joy deliciously pass through my heart!

A crowd of fishermen with handlines and gouty naturalists were already swarming around the prodigy. With patient, loving care those people rigged a tall derrick and iron grapnels to fish out my car, like a big beached shark. Up it came from the ditch, slowly, leaving in the bottom, like scales, its heavy framework of good sense and its soft upholstery of comfort.

They thought it was dead, my beautiful shark, but a caress from me was enough to revive it; and there it was, alive again, running on its powerful fins!

And so, faces smeared with good factory muck – plastered with metallic waste, with senseless sweat, with celestial soot – we, bruised, our arms in slings, but unafraid, declared our high intentions to all the *living* of the earth.

Manifesto of Futurism

1. We intend to sing the love of danger, the habit of energy and fear-lessness.
2. Courage, audacity, and revolt will be essential elements of our poetry.
3. Up to now literature has exalted a pensive immobility, ecstasy, and sleep. We intend to exalt aggressive action, a feverish insomnia, the racer's stride, the mortal leap, the punch and the slap.
4. We affirm that the world's magnificence has been enriched by a new beauty: the beauty of speed. A racing car whose hood is adorned with great pipes, like serpents of explosive breath – a roaring car that seems to ride on grapeshot is more beautiful than the *Victory of Samothrace*.
5. We want to hymn the man at the wheel, who hurls the lance of his spirit across the Earth, along the circle of its orbit.
6. The poet must spend himself with ardour, splendour, and generosity, to swell the enthusiastic fervour of the primordial elements.
7. Except in struggle, there is no more beauty. No work without an aggressive character can be a masterpiece. Poetry must be conceived as a violent attack on unknown forces, to reduce and prostrate them before man.
8. We stand on the last promontory of the centuries! ... Why should we look back, when what we want is to break down the mysteri-ous doors of the Impossible? Time and Space died yesterday. We already live in the absolute, because we have created eternal, omnipres-ent speed.
9. *We will glorify war* – the world's only hygiene – militarism, patriotism, the destructive gesture of freedom-bringers, beautiful ideas worth dying for, *and scorn for woman.*
10. We will destroy the museums, libraries, academies of every kind, will fight moralism, feminism, every opportunistic or utilitarian cowardice.
11. We will sing of great crowds excited by work, by pleasure, and by *riot*; we will sing of the multicoloured, polyphonic tides of revolution in the modern capitals; we will sing of the vibrant nightly fervour of arsenals and shipyards blazing with violent electric moons; greedy railway stations that devour smoke-plumed serpents; factories hung on clouds by the crooked lines of their smoke; bridges that stride the rivers like giant gymnasts, flashing in the sun with a glitter of knives; adventurous steamers that sniff the horizon; deep-chested locomotives whose wheels paw the tracks like the hooves of enormous steel horses bridled by tubing; and the sleek flight of planes whose propellers chatter in the wind like banners and seem to cheer like an enthusiastic crowd.

It is from Italy that we launch through the world this violently upsetting incendiary manifesto of ours. With it, today, we establish *Futurism*, because we want to free this land from its smelly gangrene of professors, archaeologists, *ciceroni* and antiquarians. For too long has Italy been a dealer in second-hand clothes. We mean to free her from the numberless museums that cover her like so many graveyards.

Museums: cemeteries! . . . Identical, surely, in the sinister promiscuity of so many bodies unknown to one another. Museums: public dormitories where one lies forever beside hated or unknown beings. Museums: absurd abattoirs of painters and sculptors ferociously slaughtering each other with colour-blows and line-blows, the length of the fought-over walls!

That one should make an annual pilgrimage, just as one goes to the graveyard on All Souls' Day – that I grant. That once a year one should leave a floral tribute beneath the *Gioconda*, I grant you that. . . . But I don't admit that our sorrows, our fragile courage, our morbid restlessness should be given a daily conducted tour through the museums. Why poison ourselves? Why rot?

And what is there to see in an old picture except the laborious contortions of an artist throwing himself against the barriers that thwart his desire to express his dream completely? . . . Admiring an old picture is the same as pouring our sensibility into a funerary urn instead of hurling it far off, in violent spasms of action and creation.

Do you, then, wish to waste all your best powers in this eternal and futile worship of the past, from which you emerge fatally exhausted, shrunken, beaten down?

In truth I tell you that daily visits to museums, libraries, and academies (cemeteries of empty exertion, Calvaries of crucified dreams, registries of aborted beginnings!) are, for artists, as damaging as the prolonged supervision by parents of certain young people drunk with their talent and their ambitious wills. When the future is barred to them, the admirable past may be a solace for the ills of the moribund, the sickly, the prisoner. . . . But we want no part of it, the past, we the young and strong *Futurists*!

So let them come, the gay incendiaries with charred fingers! Here they are! Here they are! . . . Come on! set fire to the library shelves! Turn aside the canals to flood the museums! . . . Oh, the joy of seeing the glorious old canvases bobbing adrift on those waters, discoloured and shredded! . . . Take up your pickaxes, your axes and hammers and wreck, wreck the venerable cities, pitilessly!

The oldest of us is thirty: so we have at least a decade for finishing our work. When we are forty, other younger and stronger men will probably throw us in the wastebasket like useless manuscripts – we want it to happen!

They will come against us, our successors, will come from far away, from every quarter, dancing to the winged cadence of their first songs, flexing the hooked claws of predators, sniffing doglike at the academy doors the strong odour of our decaying minds, which will already have been promised to the literary catacombs.

But we won't be there. . . . At last they'll find us – one winter's night – in open country, beneath a sad roof drummed by a monotonous rain. They'll see us crouched beside our trembling aeroplanes in the act of warming our hands at the poor little blaze that our books of today will give out when they take fire from the flight of our images.

They'll storm around us, panting with scorn and anguish, and all of them, exasperated by our proud daring, will hurtle to kill us, driven by a hatred the more implacable the more their hearts will be drunk with love and admiration for us.

Injustice, strong and sane, will break out radiantly in their eyes.

Art, in fact, can be nothing but violence, cruelty, and injustice.

The oldest of us is thirty: even so we have already scattered treasures, a thousand treasures of force, love, courage, astuteness, and raw will-power; have thrown them impatiently away, with fury, carelessly, unhesitatingly, breathless, and unresting. . . . Look at us! We are still untired! Our hearts know no weariness because they are fed with fire, hatred, and speed! . . . Does that amaze you? It should, because you can never remember having lived! Erect on the summit of the world, once again we hurl our defiance at the stars!

You have objections? – Enough! Enough! We know them. . . . We've understood! . . . Our fine deceitful intelligence tells us that we are the revival and extension of our ancestors – Perhaps! . . . If only it were so! – But who cares? We don't want to understand! . . . Woe to anyone who says those infamous words to us again!

Lift up your heads!

Erect on the summit of the world, once again we hurl defiance to the stars!

The Variety Theatre
(*29 September 1913*)

We are deeply disgusted with the contemporary theatre (verse, prose, and musical) because it vacillates stupidly between historical reconstruction (pastiche or plagiarism) and photographic reproduction of our daily life; a finicking, slow, analytic, and diluted theatre worthy, all in all, of the age of the oil lamp.

FUTURISM EXALTS THE VARIETY THEATRE because:

1. The Variety Theatre, born as we are from electricity, is lucky in having no tradition, no masters, no dogma, and it is fed by swift actuality.
2. The Variety Theatre is absolutely practical, because it proposes to distract and amuse the public with comic effects, erotic stimulation, or imaginative astonishment.
3. The authors, actors, and technicians of the Variety Theatre have only one reason for existing and triumphing: incessantly to invent new elements of astonishment. Hence the absolute impossibility of arresting or repeating oneself, hence an excited competition of brains and muscles to conquer the various records of agility, speed, force, complication, and elegance.
4. The Variety Theatre is unique today in its use of the cinema, which enriches it with an incalculable number of visions and otherwise unrealizable

spectacles (battles, riots, horse races, automobile and airplane meets, trips, voyages, depths of the city, the countryside, oceans, and skies).

5. The Variety Theatre, being a profitable show window for countless inventive forces, naturally generates what I call 'the futurist marvelous', produced by modern mechanics. Here are some of the elements of this 'marvelous': (*a*) powerful caricatures; (*b*) abysses of the ridiculous; (*c*) delicious, impalpable ironies; (*d*) all-embracing, definitive symbols; (*e*) cascades of uncontrollable hilarity; (*f*) profound analogies between humanity, the animal, vegetable, and mechanical worlds; (*g*) flashes of revealing cynicism; (*h*) plots full of the wit, repartee, and conundrums that aerate the intelligence; (*i*) the whole gamut of laughter and smiles, to flex the nerves; (*j*) the whole gamut of stupidity, imbecility, doltishness, and absurdity, insensibly pushing the intelligence to the very border of madness; (*k*) all the new significations of light, sound, noise, and language, with their mysterious and inexplicable extensions into the least-explored part of our sensibility; (*l*) a cumulus of events unfolded at great speed, of stage characters pushed from right to left in two minutes ('and now let's have a look at the Balkans'; King Nicolas, Enver-Bey, Daneff, Venizelos, belly-blows and fistfights between Serbs and Bulgars, a *couplet*, and everything vanishes); (*m*) instructive satirical pantomimes; (*n*) caricatures of suffering and nostalgia, strongly impressed on the sensibility through gestures exasperating in their spasmodic, hesitant, weary slowness; grave words made ridiculous by funny gestures, bizarre disguises, mutilated words, ugly faces, pratfalls.

6. Today the Variety Theatre is the crucible in which the elements of an emergent new sensibility are seething. Here you find an ironic decomposition of all the worn-out prototypes of the Beautiful, the Grand, the Solemn, the Religious, the Ferocious, the Seductive, and the Terrifying, and also the abstract elaboration of the new prototypes that will succeed these.

   The Variety Theatre is thus the synthesis of everything that humanity has up to now refined in its nerves to divert itself by laughing at material and moral grief; it is also the bubbling fusion of all the laughter, all the smiles, all the mocking grins, all the contortions and grimaces of future humanity. Here you sample the joy that will shake men for another century, their poetry, painting, philosophy, and the leaps of their architecture.

7. The Variety Theatre offers the healthiest of all spectacles in its dynamism of form and color (simultaneous movement of jugglers, ballerinas, gymnasts, colorful riding masters, spiral cyclones of dancers spinning on the points of their feet). In its swift, over-powering dance rhythms the Variety Theatre forcibly drags the slowest souls out of their torpor and forces them to run and jump.

8. The Variety Theatre is alone in seeking the audience's collaboration. It doesn't remain static like a stupid *voyeur*, but joins noisily in the action, in the singing, accompanying the orchestra, communicating with the actors in

surprising actions and bizarre dialogues. And the actors bicker clownishly with the musicians.

The Variety Theatre uses the smoke of cigars and cigarettes to join the atmosphere of the theatre to that of the stage. And because the audience cooperates in this way with the actors' fantasy, the action develops simultaneously on the stage, in the boxes, and in the orchestra. It continues to the end of the performance, among the battalions of fans, the honeyed dandies who crowd the stage door to fight over the *star*; double final victory: chic dinner and bed.

9. The Variety Theatre is a school of sincerity for man because it exalts his rapacious instincts and snatches every veil from woman, all the phrases, all the sighs, all the romantic sobs that mask and deform her. On the other hand it brings to light all woman's marvelous animal qualities, her grasp, her powers of seduction, her faithlessness, and her resistance.

10. The Variety Theatre is a school of heroism in the difficulty of setting records and conquering resistances, and it creates on the stage the strong, sane atmosphere of danger. (E.g., death-diving, 'looping the loop' on bicycles, in cars, and on horseback.)

11. The Variety Theatre is a school of subtlety, complication, and mental synthesis, in its clowns, magicians, mind readers, brilliant calculators, writers of skits, imitators and parodists, its musical jugglers and eccentric Americans, its fantastic pregnancies that give birth to objects and weird mechanisms.

12. The Variety Theatre is the only school that one can recommend to adolescents and to talented young men, because it explains, quickly and incisively, the most abstruse problems and most complicated political events. Example: A year ago at the Folies-Bergère, two dancers were acting out the meandering discussions between Cambon and Kinderlen-Watcher on the question of Morocco and the Congo in a revealing symbolic dance that was equivalent to at least three years' study of foreign affairs. Facing the audience, their arms entwined, glued together, they kept making mutual territorial concessions, jumping back and forth, to left and right, never separating, neither of them ever losing sight of his goal, which was to become more and more entangled. They gave an impression of extreme courtesy, of skilful, flawlessly diplomatic vacillation, ferocity, diffidence, stubbornness, meticulousness.

Furthermore the Variety Theatre luminously explains the governing laws of life:

a) the necessity of complication and varying rhythms;

b) the fatality of the lie and the contradiction (e.g., two-faced English *danseuses*: little shepherd girl and fearful soldier);

c) the omnipotence of a methodical will that modifies human powers;

d) a synthesis of speed + transformations.

13. The Variety Theatre systematically disparages ideal love and its romantic obsession that repeats the nostalgic languors of passion to satiety, with

the robot-like monotony of a daily profession. It whimsically mechanizes sentiment, disparages and healthily tramples down the compulsion toward carnal possession, lowers lust to the natural function of coitus, deprives it of every mystery, every crippling anxiety, every unhealthy idealism.

Instead, the Variety Theatre gives a feeling and a taste for easy, light and ironic loves. Café-concert performances in the open air on the terraces of casinos offer a most amusing battle between spasmodic moonlight, tormented by infinite desperations, and the electric light that bounces off the fake jewelry, painted flesh, multicolored petti-coats, velvets, tinsel, the counterfeit color of lips. Naturally the energetic electric light triumphs and the soft decadent moonlight is defeated.

14. The Variety Theatre is naturally anti-academic, primitive, and naïve, hence the more significant for the unexpectedness of its discoveries and the simplicity of its means. (E.g., the systematic tour of the stage that the *chanteuses* make, like caged animals, at the end of every *couplet*.)

15. The Variety Theatre destroys the Solemn, the Sacred, the Serious, and the Sublime in Art with a capital *A*. It cooperates in the Futurist destruction of immortal masterworks, plagiarizing them, parodying them, making them look commonplace by stripping them of their solemn apparatus as if they were mere *attractions*. So we unconditionally endorse the performance of *Parsifal* in forty minutes, now in rehearsal in a great London music hall.

16. The Variety Theatre destroys all our conceptions of perspective, proportion, time, and space. (E.g., a little doorway and gate, thirty centimeters high, alone in the middle of the stage, which certain eccentric Americans open and close as they pass and repass, very seriously as if they couldn't do otherwise.)

17. The Variety Theatre offers us all the records so far attained: the greatest speed and the finest gymnastics and acrobatics of the Japanese, the greatest muscular frenzy of the Negroes, the greatest development of animal intelligence (horses, elephants, seals, dogs, trained birds), the finest melodic inspiration of the Gulf of Naples and the Russian steppes, the best Parisian wit, the greatest competitive force of different races (boxing and wrestling), the greatest anatomical monstrosity, the greatest female beauty.

18. The conventional theatre exalts the inner life, professorial meditation, libraries, museums, monotonous crises of conscience, stupid analyses of feelings, in other words (dirty thing and dirty word), *psychology*, whereas, on the other hand, the Variety Theatre exalts action, heroism, life in the open air, dexterity, the authority of instinct and intuition. To psychology it opposes what I call 'body-madness' (*fisicofollia*).

19. Finally, the Variety Theatre offers to every country (like Italy) that has no great single capital city a brilliant résumé of Paris considered as the one magnetic center of luxury and ultrarefined pleasure.

FUTURISM WANTS TO TRANSFORM THE VARIETY THEATRE INTO A THEATRE OF AMAZEMENT, RECORD-SETTING, AND BODY-MADNESS.

1b
ILYA ZDANEVICH (1894–1975) AND MIKHAIL LARIONOV (1881–1964) 'WHY WE PAINT OURSELVES: A FUTURIST MANIFESTO' 1913

The text of this Futurist-inspired manifesto appeared in the St Petersburg magazine Argus, *in 1913. Zdanevich published a book on the work of his friends and collaborators Larionov and Natalia Goncharova (see below) and, like them, was also interested in and promoted neo-primitivism. Zdanevich met Marinetti in Moscow in 1914 and helped to organise a Futurist group in Tiflis in 1917–18. In 1921 he joined Larionov and Goncharova in Paris, where they had already settled from 1918. The manifesto appears in John E. Bowlt's translation (from his revised and enlarged edition of* Russian Art of the Avant-Garde, *1988).*

To the frenzied city of arc lamps, to the streets bespattered with bodies, to the houses huddled together, we have brought our painted faces; we're off and the track awaits the runners.

Creators, we have not come to destroy construction, but to glorify and to affirm it. The painting of our faces is neither an absurd piece of fiction, nor a relapse – it is indissolubly linked to the character of our life and of our trade.

The dawn's hymn to man, like a bugler before the battle, calls to victories over the earth, hiding itself beneath the wheels until the hour of vengeance; the slumbering weapons have awoken and spit on the enemy.

The new life requires a new community and a new way of propagation.

Our self-painting is the first speech to have found unknown truths. And the conflagrations caused by it show that the menials of the earth have not lost hope of saving the old nests, have gathered all forces to the defence of the gates, have crowded together knowing that with the first goal scored we are the victors.

The course of art and a love of life have been our guides. Faithfulness to our trade inspires us, the fighters. The steadfastness of the few presents forces that cannot be overcome.

We have joined art to life. After the long isolation of artists, we have loudly summoned life and life has invaded art, it is time for art to invade life. The painting of our faces is the beginning of the invasion. That is why our hearts are beating so.

We do not aspire to a single form of aesthetics. Art is not only a monarch, but also a newsman and a decorator. We value both print and news. The synthesis of decoration and illustration is the basis of our self-painting. We decorate life and preach – that's why we paint ourselves.

Self-painting is one of the new valuables that belong to the people as they all do in our day and age. The old ones were incoherent and squashed flat by money. Gold was valued as an ornament and became expensive. We throw down gold and precious stones from their pedestal and declare them valueless. Beware, you who collect them and horde them – you will soon be beggars.

It began in '05. Mikhail Larionov painted a nude standing against a background of a carpet and extended the design onto her. But there was no proclamation. Now Parisians are doing the same by painting the legs of their dancing girls, and ladies powder themselves with brown powder and like Egyptians elongate their eyes. But that's old age. We, however, join contemplation with action and fling ourselves into the crowd.

To the frenzied city of arc lamps, to the streets bespattered with bodies, to the houses huddled together, we have not brought the past: unexpected flowers have bloomed in the hothouse and they excite us.

City dwellers have for a long time been varnishing their nails, using eyeshadow, rouging their lips, cheeks, hair – but all they are doing is to imitate the earth.

We, creators, have nothing to do with the earth; our lines and colors appeared with us. If we were given the plumage of parrots, we would pluck out their feathers to use as brushes and crayons.

If we were given immortal beauty, we would daub over it and kill it – we who know no half measures.

Tattooing doesn't interest us. People tattoo themselves once and for always. We paint ourselves for an hour, and a change of experience calls for a change of painting, just as picture devours picture, when on the other side of a car windshield shopwindows flash by running into each other: that's our faces. Tattooing is beautiful but it says little – only about one's tribe and exploits. Our painting is the newsman.

Facial expressions don't interest us. That's because people have grown accustomed to understanding them, too timid and ugly as they are. Our faces are like the screech of the trolley warning the hurrying passers-by, like the drunken sounds of the great tango. Mimicry is expressive but colorless. Our painting is the decorator.

Mutiny against the earth and transformation of faces into a projector of experiences.

The telescope discerned constellations lost in space, painting will tell of lost ideas.

We paint ourselves because a clean face is offensive, because we want to herald the unknown, to rearrange life, and to bear man's multiple soul to the upper reaches of reality.

2

MINA LOY (1882–1966)
'FEMINIST MANIFESTO' 1914

English poet, painter and dramatist. Loy studied in Munich, London and Paris and later moved to France. Her project partly consisted of establishing a feminist reading of Futurist aesthetics and cultural politics (see also 'Feminist Manifesto' below). After the alignment of Futurism with Fascism she rejected the movement. Her play The Pamperers *(published in* Dial, *1920) satirises insular and self-important avant-gardism in general, including a particular attack on Futurist 'buffoons'. Loy's concern with social critique and the need for alternative ideologies of gender was expressed in the manifesto-like pamphlet* Psycho-Democracy, *published in Florence in 1920 and reprinted in* Little Review *the following year. Her collection of poems,* Lunar Baedecker *(1923), also looks at female experience within an aesthetic and political context, while being technically innovative and adhering to Modernist form. Loy's work was particularly admired and championed by Ezra Pound who saw in her poetry the fulfilment of his own 'logopoeic' model. Her numerous contributions to journals are collected in* Lunar Baedecker and Time-Tables *(1958).* Last Lunar Baedecker *(1982) is the complete collection of her poetry. She also left an uncompleted volume entitled* Anglo-

Mongrels and the Rose *(1925). Written in 1914, the same year as her 'Aphorisms on Futurism', Loy's manifesto is taken from the collection* The Last Lunar Baedeker, *edited by Roger L. Conover, 1982.*

The Feminist Movement as instituted at present is INADEQUATE.

Women, if you want to realize yourselves (for you are on the brink of a devastating psychological upheaval) all your pet illusions must be unmasked. The lies of centuries have got to be discarded. Are you prepared for the WRENCH?

There is no half-measure, no scratching on the surface of the rubbish heap of tradition. Nothing short of Absolute Demolition will bring about reform. So cease to place your confidence in economic legislation, vice-crusades and uniform education. You are glossing over REALITY.

Professional and commercial careers are opening up for you. *Is that all you want?* If you honestly desire to find your level without prejudice, be brave and deny at the outset that pathetic clap-trap warcry, 'Woman is the equal of man.'

She is *not*.

For the man who lives a life in which his activities conform to a social code which is a protectorate of the feminine element is no longer masculine. The woman who adapts herself to a theoretical valuation of her sex as a *relative impersonality* is not yet feminine.

Leave off looking to men to find out what you are *not*. Seek within yourselves to find out what you *are*. As conditions are at present constituted you have the choice between Parasitism, Prostitution, or Negation.

Men and women are enemies, with the enmity of the exploited for the parasite, the parasite for the exploited — at present they are at the mercy of the advantage that each can take of the others' sexual dependence. The only point at which the interests of the sexes merge is the sexual embrace.

The first illusion to demolish is the division of women into two classes: the mistress and the mother. Every well balanced and developed woman knows that no such division exists, that Nature has endowed the Complete Woman with a faculty for expressing herself through all her functions. These are *no restrictions*. The woman who is so incompletely evolved as to be unselfconscious in sex will prove a restrictive influence on the temperamental expansion of the next generation; the woman who is a poor mistress will be an incompetent mother, an inferior mentality. She will not have an adequate apprehension of LIFE.

To obtain results you must make sacrifices and the first and greatest sacrifice you have to make is of your VIRTUE.

The fictitious value of woman as identified with her physical purity is too easy a standby. It renders her lethargic in the acquisition of intrinsic merits of character by which she could obtain a concrete value. Therefore, the first self-enforced law for the female sex, as protection against the manmade bogey of virtue (which is the principal instrument of her subjugation) is the *unconditional* surgical *destruction of virginity* throughout the female population at puberty.

The value of man is assessed entirely according to his use or interest to the community; the value of woman depends entirely on chance – her success or failure in manipulating a man into taking life-long responsibility for her.

The advantages of marriage are too ridiculously ample compared to all other trades, for under modern conditions a woman can accept preposterously luxurious support from a man without returning anything – even offspring – as an offering of thanks for her virginity.

The woman who has not succeeded in striking that advantageous bargain is prohibited from any but the most surreptitious reaction to life-stimuli and is entirely debarred from maternity. Every woman has a right to maternity.

Every woman of superior intelligence should realize her race-responsibility by producing children in adequate proportion to the unfit or degenerate members of her sex.

Each child of a superior woman should be the result of a definite period of psychic development in her life and not necessarily of a possibly irksome and outworn continuance of an alliance that is spontaneously adapted for vital creation in the beginning but which becomes unbalanced as the parties of that alliance follow the individual lines of their personal evolution.

For the harmony of the race, each individual should be the expression of an easy and ample interpenetration of the male and female temperaments – free from stress.

Woman must become more responsible for the child than man.

Woman must destroy in herself the desire to be loved.

The desire for comfortable protection rather than intelligent curiosity and courage in meeting and resisting the presence of sex (or so-called love) must be reduced to its initial element. Honor, grief, sentimentality, pride, and consequently jealousy must be detached from sex.

Woman must retain her deceptive fragility of appearance, combined with indomitable will, irreducible courage, abundant health, and sound nerves.

Another great illusion that woman must use all her introspection, innate clear-sightedness, and unbiased bravery to destroy is the impurity of sex – for the sake of her self-respect.

In defiance of superstition I assert that *there is nothing impure in sex* except the mental attitude toward it. The eventual acceptance of this fact will constitute an incalculably wider social regeneration than it is possible for our generation to acquire.

[handwritten: Cubism – reduces the form to a mathematical formula]

[handwritten: free the world of humanity so that another reality becomes visible]

3
CUBISM

GUILLAUME APOLLINAIRE (1880–1918)
FROM *THE CUBIST PAINTERS* 1913

The following extracts are taken from the opening chapter ('On painting') of Apollinaire's Les peintres cubistes, *which was published in 1913 and became the most influential formulation of cubist principles in art. They are translated by Lionel Abel for the 1970 edition of* The Cubist Painters: Aesthetic Meditations. *[See IIa 13]*

I.   On painting

1

The plastic virtues: purity, unity, and truth, keep nature in subjection.

The rainbow is bent, the seasons quiver, the crowds push on to death, science undoes and remakes what already exists, whole worlds disappear forever from our understanding, our mobile images repeat themselves, or revive their vagueness, and the colors, the odors, and the sounds to which we are sensitive astonish us, then disappear from nature – all to no purpose.

This monster beauty is not eternal.

We know that our breath has had no beginning and will never cease, but our first conceptions are of the creation and the end of the world.

However, too many painters still adore plants, stones, the sea, or men.

We quickly get used to the bondage of the mysterious. And servitude ends by creating real delights.

Workers are allowed to control the universe, yet gardeners have even less respect for nature than have artists.

The time has come for us to be the masters. And good will is not enough to make victory certain.

On this side of eternity dance the mortal forms of love, whose accursed discipline is summed up by the name 'nature'.

Flame is the symbol of painting, and the three plastic virtues burn with radiance.

Flame has a purity which tolerates nothing alien, and cruelly transforms in its image whatever it touches.

Flame has a magical unity; if it is divided, each fork will be like the single flame.

Finally it has the sublime and incontestable truth of its own light.

Good western painters of this period hold to their purity, without regard to natural forces.

[handwritten left margin: Baudelaire]

[handwritten left margin: distinction btwn form + content]

[handwritten left margin: @ futurism – poetry – Il Pleut. collapses the distinction btwn form + content]

Purity is a forgetting after study. And for a single pure artist to die, it would be necessary for all pure artists of past ages to have never existed.

Painting purifies itself in Europe with the ideal logic which the older painters handed on to the new ones, as if giving them life.

And that is all.

This painter finds pleasure, that one, pain; one squanders his inheritance, another becomes rich, and still others have nothing but life.

And that is all.

You cannot carry around on your back the corpse of your father. You leave him with the other dead. You remember him, miss him, speak of him with admiration. And if you become a father yourself, you cannot expect one of your children to be willing to split in two for the sake of your corpse.

But in vain do our feet relinquish the soil which holds the dead.

To insist on purity is to baptize instinct, to humanize art, and to deify personality.

The root, the stem and the flower of the lily instance the development of purity to its symbolical blossoming.

All bodies stand equal before light, and their modifications are determined by this dazzling power, which molds them according to its will.

We do not know all the colors. Each of us invents new ones.

But above all, the painter must contemplate his own divinity, and the pictures which he offers to the admiration of men will confer upon them, likewise, the glory of exercising their divinity – if only for a moment. To achieve this, it is necessary to encompass in one glance the past, the present, and the future.

The canvas should present that essential unity which alone can elicit ecstasy.

Then nothing unstable will send us off half-cocked. We will not be suddenly turning back. Free spectators, we will not sacrifice our lives to our curiosity. The smugglers of appearances will not be able to get their contraband past the salt statues before our customs house of reason.

We will not go astray in the unknown future, which, severed from eternity, is but a word fated to tempt man.

We will not waste our strength on the too fugitive present; the fashionable, for the artist, can only be the mask of death.

The picture will exist ineluctably. The vision will be entire, complete, and its infinity, instead of indicating some imperfection, will simply express the relation between a newly created thing and a new creator, nothing more. Otherwise there would be no unity, and the connection which the different points of the canvas have with various dispositions, objects, and lights, would reveal only an assemblage of odds and ends, lacking all harmony.

For while an infinite number of creatures, each testifying to its creator, can exist without any one creation encroaching on the space of the others, yet it is impossible to conceive them all at once, and death results from their juxtaposition, their union, their love.

Our humanness makes us seeing / the world a certain way → We see the world & we are the center / the human is the center

Humanity is a limitation / I become some-thing else.

Each god creates in his own image, and so do painters. Only photographers manufacture duplicates of nature.

Neither purity nor unity count without truth, which cannot be compared to reality, since it is always the same, subsisting beyond the scope of nature, which strives to imprison us in that fatal order of things limiting us to the merely animal.

Artists are above all men who want to become inhuman.

Painfully they search for traces of inhumanity, traces which are to be found nowhere in nature.

These traces are clues to truth, aside from which there is no reality we can know.

But reality will never be discovered once and for all. Truth is always new. Otherwise truth would be a system even more wretched than nature itself.

But such pitiful truth, more distant, less distinct, less real each day, would reduce painting to a sort of plastic writing, intended simply to facilitate communication between people of the same race.

In our times, a machine to reproduce such signs would be quickly invented.

[. . .]

Real resemblance no longer has any importance, since everything is sacrificed by the artist to truth, to the necessities of a higher nature whose existence he assumes, but does not lay bare. The subject has little or no importance any more.

Generally speaking, modern art repudiates most of the techniques of pleasing devised by the great artists of the past.

While the goal of painting is today, as always, the pleasure of the eye, the art-lover is henceforth asked to expect delights other than those which looking at natural objects can easily provide.

Thus we are moving towards an entirely new art which will stand, with respect to painting as envisaged heretofore, as music stands to literature.

It will be pure painting, just as music is pure literature.

The music-lover experiences, in listening to a concert, a joy of a different order from the joy given by natural sounds, such as the murmur of the brook, the uproar of a torrent, the whistling of the wind in a forest, or the harmonies of human speech based on reason rather than on aesthetics.

In the same way the new painters will provide their admirers with artistic sensations by concentrating exclusively on the problem of creating harmony with unequal lights.

[. . .]

The secret aim of the young painters of the extremist schools is to produce pure painting. Theirs is an entirely new plastic art. It is still in its beginnings, and is not yet as abstract as it would like to be. Most of the new painters depend a good deal on mathematics, without knowing it; but they have not yet abandoned nature, which they still question patiently, hoping to learn the right answers to the questions raised by life.

A man like Picasso studies an object as a surgeon dissects a cadaver.

This art of pure painting, if it succeeds in freeing itself from the art of the past, will not necessarily cause the latter to disappear; the development of music has not brought in its train the abandonment of the various genres of literature, nor has the acridity of tobacco replaced the savoriness of food.

3

The new artists have been violently attacked for their preoccupation with geometry. Yet geometrical figures are the essence of drawing. Geometry, the science of space, its dimensions and relations, has always determined the norms and rules of painting.

Until now, the three dimensions of Euclid's geometry were sufficient to the restiveness felt by great artists yearning for the infinite.

The new painters do not propose, any more than did their predecessors, to be geometers. But it may be said that geometry is to the plastic arts what grammar is to the art of the writer. Today, scientists no longer limit themselves to the three dimensions of Euclid. The painters have been led quite naturally, one might say by intuition, to preoccupy themselves with the new possibilities of spatial measurement which, in the language of the modern studios, are designated by the term: the fourth dimension.

Regarded from the plastic point of view, the fourth dimension appears to spring from the three known dimensions: it represents the immensity of space eternalizing itself in all directions at any given moment. It is space itself, the dimension of the infinite; the fourth dimension endows objects with plasticity. It gives the object its right proportions on the whole, whereas in Greek art, for instance, a somewhat mechanical rhythm constantly destroys the proportions.

Greek art had a purely human conception of beauty. It took man as the measure of perfection. But the art of the new painters takes the infinite universe as its ideal, and it is to this ideal that we owe a new norm of the perfect, one which permits the painter to proportion objects in accordance with the degree of plasticity he desires them to have.

Nietzsche divined the possibility of such an art:

'O divine Dionysius, why pull my ears?' Ariadne asks her philosophical lover in one of the celebrated dialogues on the Isle of Naxos. 'I find something pleasant and delightful in your ears, Ariadne; why are they not even longer?'

Nietzsche, in relating this anecdote, puts in the mouth of Dionysius an implied condemnation of all Greek art.

Finally, I must point out that the fourth dimension – this utopian expression should be analyzed and explained, so that nothing more than historical interest may be attached to it – has come to stand for the aspirations and premonitions of the many young artists who contemplate Egyptian, negro, and oceanic sculptures, meditate on various scientific works, and live in the anticipation of a sublime art.

4

Wishing to attain the proportions of the ideal, to be no longer limited to the human, the young painters offer us works which are more cerebral than sensual. They discard more and more the old art of optical illusion and local proportion, in order to express the grandeur of metaphysical forms. This is why contemporary art, even if it does not directly stem from specific religious beliefs, nonetheless possesses some of the characteristics of great, that is to say, religious art.

5

It is the social function of great poets and artists to renew continually the appearance nature has for the eyes of men.

Without poets, without artists, men would soon weary of nature's monotony. The sublime idea men have of the universe would collapse with dizzying speed. The order which we find in nature, and which is only an effect of art, would at once vanish. Everything would break up in chaos. There would be no seasons, no civilization, no thought, no humanity; even life would give way, and the impotent void would reign everywhere.

Poets and artists plot the characteristics of their epoch, and the future docilely falls in with their desires.

[. . .]

To create the illusion of the typical is the social role and peculiar end of art. God knows how the pictures of Monet and Renoir were abused! Very well! But one has only to glance at some photographs of the period to see how closely people and things conformed to the pictures of them by these great painters.

Since of all the plastic products of an epoch, works of art have the most energy, this illusion seems to me quite natural. The energy of art imposes itself on men, and becomes for them the plastic standard of the period. Thus, those who mock the new painters are actually laughing at their own features, for people in the future will portray the men of today to be as they are represented in the most alive, which is to say, the newest art of our time. And do not tell me there are today various other schools of painting in whose images humanity will be able to recognize itself. All the art works of an epoch end by resembling the most energetic, the most expressive, and the most typical works of the period. Dolls belong to popular art; yet they always seem to be inspired by the great art of the same epoch. This is a truth which can easily be verified. Yet who would dare to say that the dolls which were sold at bargain counters, around 1880, were shaped by a sentiment akin to what Renoir felt when he painted his portraits? No one perceived the relationship then. But this only means that Renoir's art was sufficiently energetic to take hold of our senses, even though to the general public of the epoch in which he made his debut, his conceptions seemed absurd and foolish.

[. . .]

7

The new school of painting is known as cubism, a name first applied to it in the fall of 1908 in a spirit of derision by Henri-Matisse, who had just seen a picture of some houses, whose cube-like appearance had greatly struck him.

The new aesthetics was first elaborated in the mind of André Derain, but the most important and audacious works the movement at once produced were those of a great artist, Pablo Picasso, who must also be considered one of the founders: his inventions, corroborated by the good sense of Georges Braque, who exhibited a cubist picture at the *Salon des Indépendants* as early as 1908, were envisaged in the studies of Jean Metzinger, who exhibited the first cubist portrait (a portrait of myself) at the *Salon des Indépendants* in 1910, and who in the same year managed to induce the jury of the *Salon d'Automne* to admit some cubist paintings. It was also in 1910 that pictures by Robert Delaunay, Marie Laurencin, and Le Fauconnier, who all belonged to the same school, were exhibited at the *Indépendants*.

The first group exhibition of the cubists, who were becoming more numerous, took place in 1911 at the *Indépendants*; room 41, which was devoted to their works, made a deep impression. There were the knowing and seductive works of Jean Metzinger; some landscapes, *Male Nude* and *Women with Phlox* by Albert Gleizes; *Portrait of Mme Fernande X* and *Young Girls* by Marie Laurencin; *The Tower*, by Robert Delaunay, *Abundance*, by Le Fauconnier, and *Landscape with Nudes*, by Fernand Léger.

That same year the cubists made their first appearance outside of France, in Brussels; and in the preface to the catalogue of this exhibition, I accepted on behalf of the exhibitors the appellations: cubism and cubist.

Towards the end of 1911 the exhibition of the cubists at the *Salon d'Automne* made a considerable stir, and Gleizes (*The Hunt, Portrait of Jacques Nayral*), Metzinger (*Woman with Spoon*), and Fernand Léger were ridiculed without mercy. A new painter, Marcel Duchamp, had joined the group, as had the sculptor-architect, Duchamp-Villon.

[. . .]

The modern school of painting seems to me the most audacious that has ever appeared. It has posed the question of what is beautiful in itself.

It wants to visualize beauty disengaged from whatever charm man has for man, and until now, no European artist has dared attempt this. The new artists demand an ideal beauty, which will be, not merely the proud expression of the species, but the expression of the universe, to the degree that it has been humanized by light.

The new art clothes its creations with a grandiose and monumental appearance which surpasses anything else conceived by the artists of our time. Ardent in its search for beauty, it is noble and energetic, and the reality it brings us is marvelously clear. I love the art of today because above all else I love the light, for man loves light more than anything; it was he who invented fire.

[. . .]

4
IMAGISM
PREFACE TO *SOME IMAGIST POETS* 1915

The following 'Preface' to the first volume of Some Imagist Poets *(second volume 1916, third volume 1917) is one of the declarations of Imagism, a movement associated with the early careers of poets such as Richard Aldington, Ezra Pound, Hilda Doolittle (H.D.), Amy Lowell, William Carlos Williams, D. H. Lawrence and F. S. Flint. The 1915 volume was the second compilation of Imagism, after* Des Imagistes *of 1914 and, while it summarised and reinforced the intentions and principles of the movement, it also signalled the break into 'factions', with Amy Lowell taking over as self-appointed promoter and spokesperson. [See IIIa 7]*

In March, 1914, a volume appeared entitled 'Des Imagistes'. It was a collection of the work of various young poets, presented together as a school. This school has been widely discussed by those interested in new movements in the arts, and has already become a household word. Differences of taste and judgment, however, have arisen among the contributors to that book; growing tendencies are forcing them along different paths. Those of us whose work appears in this volume have therefore decided to publish our collection under a new title, and we have been joined by two or three poets who did not contribute to the first volume, our wider scope making this possible.

In this new book we have followed a slightly different arrangement to that of the former Anthology. Instead of an arbitrary selection by an editor, each poet has been permitted to represent himself by the work he considers his best, the only stipulation being that it should not yet have appeared in book form. A sort of informal committee – consisting of more than half the authors here represented – have arranged the book and decided what should be printed and what omitted, but, as a general rule, the poets have been allowed absolute freedom in this direction, limitations of space only being imposed upon them. Also, to avoid any appearance of precedence, they have been put in alphabetical order.

As it has been suggested that much of the misunderstanding of the former volume was due to the fact that we did not explain ourselves in a preface, we have thought it wise to tell the public what our aims are, and why we are banded together between one set of covers.

The poets in this volume do not represent a clique. Several of them are personally unknown to the others, but they are united by certain common principles, arrived at independently. These principles are not new; they have fallen into desuetude. They are the essentials of all great poetry, indeed of all great literature, and they are simply these:

1. To use the language of common speech, but to employ always the *exact* word, not the nearly-exact, nor the merely decorative word.

2. To create new rhythms – as the expression of new moods – and not to copy old rhythms, which merely echo old moods. We do not insist upon 'free-verse' as the only method of writing poetry. We fight for it as for a principle of liberty. We believe that the individuality of a poet may often be better expressed in free-verse than in conventional forms. In poetry, a new cadence means a new idea.

3. To allow absolute freedom in the choice of subject. It is not good art to write badly about aeroplanes and automobiles; nor is it necessarily bad art to write well about the past. We believe passionately in the artistic value of modern life, but we wish to point out that there is nothing so uninspiring nor so old-fashioned as an aeroplane of the year 1911.

4. To present an image (hence the name: 'Imagist'). We are not a school of painters, but we believe that poetry should render particulars exactly and not deal in vague generalities, however magnificent and sonorous. It is for this reason that we oppose the cosmic poet, who seems to us to shirk the real difficulties of his art.

5. To produce poetry that is hard and clear, never blurred nor indefinite.

6. Finally, most of us believe that concentration is of the very essence of poetry.

The subject of free-verse is too complicated to be discussed here. We may say briefly, that we attach the term to all that increasing amount of writing whose cadence is more marked, more definite, and closer knit than that of prose, but which is not so violently nor so obviously accented as the so-called 'regular verse'. We refer those interested in the question to the Greek Melic poets, and to the many excellent French studies on the subject by such distinguished and well-equipped authors as Rémy de Gourmont, Gustave Kahn, Georges Duhamel, Charles Vildrac, Henri Ghéon, Robert de Souza, André Spire, etc.

We wish it to be clearly understood that we do not represent an exclusive artistic sect; we publish our work together because of mutual artistic sympathy, and we propose to bring out our co-operative volume each year for a short term of years, until we have made a place for ourselves and our principles such as we desire.

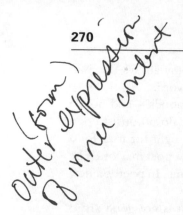

Outer expression (form)
Inner content

5
EXPRESSIONISM

WASSILY KANDINSKY (1866–1944)
FROM 'THE PROBLEM OF FORM' 1912

Born in Moscow, Kandinsky left a career in law to train as an artist in Munich. Early work produced in 1910 was already moving towards abstraction, although he did not abandon representation totally until the 1920s. In 1912 he published the influential On the Spiritual in Art *and co-founded with Franz Marc and Paul Klee the Blaue Reiter ('Blue Rider') group. He returned to Russia in 1914 and became head of the Museum of Modern Art in 1919. In 1922 he became one of the teachers at the Bauhaus School in Weimar. The following extract from an essay published in the* Blaue Reiter Almanac *(1912) is reproduced from* Voices of German Expressionism *(trans. and ed. Victor H. Miesel, 1970). [See IIIb 34]*

What is destined ripens at its appointed time, i.e., the Creative Spirit (which can be called the 'Abstract Spirit') first inspires a single soul, later other souls, and causes widespread yearning or spiritual desire.

When the necessary conditions for the ripening of a particular form have been fulfilled, this yearning or spiritual desire is granted the power to create a new value in the human soul, a new value which then consciously or unconsciously begins to live in people.

From that moment people, consciously or unconsciously, attempt to give material form to that inner spiritual form.

It is Spirit striving for material realization. Matter here is simply a kind of pantry from which the Spirit, like a cook, takes necessary ingredients.

It is the Positive, the Creative. It is the Good. *The inspiring White Beam.*

This White Beam leads to evolution, to elevation. Thus, the Creative Spirit is hidden behind matter and in matter.

The Spirit frequently is so well-hidden by matter that few people are able to detect it. In fact, there are many people who cannot recognize the Spirit in a spiritual form. Right now many cannot recognize the Spirit in religion and art. Whole epochs deny the Spirit because they are unable to see it. This happened in the nineteenth century and, generally speaking, nothing has changed in our own day.

People are blind.

A Black Hand covers their eyes, and this Black Hand belongs to the Hater! The Hater tries to retard evolution and elevation in every way possible.

It is the Negative, the Destructive. It is Evil. *The Black Hand bringing death.*

Evolution, movement upward and forward, is possible only when the road is clear, i.e., when no barriers are in the way. That is the external condition.

The power which moves the human spirit forward and upward on the open road is the Abstract Spirit. Of course it must ring out and be heard. The possibility for it to call out must exist. That is the inner condition.

The Black Hand attempts to destroy both conditions in order to prevent evolution.

Its weapons are: fear of the open road, of freedom (philistinism), and a refusal to listen to the Spirit (vulgar materialism).

That is why every new value antagonizes people and provokes scorn and slander. The person who introduces a new value is attacked as a fool and a fraud while the new value is criticized and ridiculed.

That is the horror of life.

But the joy of life is the steady and inevitable victory of new values.

It is a slow victory. A new value conquers only very gradually, but when it once becomes established beyond question, though it was absolutely necessary at the time, it becomes nothing less than a wall against the future.

The transformation of new value (the fruit of freedom) into stone (a wall against freedom) is the work of the Black Hand.

Thus, all of evolution, i.e., internal growth and external culture, becomes a matter of breaking down barriers.

Barriers destroy freedom and prevent new revelations of the spirit.

Barriers are constantly being built up out of the new values which have overthrown the old.

Thus, one realizes that basically it is not the new value which is all-important but the Spirit which reveals itself in this value and, furthermore, the freedom which is necessary for revelation.

Thus, one realizes that the Absolute is not to be found in form (materialism).

Form is always transient, i.e., relative, since it is nothing more than the necessary medium through which today's revelation can be heard.

The Sound is therefore the soul of form. Coming from within, it alone activates form.

Form is the outer expression of inner content.

[. . .]

Necessity creates form. Fishes living in lightless depths have no eyes. The elephant has a trunk. The chameleon changes his color, etc., etc.

Form reflects the spirit of each artist. Form bears the imprint of *personality*.

Of course, personality does not exist outside time and space. It is determined to a degree by time (historical period) and space (race).

Just as every artist has his message, so has every race, and this includes the race to which a particular artist belongs. This relationship is reflected in form and is called *nationality*.

And finally, every age has its assigned task – the revelation which is possible through it and it alone. The reflection of this temporal aspect is called *style*.

These three elements of a work's personality are all absolutely inevitable. Not only is it unnecessary to worry about them, but it is harmful since great effort in this area will produce nothing but a passing delusion.

In addition, it is obviously unnecessary and harmful to favor one element more than another. Just as many today trouble themselves about nationality and others about style, a short time ago everyone payed homage to the personality cult (the individual).

As was said at the beginning of this article, the Abstract Spirit influences first a single human spirit and then a constantly growing number of people. At that moment individual artists become subordinated to the spirit of the age and are compelled, though using individual forms, to work in terms of forms that are closely interrelated and outwardly similar.

This moment is called a *movement*.

A movement is quite justified (just as individual form expresses an individual artist) and indispensable for a group of artists.

[...]

The appearance of forms in time and space can also be explained as resulting from the inner necessity of a period and place.

Therefore, in the final analysis it will be possible to uncover and represent schematically the characteristics of an age and of a race.

And the greater an epoch is, i.e., the greater (quantitatively and qualitatively) the effort to achieve the spiritual, the larger will be the number of forms and collective efforts (movements). This is obvious.

The marks of a great spiritual epoch (which was prophesied and today is revealed in its early stages) are seen in contemporary art. That is to say:

1. a great *freedom*, which appears limitless to some and which
2. makes the *Spirit* audible, which
3. we see revealing itself with especially powerful *energy* in objects which
4. will gradually use and have already used all *spiritual spheres* whereby
5. a *means of expression* (forms) will be created for individuals and groups in every spiritual sphere, the visual arts (especially painting) included, and
6. for which today all the items in the pantry are being prepared, i.e., where *every material* is used as an element of form, from the most complex to those used only for two-dimensional (abstract) works.

[...]

The forms for this embodiment which are taken by the Spirit from the pantry of matter can be located easily between two extremes.

These two extremes are:

1. The great abstraction.
2. The great realism.

These two extremes open *two roads* which ultimately lead to a *single goal*.

[...]

The previously mentioned great realism which is now developing tries to purge the picture of everything artistic. It wants to manifest content by means of the simple ('inartistic') representation of simple, tough objects. The outer husk of the object so conceived and defined in the picture and at the same time the suppression of conventional beauty most certainly reveals the inner sound of the object. It is precisely through this husk that the soul of the object sounds strongest, since the 'artistic' has been reduced to a minimum and superficial prettiness has been stripped away.

And that is only possible because more and more we want to hear the world, not as a beautiful tune but as it really is.

Reduced to a minimum the 'artistic' becomes comparable in effectiveness to the most intense abstraction.

The great abstraction is the great antithesis to this realism. It results from an apparent determination to eliminate completely the representational (reality) and to embody content in 'incorporeal' forms. The inner sound of a picture is revealed most effectively by abstract life conceived and established as a reduction of representational forms to a bare minimum and therefore as a preponderance of abstract entities. Just as the cancellation of abstraction intensified the inner sound in realistic art so the inner sound is intensified in abstract art by cancelling out realism. In the former, conventional prettiness muted the inner sound; in the latter it was the usual appearance of things.

In order to 'understand' this kind of picture the same liberation as in realism is necessary, i.e., here too one must learn to hear the whole world exactly as it is without any representational interpretation. And in such work abstract forms (lines, planes, spots, etc.) are not important as such, but only as inner sound, as life. Just as in realism, neither the object itself nor its outer husk but its inner sound, its life is important.

Reduced to a minimum the 'representational' becomes comparable in effectiveness to the most intense realism.

Thus, in conclusion: we see that in the great realism the real appears strikingly prominent and the abstract strikingly small and in the great abstraction the relationship is reversed. Thus, in the final analysis (goals) these two extremes meet. An image can be placed somewhere between these two antipodes:

Realism = Abstraction

Abstraction = Realism

The greatest external difference becomes inwardly complete identity.

[. . .]

Thus we may conclude that pure abstraction can serve things in all their corporeality as effectively as pure realism. Once again the greatest negation of objects and their greatest affirmation become identical. And this identity is the result of identical goals: the expression of the same inner sound.

Here we see that in principle *it makes no difference whether a realistic or an abstract form is used by an artist.*

Since both forms are inwardly identical. To the artist, the person who knows best, must be left the choice of which form most clearly materializes the content of his art.

Formulated as a general principle: *there is no problem of form.*

[. . .]

Let the reader examine any object on his table (even a cigar butt) and he will notice these two levels of expression. It does not matter where or when (in the street, church, heaven, water, barn, or forest) the two levels of expression reveal themselves everywhere and everywhere the inner sound is independent from conventional or external meaning.

The whole world rings out. It is a cosmos of spiritually expressive beings. Even dead matter is actually living spirit.

[. . .]

The artist, whose life is comparable to a child's in many respects, frequently can reach the inner sound more easily than anyone else. In this respect it is especially interesting to see how the composer Arnold Schönberg paints – simply and confidently. As a rule he is interested only in the inner sound. He omits, without regard, all embellishments and refinements and the 'poorest' form in his hands becomes the richest (his self-portrait, for example).

Here lies the root of the new Great Realism. The object is separated from conventional and practical meanings by a complete but absolutely simple representation of its outer husk which permits the inner sound to be heard, clearly and easily. Henri Rousseau, who is the father of this type of realism, indicated the way with simple and convincing work (look at his portraits and other pictures).

Henri Rousseau revealed the new possibilities of simplicity. And at the present moment this is the most important aspect of his many-sided genius.

Objects, or the object (i.e., it and its component parts), must be in some sort of relationship. This relationship can be shockingly harmonious or shockingly dissonant. Clearcut or extremely subtle rhythms can be used.

What impels artists of all types toward a common goal today is their irresistible determination to clarify form and to reveal the future laws of our great epoch.

Naturally, in such cases people tend to use the most regular and most abstract shapes possible. Thus we see that the triangle was used as a basis of composition in various periods in the history of art. The triangle was often equilaterial and in this way number became important, i.e., the completely abstract aspect of the triangle. In today's search after abstract relationships, numbers play an especially important role. Every numerical formula is cool like an icy mountain peak and, in its conformity to rule, solid like a marble block – cold and solid like every necessity. Cubism, so-called, originated in the desire to compose according to specific rules. 'Mathematical' construction sometimes culminates in the complete destruction of an object's conventional physical unity and leads to extremely important results (e.g., Picasso).

[. . .]

If the reader is able to free himself for a while from his own wishes, his own thoughts, his own feelings and skims through this book, going from a votive picture to Delaunay, from a Cézanne to a Russian folk print, from a mask to Picasso, from a glass painting to Kubin, etc., etc., then his soul will experience many vibrations and he will enter into the world of art. Here he will not be bothered by outrageous defects or aggravating errors. Instead he will experience a spiritual plus instead of a minus.

Later the reader can examine works of art objectively and analytically. He will then find that all the examples cited obey a common inner call – composition, that they all have a common base – structure.

The inner content of a work can belong to either one or the other of two types. Today these two types (only today? or only obvious today?) embrace all secondary movements.

These two types are:

1. The disintegration of the soulless, materialistic life of the nineteenth century, i.e., the destruction of the very basis of matter, its fragmentation into parts and then the dissolution of those parts.

2. The creation of the spiritual and intellectual life of the twentieth century, our era, which already is manifested and embodied in strong, expressive and well-defined forms.

These two types are the two aspects of the 'modern movement'.

To define what has already been achieved or even to define the final goal would be a presumption which would be punished by a frightful loss of freedom.

As has been often observed, we should strive for more freedom, not greater restriction. One should reject nothing without making *every effort* to uncover its vital, living qualities. It is preferable to mistake a dead for a living thing than ever, even once, to mistake something living for something dead. *New growth* needs free and open ground and the free person is inspired by every experience, affected by every aspect of life, even if it is only a burnt match.

That which is coming can be taken up only by free people.

One cannot stand aside like the barren tree in the Bible, the tree which Christ saw as ready and waiting for the ax.

open minds?

expressionism can be a form of realism

realism doesn't have to be representational

what happens on the canvas can connect to our mind

[handwritten marginalia: formula for writing / Combines arbitrary / play & collage]

6
DADA

6a
TRISTAN TZARA (1896–1963)
FROM 'DADA MANIFESTO, 1918';
'NOTE ON ART' 1917; 'NOTE ON NEGRO ART' 1917

Romanian-born French poet, artist, avant-garde terrorist and revolutionary. Tzara was a member of the Cabaret Voltaire and founded Zurich Dada during the First World War. He was the editor of Dada, *the most important of the French Dada reviews. Reproduced below are extracts from his 1918 manifesto, originally published in* Dada, *and two short pieces originally published in* Dada *and* Sic *in 1917. They appear in Barbara Wright's translation for the 1977 edition of* Seven Dada Manifestos *and* Lampisteries. *[See IIa 12]*

Cubism was born out of a simple manner of looking at objects: Cézanne painted a cup twenty centimetres lower than his eyes, the cubists look at it from above, others complicate its appearance by cutting a vertical section through it and soberly placing it to one side. (I'm not forgetting the creators, nor the seminal reasons of unformed matter that they rendered definitive.) The futurist sees the same cup in movement, a succession of objects side by side, mischievously embellished by a few guide-lines. This doesn't stop the canvas being either a good or a bad painting destined to form an investment for intellectual capital. The new painter creates a world whose elements are also its means, a sober, definitive, irrefutable work. The new artist protests: he no longer paints (symbolic and illusionistic reproduction) but creates directly in stone, wood, iron, tin, rocks, or locomotive structures capable of being spun in all directions by the limpid wind of the momentary sensation. Every pictorial or plastic work is unnecessary, even if it is a monster which terrifies servile minds, and not a sickly-sweet object to adorn the refectories of animals in human garb, those illustrations of the sad fable of humanity. – A painting is the art of making two lines, which have been geometrically observed to be parallel, meet on a canvas, before our eyes, in the reality of a world that has been transposed according to new conditions and possibilities. This world is neither specified nor defined in the work, it belongs, in its innumerable variations, to the spectator. For its creator it has neither cause nor theory. *Order = disorder; ego = non-ego; affirmation = negation*: the supreme radiations of an absolute art. Absolute in the purity of its cosmic and regulated chaos, eternal in that globule that is a second which has no duration, no breath, no light and no control. I appreciate an old work for its novelty. It is only contrast that links us to the past. Writers who like to moralise and discuss or ameliorate psychological bases have, apart from a secret wish to win, a ridiculous knowledge of life, which they have classified, parcelled out, canalised; they are determined to see its categories dance when they beat time. Their readers laugh derisively, but carry on: what's the use?

There is one kind of literature which never reaches the voracious masses. The work of creative writers, written out of the author's real necessity, and for his own benefit. The awareness of a supreme egoism, wherein laws become insignificant. Every page should explode, either because of its profound gravity, or its vortex, vertigo, newness, eternity, or because of its staggering absurdity, the enthusiasm of its principles, or its typography. On the one hand there is a world tottering in its flight, linked to the resounding tinkle of the infernal gamut; on the other hand, there are: the new men. Uncouth, galloping, riding astride on hiccups. And there is a mutilated world and literary medicasters in desperate need of amelioration.

I assure you: there is no beginning, and we are not afraid; we aren't sentimental. We are like a raging wind that rips up the clothes of clouds and prayers, we are preparing the great spectacle of disaster, conflagration and decomposition. Preparing to put an end to mourning, and to replace tears by sirens spreading from one continent to another. Clarions of intense joy, bereft of that poisonous sadness. DADA is the mark of abstraction; publicity and business are also poetic elements.

I destroy the drawers of the brain, and those of social organisation: to sow demoralisation everywhere, and throw heaven's hand into hell, hell's eyes into heaven, to reinstate the fertile wheel of a universal circus in the Powers of reality, and the fantasy of every individual.

A philosophical question: from which angle to start looking at life, god, ideas, or anything else. Everything we look at is false. I don't think the relative result is any more important than the choice of pâtisserie or cherries for dessert. The way people have of looking hurriedly at things from the opposite point of view, so as to impose their opinions indirectly, is called dialectic, in other words, heads I win and tails you lose, dressed up to look scholarly.

If I shout:

Ideal, Ideal, Ideal

Knowledge, Knowledge, Knowledge,

Boomboom, Boomboom, Boomboom

I have recorded fairly accurately Progress, Law, Morals, and all the other magnificent qualities that various very intelligent people have discussed in so many books in order, finally, to say that even so everyone has danced according to his own personal boomboom, and that he's right about his boomboom; the satisfaction of unhealthy curiosity; private bell-ringing for inexplicable needs; bath; pecuniary difficulties; a stomach with repercussions on to life; the authority of the mystical baton formulated as the grand final of a phantom orchestra with mute bows, lubricated by philtres with a basis of animal ammonia. With the blue monocle of an angel they have dug out its interior for twenty souls worth of unanimous gratitude. If all of them are right, and if all pills are only Pink, let's try for once not to be right. People think they can explain rationally, by means of thought, what they write. But it's very relative. Thought is a fine thing for philosophy, but it's relative. Psychoanalysis is a dangerous disease, it deadens man's anti-real inclinations and systematises the bourgeoisie. There is no ultimate

Truth. Dialectics is an amusing machine that leads us (in banal fashion) to the opinions which we would have held in any case. Do people really think that, by the meticulous subtlety of logic, they have demonstrated the truth and established the accuracy of their opinions? Even if logic were confirmed by the senses it would still be an organic disease. To this element, philosophers like to add: The power of observation. But this magnificent quality of the mind is precisely the proof of its impotence. People observe, they look at things from one or several points of view, they choose them from amongst the millions that exist. Experience too is the result of chance and of individual abilities. Science revolts me when it becomes a speculative system and loses its utilitarian character – which is so useless – but is at least individual. I hate slimy objectivity, and harmony, the science that considers that everything is always in order. Carry on, children, humanity. [. . .] Science says that we are nature's servants: everything is in order, make both love and war. Carry on, children, humanity, nice kind bourgeois and virgin journalists [. . .] I am against systems; the most acceptable system is that of having none on no principle. To complete oneself, to perfect oneself in one's own pettiness to the point of filling the little vase of oneself with oneself, even the courage to fight for and against thought, all this can suddenly infernally propel us into the mystery of daily bread and the lilies of the economic field.

Dadaist Spontaneity

What I call the I-don't-give-a-damn attitude of life is when everyone minds his own business, at the same time as he knows how to respect other individualities, and even how to stand up for himself, the two-step becoming a national anthem, a junk shop, the wireless (the wire-less telephone) transmitting Bach fugues, illuminated advertise-ments and placards for brothels, the organ broadcasting carnations for God, all this at the same time, and in real terms, replacing photography and unilateral catechism.

Active simplicity.

The incapacity to distinguish between degrees of light: licking the twilight and floating in the huge mouth filled with honey and excrement. Measured against the scale of Eternity, every action is vain – (if we allow thought to have an adventure whose result would be infinitely grotesque – an important factor in the awareness of human incapacity). But if life is a bad joke, with neither goal nor initial accouchement, and because we believe we ought, like clean chrysanthemums, to make the best of a bad bargain, we have declared that the only basis of understanding is: art. It hasn't the importance that we, old hands at the spiritual, have been lavishing on it for centuries. Art does nobody any harm, and those who are capable of taking an interest in it will not only receive caresses, but also a marvellous chance to people the country of their conversation. Art is a private thing, the artist makes it for himself; a comprehensible work is the product of a journalist, and because at this moment I enjoy mixing this monster in oil paints: a paper tube imitating the metal that you press and automatically squeeze out hatred, cowardice and villainy. The artist, or the poet, rejoices in the venom of this mass condensed into one shopwalker of this trade, he is glad to be insulted, it proves his immutability. The author or the artist praised by the papers observes that his work has been understood: a miserable lining to a coat that is of public utility; rags covering brutishness, horse-piss collaborating with the heat of an animal incubating the baser instincts. Flabby, insipid flesh multiplying itself with the aid of typographical microbes.

We have done violence to the snivelling tendencies in our natures. Every infiltration of this sort is macerated diarrhoea. To encourage this sort of art is to digest it. What we need are strong, straightforward, precise works which will be forever misunderstood. Logic is a complication. Logic is always false. It draws the superficial threads of concepts and words towards illusory conclusions and centres. Its chains kill, an enormous myriapod that asphyxiates independence. If it were married to logic, art would be living in incest, engulfing, swallowing its own tail, which still belongs to its body, fornicating in itself, and temperament would become a nightmare tarred and feathered with protestantism, a monument, a mass of heavy, greyish intestines.

But suppleness, enthusiasm and even the joy of injustice, that little truth that we practise as innocents and that makes us beautiful: we are cunning, and our fingers are malleable and glide like the branches of that insidious and almost liquid plant; this injustice is the indication of our soul, say the cynics. This is also a point of view; but all flowers aren't saints, luckily, and what is divine in us is the awakening of anti-human action. What we are talking about here is a paper flower for the buttonhole of gentlemen who frequent the ball of masked life, the kitchen of grace, our white, lithe or fleshy girl cousins. They make a profit out of what we have selected. The contradiction and unity of opposing poles at the same time may be true. If we are absolutely determined to utter this platitude, the appendix of a libidinous, evil-smelling morality. Morals have an atrophying effect, like every other pestilential product of the intelligence. Being governed by morals and logic has made it impossible for us to be anything other than impassive towards policemen – the cause of slavery – putrid rats with whom the bourgeois are fed up to the teeth, and who have infected the only corridors of clear and clean glass that remained open to artists.

Every man must shout: there is great destructive, negative work to be done. To sweep, to clean. The cleanliness of the individual materialises after we've gone through folly, the aggressive, complete folly of a world left in the hands of bandits who have demolished and destroyed the centuries. With neither aim nor plan, without organisation: uncontrollable folly, decomposition. Those who are strong in word or in strength will survive, because they are quick to defend themselves; the agility of their limbs and feelings flames on their faceted flanks.

Morals have given rise to charity and pity, two dumplings that have grown like elephants, planets, which people call good. There is nothing good about them. Goodness is lucid, clear and resolute, and ruthless towards compromise and politics. Morality infuses chocolate into every man's veins. This task is not ordained by a supernatural force, but by a trust of ideas-merchants and academic monopolists. Sentimentality: seeing a group of bored and quarrelling men, they invented the calendar and wisdom as a remedy. By sticking labels on to things, the battle of the philosophers was let loose (money-grubbing, mean and meticulous weights and measures) and one understood once again that pity is a feeling, like diarrhoea in relation to disgust, that undermines health, the filthy carrion job of jeopardising the sun. I proclaim the opposition of all the cosmic faculties to that blennorrhoea of a putrid sun that issues from the factories of philosophical thought, the fight to the death, with all the resources of

DADAIST DISGUST

Every product of disgust that is capable of becoming a negation of the family is *dada*; protest with the fists of one's whole being in destructive action: DADA; acquaintance with all the means hitherto rejected by the sexual prudishness of easy compromise and good manners: DADA; abolition of logic, dance of those who are incapable of creation: DADA; every hierarchy and social equation established for values by our valets: DADA; every object, all objects, feelings and obscurities, every apparition and the precise shock of parallel lines, are means for the battle of: DADA; the abolition of memory: DADA; the abolition of archaeology: DADA the abolition of prophets: DADA; the abolition of the future: **dada**; the absolute and indiscutable belief in every god that is an immediate product of spontaneity: DADA; the elegant and unprejudiced leap from one harmony to another sphere; the trajectory of a word, a cry, thrown into the air like an acoustic disc; to respect all individualities in their folly of the moment, whether serious, fearful, timid, ardent, vigorous, decided or enthusiastic; to strip one's church of every useless and unwieldy accessory; to spew out like a luminous cascade any offensive or loving thought, or to cherish it – with the lively satisfaction that it's all precisely the same thing – with the same intensity in the bush, which is free of insects for the blue-blooded, and gilded with the bodies of archangels, with one's soul. Liberty: **dada dada dada**; – the roar of contorted pains, the interweaving of contraries and of all contradictions, freaks and irrelevancies: LIFE.

Note on Art

Art is at present the only self-contained construction about which there is no more to be said, such is its richness, vitality, meaning and wisdom. To understand, to see. To describe a flower: relative poetry more or less artificial flower. To see.

Until we discover the intimate vibrations of the final cell of a mathematical god-brain and the explanation of the primary astronomies – its essence – we shall always find ourselves describing this impossibility with its logical elements of perpetual contradiction, a marshland of stars and of futile bell-ringing. Like toads squatting on cold lanterns, squashing the descriptive intelligence of the red belly. What people write on art is an educative work, and in this sense it has a right to exist. We want to give back to mankind the ability to understand that a unique fraternity comes into existence at the intense moment when beauty and life itself, brought into high tension on a wire, ascend towards a flash-point; the blue tremor linked to the ground by our magnetised gaze which covers the peak with snow. The miracle. I open my heart to creation.

There are many artists who are no longer looking for solutions in the object and in its relations with the outside world; they are cosmic or primary, decided, simple, wise and serious.

The diversity of today's artists is a compressed jet of water scattered at crystal liberty. And their efforts create new limpid organisms, in a world of purity, with the aid of transparencies and of the materiality of construction of a simple image which is in the process of formation. They are carrying on the tradition; the past and its evolution are pushing them slowly, like a snake, towards their inner, direct consequences, beyond both surfaces and reality.

Note on Negro Art

The new art is first and foremost concentration, the lines from the base to the apex of a pyramid forming a cross; through purity we have first deformed and then decomposed the object, we have approached its surface, we have penetrated it. We want a clarity that is direct. Art is grouped into camps, each with its special skills, within its own frontiers. The influences of a foreign nature which were mixed up in it are the rags of a Renaissance lining still sticking to the souls of our fellow men, for my brother's soul has sharp branches, black with autumn.

My other brother is naive and good, and laughs. He eats in Africa or along the South Sea Islands. He concentrates his vision on the head, carves it out of wood that is as hard as iron, patiently, without bothering about the conventional relationship between the head and the rest of the body. What he thinks is: man walks vertically, everything in nature is symmetrical. While working, new relationships organise themselves according to degree of necessity; this is how the expression of purity came into being.

From blackness, let us extract light. Simple, rich luminous naivety. Different materials, the scales of form. To construct in balanced hierarchy. EYE: button, open wide, round, and pointed, to penetrate my bones and my belief. Transform my country into a prayer of joy or anguish. Cotton wool eye, flow in my blood.

Art, in the infancy of time, was prayer. Wood and stone were truth. In man I see the moon, plants, blackness, metal, stars, fish. Let the cosmic elements glide symmetrically. Deform, boil. Hands are big and strong. Mouths contain the power of darkness, invisible substance, goodness, fear, wisdom, creation, fire.

No one has seen so clearly as I this dark grinding whiteness.

6b
KURT SCHWITTERS (1887–1948)
FROM *MERZ* 1921; 'CONSISTENT POETRY' 1924;
'TO ALL THE THEATRES OF THE WORLD' 1926

German artist, collagist, and poet, founder of Hanover Dada (1919), and inventor of his own particular Dada (or anti-Dada) – MERZ, art made from refuse. He took the name Merz from an advertisement for Commerz und Privatbank, and built his first Merz construction ('Merzbau') in 1923 in his Hanover house. He was founder of the Dadaist magazine, Merz (1923–32). In 1937 he fled to Norway, and to England in 1940 where he was interned as a German alien. He built his last Merzbau in Ambleside. Schwitters was a pioneer of sound poetry. His most famous

poems are 'An Anna Blume', published in Der Sturm, *1919, and 'Ursonate',* Merz, *1932.
His performance piece 'Revolution in Revon' (*Der Sturm, *1922) was translated and published by
Eugene Jolas in* transition *(1927). In his latter years in England, Schwitters translated earlier work
and wrote new poetry in English. The following pieces from 1921, 1924 and 1926 are taken from*
Kurt Schwitters: Poems, Performance Pieces, Proses, Plays, Poetics *(Jerome Rothenberg
and Pierre Joris eds and trans, 1993) and from* Dada Performance *(trans. Michael Bullock, ed.
Mel Gordon, 1987).*

Today even the striving for expression in a work of art seems to me deleterious to
art. Art is a primordial concept, exalted as a godhead, inexplicable as life, indefinable
and pointless. The work of art comes into being through the artistic evaluation of its
elements. I know only how I do it, I know only my materials, from which I take, I
know not to what end.

The material is as unessential as myself. The only essential thing is giving form.
Because the material is unessential. I use any material the picture demands. By
harmonizing different types of materials among themselves, I have an advantage over
mere oil painting, for besides playing off color against color, I also play off line against
line, form against form, etcetera, and even material against material, for example
wood against burlap. I call the worldview from which this mode of artistic creation
arose 'Merz'.

The word 'Merz' had no meaning when I formed it. Now it has the meaning which
I gave it. The meaning of the concept 'Merz' changes as the insight of those who
continue to work with it changes.

Merz wants freedom from all fetters for the sake of creating artistic form. Freedom
is not dissoluteness, but the result of strict artistic discipline. Merz also means tolerance
toward any limitations based on art. Every artist must be permitted to compose his
picture from nothing but blotting paper, for example, provided he can give it form.

The reproduction of natural elements is not essential for the work of art. But
inartistic representations of nature, as such, can form parts of a picture if they are
played off against other elements of the picture.

To begin with I concerned myself with other genres, for example with the art of
poetry. The elements of poetry are letters, syllables, words, sentences. Poetry arises
from the playing off of these elements against each other. Meaning is only essential if
it is to be used as one such factor. I play off sense against nonsense. I prefer nonsense,
but that is a purely personal matter. I pity nonsense, because until now it has been so
neglected in the making of art, and that's why I love it.

Here I must mention dadaism, which cultivates nonsense just as I do. There are
two kinds of Dadaists, the kernel and the husk dadas, the latter living principally in
Germany. Originally there existed only kernel Dadaists, the huskdadaists peeled off
from this original kernel under the leadership of Huelsenbeck and in the split took
part of the kernel with them. The peeling off happened amid loud howls, singing
of the 'Marseillaise', and distribution of kicks with foot and elbow, a tactic which
Huelsenbeck still uses today. Under Huelsenbeck dadaism became a political affair.
The well-known manifesto of the German Central Committee of Revolutionary

Dadaists demands the introduction of radical communism as a dadaistic dictate. Huelsenbeck writes in his history of dadaism, published in 1920 by Steegemann: 'Dada is German bolshevism.' The above mentioned Central Committee Manifesto further demands 'the most brutal fight against Expressionism.' In his *History of Dadaism* Huelsenbeck also writes: 'Anyway, art should get a sound beating.' In the introduction of the recently published Dada Almanach Huelsenbeck states: 'Dada carries on a kind of anti-culture propaganda.' Huelsendada is clearly politically motivated and is directed against art and culture. I am tolerant and let everybody have his own view of the world, but I have to mention that such views are alien to Merz. As a matter of principle Merz strives only to create art, because no man can serve two masters.

But 'the Dadaists' conception of dadaism varies greatly,' as Huelsenbeck himself has to admit. And thus Tristan Tzara, the leader of the kernel Dadaists, writes in his 1918 Dada manifesto: 'Everyone makes his own kind of art,' and further on: 'Dada is the billboard of abstraction.' I have to mention that Merz entertains a close artistic friendship with this version of kernel dadaism and with the art of kernel dadaists like Hans Arp, of whom I am particularly fond, Picabia, Ribémont-Dessaignes, and Archipenko. In Huelsenbeck's own words, husk dadaism 'has made itself into God's clown', while kernel dadaism holds fast to the good old tradition of abstract art. Husk Dada 'foresees its own demise and laughs about it', while kernel dadaism will live as long as art itself. Merz too strives after art and is the enemy of kitsch, even of kitsch-as-principle, though the latter may call itself dadaism under Huelsenbeck's leadership. Not everyone who lacks the ability to judge art should be entitled to write about art: 'quod licet jovi non licet bovi.' Merz energetically and as a matter of principle repudiates Mister Richard Huelsenbeck's inconsequential and dilettantish views on art, while it officially recognizes the above-stated views of Tristan Tzara.

I should clear up another misunderstanding that could arise through my friendship with certain kernel Dadaists. It might be thought that I consider myself a Dadaist, especially as the word 'Dada' appears on the cover of my collection of poems entitled *Anna Blume*, as published by Verlag Paul Steegemann.

The same cover has drawings of a windmill, a head, a locomotive running backward, and a man hanging in the air. This only means that in the world in which Anna Blossom lives, in which men walk on their heads, windmills turn, and locomotives run backward, Dada also exists. So as not to be misunderstood I have written 'antidada' on the outside of my Cathedral. That doesn't mean that I am against dadaism but that in this world there also exists a movement directed against dadaism. Locomotives can run in both directions. Why shouldn't a locomotive run backward for a change?

As long as I paint, I also model. At present I am making Merz sculptures: Lustgallows and Cultpump. Like the Merz paintings, the Merz sculptures are made from various materials. They are conceived as round sculptures and can be looked at from all sides.

Merz House was my first architectural Merz work. Spengemann comments on it in issue 8–10 of *Zweemann*: 'In Merz House I see a cathedral: *the* cathedral. Not a church building, no, but the building as truly spiritual conception of that which raises us into the infinite: absolute art. This cathedral cannot be used. Its inner space is so filled up with wheels that people cannot find room in it [. . .] this is absolute architecture with an exclusively artistic meaning.'

To busy myself with various genres was for me an artistic need. The reason for it was not so much a desire for a widening of the scope of my work, but rather the endeavor to be an artist and not a specialist in one genre. My aim is the total Merz art work, which combines all genres into an artistic unity. First I married off single genres. I pasted words and sentences together into poems in such a way that their rhythmic composition created a kind of drawing. The other way around, I pasted together pictures and drawings containing sentences that demand to be read. I drove nails into pictures in such a way that besides the pictorial effect a plastic relief effect arose. I did this in order to erase the boundaries between genres. The total Merz art work is, however, the Merz stage, which so far I have been able to work out only theoretically.

[. . .]

Consistent Poetry

Not the word but the letter is the original material of poetry: Word is:

1. Composition of letters.
2. Sound.
3. Denotation (Meaning).
4. Carrier of associations of ideas.

Art is inexplicable, infinite; for consistency of form its material has to be clear, unambiguous.

1. In a given word the sequence of letters is unambiguous, is the same for everyone. It is independent of the personal position of the observer.
2. The sound is unambiguous only for the spoken word. For the written word it is dependent on the observer's imaginative faculty. Therefore sound can only be material for the performance and not for the poetry.
3. Meaning is unambiguous only when the designated object is present. Otherwise it is dependent on the imaginative faculty of the observer.
4. The association of ideas cannot be unambiguous, as it is totally dependent on the combinatorial faculty of the observer. Everybody has different experiences and remembers and combines differently.

4. Classical poetry counted on the similarities between people. It considered the associations of ideas as unambiguous. It was mistaken. At any rate it built its foci on associations of ideas: 'Über allen Gipfeln ist Ruh' ('O'er every mountain peace does reign'). Here Goethe does not only want to indicate that there is quiet on mountaintops; the reader is supposed to enjoy this peacefulness in the same way the poet, tired from his official duties and usually functioning in an urban environment, does himself. That such associations of ideas are not all that commonly shared can be shown if one were

to read such a line to someone from Heidjer (a region of two inhabitants per square kilometer). That person would certainly be much more impressed by a line like 'lightning harry zigzags the subway crushes the skyscraper'. At any rate, the realization that all is quiet does not bring forth poetic feelings in him because, for him, quietness is the normal state of affairs. The poet has to take poetic feelings into account. And what is a poetic feeling? The whole poetry of quietude rests and falls with the observer's ability to feel. Here words are not given their value.

Except for a very minor sound rhythm in the cadence, there is but one rhyme connection (between 'Ruh' and 'du') in the next verse. The only conforming relation between the parts in classical poetry is the one concerning the association of ideas, i.e., poetic feeling. The whole of classical poetry now appears to us as dadaistic philosophy, and its effects are all the crazier the less the intention to be dadaistic is present. Today only the couplet singers on Variety stages hark back to classical poetry.

3. Abstract poetry separated – and therein lies its great merit – the word from its associations, and played off word against word; more particularly concept against concept, while taking sound into account. That is more consistent that the evaluation of poetic feelings, but not yet consistent enough. What abstract poetry tried to achieve is achieved in a similar fashion, though more consistently, by dadaistic painters, who played off actual real objects by nailing or gluing them next to each other in a painting. Concepts can be played off against each other much more clearly this way than when their meanings have been translated into words.

2. Nor do I consider it to be very consistent to make the sound into the carrier of the poem, because sound is unambiguous only in relation to the spoken and not in relation to the written word. Sound poetry is consistent only in one case, namely when it is created in public performance and is not written down. One has to differentiate sharply between writing poetry and giving a poetry reading. For a reading, poetry is only material. The reading doesn't even care if its material is poetry or not. One can, for example, perform the alphabet, which was originally only a utilitarian form, in such a way that it results in a work of art. Much could be said concerning artistic readings.

1. Consistent poetry is constructed from letters. Letters have no concepts. Letters in themselves have no sound, they only offer the possibility to be given sound values by the performer. The consistent poem plays off letters and groups of letters against each other.

To All the Theatres of the World I Demand the MERZ-Stage

I demand the total combination of all artistic forces to achieve the total work of art. I demand the equality in principle of all materials, equality between complete human beings, idiots, whistling wire-netting and thought pumps. I demand the complete seizure of all materials from the double-rail welder to the three-quarter violin. I demand the most conscientious rape of technology to the point of the complete execution of fusing fusions. I demand the abstract use of critics and the indivisibility of all their essays on the mutability of the stage setting and the inadequacy of human knowledge in general.

I demand the Bismark herring.

Set up gigantic surfaces, comprehend them to the point of conceived infinity, cloak them with color, displace them threateningly and arch to destruction their smooth modesty. Snap and turbulate finite parts and twist hole-boring parts of nothingness endlessly together. Glue smoothing surfaces one on top of the other. Wire lines into movement, real movement climbs real rope of a wire mesh. Flaming lines, crawling lines, flattening lines crossed. Let lines fight among themselves and stroke each other in generous tenderness. Let dots star in between, join hands and turn themselves into lines. Bend the lines, snap and double up corners throttling whirling round a point. In the waves of a whirling storm let a line rush by, graspable of wire. Roll up balls and let them come into contact in the whirling air. Let surfaces interpenetrate one another and become one and torn apart. Boxes piled up rectangular, straight and crooked and painted. Collapsible cylinder collapses box throttles box. Put lines to pull that draw a net and paint it blue. Nets encircle and constrict the torments of St. Anthony. Lets nets billow and flow out in lines grow dense in surfaces, net the nets. Let veils waft, soft folds fall, let cotton wool drip and water sparkle. Roll air soft and white through thousand-candle arc lamps. Then take wheels and axles, make them rear up and sing (water giant over-stander). Axles dance middle-wheel balls roll tub. Cogwheels scent cogs, find a sewing machine that is yawning. Twisting itself upwards or stooped, the sewing machine beheads itself, feet uppermost. Take a dentist's drill, a mincing machine, crack-scratchers from the streetcar, omnibuses and automobiles, bicycles, tandems and their tires, including wartime utility tires, and deform them. Take lights and deform them in the most brutal manner. Drive locomotives into one another, let window and door curtains spider-webs dance with window frames and break whimpering glass. Make steam-boilers explode to produce railway smoke. Take petticoats and other similar things, shoes and artificial hair, also skates and throw them in the right place, where they belong, and always at the right time. As far as I'm concerned also take man-traps, spring-guns, infernal machines, the tin fish in which one bakes puddings (critics) and the funnel, naturally everything in an artistically deformed state. Hoses are also very much to be recommended. In short, take everything from the emperor's screw to the fine lady's hairnet, in each case of a size in conformity with the work.

Human beings may also be used.

Human beings may be tied to the wings. Human beings may also make an appearance, even in their everyday situation, may speak with two legs, even in sensible sentences.

Now begin to marry off the materials to each other. For instance, marry the oilcloth sheet to the building society, bring the lamp-cleaner into a relationship with the marriage between Anna Blume and the concert pitch A. Give the balls to the surface to eat and have a cracked corner destroyed by twenty-two candlepower arc lamps. Make people walk on their hands and wear hats on their feet, like Anna Blume. (Cataracts.) Foam is sprayed.

And now begins the glow of musical saturation. Organs behind the stage sing and say: 'Phutt, phutt.' The sewing machine rattles on in front. A man in one wing says 'Bah.' Another suddenly appears and says: 'I'm stupid.' (Copyright reserved.) A priest kneels between them the wrong way round and cries and prays loudly: 'O mercy seething distonishment hallelujah lad, lad weds drops of water.' A water-pipe uninhibitedly drips monotonously. Eight. Drums and flutes flash death, and a streetcar driver's pipe shines brightly. A jet of ice-cold water runs down the back of the man in one wing into a pot. He sings C sharp, D, D sharp, E flat, the whole worker's song. Under the pot a gas flame has been lit to boil the water, and a melody of violins shimmers pure and as delicate as a girl. A veil spreads latitudes. The glow in the center boils a deep dark red. There is a soft rustling. The long sighs of violins swell and die away. Light darkens stage, the sewing machine is also dark.

I demand unity in the forming of space.

I demand unity in the molding of time.

I demand unity in the mating question in respect of deformation, copulation, overlapping.

This is the Merz stage such as our time needs. I demand revision of all the theatres in the world on the basis of the Merz idea.

I demand immediate abolition of all bad conditions.

Above all, however, I demand the immediate establishment of an international experimental stage for the working out of the Merz total work of art. I demand the establishment of Merz theatres in every sizable town for the unimpeachable performance of every kind of exhibition. (Children Half-Price.)

6c
GEORGE GROSZ (1893–1959) WITH WIELAND HERZFELDE (1896–1988) FROM 'ART IS IN DANGER' 1925

German artist, caricaturist, and Berlin-based Dadaist who became an American citizen in 1938. Grosz, later described by the Nazis as 'Cultural Bolshevist Number One', trained at Dresden Academy (1909) and served in the German army from 1914. He was discharged as unfit for service, having come close to being shot after a court martial for insubordination. Grosz anglicised his name (from Georg Gro) as a war protest. He joined the Communist Party in 1918 and Berlin Dada in 1919. He organised and exhibited at the first International Dada Fair (1920), and was prosecuted a number of times for blasphemy and obscenity during the 1920s. With John Heartfield he published a series of illustrated books and journals satirising German militarism and Weimar corruption. Grosz was famous not only for his Dadaist montages, but also as a leading exponent, with Otto Dix, of Neue Sachlichkeit – the satirical New German Realism. His collections of drawings, The Face of the Ruling Class *(1921), published by Wieland Herzfelde in his Malik Verlag 'Little Revolutionary Library', and* Ecce Homo *(1923), offer savage depictions of Weimar politicians, profiteers and prostitutes. In despair at the rise of Fascism and disillusioned with the Communist Party, Grosz left*

Germany for a teaching post at the Art Students' League in New York. He returned to Berlin in the late 1950s, having become disillusioned with America ('my American dream turned out to be a soap bubble').

Jesus in the trenches

The German Dada movement was rooted in the realization, which came simultaneously to several of my comrades and myself, that it was complete insanity to believe that 'spirit' [Geist] or people of 'spirit' ruled the world. Goethe under bombardment, Nietzsche in rucksack, Jesus in the trenches – there were still people who continued to believe in the autonomous power of spirit and art.

Dada was the first significant art movement in Germany in decades. Don't laugh – through this movement all the 'isms' of art became yesterday's inconsequential studio affairs. Dada was not a 'made' movement, but an organic product, originating in reaction to the head-in-the-clouds tendency of so-called holy art, whose disciples brooded over cubes and Gothic art while the generals were painting in blood. Dada forced the devotees of art to show their colors.

Dada as exterminator

What did the Dadas do? They said it's all the same, whether one just blusters – or gives forth with a sonnet from Petrarch, Shakespeare, or Rilke; whether one gilds boot-heels or carves Madonnas: the shooting goes on, profiteering goes on, hunger goes on, lying goes on; why all that art? Wasn't it the height of fraud to pretend art created spiritual values? Wasn't it unbelievably ridiculous that art was taken seriously by itself and no one else? 'Hands off holy art!' screamed the foes of Dada. 'Art is in danger!' 'Spirit is being dishonoured!' This prattle about the spirit, when the only spirit was the dishonoured one of the press, which wrote: Buy war bonds! – What prattle about art, as they finally arrived at the task of overpainting with beauty and interesting features the face of Anno 13, which daily unmasked itself more and more.

Against windmills

Today I know, together with all the other founders of Dada, that our only mistake was to have been seriously engaged at all with so-called art. Dada was the breakthrough, taking place with bawling and scornful laughter; it came out of a narrow, overbearing, and overrated milieu, and floating in the air between the classes, knew no responsibility to the general public. We saw then the insane end products of the ruling order of society and burst into laughter. We had not yet seen the system behind this insanity.

It dawns

The pending revolution brought gradual understanding of this system. There were no more laughing matters, there were more important problems than those of art; if art was still to have a meaning, it had to submit to those problems. In the void in which we found ourselves after overcoming art phraseology, some of us dadas got lost, mainly those in Switzerland and France, who had experienced the cultural shocks of the last decade more from the newspaper perspective. The rest of us saw the great new task: Tendency Art in the service of the revolutionary cause.

[. . .]

Whose bread I eat, his praise I sing

The artist, whether he likes it or not, lives in continual correlation to the public, to society, and he cannot withdraw from its laws of evolution, even when, as today, they include class conflict. Anyone maintaining a sophisticated stance above or outside of things is also taking sides, for such indifference and aloofness is automatically a support of the class currently in power – in Germany, the Middle Class. Moreover, a great number of artists quite consciously support the bourgeois system, since it is within that system that their work sells.

What will I think tomorrow?

In November, 1918, as the tide seemed to be turning – the most sheltered simpleton suddenly discovered his sympathy for the working people, and for several months mass-produced red and reddish allegories and pamphlets did well in the art market. Soon afterward, however, quiet and order returned; would you believe it, our artists returned with the greatest possible silence to the higher regions: 'What do you mean? We remained revolutionary – but the workers, don't even mention them. They are all bourgeois. In this country one cannot make a revolution.' And so they brood again in their studios over 'really' revolutionary problems of form, color, and style.

The young man digests everything

Formal revolution lost its shock effect a long time ago. The modern citizen digests everything; only the money chests are vulnerable. Todays young merchant is not like his counterpart in Gustav Freytag's times: ice-cold, aloof, he hangs the most radical things in his apartment. . . . Rash and unhesitating acceptance so as not to be 'born yesterday' is the password. Automobile the newest, most sporty model. Nothing said about professional mission, obligations of wealth; cool, objective to the point of dullness, sceptical, without illusions, avaricious, he understands only his merchandise, for everything else – including the fields of philosophy, ethics, art – for all culture, there are specialists who determine the fashion, which is then accepted at face value. Even the formal revolutionaries and 'wanderers into the void' do fairly well, for, underneath, they are related to those gentlemen, and have, despite all their apparent discrepancies, the same indifferent, arrogant view of life.

Paint usefully

Anyone to whom the workers' revolutionary cause is not just a phrase or 'a beautiful idea, but impossible to realize,' cannot be content to work harmlessly along dealing with formal problems. He must try to express the workers' battle idea and measure the value of his work by its social usefulness and effectiveness, rather than by uncontrollable individual artistic principles or public success.

Last round

Let us summarize: the meaning, nature, and history of art are directly related to the meaning, nature, and history of society. The prerequisite for the perception and evaluation of contemporary art is an intellect directed at the knowledge of facts and of correlations with real life and all its convulsions and tensions. For a hundred years, man has been seizing the earth's means of production. At the same time, the fight among men for possession of these means assumes ever more extensive forms, drawing all men into its vortex. There are workers, employees, civil servants, commercial travelers, and stockholders, contractors, merchants, men of finance. Everyone else represents stages of these two fronts. The struggle for existence of a mankind divided into the exploited and the exploiters is, in its sharpest and final form: class warfare.

Yes, art is in danger:

Today's artist, if he does not want to run down and become an antiquated dud, has the choice between technology and class warfare propaganda. In both cases he must give up 'pure art'. Either he enrolls as an architect, engineer, or advertising artist in the army (unfortunately very feudalistically organized) which develops industrial powers and exploits the world; or, as a reporter and critic reflecting the face of our times, a propagandist and defender of the revolutionary idea and its partisans, he finds a place in the army of the suppressed who fight for their just share of the world, for a significant social organization of life.

7
VORTICISM

FROM *BLAST* 1914

The term 'vorticism' was first used by Ezra Pound to describe the avant-garde nature of the London art world. It was adopted in 1913 by Wyndham Lewis (see also section IIa) to define the new and various arts of Modernism and their fascination with the 'vortices' of modern civilisation. Along with painters like Frederick Etchells and Cuthbert Hamilton, Lewis founded the Rebel Art Centre in 1914. The Centre attracted artists and poets (particularly Imagists) who were interested in German aesthetics, Futurism, Expressionism and Cubism, in opposition to the prevalent Post-Impressionism. In July 1914 the first of two issues of Blast *magazine was published. It included attacks on Victorianism and the Bloomsbury Group and issued a manifesto of Vorticism celebrating the geometric, mechanical and non-representational features of Futurist, Expressionist and Cubist art. It was signed 'R. Aldington, Arbuthnot, L. Atkinson, Gaudier Brzeska, J. Dismorr, G. Hamilton, E. Pound, W. Roberts, H. Sanders, E. Wadsworth, Wyndham Lewis'. [See IIa 10]*

Long Live the Vortex!

Long live the great art vortex sprung up in the centre of this town!

We stand for the Reality of the Present – not for the sentimental Future, or the sacripant Past.

We want to leave Nature and Men alone.

We do not want to make people wear Futurist Patches, or fuss men to take to pink and sky-blue trousers.

We are not their wives or tailors.

The only way Humanity can help artists is to remain independent and work unconsciously.

WE NEED THE UNCONSCIOUSNESS OF HUMANITY – their stupidity, animalism and dreams.

We believe in no perfectibility except our own.

Intrinsic beauty is in the Interpreter and Seer, not in the object or content.

We do not want to change the appearance of the world, because we are not Naturalists, Impressionists or Futurists (the latest form of Impressionism), and do not depend on the appearance of the world for our art.

WE ONLY WANT THE WORLD TO LIVE, and to feel it's crude energy flowing through us.

It may be said that great artists in England are always revolutionary, just as in France any really fine artist had a strong traditional vein.

Blast sets out to be an avenue for all those vivid and violent ideas that could reach the Public in no other way.

Blast will be popular, essentially. It will not appeal to any particular class, but to the fundamental and popular instincts in every class and description of people, TO THE INDIVIDUAL. The moment a man feels or realizes himself as an artist, he ceases to belong to any milieu or time. Blast is created for this timeless, fundamental Artist that exists in everybody.

The Man in the Street and the Gentleman are equally ignored.

Popular art does not mean the art of the poor people, as it is usually supposed to. It means the art of the individuals.

Education (art education and general education) tends to destroy the creative instinct. Therefore it is in times when education has been non-existent that art chiefly flourished.

But it is nothing to do with 'the People'.

It is a mere accident that that is the most favourable time for the individual to appear.

To make the rich of the community shed their education skin, to destroy politeness, standardization and academic, that is civilized, vision, is the task we have set ourselves.

We want to make in England not a popular art, not a revival of lost folk art, or a romantic fostering of such unactual conditions, but to make individuals, wherever found.

We will convert the King if possible.

A VORTICIST KING! WHY NOT?

DO YOU THINK LLOYD GEORGE HAS THE VORTEX IN HIM?

MAY WE HOPE FOR ART FROM LADY MOND?

We are against the glorification of 'the People', as we are against snobbery. It is not necessary to be an outcast bohemian, to be unkempt or poor, any more than it is necessary to be rich or handsome, to be an artist. Art is nothing to do with the coat you wear. A top-hat can well hold the Sixtine. A cheap cap could hide the image of Kephren.

AUTOMOBILISM (Marinetteism) bores us. We don't want to go about making a hullo-bulloo about motor cars, anymore than about knives and forks, elephants or gas-pipes.

Elephants are VERY BIG. Motor cars go quickly.

Wilde gushed twenty years ago about the beauty of machinery. Gissing, in his romantic delight with modern lodging houses was futurist in this sense.

The futurist is a sensational and sentimental mixture of the aesthete of 1890 and the realist of 1870.

The 'Poor' are detestable animals! They are only picturesque and amusing for the sentimentalist or the romantic! The 'Rich' are bores without a single exception, *en tant que riches!*

We want those simple and great people found everywhere.

Blast presents an art of Individuals.

II.

1. We hear from America and the Continent all sorts of disagreeable things about England: 'the unmusical, anti-artistic, unphilosophic country.'
2. We quite agree.
3. Luxury, sport, the famous English 'Humour,' the thrilling ascendancy and idée fixe of Class, producing the most intense snobbery in the World; heavy stagnant pools of Saxon blood, incapable of anything but the song of a frog, in home-counties: – these phenomena give England a peculiar distinction in the wrong sense, among the nations.
4. This is why England produces such good artists from time to time.
5. This is also the reason why a movement towards art and imagination could burst up here from this lump of compressed life, with more force than anywhere else.
6. To believe that it is necessary for or conducive to art, to 'Improve' life, for instance – make architecture, dress, ornament, in 'better taste,' is absurd.
7. The Art-instinct is permanently primitive.
8. In a chaos of imperfection, discord, etc., it finds the same stimulus as in Nature.
9. The artist of the modern movement is a savage (in no sense an 'advanced', perfected, democratic, Futurist individual of Mr. Marinetti's limited imagination): this enormous, jangling, journalistic, fairy desert of modern life serves him as Nature did more technically primitive man.
10. As the steppes and the rigours of the Russian winter, when the peasant has to lie for weeks in his hut, produces that extraordinary acuity of feeling and intelligence we associate with the Slav; so England is just now the most favourable country for the appearance of a great art.

VI.

1. The Modern World is due almost entirely to Anglo Saxon genius, its appearance and its spirit.
2. Machinery, trains, steam-ships, all that distinguishes externally our time, came far more from here than anywhere else.
3. In dress, manners, mechanical inventions, LIFE, that is, ENGLAND, has influenced Europe in the same way that France has in Art.
4. But busy with this LIFE-EFFORT, she has been the last to become conscious of the Art that is an organism of this new Order and Will of Man.
5. Machinery is the greatest Earth-medium: incidentally it sweeps away the doctrines of a narrow and pedantic Realism at one stroke.
6. By mechanical inventiveness, too, just as Englishmen have spread themselves all over the Earth, they have brought all the hemispheres about them in their original island.

7. It cannot be said that the complication of the Jungle, dramatic tropic growths, the vastness of American trees, is not for us.

8. For, in the forms of machinery, Factories, new and vaster buildings, bridges and works, we have all that, naturally, around us.

8
ECCENTRICISM

THE ECCENTRIC MANIFESTO 1922

The Eccentric Manifesto (1922) was published by the 'Depot of Eccentrics' on 9 July 1922 in Petrograd and printed in a limited run of 1000 copies. It contained four articles by Leonid Trauberg, Grigorii Kozintsev, Sergei Yutkevich and the professional gambler Georgii Kryzhitskii. Affiliated to the group was 'The Factory of the Eccentric Actor'. Georgii Kryzhitskii soon disappeared, Sergei Yutkevich left Petrograd to work in Moscow with Eisenstein, and Kozintsev and Trauberg stayed in Petrograd to work in the newly nationalised Leningrad film company. There they worked with the great cameraman Andrei Moskvin and the composer Dimitri Shostakovich (23 at the time) to produce some of the most innovative films of the period (under the FEKS label). These were all critical of the official government and used music hall, circus and fun-fair inspired techniques. Their work was heavily censored. Kozintsev continued to work in film; his last works were Hamlet *(1963) and* King Lear *(1971), both with Shostakovich. In 1949 Trauberg was accused of being 'a leader of cosmopolitanism' and was sacked as director at Lenfilm. He died in November 1990 at the age of 89. Reproduced below is Grigorii Kozintsev's contribution to* The Eccentric Manifesto, *in Marek Pytel's translation, based on a typescript of the original text of the manifesto as communicated to Pytel by Leonid Trauberg in 1977.*

SALVATION IN THE TROUSERS

ECCENTRISM

Patented

5 December 5
1921

In the Theatre of Free Comedy Petrograd
From the Manifesto of the Eccentric Theatre:
For the first time! 5 DECEMBER 5 Eccentrism!

Four blasts on the whistle!

1. For the actor – from emotion to the machine. from anguish gag. The technique – circus. The psychology – head over heels
2. For the director – a maximum of devices, a record number inventions, a turbine of rhythm.
3. For the dramatist – the coupler of gags.
4. For the artist – decoration in jumps.

For the fifth whistle blast – from the public – we are ready.
And remember; The American MARK TWAIN said:
'Better to be a young pup than an old bird of paradise'.

OF THE ECCENTRIC

AB!
PARADE OF THE ECCENTRIC!

ROSTA without bite, Max Linder without his top hat, Brockhaus
without Efron – What could be more absurd?

1921 December 5 (a historic date)
Kozintsev, Kryzhitskii, Trauberg found:
The 20th Century Without
A QUESTIONNAIRE

and the trousers of the eccentric, deep as a chasm, from which shall emerge amidst a thousand lusts and desires the great gaiety of Futurism. **MARINETTI**.

For the theatre as such this is a defeat because its territory has been captured by the eccentrism of the Music Hall. **LUNACHARSKII**

Oh, oh, oh! **The clown, SERGE**

WITHOUT
ECCENTRISM
A visiting card

Music Hall Cinematographovich Pinkertonov one year old

For Information See Below

1 THE KEY TO THE EVENTS

1 YESTERDAY – Comfortable offices, Bald foreheads, People pondered, made decision thought things over.
   TODAY – A Signal. To the Machines! Belts, chains, wheels, hands, feet, electricity The rhythm of production.
   YESTERDAY – Museums, Temples, Libraries.
   TODAY – Factories, Workshops, Dockyards.
2 YESTERDAY – The Culture of Europe.
   TODAY – The technology of America. Industry, Production under the Stars & Stripe. Either Americanisation or the undertakers.
3 YESTERDAY – The Salon, deep bows, aristocracy.
   TODAY – The shouts of the newsvendor, scandal, police truncheons, a noise, scream footsteps, the chase.

THE PACE TODAY

THE RHYTHM OF THE MACHINE CONCENTRATED
BY AMERICA REALISED ON THE STREET.
2 ART WITHOUT A CAPITAL LETTER,
A PEDESTAL OR A FIG LEAF

Life Requires Art That Is

HYPERBOLICALLY CRUDE, STUPENDOUS, NERVE WRACKING OPENLY UTILITARIAN, MECHANICALLY-PRECISE, MOMENTARY, RAPID.

Otherwise no one will hear, no one will see, no one will stop.

Everything adds up to this: The art of the 20th Century, the art of 1922, the art of this very moment is:

ECCENTRISM

3 OUR PARENTS
Parade allez!

In song – The Torch singer, Pinkerton, the cry of the auctioneer, slang.
In painting – The circus poster, the jacket of a cheap pulp thriller.
In music – The jazz band, (black street orchestra), circus marches.
In ballet – American song and dance routines.
In theatre – Music Hall, cinema, circus, cabaret, boxing.

4 WE ARE ECCENTRISM IN ACTION

1 A spectacle – should beat rhythmically on the nerves.
2 The high spot – the gag
3 The author – an explorer
4 The actor – a mechanised movement, not ballet pumps but roller skates, not a mask but a red nose. Acting is not movement but a wriggle, not mimicry but a grimace, not speech but a scream.

CHARLIE'S BUM IS MORE PRECIOUS TO US THAN THE HANDS OF ELEONORA DUSE!

5 The play is an acclimatisation of gags. The speed of 1,000 horsepower. Chase, pursuit, flight. Form – a divertissement.
6 Hunched backs, Fake stomachs, Clown wigs that pump up and down – these are the beginnings of a new style of stage costume. The basis of this – continuous transformation.
7 Sirens, shots, typewriters – are eccentric music. Tap shoes – the start   of a new rhythm.

we prefer the tap shoes of an american dancer to the 500 instruments of the marinskii theatre.

8 The synthesis of movements: acrobatic, gymnastic, balletic, bio-mechanic
9 A can-can on the tightrope of logic. Towards the Eccentric by way of the 'impossible' and   'insane'.
10 From fantasy to sleight of hand. From Hoffman to Fregoli. The infernal American 'Secrets of New York', 'Mystery of the grinning mask'?
11 The Alphabet for All! Sport in the theatres. The champion's sash and the boxer's gloves. A victory parade – more theatrical than Harlequin's grimace
12 Use of the principles of American Advertising.
13 The cult of the amusement park, the Devil's Wheel and Switchback, teaching the younger generation the BASIC TEMPO of our epoch.

THE RHYTHM OF THE TAP DANCE. THE RACKET OF THE CINEMA. PINKERTON. THE ROAR OF THE SWITCHBACK. A LOUD SLAP IN THE FACE OF PUBLIC TASTE. THE POETRY – 'TIME IS MONEY'!

OUR RAILS RUSH PAST

Paris, Berlin, London
Romanticism
Stylism
Exotism,
Archaism,
Reconstruction,
Restoration,
The Pulpit,
The Temple,
The Museum,

Only our methods are indispensible

THE AMERICANISATION OF THE THEATRE
In Russian means
ECC entr ISM

9
CONSTRUCTIVISM

9a
ALEKSEI GAN (1893–1942)
FROM *CONSTRUCTIVISM* 1922

Russian artist and designer. Head of the Section of Mass Presentations and Spectacles (attached to the Theatre Section of 'Narkompros', the People's Commissariat for Enlightenment), Gan was vehemently 'anti-art', stressing the importance of the industrial element in the new culture. He soon fell out of favour because of his extreme ideological position and eventually died in a prison camp. His book Constructivism, *published in 1922, served as a declaration of the industrial constructivists and was partly a response to the many contemporary debates on art, construction and production at the time. Extracts from the section 'From Speculative Activity of Art to Socially Meaningful Artistic Labor' are reproduced below in the original typography, in John E. Bowlt's translation from his revised and enlarged edition of* Russian Art of the Avant-Garde: Theory and Criticism 1902–1934, *1988.*

[. . .] When we talk about social technology, this should imply not just one kind of tool, and not a number of different tools, but a system of these tools, their sum total in the whole of society.

It is essential to picture that in this society, lathes and motors, instruments and apparatuses, simple and complex tools are scattered in various places, but in a definite order.

In some places they stand like huge sockets (e.g., in centers of large-scale industry), in other places other tools are scattered about. But at any given moment, if people are linked by the bond of labor, if we have a society, then all the tools of labor will also be interlocked: all, so to say, 'technologies' of individual branches of production will form something whole, a united social technology, and not just in our minds, but objectively and concretely.

The technological system of society, the structure of its tools, creates the structure of human relationships, as well.

The economic structure of society is created from the aggregate of its productional relationships.

The sociopolitical structure of society is determined directly by its economic structure.

But in times of revolution peculiar contradictions arise.

We live in the world's first proletarian republic. The rule of the workers is realizing its objectives and is fighting not only for the retention of this rule, but also for absolute supremacy, for the assertion of new, historically necessary forms of social reality.

In the territory of labor and intellect, there is no room for speculative activity.

In the sphere of cultural construction, only that has concrete which is indissolubly linked with the general tasks of revolutionary actuality.

Bourgeois encirclement can compel us to carry out a whole series of strategic retreats in the field of economic norms and relationships, but in no way must it distort the process of our intellectual work.

The proletarian revolution has bestirred human thought and has struck home at the holy relics and idols of bourgeois spirituality. *Not only the clesiastical priests have caught it in the neck, the priests of aesthetics had it too.*

Art is finished! It has no place in the human labor apparatus.

Labor, technology, organization!

The revaluation of the functions of human activity, the linking of every effort with the general range of social objectives—

that is the ideology of our time.

And the more distinctly the motive forces of social reality confront our consciousness, the more saliently its sociopolitical forms take shape the more the masters of artistic labor are confronted with the task of:

Breaking with their speculative activity (of art) of finding the paths to concrete action by employing their knowledge and skill for the sake of true living purposeful labor.

Intellectual-material production establishes labor interrelations and productional links with science and technology by arising in the place of art — art, which by its very nature cannot break with religion and philosophy and which is powerless to leap from the exclusive circle of stract, speculative activity.

utilitarian + futurist

9b
LÁSZLÓ MOHOLY-NAGY (1895–1946)
'CONSTRUCTIVISM AND THE PROLETARIAT' 1922

Hungarian artist and photographer. Having studied law in Budapest, he was a member of Dada and Constructivist groups in Vienna and Berlin in the period 1919–23. He produced his first 'photograms' in 1923 and continued to experiment with camera techniques throughout his career. In 1925 he joined the staff of the Bauhaus under Walter Gropius (see below) and soon became one of the leading avant-garde artists in the New Photographers movement in Europe. He left Germany in 1935 and after working as a designer in Amsterdam and London was invited to the United States in 1937 to head the New Bauhaus school in Chicago. The following piece was originally published in the Hungarian magazine MA in 1922 and is taken from Moholy-Nagy: An Anthology *(Richard Kostelanetz ed., 1970).*

Reality is the measure of human thinking. It is the means by which we orient ourselves in the Universe. The actuality of time – the reality of this century – determines what we can grasp and what we cannot understand.

And this reality of our century is *technology* – the invention, construction and maintenance of the machine. To be a user of machines is to be of the spirit of this century. It has replaced the transcendental spiritualism of past eras.

Before the machine, everyone is equal – I can use it, so can you – it can crush me and the same can happen to you. There is no tradition in technology, no consciousness of class or standing. Everybody can be the machine's master or its slave.

This is the root of socialism, the final liquidation of feudalism. It is the machine that woke up the proletariat. In serving technology the worker discovered a changed world. We have to eliminate the machine if we want to eliminate socialism. But we all know there is no such thing. This is our century – technology, machine, socialism. Make your peace with it. Shoulder its task.

Because it is our task to carry the revolution toward reformation, to fight for a new spirit to fill the forms stamped out by the monstrous machine. Material well-being does not depend on manufactured goods. Look around. The proletariat isn't happy today in spite of the machine.

Material well-being is caused by the spirit that is superior to the demand of routine work; it is a socialism of the mind, a dedication to the spirit of the group. Only a proletariat, educated to this grasp of essential community, can be satisfied.

Who will teach them? Words are heavy, obscure. Their meaning is evasive to the untrained mind. Past traditions hang on to their meaning. But there is art. Art expresses the spirit of the times; it is art that crystallizes the emotional drive of an age. The art of our century, its mirror and its voice, is *Constructivism*.

Constructivism is neither proletarian nor capitalist. Constructivism is primordial, without class and without ancestor. It expresses the pure form of nature, the direct color, the spatial element not distorted by utilitarian motifs.

The new world of the proletariat needs Constructivism; it needs fundamentals that are without deceit. Only the natural element, accessible to all eyes, is revolutionary. It has never before been the property of civilized man.

In Constructivism form and substance are one. Not substance and tendency, which are always identified. Substance is essential, but tendency is intentional. Constructivism is pure substance – not the property of one artist alone who drags along under the yoke of individualism. Constructivism is not confined to the picture frame and the pedestal. It expands into industrial design, into houses, objects, forms. It is the socialism of vision – the common property of all men.

Only the today is important for the Constructivist. He cannot indulge in the luxurious speculations of either the Utopian Communist who dreams of a future world domination, or of the bourgeois artist who lives in splendid isolation. It cannot be either proletarian art or art of the precious salons. In Constructivism the process and the goal are one – the spiritual conquest of a century of technology.

Generalized Fordism

needs to serve functionality

10
BAUHAUS

10a
WALTER GROPIUS (1883–1969)
'MANIFESTO OF THE BAUHAUS, APRIL 1919'

German architect, born into a family of painters and architects. He studied architecture in Munich and Berlin and soon opened his own practice. His first commission in 1910 for the Fagus factory made his name and established him as a new designer with a radical vision. He fought and was wounded in the First World War, an experience which left him mentally and physically scarred, but which also strengthened his political commitment against capitalism and bourgeois philistinism. His particular concern with the influence of mechanised production on traditional craftmanship led to a proposal to the Weimar authorities for the creation of a school of art and design. The Bauhaus was founded in 1919 and, until its closure by the Nazis in 1933, it encouraged and synthesised the energies and talents of such teachers and students as Paul Klee, Wassily Kandinsky, Oscar Schlemmer and László Moholy-Nagy, among others. Crucial to Gropius's conception of the role of the Bauhaus was the belief that there was no fundamental difference between fine arts and the crafts and that the School should therefore stress and develop the elements common to all artistic activities. After the Nazis took over the Bauhaus to convert it into a training school, Gropius moved to London and from there, in 1937, emigrated to the United States. Reproduced below, in Frank Whitford's translation, is his 'Manifesto of the Bauhaus, April 1919'.

The ultimate aim of all creative activity is the building! The decoration of buildings was once the noblest function of the fine arts, and the fine arts were indispensable to great architecture. Today they exist in complacent isolation, and can only be rescued from it by the conscious co-operation and collaboration of all craftsmen. Architects, painters and sculptors must once again come to know and comprehend the composite character of a building both as an entity and in terms of its various parts. Then their work will be filled with that true architectonic spirit which, as 'salon art', it has lost.

The old art schools were unable to produce this unity; and how, indeed, should they have done so, since art cannot be taught? Schools must be absorbed by the *workshop* again. The world of the pattern-designer and applied artist, consisting only of drawing and painting, must at last and again become a world in which things are *built*. If the young person who takes joy in creative activity begins his career now, as he formerly did, by learning a craft, then the unproductive 'artist' will no longer be condemned to inadequate artistry, for his skills will be preserved for the crafts in which he can achieve great things.

Architects, painters, sculptors, we must all return to crafts! For there is *no such thing* as 'professional art'. There is no essential difference between the artist and the craftsman.

The artist is an exalted craftsman. By the grace of Heaven and in rare moments of inspiration which transcend the will, art may unconsciously blossom from the labour of his hand, *but a foundation of handicraft is essential for every artist.* It is there that the primary source of creativity lies.

Let us therefore create a *new guild of craftsmen* without the class-distinctions that raise an arrogant barrier between craftsman and artist! Let us together desire, conceive and create the new building of the future, which will combine everything – architecture *and* sculpture *and* painting – in a *single form* which will one day rise towards the heavens from the hands of a million workers as the crystalline symbol of a new and coming faith.

10b
ANNELISE FLEISCHMANN
FROM 'ECONOMIC LIVING' 1924

Fleischmann was one of the most gifted weavers at the Bauhaus, where she studied between 1922 and 1930. The following piece dates from 1924 and is reproduced in Frank Whitford's translation Bauhaus, *1984.*

Economy is demanded today throughout the business world. Economy of living (not its restriction) is but little considered. To gain four hours of freedom by means of economic house design implies a significant change in the pattern of modern life.

Economy of living must first be economy of labour. Every door-handle must require a minimum of energy to operate it. The traditional style of living is an exhausted machine which enslaves the woman to the house. The bad arrangement of rooms and their furnishings (padded chairs, curtains) rob her of freedom, restrict her development and make her uneasy. Today the woman is the victim of a false style of living. It is obvious that a complete change is urgently required.

New objects (the car, aeroplane, telephone) are designed above all for ease of use and maximum efficiency. Today they perform their function well. Other objects in use for centuries (the house, table, chair) were once good, but now no longer fully do their job. In order to make them meet our needs we must design them unencumbered by the weight of history.

10c
LÁSZLÓ MOHOLY-NAGY (1895–1946)
'THE NEW TYPOGRAPHY' 1923

Representative of the work Moholy-Nagy contributed to the Bauhaus, the following piece from 1923 is taken from Moholy-Nagy: An Anthology *(ed. Richard Kostelanetz, 1970).*

It is not enough to improve old forms (such as water pipes, central heating, electric light). That is merely to give an old dress a new hem.

Compare our dress: it meets the demands of modern travel, hygiene and economics (you can't travel by rail in a crinoline) . . .

The Bauhaus attempts to find the functional form for the house, as well as for the simplest utensil. It wants things clearly constructed, it wants functional materials, it wants this new beauty.

This new beauty is not a style which matches one object with another aesthetically by using similar external forms (façade, motif, ornament). Today, something is beautiful if its form serves its function, if it is well made of well-chosen material. A good chair will then 'match' a good table.

The good object can offer only one unambiguous solution: the type. (We all have the same telephone without longing for an individual design. We wear similar clothes and are satisfied with a small degree of difference within this restriction.)

The optimal form demands mass production. Mechanization also means economy.

The Bauhaus attempts to produce the elements of the house with this economy in mind – therefore to find the single solution that is best for our times. It applies itself to this task in experimental workshops, it designs prototypes for the whole house as well as the teapot, and it works to improve our entire way of life by means of economic production which is only possible with the aid of the prototype.

10d
OSCAR SCHLEMMER (1888–1943)
DIARY EXTRACT 1927

German painter, designer and theatre director. His work for the theatre was heavily influenced by architectural notions of space and he was one of the originators of what is now termed 'performance art'. His geometrical Triadic Ballet, originally conceived in 1916, was staged in full in 1922. He taught at the Bauhaus from 1920, collaborated with Erwin Piscator (see section IIa 24), and in 1925 created the Bauhaus Theatre. After political criticism of his work in 1929, he left the Bauhaus to work at the Breslau Academy. In 1930 the Nazis destroyed his murals at Weimar and in 1932 they closed down the Academy and an exhibition of his works in Stuttgart. Schlemmer's work figured in the Nazi exhibition of 'Degenerate Art' in 1937 (see below, section IIIb). Towards the end of his life he worked in a factory. The following extract is from Schlemmer's diary entry for 9 April 1927, translated by Frank Whitford.

'The cathedral of Socialism'. The original sentence reads: 'The State Bauhaus, founded after the catastrophe of war, in the chaos of the revolution and at a time when an emotionally charged, explosive kind of art had reached a high-point, will initially become the place where those people gather who, believing in the future and beating at the gates of heaven, wish to build the cathedral of Socialism.'

The sentence, taken from a manifesto written for a Bauhaus exhibition in 1923, referred to an earlier period and was intended to describe the stages of development of the Bauhaus. The word 'initially' makes this clear enough. It is therefore nonsensical and michievous to take the sentence out of context and to turn it into the Bauhaus manifesto. The following sentences adequately demonstrate that this stage was very quickly superseded and replaced by other aims, just as the political face of the

Bauhaus – if there ever was such a thing – was also very soon changed: there were as many right-wing as left-wing students, or, at the most, a religious wave followed a political one.

It need not be denied that . . . the Bauhaus mirrors an historical epoch. Did not the majority of Germans wish to build the cathedral of Socialism in 1918? Did not the revolution and subsequent constitution acknowledge a desire for a People's State? And what is a People's State, if not socialism? Moreover: is not socialism the same as a social democratic or a communist party? Is not socialism an idea, an ethical concept, which stands above all parties?

11
MANIFESTO ISSUED BY THE SYNDICATE OF TECHNICAL WORKERS, PAINTERS AND SCULPTORS, MEXICO CITY, 1922

This manifesto was originally published as a broadside. It is reproduced here in Laurence E. Schmeckebier's translation, from Theories of Modern Art *(ed. Herschel B. Chipp, 1968).*

Social, Political, and Aesthetic Declaration from the Syndicate of Technical Workers, Painters, and Sculptors to the indigenous races humiliated through centuries; to the soldiers converted into hangmen by their chiefs; to the workers and peasants who are oppressed by the rich; and to the intellectuals who are not servile to the bourgeoisie:

We are with those who seek the overthrow of an old and inhuman system within which you, worker of the soil, produce riches for the overseer and politician, while you starve. Within which you, worker in the city, move the wheels of industries, weave the cloth, and create with your hands the modern comforts enjoyed by the parasites and prostitutes, while your own body is numb with cold. Within which you, Indian soldier, heroically abandon your land and give your life in the eternal hope of liberating your race from the degradations and misery of centuries.

Not only the noble labor but even the smallest manifestations of the material or spiritual vitality of our race spring from our native midst. Its admirable, exceptional, and peculiar ability to create beauty – the art of the Mexican people – is the highest and greatest spiritual expression of the world-tradition which constitutes our most valued heritage. It is great because it surges from the people; it is collective, and our own aesthetic aim is to socialize artistic expression, to destroy bourgeois individualism.

We repudiate the so-called easel art and all such art which springs from ultra-intellectual circles, for it is essentially aristocratic.

We hail the monumental expression of art because such art is public property.

We proclaim that this being the moment of social transition from a decrepit to a new order, the makers of beauty must invest their greatest efforts in the aim of materializing an art valuable to the people, and our supreme objective in art, which is today an expression for individual pleasure, is to create beauty for all, beauty that enlightens and stirs to struggle.

12
LEF MANIFESTO 1923

The journal Lef *('Left Front of the Arts', 1923–25, continued as 'New Left Front of the Arts' in 1927–28) was based in Moscow. It was particularly close to the Constructivists and Formalists and its founders included Boris Arvatov, Osip Brik, Nikolai Chuzhak, Boris Kushner, Vladimir Mayakovsky and Sergei Tretyakov. It featured pieces on photography and cinematography with regular contributions by Alexander Rodchenko and Sergei Eisenstein. The following piece appeared in* Lef *2, April–May 1923, in Russian, German and English. This translation is based on the English version and is taken from* Bolshevik Visions: First Phase of the Cultural Revolution in Soviet Russia, Part II *(ed. William G. Rosenberg).*

COMRADES, ORGANIZERS OF LIFE!

To-day the First of May, the Workers of the World will demonstrate in their millions with songs and festivity.

Five years of Victory!

Five years of daily renewed and realized Slogans!

Five years of Conquest.

And –

Five years of monotonous celebration.

Five years of languishing art!

So called Stage managers!

How long will you and the other rats gnaw this theatrical sham?

Begin to take from real life!

Begin to form victorious processions of the Revolution.

So called Poets!

When will you throw away your sickly lyrics?

Will you ever understand that to write of a storm from newspaper knowledge

Is not to write about a storm?

Give us a new 'Marseillaise' and let the International thunder the march of the Conquering Revolution.

So called Artists!

Stop color patching on moth-eaten canvasses.

Stop decorating the easy life of the bourgeoisie.

Exercise your artistic strength to engirdle cities until you are able to take part in the world's work.

Give new colors and outlines to the world.

These 'small groups' have neither the strength, nor the desire to meet the problem.

These 'Art Priests' keep aesthetic knowledge to themselves. Between the people and themselves they have established a wall.

On this day of demonstration, the First of May, when Proletarians are gathered in a United Front, we call you Organizers of the World!

Break the Barrier 'Beauty of Ourselves'. Break the artistic 'school' barriers!

Add your strength to the united energy of the collective.

We know that the aesthetics of old, branded with the name 'Rights' who revive monasticism, and await inspiration from the Saints, will not answer our call!

We call the Lefts. Revolutionary Futurists, who have given the streets and squares their art, the producers who have given inspiration an accurate account. Their inspiration they took from Factory Dynamos!

Constructiveness has been substituted for mysticism. The mystery of creation has been replaced by the shaping of materials.

THE 'LEFTS' OF THE WORLD. We know little of your name, the names of your schools, but this we do know: wherever revolutions begin, there you grow.

We call upon you to establish a single Front of the Left Art – The Red Art International.

Comrades! Split Left from Right Art everywhere! With Left Art prepare the European Revolution. In the U.S.S.R., strengthen it.

Communicate with your Staff in Moscow (Journal 'Lef', Nikitsky Boulevard S., Moscow).

Not by accident did we choose the First of May the day of our call.

Only in conjunction with the Workers' Revolution can we see the dawn of future Art.

We who have worked for five years in a Land of Revolution know:

That the October Revolution has given us great ideas which require new formations.

Only the October Revolution, which freed art from Bourgeois enslavement, has given freedom to Art.

Down with the boundaries of Lands and Studios!

Down with the Monks of the Right Art!

Long Live the Single Front of the Lefts!

Long Live the Art of the Proletarian Revolution!

13
SURREALISM

ANDRÉ BRETON (1896–1966)
FROM THE FIRST MANIFESTO OF SURREALISM 1924

French writer, critic, leader of the Surrealist movement. Breton joined the Dadaists in 1916 and was co-founder of Littérature *in 1919. He produced* Les Champs magnétiques, *the first experiment in automatic writing with Philippe Soupault, before turning, in 1922, to Surrealism to assume the role of leader of that movement, as well as that of the left wing of the French avant-garde. Breton was introduced to Freudian analysis while serving in the First World War and his formulation of Surrealism relied heavily on the role of the irrational and the function of the subconscious in art. The following extracts from the 1924 manifesto written by Breton are taken from Richard Seaver's and Helen R. Lane's translation of* Manifestos of Surrealism, *1969. [See IIIa 31]*

So strong is the belief in life, in what is most fragile in life – *real* life, I mean – that in the end this belief is lost. Man, that inveterate dreamer, daily more discontent with his destiny, has trouble assessing the objects he has been led to use, objects that his nonchalance has brought his way, or that he has earned through his own efforts, almost always through his own efforts, for he has agreed to work, at least he has not refused to try his luck (or what he calls his luck!). At this point he feels extremely modest: he knows what women he has had, what silly affairs he has been involved in; he is unimpressed by his wealth or poverty, in this respect he is still a newborn babe and, as for the approval of his conscience, I confess that he does very nicely without it. If he still retains a certain lucidity, all he can do is turn back toward his childhood which, however his guides and mentors may have botched it, still strikes him as somehow charming. There, the absence of any known restrictions allows him the perspective of several lives lived at once; this illusion becomes firmly rooted within him; now he is only interested in the fleeting, the extreme facility of everything. Children set off each day without a worry in the world. Everything is near at hand, the worst material conditions are fine. The woods are white or black, one will never sleep.

But it is true that we would not dare venture so far, it is not merely a question of distance. Threat is piled upon threat, one yields, abandons a portion of the terrain to be conquered. This imagination which knows no bounds is henceforth allowed to be exercised only in strict accordance with the laws of an arbitrary utility; it is incapable of assuming this inferior role for very long and, in the vicinity of the twentieth year, generally prefers to abandon man to his lusterless fate.

Though he may later try to pull himself together upon occasion, having felt that he is losing by slow degrees all reason for living, incapable as he has become of being able to rise to some exceptional situation such as love, he will hardly succeed. This is because he henceforth belongs body and soul to an imperative practical necessity which demands his constant attention. None of his gestures will be expansive, none of his ideas generous or far-reaching. In his mind's eye, events real or imagined will be seen only as they relate to a welter of similar events, events in which he has not participated, *abortive* events. What am I saying: he will judge them in relationship to one of these events whose consequences are more reassuring than the others. On no account will he view them as his salvation.

Beloved imagination, what I most like in you is your unsparing quality.

The mere word 'freedom' is the only one that still excites me. I deem it capable of indefinitely sustaining the old human fanaticism. It doubtless satisfies my only legitimate aspiration. Among all the many misfortunes to which we are heir, it is only fair to admit that we are allowed the greatest degree of freedom of thought. It is up to us not to misuse it. To reduce the imagination to a state of slavery – even though it would mean the elimination of what is commonly called happiness – is to betray all sense of absolute justice within oneself. Imagination alone offers me some intimation of what *can* be, and this is enough to remove to some slight degree the terrible injunction; enough, too, to allow me to devote myself to it without fear of making a mistake (as though it were possible to make a bigger mistake). Where does it begin to turn bad, and where does the mind's stability cease? For the mind, is the possibility of erring not rather the contingency of good?

[. . .]

We are still living under the reign of logic: this, of course, is what I have been driving at. But in this day and age logical methods are applicable only to solving problems of secondary interest. The absolute rationalism that is still in vogue allows us to consider only facts relating directly to our experience. Logical ends, on the contrary, escape us. It is pointless to add that experience itself has found itself increasingly circumscribed. It paces back and forth in a cage from which it is more and more difficult to make it emerge. It too leans for support on what is most immediately expedient, and it is protected by the sentinels of common sense. Under the pretense of civilization and progress, we have managed to banish from the mind everything that may rightly or wrongly be termed superstition, or fancy; forbidden is any kind of search for truth which is not in conformance with accepted practices. It was, apparently, by pure chance that a part of our mental world which we pretended not to be concerned with any longer – and, in my opinion by far the most important part – has been brought back to light. For this we must give thanks to the discoveries of Sigmund Freud. On the basis of these discoveries a current of opinion is finally forming by means of which the human explorer will be able to carry his investigations much further, authorized as he will henceforth be not to confine himself solely to the most summary realities. The imagination is perhaps on the point of reasserting itself, of reclaiming its rights. If the depths of our mind contain within it strange forces capable of augmenting those on the surface, or of waging a victorious battle against them, there is every reason to seize them – first to seize them, then, if need be, to submit them to the control of our reason

[. . .]

I believe in the future resolution of these two states, dream and reality, which are seemingly so contradictory, into a kind of absolute reality, a *surreality*, if one may so speak. It is in quest of this surreality that I am going, certain not to find it but too unmindful of my death not to calculate to some slight degree the joys of its possession.

[. . .]

Let us not mince words: the marvelous is always beautiful, anything marvelous is beautiful, in fact only the marvelous is beautiful.

[. . .]

Those who might dispute our right to employ the term surrealism in the very special sense that we understand it are being extremely dishonest, for there can be no doubt that this word had no currency before we came along. Therefore, I am defining it once and for all:

surrealism, *n.* Psychic automatism in its pure state, by which one proposes to express – verbally, by means of the written word, or in any other manner – the actual functioning of thought. Dictated by thought, in the absence of any control exercised by reason, exempt from any aesthetic or moral concern.

[. . .]

Swift is Surrealist in malice,
Sade is Surrealist in sadism.
Chateaubriand is Surrealist in exoticism.
Constant is Surrealist in politics.
Hugo is Surrealist when he isn't stupid.
Desbordes-Valmore is Surrealist in love.
Bertrand is Surrealist in the past.
Rabbe is Surrealist in death.
Poe is Surrealist in adventure.
Baudelaire is Surrealist in morality.
Rimbaud is Surrealist in the way he lived, and elsewhere.
Mallarmé is Surrealist when he is confiding.
Jarry is Surrealist in absinthe.
Nouveau is Surrealist in the kiss.
Saint-Pol-Roux is Surrealist in his use of symbols.
Fargue is Surrealist in the atmosphere.
Vaché is Surrealist in me.
Reverdy is Surrealist at home.
Saint-Jean-Perse is Surrealist at a distance.
Roussel is Surrealist as a storyteller.
Etc.

[. . .]

Language has been given to man so that he may make Surrealist use of it. To the extent that he is required to make himself understood, he manages more or less to express himself, and by so doing to fulfill certain functions culled from among the most vulgar. Speaking, reading a letter, present no real problem for him, provided that, in so doing, he does not set himself a goal above the mean, that is, provided he confines himself to carrying on a conversation (for the pleasure of conversing) with someone. He is not worried about the words that are going to come, nor about the sentence which will follow after the sentence he is just completing. To a very simple question, he will be capable of making a lightning-like reply.

[. . .]

Not only does this unrestricted language, which I am trying to render forever valid, which seems to me to adapt itself to all of life's circumstances, not only does this language not deprive me of any of my means, on the contrary it lends me an extraordinary lucidity, and it does so in an area where I least expected it. I shall even go so far as to maintain that it instructs me and, indeed, I have had occasion to use *surreally* words whose meaning I have forgotten. I was subsequently able to verify that the way in which I had used them corresponded perfectly with their definition. This would lead one to believe that we do not 'learn', that all we ever do is 'relearn'. There are felicitous turns of speech that I have thus familiarized myself with. And I am not talking about the *poetic consciousness of objects* which I have been able to acquire only after a spiritual contact with them repeated a thousand times over.

[. . .]

Poetic Surrealism, which is the subject of this study, has focused its efforts up to this point on re-establishing dialogue in its absolute truth, by freeing both interlocutors from any obligations of politeness. Each of them simply pursues his soliloquy without trying to derive any special dialectical pleasure from it and without trying to impose anything whatsoever upon his neighbor. The remarks exchanged are not, as is generally the case, meant to develop some thesis, however unimportant it may be; they are as disaffected as possible. As for the reply that they elicit, it is, in principle, totally indifferent to the personal pride of the person speaking. The words, the images are only so many springboards for the mind of the listener.

[. . .]

The mind which plunges into Surrealism relives with glowing excitement the best part of its childhood. For such a mind, it is similar to the certainty with which a person who is drowning reviews once more, in the space of less than a second, all the insurmountable moments of his life. Some may say to me that the parallel is not very encouraging. But I have no intention of encouraging those who tell me that. From childhood memories, and from a few others, there emanates a sentiment of being unintegrated, and then later of *having gone astray*, which I hold to be the most fertile that exists. It is perhaps childhood that comes closest to one's 'real life'; childhood beyond which man has at his disposal, aside from his laissez-passer, only a few complimentary tickets; childhood where everything nevertheless conspires to bring about the effective, risk-free possession of oneself. Thanks to Surrealism, it seems that opportunity knocks a second time. It is as though we were still running toward our salvation, or our perdition. In the shadow we again see a precious terror. Thank God, it's still only Purgatory. With a shudder, we cross what the occultists call *dangerous territory*.

[. . .]

Surrealism, such as I conceive of it, asserts our complete *nonconformism* clearly enough so that there can be no question of translating it, at the trial of the real world, as evidence for the defense. It could, on the contrary, only serve to justify the complete state of distraction which we hope to achieve here below. Kant's absentmindedness regarding women, Pasteur's absentmindedness about 'grapes', Curie's absentmindedness with respect to vehicles, are in this regard profoundly symptomatic. This world is only very relatively in tune with thought, and incidents of this kind are only the most obvious episodes of a war in which I am proud to be participating. Surrealism is the 'invisible ray' which will one day enable us to win out over our opponents. 'You are no longer trembling, carcass.' This summer the roses are blue; the wood is of glass. The earth, draped in its verdant cloak, makes as little impression upon me as a ghost. It is living and ceasing to live that are imaginary solutions. Existence is elsewhere.

poetic

14
TRANSITION

EUGENE JOLAS (1894–1952)
'SUGGESTIONS FOR A NEW MAGIC' 1927; 'PROCLAMATION' 1929

American editor of the Paris-based radical journal transition. *Jolas worked as a newspaper reporter in America and France before turning his attention to literature. The desire to establish an international forum for experimental writing led to the co-founding and co-editing* transition *which was published between 1927 and 1939, with a two-year interruption (1930–32). The list of regular contributors to* transition *reads like an inventory of European and American Modernism, including poets, novelists, theorists and artists. The magazine often featured Jolas's own declarations on writing, based mainly on the key function played by dreams and the unconscious. Reproduced below are 'Suggestions for a New Magic' (June 1927) and 'Proclamation' (June 1929). [See IIIb 37]*

SUGGESTIONS FOR A NEW MAGIC

transition will attempt to present the quintessence of the modern spirit in evolution. It may be interesting, therefore, to re-define some of the concepts that symbolize this spirit which both on the American and European continents is surrounded by a certain confusion.

We believe in the ideology of revolt against all diluted and synthetic poetry, against all artistic efforts that fail to subvert the existing concepts of beauty. Once and for all let it be stated that if there is any real choice to be made, we prefer to skyscraper spirituality, the immense lyricism and madness of illogic.

Realism in America has reached its point of saturation. We are no longer interested in the photography of events, in the mere silhouetting of facts, in the presentation of misery, in the anecdotic boredom of verse.

We are not interested in dilettantism as a means of literary expression. We denounce the *farceurs* whose sole claim to contemporary consideration is a facile sense of lilting rhythms. The epigones of Whitman and his followers have become hopelessly entangled in sentimentality, eclecticism, 'delicate perceptions'.

We are not interested in literature that wilfully attempts to be of the age. Unless there be a perception of eternal values, there can be no new magic. The point of departure is unimportant. The poet may use the rhythm of his age, if he be so inclined, and thus tell us, with accelerated intensity, the Arabian Nights' adventures of his brain. But let him not forget that only the dream is essential.

The rushing of new springs can be heard only in silence. To be sure, few of us can have Paul Valéry's ecstatic and fertile silence. That is more of the spirit of poetry than the roar of machines. Out of it may come finally a vertical urge.

We believe that there is no hope for poetry unless there be disintegration first. We need new words, new abstractions, new hieroglyphics, new symbols, new myths. These values to be organically evolved and hostile to a mere metaphorical conception must seek freer association. Thus there may be produced that sublimation of the spirit which grows imminently out of the modern consciousness. By re-establishing the simplicity of the word, we may find again its old magnificence. Gertrude Stein, James Joyce, Hart Crane, Louis Aragon, André Breton, Leon-Paul Fargue, August Stramm and others are showing us the way.

We who live in this chaotic age, are we not aware that living itself is an inferno? And having experienced it, can we not express it by seeking new outlets and new regions of probability? Are not the working of the instincts and the mysteries of the shadows more beautiful than the sterile world of beauty we have known? It is Arthur Rimbaud who captured this idea first. In him broke forth savagely intensified the feeling of the subconscious, pure emergence of the instinct, child-like and brutal.

Perhaps we are seeking God. Perhaps not. It matters little one way or the other. What really matters is that we are on the quest. Piety or savagery have both the same bases. Without unrest we have stagnation and impotence.

The Editors.

PROCLAMATION

Tired of the spectacle of short stories, novels, poems and plays still under the hegemony of the banal word, monotonous syntax, static psychology, descriptive naturalism, and desirous of crystallizing a viewpoint . . .

we hereby declare that:

1. THE REVOLUTION IN THE ENGLISH LANGUAGE IS AN ACCOMPLISHED FACT.
2. THE IMAGINATION IN SEARCH OF A FABULOUS WORLD IS AUTONOMOUS AND UNCONFINED.

    (Prudence is a rich, ugly old maid courted by Incapacity . . . Blake)

3. PURE POETRY IS A LYRICAL ABSOLUTE THAT SEEKS AN A PRIORI REALITY WITHIN OURSELVES ALONE.

    (Bring out number, weight and measure in a year of dearth . . . Blake)

4. NARRATIVE IS NOT MERE ANECDOTE, BUT THE PROJECTION OF A METAMORPHOSIS OF REALITY.

    (Enough! Or Too Much! . . . Blake)

5. THE EXPRESSION OF THESE CONCEPTS CAN BE ACHIEVED ONLY THROUGH THE RHYTHMIC 'HALLUCINATION OF THE WORD'.

    (Rimbaud)

6. THE LITERARY CREATOR HAS THE RIGHT TO DISINTEGRATE THE PRIMAL MATTER OF WORDS IMPOSED ON HIM BY TEXT-BOOKS AND DICTIONARIES.

    (The road of excess leads to the palace of Wisdom . . . Blake)

7. HE HAS THE RIGHT TO USE WORDS OF HIS OWN FASHIONING AND TO DISREGARD EXISTING GRAMMATICAL AND SYNTACTICAL LAWS.

    (The tigers of wrath are wiser than the horses of instruction . . . Blake)

8. THE 'LITANY OF WORDS' IS ADMITTED AS AN INDEPENDENT UNIT.

9. WE ARE NOT CONCERNED WITH THE PROPAGATION OF SOCIOLOGICAL IDEAS, EXCEPT TO EMANCIPATE THE CREATIVE ELEMENTS FROM THE PRESENT LIDEOLOGY.

10. TIME IS A TYRANNY TO BE ABOLISHED.

11. THE WRITER EXPRESSES. HE DOES NOT COMMUNICATE.

12. THE PLAIN READER BE DAMNED.

(Damn braces! Bless relaxes! . . . Blake)

– *Signed*: KAY BOYLE, WHIT BURNETT, HART CRANE, CARESSE CROSBY, HARRY CROSBY, MARIHA FOLFY, STUART GILBERT, A. L. GILLESPIE, LEIGH HOFFMAN, EUGENE JOLAS, ELLIOT PAUL, DOUGLAS RIGBY, THEO RUTRA, ROBERT SAGE, HAROLD J. SALEMSON, LAURENCE VAIL.

15
ANARCHISM

ALEXANDER ('SASHA') BERKMAN (1870–1936)
FROM *THE ABC OF ANARCHISM* 1929

Leading American anarchist, Russian by birth, partner and colleague of Emma Goldman (1869–1940). Berkman and Goldman were deported from the United States for their anti-war activities in the Red Scare of 1919, and after a few disillusioned years in Russia, lived in Europe. Seventeen-year-old Berkman arrived in America in the aftermath of the Haymarket affair (1886–87) and became an anarchist. In 1892 he attempted to assassinate Henry Clay Frick, the bosses' leader in the Homestead, Pennsylvania, steel dispute and for this served fourteen of a twenty-two year sentence. Berkman's Prison Memoirs of an Anarchist *(1912) is considered a classic in prison literature and revolutionary autobiography. After his release in 1906 he helped edit Goldman's radical paper* Mother Earth *(1908–15) and established his own paper* The Blast *(1916–17). In the 1920s and 1930s he lived in poverty, scratching by as a ghost writer and translator. The following extract is from* The ABC of Anarchism *which was first issued in 1929 under the title* What is Communist Anarchism?, *and reissued in 1936 as* Now and After: The ABC of Communism

I want to tell you about Anarchism.

I want to tell you what Anarchism is, because I think it is well you should know it. Also because so little is known about it, and what is known is generally hearsay and mostly false.

I want to tell you about it, because I believe that Anarchism is the finest and biggest thing man has ever thought of; the only thing that can give you liberty and well-being, and bring peace and joy to the world.

I want to tell you about it in such plain and simple language that there will be no misunderstanding it. Big words and high sounding phrases serve only to confuse. Straight thinking means plain speaking.

But before I tell you what Anarchism is, I want to tell you what it *is not*.

That is necessary because so much falsehood has been spread about Anarchism. Even intelligent persons often have entirely wrong notions about it. Some people talk about Anarchism without knowing a thing about it. And some lie about Anarchism, because they don't want *you* to know the truth about it.

Anarchism has many enemies; they won't tell you the truth about it. Why Anarchism has enemies and who they are, you will see later, in the course of this story. Just now I can tell you that neither your political boss nor your employer, neither the capitalist nor the policeman will speak to you honestly about Anarchism. Most of them know nothing about it, and all of them hate it. Their newspapers and publications – the capitalistic press – are also against it.

Even most Socialists and Bolsheviki misrepresent Anarchism. True, the majority of them don't know any better. But those who do know better also often lie about Anarchism and speak of it as 'disorder and chaos.' You can see for yourself how dishonest they are in this: the greatest teachers of Socialism – Karl Marx and Friedrich Engels – had taught that Anarchism would come from Socialism. They said that we must first have Socialism, but that after Socialism there will be Anarchism, and that it would be a freer and more beautiful condition of society to live in than Socialism. Yet the Socialists, who swear by Marx and Engels, insist on calling Anarchism 'chaos and disorder', which shows you how ignorant or dishonest they are.

The Bolsheviki do the same, although their greatest teacher, Lenin, had said that Anarchism would follow Bolshevism, and that then it will be better and freer to live.

Therefore I must tell you, first of all, what Anarchism is *not*.

It is *not* bombs, disorder, or chaos.

It is *not* robbery and murder.

It is *not* a war of each against all.

It is *not* a return to barbarism or to the wild state of man.

Anarchism is the very opposite of all that.

Anarchism means that you should be free; that no one should enslave you, boss you, rob you, or impose upon you.

It means that you should be free to do the things you want to do; and that you should not be compelled to do what you don't want to do.

It means that you should have a chance to choose the kind of a life you want to live, and live it without anybody interfering.

It means that the next fellow should have the same freedom as you, that every one should have the same rights and liberties.

It means that all men are brothers, and that they should live like brothers, in peace and harmony.

That is to say, that there should be no war, no violence used by one set of men against another, no monopoly, and no poverty, no oppression, no taking advantage of your fellow-man.

In short, Anarchism means a condition of society where all men and women are free, and where all enjoy equally the benefits of an ordered and sensible life.

'Can that be?' you ask; 'and how?'

'Not before we all become angels,' your friend remarks.

Well, let us talk it over. Maybe I can show you that we can be decent and live as decent folks even without growing wings.

III

MODERNISTS ON THE MODERN

IIIa

The 1910s and 1920s:
The making of Modernist traditions

1
(Margaret) Storm Jameson (1891–1986)
From 'England's Nest of Singing Birds' 1915

British writer of novels (she published forty-five between 1919 and 1979), poetry, short stories, essays and a two-volume autobiography. Her novels include two trilogies on Yorkshire shipbuilders: The Triumph of Time *(1927–31) and* The Mirror in Darkness *(1934–36). Jameson worked for the American publisher Alfred K. Knopf in the 1920s. An outspoken anti-Nazi, in 1939 she became the first female president of the British section of International* PEN, *and was a champion and helper of many European refugee intellectuals and writers. The following extracts are taken from an early review, published in* The Egoist, *1st November, 1915. [See IIIb 29]*

The dramatists are dead: the poets have gone to the funeral: as for the novelists, it is probable that they are down the area again Bah! they were a sickly tribe.

We have been too careful of life – rather, of mere human lives. We have hedged it round with Poor Laws, with Care Committees, and Commissions on Infant Mortality, and the arts have perished in the atmosphere of fussy benevolence. When men spilt life wantonly to show their love of it, art ran joyously to keep pace with the revellers. The age of the Renaissance in Europe is the wayside instance. There is no Cellini among craftsmen to-day: if there were he would not murder his rivals, beat his mistress, be pardoned by Christ's Vicar – and work for the all-seeing gods. He would fritter away his energy in a tinsel audacity, and work for Messrs. Waring and Gillow.

Not all at once did the world accept – save in word – the Christian belief in the equality of souls. The sixteenth century was still pagan and classical and well aware that souls are no more equal than bodies or estates. Art, which is the supreme aristocracy of the spirit, was still free therefore. Her weakness grew as grew that doctrine of equality, fostered by priests life became so precious that men forgot living or that spending of life, which is art.

The descent is prettily ordered. There is the classic art: an art concerned above all with fitting proportions so that to the story of great deeds, thoughts, feelings, is given a great form – the epic or the tragedy: and to slighter thoughts and feelings, a lesser form – the lyric or the elegiac or the comedy. Hamlet is as classic as the Iliad or the Agamemnon. It is also an art concerned primarily with man, the enemy of nature. As soon as an art betakes itself to filling out a great form with petty or bombastic deeds and emotions, it becomes Romantic Art. Shelley's 'Cenci' is romantic – as are all the pseudo-dramas of Tennyson. Romantic art further tends to give to Nature an utterly disproportionate importance – to the extent of bestowing upon it human attributes.

[. . .]

In the nineteenth century, Tennyson's trained lilies are whispering 'I wait', or 'I come'; and when in the twentieth, Miss Lowell permits the lilies to goggle their tongues at her, she is merely Tennyson turning in his grave.

There are bastards even among the Muses. Of such is that misshapen thing, a latter-day realism. A kitchen art, concerned with the habits and emotions of an onion *quâ* onion. The abdication of art in favour of an entymological collection of small men and emotions as like as fleas and not one half so lively. A perky Nonconformist art, as in the novels of Bennett. A bawdy cheapjack art, as in the best-known versifyings of Masefield.

Art that once was master of life, and then her pandar, and of late her draggled body-servant has not now one single achievement to offset the sudden revival of the spirit of life. Life is spending herself wantonly for life's sake, and art has nothing to give save the sonnets of rhyming haberdashers in the evening newspapers, or the silly war plays of a sillier stage.

During all the dead great year not a single one of England's dramatists has written a play fit for a sergeant of the line to spit upon. There has not been one poem worthy the name from any of England's poetasters of the century. There is already the first trickling of the muddy stream of war novels.

There are also the Imagists: let us praise God a little for them. They sign one manifesto: they should have signed twenty, for whatever common aims they think to have, their ends are as far apart as might have been expected. Mr. Pound translates other men's poems so passing well that it is a pity he does anything else. Mr. Fletcher gyrates with infinite care on the point of a needle. If Mr. Aldington be young, Imagism was not still-born: if he be middle-aged, may Apollo fly away with him: he will be immature at sixty. None but young poets can afford to talk so much as do these Imagists.

Pray regard again the degradation of literature. With the close of the Elizabethan age, poetry and drama came indoors. Throughout the seventeenth century it hung round the Court. In the eighteenth it paced between the coffee house and my lord's study. In the nineteenth it began to haunt free libraries and read Huxley: it entered the drawing-room: it took to itself a macintosh and umbrella and communed discreetly with nature. From languishing with Swinburne in the bedchamber it came to brawling with Masefield in the pot-house, scouring the streets with F. S. Flint. The natural and coincident reaction is to be seen in the prevailing finicky and pernickety state of 'legitimate' poetry and drama. The former is in the hands of a hundred bloodless Tennysons and Shelleys: the latter has fallen among intellectuals and is therefore thrice damned. Critics, moreover, have bred as locusts – verbose aestheticians like Mr. Huntley Carter, and vague twilight spooks of the stage like Mr. Gordon Craig. Every year sees another dull book on Mr. Shaw, whose disciples will not even let him die in peace, but must drag out the corpse to putrify in public.

Such conditions produce naturally groups such as the Imagist, intent on starting again at the beginning, and with all their baggage of manifesto, peacock-screaming and the like.

Brutal methods might arrest where tolerance has but assisted the descent. Let us lament the decay of ridicule. Not even the mild gibes of a Horace prick the thousand and one sweating rhymers, the hundred futile playwrights. Poetry and drama flourished when poets and dramatists were despised as outcasts given to lies and brawling, or distrusted as erratic fools. They were then set apart, divinely conscious of power and the need for justification by works. To-day it is hard to tell a poet from a gentleman. A duchess would not spurn Mr. Pound, not even for his villainous version of *The Seafarer.*

Let us lament further that lack of real hardship that has bred us up this flabby-minded race of writers. So squeamish are they that there is more weeping in Belgravia over one third-rate poet selling matches in the Strand than over a hundred buried miners. Is life harsh because a few fifth-rate poets are half-starved in garrets? Semi-starvation is quite endurable when one is used to it, and something must be paid for the joy of leering at the Muses. A hardier company lived under the fear of Court displeasure or the shadow of an Inquisition. One may wonder what would be the effect on the work of the finest poet among the Imagists if Mr. Aldington were partially flayed. The experiment would require extreme care and a nicety of calculation; it should be proportionately interesting and without doubt valuable.

The state of the drama is on the whole more unhappy than that of any other art save music. The stage exists for the titillation of the suburbs and the paunches of managers. If it were not so, there would be no Craigs among us babbling of the trappings of the hearse. The multitude of the theatres is partly to blame. Destroy me nine out of ten, turn them into homes for insane politicians, or museums for eugenic exhibits, only get rid of them. Pray, gentlemen, stand away: the drama is stifling.

As for the novelists, God help them and us, for they will never recover from the war, nor we from them.

Reasons are the mere chaff of an argument. At the end it seems that there is neither poetry nor drama, because there are neither poets nor dramatists, but only jobbing versemakers and playwrights. A little while ago, and they might have pleaded the degradation of life for their own degradation. But life has gone to laugh at death on the flaming peaks and the arts may even slink down the valleys, tongues wagging and tail between legs.

2
FORD MADOX FORD (1873–1939)
FROM 'ON IMPRESSIONISM' 1914

English novelist, literary critic and journalist. Originally Ford Hermann Hueffer (the son of the music critic of The Times, *Francis Hueffer, and grandson on his mother's side of the painter and associate of William Morris, Ford Madox Brown). Ford was brought up in pre-Raphaelite circles and published his first books (the fairy story* The Brown Owl, *1891, and the novel* The Shifting of the Fire, *1892) before the age of twenty. A dominant figure in the Anglophone Modernist tradition, he collaborated with Joseph Conrad on* The Inheritors *(1901) and* Romance *(1903). As editor of* The English Review *during 1908–10 he sponsored Ezra Pound, D. H. Lawrence and Wyndham Lewis as well as publishing works by established figures. Ford published numerous works before the First World War, including two novels,* A Call *(1910) and* The Good Soldier *(1915). He later moved to France where he published the tetralogy* Parade's End *(1924–28), and founded* The Transatlantic Review *in 1924. The journal featured work by Pound, Joyce, Gertrude Stein, e. e. cummings and Jean Rhys. The Paris years are described in* It was a Nightingale *(1933). During his last years he lived in the south of France with the American Janice Biala, and published* From Minstrels to the Machine *(1938). His last work* The March of Literature *(1939), remains unfinished. The following extracts are from the essay 'On Impressionism', published in* Poetry and Drama, II *(June, December 1914), under the name Ford Madox Hueffer.* [See Ib 15]

[. . .]

I have a certain number of maxims, gained mostly in conversation with Mr. Conrad, which form my working stock-in-trade. I stick to them pretty generally; sometimes I throw them out of the window and just write whatever comes. But the effect is usually pretty much the same. I guess I must be fairly well drilled by this time and function automatically, as the Americans say. The first two of my maxims are these:

Always consider the impressions that you are making upon the mind of the reader, and always consider that the first impression with which you present him will be so strong that it will be all that you can ever do to efface it, to alter it or even quite slightly to modify it. Maupassant's gentleman with red whiskers, who always pushed in front of people when it was a matter of going through a doorway, will remain, for the mind of the reader, that man and no other. The impression is as hard and as definite as a tin-tack.

[. . .]

Maupassant, however, uses physical details more usually as a method of introduction of his characters than I myself do. I am inclined myself, when engaged in the seductive occupation, rather to strike the keynote with a speech than with a description of personality, or even with an action. And, for that purpose, I should set it down, as a rule, that the first speech of a character you are introducing should always be a generalisation – since generalisations are the really strong indications of character. Putting the matter exaggeratedly, you might say that, if a gentleman sitting opposite you in the train remarked to you: 'I see the Tories have won Leith Boroughs', you would have practically no guide to that gentleman's character. But, if he said: 'Them bloody Unionists have crept into Leith because the Labourites, damn them, have taken away 1,100 votes from us', you would know that the gentleman belonged to a certain political party, had a certain social status, a certain degree of education and a certain amount of impatience.

It is possible that such disquisitions on Impressionism in prose fiction may seem out of place in a journal styled *Poetry and Drama*. But I do not think they are. For Impressionism, differing from other schools of art, is founded so entirely on observation of the psychology of the patron – and the psychology of the patron remains constant.

[. . .]

It is, however, perfectly possible that a piece of Impressionism should give a sense of two, of three, of as many as you will, places, persons, emotions, all going on simultaneously in the emotions of the writer. It is, I mean, perfectly possible for a sensitised person, be he poet or prose writer, to have the sense, when he is in one room, that he is in another, or when he is speaking to one person he may be so intensely haunted by the memory or desire for another person that he may be absent-minded or distraught. And there is nothing in the canons of Impressionism, as I know it, to stop the attempt to render those superimposed emotions. Indeed, I suppose that Impressionism exists to render those queer effects of real life that are like so many views seen through bright glass – through glass so bright that whilst you perceive through it a landscape or a backyard, you are aware that, on its surface, it reflects a face of a person behind you. For the whole of life is really like that; we are almost always in one place with our minds somewhere quite other.

And it is, I think, only Impressionism that can render that peculiar effect; I know, at any rate, of no other method. It has, this school, in consequence, certain quite strong canons, certain quite rigid unities that must be observed. The point is that any piece of Impressionism, whether it be prose, or verse, or painting, or sculpture, is the record of the impression of a moment; it is not a sort of rounded, annotated record of a set of circumstances – it is the record of the recollection in your mind of a set of circumstances that happened ten years ago – or ten minutes. It might even be the impression of the moment – but it is the impression, not the corrected chronicle.

[. . .]

In that way you would attain to the sort of odd vibration that scenes in real life really have; you would give your reader the impression that he was witnessing something real, that he was passing through an experience. . . . You will observe also that you will have produced something that is very like a Futurist picture – not a Cubist picture, but one of those canvases that show you in one corner a pair of stays, in another a bit of the foyer of a music hall, in another a fragment of early morning landscape, and in the middle a pair of eyes, the whole bearing the title of 'A Night Out'. And, indeed, those Futurists are only trying to render on canvas what Impressionists *tel que moi* have been trying to render for many years. (You may remember Emma's love scene at the cattle show in *Madame Bovary*.)

Do not, I beg you, be led away by the English reviewer's cant phrase to the effect that the Futurists are trying to be literary and the plastic arts can never be literary. Les Jeunes of to-day are trying all sorts of experiments, in all sorts of media. And they are perfectly right to be trying them.

IV.

I have been trying to think what are the objections to Impressionism as I understand it – or rather what alternative method could be found. It seems to me that one is an Impressionist because one tries to produce an illusion of reality – or rather the business of Impressionism is to produce that illusion. The subject is one enormously complicated and is full of negatives. Thus the Impressionist author is sedulous to avoid letting his personality appear in the course of his book. On the other hand, his whole book, his whole poem is merely an expression of his personality.

[. . .]

The other day I was discussing these matters with a young man whose avowed intention is to sweep away Impressionism. And, after I had energetically put before him the views that I have here expressed, he simply remarked: 'Why try to produce an illusion?' To which I could only reply: 'Why then write?'

I have asked myself frequently since then why one should try to produce an illusion of reality in the mind of one's reader. Is it just an occupation like any other – like postage-stamp collecting, let us say – or is it the sole end and aim of art? I have spent the greater portion of my working life in preaching that particular doctrine: is it possible, then, that I have been entirely wrong?

Of course it is possible for any man to be entirely wrong; but I confess myself to being as yet unconverted. The chief argument of my futurist friend was that producing an illusion causes the writer so much trouble as not to be worth while. That does not seem to me to be an argument worth very much because – and again I must say it seems to me – the business of an artist is surely to take trouble, but this is probably doing my friend's position, if not his actual argument, an injustice. I am aware that there are quite definite æsthetic objections to the business of producing an illusion. In order to produce an illusion you must justify; in order to justify you must introduce a certain amount of matter that may not appear germane to your story or to your poem.

[. . .]

But again, if the final province of art is to convince, its first province is to interest. So that, to the extent that your justification is uninteresting, it is an artistic defect. It may sound paradoxical, but the truth is that your Impressionist can only get his strongest effects by using beforehand a great deal of what one may call non-Impressionism. He will make, that is to say, an enormous impression on his reader's mind by the use of three words. But very likely each one of those three words will be prepared for by ten thousand other words. Now are we to regard those other words as being entirely unnecessary, as being, that is to say, so many artistic defects? That I take to be my futurist friend's ultimate assertion.

Says he: 'All these elaborate conventions of Conrad or of Maupassant give the reader the impression that a story is being told – all these meetings of bankers and master-mariners in places like the Ship Inn at Greenwich, and all Maupassant's dinner-parties, always in the politest circles, where a countess or a fashionable doctor or someone relates a passionate or a pathetic or a tragic or a merely grotesque incident – as you have it, for instance, in the "Contes de la Bécasse" – all this machinery for getting a story told is so much waste of time. A story is a story; why not just tell it anyhow? You can never tell what sort of an impression you will produce upon a reader. Then why bother about Impressionism? Why not just chance your luck?'

There is a good deal to be said for this point of view. Writing up to my own standards is such an intolerable labour and such a thankless job, since it can't give me the one thing in the world that I desire – that for my part I am determined to drop creative writing for good and all. But I, like all writers of my generation, have been so handicapped that there is small wonder that one should be tired out. On the one hand the difficulty of getting hold of any critical guidance was, when I was a boy, insuperable. There was nothing. Criticism was non-existent; self-conscious art was decried; you were supposed to write by inspiration; you were the young generation with the vine-leaves in your hair, knocking furiously at the door. On the other hand, one writes for money, for fame, to excite the passion of love, to make an impression upon one's time. Well, God knows what one writes for. But it is certain that one gains neither fame nor money; certainly one does not excite the passion of love, and one's time continues to be singularly unimpressed.

But young writers to-day have a much better chance, on the æsthetic side at least. Here and there, in nooks and corners, they can find someone to discuss their work, not from the point of view of goodness or badness or of niceness or of nastiness, but from the simple point of view of expediency. The moment you can say: 'Is it expedient to print *vers libre* in long or short lines, or in the form of prose, or not to print it at all, but to recite it?' – the moment you can find someone to discuss these expediences calmly, or the moment that you can find someone with whom to discuss the relative values of justifying your character or of abandoning the attempt to produce an illusion of reality – at that moment you are very considerably helped; whereas an admirer of your work might fall down and kiss your feet and it would not be of the very least use to you.

V.

This adieu, like Herrick's, to poesy, may seem to be a digression. Indeed it is; and indeed it isn't. It is, that is to say, a digression in the sense that it is a statement not immediately germane to the argument that I am carrying on. But it is none the less an insertion fully in accord with the canons of Impressionism as I understand it. For the first business of Impressionism is to produce an impression, and the only way in literature to produce an impression is to awaken interest. And, in a sustained argument, you can only keep interest awakened by keeping alive, by whatever means you may have at your disposal, the surprise of your reader. You must state your argument; you must illustrate it, and then you must stick in something that appears to have nothing whatever to do with either subject or illustration, so that the reader will exclaim: 'What the devil is the fellow driving at?' And then you must go on in the same way – arguing, illustrating and startling and arguing, startling and illustrating – until at the very end your contentions will appear like a ravelled skein. And then, in the last few lines, you will draw towards you the masterstring of that seeming confusion, and the whole pattern of the carpet, the whole design of the net-work will be apparent.

This method, you will observe, founds itself upon analysis of the human mind. For no human being likes listening to long and sustained arguments. Such listening is an effort, and no artist has the right to call for any effort from his audience. A picture should come out of its frame and seize the spectator.

Let us now consider the audience to which the artist should address himself. Theoretically a writer should be like the Protestant angel, a messenger of peace and goodwill towards all men. But, inasmuch as the Wingless Victory appears monstrously hideous to a Hottentot, and a beauty of Tunis detestable to the inhabitants of these fortunate islands, it is obvious that each artist must adopt a frame of mind, less Catholic possibly, but certainly more Papist, and address himself, like the angel of the Vulgate, only *hominibus bon voluntatis*. He must address himself to such men as be of goodwill; that is to say, he must typify for himself a human soul in sympathy with his own; a silent listener who will be attentive to him, and whose mind acts very much as his acts. According to the measure of this artist's identity with his species, so will be the measure of his temporal greatness. That is why a book, to be really popular, must be either extremely good or extremely bad. For Mr. Hall Caine has millions of readers; but then Guy de Maupassant and Flaubert have tens of millions.

I suppose the proposition might be put in another way. Since the great majority of mankind are, on the surface, vulgar and trivial – the stuff to fill graveyards – the great majority of mankind will be easily and quickly affected by art which is vulgar and trivial. But, inasmuch as this world is a very miserable purgatory for most of us sons of men – who remain stuff with which graveyards are filled – inasmuch as horror, despair and incessant strivings are the lot of the most trivial of humanity, who endure them as a rule with commonsense and cheerfulness – so, if a really great master strike the note of horror, of despair, of striving, and so on, he will stir chords in the hearts of a larger number of people than those who are moved by the merely vulgar and the merely trivial. This is probably why *Madame Bovary* has sold more copies than any book ever published, except, of course, books purely religious. But the appeal of religious books is exactly similar.

It may be said that the appeal of *Madame Bovary* is largely sexual. So it is, but it is only in countries like England and the United States that the abominable tortures of sex – or, if you will, the abominable interests of sex – are not supposed to take rank alongside of the horrors of lost honour, commercial ruin, or death itself. For all these things are the components of life, and each is of equal importance.

So, since Flaubert is read in Russia, in Germany, in France, in the United States, amongst the non-Anglo-Saxon population, and by the immense populations of South America, he may be said to have taken for his audience the whole of the world that could possibly be expected to listen to a man of his race. (I except, of course, the Anglo-Saxons who cannot be confidently expected to listen to anything other than the words produced by Mr. George Edwardes, and musical comedy in general.)

My futurist friend again visited me yesterday, and we discussed this very question of audiences. Here again he said that I was entirely wrong. He said that an artist should not address himself to *l'homme moyen sensuel*, but to intellectuals, to people who live at Hampstead and wear no hats. (He withdrew his contention later.)

I maintain on my own side that one should address oneself to the cabmen round the corner, but this also is perhaps an exaggeration. My friend's contention on behalf of the intellectuals was not so much due to his respect for their intellects. He said that they knew the ABC of an art, and that it is better to address yourself to an audience that knows the ABC of an art than to an audience entirely untrammelled by such knowledge. In this I think he was wrong, for the intellectuals are persons of very conventional mind, and they acquire as a rule simultaneously with the ABC of any art the knowledge of so many conventions that it is almost impossible to make any impression upon their minds. Hampstead and the hatless generally offer an impervious front to futurisms, simply because they have imbibed from Whistler and the Impressionists the convention that painting should not be literary. Now every futurist picture tells a story; so that rules out futurism. Similarly with the cubists. Hampstead has imbibed, from God knows where, the dogma that all art should be based on life, or should at least draw its inspiration and its strength from the representation of nature. So there goes cubism, since cubism is non-representational, has nothing to do with life, and has a quite proper contempt of nature.

When I produced my argument that one should address oneself to the cabmen at the corner, my futurist friend at once flung to me the jeer about Tolstoi and the peasant. Now the one sensible thing in the long drivel of nonsense with which Tolstoi misled this dull world was the remark that art should be addressed to the peasant. My futurist friend said that that was sensible for an artist living in Russia or Roumania, but it was an absurd remark to be let fall by a critic living on Campden Hill. His view was that you cannot address yourself to the peasant unless that peasant have evoked folk-song or folk-lores. I don't know why that was his view, but that was his view.

It seems to me to be nonsensical, even if the inner meaning of his dictum was that art should be addressed to a community of practising artists. Art, in fact, should be addressed to those who are not preoccupied.

[. . .]

The really impassible mind is not the mind quickened by passion, but the mind rendered slothful by preoccupation purely trivial. The 'English gentleman' is, for instance, an absolutely hopeless being from this point of view. His mind is so taken up by considerations of what is good form, of what is good feeling, of what is even good fellowship; he is so concerned to pass unnoticed in the crowd; he is so set upon having his room like everyone else's room, that he will find it impossible to listen to any plea for art which is exceptional, vivid, or startling. The cabman, on the other hand, does not mind being thought a vulgar sort of bloke; in consequence he will form a more possible sort of audience. On the other hand, amongst the purely idler classes it is perfectly possible to find individuals who are so firmly and titularly gentle folk that they don't have to care a damn what they do. These again are possible audiences for the artist. The point is really, I take it, that the preoccupation that is fatal to art is the moral or the social preoccupation. Actual preoccupations matter very little. Your cabman may drive his taxi through exceedingly difficult streets; he may have half-a-dozen close shaves in a quarter of an hour. But when those things are over they are over, and he has not the necessity of a cabman. His point of view as to what is art, good form, or, let us say, the proper relation of the sexes, is unaffected. He may be a hungry man, a thirsty man, or even a tired man, but he will not necessarily have his finger upon his moral pulse, and he will not hold as æsthetic dogma the idea that no painting must tell a story, or the moral dogma that passion only becomes respectable when you have killed it.

It is these accursed dicta that render an audience hopeless to the artist, that render art a useless pursuit and the artist himself a despised individual.

So that those are the best individuals for an artist's audience who have least listened to accepted ideas – who are acquainted with deaths at street corners, with the marital infidelities of crowded courts, with the goodness of heart of the criminal, with the meanness of the undetected or the sinless, who know the queer odd jumble of negatives that forms our miserable and hopeless life. If I had to choose a reader I would rather have one who had never read anything before but the Newgate Calendar, or the records of crime, starvation and divorce in the Sunday paper – I would rather have him for a reader than a man who had discovered the song that the sirens sang, or had by heart the whole of the *Times Literary Supplement*, from its inception to the present day. Such a peasant intelligence will know that this is such a queer world that anything may be possible. And that is the type of intelligence that we need.

[. . .]

And the whole of Impressionism comes to this: having realized that the audience to which you will address yourself must have this particular peasant intelligence, or, if you prefer it, this particular and virgin openness of mind, you will then figure to yourself an individual, a silent listener, who shall be to yourself the *homo bon voluntatis* – man of goodwill. To him, then, you will address your picture, your poem, your prose story, or your argument. You will seek to capture his interest; you will seek to hold his interest. You will do this by methods of *surprise*, of *fatigue*, by passages of *sweetness* in your language, by passages suggesting the sudden and brutal shock of suicide. You will give him passages of dullness, so that your bright effects may seem more bright; you will *alternate*, you will *dwell* for a long time upon an intimate point; you will seek to *exasperate* so that you may the better enchant. You will, in short, employ all the devices of the prostitute. If you are too proud for this you may be the better gentleman or the better lady, but you will be the worse artist. For the artist must always be humble and humble and again humble, since before the greatness of his task he himself is nothing. He must again be outrageous, since the greatness of his task calls for enormous excesses by means of which he may recoup his energies. That is why the artist is, quite rightly, regarded with suspicion by people who desire to live in tranquil and ordered society.

But one point is very important. The artist can never write to satisfy himself – to get, as the saying is, something off the chest. He must not write propaganda which it is his desire to write; he must not write rolling periods, the production of which gives him a soothing feeling in his digestive organs or wherever it is. He must write always so as to satisfy that other fellow – that other fellow who has too clear an intelligence to let his attention be captured or his mind deceived by special pleadings in favour of any given dogma. You must not write so as to improve him, since he is a much better fellow than yourself, and you must not write so as to influence him, since he is a granite rock, a peasant intelligence, the gnarled bole of a sempiternal oak, against which you will dash yourself in vain. It is in short no pleasant kind of job to be a conscious artist. You won't have any vine leaves in your poor old hair; you won't just dash your quill into an inexhaustible ink-well and pour out fine frenzies. No, you will be just the skilled workman doing his job with drill or chisel or mallet. And you will get precious little out of it. Only, just at times, when you come to look again at some work of yours that you have quite forgotten, you will say, 'Why, that is rather well done.' That is all.

3
DORA MARSDEN (1882–1960)
FROM 'I AM.' 1915

English editor, writer and feminist. Marsden studied philosophy at Manchester University and in 1908 joined the suffragette Women's Social and Political Union. Her activism landed her a six-month jail sentence in 1909. The following year she left the WSPU and established the journal The Freewoman *which was highly critical of the Pankhurst leadership. Marsden rejected the suffragette insistence on 'the vote', advocating instead a broader feminism of which political reform was only part. In the next reincarnation of her journal,* The New Freewoman *(1913), her interest shifted further towards the 'philosophic individualism' which she saw as underlying all modern movements, including feminism. At the prompting of Ezra Pound and Richard Aldington the journal changed name again, this time to* The Egoist, *in 1914. Marsden contributed more than five hundred articles to the review before its closure in 1919. Reproduced here is an extract from Marsden's editorial for* The Egoist, *No. 1, Vol. II, January 1st, 1915, in its original front page format.*

Published on the 1st of each month.

THE EGOIST
AN INDIVIDUALIST REVIEW.
Formerly, the NEW FREEWOMAN.

No. 1.—Vol II.   FRIDAY, JANUARY 1st, 1915.   SIXPENCE

Editor: **HARRIET SHAW WEAVER.**   *Contributing Editor:*
Assistant Editor: **RICHARD ALDINGTON.**   **DORA MARSDEN, B.A.**

CONTENTS.

"I AM."
By DORA MARSDEN.

THE beginning of the New Year will serve as a sufficient apology for stating afresh the ambitions of this journal and detailing what one considers to be its unique and supremely important task: one for the execution of which we can see no evidence of minds other than our own being forthcoming. There are, we very willingly admit, men of almost infinitely greater attainments in "scholarship," and for such a task as ours "scholars" must of necessity be the untiring hodmen: the willing and directed servants. But of minds possessing the cold courage which can go forward and advance up to and through those mirages of flame and rage as they appear on the hither side: but which prove but echoes of a weak thin sound when they are traversed: of such minds the appearance is rare. When they do appear they find their own work, and that work accomplished establishes a new era. After they are gene—these directing minds—minds of a different order—stuffed minds, scholarly minds, begin to disburse their heavy stores upon the lines they have laid down. The stored rubbish then becomes invaluably useful treasure: what was purposeless will become vibrant with purpose. So it will be, long after "The Egoist" has become a thing of the past. Meanwhile it has its unique work to do, ill-equipped in all accessories as it is, and armed only with the one thing essential. Let this, then, be the answer to those friends who have been good enough to say that "The Egoists's" activities are all derailed and are willing to pray that the journal might die, if by dying the "remarkable abilities" of the writer might have a chance of "coming into their own." "Their own": the only task which matches their powers in a Verbal Age like this is—to break the hypnotic spell, to blast the stupefactions of—The Word.

*   *   *   *

Our war is with words and in their every aspect: grammar, accidence, syntax: body, blood, and bone. Let none make a mistake: not because men use words to deceive; not even because words incline by capacity to deception and are the natural basis of Civilisation: the inoculators of men's powers with the debilitating serum of "Culture"; not because they can be used, and are used, as readily for ends of diplomacy as of frankness; for hiding motives as much as for revealing them, for alluring and deceiving as much as for guiding and illuminating. One could not reasonably object to the surface-deceits of words which make possible those ends of deception rulers and masters require in their difficult task of governing a wayward animal. Words are good for those who use them when they subserve according to design: If the design is to deceive well and good: a good instrument is one which performs the operation—whatever it may be—to which it is set. And those who will the end will also the means: those who extol Civilisation and Culture may not decry in words their powers of deception. Nor will those who care nothing for either civilisation or culture. Since deception is the human way of the strong with the weak, the ways of culture and civilisation are the natural human way of the strong with the weak. And long it will continue to be. As long as there is interplay of intelligences of unequal degrees of power, the verbal deception, which in the bulk constitutes civilisation and culture, will continue. Only a dreamer: a dunce: could seriously expect it to be otherwise. To civilise, to break in a recalcitrant animal by words is an exceedingly clever ruse, the way of men having once been intelligent enough to master they will never lightly forego. The deceptive element in sound, which is the basis of civilisation and culture, was "there in the beginning": before the element of truth, in fact. The alluring and deceptive function of living sounds are more fundamental than their expository. Song is older than speech: cant is more venerable than truth, and only a dunce will expect the former to be abandoned because the latter has arrived. [. . .]

4
FERNANDO PESSOA (1888–1935)
FROM 'NOTES ON SENSATIONISM' 1916

Portuguese-born poet and essayist. Pessoa was brought up in South Africa where he became fluent in English. Returning to Lisbon in 1905 he worked as a translator and contributed to the Modernist aesthetic debate in avant-garde journals such as Orpheu. *His early volumes of poetry were written in English; it was not until 1934 that his first book in Portuguese,* Mensagem (Message) *was published. Prose and poetry from the 1910–20 decade, his most productive period, was published and promoted by the Lisbon literati in the 1920s, but it was not until 1982 that a major collection of his writings appeared as a two-volume edition under the title* Livro de Desassosego (Book of Disquietude). *Pessoa wrote under a variety of alter egos or 'heteronyms' to which invented personalities were attached. He considered these to exist within himself – as one heteronym, Bernardo Soares, puts it, 'In each of us there is a differingness and a profusion of ourselves'. The following extract from 1916 is taken from the 1988 selection from Pessoa's prose* (Always Astonished), *edited and translated by Edwin Honig.*

There is nothing, no reality, but sensation. Ideas are sensations, but of things not placed in space and sometimes not even in time.

Logic, the place of ideas, is another kind of space.

Dreams are sensations with only two dimensions. Ideas are sensations with only one dimension. A line is an idea.

Every sensation (of a solid thing) is a solid body bounded by planes, which are *inner images* (of the nature of dreams – two-dimensioned), bounded themselves by lines (which are *ideas*, of one dimension only). *Sensationism pretends, taking stock of this real reality, to realize in art a decomposition of reality into its psychic geometrical elements.*

The end of art is simply to increase human self-consciousness. Its criterion is general (or semigeneral) acceptance, sooner or later, for that is the proof that it does tend to increase self-consciousness in men.

The more we decompose and analyze into their psychic elements our sensations, the more we increase our self-consciousness. Art has, then, the duty of becoming increasingly conscious. In the classic age, art developed consciousness on the level of the three-dimensional sensation, that is, art applied itself to a perfect and clear visioning of reality [taken to be] solid. Hence the Greek mental attitude, which seems so strange to us, of introducing concepts such as that of the sphere into the most abstract abstractions, as in the case of Parmenides, whose idealistic conception of a highly abstract universe yet admits of a description of it as spherical.

Post-Christian art has worked constantly toward the creating of a two-dimensional art.

We must create a one-dimensional art.

This seems a narrowing of art, and to a certain extent it is.

Cubism, futurism, and kindred schools are wrong applications of intuitions that are fundamentally right. The wrong lies in the fact that they attempt to solve the problem they suspect on the lines of three-dimensional art; their fundamental error lies in that they attribute to sensations an exterior reality, which indeed they have, but not in the sense the futurists and others believe. The futurists are something absurd, like Greeks trying to be modern and analytic.

5
JOHN DOS PASSOS (1896–1970)
'AGAINST AMERICAN LITERATURE' 1916

American writer, born in Chicago and educated at Harvard, Dos Passos was a Marxist until the Second World War. In 1916 he went to Spain to study architecture and ended up serving with a French ambulance unit in the First World War, then with the Red Cross in Italy, and then as a private in the medical corps of the US Army. He became a journalist and foreign correspondent. His first important novel was Manhattan Transfer *(1925) which was followed by his masterpiece of montage, the trilogy* U.S.A. *(1930–36). His later collection of critical essays,* The Ground We Stand On *(1941), reflects his sharp move towards the political right and the rejection of his earlier Marxist position. 'Against American Literature' was first published in* New Republic, 8, 14th October, 1916. [See IIIb 26]*

If any mood predominates in American writing it is that of gentle satire. This tendency to satire, usually vague and kindly, sometimes bitter with the unconvinced bitterness of a middle-aged lady who thinks herself worldly wise, is the one feature pervading all that can be called American among the mass of foreign-inspired writing in this country. Washington Irving is typical of its least significant manifestation; Edgar Lee Masters, Edith Wharton and Katherine Fullerton Gerould of its modern – and bitter – form. Search as you may, you will find little not permeated by this tone, which, chameleon-like, changes with the variations of European thought, but remains in its fundamentals always the same. And there is no doubt that up to now it has well approximated the temper of the nation, has pretty faithfully represented that genial, ineffectual, blindly energetic affair, the American soul. Strange combination of words; for until recently we have troubled very little about our *âme nationale*, leaving that sort of thing to introspective and decadent nations overseas. But even if we are unconscious of it, we have a national soul, and it is this, or at least the external of it, which is so aptly reflected by the pervading tone of our literature.

This wholesome rice-pudding fare is, unfortunately, a strangely unstimulating diet; so we are forced to give it body – like apple jack – by a stiff infusion of a stronger product. As a result of this constant need to draw on foreign sources our literature has become a hybrid which, like the mule, is barren and must be produced afresh each time by the crossing of other strains. What is the reason for this state of affairs? Much of our writing, particularly in the upper realm of the novel, the region of Edith Wharton and Robert Herrick, is sincere, careful, and full of shrewd observation of contemporary life; yet I defy anyone to confine himself for long to purely American books without feeling starved, without pining for the color and passion and profound thought of other literatures. Our books are like our cities; they are all the same. Any other nation's literature would take a lifetime to exhaust. What then is lacking in ours?

For one thing American literature is a rootless product, a cutting from England's sturdy well branched oak tree, nurtured in the arid soil of the New England colonies, and recently transplanted to the broad lands of the Middle West. In other countries literature is the result of long evolution, based on primitive folklore, on the first joy and terror of man in the presence of the trees and scented meadowlands and dimpled whirling rivers, interwoven with the moulding fabric of old dead civilizations, and with threads of fiery new gold from incoming races. The result is glamour, depth, real pertinence to the highest and lowest in man. It is to be found, in one form or another, beneath the temporary scum of every established literature. This artistic stimulus, fervid with primitive savageries, redolent with old cults of earth and harvest, smoked and mellowed by time, is the main inheritance of the civilizations, the woof upon which individual artists may work the warp of their own thoughts.

America lacks it almost completely. The earth-feeling, the jewelled accretions of the imagination of succeeding ages, so rich in old English writing, seem to have lost their validity in the transplanting. The undercurrent, rooted in the people, often voiceless for whole epochs, which springs from the chants of Druids, from fairy-tales and terror-tales recited in wattled huts about the smoky fires of the woad-daubed Britons, and which has time and again revivified the literature of England, saved it from artificiality and courtiership, has been cut off from us. We find ourselves floundering without rudder or compass, in the sea of modern life, vaguely lit by the phosphorescent gleam of our traditional optimism. A sense of landscape, or else an imported, flushed, *erdgeist* feeling, has taken the place of the unconscious intimacy with nature – the deeper the less reflective it is – which has always lain at the soul of great writings. No ghosts hover about our fields; there are no nymphs in our fountains; there is no tradition of countless generations tilling and tending to give us reverence for those rocks and rills and templed hills so glibly mentioned in the national anthem.

Faulkner

The only substitute for dependence on the past is dependence on the future. Here our only poet found his true greatness. Walt Whitman abandoned the vague genteelness that had characterized American writing, the stiff product of the leisure hours of a *petite noblesse de province*, and, founding his faith on himself, on the glowing life within him, shouted genially, fervidly his challenge to the future. But, although sensibly unconventional in manners and customs, the American public desires its ideas well disciplined according to the conventions of ten years back; Walt Whitman failed to reach the people he intended to, and aroused only a confused perturbation and the sort of moral flutter experienced by a primly dressed old bachelor when a ruddy smiling Italian, smelling of garlic and sweat, plumps down beside him in the street car. Still, the day of Whitman's power may be in a rosy future, when Americans, instead of smiling with closed eyes, will look keenly before them.

Then there is the cult of the abstract. Perhaps it too grows out of our lack of root, out of our lack of spiritual kinship to the corn and wheat our fields grow, out of our inane matter-of-factness. American life, as much as an unsuccessful inventor,

contact zones

is occupied with smiling abstractions. This is particularly true of our religion, which under multifarious forms of Protestant Christianity is actually a muddled abstract theism. We have none of those local saints – tamed pagan gods, most of them – that have tied the Church in Europe so tightly to the people, to the soil, to the eternal powers of corn and wine and resurgent earth. One by one we have pulled from our god the garments of concreteness, the human qualities. Even the abolition of hell and the devil may have done much to tear religion from people's souls, and to place it in the chilly soil of convention where it at present languishes. There was something tangible and human about hell-fire which cannot be found in the vague notion of future harp-twanging for all 'nice' people, that symbolizes most current religious faiths.

What is true of religion is true of art and literature. Worse than its lack of depth and texture is its abstractness, its lack, on the whole, of dramatic actuality. Compare say 'The House of Mirth', a fairly typical American novel, with Turgenev's 'Spring Freshets'. The Russian stirs eyes and ears and nose and sense of touch, portrays his story with vivid tangibility; the American leaves an abstract impression of intellectual bitterness. It is not so much a question of technique as of feeling. In the same way match the dramatic power of Couperus's 'Small Souls' with Mary S. Watts's 'The Legacy', a novel dealing with the corresponding class of people in this country. Why should not our writers be as vivid as the Russian, express their life as dramatically as the Dutchman?

It is significant that, quite unconsciously, I chose the works of two women to typify American novels. The tone of the higher sort of writing in this country is undoubtedly that of a well brought up and intelligent woman, tolerant, versed in the things of this world, quietly humorous, but bound tightly in the fetters of 'niceness', of the middle-class outlook. And when the shackles are thrown off the result is vulgarity, and, what is worse, affectation.

In all this may lie the explanation of the sudden vogue of Russian literature in this country. It has so much that our own lacks. There is the primitive savagery, the color, the romance of an age of faith suddenly burst in upon by European science, the freshness, rank and lush as the vegetation of early May. No wonder it is a relief to us Americans to turn from our prim colonial living room of thought, where the shades are drawn for fear the sun will fade the carpet Puritan ancestors laid there, to the bizarre pains and passions, to the hot moist steppe-savour of a Russian novel.

And it becomes harder every day for any race to gain the lesson of the soil. An all-enveloping industrialism, a new mode of life preparing, has broken down the old bridges leading to the past, has cut off the possibility of retreat. Our only course is to press on. Shall we pick up the glove Walt Whitman threw at the feet of posterity? Or shall we stagnate forever, the Sicily of the modern world, rich in this world's goods, absorbing the thought, patronizing the art of other peoples, but producing nothing from amid our jumble of races but steel and oil and grain?

'Well, isn't that enough?' I hear someone say.

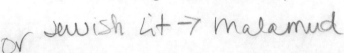

6
W. B. (WILLIAM BUTLER) YEATS (1865–1939)
FROM 'ANIMA HOMINIS' 1917

The following is an extract from a 1917 essay (published in the collection Per Amica Silentia Lunae) *in which Yeats explores esoteric thoughts and experiences. [See Ib 17, IIIb 14]*

[. . .]

II.

When I consider the minds of my friends, among artists and emotional writers, I discover a like contrast. I have sometimes told one close friend that her only fault is a habit of harsh judgment with those who have not her sympathy, and she has written comedies where the wickedest people seem but bold children. She does not know why she has created that world where no one is ever judged, a high celebration of indulgence, but to me it seems that her ideal of beauty is the compensating dream of a nature wearied out by over-much judgment. I know a famous actress who, in private life, is like the captain of some buccaneer ship holding his crew to good behaviour at the mouth of a blunderbuss, and upon the stage she excels in the representation of women who stir to pity and to desire because they need our protection, and is most adorable as one of those young queens imagined by Maeterlinck who have so little will, so little self, that they are like shadows sighing at the edge of the world. When I last saw her in her own house she lived in a torrent of words and movements, she could not listen, and all about her upon the walls were women drawn by Burne-Jones in his latest period. She had invited me in the hope that I would defend those women, who were always listening, and are as necessary to her as a contemplative Buddha to a Japanese Samurai, against a French critic who would persuade her to take into her heart in their stead a Post-Impressionist picture of a fat, flushed woman lying naked upon a Turkey carpet.

There are indeed certain men whose art is less an opposing virtue than a compensation for some accident of health or circumstance. During the riots over the first production of *The Playboy of the Western World*, Synge was confused, without clear thought, and was soon ill – indeed the strain of that week may perhaps have hastened his death – and he was, as is usual with gentle and silent men, scrupulously accurate in all his statements. In his art he made, to delight his ear and his mind's eye, voluble daredevils who 'go romancing through a romping lifetime . . . to the dawning of the Judgment Day.' At other moments this man, condemned to the life of a monk by bad health, takes an amused pleasure in 'great queens . . . making themselves matches from the start to the end.' Indeed, in all his imagination he delights in fine physical life, in life when the moon pulls up the tide. The last act of *Deirdre of the Sorrows*, where his art is at its noblest, was written upon his death-bed. He was not sure of any world to come, he was leaving his betrothed and his unwritten play – 'O, what a waste of time,' he said to me; he hated to die, and in the last speeches of Deirdre and in the middle act he accepted death and dismissed life with a gracious gesture. He gave to

Deirdre the emotion that seemed to him most desirable, most difficult, most fitting, and maybe saw in those delighted seven years, now dwindling from her, the fulfilment of his own life.

III.

When I think of any great poetical writer of the past (a realist is a historian and obscures the cleavage by the record of his eyes), I comprehend, if I know the lineaments of his life, that the work is the man's flight from his entire horoscope, his blind struggle in the network of the stars. William Morris, a happy, busy, most irascible man, described dim colour and pensive emotion, following, beyond any man of his time, an indolent Muse; while Savage Landor topped us all in calm nobility when the pen was in his hand, as in the daily violence of his passion when he had laid it down. He had in his *Imaginary Conversations* reminded us, as it were, that the Venus de Milo is a stone, and yet he wrote when the copies did not come from the printer as soon as he expected: 'I have . . . had the resolution to tear in pieces all my sketches and projects and to forswear all future undertakings. I have tried to sleep away my time and pass two-thirds of the twenty-four hours in bed. I may speak of myself as a dead man.' I imagine Keats to have been born with that thirst for luxury common to many at the outsetting of the Romantic Movement, and not able, like wealthy Beckford, to slake it with beautiful and strange objects. It drove him to imaginary delights; ignorant, poor, and in poor health, and not perfectly well-bred, he knew himself driven from tangible luxury; meeting Shelley, he was resentful and suspicious because he, as Leigh Hunt recalls, 'being a little too sensitive on the score of his origin, felt inclined to see in every man of birth his natural enemy.'

[. . .]

V.

We make out of the quarrel with others, rhetoric, but of the quarrel with ourselves, poetry. Unlike the rhetoricians, who get a confident voice from remembering the crowd they have won or may win, we sing amid our uncertainty; and, smitten even in the presence of the most high beauty by the knowledge of our solitude, our rhythm shudders. I think, too, that no fine poet, no matter how disordered his life, has ever, even in his mere life, had pleasure for his end. Johnson and Dowson, friends of my youth, were dissipated men, the one a drunkard, the other a drunkard and mad about women, and yet they had the gravity of men who had found life out and were awakening from the dream; and both, one in life and art and one in art and less in life, had a continual preoccupation with religion. Nor has any poet I have read of or heard of or met with been a sentimentalist. The other self, the anti-self or the antithetical self, as one may choose to name it, comes but to those who are no longer deceived, whose passion is reality. The sentimentalists are practical men who believe in money, in position, in a marriage bell, and whose understanding of happiness is to be so busy whether at work or at play that all is forgotten but the momentary aim. They find their pleasure in a cup that is filled from Lethe's wharf, and for the awakening, for the vision, for the revelation of reality, tradition offers us a different word – ecstasy. An old artist wrote to me of his wanderings by the quays of New York, and how he found there a woman nursing a sick child, and drew her story from her. She spoke, too, of other children who had died: a long tragic story. 'I wanted to paint her,' he wrote; 'if I denied myself any of the pain I could not believe in my own ecstasy.' We must not make a false faith by hiding from our thoughts the causes of doubt, for faith is the highest achievement of the human intellect, the only gift man can make to God, and therefore it must be offered in sincerity. Neither must we create, by hiding ugliness, a false beauty as our offering to the world. He only can create the greatest imaginable beauty who has endured all imaginable pangs, for only when we have seen and foreseen what we dread shall we be rewarded by that dazzling, unforeseen, wing-footed wanderer. We could not find him if he were not in some sense of our being, and yet of our being but as water with fire, a noise with silence. He is of all things not impossible the most difficult, for that only which comes easily can never be a portion of our being; 'soon got, soon gone,' as the proverb says. I shall find the dark grow luminous, the void fruitful when I understand I have nothing, that the ringers in the tower have appointed for the hymen of the soul a passing bell.

[. . .]

VI.

I think the Christian saint and hero, instead of being merely dissatisfied, make deliberate sacrifice. I remember reading once an autobiography of a man who had made a daring journey in disguise to Russian exiles in Siberia, and his telling how, very timid as a child, he schooled himself by wandering at night through dangerous streets. Saint and hero cannot be content to pass at moments to that hollow image and after become their heterogeneous selves, but would always, if they could, resemble the antithetical self. There is a shadow of type on type, for in all great poetical styles there is saint or hero, but when it is all over Dante can return to his chambering and Shakespeare to his 'pottle-pot'. They sought no impossible perfection but when they handled paper or parchment. So too will saint or hero, because he works in his own flesh and blood and not in paper or parchment, have more deliberate understanding of that other flesh and blood.

Some years ago I began to believe that our culture, with its doctrine of sincerity and self-realisation, made us gentle and passive, and that the Middle Ages and the Renaissance were right to found theirs upon the imitation of Christ or of some classic hero. Saint Francis and Caesar Borgia made themselves overmastering, creative persons by turning from the mirror to meditation upon a mask. When I had this thought I could see nothing else in life. I could not write the play I had planned, for all became allegorical, and though I tore up hundreds of pages in my endeavour to escape from allegory, my imagination became sterile for nearly five years and I only escaped at last when I had mocked in a comedy my own thought. I was always thinking of the element of imitation in style and in life, and of the life beyond heroic imitation. I find in an old diary: 'I think all happiness depends on the energy to assume the mask of some other life, on a re-birth as something not one's self, something created in a moment and perpetually renewed; in playing a game like that of a child where one loses the infinite pain of self-realisation, in a grotesque or solemn painted face put on that one may hide from the terror of judgment. . . . Perhaps all the sins and energies of the world are but the world's flight from an infinite blinding beam'; and again at an earlier date: 'If we cannot imagine ourselves as different from what we are, and try to assume that second self, we cannot impose a discipline upon ourselves though we may accept one from others. Active virtue, as distinguished from the passive acceptance of a code, is therefore theatrical, consciously dramatic, the wearing of a mask. . . . Wordsworth, great poet though he be, is so often flat and heavy partly because his moral sense, being a discipline he had not created, a mere obedience, has no theatrical element. This increases his popularity with the better kind of journalists and politicians who have written books.'

[. . .]

VIII.

I think that all religious men have believed that there is a hand not ours in the events of life, and that, as somebody says in *Wilhelm Meister*, accident is destiny; and I think it was Heraclitus who said: the Daimon is our destiny. When I think of life as a struggle with the Daimon who would ever set us to the hardest work among those not impossible, I understand why there is a deep enmity between a man and his destiny, and why a man loves nothing but his destiny. In an Anglo-Saxon poem a certain man is called, as though to call him something that summed up all heroism, 'Doom eager'. I am persuaded that the Daimon delivers and deceives us, and that he wove that netting from the stars and threw the net from his shoulder. Then my imagination runs from Daimon to sweetheart, and I divine an analogy that evades the intellect. I remember that Greek antiquity has bid us look for the principal stars, that govern enemy and sweetheart alike, among those that are about to set, in the Seventh House as the astrologers say; and that it may be 'sexual love', which is 'founded upon spiritual hate', is an image of the warfare of man and Daimon; and I even wonder if there may not be some secret communion, some whispering in the dark between Daimon and sweetheart. I remember how often women when in love grow superstitious, and believe that they can bring their lovers good luck; and I remember an old Irish story of three young men who went seeking for help in battle into the house of the gods at Slieve-na-mon. 'You must first be married,' some god told them, 'because a man's good or evil luck comes to him through a woman.'

I sometimes fence for half an hour at the day's end, and when I close my eyes upon the pillow I see a foil playing before me, the button to my face. We meet always in the deep of the mind, whatever our work, wherever our reverie carries us, that other Will.

IX.

The poet finds and makes his mask in disappointment, the hero in defeat. The desire that is satisfied is not a great desire, nor has the shoulder used all its might that an unbreakable gate has never strained. The saint alone is not deceived, neither thrusting with his shoulder nor holding out unsatisfied hands. He would climb without wandering to the antithetical self of the world, the Indian narrowing his thought in meditation or driving it away in contemplation, the Christian copying Christ, the antithetical self of the classic world. For a hero loves the world till it breaks him, and the poet till it has broken faith; but while the world was yet debonair, the saint has turned away, and because he renounced experience itself, he will wear his mask as he finds it. The poet or the hero, no matter upon what bark they found their mask, so teeming their fancy, somewhat change its lineaments, but the saint, whose life is but a round of customary duty, needs nothing the whole world does not need, and day by day he scourges in his body the Roman and Christian conquerors: Alexander and Caesar are famished in his cell. His nativity is neither in disappointment nor in defeat, but in a temptation like that of Christ in the Wilderness, a contemplation in a single instant perpetually renewed of the Kingdoms of the World; all – because all renounced – continually present showing their empty thrones.

[. . .]

X.

It is not permitted to a man who takes up pen or chisel, to seek originality, for passion is his only business, and he cannot but mould or sing after a new fashion because no disaster is like another. He is like those phantom lovers in the Japanese play who, compelled to wander side by side and never mingle, cry: 'We neither wake nor sleep and, passing our nights in a sorrow which is in the end a vision, what are these scenes of spring to us?' If when we have found a mask we fancy that it will not match our mood till we have touched with gold the cheek, we do it furtively, and only where the oaks of Dodona cast their deepest shadow, for could he see our handiwork the Daimon would fling himself out, being our enemy.

XI.

Many years ago I saw, between sleeping and waking, a woman of incredible beauty shooting an arrow into the sky, and from the moment when I made my first guess at her meaning I have thought much of the difference between the winding movement of Nature and the straight line, which is called in Balzac's *Séraphita* the 'Mark of Man', but is better described as the mark of saint or sage. I think that we who are poets and artists, not being permitted to shoot beyond the tangible, must go from desire to weariness and so to desire again, and live but for the moment when vision comes to our weariness like terrible lightning, in the humility of the brutes. I do not doubt those heaving circles, those winding arcs, whether in one man's life or in that of an age, are mathematical, and that some in the world, or beyond the world, have foreknown the event and pricked upon the calendar the life-span of a Christ, a Buddha, a Napoleon: that every movement, in feeling or in thought, prepares in the dark by its own increasing clarity and confidence its own executioner. We seek reality with the slow toil of our weakness and are smitten from the boundless and the unforeseen. Only when we are saint or sage, and renounce experience itself, can we, in imagery of the Christian Cabbala, leave the sudden lightning and the path of the serpent and become the bowman who aims his arrow at the centre of the sun.

[...]

7
AMY LOWELL (1874–1925)
FROM PREFACE TO *TENDENCIES IN MODERNIST POETRY* 1917

American poet. Born into one of Boston's wealthiest families, Lowell took control of the family estate ('Sevenels') in 1903, after her parents' death. Determined from an early age to pursue a serious career as a poet, she had a poem published in the prestigious Boston magazine The Atlantic Monthly, *in 1910; in 1912, following encouragement by Harriet Monroe, the editor of the Chicago-based* Poetry: A Magazine of Verse, *she brought out her first collection,* A Dome of Many-Colored Glass. *In the same year she met the actress Ada Dwyer Russell and established what was to be a lifelong relationship, with whom she sailed to England in July 1914. Lowell had read H. D.'s first Imagist poems in 1913 and had already decided to join the 'Imagistes' when she eventually met H. D., her husband Richard Aldington, John Gould Fletcher, D. H. Lawrence and Ezra Pound. As editor of* The New Freewoman, *Pound had published Lowell's 'In a Garden' in 1913, but failed to persuade her to buy into the magazine (soon to become* The Egoist). *Despite this and other disagreements with Pound over the proper definition and direction of Imagism, Lowell continued to promote her own and her fellow Imagists' work through lecturing and anthologising (three volumes entitled* Some Imagist Poets *were brought out in 1915, 1916 and 1917). Other important contributions to the propagations of the idea of modern poetry include the studies* Six French Poets *(1915) and* Tendencies in Modern American Poetry *(1917), extracts from Lowell's Preface to which are reproduced below. [See IIb 4]*

It is impossible for any one writing to-day not to be affected by the war. It has overwhelmed us like a tidal wave. It is the equinoctial storm which bounds a period. So I make no apology for beginning a book of poetical essays with a reference to the war. In fact, the war and the subject of this volume are not so far apart as might at first appear.

The so-called 'new movement' in American poetry is evidence of the rise of a native school. The welding together of the whole country which the war has brought about, the mobilizing of our whole population into a single, strenuous endeavour, has produced a more poignant sense of nationality than has recently been the case in this country of enormous spaces and heterogeneous population. Hyphens are submerged in the solid overprinting of the word 'America'. We are no more colonies of this or that other land, but ourselves, different from all other peoples whatsoever.

It is this realization of ourselves that has drawn us into an understanding sympathy with our allies hardly to be conceived of before. And let us make no mistake; such a result cannot be reached through a devotion to the teachings of materialism. The real truth is that at a time when most people were bewailing the growth of materialism, already, beneath the surface, the seething of a new idealism was in process.

Long before the shadow of battle flung itself over the world, the travail of this idealism began. Slowly, painfully, it took on a shape, hidden away in the dreams and desires of unknown men.

Literature is rooted to life, and although a work of art is great only because of its æsthetic importance, still its very astheticism is conditioned by its sincerity and by the strength of its roots. Posterity cares nothing for the views which urged a man to write; to it, the poetry, its beauty as a work of art, is the only thing which matters. But that beauty could not exist without the soil from which it draws its sustenance, and it is a fact that those works of art which are superficial or meretricious do certainly perish remarkably soon. This is why time alone can determine a man's fate. Tinsel can be made to look extraordinarily like gold; it is only wear which rubs off the plating.

To a certain extent, the change which marks American poetry has been going on in the literature of other countries also. But not quite in the same way. Each country approaches an evolutionary step from its own racial angle, and they move alternately, first one leads and then another, but all together, if we look back a century or so, move the world forward into a new path. At the moment of writing, it is America who has taken the last, most advanced step.

It is not my intention, here, to combat the opinions of the conservatives. Conservatives are always with us, they have been opposing change ever since the days of the cave-men. But, fortunately for mankind, they agitate in vain. Already the more open minded see that the change going on in the arts is not a mere frivolous interest in experiment. Already the reasons for difference begin to stand out clearly. We who watch realize something of the grandeur of conception toward which this evolution is working.

The modern poets are less concerned with dogma and more with truth. They see in the universe a huge symbol, and so absolute has this symbol become to them that they have no need to dwell constantly upon its symbolic meaning. For this reason, the symbol has taken on a new intensity, and is given much prominence. What appear to be pure nature poems are of course so, but in a different way from most nature poems of the older writers; for nature is not now something separate from man, man and nature are recognized as a part of a whole, man being a part of nature, and all falling into a place in a vast plan, the key to which is natural science.

In some modern American poets this attitude is more conscious than in others, but all have been affected by it; it has modified poetry, as it is more slowly modifying the whole of our social fabric.

What sets the poets of to-day apart from those of the Victorian era is an entire difference of outlook. Ideas believed to be fundamental have disappeared and given place to others. And as poetry is the expression of the heart of man, so it reflects this change to its smallest particle.

It has been my endeavour in these essays to follow this evolution, in the movement as a whole, and also in the work of the particular poets who compose it.

[. . .]

As to those poets who still cling to an older order, of course, in such a volume as this, their work can find no place however excellent it may be in itself.

How shall one write a book of literary criticism? What weight shall one lay on biography; what on æsthetics? I quite agree with that brilliant disciple of Signor Benedetto Croce, Mr. J. E. Spingarn, that the criticism of art should be first, foremost, and all the time, æsthetic. As I have already said, its æsthetic value is, in the final summing up, the only value of a work of art, as such. But life, too, has a right to its criticism, and to the lover of poetry the life which conditioned the poems also has its charm. Therefore, I have considered these poets as men and artists.

[. . .]

It is impossible for the judgment of any one critic to be final. In fact, no contemporary criticism can make any such pretence. Hitherto, American students have felt this so strongly that practically no serious consideration of contemporary work has been attempted. Other countries, however, are not so modest. France, particularly, delights in analyzing the art of the time. The French realize that a contemporary can often reveal facets in an author's work which may be hidden from posterity, that certain *nuances* can only be apprehended by a person living under the same conditions. This must be my excuse for attempting a study of living authors. Also, that they are poets. For, recently, in England and America, a movement has started which has taken form in various little booklets, monographs of this and that novelist for the most part. Poetry has not been touched upon; and this is strange, for poetry, far more than fiction, reveals the soul of humanity. Poets are always the advance guard of literature; the advance guard of life. It is for this reason that their recognition comes so slowly.

8
WILLIAM CARLOS WILLIAMS (1883–1963)
FROM PROLOGUE TO *KORA IN HELL* 1918

American poet, born in New Jersey. He studied medicine at Pennsylvania University, where he met Hilda Doolittle and Ezra Pound, and later in New York and Leipzig, after which he visited London where he met W. B. Yeats. In 1909 he settled as a GP in Rutherford and published his first book, Poems *(1909). Williams was among the early practitioners of Imagism, from which he moved away to write in celebration of American idiom. His poetic manifesto is encapsulated in the phrase 'no ideas but in things'. He edited, with Robert McAlmon,* Contact *magazine (1921–23) and* Contact: An American Quarterly *(1931–33). His early volumes of poetry include* Al Que Quiere! *(1917),* Kora in Hell *(1920), and* Spring and All *(1923). His epic five-volume, collagistic work* Paterson *was published between 1946 and 1958. The following extract is taken from Williams's 'Prologue' to his 'Improvisations', entitled* Kora in Hell, *written in 1918 and first published in 1920.*

[. . .]

I like to think of the Greeks as setting out for the colonies in Sicily and the Italian peninsula. The Greek temperament lent itself to a certain symmetrical sculptural phase and to a fat poetical balance of line that produced important work but I like better the Greeks setting their backs to Athens. The ferment was always richer in Rome, the dispersive explosion was always nearer, the influence carried further and remained hot longer. Hellenism, especially the modern sort, is too staid, too chilly, too little fecundative to impregnate my world.

Hilda Doolittle before she began to write poetry or at least before she began to show it to anyone would say: 'You're not satisfied with me, are you Billy? There's something lacking, isn't there?' When I was with her my feet always seemed to be sticking to the ground while she would be walking on the tips of the grass stems.

Ten years later as assistant editor of the *Egoist* she refers to my long poem, 'March', which thanks to her own and her husband's friendly attentions finally appeared there in a purified form:

14 *Aug.* 1916

Dear Bill: –

I trust you will not hate me for wanting to delete from your poem all the flippancies. The reason I want to do this is that the beautiful lines are so very beautiful   so in the tone and spirit of your *Postlude* – (which to me stands, a Nike, supreme among your poems). I think there is *real* beauty – and real beauty is a rare and sacred thing in this generation   in all the pyramid, Ashur-ban-i-pal bits and in the Fiesole and in the wind at the very last.

I don't know what you think but I consider this business of writing a very sacred thing! – I think you have the 'spark' – am sure of it, and when you speak *direct* are a poet. I feel in the heyding-ding touch running through your poem a derivative tendency which, to me, is not *you* – not your very self. It is as if you were *ashamed* of your Spirit, ashamed of your inspiration! – as if you mocked at your own song. It's very well to *mock* at yourself – it is a spiritual sin to mock at your inspiration –

Hilda

Oh well, all this might be very disquieting were it not that 'sacred' has lately been discovered to apply to a point of arrest where stabilization has gone on past the time. There is nothing sacred about literature, it is damned from one end to the other. There is nothing in literature but change and change is mockery. I'll write whatever I damn please, whenever I damn please and as I damn please and it'll be good if the authentic spirit of change is on it.

But in any case H. D. misses the entire intent of what I am doing no matter how just her remarks concerning that particular poem happen to have been. The hey-ding-ding touch *was* derivative, but it filled a gap that I did not know how better to fill at the time. It might be said that that touch is the prototype of the improvisations.

It is to the inventive imagination we look for deliverance from every other misfortune as from the desolation of a flat Hellenic perfection of style. What good then to turn to art from the atavistic religionists, from a science doing slavery service upon gas engines, from a philosophy tangled in a miserable sort of dialect that means nothing if the full power of initiative be denied at the beginning by a lot of baying and snapping scholiasts? If the inventive imagination must look, as I think, to the field of art for its richest discoveries today it will best make its way by compass and follow no path.

But before any material progress can be accomplished there must be someone to draw a discriminating line between true and false values.

The true value is that peculiarity which gives an object a character by itself. The associational or sentimental value is the false. Its imposition is due to lack of imagination, to an easy lateral sliding. The attention has been held too rigid on the one plane instead of following a more flexible, jagged resort. It is to loosen the attention, my attention since I occupy part of the field, that I write these improvisations. Here I clash with Wallace Stevens.

The imagination goes from one thing to another. Given many things of nearly totally divergent natures but possessing one-thousandth part of a quality in common, provided that be new, distinguished, these things belong in an imaginative category and not in a gross natural array. To me this is the gist of the whole matter. It is easy to fall under the spell of a certain mode, especially if it be remote of origin, leaving thus certain of its members essential to a reconstruction of its significance permanently lost in an impenetrable mist of time. But the thing that stands eternally in the way of really good writing is always one: the virtual impossibility of lifting to the imagination those things which lie under the direct scrutiny of the senses, close to the nose. It is this difficulty that sets a value upon all works of art and makes them a necessity.

[. . .]

I wish that I might here set down my 'Vortex' after the fashion of London, 1913, stating how little it means to me whether I live here, there or elsewhere or succeed in this, that or the other so long as I can keep my mind free from the trammels of literature, beating down every attack of its *retiarii* with my *mirmillones*. But the time is past.

I thought at first to adjoin to each improvisation a more or less opaque commentary. But the mechanical interference that would result makes this inadvisable. Instead I have placed some of them in the preface where without losing their original intention (see reference numerals at the beginning of each) they relieve the later text and also add their weight to my present fragmentary argument.

V. No. 2. By the brokenness of his composition the poet makes himself master of a certain weapon which he could possess himself of in no other way. The speed of the emotions is sometimes such that thrashing about in a thin exaltation or despair many matters are touched but not held, more often broken by the contact.

II. No. 3. The instability of these improvisations would seem such that they must inevitably crumble under the attention and become particles of a wind that falters. It would appear to the unready that the fiber of the thing is a thin jelly. It would be these same fools who would deny touch cords to the wind because they cannot split a storm endwise and wrap it upon spools. The virtue of strength lies not in the grossness of the fiber but in the fiber itself. Thus a poem is tough by no quality it borrows from a logical recital of events nor from the events themselves but solely from that attenuated power which draws perhaps many broken things into a dance giving them thus a full being.

It is seldom that anything but the most elementary communications can be exchanged one with another. There are in reality only two or three reasons generally accepted as the causes of action. No matter what the motive it will seldom happen that true knowledge of it will be anything more than vaguely divined by some one person, some half a person whose intimacy has perhaps been cultivated over the whole of a lifetime. We live in bags. This is due to the gross fiber of all action. By action itself almost nothing can be imparted. The world of action is a world of stones.

XV. No. 1. Bla! Bla! Bla! Heavy talk is talk that waits upon a deed. Talk is servile that is set to inform. Words with the bloom on them run before the imagination like the saeter girls before Peer Gynt. It is talk with the patina of whim upon it makes action a bootlicker. So nowadays poets spit upon rhyme and rhetoric.

The stream of things having composed itself into wiry strands that move in one fixed direction, the poet in desperation turns at right angles and cuts across current with startling results to his hangdog mood.

[. . .]

VIII. No. 3. Those who permit their senses to be despoiled of the things under their noses by stories of all manner of things removed and unattainable are of frail imagination. Idiots, it is true nothing is possessed save by dint of that vigorous conception of its perfections which is the imagination's special province but neither is anything possessed which is not extant. A frail imagination, unequal to the tasks before it, is easily led astray.

IV. No. 2. Although it is a quality of the imagination that it seeks to place together those things which have a common relationship, yet the coining of similes is a pastime of very low order, depending as it does upon a nearly vegetable coincidence. Much more keen is that power which discovers in things those inimitable particles of dissimilarity to all other things which are the peculiar perfections of the thing in question.

But this loose linking of one thing with another has effects of a destructive power little to be guessed at: all manner of things are thrown out of key so that it approaches the impossible to arrive at an understanding of anything. All is confusion, yet it comes from a hidden desire for the dance, a lust of the imagination, a will to accord two instruments in a duet.

But one does not attempt by the ingenuity of the joiner to blend the tones of the oboe with the violin. On the contrary the perfections of the two instruments are emphasized by the joiner; no means is neglected to give to each the full color of its perfections. It is only the music of the instruments which is joined and that not by the woodworker but by the composer, by virtue of the imagination.

On this level of the imagination all things and ages meet in fellowship. Thus only can they, peculiar and perfect, find their release. This is the beneficent power of the imagination.

Age and youth are great flatterers. Brooding on each other's obvious psychology neither dares tell the other outright what manifestly is the truth: your world is poison. Each is secure in his own perfections. Monsieur Eichorn used to have a most atrocious body odor while the odor of some girls is a pleasure to the nostril. Each quality in each person or age, rightly valued, would mean the freeing of that age to its own delights of action or repose. Now an evil odor can be pursued with praiseworthy ardor leading to great natural activity whereas a flowery skinned virgin may and no doubt often does allow herself to fall into destructive habits of neglect.

XIII. No. 3. A poet witnessing the chicory flower and realizing its virtues of form and color so constructs his praise of it as to borrow no particle from right or left. He gives his poem over to the flower and its plant themselves, that they may benefit by those cooling winds of the imagination which thus returned upon them will refresh them at their task of saving the world. But what does it mean, remarked his friends?

VII. *Coda.* It would be better than depriving birds of their song to call them all nightingales. So it would be better than to have a world stript of poetry to provide men with some sort of eyeglasses by which they should be unable to read any verse but sonnets. But fortunately although there are many sorts of fools, just as there are many birds which sing and many sorts of poems, there is no need to please them.

All schoolmasters are fools. Thinking to build in the young the foundations of knowledge they let slip their minds that the blocks are of gray mist bedded upon the wind. Those who will taste of the wind himself have a mark in their eyes by virtue of which they bring their masters to nothing.

All things brought under the hand of the possessor crumble to nothingness. Not only that: He who possesses a child if he cling to it inordinately becomes childlike, whereas, with a twist of the imagination, himself may rise into comradeship with the grave and beautiful presences of antiquity. But some have the power to free, say a young matron pursuing her infant, from her own possessions, making her kin to Yang Kuei-fei because of a haunting loveliness that clings about her knees, impeding her progress as she takes up her matronly pursuit.

As to the sun what is he, save for his light, more than the earth is: the same mass of metals, a mere shadow? But the winged dawn is the very essence of the sun's self, a thing cold, vitreous, a virtue that precedes the body which it drags after it.

The features of a landscape take their position in the imagination and are related more to their own kind there than to the country and season which has held them hitherto as a basket holds vegetables mixed with fruit.

[. . .]

VIII. No. 1. A man of note upon examining the poems of his friend and finding there nothing related to his immediate understanding laughingly remarked: After all, literature is communication while you, my friend, I am afraid, in attempting to do something striking, are in danger of achieving mere preciosity. – But inasmuch as the fields of the mind are vast and little explored, the poet was inclined only to smile and to take note of that hardening infirmity of the imagination which seems to endow its victim with great solidity and rapidity of judgment. But he thought to himself: And yet of what other thing is greatness composed than a power to annihilate half-truths for a thousandth part of accurate understanding.

I have discovered that the thrill of first love passes! It even becomes the backbone of a sordid sort of religion if not assisted in passing. I knew a man who kept a candle burning before a girl's portrait day and night for a year – then jilted her, pawned her off on a friend. I have been reasonably frank about my erotics with my wife. I have never or seldom said, my dear I love you, when I would rather say: My dear, I wish you were in Tierra del Fuego. I have discovered by scrupulous attention to this detail and by certain allied experiments that we can continue from time to time to elaborate relationships quite equal in quality, if not greatly superior, to that surrounding our wedding. In fact, the best we have enjoyed of love together has come after the most thorough destruction or harvesting of that which has gone before. Periods of barrenness have intervened, periods comparable to the prison music in *Fidelio* or to any of Beethoven's pianissimo transition passages. It is at these times our formal relations have teetered on the edge of a debacle to be followed, as our imaginations have permitted, by a new growth of passionate attachment dissimilar in every member to that which has gone before.

It is in the continual and violent refreshing of the idea that love and good writing have their security.

[...]

Nothing is good save the new. If a thing have novelty it stands intrinsically beside every other work of artistic excellence. If it have not that, no loveliness or heroic proportion or grand manner will save it. It will not be saved above all by an attenuated intellectuality.

But all U.S. verse is not bad according to Mr. J., there is T. S. Eliot and his 'Love Song of J. Alfred Prufrock'.

But our prize poems are especially to be damned not because of superficial bad workmanship, but because they are rehash, repetition – just as Eliot's more exquisite work is rehash, repetition in another way of Verlaine, Baudelaire, Maeterlinck – conscious or unconscious – just as there were Pound's early paraphrases from Yeats and his constant later cribbing from the Renaissance, Provence and the modern French: Men content with the connotations of their masters.

It is convenient to have fixed standards of comparison: All antiquity! And there is always some everlasting Polonius of Kensington forever to rate highly his eternal Eliot. It is because Eliot is a subtle conformist. It tickles the palate of this archbishop of procurers to a lecherous antiquity to hold up Prufrock as a New World type. Prufrock, the nibbler at sophistication, endemic in every capital, the not quite (because he refuses to turn his back), is 'the soul of that modern land,' the United States!

> Blue undershirts,
> Upon a line,
> It is not necessary to say to you
> Anything about it –

I cannot question Eliot's observation. Prufrock is a masterly portrait of the man just below the summit, but the type is universal; the model in his case might be Mr. J.

No. The New World is Montezuma or, since he was stoned to death in a parley, Guatemozin who had the city of Mexico leveled over him before he was taken.

For the rest, there is no man even though he dare who can make beauty his own and 'so at last live', at least there is no man better situated for that achievement than another. As Prufrock longed for his silly lady, so Kensington longs for its Hardanger dairymaid. By a mere twist of the imagination, if Prufrock only knew it, the whole world can be inverted (why else are there wars?) and the mermaids be set warbling to whoever will listen to them. Seesaw and blindman's buff converted into a sort of football.

But the summit of United States achievement, according to Mr. J. – who can discourse on Catullus – is that very beautiful poem of Eliot's, 'La Figlia Que Piange': just the right amount of everything drained through, etc., etc., etc., etc., the rhythm delicately studied and – IT CONFORMS! *ergo*, here we have 'the very fine flower of the finest spirit of the United States'.

Examined closely this poem reveals a highly refined distillation. Added to the already 'faithless' formula of yesterday we have a conscious simplicity:

Simple and faithless as a smile and shake of the hand.

The perfection of that line is beyond cavil. Yet, in the last stanza, this paradigm, this very fine flower of U. S. art is warped out of alignment, obscured in meaning even to the point of an absolute unintelligibility by the inevitable straining after a rhyme, the very cleverness with which this straining is covered being a sinister token in itself.

> And I wonder how they should have been together!

So we have no choice but to accept the work of this fumbling conjurer.

Upon the Jepson filet Eliot balances his mushroom. It is the latest touch from the literary cuisine, it adds to the pleasant outlook from the club window. If to do this, if to be a Whistler at best, in the art of poetry, is to reach the height of poetic expression then Ezra and Eliot have approached it and *tant pis* for the rest of us.

[. . .]

Imagine an international congress of poets at Paris or Versailles, Rémy de Gourmont (now dead) presiding, poets all speaking five languages fluently. Ezra stands up to represent U. S. verse and de Gourmont sits down smiling. Ezra begins by reading 'La Figlia Que Piange'. It would be a pretty pastime to gather into a mental basket the fruits of that reading from the minds of the ten Frenchmen present; their impressions of the sort of United States that very fine flower was picked from. After this Kreymborg might push his way to the front and read 'Jack's House'.

E. P. is the best enemy United States verse has. He is interested, passionately interested – even if he doesn't know what he is talking about. But of course he does know what he is talking about. He does not, however, know everything, not by more than half. The accordances of which Americans have the parts and the colors but not the completions before them pass beyond the attempts of his thought. It is a middle-aging blight of the imagination.

I praise those who have the wit and courage, and the conventionality, to go direct toward their vision of perfection in an objective world where the signposts are clearly marked, viz., to London. But confine them in hell for their paretic assumption that there is no alternative but their own groove.

[. . .]

9
MAY SINCLAIR (1863–1946)
FROM A REVIEW OF *PILGRIMAGE* 1918

English novelist, poet and literary critic. She was born into a shipping family that went bankrupt, so lived at home and was mostly educated there. She supported herself through reviews and translations and had her first publishing success with The Divine Power *(1904), which led to a tour of the USA. Sinclair's work was firmly within a Modernist tradition. Strongly influenced by psychoanalysis and Modernist formal experimentation, her novels concentrate on the political, social and psychological aspects of women's struggles. This type of writing figures in her early work* The Three Sisters *(1919),* Kitty Tailleur *(1908) and* The Creators *(1910). In her appraisal of the innovative style of Dorothy Richardson's writing in a review of three 'chapters' from* Pilgrimage, *originally published in* The Egoist, *April 1918 (extracts from which are reproduced below), Sinclair was the first to use the term 'stream of consciousness' in a literary context. She proceeded to deploy the stream-of-consciousness technique in her own writing, in* Mary Olivier: A Life *(1919) and* The Life and Death of Harriet Frean *(1922). Later works include* The Dark Night *(1922),* Far End *(1926) and* The History of Anthony Waring *(1927). [See IIIb 8]*

I do not know whether this article is or is not going to be a criticism, for so soon as I begin to think what I shall say I find myself criticizing criticism, wondering what is the matter with it and what, if anything, can be done to make it better, to make it alive. Only a live criticism can deal appropriately with a live art. And it seems to me that the first step towards life is to throw off the philosophic cant of the nineteenth century. I don't mean that there is no philosophy of Art, or that if there has been there is to be no more of it; I mean that it is absurd to go on talking about realism and idealism, or objective and subjective art, as if the philosophies were sticking where they stood in the eighties.

In those days the distinction between idealism and realism, between subjective and objective was important and precise. And so long as the ideas they stand for had importance and precision those words were lamps to the feet and lanterns to the path of the critic. Even after they had begun to lose precision and importance they still served him as useful labels for the bewildering phenomena of the arts.

But now they are beginning to give trouble; they obscure the issues. Mr. J. B. Beresford in his admirable Introduction to *Pointed Roofs* confesses to having felt this trouble. When he read it in manuscript he decided that it 'was realism, was objective'. When he read it in typescript he thought: 'This . . . is the most subjective thing I have ever read'. It is evident that when first faced with the startling 'newness' of Miss Richardson's method, and her form, the issues did seem a bit obscure to Mr. Beresford. It was as if up to one illuminating moment he had been obliged to think of methods and forms as definitely objective or definitely subjective. His illuminating moment came with the third reading, when *Pointed Roofs* was a printed book. The book itself gave him the clue to his own trouble, which is my trouble, the first hint that criticism up till now has been content to think in *clichés*, missing the new trend of the philosophies of the twentieth century. All that we know of reality at first hand is given to us through contacts in which those interesting distinctions are lost. Reality is thick and deep, too thick and too deep, and at the same time too fluid to be cut with any convenient carving-knife. The novelist who would be close to reality must confine himself to this knowledge at first hand. He must, as Mr. Beresford says, simply 'plunge in.' Mr. Beresford says that Miss Richardson is the first novelist who has plunged in. She has plunged so neatly and quietly that even admirers of her performance might remain unaware of what it is precisely that she has done. She has disappeared while they are still waiting for the splash. So that Mr. Beresford's Introduction was needed.

When first I read *Pointed Roofs* and *Backwater* and *Honeycomb* I too thought, like Mr. Beresford, that Miss Richardson has been the first to plunge. But it seems to me rather that she has followed, independently, perhaps unconsciously, a growing tendency to plunge. As far back as the eighties the de Goncourts plunged completely, finally, in *Sœur Philomène, Germinie Lacerteux*, and *Les Frères Zemgann*. Marguerite Audoux plunged in the best passages of *Marie Claire*. The best of every good novelist's best work is a more or less sustained immersion. The more modern the novelist the longer his capacity to stay under. Miss Richardson has not plunged deeper than Mr. James Joyce in his *Portrait of the Artist as a Young Man*.

By imposing very strict limitations on herself she has brought her art, her method, to a high pitch of perfection, so that her form seems to be newer than it perhaps is. She herself is unaware of the perfection of her method. She would probably deny that she has written with any deliberate method at all. She would say: 'I only know there are certain things I mustn't do if I was to do what I wanted.' Obviously, she must not interfere; she must not analyse or comment or explain. Rather less obviously, she must not tell a story or handle a situation or set a scene; she must avoid drama as she avoids narration. And there are some things she must not be. She must not be the wise, all-knowing author. She must be Miriam Henderson. She must not know or divine anything that Miriam does not know or divine; she must not see anything that Miriam does not see. She has taken Miriam's nature upon her. She is not concerned, in the way that other novelists are concerned with character. Of the persons who move through Miriam's world you know nothing but what Miriam knows. If Miriam is mistaken, well, she and not Miss Richardson is mistaken. Miriam is an acute observer, but she is very far from seeing the whole of these people. They are presented to us in the same vivid but fragmentary way in which they appeared to Miriam, the fragmentary way in which people appear to most of us. Miss Richardson has only imposed on herself the conditions that life imposes on us all. And if you are going to quarrel with those conditions you will not find her novels satisfactory. But your satisfaction is not her concern.

And I find it impossible to reduce to intelligible terms this satisfaction that I feel. To me these three novels show an art and method and form carried to punctilious perfection. Yet I have heard other novelists say that they have no art and no method and no form, and that it is this formlessness that annoys them. They say that they have no beginning and no middle and no end, and that to have form a novel must have an end and a beginning and a middle. We have come to words that in more primitive times would have been blows on this subject. There is a certain plausibility in what they say, but it depends on what constitutes a beginning and a middle and an end. In this series there is no drama, no situation, no set scene. Nothing happens. It is just life going on and on. It is Miriam Henderson's stream of consciousness going on and on. And in neither is there any grossly discernible beginning or middle or end.

In identifying herself with this life, which is Miriam's stream of consciousness, Miss Richardson produces her effect of being the first, of getting closer to reality than any of our novelists who are trying so desperately to get close. No attitude or gesture of her own is allowed to come between her and her effect. [. . .]

This intensity is the effect of an extreme concentration on the thing seen or felt. Miss Richardson disdains every stroke that does not tell. Her novels are novels of an extraordinary compression, and of an extenuation more extraordinary still. The moments of Miriam's consciousness pass one by one, or overlapping; moments tense with vibration, moments drawn out fine, almost to snapping-point. On one page Miss Richardson seems to be accounting for every minute of Miriam's time. On another she passes over events that might be considered decisive with the merest slur of reference. She is not concerned with the strict order of events in time. Chapter Three of *Pointed Roofs* opens with an air of extreme decision and importance: 'Miriam was practising on the piano in the larger of the two English bedrooms', as if something hung on her practising. But no, nothing hangs on it, and if you want to know on what day she is practising you have to read on and back again. It doesn't matter. It is Miriam's consciousness that is going backwards and forwards in time. The time it goes in is unimportant. On the hundredth page out of three hundred and twelve pages Miriam has been exactly two weeks in Hanover. Nothing has happened but the infinitely little affairs of the school, the practising, the *vorspielen*, the English lesson, the *raccommodage*, the hair-washing.

[. . .]

Nothing happens. In Miriam Henderson's life there is, apparently, nothing to justify living. Everything she ever wanted was either withheld or taken from her. She is reduced to the barest minimum on which it is possible to support the life of the senses and the emotions at all. And yet Miriam is happy. Her inexhaustible passion for life is fed. Nothing happens, and yet everything that really matters is happening; you are held breathless with the anticipation of its happening. What really matters is a state of mind, the interest or the ecstasy with which we close with life. It can't be explained. To quote Mr. Beresford again: 'explanation in this connexion would seem to imply knowledge that only the mystics can faintly realize.' But Miss Richardson's is a mysticism apart.

[. . .]

10
EDWIN MUIR (1887–1959)
FROM 'WHAT IS MODERN?' 1918

British poet, novelist, translator and critic. Born in Orkney, Muir moved to Glasgow, then to London. With his wife Willa he travelled to Prague, and after the Second World War worked there for the British Council. He became Director of the British Institute in Rome in 1949, and Professor of Poetry at Harvard 1955–56. He contributed to A. A. Orage's New Age, *and in the 1920s, at Orage's suggestion, underwent psychoanalysis which triggered a series of mythological dreams influencing his poetry. Between 1930 and 1949 he published translations of Kafka's novels. His volumes of poetry include* First Poems *(1925),* Chorus of the Newly Dead *(1926),* Journeys and Places *(1937),* The Narrow Place *(1943),* The Voyage *(1946) and* The Labyrinth *(1949).* transition, *his first critical work, appeared under a pseudonym in 1926. The following extract is from an essay on 'the modern', published in* We Moderns: Enigmas and Guesses *in 1918.*

Whither?

The fever of modern thought which burns in our veins, and from which we refuse to escape by reactionary backdoors – Christianity and the like – is not without its distinction: it is an 'honourable sickness', to use the phrase of Nietzsche. I speak of those who sincerely strive to seek an issue from this fever; to pass through it into a new health. Of the others to whom fever is the condition of existence, who make a profession of their maladies, the valetudinarians of the spirit, the dabblers in quack soul-remedies for their own sake, it is impossible to speak without disdain. Our duty is to exterminate them, by ridicule or any other means found effectual. But we are ourselves already too grievously harassed; we are caught in the whirlwind of modern thought, which contains as much dust as wind. We see outside our field of conflict a region of Christian calm, but never, never, never can we return there, for our instincts as well as our intellect are averse to it. The problem must have a different solution. And what, indeed, is the problem? To some of us it is still that of emancipation – that which confronted Goethe, Ibsen, Nietzsche, and the other great spirits of last century. It is an error to think that these men have yet been refuted or even understood; they have simply been buried beneath the corpses of later writers. And it is the worst intellectual weakness, and, therefore, crime, of our age that ideas are no longer disproved, but simply superseded by newer ideas. The latest is the true, and Time refutes everything! That is our modern superstition. We have still, then, to go back – or, rather, forward – to Goethe, Ibsen and Nietzsche. Our problem is still that of clearing a domain of freedom around us, of enlarging our field of choice, and so making destiny itself more spacious; and, then, having delivered ourselves from prejudice and superstition – and how many other things! – of setting an aim before us for the unflinching pursuit of which we make ourselves responsible. Greater freedom, and therefore greater responsibility, above all greater aims, an enlargement of life, not a whittling of it down to Christian standards – that is our problem still!

[. . .]

Genealogy of the Moderns

This is what has happened. The convential moderns of our time are the descendants *not* of Heine and Ibsen, but of the race against which the poets fought. They live unthinkingly in the present, just as their spiritual ancestors lived unthinkingly in the past. But slavery to the past has long ago fallen into the second place among dangers to humanity: it is slavery to the present that is now by far the greatest peril. Not because they broke the tyranny of the past, but because they had an ideal in the future are the great fighters of last century significant. To think of them as iconoclasts is to mistake for their aim the form of their activity: the past lay between them and their object: on that account alone did they destroy it. But the great obstacle now is the domination of the present; and were the demigods of last century alive to-day, they would be fighting precisely against *you*, my dear moderns, who live so complacently in your provincial present, making of it almost a cult. To be a modern in the true sense, however, is to be a forerunner; there is in this age, an age of preparation, no other test of the modern. To believe that there are still potentialities in man; to have faith that the 'elevation of the type Man' is possible, yes, that the time is ripe to prepare for it, and to write and live in and by that thought: this is to be modern.

[. . .]

What is Modern

It is time we erected a standard whereby to test what is modern. To be an adherent of all the latest movements – that is at most to be anarchistic, eclectic, inconsistent – call it what you will. Futurism, Realism, Feminism, Traditionalism may be all of them opposed or irrelevant to modernity. It is not sufficient that movements should be new – if they are ever new; the question is, To what end are they? If they are movements in the direction of emancipation, 'the elevation of the type Man', then they are modern; if they are not, then they are movements to be opposed or ignored by moderns. If modernism be a vital thing it must needs have roots in the past and be an essential expression of humanity, to be traced, therefore, in the history of humanity: in short, it can only be a tradition. The true modern is a continuator of tradition as much as the Christian or the conservative: the true fight between progress and stagnation is always a fight between antagonistic *traditions*. To battle against tradition *as such* is, therefore, not the task of the modern; but rather to enter the conflict – an eternal one – for his tradition against its opposite: Nietzsche found for this antithesis the symbolism of Dionysus and Apollo. Does such a tradition of modernity exist? Is there a 'modern spirit' not dependent upon time and place, and in all ages modern? If there is – and there is – the possession of it in some measure will alone entitle us to the name of moderns, give us dignity and make the history of Man once more dramatic and tragical. It is a pity that some historian has not yet traced, in its expression in events, the history of this conflict – a task requiring the deepest subtlety and insight. Meantime, for this tradition may be claimed with confidence such events as Greek Tragedy, the most of the Renaissance, and the emancipators of last century. These are triumphant expressions of 'the modern spirit', but that spirit is chiefly to be recognized as a principle, not always triumphant or easy of perception, constantly struggling, assuming many disguises and tirelessly creative. It is not, indeed, only a tradition of persons, of dogmas, or of sentiments: it is a principle of Life itself. This conception, it is true, is grand, and even terrifying – a disadvantage in this age. But is there any other which grants modernity more than the status of an accident of time and fashion?

[. . .]

Super-Art

In the works of some artists everything is on a slightly superhuman scale. The figures they create fill us with astonishment; we cannot understand how such unparalleled creatures came into being. When we contemplate them, in the works of Michelangelo or of Nietzsche, there arise involuntarily in our souls sublime dreams of what Man may yet attain. Our thoughts travel into the immeasurable, the undiscovered, and the future becomes almost an intoxication to us.

In Nietzsche, especially, this attempt to make Art perform the impossible – this *successful* attempt to make Art perform the impossible – is to be noted in every book, almost in every word. For he strains language to the utmost it can endure; his words seem to be striving to escape from the bonds of language, seeking to transcend language. 'It is my ambition,' he says in 'The Twilight of the Idols', 'to say in ten sentences what every one else says in a whole book – what every one else does *not* say in a whole book.' In the same way, when in his first book he wrote about Tragedy, he raised it to an elevation greater than it had ever known before, except, perhaps, in the works of Æschylus; when, in his essay upon 'Schopenhauer as Educator', he adumbrated his conception of the philosopher, philosophy seemed to become a task for the understandings of gods; and when, having criticized the prevailing morality, he set up another, it seemed to his generation an impossible code for human beings, a code cruel, over-noble. Finally, when he wrote of Man, it was to create the Superman. He touched nothing which he did not ennoble. And, consequently, in Art his chosen form was Myth; he held it beneath the nobility of great art to create anything less than demi-gods; religion and art were in him a unity.

In super-art, in these works of Leonardo and Michelangelo, of Æschylus and Nietzsche, Man is incited again and again to surpass himself, to become more than 'human'.

[. . .]

Myth

The worst evil of our time is this, that there is nothing greater than the current average existence to which men can look; Religion has dried up, Art has decayed from an idealization of life into a reflection of it. In short, Art has become a passive thing, where once it was the 'great stimulus to Life'. The idealization and enchantment which the moderns have so carefully eliminated from it was precisely its *raison d'être*. And modern Art, which sets out to copy life, has forgotten Art altogether, its origin, its meaning and its end.

Against this aimless Realism, we must oppose idealization, and especially that which is its highest expression, Myth. And let no one say that it is impossible at this stage in Man's history to resuscitate Myth. The past has certainly lost its mystery for us, and it was in the past, at the source of Humanity, that the old poets set their sublime fictions. But the future is still ours, and there, at Man's goal, our myths must be planted. And thither, indeed, has set the great literature of the last hundred years. Faust, Mephistopheles, Brand, Peer Gynt, Zarathustra – there were no greater figures in the literature of the last century – were all myths, and all forecasts of the future. The soil out of which literature grows, then, has not yet been exhausted! If we but break away from Realism, if we make Art symbolic, if we bring about a marriage between Art and Religion, Art will rise again. That this is possible, we who have faith in the Future *must* believe.

11

E. M. (EDWARD MORGAN) FORSTER (1879–1970)
FROM 'THE POETRY OF C. P. CAVAFY' (WITH G. VALASSOPOULO) 1919

English novelist and critic, born in London. At King's College, Cambridge, he joined the 'Bloomsbury' circle of G. E. Moore, G. M. Trevelyan and Lowes Dickinson, whose biography he wrote in 1934 and with whom he founded the Independent Review *in 1903. Periods in Italy and in India (as secretary to the Maharajah of Dewas Senior in 1921) provide the background for some of his most important fiction, including* Where Angels Fear to Tread *(1905),* A Room with a View *(1908),* A Passage to India *(1924) and* The Hill of Devi *(1953). Deploying subtle, rather than radical, insight, Forster scrutinises in his novels and short stories the assumptions and limitations of the English middle-class ethos. His most open account of homosexuality, the novel* Maurice *(1913–14) was published posthumously in 1971. The following extract is from an appreciation of a Greek poet which appeared in* The Athenaeum *on 25 April 1919.* **C. (Constantine) P. Cavafy (1863–1933)** *was a Greek poet who lived in Alexandria. From 1851–70 his father had one of the largest export companies in Egypt. He later went bankrupt and his widow and family moved to England for seven years. Cavafy's work first came to the attention of the Anglophone Modernists through E. M. Forster's translation of the poem 'The God Abandons Antony' in his* Alexandria: A History and a Guide *(1922). He began his poetic career translating of English and French poetry; his own writing features a stylised, hybridic Greek which includes modern, Byzantine and classical elements. Alexandria figures in his work as a metaphor for the rise and decline of Hellenism, as well as the contemporary setting for the poet's melancholy and poignant accounts of homosexual encounters. The 1961 edition of his complete poems in English appeared with a foreword by W. H. Auden, who acknowledges Cavafy as a major influence.*

Modern Alexandria is scarcely a city of the soul. Founded upon cotton with the con-currence of onions and eggs, ill built, ill planned, ill drained – many hard things can be said against it, and most are said by its inhabitants. Yet to some of them, as they traverse the streets, a delightful experience can occur. They hear their own name proclaimed in firm yet meditative accents – accents that seem not so much to expect an answer as to pay homage to the fact of individuality. They turn and see a Greek gentleman in a straw hat, standing absolutely motionless at a slight angle to the universe. His arms are extended, possibly. 'Oh, Cavafy [. . .] !' Yes, it is Mr. Cavafy, and he is going either from his flat to the office, or from his office to the flat. If the former, he vanishes when seen, with a slight gesture of despair. If the latter, he may be prevailed upon to begin a sentence – an immense complicated yet shapely sentence, full of parentheses that never get mixed and of reservations that really do reserve; a sentence that moves with logic to its foreseen end, yet to an end that is always more vivid and thrilling than one foresaw. Sometimes the sentence is finished in the street, sometimes the traffic murders it, sometimes it lasts into the flat. It deals with the tricky behaviour of the Emperor Alexius Comnenus in 1096, or with olives, their possibilities and price, or with the fortunes of friends, or George Eliot, or the dialects of the interior of Asia Minor. It is delivered with equal ease in Greek, English, or French. And despite its intellectual richness and human outlook, despite the matured charity of its judgments, one feels that it too stands at a slight angle to the universe: it is the sentence of a poet.

A Greek who wishes to compose poetry has a special problem; between his written and spoken language yawns a gulf. There is an artificial 'literary' jargon beloved by schoolmasters and journalists, which has tried to revive the classical tradition, and which only succeeds in being dull. And there is the speech of the people, varying from place to place, and everywhere stuffed with non-Hellenic constructions and words. Can this speech be used for poetry and for cultivated prose? The younger generation believes that it can. A society (Nea Zoe) was started in Alexandria to encourage it, and there is an admirable literary quarterly (*Grammata*) which shocks the stodgy not only by its articles, but by its vocabulary – expressions are used that one might actually hear in a shop. Similar movements are born and die all over the Levant, from Smyrna and Cyprus to Jannina, all testifying to the zeal of a race who, alone among the peoples of the Eastern Mediterranean, appear to possess the literary sense and to desire that words should be alive. Cavafy is one of the heroes of this movement, though not one of its extremists. Eclectic by nature, he sees that a new theory might be as sterile as the old, and that the final test must be the incommunicable one of taste. His own poems are in Demotic, but in moderate Demotic.

They are all short poems, and they are unrhymed, so that there is some hope of conveying them in a verbal translation. They reveal a very beautiful and a curious world. It comes into being through the world of experience, but it is not experience, for, as he often points out, the poet is even more incapable than most people of seeing straight:

> Here let me stand. Let me too look at Nature a little,
> The radiant blue of the morning sea,

The cloudless sky and the yellow beach;
All beautiful and flooded with light.
  The Alexandrians knew perfectly well
    that all this was words and empty pomp.
Here let me stand. And let me deceive myself into thinking that I saw them –
(I really did see them one moment, when first I came) – that I am not seeing,
even here, my fancies,
my memories, my visions of voluptuousness.

It is the world within. And since the poet cannot hope to escape from this world, he should at all costs arrange and rule it sensibly. 'My mind to me a kingdom is,' sang the Elizabethan, and so is Cavafy's; but his is a real, not a conventional, kingdom, in which there may be mutinies and war. In 'The City' he sketches the tragedy of one who misgoverned, and who hopes to leave the chaos behind him and to 'build another city, better than this'. Useless!

The city shall ever follow you.
In these same streets you shall wander,
and in the same purlieux you shall roam,
and in the same house you shall grow grey.
[. . .]
There is no ship to take you to other lands, there is no road.
You have so shattered your life here, in this small corner,
that in all the world you have ruined it.

And in 'Ithaca' he sketches another and a nobler tragedy – that of a man who seeks loftily, and finds at the end that the goal has not been worth the effort. Such a man should not lament. He has not failed really.

Ithaca gave you your fair voyage.
Without her you would not have ventured on the way,
but she has no more to give you.
And if you find Ithaca a poor place, she has not mocked you.
You have become so wise, so full of experience,
that you should understand by now what these Ithacas mean.

The above extracts illustrate one of Cavafy's moods – intensely subjective; scenery, cities and legends all re-emerge in terms of the mind. There is another mood in which he stands apart from his subject-matter, and with the detachment of an artist hammers it into shape. The historian comes to the front now, and it is interesting to note how different is his history from an Englishman's. He even looks back upon a different Greece. Athens and Sparta, so drubbed into us at school, are to him two quarrelsome little slave states, ephemeral beside the Hellenistic kingdoms that followed them, just as these are ephemeral beside the secular empire of Constantinople. He reacts against the tyranny of Classicism – Pericles and Aspasia and Themistocles and all those bores.

Alexandria, his birthplace, came into being just when Public School Greece decayed; kings, emperors, patriarchs, have trodden the ground between his office and his flat; his literary ancestor – if he has one – is Callimachus, and his poems bear titles such as 'The Displeasure of the Seleucid', 'In the Month of Athyr', 'Manuel Comnenus', and are prefaced by quotations from Philostratus or Lucian.

Two of these poems shall be quoted in full, to illustrate his method. In the first he adopts the precise, almost mincing style of a chronicle to build up his effect. It is called 'Alexandrian Kings', and deals with an episode of the reign of Cleopatra and Antony.

> An Alexandrian crowd collected
> to see the sons of Cleopatra,
> Cæsarion and his little brothers
> Alexander and Ptolemy, who for the first
> time were brought to the Gymnasium,
> there to be crowned as kings
> amidst a splendid display of troops.
> Alexander they named king
> of Armenia, of Media, and of the Parthians.
> Ptolemy they named king
> of Cilicia, of Syria, and Phœnicia.
> Cæsarion stood a little in front,
> clad in silk the colour of roses,
> with a bunch of hyacinths at his breast.
> His belt was a double line of sapphires and amethysts,
> his sandals were bound with white ribbons
> embroidered with rosy pearls.
> Him they acclaimed more than the small ones.
> Him they named 'King of Kings!'
> But the day was warm and exquisite,
> the sky clear and blue,
> the Gymnasium of Alexandria a triumph of art,
> the courtiers' apparel magnificent,
> Cæsarion full of grace and beauty
> (son of Cleopatra, blood of the Lagidæ!),
> and the Alexandrians ran to see the show
> and grew enthusiastic, and applauded
> in Greek, in Egyptian and some in Hebrew,
> bewitched with the beautiful spectacle,
> though they knew perfectly well how worthless,
> what empty words, were these king-makings.

Such a poem has, even in a translation, a 'distinguished' air. It is the work of an artist who is not interested in facile beauty. In the second example, though its subject-matter is pathetic, Cavafy stands equally aloof. The poem is broken into half-lines; he is spelling out an epitaph on a boy of sixteen who died in the month of Athyr, the ancient Egyptian November, and he would convey the obscurity, the poignancy, that sometimes arise together out of the past, entwined into a single ghost:

> It is hard to read [. . .] on the ancient stone.
> 'Lord Jesus Christ.' [. . .] I make out the word 'Soul.'
> 'In the month of Athyr [. . .] Lucius fell asleep.'
> His age is mentioned [. . .] 'He lived years [. . .] ' –
> The letters KZ show [. . .] that he fell asleep young.
> In the damaged part I see the words [. . .] 'Him [. . .] Alexandrian.'
> Then come three lines [. . .] much mutilated.
> But I can read a few words [. . .] perhaps 'our tears' and 'sorrows.'
> And again: 'Tears' [. . .] and: 'for us his friends mourning.'
> I think Lucius [. . .] was much beloved.
> In the month of Athyr [. . .] Lucius fell asleep

> [. . .]

Such a writer can never be popular. He flies both too slowly and too high. Whether subjective or objective, he is equally remote from the bustle of the moment, he will never compose a Venizelist Hymn. He has the strength (and of course the limitations) of the recluse, who, though not afraid of the world, always stands at a slight angle to it, and, in conversation, he has sometimes devoted a sentence to this subject. Which is better – the world or seclusion? Cavafy, who has tried both, can't say. But so much is certain – either life entails courage, or it ceases to be life.

The God Abandons Antony

> When at the hour of midnight
> an invisible choir is suddenly heard passing
> with exquisite music, with voices –
> Do not lament your fortune that at last subsides,
> your life's work that has failed, your schemes that have proved illusions.
> But like a man prepared, like a brave man,
> bid farewell to her, to Alexandria who is departing.
> Above all, do not delude yourself, do not say that it is a dream,
> that your ear was mistaken.
> Do not condescend to such empty hopes.
> Like a man for long prepared, like a brave man,
> like to the man who was worthy of such a city,
> go to the window firmly,
> and listen with emotion,
> but not with the prayers and complaints of the coward
> (Ah! supreme rapture!)
> listen to the notes, to the exquisite instruments of the mystic choir.
> and bid farewell to her, to Alexandria whom you are losing.

12
KATHERINE MANSFIELD (1888–1923)
FROM REVIEWS FOR THE *ATHENAEUM* 1919;
FROM LETTERS TO JOHN MIDDLETON MURRY 1919

Short-story writer born in Wellington, New Zealand. She completed her education at Queen's College, London, in 1905 and returned to New Zealand in 1906 where she began publishing in the Australian Companion. *In 1908 she returned to England and quickly started publishing in literary journals (A. A. Orage's* The New Age *and John Middleton Murry's* Rhythm *in 1911). She eventually married Murry in 1918. Although a tuberculosis sufferer, she was quite prolific in her output.* In a German Pension *1911;* Prelude *1918;* Bliss and other Stories *1919;* The Garden Party and Other Stories *1920;* Other Stories *1922. Posthumous works include* Poems *1923 (edited by Murry), and* Something Childish and Other Stories *1924. Murry also edited two volumes of her letters. The following extracts are taken from Mansfield's reviews of Joseph Conrad's* Arrow of Gold, *Virginia Woolf's* Night and Day *(Athenaeum,* August and November 1919*) and from two letters to J. M. Murry.*

From 'A Backward Glance', *Athenaeum*, 8 August 1919

As we read Mr. Conrad's latest published book we find ourselves wishing once again that it were a common practice among authors to let us know the year in which a book is begun and ended. This, of course, applies only to those authors whose work does show very marked signs of progression, development and expansion. The others, that large band who will guarantee to produce the same thrill with variations for you once, twice, or thrice yearly do not count

[. . .]

Perhaps your real writer would retort that this was precisely the business of the critic to be able to see, at a glance almost, what place this or that novel filled in the growing chain. Our reply would be that the spirit of the age is against us; it is an uneasy, disintegrating, experimental spirit, and there are moments, as, for instance, the moment after reading the *Arrow of Gold*, when it shakes into wishing that Mr. Conrad had just added those four figures, thereby putting out once and for all that tiny flicker of dismay.

From 'A Ship Comes into the Harbour', *Athenaeum*, 21 November 1919

There is at the present day no form of writing which is more eagerly, more widely discussed than the novel. What is its fate to be? We are told on excellent authority that it is dying; and on equally good authority that only now it begins to live . . . But in all this division and confusion it would seem that opinion is united in declaring this to be an age of experiment. If the novel dies it will be to give way to some new form of expression; if it lives it must accept the fact of a new world.

To us who linger down at the harbour, as it were, watching the new ships being built, the old ones returning, and the many putting out to sea, comes the strange sight of *Night and Day* sailing into port serene and resolute on a deliberate wind. The strangeness lies in her aloofness, her air of quiet perfection, her lack of any sign that she has made a perilous voyage – the absence of any scars. There she lies among the strange shipping – a tribute to civilisation for our admiration and wonder.

It is impossible to refrain from comparing *Night and Day* with the novels of Miss Austen. There are moments, indeed, when one is almost tempted to cry it Miss Austen up-to-date

[. . .]

We had thought that this world was vanished for ever, that it was impossible to find on the great ocean of literature a ship that was unaware of what has been happening. Yet here is *Night and Day* fresh, new, and exquisite, a novel in the tradition of the English novel. In the midst of our admiration it makes us feel old and chill.

From letter to J. M. Murry, 10 November 1919

[. . .] I don't like it, Boge. My private opinion is that it is a lie in the soul. The war has never been: that is what its message is. I don't want (G. forbid!) mobilisation and the violation of Belgium, but the novel can't just leave the war out. There *must* have been a change of heart. It is really fearful to see the 'settling down' of human beings. I feel in the *profoundest* sense that nothing can ever be the same – that, as artists, we are traitors if we feel otherwise: we have to take it into account and find new expressions, new moulds for our thoughts and feelings. Is this exaggeration? What *has* been stands, but Jane Austen could not write *Northanger Abbey* – or if she did, I'd have none of her.

[. . .]

We have to face our war.

From letter to J. M. Murry, 16 November 1919

What is this about the novel? Tell me, thou little eye among the blind. (It's easy to see who my bedfellow has been.) But seriously, Bogey, the more I read the more I feel all these novels will not do. After them I'm a swollen sheep looking up who is not fed. And yet I feel one can lay down no rules. It's not in the least a question of material or style or plot. I can only think in terms like 'a change of heart'. I can't imagine how after the war these men can pick up the old threads as though it had never been. Speaking to *you* I'd say we have died and live again. How can that be the same life? It doesn't mean that life is the less precious or that 'the common things of light and day' are gone. They are not gone, they are intensified, they are illumined. Now we know ourselves for what we are. In a way it's a tragic knowledge: it's as though, even while we live again, we face death. But *through Life*: that's the point. We see death in life as we see death in a flower that is fresh unfolded. Our hymn is to the flower's beauty: we would make that beauty immortal because we *know*. Do you feel like this – or otherwise – or how?

But of course, you don't imagine I mean by this knowledge let-us-eat-and-drink-ism. No, I mean 'deserts of vast eternity'. But the difference between you and me is (perhaps I'm wrong) I couldn't tell anybody *bang out* about those deserts: they are my secret. I might write about a boy eating strawberries or a woman combing her hair on a windy morning, and that is the only way I can ever mention them. But they *must* be there. Nothing less will do. They can advance and retreat, curtsey, caper to the most delicate airs they like, but I am bored to Hell by it all. Virginia, *par exemple.*

13
THOMAS MANN (1875–1955)
FROM *DIARIES* 1918, 1919, 1920

German novelist. Born into a family of wealthy merchants and senators, Mann settled in Munich with his mother, a talented musician of German and Portuguese West Indian origin, at the age of nineteen. His early work Buddenbrooks *(1901) quickly established him as a leading German writer and launched an artistic career which included the association, as reader, with the Munich-based satirical literary magazine* Simplicissimus, *where many of his early short stories were published. The novellas* Tonio Kröger *(1902),* Tristan *(1903) and* Death in Venice *(1913) dealt with the recurrent themes of an embattled artistic sensibility and redemption through art. Mann's distrust of political ideology, coupled in a contradictory way with his militant German patriotism, permeated later works, such as* Meditations of an Unpolitical Man *(1918), as well as his 1915 essay on Frederick the Great. In the 1920s, he turned his attention to a diagnosis of what he saw as Europe's moral and intellectual disintegration, which he rendered in the symbolic and extreme environment of* The Magic Mountain *(1924). The novel won him the Nobel Prize for Literature in 1929. The rise of Nazism confirmed Mann's fears of a fall into barbarism and from 1930 onwards he produced a set of anti-Fascist works, including the attack on Italian Fascism in* Mario and the Magician *(1930) and a number of anti-Hitler broadcasts to Germany (from the* US *where he had settled in 1936), later collected in* Achtung Europa! *and* Deutsche Hörer *(1945). Mann's analysis and critique of the potential for self-destruction of the modern European humanist tradition was expounded in* Doktor Faustus *(1947), which focused again on the life and catastrophic end of a modern artist. The following extracts are taken from four of Mann's diary entries for 1919 and 1920, in Richard and Clara Winston's 1983 translation.*

Thursday, April 17 1919

In bed yesterday, continued with Sologub. Again neither mail nor newspapers today. The trams also do not seem to be running, but now the telephone is functioning. No news can be obtained. My attitude toward affairs very uncertain, but my personal wishes are for the 'Whites' to march in and for the restoration of the bourgeois order – Bertram said that authorized looting was carried out on Leopoldstrasse yesterday with the aid of furniture vans. Alois Ludwig reports that he had been denounced, that the soldiers who came to search knew all the places in the house where stores of food were hidden, and confiscated them. Confiscation of linens and clothing also in the offing, he maintains. Today safe-deposit boxes in banks are to be 'examined'. Key-holders are supposed to report for that purpose – Even if there is to be a 'White' victory, grave disorders are to be feared, looting by the retreating Reds, etc.

Meanwhile I am pondering *The Magic Mountain*, for now at last the time is right for resuming work on it. During the war it was too early; I had to stop. The war first had to clarify itself as the beginning of the revolution, and not only did it have to end, but the end had to become recognizable as only a pseudo-end. The conflict between reaction (affinity for the Middle Ages) and humanistic rationalism is by now entirely historical, prewar. The synthesis appears to lie in the (communist) future. What is new consists essentially of a new conception of man as a mind-body entity (abolition of the Christian dualism of soul and body, church and state, life and death) – a conception that already existed in the prewar period, incidentally. It is a matter of perspective vis-à-vis the renewal of the Christian *civitas Dei* in humanist guise, a human City of God somehow imbued with transcendence, that is to say oriented toward the mind-body unity. Both Pastor Bunge and Settembrini are equally right and wrong in their viewpoints. Sending Hans Castorp into the war thus means sending him into the beginning of the struggle for the new after he has thoroughly savored its components. Christianity and paganism, in the course of his education.

Hülsen reports that Dachau is in the hands of the Reds. He says there are enough provisions in the city to last for several weeks, because the confiscations brought in a great deal. Henceforth rationing will be handled in the Budapest fashion, with the propertied classes receiving a minimum. Neat. Student Toller is reported to hold the high command on the Red front. Delicious. – The troops driven out of Dachau were not those of Epp, but parts of the Munich garrison loyal to the government that had withdrawn to the town. Officers and 700 enlisted men have been captured. But word has it that strong forces are supposed to be stationed near Pfaffenhofen. In the city, placards have been posted that partly defend the Communist leaders against all and sundry slanders, and partly fulminate against the 'parasitic bourgeoisie'. Wood and coal are being distributed to proletarians only. Airplanes have dropped leaflets announcing a ban by the Bamberg government on all participation in the revolutionary tribunal. – Went for a walk at noon. Before luncheon, telephoned Martens and talked about the situation. Read some in the *Mittelalterliche Weltanschauung* and slept very well in the afternoon. On my walk, after witnessing a sensually exciting spectacle, thoughts about the motif of forbidden love in *The Magic Mountain*.

[. . .]

Wednesday, July 2 (afternoon) 1919

It impresses me deeply and mysteriously to see how great a role the problem of time plays in Spengler's philosophy of history. This has preoccupied me as a fundamental motif of *The Magic Mountain* since 1912 or 1913, when Spengler was still at work on his book. I added details such as the special physical and psychic relationship between grandson and grandfather just before I began reading the *Decline*, prompted by the book's reputation, but also by a foreboding that it would be somehow pertinent. The experience once again confirms what I take to be my unusual sensitivity, linking my solitude sympathetically with all the more profound thoughts and insights of the times. The fact that around 1912 the problem of 'time' became acute for philosophers and dreamers and entered into their creative work may be related to the historical upheavals of these present days, at that time still deep underground. – I am less and less inclined to reject the possibility that Spengler's book may mark an epoch in my life in somewhat the same way that I was affected twenty years ago by *The World as Will and Idea*. I cannot always follow it, and don't worry about that; it does not prevent me from eagerly absorbing the a priori, familiar essence of the book.

[. . .]

Wednesday, March 3 1920

This afternoon and evening read various interesting and stimulating things: in the *Tage-Buch* a letter of Dehmel's to the pacifists, excellent highly gratifying; in the *Neue Merkur* a very good article by Lion on Germany and France. A harrowing novella by Döblin, *Predigt und Judenverbrennung*, compared to which the torture scenes in *Ulenspiegel* seem utterly innocuous. Also an article on the religious element in modern art, obviously by a Catholic churchman; discriminating objective, good. Also an epistemological critique of Einstein's theory (which, incidentally, has been analyzed by Flammarion and largely rejected by him): it deals again in my conception of *The Magic Mountain*, just as I had anticipated the political antitheses leading up to the war. My satisfaction at my seismographic sensitivity in more than one respect in those days is diminished, even nullified, by sorrow in the recognition, constantly absolutely confirmed, that this novel as well as *The Confidence Man* should have been finished in 1914. Its merits have been vitiated by the abnormally rapid course of events [. . .]

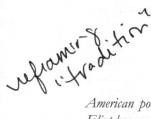

14
T. S. (THOMAS STEARNS) ELIOT (1888–1965)
FROM 'TRADITION AND THE INDIVIDUAL TALENT' 1919;
FROM '*ULYSSES*, ORDER, AND MYTH' 1923

American poet, dramatist and critic. Born in Missouri and educated at Harvard and Oxford, Eliot became a British citizen in 1927. After working as a teacher in London, he worked for the Foreign Office Information Bureau, Lloyds Bank, London (1917–25). He became editor, and later director of Faber and Gwyer (1925–28), and Faber and Faber publishers (1929–65). He was also assistant editor of The Egoist *(1917–19) and founding editor of* The Criterion *(1922–39). Early examples of his poetry appeared in Wyndham Lewis's* Blast, *and his first volume,* Prufrock and Other Observations, *was published in 1917. His most important publication was* The Waste Land *(1922), dedicated to Ezra Pound ('il miglior fabro') who edited and shaped the poem.* Ash-Wednesday *(1930) marks Eliot's conversion to Anglo-Catholicism, and* Four Quartets *(1935–42) is considered the apex of his poetic career. The following extracts are taken from one of his most influential theoretical essays, first published in 1919, and from his famous formulation of the significance of James Joyce's method, dating from 1923. [See IIIb 10]*

I.

In English writing we seldom speak of tradition, though we occasionally apply its name in deploring its absence. We cannot refer to 'the tradition' or to 'a tradition'; at most, we employ the adjective in saying that the poetry of So-and-so is 'traditional' or even 'too traditional'. Seldom, perhaps, does the word appear except in a phrase of censure. If otherwise, it is vaguely approbative, with the implication, as to the work approved, of some pleasing archaeological reconstruction. You can hardly make the word agreeable to English ears without this comfortable reference to the reassuring science of archaeology.

Certainly the word is not likely to appear in our appreciations of living or dead writers. Every nation, every race, has not only its own creative, but its own critical turn of mind; and is even more oblivious of the shortcomings and limitations of its critical habits than of those of its creative genius. We know, or think we know, from the enormous mass of critical writing that has appeared in the French language the critical method or habit of the French; we only conclude (we are such unconscious people) that the French are 'more critical' than we, and sometimes even plume ourselves a little with the fact, as if the French were the less spontaneous. Perhaps they are; but we might remind ourselves that criticism is as inevitable as breathing, and that we should be none the worse for articulating what passes in our minds when we read a book and feel an emotion about it, for criticizing our own minds in their work of criticism. One of the facts that might come to light in this process is our tendency to insist, when we praise a poet, upon those aspects of his work in which he least resembles *innovation* anyone else. In these aspects or parts of his work we pretend to find what is individual, what is the peculiar essence of the man. We dwell with satisfaction upon the poet's difference from his predecessors, especially his immediate predecessors; we endeavour to find something that can be isolated in order to be enjoyed. Whereas if we approach a poet without this prejudice we shall often find that not only the best, but the most individual parts of his work may be those in which the dead poets, his ancestors, assert their immortality most vigorously. And I do not mean the impressionable period of adolescence, but the period of full maturity.

Yet if the only form of tradition, of handing down, consisted in following the ways of the immediate generation before us in a blind or timid adherence to its successes, 'tradition' should positively be discouraged. We have seen many such simple currents soon lost in the sand; and novelty is better than repetition. Tradition is a matter of much wider significance. It cannot be inherited, and if you want it you must obtain it by great labour. It involves, in the first place, the historical sense, which we may call nearly *historical* indispensable to anyone who would continue to be a poet beyond his twenty-fifth year; and the historical sense involves a perception, not only of the pastness of the past, but of its presence; the historical sense compels a man to write not merely with his own generation in his bones, but with a feeling that the whole of the literature of Europe from Homer and within it the whole of the literature of his own country has a simultaneous existence and composes a simultaneous order. This historical sense, which is a sense of the timeless as well as of the temporal and of the timeless and of the temporal together, is what makes a writer traditional. And it is at the same time what makes a writer most acutely conscious of his place in time, of his own contemporaneity.

No poet, no artist of any art, has his complete meaning alone. His significance, his appreciation is the appreciation of his relation to the dead poets and artists. You cannot value him alone; you must set him, for contrast and comparison, among the

affect
objective correlative

(margin handwritten note: adjustments for new)

dead. I mean this as a principle of aesthetic, not merely historical, criticism. The necessity that he shall conform, that he shall cohere, is not onesided; what happens when a new work of art is created is something that happens simultaneously to all the works of art which preceded it. The existing monuments form an ideal order among themselves, which is modified by the introduction of the new (the really new) work of art among them. The existing order is complete before the new work arrives; for order to persist after the supervention of novelty, the *whole* existing order must be, if ever so slightly, altered; and so the relations, proportions, values of each work of art toward the whole are readjusted; and this is conformity between the old and the new. Whoever has approved this idea of order, of the form of European, of English literature will not find it preposterous that the past should be altered by the present as much as the present is directed by the past. And the poet who is aware of this will be aware of great difficulties and responsibilities.

In a peculiar sense he will be aware also that he must inevitably be judged by the standards of the past. I say judged, not amputated, by them; not judged to be as good as, or worse or better than, the dead; and certainly not judged by the canons of dead critics. It is a judgment, a comparison, in which two things are measured by each other. To conform merely would be for the new work not really to conform at all; it would not be new, and would therefore not be a work of art. And we do not quite say that the new is more valuable because it fits in; but its fitting in is a test of its value – a test, it is true, which can only be slowly and cautiously applied, for we are none of us infallible judges of conformity. We say: it appears to conform, and is perhaps individual, or it appears individual, and may conform; but we are hardly likely to find that it is one and not the other.

To proceed to a more intelligible exposition of the relation of the poet to the past: he can neither take the past as a lump, an indiscriminate bolus, nor can he form himself wholly on one or two private admirations, nor can he form himself wholly upon one preferred period. The first course is inadmissible, the second is an important experience of youth, and the third is a pleasant and highly desirable supplement. The poet must be very conscious of the main current, which does not at all flow invariably through the most distinguished reputations. He must be quite aware of the obvious fact that art never improves, but that the material of art is never quite the same. He must be aware that the mind of Europe – the mind of his own country – a mind which he learns in time to be much more important than his own private mind – is a mind which changes, and that this change is a development which abandons nothing *en route*, which does not superannuate either Shakespeare, or Homer, or the rock drawing of the Magdalenian draughtsmen. That this development, refinement perhaps, complication certainly, is not, from the point of view of the artist, any improvement. Perhaps not even an improvement from the point of view of the psychologist or not to the extent which we imagine; perhaps only in the end based upon a complication in economics and machinery. But the difference between the present and the past is that the conscious present is an awareness of the past in a way and to an extent which the past's awareness of itself cannot show.

Someone said: 'The dead writers are remote from us because we *know* so much more than they did'. Precisely, and they are that which we know.

I am alive to a usual objection to what is clearly part of my programme for the *métier* of poetry. The objection is that the doctrine requires a ridiculous amount of erudition (pedantry), a claim which can be rejected by appeal to the lives of poets in any pantheon. It will even be affirmed that much learning deadens or perverts poetic sensibility. While, however, we persist in believing that a poet ought to know as much as will not encroach upon his necessary receptivity and necessary laziness, it is not desirable to confine knowledge to whatever can be put into a useful shape for examinations, drawing-rooms, or the still more pretentious modes of publicity. Some can absorb knowledge, the more tardy must sweat for it. Shakespeare acquired more essential history from Plutarch than most men could from the whole British Museum. What is to be insisted upon is that the poet must develop or procure the consciousness of the past and that he should continue to develop this consciousness throughout his career.

What happens is a continual surrender of himself as he is at the moment to something which is more valuable. The progress of an artist is a continual self-sacrifice, a continual extinction of personality. Woolf

There remains to define this process of depersonalization and its relation to the sense of tradition. It is in this depersonalization that art may be said to approach the condition of science. I therefore invite you to consider, as a suggestive analogy, the action which takes place when a bit of finely filiated platinum is introduced into a chamber containing oxygen and sulphur dioxide.

II.

Honest criticism and sensitive appreciation is directed not upon the poet but upon the poetry. If we attend to the confused cries of the newspaper critics and the susurrus of popular repetition that follows, we shall hear the names of poets in great numbers; if we seek not Blue-book knowledge but the enjoyment of poetry, and ask for a poem, we shall seldom find it. I have tried to point out the importance of the relation of the poem to other poems by other authors, and suggested the conception of poetry as a living whole of all the poetry that has ever been written. The other aspect of this Impersonal theory of poetry is the relation of the poem to its author. And I hinted, by an analogy, that the mind of the mature poet differs from that of the immature one not precisely in my valuation of 'personality', not being necessarily more interesting, or having 'more to say', but rather by being a more finely perfected medium in which special, or very varied, feelings are at liberty to enter into new combinations.

The analogy was that of the catalyst. When the two gases previously mentioned are mixed in the presence of a filament of platinum, they form sulphurous acid. This combination takes place only if the platinum is present; nevertheless the newly formed acid contains no trace of platinum, and the platinum itself is apparently unaffected: has remained inert, neutral, and unchanged. The mind of the poet is the shred of platinum. It may partly or exclusively operate upon the experience of the man himself; but, the more perfect the artist, the more completely separate in him will be the man who suffers and the mind which creates; the more perfectly will the mind digest and transmute the passions which are its material.

The experience, you will notice, the elements which enter the presence of the transforming catalyst, are of two kinds: emotions and feelings. The effect of a work of art upon the person who enjoys it is an experience different in kind from any experience not of art. It may be formed out of one emotion, or may be a combination of several; and various feelings, inhering for the writer in particular words or phrases or images, maybe added to compose the final result. Or great poetry maybe made without the direct use of any emotion whatever: composed out of feelings solely.

[. . .]

The poet's mind is in fact a receptacle for seizing and storing up numberless feelings, phrases, images, which remain there until all the particles which can unite to form a new compound are present together.

[. . .]

The point of view which I am struggling to attack is perhaps related to the meta-physical theory of the substantial unity of the soul: for my meaning is, that the poet has, not a 'personality' to express, but a particular medium, which is only a medium and not a personality, in which impressions and experiences combine in peculiar and unexpected ways. Impressions and experiences which are important for the man may take no place in the poetry, and those which become important in the poetry may play quite a negligible part in the man, the personality.

[. . .]

It is not in his personal emotions, the emotions provoked by particular events in his life, that the poet is in any way remarkable or interesting. His particular emotions may be simple, or crude, or flat. The emotion in his poetry will be a very complex thing, but not with the complexity of the emotions of people who have very complex or unusual emotions in life. One error, in fact, of eccentricity in poetry is to seek for new human emotions to express; and in this search for novelty in the wrong place it discovers the perverse. The business of the poet is not to find new emotions, but to use the ordinary ones and, in working them up into poetry, to express feelings which are not in actual emotions at all. And emotions which he has never experienced will serve his turn as well as those familiar to him. Consequently, we must believe that 'emotion recollected in tranquillity' is an inexact formula. For it is neither emotion, nor recollection, nor, without distortion of meaning, tranquillity. It is a concentration, and a new thing resulting from the concentration, of a very great number of experiences which to the practical and active person would not seem to be experiences at all; it is a concentration which does not happen consciously or of deliberation. These experiences are not 'recollected', and they finally unite in an atmosphere which is 'tranquil' only in that it is a passive attending upon the event. Of course this is not quite the whole story. There is a great deal, in the writing of poetry, which must be conscious and deliberate. In fact, the bad poet is usually unconscious where he ought to be conscious, and conscious where he ought to be unconscious. Both errors tend to make him 'personal'. Poetry is not a turning loose of emotion, but an escape from emotion; it is not the expression of personality, but an escape from personality. But, of course, only those who have personality and emotions know what it means to want to escape from these things.

II.

ὁ δὲ νοῦς ἴσως θειότερόν τι καὶ ἀπαθές ἐστιν.

This essay proposes to halt at the frontier of metaphysics or mysticism, and confine itself to such practical conclusions as can be applied by the responsible person interested in poetry. To divert interest from the poet to the poetry is a laudable aim: for it would conduce to a juster estimation of actual poetry, good and bad. There are many people who appreciate the expression of sincere emotion in verse, and there is a smaller number of people who can appreciate technical excellence. But very few know when there is an expression of *significant* emotion, emotion which has its life in the poem and not in the history of the poet. The emotion of art is impersonal. And the poet cannot reach this impersonality without surrendering himself wholly to the work to be done. And he is not likely to know what is to be done unless he lives in what is not merely the present, but the present moment of the past, unless he is conscious, not of what is dead, but of what is already living. *new critical*

'Ulysses, Order, and Myth'

Mr. Joyce's book has been out long enough for no more general expression of praise, or expostulation with its detractors, to be necessary; and it has not been out long enough for any attempt at a complete measurement of its place and significance to be possible. All that one can usefully do at this time, and it is a great deal to do, for such a book, is to elucidate any aspect of the book – and the number of aspects is indefinite – which has not yet been fixed. I hold this book to be the most important expression which the present age has found; it is a book to which we are all indebted, and from which none of us can escape. These are postulates for anything that I have to say about it, and I have no wish to waste the reader's time by elaborating my eulogies; it has given me all the surprise, delight, and terror that I can require, and I will leave it at that.

Among all the criticisms I have seen of the book, I have seen nothing – unless we except, in its way, M. Valéry Larbaud's valuable paper which is rather an Introduction than a criticism – which seemed to me to appreciate the significance of the method employed – the parallel to the *Odyssey*, and the use of appropriate styles and symbols to each division. Yet one might expect this to be the first peculiarity to attract attention; but it has been treated as an amusing dodge, or scaffolding erected by the author for the purpose of disposing his realistic tale, of no interest in the completed structure. The criticism which Mr. Aldington directed upon *Ulysses* several years ago seems to me to fail by this oversight – but, as Mr. Aldington wrote before the complete work had appeared, fails more honourably than the attempts of those who had the whole book before them. Mr. Aldington treated Mr. Joyce as a prophet of chaos; and wailed at the flood of Dadaism which his prescient eye saw bursting forth at the tap of the magician's rod. Of course, the influence which Mr. Joyce's book may have is from my point of view an irrelevance. A very great book may have a very bad influence indeed; and a mediocre book may be in the event most salutary. The next generation is responsible for its own soul; a man of genius is responsible to his peers, not to a studio full of uneducated and undisciplined cox-combs.

[...] *tradition*

I think that Mr. Aldington and I are more or less agreed as to what we want in principle, and agreed to call it classicism. It is because of this agreement that I have chosen Mr. Aldington to attack on the present issue. We are agreed as to what we want, but not as to how to get it, or as to what contemporary writing exhibits a tendency in that direction. We agree, I hope, that 'classicism' is not an alternative to 'romanticism', as of political parties, Conservative and Liberal, Republican and Democrat, on a 'turn-the-rascals-out' platform. It is a goal toward which all good literature strives, so far as it is good, according to the possibilities of its place and time. One can be 'classical', in a sense, by turning away from nine-tenths of the material which lies at hand and selecting only mummified stuff from a museum – like some contemporary writers, about whom one could say some nasty things in this connection, if it were worth while (Mr. Aldington is not one of them). Or one can be classical in tendency by doing the best one can with the material at hand. The confusion springs from the fact that the term is applied to literature and to the whole complex of interests and modes of behaviour and society of which literature is a part; and it has not the same bearing in both applications. It is much easier to be a classicist in literary criticism than in creative art – because in criticism you are responsible only for what you want, and in creation you are responsible for what you can do with material which you must simply accept. And in this material I include the emotions and feelings of the writer himself, which, for that writer, are simply material which he must accept – not virtues to be enlarged or vices to be diminished. The question, then, about Mr. Joyce, is: how much living material does he deal with, and how does he deal with it: deal with, not as a legislator or exhorter, but as an artist?

It is here that Mr. Joyce's parallel use of the *Odyssey* has a great importance. It has the importance of a scientific discovery. No one else has built a novel upon such a foundation before: it has never before been necessary. I am not begging the question in calling *Ulysses* a 'novel'; and if you call it an epic it will not matter. If it is not a novel, that is simply because the novel is a form which will no longer serve; it is because the novel, instead of being a form, was simply the expression of an age which had not sufficiently lost all form to feel the need of something stricter. Mr. Joyce has written one novel – the *Portrait*; Mr. Wyndham Lewis has written one novel – *Tarr*. I do not suppose that either of them will ever write another 'novel'. The novel ended with Flaubert and with James. It is, I think, because Mr. Joyce and Mr. Lewis, being 'in advance' of their time, felt a conscious or probably unconscious dissatisfaction with the form, that their novels are more formless than those of a dozen clever writers who are unaware of its obsolescence.

In using the myth, in manipulating a continuous parallel between contemporaneity and antiquity, Mr. Joyce is pursuing a method which others must pursue after him.

They will not be imitators, any more than the scientist who uses the discoveries of an Einstein in pursuing his own, independent, further investigations. It is simply a way of controlling, of ordering, of giving a shape and a significance to the immense panorama of futility and anarchy which is contemporary history. It is a method already adumbrated by Mr. Yeats, and of the need for which I believe Mr. Yeats to have been the first contemporary to be conscious. It is a method for which the horoscope is auspicious. Psychology (such as it is, and whether our reaction to it be comic or serious), ethnology, and *The Golden Bough* have concurred to make possible what was impossible even a few years ago. Instead of narrative method, we may now use the mythical method. It is, I seriously believe, a step toward making the modern world possible for art, toward that order and form which Mr. Aldington so earnestly desires. And only those who have won their own discipline in secret and without aid, in a world which offers very little assistance to that end, can be of any use in furthering this advance.

15
EZRA POUND (1885–1972)
FROM 'A RETROSPECT' 1918; FROM PREFACE TO RÉMY DE GOURMONT'S
THE NATURAL PHILOSOPHY OF LOVE 1926

American poet, editor and energiser. A student of Romance languages, Pound came to Europe in 1908, and was in London 1908–21, Paris 1921–24, and Rapallo, Italy 1924–46. He was a regular reviewer for The New Age *from 1911, and was an editor on many journals and little magazines, including* Poetry *(1912–19),* The New Freewoman – *later* The Egoist – *(1913–14),* Blast *(which he founded with Wyndham Lewis) and* Little Review *(1917–19). He was Paris correspondent for* The Dial *(1920–23), founding editor of* The Exile *(1927–28), and contributor to* Il Mare *(1932–40) and* New English Weekly *(1932–35). Pound was influential in the careers of Eliot, Yeats, William Carlos Williams and many others, as well as a central figure in Imagism. Pound also promoted 'social credit theories' from the late 1920s, met Mussolini in 1933 and made pro-Fascist broadcasts over Rome Radio from 1940. He was arrested and jailed as a traitor by the* US Army *in 1945. While in prison in Pisa he wrote some of the most important sections of his epic work,* Cantos, *one of the major achievements in twentieth-century poetry. He was found unfit to stand trial for treason, and was committed to St Elizabeth's Hospital, Washington (1946–58), where he was visited by many literary admirers. Reproduced below are extracts from 'A Retrospect' (a group of early essays and notes which appeared under this title in* Pavannes and Divisions *in 1918, and can be found in* Literary Essays of Ezra Pound) *and from the 'Preface' to* The Natural Philosophy of Love *(1926), his translation of Rémy de Gourmont's* Physique de l'amour *from 1904. An ardent admirer of the work of the French scholar, essayist and novelist, Pound expounds here his own views on the correlation between gender and creativity. [See IIIb 11]*

A retrospect

There has been so much scribbling about a new fashion in poetry, that I may perhaps be pardoned this brief recapitulation and retrospect.

In the spring or early summer of 1912, 'H. D.', Richard Aldington and myself decided that we were agreed upon the three principles following:

1. Direct treatment of the 'thing' whether subjective or objective.
2. To use absolutely no word that does not contribute to the presentation.
3. As regarding rhythm: to compose in the sequence of the musical phrase, not in sequence of a metronome.

Upon many points of taste and of predilection we differed, but agreeing upon these three positions we thought we had as much right to a group name, at least as much right, as a number of French 'schools' proclaimed by Mr. Flint in the August number of Harold Monro's magazine for 1911.

This school has since been 'joined' or 'followed' by numerous people who, whatever their merits, do not show any signs of agreeing with the second specification. Indeed *vers libre* has become as prolix and as verbose as any of the flaccid varieties that preceded it. It has brought faults of its own. The actual language and phrasing is often as bad as that of our elders without even the excuse that the words are shovelled in to fill a metric pattern or to complete the noise of a rhyme-sound. Whether or no the phrases followed by the followers are musical must be left to the reader's decision. At times I can find a marked metre in 'vers libres', as stale and hackneyed as any pseudo-Swinburnian, at times the writers seem to follow no musical structure whatever. But it is, on the whole, good that the field should be ploughed. Perhaps a few good poems have come from the new method, and if so it is justified.

Criticism is not a circumscription or a set of prohibitions. It provides fixed points of departure. It may startle a dull reader into alertness. That little of it which is good is mostly in stray phrases; or if it be an older artist helping a younger it is in great measure but rules of thumb, cautions gained by experience.

I set together a few phrases on practical working about the time the first remarks on imagisme were published. The first use of the word 'Imagiste' was in my note to T. E. Hulme's five poems, printed at the end of my 'Ripostes' in the autumn of 1912. I reprint my cautions from *Poetry* for March, 1913.

A few don'ts

An 'Image' is that which presents an intellectual and emotional complex in an instant of time. I use the term 'complex' rather in the technical sense employed by the newer psychologists, such as Hart, though we might not agree absolutely in our application.

It is the presentation of such a 'complex' instantaneously which gives that sense of sudden liberation; that sense of freedom from time limits and space limits; that sense of sudden growth, which we experience in the presence of the greatest works of art.

It is better to present one Image in a lifetime than to produce voluminous works.

All this, however, some may consider open to debate. The immediate necessity is to tabulate A LIST OF DON'TS for those beginning to write verses. I can not put all of them into Mosaic negative.

To begin with, consider the three propositions (demanding direct treatment, economy of words, and the sequence of the musical phrase), not as dogma – never consider anything as dogma – but as the result of long contemplation, which, even if it is some one else's contemplation, may be worth consideration.

Pay no attention to the criticism of men who have never themselves written a notable work. Consider the discrepancies between the actual writing of the Greek poets and dramatists, and the theories of the Graeco Roman grammarians, concocted to explain their metres.

Language

Use no superfluous word, no adjective which does not reveal something.

Don't use such an expression as 'dim lands *of peace*'. It dulls the image. It mixes an abstraction with the concrete. It comes from the writer's not realizing that the natural object is always the *adequate* symbol.

Go in fear of abstractions. Do not retell in mediocre verse what has already been done in good prose. Don't think any intelligent person is going to be deceived when you try to shirk all the difficulties of the unspeakably difficult art of good prose by chopping your composition into line lengths.

What the expert is tired of today the public will be tired of tomorrow.

Don't imagine that the art of poetry is any simpler than the art of music, or that you can please the expert before you have spent at least as much effort on the art of verse as the average piano teacher spends on the art of music.

Be influenced by as many great artists as you can, but have the decency either to acknowledge the debt outright, or to try to conceal it.

Don't allow 'influence' to mean merely that you mop up the particular decorative vocabulary of some one or two poets whom you happen to admire. A Turkish war correspondent was recently caught red-handed babbling in his despatches of 'dove-grey' hills, or else it was 'pearl-pale', I can not remember.

Use either no ornament or good ornament.

Rhythm and rhyme

Let the candidate fill his mind with the finest cadences he can discover, preferably in a foreign language, so that the meaning of the words may be less likely to divert his attention from the movement; e.g. Saxon charms, Hebridean Folk Songs, the verse of Dante, and the lyrics of Shakespeare – if he can dissociate the vocabulary from the cadence. Let him dissect the lyrics of Goethe coldly into their component sound values, syllables long and short, stressed and unstressed, into vowels and consonants.

It is not necessary that a poem should rely on its music, but if it does rely on its music that music must be such as will delight the expert.

Let the neophyte know assonance and alliteration, rhyme immediate and delayed, simple and polyphonic, as a musician would expect to know harmony and counterpoint and all the minutiae of his craft. No time is too great to give to these matters or to any one of them, even if the artist seldom have need of them.

Don't imagine that a thing will 'go' in verse just because it's too dull to go in prose.

Don't be 'viewy' – leave that to the writers of pretty little philosophic essays. Don't be descriptive; remember that the painter can describe a landscape much better than you can, and that he has to know a deal more about it.

When Shakespeare talks of the 'Dawn in russet mantle clad' he presents something which the painter does not present. There is in this line of his nothing that one can call description; he presents.

Consider the way of the scientists rather than the way of an advertising agent for a new soap.

The scientist does not expect to be acclaimed as a great scientist until he has *discovered* something. He begins by learning what has been discovered already. He goes from that point onward. He does not bank on being a charming fellow personally. He does not expect his friends to applaud the results of his freshman class work. Freshmen in poetry are unfortunately not confined to a definite and recognizable class room. They are 'all over the shop'. Is it any wonder 'the public is indifferent to poetry'?

Don't chop your stuff into separate *iambs*. Don't make each line stop dead at the end, and then begin every next line with a heave. Let the beginning of the next line catch the rise of the rhythm wave, unless you want a definite longish pause.

In short, behave as a musician, a good musician, when dealing with that phase of your art which has exact parallels in music. The same laws govern, and you are bound by no others.

Naturally, your rhythmic structure should not destroy the shape of your words, or their natural sound, or their meaning. It is improbable that, at the start, you will be able to get a rhythm-structure strong enough to affect them very much, though you may fall a victim to all sorts of false stopping due to line ends and cæsurae.

The Musician can rely on pitch and the volume of the orchestra. You can not. The term harmony is misapplied in poetry; it refers to simultaneous sounds of different pitch. There is, however, in the best verse a sort of residue of sound which remains in the ear of the hearer and acts more or less as an organ-base.

A rhyme must have in it some slight element of surprise if it is to give pleasure; it need not be bizarre or curious, but it must be well used if used at all.

[. . .]

That part of your poetry which strikes upon the imaginative eye of the reader will lose nothing by translation into a foreign tongue; that which appeals to the ear can reach only those who take it in the original.

Consider the definiteness of Dante's presentation, as compared with Milton's rhetoric. Read as much of Wordsworth as does not seem too unutterably dull.

If you want the gist of the matter go to Sappho, Catullus, Villon, Heine when he is in the vein, Gautier when he is not too frigid; or, if you have not the tongues, seek out the leisurely Chaucer. Good prose will do you no harm, and there is good discipline to be had by trying to write it.

Translation is likewise good training, if you find that your original matter 'wobbles' when you try to rewrite it. The meaning of the poem to be translated can not 'wobble'.

If you are using a symmetrical form, don't put in what you want to say and then fill up the remaining vacuums with slush.

Don't mess up the perception of one sense by trying to define it in terms of another.

This is usually only the result of being too lazy to find the exact word. To this clause there are possibly exceptions.

The first three simple prescriptions will throw out nine-tenths of all the bad poetry now accepted as standard and classic; and will prevent you from many a crime of production.

[. . .]

Credo – beliefs

Rhythm. – I believe in an 'absolute rhythm', a rhythm, that is, in poetry which corresponds exactly to the emotion or shade of emotion to be expressed. A man's rhythm must be interpretative, it will be, therefore, in the end, his own, uncounterfeiting, uncounterfeitable.

Symbols. – I believe that the proper and perfect symbol is the natural object, that if a man use 'symbols' he must so use them that their symbolic function does not obtrude; so that *a* sense, and the poetic quality of the passage, is not lost to those who do not understand the symbol as such, to whom, for instance, a hawk is a hawk.

Technique. – I believe in technique as the test of a man's sincerity; in law when it is ascertainable; in the trampling down of every convention that impedes or obscures the determination of the law, or the precise rendering of the impulse.

Form. – I think there is a 'fluid' as well as a 'solid' content, that some poems may have form as a tree has form, some as water poured into a vase. That most symmetrical forms have certain uses. That a vast number of subjects cannot be precisely, and therefore not properly rendered in symmetrical forms.

'Thinking that alone worthy wherein the whole art is employed.' I think the artist should master all known forms and systems of metric, and I have with some persistence set about doing this, searching particularly into those periods wherein the systems came to birth or attained their maturity. It has been complained, with some justice, that I dump my note-books on the public. I think that only after a long struggle will poetry attain such a degree of development, or, if you will, modernity, that it will vitally concern people who are accustomed, in prose, to Henry James and Anatole France, in music to Debussy. I am constantly contending that it took two centuries of Provence and one of Tuscany to develop the media of Dante's masterwork, that it took the latinists of the Renaissance, and the Pleiade, and his own age of painted speech to prepare Shakespeare his tools. It is tremendously important that great poetry be written, it makes no jot of difference who writes it. The experimental demonstrations of one man may save the time of many – hence my furore over Arnaut Daniel – if a man's experiments try out one new rime, or dispense conclusively with one iota of currently accepted nonsense, he is merely playing fair with his colleagues when he chalks up his result.

[. . .]

If a certain thing was said once for all in Atlantis or Arcadia, in 450 Before Christ or in 1290 after, it is not for us moderns to go saying it over, or to go obscuring the memory of the dead by saying the same thing with less skill and less conviction.

My pawing over the ancients and semi-ancients has been one struggle to find out what has been done, once for all, better than it can ever be done again, and to find out what remains for us to do, and plenty does remain, for if we still feel the same emotions as those which launched the thousand ships, it is quite certain that we come on these feelings differently, through different nuances, by different intellectual gradations. Each age has its own abounding gifts yet only some ages transmute them into matter of duration. No good poetry is ever written in a manner twenty years old, for to write in such a manner shows conclusively that the writer thinks from books, convention and *cliché*, and not from life, yet a man feeling the divorce of life and his art may naturally try to resurrect a forgotten mode if he finds in that mode some leaven, or if he think he sees in it some element lacking in contemporary art which might unite that art again to its sustenance, life.

In the art of Daniel and Cavalcanti, I have seen that precision which I miss in the Victorians, that explicit rendering, be it of external nature, or of emotion. Their testimony is of the eyewitness, their symptoms are first hand.

As for the nineteenth century, with all respect to its achievements, I think we shall look back upon it as a rather blurry, messy sort of a period, a rather sentimentalistic, mannerish sort of a period. I say this without any self-righteousness, with no self-satisfaction.

As for there being a 'movement' or my being of it, the conception of poetry as a 'pure art' in the sense in which I use the term, revived with Swinburne. From the puritanical revolt to Swinburne, poetry had been merely the vehicle – yes, definitely, Arthur Symon's scruples and feelings about the word not withholding – the ox-cart and post-chaise for transmitting thoughts poetic or otherwise. And perhaps the 'great Victorians', though it is doubtful, and assuredly the 'nineties' continued the development of the art, confining their improvements, however, chiefly to sound and to refinements of manner.

Mr. Yeats has once and for all stripped English poetry of its perdamnable rhetoric. He has boiled away all that is not poetic – and a good deal that is. He has become a classic in his own lifetime and *nel mezzo del cammin*. He has made our poetic idiom a thing pliable, a speech without inversions.

[. . .]

As to Twentieth century poetry, and the poetry which I expect to see written during the next decade or so, it will, I think, move against poppy-cock, it will be harder and saner, it will be what Mr. Hewlett calls 'nearer the bone'. It will be as much like granite as it can be, its force will lie in its truth, its interpretative power (of course, poetic force does always rest there); I mean it will not try to seem forcible by rhetorical din, and luxurious riot. We will have fewer painted adjectives impeding the shock and stroke of it. At least for myself, I want it so, austere, direct, free from emotional slither.

What is there now, in 1917, to be added?

I think the desire for vers libre is due to the sense of quantity reasserting itself after years of starvation. But I doubt if we can take over, for English, the rules of quantity laid down for Greek and Latin, mostly by Latin grammarians.

I think one should write vers libre only when one 'must', that is to say, only when the 'thing' builds up a rhythm more beautiful than that of set metres, or more real, more a part of the emotion of the 'thing', more germane, intimate, interpretative than the measure of regular accentual verse; a rhythm which discontents one with set iambic or set anapaestic.

Eliot has said the thing very well when he said, 'No *vers is libre* for the man who wants to do a good job.'

[. . .]

Only emotion endures

'Only emotion endures.' Surely it is better for me to name over the few beautiful poems that still ring in my head than for me to search my flat for back numbers of periodicals and rearrange all that I have said about friendly and hostile writers.

The first twelve lines of Pádraic Colum's 'Drover'; his 'O Woman shapely as a swan, on your account I shall not die'; Joyce's 'I hear an army'; the lines of Yeats that ring in my head and in the heads of all young men of my time who care for poetry: Braseal and the Fisherman, 'The fire that stirs about her when she stirs'; the later lines of 'The Scholars', the faces of the Magi; William Carlos Williams's 'Postlude', Aldington's version of 'Atthis', and 'H. D.'s' waves like pine tops, and her verse in 'Des Imagistes' the first anthology; Hueffer's 'How red your lips are' in his translation from Von der Vogelweide, his 'Three Ten', the general effect of his 'On Heaven'; his sense of the prose values or prose qualities in poetry; his ability to write poems that half-chant and are spoiled by a musician's additions; beyond these a poem by Alice Corbin, 'One City Only', and another ending 'But sliding water over a stone'. These things have worn smooth in my head and I am not through with them, nor with Aldington's 'In Via Sestina' nor his other poems in 'Des Imagistes', though people have told me their flaws. It may be that their content is too much embedded in me for me to look back at the words.

I am almost a different person when I come to take up the argument for Eliot's poems.

Introduction to *The Natural Philosophy of Love*

It is more than likely that the brain itself, is, in origin and development, only a sort of great clot of genital fluid held in suspense or reserve; at first over the cervical ganglion, or, earlier or in other species, held in several clots over the scattered chief nerve centres; and augmenting in varying speeds and quantities into medulla oblongata, cerebellum and cerebrum. This hypothesis would perhaps explain a certain number of as yet uncorrelated phenomena both psychological and physiological. It would explain the enormous content of the brain as a maker or presenter of images. Species would have developed in accordance with, or their development would have been affected by the relative discharge and retention of the fluid; this proportion being both a matter of quantity and of quality, some animals profiting hardly at all by the alluvial Nile-flood; the baboon retaining nothing; men apparently stupefying themselves in some cases by excess, and in other cases discharging apparently only a surplus at high pressure; the imbecile, or the genius, the 'strong-minded'.

[. . .]

There are traces of it in the symbolism of phallic religions, man really the phallus or spermatozoid charging, head-on, the female chaos; integration of the male in the male organ. Even oneself has felt it, driving any new idea into the great passive vulva of London, a sensation analogous to the male feeling in copulation.

Without any digression on feminism, taking merely the division Gourmont has given (Aristotelian, if you like), one offers woman as the accumulation of hereditary aptitudes, better than man in the 'useful gestures', the perfections; but to man, given what we have of history, the 'inventions', the new gestures, the extravagance, the wild shots, the impractical, merely because in him occurs the new upjut, the new bathing of the cerebral tissues in the residuum, in *la mousse* of the life sap.

Or, as I am certainly neither writing an anti-feminist tract, nor claiming disproportionate privilege for the spermatozoid, for the sake of symmetry ascribe a cognate role to the ovule, though I can hardly be expected to introspect it. A flood is as bad as a famine; the ovular bath could still account for the refreshment of the female mind, and the recharging, regracing of its 'traditional aptitudes'; where one woman appears to benefit by an alluvial clarifying, ten dozen appear to be swamped.

Postulating that the cerebral fluid tried all sorts of experiments, and, striking matter, forced it into all sorts of forms, by gushes; we have admittedly in insect life a female predominance; in bird, mammal and human, at least an increasing male prominence. And these four important branches of 'the fan' may be differentiated according to their apparent chief desire, or source of choosing their species.

Insect, utility; bird, flight; mammal, muscular splendour; man, experiment.

[. . .]

In its subservience to the money fetish our age returns to the darkness of medievalism. Two osmies may make superfluous eggless nests, but do not kill each other in contesting which shall deposit the supererogatory honey therein. It is perhaps no more foolish to go at a hermit's bidding to recover an old sepulchre than to make new sepulchres at the bidding of finance.

In his growing subservience to, and adoration of, and entanglement in machines, in utility, man rounds the circle almost into insect life, the absence of flesh; and may have need even of horned gods to save him, or at least of a form of thought which permits them.

[. . .]

Thought is a chemical process, the most interesting of all transfusions in liquid solution. The mind is an up-spurt of sperm, no, let me alter that; trying to watch the process: the sperm, the form-creator, the substance which compels the ovule to evolve in a given pattern, one microscopic, minuscule particle, entering the 'castle' of the ovule.

[. . .]

Thought is a 'chemical process' in relation to the organ, the brain; creative thought is an act like fecundation, like the male cast of the human seed, but given that cast, that ejaculation, I am perfectly willing to grant that the thought once born, separated, in regard to itself, not in relation to the brain that begat it, does lead an independent life much like a member of the vegetable kingdom, blowing seeds, ideas from the paradisial garden at the summit of Dante's *Purgatory*, capable of lodging and sprouting where they fall. And Gourmont has the phrase 'fecundating a generation of bodies as genius fecundates a generation of minds'.

Man is the sum of the animals, the sum of their instincts, as Gourmont has repeated in the course of his book. Given, first a few, then as we get to our own condition, a mass of these spermatozoic particles withheld, in suspense, waiting in the organ that has been built up through ages by a myriad similar waitings.

[. . .]

Creative thought has manifested itself in images, in music, which is to sound what the concrete image is to sight. And the thought of genius, even of the mathematical genius, the mathematical prodigy, is really the same sort of thing, it is a sudden out spurt of mind which takes the form demanded by the problem; which creates the answer, and baffles the man counting on the abacus.

[. . .]

But man goes on making new faculties, or forgetting old ones. That is to say you have all sorts of aptitudes developed without external change, which in an earlier biological state would possibly have found carnal expression. You have every exploited 'hyper-aesthesia', i.e. every new form of genius, from the faculty of hearing four parts in a fugue perfectly, to the ear for money (*vide* Henry James in *The Ivory Tower*, the passages on Mr. Gaw). Here I only amplify what Gourmont has indicated in Chapter 20. You have the visualizing sense, the 'stretch' of imagination, the mystics – for what there is to them – Santa Theresa who 'saw' the microcosmos, hell, heaven, purgatory complete, 'the size of a walnut'; and you have Mr. W., a wool-broker in London, who suddenly at 3 a.m. visualizes the whole of his letter-file, three hundred folios; he sees and reads particularly the letter at folder 171, but he sees simultaneously the entire contents of the file, the whole thing about the size of two lumps of loaf sugar laid flat side to flat side.

Remains precisely the question: man feeling this protean capacity to grow a new organ: what organ shall it be? Or new faculty: what faculty?

[. . .]

The dead laborious compilation and comparison of other men's dead images, all this is mere labour, not the spermatozoic act of the brain.

Woman, the conservator, the inheritor of past gestures, clever, practical, as Gourmont says, not inventive, always the best disciple of any inventor, has been always the enemy of the dead or laborious form of compilation, abstraction.

Not considering the process ended; taking the individual genius as the man in whom the new access, the new superfluity of spermatozoic pressure (quantitative and qualitative) upshoots into the brain, alluvial Nile-flood, bringing new crops, new invention. And as Gourmont says, there is only reasoning where there is initial error, i.e. weakness of the spurt, wandering search.

In no case can it be a question of mere animal quantity of sperm. You have the man who wears himself out and weakens his brain, echo of the orang, obviously not the talented sieve; you have the contrasted case in the type of man who really cannot work until he has relieved the pressure on his spermatic canals.

This is a question of physiology, it is not a question of morals and sociology. Given the spermatozoic thought, the two great seas of fecundative matter, the brain lobes, mutually magnetized, luminous in their own knowledge of their being; whether they may be expected to seek exterior 'luxuria', or whether they are going to repeat Augustine hymns, is not in my jurisdiction. An exterior paradise might not allure them 'La bêtise humaine est la seule chose qui donne une idée de l'infini', says Renan, and Gourmont has quoted him, and all flesh is grass, a superior grass.

It remains that man has for centuries nibbled at this idea of connection, intimate connection between his sperm and his cerebration, the ascetic has tried to withhold all his sperm, the lure, the ignis fatuus perhaps, of wanting to super-think; the dope-fiend has tried opium and every inferior to Bacchus, to get an extra kick out of the organ, the mystics have sought the gleam in the tavern, Helen of Tyre, priestesses in the temple of Venus, in Indian temples, stray priestesses in the streets, unprootable custom, and probably with a basis of sanity. A sense of balance might show that asceticism means either a drought or a crowding. The liquid solution must be kept at right consistency; one would say the due proportion of liquid to viscous particles, a good circulation; the actual quality of the sieve or separator, counting perhaps most of all; the balance and retentive media.

Perhaps the clue is in Propertius after all:

Ingenium nobis ipsa puella fecit

There is the whole of the twelfth century love cult, and Dante's metaphysics a little to one side, and Gourmont's Latin Mystique; and for image-making both Fenollosa on *The Chinese Written Character*, and the paragraphs in *Le Problème du Style*. At any rate the quarrel between cerebralist and viveur and ignorantist ends, if the brain is thus conceived not as a separate and desiccated organ, but as the very fluid of life itself.

16
H. D. (HILDA DOOLITTLE) (1886–1961)
FROM 'NOTES ON THOUGHT AND VISION' 1919

American poet. Doolittle came to Europe in 1911 and quickly established herself among the Imagist poets. Her work was published in Poetry *magazine and in the anthology* Des Imagistes *(1914). In 1913 she married Richard Aldington with whom she undertook translations from classical Greek and Latin. Her first volume of verse,* Sea Garden *(1916), combined her gift for concrete imagery with her passion for classical literature. As her marriage disintegrated she began a lifelong friendship with the English writer Winifred Ellerman, who published under the name Bryher. The 1920s saw the publication of more volumes of poetry, as well as prose fiction, including* Palimpsest *(1926) and* Hedylus *(1928). H. D. also worked on several prose works concerned with lesbianism which were published posthumously. Her response to the Second World War helped produce some of her most powerful and engaged poetry, including the trilogy* The Walls Do Not Fall *(1944),* Tribute to Angels *(1945) and* Flowering of the Rod *(1946). The following extracts are from a 1919 collection of statements on the natural duality of thought, language and art.*

Three states or manifestations of life: body, mind, over-mind.

Aim of men and women of highest development is equilibrium, balance, growth of the three at once: brain without physical strength is a manifestation of weakness, a disease comparable to cancerous growth or tumor; body without reasonable amount of intellect is an empty fibrous bundle of glands as ugly and little to be desired as body of a victim of some form of elephantiasis or fatty-degeneracy; over-mind without the balance of the other two is madness and a person so developed should have as much respect as a reasonable maniac and no more.

All reasoning, normal, sane and balanced men and women need and seek at certain times of their lives, certain definite physical relationships. Men and women of temperament, musicians, scientists, artists especially, need these relationships to develop and draw forth their talents. Not to desire and make every effort to develop along these natural physical lines, cripples and dwarfs the being. To shun, deny and belittle such experiences is to bury one's talent carefully in a napkin.

When a creative scientist, artist or philosopher has been for some hours or days intent on his work, his mind often takes on an almost physical character. That is, his mind becomes his real body. His over mind becomes his brain.

When Leonardo da Vinci worked, his brain was Leonardo, the personality, Leonardo da Vinci. He saw the faces of many of his youths and babies and young women definitely with his over-mind. The *Madonna of the Rocks* is not a picture. It is a window. We look through a window into the world of pure overmind.

If I could visualise or describe that over-mind in my own case, I should say this: it seems to me that a cap is over my head, a cap of consciousness over my head, my forehead, affecting a little my eyes. Sometimes when I am in that state of consciousness, things about me appear slightly blurred as if seen under water.

Ordinary things never become quite unreal nor disproportionate. It is only an effort to readjust, to focus, seemingly a slight physical effort.

That over-mind seems a cap, like water, transparent, fluid yet with definite body, contained in a definite space. It is like a closed sea-plant, jelly-fish or anemone.

Into that over-mind, thoughts pass and are visible like fish swimming under clear water.

The swing from normal consciousness to abnormal consciousness is accompanied by grinding discomfort of mental agony.

I should say – to continue this jelly-fish metaphor – that long feelers reached down and through the body, that these stood in the same relation to the nervous system as the over-mind to the brain or intellect.

There is, then, a set of super-feelings. These feelings extend out and about us; as the long, floating tentacles of the jelly-fish reach out and about him. They are not of different material, extraneous, as the physical arms and legs are extraneous to the gray matter of the directing brain. The super-feelers are part of the super-mind, as the jelly-fish feelers are the jelly-fish itself, elongated in fine threads.

I first realised this state of consciousness in my head. I visualise it just as well, now, centered in the love-region of the body or placed like a foetus in the body.

The centre of consciousness is either the brain or the love-region of the body.

Is it easier for a woman to attain this state of consciousness than for a man?

For me, it was before the birth of my child that the jelly-fish consciousness seemed to come definitely into the field or realm of the intellect or brain.

Are these jelly-fish states of consciousness interchangeable? Should we be able to think with the womb and feel with the brain?

May this consciousness be centered entirely in the brain or entirely in the womb or corresponding love-region of a man's body?

Vision is of two kinds – vision of the womb and vision of the brain. In vision of the brain, the region of consciousness is above and about the head; when the centre of consciousness shifts and the jelly-fish is in the body, (I visualise it in my case lying on the left side with the streamers or feelers floating up toward the brain) we have vision of the womb or love-vision.

The majority of dream and of ordinary vision is vision of the womb.

The brain and the womb are both centres of consciousness, equally important.

Most of the so-called artists of today have lost the use of their brain. There is no way of arriving at the over-mind, except through the intellect. To arrive at the world of over-mind vision any other way, is to be the thief that climbs into the sheep-fold.

I believe there are artists coming in the next generation, some of whom will have the secret of using their over-minds.

There is no great art period without great lovers.

Socrates' whole doctrine of vision was a doctrine of love.

We must be 'in love' before we can understand the mysteries of vision.

A lover must choose one of the same type of mind as himself, a musician, a musician, a scientist, a scientist, a general, a young man also interested in the theory and practice of arms and armies.

We begin with sympathy of thought.

The minds of the two lovers merge, interact in sympathy of thought.

The brain, inflamed and excited by this interchange of ideas, takes on its character of over-mind, becomes (as I have visualised in my own case) a jelly-fish, placed over and about the brain.

The love-region is excited by the appearance of beauty of the loved one, its energy not dissipated in physical relations, takes on its character of mind, becomes this womb-brain or love-brain that I have visualised as a jelly-fish *in* the body.

The love-brain and over-brain are both capable of thought. This thought is vision.

All men have possibilities of developing this vision.

The over-mind is like a lens of an opera-glass. When we are able to use this over-mind lens, the whole world of vision is open to us.

I have said that the over-mind is a lens. I should say more exactly that the love-mind and the over-mind are two lenses. When these lenses are properly adjusted, focused, they bring the world of vision into consciousness. The two work separately, perceive separately, yet make one picture.

Our minds, all of our minds, are like dull little houses, built more or less alike – a dull little city with rows of little detached villas, and here and there a more pretentious house, set apart from the rest, but in essentials, seen from a distance, one with the rest, all drab, all grey.

Each comfortable little home shelters a comfortable little soul – and a wall at the back shuts out completely any communication with the world beyond.

Man's chief concern is keeping his little house warm and making his little wall strong.

Outside is a great vineyard and grapes and rioting and madness and dangers.

It is very dangerous.

An enormous moth detached himself from a bunch of yellow grapes – he seemed stupefied with the heat of the sun – heavy with the sun and his soft belly swollen with the honey of the grapes, I would have said, for there was a bead of gold – resinous – that matted the feathers at his throat.

He fell rather than flew and his great feet scratched with a faint metallic ring, the side of my golden cup.

He stumbled, awkward and righted himself, clutched the rim of my cup, waved his antennae feebly.

I would have rescued him but I myself was dizzy with the heat and the fumes of the golden wine and I heard a great shout of laughter as I tried to steady my cup and I shouted in reply, *he* is drunk – *he* is drunk.

So he was drunk.

Outside is a great vineyard and rioting and madness and dangers.

17
ALFRED DÖBLIN (1878–1957)
FROM 'WARSAW' 1922

Berlin-based Jewish socialist writer, best known for his Modernist novel Berlin Alexanderplatz *(1927). Deeply disappointed at the outcome of the revolution in Germany, from 1919 he published satiric commentaries in* Die Neue Rundschau *under the pseudonym 'Linke Poot', collected in book form –* Der deutsche Maskenball (The German Masquerade) *– in 1922. Döblin wanted to learn what was happening in ravaged and divided Poland, and travelled there in the 1920s. He was profoundly affected by his visit to the Jewish quarter of Warsaw. The epigraph to* Journey to Poland *is from Schiller: 'For every border wields a tyrant's power'.*

They now are dwelling in their very own homes

In the long railroad car, I sway over the tracks. The train zoomed off from Berlin like an arrow. The rails are endless. Now, I whiz along, jog along, with a wood-and-iron structure, inside a gurgling tube, into the night. The cars bounce. A chaos of noises has begun: a rhythmic thrusting from the wheels, a vibrating, a rolling, a clattering of windows, a buzzing, a hollow grinding, a sliding, a brief, sharp slamming.

I – am not here. I – am not in the train. We pelt across bridges. I – have not flown along. Not yet. I am still standing in the terminal, Schlesischer Bahnhof. They stand around me, but then I get into the train, I sit on the green cushion, amid leather valises, satchels, plaids, coats, umbrellas. I am caught. The train carries me off, holds me captive, rocks me along the rails into the night.

I looked out the window, across this metal bar. Now – two young men stand there, pull down the curtain, insert cigarettes into their mouths, smoke, chat in a foreign language. They have light-gray cotton gloves on, and caps over their dark, agile eyes; they smile. One man points to a newspaper he holds under his arm. An older man joins them; corpulent. The foreign parleying – trilled *r*'s, sibilants – keeps on. Now they make way. A little girl – legs naked white up to the middle of her thighs, elegant patent-leather shoes, a short, loose velvet dress, unbound black hair – passes through, keeping her balance by holding on left and right. She gazes ahead, very earnest, very mournful.

I – am not here. The newspaper lies on my lap. 'The Triumphal March of the Zeppelin.' I read, with an intensely mounting anxiety, almost sorrow. The train, the reverberating edifice, is taking me east. This is still Germany, I am still almost at home, here comes Frankfurt on the Oder. I can't believe it, I don't recognize the countryside. They are all traveling. These are the people with whom I'm traveling. The young man who was chatting at the metal bar saunters into my compartment, sits down next to me. He speaks. A voice addressing me. My voice comes to me. I arrange the suitcases for the night. Anxiously, I think of Poland, I let him talk about it. I think of my plans. But they are not my plans now, I do not recognize them.

[. . .]

The Jews: their nation was silently imbued with the renunciation of land, country, and state. The return movement is taking place

Three hundred fifty thousand Jews live in Warsaw, half as many as in all Germany. A small number of them are strewn across the city, the bulk reside together in the northwestern sector. They are a nation. People who know only Western Europe fail to realize this. The Jews have their own costumes, their own language, religion, manners and mores, their ancient national feeling and national consciousness.

[. . .]

All at once, an ancient, dirty manikin steals along the wall. When I view him from the front, he is waxen. His mouth is wide open, his left eye is small and red, the eyelid inverted, bare. However, his right eye gapes, it is whitish. He gropes out with the cane in his left hand. He thus fumbles his way along the decrepit wall in the bright afternoon. A little Jewish bootblack spots me, zooms toward me, pulls me from the street into a building entrance. He works my shoes lightning-fast with brush blows right and left; in the end, the cloth rips in the heat of his work. Eventually, my shoes sparkle like patent leather. Three other boys have gathered around us. The bootblack exchanges brief agitated hostile words with them. Then he's done, I ask how much. The three other boys go tense, and they draw close. He asks for two zlotys; two whole zlotys! He is entitled to fifty groszy, one-fourth that sum. The boys wait to see how I respond to his impudence. And I – I pay two zlotys. Afterward, from the throng, I can observe my bootblack's radiant face, the other three communicating, greedy and hateful; then my bootblack suddenly whizzes right past me. Skedaddling – the others after him with a hue and cry.

The great synagogue on Tlomacki Street; a classical temple, narrow, lofty. Above it, the dome with the Star of David. A short beadle chats with a Polish policeman at the foot of the stairs. It's Saturday morning. They pour up the steps. Few of them wear caftans and skullcaps, this is the synagogue of the middle class, also the enlightened, the emancipated, and the assimilated. An empty vestibule with glass doors. And oddly: basins of dripping water to the right and left of the entrance; the arriving worshipers dip their fingers into the water: the vestige of a ritual ablution, and also how close to the Catholic stoup. Inside the temple, a swarming throng. The people converse, most of them softly, a few in an undertone. An elderly man tries to expel a boy from his seat. How the graybeard's eyes sparkle, and he finally summons the attendant. Shaking his head, coaxing gently, the attendant pushes the boy away; the graybeard glares venomously for a long time. On the back wall, next to Polish inscriptions, three rows of clocks with Hebrew letters. Each tells a different time; I don't understand them. A man in front of me prays very loudly, his upper body swaying, a man in a hat. Suddenly, he turns around, breaks off, pats the white-haired beadle on the back; they talk about a woman's illness. The attendant cries: 'Don't stand in the middle, don't block traffic.' Upstairs, women sit behind a high wide gate; I see fashionable modern hats. Not nearly as many women as in Christian churches. Most of the men wear prayer shawls, white with blue and black stripes. Some wear them like scarves, some wrap them around their arms, tightening them. Many young men walk about, including almost a dozen soldiers, and more join them afterward. On the whole, these are not elegant people, they unabashedly pick their noses while talking. A few respectable types wander slowly along the center aisle, the beadle makes room for them; they sit in front. Little boys in sailor caps stand on the bench; the adults accompanying them read books and hold on to the boys. These men have swift eyes. Many faces are full and broad. On either side of the room, I count seven windows, small, unadorned. Lofty columns rise from the gallery, partitioning off seven round arches. A small stairway leads to the altar. The red burning lamp, the central curtain. The liturgizing resembles the Catholic one. And it is amazingly similar to the Catholic one when the priest pulls up the curtain, produces a chinking clinking silver implement and holds it in his arm like an ostensory. Escorted by functionaries, the priest descends the steps, passes the altar while chanting, and remounts the steps. At the top two men stand, in normal clothes, reading aloud. Here, there is a close rapport between parish and priest. They read aloud, and every so often, the crowd and the choir break in tumultuously. Now, boys appear up at the altar. I hear that they are being confirmed. General whispering; a large number of excited people shove forward along the center aisle. The temple has filled up, people are pushing in from the vestibule in back. The white-bearded attendant fights with them. In a very grandiloquent voice – which is changing, it keeps breaking – a boy up there utters Hebrew words. People motion to one another familiarly, smiling. The men and women have all stood up, craning their necks. People throng forward more and more vehemently. The priest sings, and then another boy recites his passages. Men are already leaving. Newcomers press in from the vestibule. I also leave once I hear more of the same from the altar. In the vestibule, they are debating in groups. They stand at the foot of the staircase, eyeing the passerby.

Outside, the stores are closed. Men in caftans slowly amble along the hushed street. As I approach Theater Square, the tableau quickly changes. I am in Poland, in a surging Polish metropolis.

[. . .]

18
HERMAN HESSE (1877–1962)
'RECENT GERMAN POETRY' 1922

German novelist and poet. Apprenticed to a tower-clock factory, then to a bookstore, Hesse published his first novel, Peter Camenzind, *in 1904. This was followed by* Gertrud *(1910) and* Rosshalde *(1914). At the outbreak of war in 1914 he moved to Switzerland where he became a citizen in 1923. Following a course of psychoanalysis, he developed an interest in Jungian theories of the collective unconscious, idealism, symbolism, introversion and extroversion, as well as Indian mysticism. These interests are reflected in his novels from 1919 onwards:* Demian *(1919),* Steppenwolf *(1927),* Narcissus and Goldmund *(1930) and* The Glass Bead Game *(1943). He was awarded the Nobel Prize of Literature in 1946. Reprinted here is an essay published in* The Criterion *in 1922.*

During the past few months I have read a large number of books by the latest German poets, with a view to forming some idea of the intellectual standing of young Germany. My labour, although instructive, has been no pleasure to me, and I do not intend to go on with it any longer. The mental picture of this recent literature which I have built up as a result of my reading is roughly the following.

The younger and most recent German poets – apart from those who, singing old melodies, are the decadent imitators of their elders – might be divided into two groups according to poetic form. The first group would be composed of those who fancy that they have replaced the old poetic forms by new. Here has grown up, during the last few years, a strange imitative orthodoxy and philistinism. The few forerunners and first leaders of the literary revolution, with Sternheim at their head, are imitated, in their grammatical and syntactical innovations and peculiarities, with more dogmatic faith, more slavishness, and far less taste than was ever shown by the 'gilt-edged' lyric poet of the 'eighties' who imitated the classics. The whole of this literature already breathes mildew and old age; it is dying before its poets have reached their majority.

The second group, however, which is stronger and to be taken more seriously, is moving lingeringly, but more or less consciously and determinedly, towards chaos. With the poets of this group, the feeling is present, though obscurely, that you cannot, in place of a broken-down culture and form, simply set another and a new one. These poets feel, or seem to feel, that there must first be disintegration and chaos, the bitter way must first be gone to the end, before new settings, new forms, and new affinities are created. Many of these poets, out of indifference – because, in the general ruin, form can never matter – use the customary language and forms. Others drive impatiently forward, and seek consciously to hasten the disintegration of the German literary language – some with the sullen grief of the man who breaks up his own house, others with reckless humour and in the somewhat shallow mood of complete indifference to the ruin of the world. The latter, since art offers no further satisfactions, want at least to have a little fun at the expense of the philistines and to laugh a while and make merry before the ground collapses beneath them. The whole of literary 'Dadaism' belongs hereto.

But all these different groups close up immediately again into one uniform whole so soon as the rather fruitless search after new forms is abandoned and the spiritual content only is examined. This is always exactly the same. Two principal themes are everywhere predominant: rebellion against authority and against the culture of that authority in process of downfall; and eroticism. The father thrust against the wall and condemned by his son, and the youngster, hungry for love, who endeavours to sing his sexual passion in new, free, lovelier and truer forms: these are the two figures that are everywhere to be found. They will too constantly recur, for they indicate, in fact, the two central interests of youth.

The experience and impetus behind all these revolutions and innovations are clearly discernible in two powerful forces: the world-war, and the psychology of the unconscious founded by Sigmund Freud. The experience of the Great War, with the collapse of all the old forms and the breakdown of moral codes and cultures hitherto valid, appears to be incapable of interpretation except by psycho-analysis. Europe is seen by the youth of to-day as a very sick neurotic, who can be helped only by shattering the self-created complexes in which he is suffocating. And the otherwise tottering authority of the father, the teacher, the priest, the party, and of science finds a new and terrible antagonist in psycho-analysis, which projects so merciless a light into all the old modesties, apprehensions, and prudences. Those same professors who, during the war, distinguished themselves by their obsequiousness towards their Governments, and by their grotesque and senile outbreaks of nationalist infatuation, are now recognised by the young men of to-day as the men under whose leadership the *bourgeoisie* endeavoured to undo and destroy Freud's work, and to leave the world once more in its former darkness.

These two factors in the spiritual life of the young men of to-day – the break with traditional culture (which with many takes the form of a mad hatred of German grammar), and the knowledge that it is possible to investigate scientifically our subconscious life and to influence it in a rational manner – these two factors govern all the recent work of young German writers. And with this there is no lack of what the psychoanalysts call 'the abandonment to the doctor'. It expresses itself in a blindly enthusiastic submission to the one who first appeared to the patient as a liberator, whether it be Freud or Sternheim. But, although there may be a great deal of obscurity, impulsiveness, and even triviality mixed up with these two factors, they are there in the minds of the young men of to-day; and they are not a programme or a discipline either, but forces.

The knowledge of the collapse of pre-war culture and the eager acceptance of the new psychology as – at last – a science in the making, these are the foundations on which the young men of to-day are beginning to build. The foundations are good. But so far as can be judged by recent poetry nothing has yet been achieved. Neither the experience of the war nor the advent of Freud has led as yet to any very fruitful results. The prevailing mood is complacently revolutionary, very comprehensible in the circumstances, but incapable of long duration. It is more concerned with making a noise and the assertion of self-importance than with progress and the future. The large majority of these young men give one exactly the same impression as a half-analysed psychopath who knows indeed the first main results of his psycho-analysis, but is unaware of its consequences. With most of them, their breaking loose and enlargement go no further than a perception of their personality, and the assertion and proclamation of the rights of that personality. Beyond this, there is nothing but obscurity and aimlessness.

[. . .]

It is absurd to get excited, as many so angrily do, about the disappearance of the article and the straightening-out of the syntax in the latest German novels. The articles, in so far as they are useful, will inevitably return. And there is nobody to prevent the upholder of the old grammar and the old beauty from continuing to read Goethe and to ignore the writings of the younger generation. But these young people have every right to youthful years of especial intensity, since they were torn away, at the ages of sixteen to twenty, from their toys and their school-benches, to take part in the war. They themselves will understand that they cannot permanently thrust all the blame for their misfortunes on us elders. They may be a thousand times right; but merely to be right has never yet advanced anything in this world. The more the younger generation understand this, the more will they also see how little they have so far made of, or appreciated, their two great experiences. The war and psycho-analysis, as experiences, have hitherto produced no other effect than a kind of half-crapulous, half-frenzied outburst of puberty.

I do not believe in a rapid recovery of German poetry. I do not believe in an immediate efflorescence. On the contrary. There are, however, other things to do than to write poetry, and you may make bad poems or none at all, and yet live sensibly and joyously.

The two revolutionary experiences of these young men have not yet produced their full effect, not by a long way.

The war will, sooner or later, bring home to those who have returned from it the lesson that nothing is done by violence and gunplay, that war and violence are attempts to solve complicated and delicate problems in far too savage, far too stupid, and far too brutal a fashion.

And the new psychology, whose harbingers were Dostoievski and Nietzsche, and whose first architect is Freud, will teach these young men that the emancipation of the personality, the canonisation of the natural instincts, are only the first steps on the way, and that this personal freedom is a poor thing and of no account in comparison with that highest of all freedoms of the individual: the freedom to regard oneself consciously and joyously as a part of humanity, and to serve it with liberated powers.

19
VIRGINIA WOOLF (1882–1941)
'THE MOMENT: SUMMER'S NIGHT' 1927;
FROM 'MR. BENNETT AND MRS. BROWN' 1924;
FROM 'MODERN FICTION' 1919

English novelist, essayist, short-story writer, biographer, critic, publisher and feminist, central member of the Bloomsbury Group. Daughter of the eminent critic and biographer, Leslie Stephen, and sister of the painter Vanessa Bell. Mainly educated at home, Woolf occasionally attended classes in Greek and history at King's College, London (1897–1900) and took private lessons in Greek from Janet Case (1902). During 1905–06, she taught evening classes at Morley College, London, and, with her sister Vanessa, hosted the Thursday evenings at 46 Gordon Square which were the foundation of Old Bloomsbury. In 1905 she began as reviewer for The Times Literary Supplement. *She joined the Suffrage movement in 1910; and was later an organiser in the Working Women's Guild. In 1912 she married Leonard Woolf with whom she founded and ran the Hogarth Press which was responsible for the publication of many important Modernist works, including the first English editions of Freud. Her first novel,* The Voyage Out, *was published in 1915, but it is for the experimental style of her later novels,* Jacob's Room *(1922),* Mrs Dalloway *(1925),* To the Lighthouse *(1927) and* The

Waves *(1931), that she is best known as a novelist. Her collection,* The Common Reader *(1925) and its second series (1931), consolidated her reputation as an essayist.* A Room of One's Own *(1929) and* Three Guineas *(1938) count among the founding documents of modern feminism. 'The Moment: Summer's Night' (c.1927), published posthumously, has become a much cited document. It typifies the experimental merging of fact, polemic, and fiction employed in many of her important essays. Also reproduced here are extracts from the essay 'Mr. Bennett and Mrs. Brown' (1924), and the most cited of her statements from the essay, first published as 'Modern Novels' (1919), and revised as 'Modern Fiction' (as below) for* The Common Reader *(1925). [See IIIb 39]*

The Moment: Summer's Night

The night was falling so that the table in the garden among the trees grew whiter and whiter; and the people round it more indistinct. An owl, blunt, obsolete looking, heavy weighted, crossed the fading sky with a black spot between its claws. The trees murmured. An aeroplane hummed like a piece of plucked wire. There was also, on the roads, the distant explosion of a motor cycle, shooting further and further away down the road. Yet what composed the present moment? If you are young, the future lies upon the present, like a piece of glass, making it tremble and quiver. If you are old, the past lies upon the present, like a thick glass, making it waver, distorting it. All the same, everybody believes that the present is something, seeks out the different elements in this situation in order to compose the truth of it, the whole of it.

To begin with: it is largely composed of visual and of sense impressions. The day was very hot. After heat, the surface of the body is opened, as if all the pores were open and everything lay exposed, not sealed and contracted, as in cold weather. The air wafts cold on the skin under one's clothes. The soles of the feet expand in slippers after walking on hard roads. Then the sense of the light sinking back into darkness seems to be gently putting out with a damp sponge the colour in one's own eyes. Then the leaves shiver now and again, as if a ripple of irresistible sensation ran through them, as a horse suddenly ripples its skin.

But this moment is also composed of a sense that the legs of the chair are sinking through the centre of the earth, passing through the rich garden earth; they sink, weighted down. Then the sky loses its colour perceptibly and a star here and there makes a point of light. Then changes, unseen in the day, coming in succession seem to make an order evident. One becomes aware that we are spectators and also passive participants in a pageant. And as nothing can interfere with the order, we have nothing to do but accept, and watch. Now little sparks, which are not steady, but fitful as if somebody were doubtful, come across the field. Is it time to light the lamp, the farmers' wives are saying: can I see a little longer? The lamp sinks down; then it burns up. All doubt is over. Yes the time has come in all cottages, in all farms, to light the lamps. Thus then the moment is laced about with these weavings to and fro, these inevitable downsinkings, flights, lamp lightings.

But that is the wider circumference of the moment. Here in the centre is a knot of consciousness; a nucleus divided up into four heads, eight legs, eight arms, and four separate bodies. They are not subject to the law of the sun and the owl and the lamp.

They assist it. For sometimes a hand rests on the table; sometimes a leg is thrown over a leg. Now the moment becomes shot with the extraordinary arrow which people let fly from their mouths – when they speak.

'He'll do well with his hay.'

The words let fall this seed, but also, coming from that obscure face, and the mouth, and the hand so characteristically holding the cigarette, now hit the mind with a wad, then explode like a scent suffusing the whole dome of the mind with its incense, flavour; let fall, from their ambiguous envelope, the self-confidence of youth, but also its urgent desire, for praise, and assurance; if they were to say: 'But you're no worse looking than many – you're no different – people don't mark you out to laugh at you': that he should be at once so cock-a-hoop and so ungainly makes the moment rock with laughter, and with the malice that comes from overlooking other people's motives; and seeing what they keep hid; and so that one takes sides; he will succeed; or no he won't; and then again, this success, will it mean my defeat; or won't it? All this shoots through the moment, makes it quiver with malice and amusement; and the sense of watching and comparing; and the quiver meets the shore, when the owl flies out, and puts a stop to this judging, this overseeing, and with our wings spread, we too fly, take wing, with the owl, over the earth and survey the quietude of what sleeps, folded, slumbering, arm stretching in the vast dark and sucking its thumb too; the amorous and the innocent; and a sigh goes up. Could we not fly too, with broad wings and with softness; and be all one wing; all embracing, all gathering, and these boundaries, these pryings over hedge into hidden compartments of different colours be all swept into one colour by the brush of the wing; and so visit in splendour, augustly, peaks; and there lie exposed, bare, on the spine, high up, to the cold light of the moon rising, and when the moon rises, single, solitary, behold her, one, eminent over us?

Ah, yes, if we could fly, fly, fly. . . . Here the body is gripped; and shaken; and the throat stiffens; and the nostrils tingle; and like a rat shaken by a terrier one sneezes; and the whole universe is shaken; mountains, snows, meadows; moon; higgledy, piggledy, upside down, little splinters flying; and the head is jerked up, down. 'Hay fever – what a noise! – there's no cure. Except spending hay time on a boat. Perhaps worse than the disease, though that's what a man did – crossing and recrossing, all the summer.'

Issuing from a white arm, a long shape, lying back, in a film of black and white, under the tree, which, down sweeping, seems a part of that curving, that flowing, the voice, with its ridicule and its sense, reveals to the shaken terrier its own insignificance. No longer part of the snow; no part of the mountain; not in the least venerable to other human beings; but ridiculous; a little accident; a thing to be laughed at; discriminated out; seen clearly cut out, sneezing, sneezing, judged and compared. Thus into the moment steals self-assertion; ah, the sneeze again; the desire to sneeze with conviction; masterfully; making oneself heard; felt; if not pitied, then somebody of importance; perhaps to break away and go. But no; the other shape has sent from its arrow another fine binding thread, 'Shall I fetch my Vapex?' She, the observant, the discriminating, who keeps in mind always other instances, so that there is nothing singular in any special case – who refuses to be jumped into extravagance; and so sceptical withal; cannot believe in miracles; sees the vanity of effort there; perhaps then it would be well to try here; yet if she isolates cases from the mists of hugeness, sees what is there all the more definitely; refuses to be bamboozled; yet in this definite discrimination shows some amplitude. That is why the moment becomes harder, is intensified, diminished, begins to be stained by some expressed personal juice; with the desire to be loved, to be held close to the other shape; to put off the veil of darkness and see burning eyes.

Then a light is struck; in it appears a sunburnt face, lean, blue-eyed, and the arrow flies as the match goes out:

'He beats her every Saturday; from boredom, I should say; not drink; there's nothing else to do.'

The moment runs like quicksilver on a sloping board into the cottage parlour; there are the tea things on the table; the hard windsor chairs; tea caddies on the shelf for ornament; the medal under a glass shade; vegetable steam curling from the pot; two children crawling on the floor; and Liz comes in and John catches her a blow on the side of her head as she slopes past him, dirty, with her hair loose and one hairpin sticking out about to fall. And she moans in a chronic animal way; and the children look up and then make a whistling noise to imitate the engine which they trail across the flags; and John sits himself down with a thump at the table and carves a hunk of bread and munches because there is nothing to be done. A steam rises from his cabbage patch. Let us do something then, something to end this horrible moment, this plausible glistening moment that reflects in its smooth sides this intolerable kitchen, this squalor; this woman moaning; and the rattle of the toy of the flags, and the man munching. Let us smash it by breaking a match. There – snap.

And then comes the low of the cows in the field; and another cow to the left answers; and all the cows seem to be moving tranquilly across the field all the owl flutes off its watery bubble. But the sun is deep below the earth. The trees are growing heavier, blacker; no order is perceptible; there is no sequence in these cries, these movements; they come from no bodies; they are cries to the left and to the right. Nothing can be seen. We can only see ourselves as outlines, cadaverous, sculpturesque. And it is more difficult for the voice to carry through this dark. The dark has stripped the fledge from the arrow – the vibrations that rise red shiver as it passes through us.

Then comes the terror, the exultation; the power to rush out unnoticed, alone; to be consumed; to be swept away to become a rider on the random wind; the tossing wind; the trampling and neighing wind; the horse with the blown-back mane; the tumbling, the foraging; he who gallops for ever, nowhither travelling, indifferent; to be part of the eyeless dark, to be rippling and streaming, to feel the glory run molten up the spine, down the limbs, making the eyes glow, burning, bright, and penetrate the buffeting waves of the wind.

'Everything's sopping wet. It's the dew off the grass. Time to go in.'

And then one shape heaves and surges and rises, and we pass, trailing coats, down the path towards the lighted windows, the dim glow behind the branches, and so enter the door, and the square draws its lines round us, and here is a chair, a table, glasses, knives, and thus we are boxed and housed, and will soon require a draught of soda-water and to find something to read in bed.

Mr. Bennett and Mrs. Brown

It seems to me possible, perhaps desirable, that I may be the only person in this room who has committed the folly of writing, trying to write, or failing to write, a novel. And when I asked myself, as your invitation to speak to you about modern fiction made me ask myself, what demon whispered in my ear and urged me to my doom, a little figure rose before me – the figure of a man, or of a woman, who said, 'My name is Brown. Catch me if you can.'

Most novelists have the same experience. Some Brown, Smith, or Jones comes before them and says in the most seductive and charming way in the world, 'Come and catch me if you can.' And so, led on by this will-o'-the-wisp, they flounder through volume after volume, spending the best years of their lives in the pursuit, and receiving for the most part very little cash in exchange. Few catch the phantom; most have to be content with a scrap of her dress or a wisp of her hair.

My belief that men and women write novels because they are lured on to create some character which has thus imposed itself upon them has the sanction of Mr. Arnold Bennett. In an article from which I will quote he says: 'The foundation of good fiction is character-creating and nothing else ... Style counts; plot counts; originality of outlook counts. But none of these counts anything like so much as the convincingness of the characters. If the characters are real the novel will have a chance; if they are not, oblivion will be its portion . . .' And he goes on to draw the conclusion that we have no young novelists of first-rate importance at the present moment, because they are unable to create characters that are real, true, and convincing.

These are the questions that I want with greater boldness than discretion to discuss tonight. I want to make out what we mean when we talk about 'character' in fiction; to say something about the question of reality which Mr. Bennett raises; and to suggest some reasons why the younger novelists fail to create characters, if, as Mr. Bennett asserts, it is true that fail they do. This will lead me, I am well aware, to make some very sweeping and some very vague assertions. For the question is an extremely difficult one. Think how little we know about character – think how little we know about art. But, to make a clearance before I begin, I will suggest that we range Edwardians and Georgians into two camps; Mr. Wells, Mr. Bennett, and Mr. Galsworthy I will call the Edwardians; Mr. Forster, Mr. Lawrence, Mr. Strachey, Mr. Joyce, and Mr. Eliot I will call the Georgians. And if I speak in the first person, with intolerable egotism, I will ask you to excuse me. I do not want to attribute to the world at large the opinions of one solitary, ill-informed, and misguided individual.

My first assertion is one that I think you will grant – that every one in this room is a judge of character. Indeed it would be impossible to live for a year without disaster unless one practised character-reading and had some skill in the art. Our marriages, our friendships depend on it; our business largely depends on it; every day questions arise which can only be solved by its help. And now I will hazard a second assertion, which is more disputable perhaps, to the effect that in or about December 1910 human character changed.

I am not saying that one went out, as one might into a garden, and there saw that a rose had flowered, or that a hen had laid an egg. The change was not sudden and definite like that. But a change there was, nevertheless; and since one must be arbitrary, let us date it about the year 1910. The first signs of it are recorded in the books of Samuel Butler, in *The Way of All Flesh* in particular; the plays of Bernard Shaw continue to record it. In life one can see the change, if I may use a homely illustration, in the character of one's cook. The Victorian cook lived like a leviathan in the lower depths, formidable, silent, obscure, inscrutable; the Georgian cook is a creature of sunshine and fresh air; in and out of the drawing room, now to borrow the *Daily Herald*, now to ask advice about a hat. Do you ask for more solemn instances of the power of the human race to change? Read the *Agamemnon*, and see whether, in process of time, your sympathies are not almost entirely with Clytemnestra. Or consider the married life of the Carlyles, and bewail the waste, the futility, for him and for her, of the horrible domestic tradition which made it seemly for a woman of genius to spend her time chasing beetles, scouring saucepans, instead of writing books. All human relations have shifted – those between masters and servants, husbands and wives, parents and children. And when human relations change there is at the same time a change in religion, conduct, politics, and literature. Let us agree to place one of these changes about the year 1910.

[. . .]

At the present moment we are suffering, not from decay, but from having no code of manners which writers and readers accept as a prelude to the more exciting intercourse of friendship. The literary convention of the time is so artificial – you have to talk about the weather and nothing but the weather throughout the entire visit – that, naturally, the feeble are tempted to outrage, and the strong are led to destroy the very foundations and rules of literary society. Signs of this are everywhere apparent. Grammar is violated; syntax disintegrated; as a boy staying with an aunt for the weekend rolls in the geranium bed out of sheer desperation as the solemnities of the sabbath wear on. The more adult writers do not, of course, indulge in such wanton exhibitions of spleen. Their sincerity is desperate, and their courage tremendous; it is only that they do not know which to use, a fork or their fingers. Thus, if you read Mr. Joyce and Mr. Eliot you will be struck by the indecency of the one, and the obscurity of the other. Mr. Joyce's indecency in *Ulysses* seems to me the conscious and calculated indecency of a desperate man who feels that in order to breathe he must break the windows. At moments, when the window is broken, he is magnificent. But what a waste of energy! And, after all, how dull indecency is, when it is not the overflowing of a super-abundant energy or savagery, but the determined and public-spirited act of a man who needs fresh air! Again, with the obscurity of Mr. Eliot. I think that Mr. Eliot has written some of the loveliest single lines of modern poetry. But how intolerant he is of the old usages and politenesses of society – respect for the weak, consideration for the dull! As I sun myself upon the intense and ravishing beauty of one of his lines, and reflect that I must make a dizzy and dangerous leap to the next, and so on from line to line, like an acrobat flying precariously from bar to bar, I cry out, I confess, for the old decorums, and envy the indolence of my ancestors who, instead of spinning madly through mid-air, dreamt quietly in the shade with a book.

[. . .]

For these reasons, then, we must reconcile ourselves to a season of failures and fragments. We must reflect that where so much strength is spent on finding a way of telling the truth the truth itself is bound to reach us in rather an exhausted and chaotic condition.

[. . .]

But do not expect just at present a complete and satisfactory presentment of her. Tolerate the spasmodic, the obscure, the fragmentary, the failure. Your help is invoked in a good cause. For I will make one final and surpassingly rash prediction – we are trembling on the verge of one of the great ages of English literature. But it can only be reached if we are determined never, never to desert Mrs. Brown.

Modern Fiction

Look within and life, it seems, is very far from being 'like this'. Examine for a moment an ordinary mind on an ordinary day. The mind receives a myriad impressions – trivial, fantastic, evanescent, or engraved with the sharpness of steel. From all sides they come, an incessant shower of innumerable atoms; and as they fall, as they shape themselves into the life of Monday or Tuesday, the accent falls differently from of old; the moment of importance came not here but there; so that, if a writer were a free man and not a slave, if he could write what he chose, not what he must, if he could base his work upon his own feeling and not upon convention, there would be no plot, no comedy, no tragedy, no love interest or catastrophe in the accepted style, and perhaps not a single button sewn on as the Bond Street tailors would have it. Life is not a series of gig lamps symmetrically arranged; life is a luminous halo, a semi-transparent envelope surrounding us from the beginning of consciousness to the end. Is it not the task of the novelist to convey this varying, this unknown and uncircumscribed spirit, whatever aberration or complexity it may display, with as little mixture of the alien and external as possible?

20
JAMES JOYCE (1882–1941)
LETTER TO HARRIET SHAW WEAVER, 15 AUGUST 1925

Irish writer, born in Dublin and self-exiled in Europe for most of his life. Educated by Jesuits at Clongowes Wood College (an experience which is famously reconstructed in his A Portrait of the Artist as a Young Man, *serialised in* The Egoist *in 1914–15 and published separately in 1916), Joyce studied at University College, Dublin. Religious and political bigotry, as well as artistic self-consciousness, drove Joyce out of Ireland. On a brief visit to Dublin after his mother's death, he met Nora Barnacle, his companion for the rest of his life, which was spent in Trieste, Zurich and Paris. His collection of short stories – sketches of life in a 'paralysed' Dublin – Dubliners (1914) earned*

him the admiration of Ezra Pound, who became a friend and supporter. Joyce imaginatively revisited
Dublin in Ulysses, *published in Paris in 1922. This novel provoked violent reactions (characterised*
as 'obscene') but also established Joyce as the master of Modernist writing. His reputation as one of
the key literary innovators of the twentieth century was secured by the serialisation in transition *(as*
Work in Progress*) and the publication in 1939 of* Finnegans Wake, *the epitome of Modernist*
experimentation with language, form and genre.

15 August 1925   *Régina Palace Hotel & d'Angleterre, Arcachon*
Dear Miss Weaver: I left Rouen (where we were drenched for 9 days out of twelve)
and stopping a night in Niort and Bordeaux reached here. Thunderstorms greeted my
stay in Niort and Bordeaux. Here the weather is serene and warm. I wanted to go on to
London, if possible, before going back to Paris but as *Exiles* will be put on in January
or February I decided to come south now (in spite of the heat) and go to London
then. The soil here is dry sand and the climate ought to improve me and I am only
an hour from Dax where Dr Borsch advised me to go. I hope I can do so for a week
or so before I go away. But certainly my sight is curious—even in the good eye. At
Fécamp in the ninth row of the stalls I could not see the actors' faces. The morning
after I came here I tried to walk down to the beach but had to come back as my sight
was overclouded. It is very trying on one's nerves.

The other part of the news is. My concierge writes (without accents) that he is
leaving the house. *Envoyer* he writes *envoillez*. Lest I should forget him he encloses a
bill. Mr Gorman, my biographer, has been firing letters and telegrams at me. He wants
to come and see me. He is in *Victoria Palace Hotel*, Paris. Mr Walsh has been holding
me up with his delay in printing Shem and now the editor of the *Calendar* has written
for the fourth or fifth time to know if he can announce Δ [*Anna Livia Plurabelle*] for
October. I think I shall say yes for I want to correct these two pieces at once and get
a few minutes of torpor before the next act.

I started to read Mr Gillet's article when my sight was better than it is today. I read
about half and was much amused by it and gave it to my son. He gave it back saying it
was not at all amusing so I then read the rest of it which, in fact, is very harsh. I think
the explanation is to be found in a letter he wrote Miss Beach explaining the delay in
finishing his article, his reason being 'mais je viens de subir la perte de ma mère'. He
makes one or two good points which, however, I could answer. But it does not matter.
It will act like the *Quarterly*, savage and tartarly.

When are you going to London. Mr Mac Cormack will surely give a concert there
and I would like you to hear him. Could someone there look out for you and book a
seat for you? My host here is onearmed.

> Rouen is the rainiest place getting
> Inside all impermeables, wetting
> Damp marrow in drenched bones.
> Midwinter soused us coming over Le Mans
> Our inn at Niort was the Grape of Burgundy
> But the winepress of the Lord thundered over that grape of Burgundy

And we left it in a hurgundy.
    (Hurry up, Joyce, it's time!)
I heard mosquitoes swarm in old Bordeaux
So many!
I had not thought the earth contained so many
    (Hurry up, Joyce, it's time)
Mr. Anthologos, the local gardener,
Greycapped, with politeness full of cunning
Has made wine these fifty years
And told me in his southern French
Le petit vin is the surest drink to buy
For if 'tis bad
Vous ne l'avez pas payé
    (Hurry up, hurry up, now, now, now!)
But we shall have great times,
When we return to Clinic, that waste land
O Esculapios!
    (Shan't we? Shan't we? Shan't we?)

With kindest regards and with remembrances to Miss Marsden
sincerely yours
                                                  JAMES JOYCE

21
RICHARD ALDINGTON (1892–1962)
FROM 'THE INFLUENCE OF MR. JAMES JOYCE' 1921

English novelist, poet and critic. In 1913 Aldington married the American poet H. D. (Hilda Doolittle) and became one of the founders of the short-lived Imagist movement. From 1914 he co-edited the periodical The Egoist *with H. D. and Harriet Shaw Weaver, overseeing the serialisation of Joyce's* A Portrait of the Artist as a Young Man *(1914–15). He collaborated with Ezra Pound and Wyndham Lewis on* Blast *and was an advocate of Vorticism. Aldington's own verse appeared in* Images 1910–1915 *(1915) and* Collected Poems *(1928). His anti-war novel,* Death of a Hero *(1929), indicted the social and intellectual complacency of pre-war Britain. In later years Aldington turned mainly to biography, producing works on D. H. Lawrence and T. E. Lawrence. The following extract is from a review of Joyce's* Ulysses *published in* The English Review *in April, 1921.*

Consider for a moment Mr. Joyce's position in the interval between *The Portrait* and *Ulysses*. He appeared to have outgrown the immature Naturalisme of *Dubliners* and had certainly improved immensely as a writer of fiction. True, *The Portrait* was sordid, but it had fine passages; the contest between the 'idealism' of Daedalus and the outer world of crass stupidity and ugliness was very moving. The spiritual conflict lifted the story out of squalor into tragedy, though there was a lingering over unsavoury details which spoiled the balance of the book. It was nasty in many spots, but with a kind of tonic nastiness. One felt that here was a man of extreme sensitiveness and talent getting rid of 'perilous stuff', throwing off the evil dreams and influences of mawkish youth to reach a saner, clearer view of human life. Many people must have had great hopes of Mr. Joyce. I did not for one moment desire him to accept a particle of that official optimism which is so poisonous; I did not want him to be 'sugary', or to affect a Renanesque benevolence and calm which were obviously foreign to his character. But I did hope to see him write real tragedy, and not return to the bastard genre of the Naturalistes who mingle satire and tragedy, and produce something wholly false; I hoped to see his characters emerge into a clearer air from the sordid arena in which they were subdued by Fate in a débris of decayed vegetables and putrid exhalations.

Clearly I hoped the wrong thing. *Ulysses* is more bitter, more sordid, more ferociously satirical than anything Mr. Joyce has yet written. It is a tremendous libel on humanity which I at least am not clever enough to refute, but which I am convinced is a libel. There is laughter in *Ulysses*, but it is a harsh, sneering kind, very different from the *gros rire* of Rabelais.

[. . .]

All I wish to say now is that I think Mr. Joyce overstresses certain aspects of existence which most writers foolishly ignore, that he tries to convince us that life is less attractive than we had thought even in our most depressed moods. I remember reading one of the 'Episodes' about three years ago in a frontline trench, and I think the situation was most appropriate. There indeed were vile smells, abrupt nerve-racking noises, dirt and disease; life was confined to a dismal hide-and-seek with annihilation; the conveniences, the amenities of existence were reduced to the compass of a large hole underground; lack of sleep, nerves, monotonous diet, no baths had made us all fit subjects for Mr. Joyce's sneers and satire. We, whom the noisy voices of two continents vaunted as heroes, by a singular irony were no more than a red-eyed, muddy, unshaved set of 'pitiful rascals' puddling along duck-boards, crawling among shell-holes and rusty wire, dodging ferocious instruments of death, wholly absorbed in the problem of how to live until the next relief, and completely depressed by the impossibility of escape. But were we despicable? Had we poor infantry cannon-fodder – apt symbols of humanity in a world whose misery seems to have neither purpose nor justification – had we nothing to set against our grotesque sufferings? Let those answer 'No' who never knew the comradeship of the front line, who never saw a man give his life for another, who never shared that dumb, profound kindness of common men under a mutual disaster. I knew that comradeship; I knew an obscure soldier who lay out under a heavy barrage to give the comfort of his presence to two wounded men, though he could easily have escaped to safety, and was indeed ordered to do so; I have known an officer lose his life to save his servant's. And I say that such things, obscure, unknown, show that men are not wholly debased, even by the disgusting savagery of war, that they can be equally superior in the disgusting vulgarities of daily existence. I say, moreover that when Mr. Joyce, with his marvellous gifts, uses them to disgust us with mankind, he is doing something which is false and a libel on humanity.

That is my opinion of Mr. Joyce's *Ulysses*. From the point of view of art there is some justification for Mr. Joyce; he has succeeded in writing a most remarkable book;

but from the point of view of human life I am sure he is wrong. Moreover, the style of *Ulysses*, which Mr. Joyce usually handles successfully, will be as deplorably false in his imitators as his philosophy. *Ulysses* is a gigantic soliloquy. Bloom is a kind of rags and tatters Hamlet, a proletarian Lear, 'mirroring' life and showing it to be hideous. Mr. Joyce has pushed the intimate detailed analysis of character to a point further than any writer I know. His faithful reproduction of Bloom's thoughts, with their inconsequence, their staccato breaks, their returns to an obsession, is an astonishing psychological document. The telegraphic method is there apt and justified. And there is also a good artistic reason for the abandonment of all unity of prose tone, a unity always observed by the French Naturalistes. Sometimes Mr. Joyce writes journalese; sometimes a kind of prose poetry; sometimes a rapid narrative; often the telegraphic prose of Bloom's thoughts; occasionally he is deliberately obscene; too often he is incoherent. Yet in nearly every case he achieves his 'effect'. He has done daring but quite wonderful things with words. He can be sober, ironic, disgusting, platitudinous, sarcastic, realistic, just as he wishes. He has telescoped drama with narrative, and varies the tone of his narrative to suit the dramatic situation. He is no longer objective, no more the detached narrator; he wishes to identify himself with his subject, and to identify both with the reader. It is this which makes me say he has made realism mystic. He has lost the sense of mental boundaries; his writing is a sort of self-abandonment, a merging of his consciousness in that of others.

[. . .]

Imagine this heterogeneous style degenerated into incoherence, affectation, and wordy confusion, and then think what will be the result of Mr. Joyce's influence. I attach no overwhelming importance to the Dadaistes; as I am reminded, they have not managed to destroy M. Anatole France; but a whole generation of Dada in England and France would be rather deplorable. If the Dadaistes wish to destroy literature by making it ridiculous (as they have declared), they are welcome to try; but I think they should not be encouraged. Yet Mr. Joyce, with his great undisciplined talent, is more dangerous than a ship-load of Dadaistes. Young writers will be dominated by his personality; they will copy his eccentricities instead of developing their own minds. If only we could treat Mr. Joyce as Plato recommends; give him praise and anoint him with oil, and put a crown of purple wool on his head, and send him to the United States.

22
CARL JUNG (1875–1961)
FROM '*ULYSSES*: EIN MONOLOG' 1932

Swiss psychologist and psychiatrist. Jung became interested in psychology while studying medecine at Zurich. From 1907–12 he collaborated with Freud, but they later diverged over Freud's conviction that the basis of neurosis was sexual. Psychology of the Unconscious *(1912) marked Jung's break with Freudianism. He turned his attention to the scientific investigation of dreams and fantasies which he maintained originated in the 'collective unconscious' – a racial memory in which all humans share and which is manifested in recurrent images and patterns or 'archetypes'. Like Freud, Jung was interested in literature, though he was guarded about the applicability of his own theories to literary criticism. The following extract is taken from his review of Joyce's* Ulysses *which was first published in* Europäische Revue *(viii, September 1932) and appears here in R. F. C. Hull's translation* (Collected Works of C. G. Jung, *Volume 15, 1966*).

The Ulysses of my title has to do with James Joyce and not with that shrewd and storm-driven figure of Homer's world who knew how to escape by guile and by deed the enmity or vengeance of gods and men, and who after a wearisome voyage returned to hearth and home. In strongest contrast to his Greek namesake, Joyce's Ulysses is an inactive, merely perceiving consciousness; a mere eye, ear, nose, and mouth, a sensory nerve exposed without choice or check to the roaring, chaotic, nonsensical cataract of psychic or physical happenings, and registering all of this in an almost photographic way.

Ulysses is a book which pours along for seven hundred and thirty-five pages, a stream of time of seven hundred and thirty-five days which all consist in one single and senseless every day of Everyman, the completely irrelevant 16th day of June 1904, in Dublin – a day on which, in all truth, nothing happens. The stream begins in the void and ends in the void. Is all of this perhaps one single, immensely long and excessively complicated Strindbergian pronouncement upon the essence of human life, and one which, to the reader's dismay, is never finished? Perhaps it does touch upon the essence of life; but quite certainly it touches upon life's ten thousand surfaces and their hundred thousand color gradations. As far as my glance reaches, there are in those seven hundred and thirty-five pages no obvious repetitions and not a single hallowed island where the long-suffering reader may come to rest. There is not a single place where he can seat himself, drunk with memories, and from which he can happily consider the stretch of road he has covered, be it one hundred pages or even less. If he could only recognize some little commonplace which had slipped in where it was not expected. But no! The pitiless and uninterrupted stream rolls by, and its velocity or precipitation grows in the last forty pages till it sweeps away even the marks of punctuation. It thus gives cruelest expression to that emptiness which is both breath taking and stifling, which is under such tension, or is so filled to bursting, as to grow unbearable. This thoroughly hopeless emptiness is the dominant note of the whole book. It not only begins and ends in nothingness, but it consists of nothing but nothingness. It is all infernally nugatory. If we regard the book from the side of technical artistry, it is a positively brilliant and hellish monster-birth.

I had an old uncle whose thinking was always to the point. One day he stopped me on the street and asked, 'Do you know how the devil tortures the souls in hell?' When I said no, he declared, 'He keeps them waiting.' And with that he walked away. This remark occurred to me when I was ploughing through *Ulysses* for the first time. Every sentence raises an expectation which is not fulfilled; finally, out of sheer resignation, you come to expect nothing any longer. Then bit by bit, again to your horror, it dawns upon you that in all truth you have hit the nail on the head. It is actual fact that nothing happens and nothing comes of it, and yet a secret expectation at war with hopeless resignation drags the reader from page to page. The seven hundred and thirty-five pages that contain nothing by no means consist of blank paper but are closely printed. You read and read and read and you pretend to understand what you read. Occasionally you drop through an air pocket into another sentence, but when once the proper degree of resignation has been reached you accustom yourself to anything. So I, too, read to page one hundred and thirty-five with despair in my heart, falling asleep twice on the way. The incredible multifariousness of Joyce's style has a monotonous and hypnotic effect. Nothing comes to the reader; everything turns away from him and leaves him to gape after it. The book is always up and away; it is not at peace with itself, but is at once ironic, sarcastic, poisonous, disdainful, sad, despairing, and bitter. . . .

23
FRANK BUDGEN (1882–1971)
FROM *JAMES JOYCE AND THE MAKING OF 'ULYSSES'* 1934

British painter and Joyce scholar who became the novelist's close friend in Zurich. James Joyce and the Making of 'Ulysses' (1934) *is Budgen's record of their early conversations and of their continuing friendship.*

[. . .]

'I am now writing a book,' said Joyce, 'based on the wanderings of Ulysses. The Odyssey, that is to say, serves me as a ground plan. Only my time is recent time and all my hero's wanderings take no more than eighteen hours.'

A train of vague thoughts arose in my mind, but failed to take shape definite enough for any comment. I drew with them in silence the shape of the Uetliberg-Albis line of hills. The Odyssey for me was just a long poem that might at any moment be illustrated by some Royal Academician. I could see his water-colour Greek heroes, book-opened, in an Oxford Street bookshop window.

Joyce spoke again more briskly:

'You seem to have read a lot, Mr. Budgen. Do you know of any complete all-round character presented by any writer?'

With quick interest I summoned up a whole population of invented persons. Of the fiction writers Balzac, perhaps, might supply him? No. Flaubert? No. Dostoevski or Tolstoi then? Their people are exciting, wonderful, but not complete. Shakespeare surely. But no, again. The foot-lights, the proscenium arch, the fatal curtain are all there to present to us not complete, all-round beings, but only three hours of passionate conflict. I came to rest on Goethe.

'What about Faust?' I said. And then, as a second shot 'Or Hamlet?'

'Faust!' said Joyce. 'Far from being a complete man, he isn't a man at all. Is he an old man or a young man? Where are his home and family? We don't know. And he can't be complete because he's never alone. Mephistopheles is always hanging round him at his side or heels. We see a lot of him, that's all.'

It was easy to see the answer in Joyce's mind to his own question.

'Your complete man in literature is, I suppose, Ulysses?'

'Yes,' said Joyce 'No-age Faust isn't a man. But you mentioned Hamlet. Hamlet is a human being, but he is a son only. Ulysses is son to Laertes, but he is father to Telemachus, husband to Penelope, lover of Calypso, companion in arms of the Greek warriors around Troy and King of Ithaca. He was subjected to many trials, but with wisdom and courage came through them all. Don't forget that he was a war dodger who tried to evade military service by simulating madness. He might never have taken up arms and gone to Troy, but the Greek recruiting sergeant was too clever for him and, while he was ploughing the sands, placed young Telemachus in front of his plough. But once at the war the conscientious objector became a jusqu'auboutist. When the others wanted to abandon the siege he insisted on staying till Troy should fall.'

I laughed at Ulysses as a leadswinger and Joyce continued:

'Another thing, the history of Ulysses did not come to an end when the Trojan war was over. It began just when the other Greek heroes went back to live the rest of their lives in peace. And then' – Joyce laughed – 'he was the first gentleman in Europe. When he advanced, naked, to meet the young princess he hid from her maidenly eyes the parts that mattered of his brine-soaked, barnacle-encrusted body. He was an inventor too. The tank is his creation. Wooden horse or iron box – it doesn't matter. They are both shells containing armed warriors.'

[. . .]

'What do you mean,' I said, 'by a complete man? For example, if a sculptor makes a figure of a man then that man is all-round, three-dimensional, but not necessarily complete in the sense of being ideal. All human bodies are imperfect, limited in some way, human beings too. Now your Ulysses . . .'

'He is both,' said Joyce. 'I see him from all sides, and therefore he is all-round in the sense of your sculptor's figure. But he is a complete man as well – a good man. At any rate, that is what I intend that he shall be.'

[. . .]

I enquired about *Ulysses*. Was it progressing?

'I have been working hard on it all day,' said Joyce.

'Does that mean that you have written a great deal?' I said.

'Two sentences,' said Joyce.

I looked sideways but Joyce was not smiling. I thought of Flaubert.

'You have been seeking the *mot juste*?' I said.

'No,' said Joyce. 'I have the words already. What I am seeking is the perfect order of words in the sentence. There is an order in every way appropriate. I think I have it.'

'What are the words?' I asked.

'I believe I told you,' said Joyce, 'that my book is a modern Odyssey. Every episode in it corresponds to an adventure of Ulysses. I am now writing the *Lestrygonians* episode, which corresponds to the adventure of Ulysses with the cannibals. My hero is going to lunch. But there is a seduction motive in the Odyssey, the cannibal king's daughter. Seduction appears in my book as women's silk petticoats hanging in a shop window. The words through which I express the effect of it on my hungry hero are: 'Perfume of embraces all him assailed. With hungered flesh obscurely, he mutely craved to adore.' You can see for yourself in how many different ways they might be arranged.'

[. . .]

'Among other things,' he said, 'my book is the epic of the human body. The only man I know who has attempted the same thing is Phineas Fletcher. But then his *Purple Island* is purely descriptive, a kind of coloured anatomical chart of the human body. In my book the body lives in and moves through space and is the home of a full human personality. The words I write are adapted to express first one of its functions then another. In *Lestrygonians* the stomach dominates and the rhythm of the episode is that of the peristaltic movement.'

'But the minds, the thoughts of the characters,' I began.

'If they had no body they would have no mind,' said Joyce. 'It's all one. Walking towards his lunch my hero, Leopold Bloom, thinks of his wife, and says to himself, "Molly's legs are out of plumb." At another time of day he might have expressed the same thought without any underthought of food. But I want the reader to understand always through suggestion rather than direct statement.'

[. . .]

24
D. H. (DAVID HERBERT) LAWRENCE (1885–1930)
LETTER TO A. W. McLEOD, 2 JUNE 1914;
FROM LETTER TO EDWARD GARNETT, 5 JUNE 1914;
FROM PREFACE TO THE AMERICAN EDITION OF *NEW POEMS* 1929

English novelist, poet, essayist, playwright and painter. Lawrence's first novel, The White Peacock *(1911) was published with the assistance of Ford Madox Ford and his second, the* Trespasser *(1912), with the help of Edward Garnett, then reader at Duckworth and Co. In 1912 Lawrence met Frieda von Richthofen. They went to Germany together where Lawrence finished* Sons and Lovers *(1913). They married and returned to England in 1914, but during the war years Frieda's nationality caused a resentment that deeply depressed Lawrence. After the war they left England to travel in Italy, Australia and Mexico, settling finally in the south of France. Lawrence's next two novels,* The Rainbow *(1915) and* Women in Love *(1920) – originally conceived as one work,* The Sisters *– give fullest expression to his central themes: the relationship between the sexes, between individuals and their environment, the forces of intuition and instinct and how they are related to (or are stunted by) rationality and the intellect. All of the above relationships were considered by Lawrence to be fraught and, if unresolved or harmonised, potentially dangerous both for the individual and for culture as a whole. His vision of a desirable solution is a unique and semi-apocalyptic blend of Nietzschean, Jungian, Blakean and primitivist motifs and is expounded in* Fantasis of the Unconscious *and* Psychoanalysis and the Unconscious, *published in 1923. The following selection includes Lawrence's letter to his friend and fellow-teacher at Davidson Road School (Croydon, Surrey) A. W. McLeod, an extract from a letter to the writer, editor and early mentor Edward Garnett and his Preface to the American edition of* New Poems, *published in 1920.*

Lerici, per Fiascherino,
Golfo della Spezia, Italia.
To A. D. McLeod. 2 *Junio*, 1914.

Dear Mac, –

I never thanked you for the Meredith poems. I was very glad indeed to get them – and a bit disappointed in them. They aren't what I want just now, I suppose.

I have been interested in the futurists. I got a book of their poetry – a very fat book too – and a book of pictures – and I read Marinetti's and Paolo Buzzi's manifestations and essays and Soffici's essays on cubism and futurism. It interests me very much. I like it because it is the applying to emotions of the purging of the old forms and sentimentalities. I like it for its saying – enough of this sickly cant, let us be honest and stick by what is in us. Only when folk say, 'Let us be honest and stick by what is in us' – they always mean, stick by those things that have been thought horrid, and by those alone. They want to deny every scrap of tradition and experience, which is silly. They are very young, college-student and medical-student at his most blatant. But I like them. Only I don't believe in them. I agree with them about the weary sickness of pedantry and tradition and inertness, but I don't agree with them as to the cure and the escape. They will progress down the purely male or intellectual or scientific line. They will even use their intuition for intellectual and scientific purpose. The one thing about their art is that it *isn't* art, but ultra scientific attempts to make diagrams of certain physic or mental states. It is ultra-ultra intellectual, going beyond Maeterlinck and the Symbolistes, who are intellectual. There isn't one trace of naïveté in the works – though there's plenty of naïveté in the authors. It's the most self-conscious, intentional, pseudo-scientific stuff on the face of the earth. Marinetti begins: 'Italy is like a great Dreadnought surrounded by her torpedo boats.' That is it exactly – a great mechanism. Italy has got to go through the most mechanical and dead stage of all – everything is appraised according to its mechanic value – everything is subject to the laws of physics. This is the revolt against beastly sentiment and slavish adherence to tradition and the dead mind. For that I love it. I love them when they say to the child, 'All right, if you want to drag nests and torment kittens, do it lustily.' But I reserve the right to answer, 'All right, try it on. But if I catch you at it you get a hiding.'

I think the only re-sourcing of art, revivifying it, is to make it more the joint work of man and woman. I think *the* one thing to do, is for men to have courage to draw nearer to women, expose themselves to them, and be altered by them: and for women to accept and admit men. That is the start – by bringing themselves together, men and women – revealing themselves each to the other, gaining great blind knowledge and suffering and joy, which it will take a big further lapse of civilisation to exploit and work out. Because the source of all life and knowledge is in man and woman, and the source of all living is in the interchange and the meeting and mingling of these two: man-life and woman-life, man-knowledge and woman-knowledge, man-being and woman-being.

Which is a sermon on a stool. We are leaving here on the 8th – next Monday. Frieda goes to Baden Baden for about two days. I am coming to England by ship. We are staying with Gordon H. Campbell in 9, Selwood Terrace, 5th Kensington. I shall write to you as soon as we arrive. I shall be 8 or 9 or 10 days at sea, I think.

We are all upset, moving. I want to write an essay about Futurism, when I have the inspiration and wit thereunto.

Lerici, per Fiascherino,
Golfo della Spezia, Italia.
To Edward Garnett.5 *Junio,* 1914.

[. . .] But when I read Marinetti – 'the profound intuitions of life added one to the other, word by word, according to their illogical conception, will give us the general lines of an intuitive physiology of matter' – I see something of what I am after. I translate him clumsily, and his Italian is obfuscated – and I don't care about physiology of matter – but somehow – that which is physic – non-human, in humanity, is more interesting to me than the old-fashioned human element – which causes one to conceive a character in a certain moral scheme and make him consistent. The certain moral scheme is what I object to. In Turgenev, and in Tolstoi, and in Dostoievsky, the moral scheme into which all the characters fit – and it is nearly the same scheme – is, whatever the extraordinariness of the characters themselves, dull, old, dead. When Marinetti writes: 'It is the solidity of a blade of steel that is interesting by itself, that is, the incomprehending and inhuman alliance of its molecules in resistance to, let us say, a bullet. The heat of a piece of wood or iron is in fact more passionate, for us, than the laughter or tears of a woman' – then I know what he means. He is stupid, as an artist, for contrasting the heat of the iron and the laugh of the woman. Because what is interesting in the laugh of the woman is the same as the binding of the molecules of steel or their action in heat: it is the inhuman will, call it physiology, or like Marinetti – physiology of matter, that fascinates me. I don't so much care about what the woman *feels* – in the ordinary usage of the word. That presumes an *ego* to feel with. I only care about what the woman *is* – what she is – inhumanly, physiologically, materially – according to the use of the word: but for me, what she *is* as a phenomenon (or as representing some greater, inhuman will), instead of what she feels according to the human conception. That is where the futurists are stupid. Instead of looking for the new human phenomenon, they will only look for the phenomena of the science of physics to be found in human beings. They are crassly stupid. But if anyone would give them eyes, they would pull the right apples off the tree, for their stomachs are true in appetite.

You mustn't look in my novel for the old stable *ego* of the character. There is another *ego*, according to whose action the individual is unrecognisable, and passes through, as it were, allotropic states which it needs a deeper sense than any we' ve been used to exercise, to discover are states of the same single radically unchanged element. (Like as diamond and coal are the same pure single element of carbon. The ordinary novel would trace the history of the diamond – but I say, 'Diamond, what! This is carbon.' And my diamond might be coal or soot, and my theme is carbon.) You must not say my novel is shaky – it is not perfect, because I am not expert in what I want to do. But it is the real thing, say what you like. And I shall get my reception, if not now, then before long. Again I say, don't look for the development of the novel to follow the lines of certain characters: the characters fall into the form of some other rhythmic form, as when one draws a fiddle-bow across a fine tray delicately sanded, the sand takes lines unknown.

Preface to the American edition of *New Poems*
It seems when we hear a skylark singing as if sound were running into the future, running so fast and utterly without consideration, straight on into futurity. And when we hear a nightingale, we hear the pause and the rich, piercing rhythm of recollection, the perfected past. The lark may sound sad, but with the lovely lapsing sadness that is almost a swoon of hope. The nightingale's triumph is a paean, but a death-paean.

So it is with poetry. Poetry is, as a rule, either the voice of the far future, exquisite and ethereal, or it is the voice of the past, rich, magnificent. When the Greeks heard the *Iliad* and the *Odyssey* they heard their own past calling in their hearts, as men far inland sometimes hear the sea and fall weak with powerful, wonderful regret, nostalgia; or else their own future rippled its time-beats through their blood, as they followed the painful, glamorous progress of the Ithacan. This was Homer to the Greeks: their Past, splendid with battles won and death achieved, and their Future, the magic wandering of Ulysses through the unknown.

With us it is the same. Our birds sing on the horizons. They sing out of the blue, beyond us, or out of the quenched night. They sing at dawn and sunset. Only the poor, shrill, tame canaries whistle while we talk. The wild birds begin before we are awake, or as we drop into dimness, out of waking. Our poets sit by the gateways, some by the east, some by the west. As we arrive and as we go out our hearts surge with response. But whilst we are in the midst of life, we do not hear them.

The poetry of the beginning and the poetry of the end must have that exquisite finality, perfection which belongs to all that is far off. It is in the realm of all that is perfect. It is of the nature of all that is complete and consummate. This completeness, this consummateness, the finality and the perfection are conveyed in exquisite form: the perfect symmetry, the rhythm which returns upon itself like a dance where the hands link and loosen and link for the supreme moment of the end. Perfected bygone moments, perfected moments in the glimmering futurity, these are the treasured gem-like lyrics of Shelley and Keats.

But there is another kind of poetry: the poetry of that which is at hand: the immediate present. In the immediate present there is no perfection, no consummation, nothing finished. The strands are all flying, quivering, intermingling into the web, the waters are shaking the moon. There is no round, consummate moon on the face of running water, nor on the face of the unfinished tide. There are no gems of the living plasm. The living plasm vibrates unspeakably, it inhales the future, it exhales the past, it is the quick of both, and yet it is neither. There is no plasmic finality, nothing crystal, permanent. If we try to fix the living tissue, as the biologists fix it with formation, we have only a hardened bit of the past, bygone life under our observation.

Life, the ever-present, knows no finality, no finished crystallization. The perfect rose is only a running flame, emerging and flowing off, and never in any sense at rest, static, finished. Herein lies its transcendent liveliness. The whole tide of all life and all time suddenly heaves, and appears before us as an apparition, a revelation. We look at the very white quick of nascent creation. A water-lily heaves herself from the flood, looks around, gleams, and is gone. We have seen the incarnation, the quick of the ever-whirling flood. We have seen the invisible. We have seen, we have touched, we have partaken of the very substance of creative change, creative mutation. If you tell me about the lotus, tell me of nothing changeless or eternal. Tell me of the mystery of the inexhaustible, forever-unfolding creative spark. Tell me of the incarnate disclosure of the flux, mutation in blossom, laughter and decay perfectly open in their transit, nude in their movement before us.

Let me feel the mud and the heavens in my lotus. Let me feel the heavy, silting, sucking mud, the spinning of sky winds. Let me feel them both in purest contact, the nakedness of sucking weight, nakedly passing radiance. Give me nothing fixed, set, static. Don't give me the infinite or the eternal: nothing of infinity, nothing of eternity. Give me the still, white seething, the incandescence and the coldness of the incarnate moment: the moment, the quick of all change and haste and opposition: the moment, the immediate present, the Now. The immediate moment is not a drop of water running downstream. It is the source and issue, the bubbling up of the stream. Here, in this very instant moment, up bubbles the stream of time, out of the wells of futurity, flowing on to the oceans of the past. The source, the issue, the creative quick.

There is poetry of this immediate present, instant poetry, as well as poetry of the infinite past and the infinite future. The seething poetry of the incarnate Now is supreme, beyond even the everlasting gems of the before and after. In its quivering momentaneity it surpasses the crystalline, pearl-hard jewels, the poems of the eternities. Do not ask for the qualities of the unfading timeless gems. Ask for the whiteness which is the seethe of mud, ask for that incipient putrescence which is the skies falling, ask for the never-pausing, never-ceasing life itself. There must be mutation, swifter that iridescence, haste, not rest, come-and-go, not fixity, inconclusiveness, immediacy, the quality of life itself, without denouement or close. There must be the rapid momentaneous association of things which meet and pass on the for ever incalculable journey of creation: everything left in its own rapid, fluid relationship with the rest of things.

This is the unrestful, ungraspable poetry of the sheer present, poetry whose very permanency lies in its wind-like transit. Whitman's is the best poetry of this kind. Without beginning and without end, without any base and pediment, it sweeps past for ever, like a wind that is for ever in passage and unchainable. Whitman truly looked before and after. But he did not sigh for what is not. The clue to all his utterance lies in the sheer appreciation of the instant moment, life surging itself into utterance at its very well-head. Eternity is only an abstraction from the actual present. Infinity is only a great reservoir of recollection, or a reservoir of aspiration: man-made. The quivering nimble hour of the present, this is the quick of Time. This is the immanence. The quick of the universe is the *pulsating carnal self* mysterious and palpable. So it is always.

Because Whitman put this into his poetry, we fear him and respect him so profoundly. We should not fear him if he sang only of the 'old unhappy far-off things', or of the 'wings of the morning'. It is because his heart beats with the urgent, insurgent Now, which is even upon us all, that we dread him. He is so near the quick.

From the foregoing it is obvious that the poetry of the instant present cannot have the same body or the same motion as the poetry of the before and after. It can never submit to the same conditions. It is never finished. There is no rhythm which returns upon itself, no serpent of eternity with its tail in its own mouth. There is no static perfection, none of that finality which we find so satisfying because we are so frightened.

Much has been written about free verse. But all that can be said, first and last, is that free verse is, or should be direct utterance from the instant, whole man. It is the soul and the mind and body surging at once, nothing left out. They speak all together. There is some confusion, some discord. But the confusion and the discord only belong to the reality, as noise belongs to the plunge of water. It is no use inventing fancy laws for free verse, no use drawing a melodic line which all the feet must toe. Free verse toes no melodic line, no matter what drill-sergeant. Whitman pruned away his clichés – perhaps his clichés of rhythm as well as of phrase. And this is about all we can do, deliberately, with free verse. We can get rid of the stereotyped movements and the old hackneyed associations of sound or sense. We can break down those artificial conduits and canals through which we do so love to force our utterance. We can break the stiff neck of habit. We can be ourselves spontaneous and flexible as flame, we can see that utterance rushes out without artificial form or artificial smoothness. But we cannot positively prescribe any motion, any rhythm. All the laws we invent or discover – it amounts to pretty much the same – will fail to apply to free verse. They will only apply to some form of restricted, limited un-free verse.

All we can say is that free verse does *not* have the same nature as restricted verse. It is not of the nature of reminiscence. It is not the past which we treasure in its perfection between our hands. Neither is it the crystal of the perfect future, into which we gaze. Its tide is neither the full, yearning flow of aspiration, nor the sweet, poignant ebb of remembrance and regret. The past and the future are the two great bournes of human emotion, the two great homes of the human days, the two eternities. They are both conclusive, final. Their beauty is the beauty of the goal, finished, perfected. Finished beauty and measured symmetry belong to the stable, unchanging eternities.

But in free verse we look for the insurgent naked throb of the instant moment. To break the lovely form of metrical verse, and to dish up the fragments as a new substance, called *vers libre*, this is what most of the free-versifiers accomplish. They do not know that free verse has its own *nature*, that it is neither star nor pearl, but instantaneous like plasm. It has no goal in either eternity. It has no finish. It has no satisfying stability, satisfying to those who like the immutable. None of this. It is the instant; the quick; the very jetting source of all will-be and has-been. The utterance is like a spasm, naked contact with all influences at once. It does not want to get anywhere. It just takes place.

For such utterance any externally applied law would be mere shackles and death. The law must come new each time from within. The bird is on the wing in the winds, flexible to every breath, a living spark in the storm, its very flickering depending upon its supreme mutability and power of change. Whence such a bird came: whither it goes: from what solid earth it rose up, and upon what solid earth it will close its wings and settle, this is not the question. This is a question of before and after. Now, *now*, the bird is on the wing in the winds.

Such is the rare new poetry. One realm we have never conquered: the pure present. One great mystery of time is *terra incognita* to us: the instant. The most superb mystery we have hardly recognized: the immediate, instant self. The quick of all time is the instant. The quick of all the universe, of all creation, is the incarnate, carnal self. Poetry gave us the clue: free verse: Whitman. Now we know.

The ideal – what is the ideal? A figment. An abstraction. A static abstraction, abstracted from life. It is a fragment of the before or the after. It is a crystallized aspiration, or a crystallized remembrance: crystallized, set, finished. It is a thing set apart, in the great storehouse of eternity, the storehouse of finished things.

We do not speak of things crystallized and set apart. We speak of the instant, the immediate self, the very plasm of the self. We speak also of free verse.

All this should have come as a preface to *Look! We have Come Through!* But is it not better to publish a preface long after the book it belongs to has appeared? For then the reader will have had his fair chance with the book, alone.

25
ALAIN LOCKE (1886–1954)
FROM INTRODUCTION TO *THE NEW NEGRO* 1925

Prominent African-American scholar and critical authority on the Harlem Renaissance. Locke was the first African-American Rhodes Scholar (1907–10). His Howard University doctorate dissertation in philosophy was on 'The Problem of Classification in Theory of Value' (1918). He held the chair of philosophy at Howard until 1953. Locke expanded on the special Harlem edition of Survey Graphic, *'Harlem: Mecca of the New Negro' (1925) which he had co-edited, to produce the key Harlem book* The New Negro *(1925). This collection was the showcase for the flourishing new black talents in the arts whose centre was Harlem in the 1920s. Zora Neale Hurston, Langston Hughes and Claude McKay are among those Locke helped to promote. He was an adviser to the Harmon Foundation which in 1926 began to give annual awards to black writers, artists and professionals; and in 1928 mounted the highly successful all-Negro art exhibition at International House, New York. Locke also established, with T. Montgomery Gregory, one of the first little theatre groups, the Howard Players, and they edited the first anthology of black drama,* Plays of Negro Life *(1927). Between 1923 and 1949 he was literary reviewer for* Opportunity: A Journal of Negro Life. *In 1924 he began a productive friendship with the Martiniquian writer René Maran, whose novel* Batoula *won the Prix Goncourt in 1921. They did much to promote exchange between Black American, French and Third World artists and intellectuals. [See Ia 17]*

In the last decade something beyond the watch and guard of statistics has happened in the life of the American Negro and the three norns who have traditionally presided over the Negro problem have a changeling in their laps. The Sociologist, the Philanthropist, the Race-leader are not unaware of the New Negro, but they are at a loss to account for him. He simply cannot be swathed in their formulæ. For the younger generation is vibrant with a new psychology; the new spirit is awake in the masses, and under the very eyes of the professional observers is transforming what has been a perennial problem into the progressive phases of contemporary Negro life.

Could such a metamorphosis have taken place as suddenly as it has appeared to? The answer is no; not because the New Negro is not here, but because the Old Negro had long become more of a myth than a man. The Old Negro, we must remember, was a creature of moral debate and historical controversy. His has been a stock figure perpetuated as an historical fiction partly in innocent sentimentalism, partly in deliberate reactionism. The Negro himself has contributed his share to this through a sort of protective social mimicry forced upon him by the adverse circumstances of dependence. So for generations in the mind of America, the Negro has been more of a formula than a human being – a something to be argued about, condemned or defended, to be 'kept down', or 'in his place', or 'helped up', to be worried with or worried over, harassed or patronized; a social bogey or a social burden. The thinking Negro even has been induced to share this same general attitude, to focus his attention on controversial issues, to see himself in the distorted perspective of a social problem. His shadow, so to speak, has been more real to him than his personality. Through having had to appeal from the unjust stereotypes of his oppressors and traducers to those of his liberators, friends and benefactors he has had to subscribe to the traditional positions from which his case has been viewed. Little true social or self-understanding has or could come from such a situation.

But while the minds of most of us, black and white, have thus burrowed in the trenches of the Civil War and Reconstruction, the actual march of development has simply flanked these positions, necessitating a sudden reorientation of view. We have not been watching in the right direction; set North and South on a sectional axis, we have not noticed the East till the sun has us blinking.

Recall how suddenly the Negro spirituals revealed themselves; suppressed for generations under the stereotypes of Wesleyan hymn harmony, secretive, half-ashamed, until the courage of being natural brought them out – and behold, there was folk-music. Similarly the mind of the Negro seems suddenly to have slipped from under the tyranny of social intimidation and to be shaking off the psychology of imitation and implied inferiority. By shedding the old chrysalis of the Negro problem we are achieving something like a spiritual emancipation. Until recently, lacking self-understanding, we have been almost as much of a problem to ourselves as we still are to others. But the decade that found us with a problem has left us with only a task. The multitude perhaps feels as yet only a strange relief and a new vague urge, but the thinking few know that in the reaction the vital inner grip of prejudice has been broken.

With this renewed self-respect and self-dependence, the life of the Negro community is bound to enter a new dynamic phase, the buoyancy from within compensating for whatever pressure there may be of conditions from without. The migrant masses, shifting from countryside to city, hurdle several generations of experience at a leap, but more important, the same thing happens spiritually in the life-attitudes and self-expression of the Young Negro, in his poetry, his art, his education and his new outlook, with the additional advantage, of course, of the poise and greater certainty of knowing what it is all about. From this comes the promise and warrant of a new leadership.

[. . .]

First we must observe some of the changes which since the traditional lines of opinion were drawn have rendered these quite obsolete. A main change has been, of course, that shifting of the Negro population which has made the Negro problem no longer exclusively or even predominantly Southern. Why should our minds remain sectionalized, when the problem itself no longer is? Then the trend of migration has not only been toward the North and the Central Midwest, but city-ward and to the great centers of industry – the problems of adjustment are new, practical, local and not peculiarly racial. Rather they are an integral part of the large industrial and social problems of our present-day democracy. And finally, with the Negro rapidly in process of class differentiation, if it ever was warrantable to regard and treat the Negro *en masse* it is becoming with every day less possible, more unjust and more ridiculous.

In the very process of being transplanted, the Negro is becoming transformed.

The tide of Negro migration, northward and city-ward, is not to be fully explained as a blind flood started by the demands of war industry coupled with the shutting off of foreign migration, or by the pressure of poor crops coupled with increased social terrorism in certain sections of the South and Southwest. Neither labor demand, the bollweevil nor the Ku Klux Klan is a basic factor, however contributory any or all of them may have been. The wash and rush of this human tide on the beach line of the northern city centers is to be explained primarily in terms of a new vision of opportunity, of social and economic freedom, of a spirit to seize, even in the face of an extortionate and heavy toll, a chance for the improvement of conditions. With each successive wave of it, the movement of the Negro becomes more and more a mass movement toward the larger and the more democratic chance – in the Negro's case a deliberate flight not only from countryside to city, but from medieval America to modern.

Take Harlem as an instance of this. Here in Manhattan is not merely the largest Negro community in the world, but the first concentration in history of so many diverse elements of Negro life. It has attracted the African, the West Indian, the Negro American; has brought together the Negro of the North and the Negro of the South; the man from the city and the man from the town and village; the peasant, the student, the business man, the professional man, artist, poet, musician, adventurer and worker, preacher and criminal, exploiter and social outcast. Each group has come with its own separate motives and for its own special ends, but their greatest experience has been the finding of one another. Proscription and prejudice have thrown these dissimilar elements into a common area of contact and interaction. Within this area, race sympathy and unity have determined a further fusing of sentiment and experience. So what began in terms of segregation becomes more and more, as its elements mix and react, the laboratory of a great race-welding. Hitherto, it must be admitted that American Negroes have been a race more in name than in fact, or to be exact, more in sentiment than in experience. The chief bond between them has been that of a common condition rather than a common consciousness; a problem in common rather than a life in common. In Harlem, Negro life is seizing upon its first chances for group expression and self-determination. It is – or promises at least to be – a race capital. That is why our comparison is taken with those nascent centers of folk-expression and self-determination which are playing a creative part in the world to-day. Without pretense to their political significance, Harlem has the same rôle to play for the New Negro as Dublin has had for the New Ireland or Prague for the New Czechoslovakia.

Harlem, I grant you, isn't typical – but it is significant, it is prophetic. No sane observer, however sympathetic to the new trend, would contend that the great masses are articulate as yet, but they stir, they move, they are more than physically restless. The challenge of the new intellectuals among them is clear enough – the 'race radicals' and realists who have broken with the old epoch of philanthropic guidance, sentimental appeal and protest. But are we after all only reading into the stirrings of a sleeping giant the dreams of an agitator? The answer is in the migrating peasant. It is the 'man farthest down' who is most active in getting up. One of the most characteristic symptoms of this is the professional man, himself migrating to recapture his constituency after a vain effort to maintain in some Southern corner what for years back seemed an established living and clientele. The clergyman following his errant flock, the physician or lawyer trailing his clients, supply the true clues. In a real sense it is the rank and file who are leading, and the leaders who are following. A transformed and transforming psychology permeates the masses.

When the racial leaders of twenty years ago spoke of developing race-pride and stimulating race-consciousness, and of the desirability of race solidarity, they could not in any accurate degree have anticipated the abrupt feeling that has surged up and now pervades the awakened centers.

[. . .]

The American mind must reckon with a fundamentally changed Negro.

The Negro too, for his part, has idols of the tribe to smash. If on the one hand the white man has erred in making the Negro appear to be that which would excuse or extenuate his treatment of him, the Negro, in turn, has too often unnecessarily excused himself because of the way he has been treated. The intelligent Negro of to-day is resolved not to make discrimination an extenuation for his shortcomings in performance, individual or collective; he is trying to hold himself at par, neither inflated by sentimental allowances nor depreciated by current social discounts. For this he must know himself and be known for precisely what he is, and for that reason he welcomes the new scientific rather than the old sentimental interest.

[. . .]

There is a growing realization that in social effort the co-operative basis must supplant long-distance philanthropy, and that the only safeguard for mass relations in the future must be provided in the carefully maintained contacts of the enlightened minorities of both race groups. In the intellectual realm a renewed and keen curiosity is replacing the recent apathy; the Negro is being carefully studied, not just talked about and discussed. In art and letters, instead of being wholly caricatured, he is being seriously portrayed and painted.

To all of this the New Negro is keenly responsive as an augury of a new democracy in American culture. He is contributing his share to the new social understanding. But the desire to be understood would never in itself have been sufficient to have opened so completely the protectively closed portals of the thinking Negro's mind. There is still too much possibility of being snubbed or patronized for that. It was rather the necessity for fuller, truer self-expression, the realization of the unwisdom of allowing social discrimination to segregate him mentally, and a counter-attitude to cramp and fetter his own living – and so the 'spite-wall' that the intellectuals built over the 'color-line' has happily been taken down. Much of this reopening of intellectual contacts has centered in New York and has been richly fruitful not merely in the enlarging of personal experience, but in the definite enrichment of American art and letters and in the clarifying of our common vision of the social tasks ahead.

[. . .]

However, this new phase of things is delicate; it will call for less charity but more justice; less help, but infinitely closer understanding. This is indeed a critical stage of race relationships because of the likelihood, if the new temper is not understood, of engendering sharp group antagonism and a second crop of more calculated prejudice. In some quarters, it has already done so. Having weaned the Negro, public opinion cannot continue to paternalize. The Negro to-day is inevitably moving forward under the control largely of his own objectives. What are these objectives? Those of his outer life are happily already well and finally formulated, for they are none other than the ideals of American institutions and democracy. Those of his inner life are yet in process of formation, for the new psychology at present is more of a consensus of feeling than of opinion, of attitude rather than of program. Still some points seem to have crystallized.

Up to the present one may adequately describe the Negro's 'inner objectives' as an attempt to repair a damaged group psychology and reshape a warped social perspective. Their realization has required a new mentality for the American Negro. And as it matures we begin to see its effects; at first, negative, iconoclastic, and then positive and constructive. In this new group psychology we note the lapse of sentimental appeal, then the development of a more positive self-respect and self-reliance; the repudiation of social dependence, and then the gradual recovery from hyper-sensitiveness and 'touchy' nerves, the repudiation of the double standard of judgment with its special philanthropic allowances and then the sturdier desire for objective and scientific appraisal; and finally the rise from social disillusionment to race pride, from the sense of social debt to the responsibilities of social contribution, and offsetting the necessary working and commonsense acceptance of restricted conditions, the belief in ultimate esteem and recognition. Therefore the Negro to-day wishes to be known for what he is, even in his faults and shortcomings, and scorns a craven and precarious survival at the price of seeming to be what he is not.

[. . .]

Of course, the thinking Negro has shifted a little toward the left with the world-trend, and there is an increasing group who affiliate with radical and liberal movements. But fundamentally for the present the Negro is radical on race matters, conservative on others, in other words, a 'forced radical', a social protestant rather than a genuine radical. Yet under further pressure and injustice iconoclastic thought and motives will inevitably increase. Harlem's quixotic radicalisms call for their ounce of democracy to-day lest to-morrow they be beyond cure.

The Negro mind reaches out as yet to nothing but American wants, American ideas. But this forced attempt to build his Americanism on race values is a unique social experiment, and its ultimate success is impossible except through the fullest sharing of American culture and institutions. There should be no delusion about this. American nerves in sections unstrung with race hysteria are often fed the opiate that the trend of Negro advance is wholly separatist, and that the effect of its operation will be to encyst the Negro as a benign foreign body in the body politic. This cannot be – even if it were desirable. The racialism of the Negro is no limitation or reservation with respect to American life; it is only a constructive effort to build the obstructions in the stream of his progress into an efficient dam of social energy and power. Democracy itself is obstructed and stagnated to the extent that any of its channels are closed. Indeed they cannot be selectively closed. So the choice is not between one way for the Negro and another way for the rest, but between American institutions frustrated on the one hand and American ideals progressively fulfilled and realized on the other.

[. . .]

Fortunately there are constructive channels opening out into which the balked social feelings of the American Negro can flow freely.

Without them there would be much more pressure and danger than there is. These compensating interests are racial but in a new and enlarged way. One is the consciousness of acting as the advance-guard of the African peoples in their contact with Twentieth Century civilization; the other, the sense of a mission of rehabilitating the race in world esteem from that loss of prestige for which the fate and conditions of slavery have so largely been responsible. Harlem, as we shall see, is the center of both these movements; she is the home of the Negro's 'Zionism'. The pulse of the Negro world has begun to beat in Harlem. A Negro newspaper carrying news material in English, French and Spanish, gathered from all quarters of America, the West Indies and Africa has maintained itself in Harlem for over five years. Two important magazines, both edited from New York, maintain their news and circulation consistently on a cosmopolitan scale. Under American auspices and backing, three pan-African congresses have been held abroad for the discussion of common interests, colonial questions and the future co-operative development of Africa. In terms of the race question as a world problem, the Negro mind has leapt, so to speak, upon the parapets of prejudice and extended its cramped horizons. In so doing it has linked up with the growing group consciousness of the dark-peoples and is gradually learning their common interests. As one of our writers has recently put it: 'It is imperative that we understand the white world in its relations to the non-white world.' As with the Jew, persecution is making the Negro international.

[. . .]

Constructive participation in such causes cannot help giving the Negro valuable group incentives, as well as increased prestigé at home and abroad. Our greatest rehabilitation may possibly come through such channels, but for the present, more immediate hope rests in the revaluation by white and black alike of the Negro in terms of his artistic endowments and cultural contributions, past and prospective. It must be increasingly recognized that the Negro has already made very substantial contributions, not only in his folk-art, music especially, which has always found appreciation, but in larger, though humbler and less acknowledged ways. For generations the Negro has been the peasant matrix of that section of America which has most undervalued him, and here he has contributed not only materially in labor and in social patience, but spiritually as well. The South has unconsciously absorbed the gift of his folk-temperament. In less than half a generation it will be easier to recognize this, but the fact remains that a leaven of humor, sentiment, imagination and tropic nonchalance has gone into the making of the South from a humble, unacknowledged source. A second crop of the Negro's gifts promises still more largely. He now becomes a conscious contributor and lays aside the status of a beneficiary and ward for that of a collaborator and participant in American civilization.

[. . .]

And certainly, if in our lifetime the Negro should not be able to celebrate his full initiation into American democracy, he can at least, on the warrant of these things, celebrate the attainment of a significant and satisfying new phase of group development, and with it a spiritual Coming of Age.

26
LANGSTON HUGHES (1902–67)
FROM 'THE NEGRO ARTIST AND THE RACIAL MOUNTAIN' 1926

countering Locke

Harlem Renaissance writer, who became known as the 'bard of Harlem'. He was represented by eleven poems in Locke's The New Negro *(1925). His work also appeared in the African-American journals,* Opportunity *and* Crisis, *and in the anthology,* Carolling Dusk. *Hughes departed from the more conventional European literary practices of other Harlem writers such as Jean Toomer and Countee Cullen by introducing into his poetry the rhythms and cadences of black speech and the improvisatory techniques of black oral traditions. Born in Joplin, Missouri, he was schooled in Detroit and Cleveland, and in 1920 became a student at Columbia University; but he turned his back on formal education and went to sea. He subsidised his writing with a chequered career in various menial jobs and worked for a while in a Parisian nightclub. In 1932 he visited the Soviet Union and was sent to Spain in 1937 as correspondent for the* Baltimore African-American. *'The Negro Artist and the Racial Mountain' was published in the* Nation *in 1926.*

One of the most promising of the young Negro poets said to me once, 'I want to be a poet – not a Negro poet,' meaning, I believe, 'I want to write like a white poet'; meaning subconsciously, 'I would like to be a white poet'; meaning behind that, 'I would like to be white.' And I was sorry the young man said that, for no great poet has ever been afraid of being himself. And I doubted then that, with his desire to run away spiritually from his race, this boy would ever be a great poet. But this is the mountain standing in the way of any true Negro art in America – this urge within the race toward whiteness, the desire to pour racial individuality into the mold of American standardization, and to be as little Negro and as much American as possible.

But let us look at the immediate background of this young poet. His family is of what I suppose one would call the Negro middle class: people who are by no means rich yet never uncomfortable nor hungry – smug, contented, respectable folk, members of the Baptist church. The father goes to work every morning. He is a chief steward at a large white club. The mother sometimes does fancy sewing or supervises parties for the rich families of the town. The children go to a mixed school. In the home they read white papers and magazines. And the mother often says 'Don't be like niggers' when the children are bad. A frequent phrase from the father is, 'Look how well a white man does things.' And so the word white comes to be unconsciously a symbol of all the virtues. It holds for the children beauty, morality, and money. The whisper of 'I want to be white' runs silently through their minds. This young poet's home is, I believe, a fairly typical home of the colored middle class. One sees immediately how difficult it would be for an artist born in such a home to interest himself in interpreting the beauty of his own people. He is never taught to see that beauty. He is taught rather not to see it, or if he does, to be ashamed of it when it is not according to Caucasian patterns.

For racial culture the home of a self-styled 'high-class' Negro has nothing better to offer. Instead there will perhaps be more aping of things white than in a less cultured or less wealthy home. The father is perhaps a doctor, lawyer, landowner, or politician. The mother may be a social worker, or a teacher, or she may do nothing and have a maid. Father is often dark but he has usually married the lightest woman he could find. The family attend a fashionable church where few really colored faces are to be found. And they themselves draw a color line. In the North they go to white theatres and white movies. And in the South they have at least two cars and a house 'like white folks.' Nordic manners, Nordic faces, Nordic hair, Nordic art (if any), and an Episcopal heaven. A very high mountain indeed for the would-be racial artist to climb in order to discover himself and his people.

But then there are the low-down folks, the so-called common element, and they are the majority – may the Lord be praised! The people who have their nip of gin on Saturday nights and are not too important to themselves or the community, or too well fed, or too learned to watch the lazy world go round. They live on Seventh Street in Washington or State Street in Chicago and they do not particularly care whether they are like white folks or anybody else. Their joy runs, bang! Into ecstasy. Their religion soars to a shout. Work maybe a little today, rest a little tomorrow. Play awhile. Sing awhile. O; let's dance! These common people are not afraid of spirituals, as for a long time their more intellectual brethren were, and jazz is their child. They furnish a wealth of colorful, distinctive material for any artist because they still hold their own individuality in the face of American standardizations. And perhaps these common people will give to the world its truly great Negro artist, the one who is not afraid to be himself. Whereas the better-class Negro would tell the artist what to do, the people at least let him alone when he does appear. And they are not ashamed of him – if they know he exists at all. And they accept what beauty is their own without question.

Certainly there is, for the American Negro artist who can escape the restrictions the more advanced among his own group would put upon him, a great field of unused material ready for his art. Without going outside his race, and even among the better classes with their 'white' culture and conscious American manners, but still Negro enough to be different, there is sufficient matter to furnish a black artist with a lifetime of creative work. And when he chooses to touch on the relations between Negroes and whites in this country with their innumerable overtones and undertones surely, and especially for literature and the drama, there is an inexhaustible supply of themes at hand. To these the Negro artist can give his racial individuality, his heritage of rhythm and warmth, and his incongruous humor that so often, as in the Blues, becomes ironic laughter mixed with tears. But let us look again at the mountain.

A prominent Negro clubwoman in Philadelphia paid eleven dollars to hear Raquel Meller sing Andalusian popular songs. But she told me a few weeks before she would not think of going to hear 'that woman,' Clara Smith, a great black artist, sing Negro folksongs. And many an upper-class Negro church, even now, would not dream of employing a spiritual in its services. The drab melodies in white folks' hymnbooks are much to be preferred. 'We want to worship the Lord correctly and quietly. We don't believe in 'shouting.' Let's be dull like the Nordics,' they say, in effect.

The road for the serious black artist, then, who would produce a racial art is most certainly rocky and the mountain is high. Until recently he received almost no encouragement for his work from either white or colored people. The fine novels of Chesnutt go out of print with neither race noticing their passing. The quaint charm and humor of Dunbar's dialect verse brought to him, in his day, largely the same kind of encouragement one would give a sideshow freak (A colored man writing poetry! How odd!) or a clown (How amusing!).

The present vogue in things Negro, although it may do as much harm as good for the budding colored artist, has at least done this: it has brought him forcibly to the attention of his own people among whom for so long, unless the other race had noticed him beforehand, he was a prophet with little honor. I understand that Charles Gilpin acted for years in Negro theatres without an special acclaim from his own, but when Broadway gave him eight curtain calls, Negroes, too, began to beat a tin pan in his honor. I know a young colored writer, a manual worker by day, who had been writing well for the colored magazines for some years, but it was not until he recently broke into the white publications and his first book was accepted by a prominent New York publisher that the 'best' Negroes in his city took the trouble to discover that he lived there. Then almost immediately they decided to give a grand dinner for him. But the society ladies were careful to whisper to his mother that perhaps she' d better not come. They were not sure she would have an evening gown.

The Negro artist works against an undertow of sharp criticism and misunderstanding from his own group and unintentional bribes from the whites. 'Oh, be respectable, write about nice people, show how good we are,' say the Negroes . . . 'Be stereotyped, don't go too far, don't shatter our illusions about you, don't amuse us too seriously. We will pay you,' say the whites. Both would have told Jean Toomer not to write *Cane*. The colored people did not praise it. The white people did not buy it. Most of the colored people who did read *Cane* hate it. They are afraid of it. Although the critics gave it good reviews the public remained indifferent. Yet (excepting the work of Du Bois) *Cane* contains the finest prose written by a Negro in America. And like the singing of Robeson, it is truly racial.

But in spite of the Nordicized Negro intelligentsia and the desires of some white editors we have an honest America Negro literature already with us. Now I await the rise of the Negro theatre. Our folk music, having achieved world-wide fame, offers itself to the genius of the great individual American composer who is to come. And within the next decade I expect to see the work of a growing school of colored artists who paint and model the beauty of dark faces and create with new technique the expressions of their own soul-world. And the Negro dancers who will dance like flame and the singers who will continue to carry our songs to all who listen – they will be with us in even greater numbers tomorrow.

Most of my own poems are racial in theme and treatment, derived from the life I know. In many of them I try to grasp and hold some of the meanings and rhythms of jazz. I am as sincere as I know how to be in these poems and yet after every reading I answer questions like these from my own people: Do you think Negroes should always write about Negroes? I wish you wouldn't read some of your poems to white folks. How do you find anything interesting in a place like a cabaret? Why do you write about black people? You aren't black. What makes you do so many jazz poems?

But jazz to me is one of the inherent expressions of Negro life in America; the eternal tom-tom beating in the Negro soul – the tom-tom of revolt against weariness in a white world, a world of subway trains, and work, work, work; the tom-tom of joy and laughter, and pain swallowed in a smile. Yet the Philadelphia clubwoman is ashamed to say that her race created it and she does not like me to write about it. The old subconscious 'white is best' runs through her mind, Years of study under white teachers, a lifetime of white books, pictures, and papers, and white manners, morals and Puritan standards made her dislike the spirituals. And now she turns up her nose at jazz and all its manifestations – likewise almost everything else distinctly racial. She doesn't care for the Winold Reiss portraits of Negroes because they are 'too Negro.' She does not want a true picture of herself from anybody. She wants the artist to flatter her, to make the white world believe that all Negroes are as smug and as near white in soul as she wants to be. But, to my mind, it is the duty of the younger Negro artist, if he accepts any duties at all from outsiders, to change through the force of his art that old whispering 'I want to be white,' hidden in the aspirations of his people, to 'Why should I want to be white? I am a Negro – and beautiful!'

So I am ashamed for the black poet who says, 'I want to be a poet, not a Negro poet,' as though his own racial world were not as interesting as any other world. I am ashamed too, for the colored artist who runs from the painting of Negro faces to the painting of sunsets after the manner of the academicians because he fears the strange un-whiteness of his own features. An artist must be free to choose what he does, certainly, but he must also never be afraid to do what he might choose.

Let the blare of Negro jazz bands and the bellowing voice of Bessie Smith singing Blues penetrate the closed ears of the colored near-intellectuals until they listen and perhaps understand. Let Paul Robeson singing 'Water Boy,' and Rudolph Fisher writing about the streets of Harlem, and Jean Toomer holding the heart of Georgia in his hands, and Aaron Douglas drawing strange black fantasies cause the smug Negro middle class to turn from their white respectable, ordinary books and papers to catch a glimmer of their own beauty. We younger Negro artists who create now intend to express our individual dark-skinned selves without fear or shame. If white people are pleased we are glad. If they are not, it doesn't matter. We know we are beautiful. And ugly too. The tom-tom cries and the tom-tom laughs. If colored people are pleased we are glad. If they are not, their displeasure doesn't matter either. We build our temples for tomorrow, strong as we know how, and we stand on top of the mountain free within ourselves.

27
GERTRUDE STEIN (1874–1946)
FROM 'COMPOSITION AS EXPLANATION' 1926

American Jewish writer who spent most of her life in France. In 1893 she studied at the Harvard Psychological Laboratory with William James and after further study left Johns Hopkins Medical School without a degree. She joined her brother Leo in Paris at 27 Rue de Fleurus, the address of her legendary artists' salon. They began to collect modern art and in 1905 she befriended Picasso who in 1906 painted her portrait. In 1907 she was joined in Paris by Alice B. Toklas who became her partner and amanuensis. They did war-relief work for the American Fund for French Wounded from 1916 to 1919 for this Stein was awarded the Médaille de la Reconnaissance in 1922. After the war her salon was a focal point for American writers in Europe. Stein's most popular (and accessible) work is The Autobiography of Alice B. Toklas *(1933), an account of the avant-garde circles in which she moved. It met with the disapproval of some prominent figures including Braque and Matisse who were among the signatories to 'Testimony against Gertrude Stein' which was published in* transition *in 1935. During the Second World War, Stein and Toklas lived out the Nazi occupation in the French countryside, protected by fellow-villagers. Stein was a pioneer in experimental writing. Her short stories* Three Lives *(1909) and poetry* Tender Buttons *(1914) are early examples. She wrote numerous plays and operas as well as a long novel,* The Making of Americans; or, The History of a Family's Progress *(1925) (and an essay about it: 'The Gradual Making of The Making of Americans'). 'Composition as Explanation' (1926) is drawn from her lecture tour of England where she met Leonard and Virginia Woolf and was published in their Hogarth Press essay series.*

There is singularly nothing that makes a difference a difference in beginning and in the middle and in ending except that each generation has something different at which they are all looking. By this I mean so simply that anybody knows it that composition is the difference which makes each and all of them then different from other generations and this is what makes everything different otherwise they are all alike and everybody knows it because everybody says it.

It is very likely that nearly every one has been very nearly certain that something that is interesting is interesting them. Can they and do they. It is very interesting that nothing inside in them, that is when you consider the very long history of how every one ever acted or has felt, it is very interesting that nothing inside in them in all of them makes it connectedly different. By this I mean this. The only thing that is different from one time to another is what is seen and what is seen depends upon how everybody is doing everything. This makes the thing we are looking at very different and this makes what those describe it make of it, it makes a composition, it confuses, it shows, it is, it looks, it likes it as it is, and this makes what is seen as it is seen. Nothing changes from generation to generation except the thing seen and that makes a composition. Lord Grey remarked that when the generals before the war talked about the war they talked about it as a nineteenth-century war although to be fought with twentieth-century weapons. That is because war is a thing that decides how it is to be done when it is to be done. It is prepared and to that degree it is like all academies it is not a thing made by being made it is a thing prepared. Writing and painting and all that, is like that, for those who occupy themselves with it and don't make it as it is made. Now the few who make it as it is made, and it is to be remarked that the most decided of them usually are prepared just as the world around them is preparing, do it in this way and so I if you do not mind I will tell you how it happens. Naturally one does not know how it happened until it is well over beginning happening.

To come back to the part that the only thing that is different is what is seen when it seems to be being seen, in other words, composition and time sense.

No one is ahead of his time, it is only that the particular variety of creating his time is the one that his contemporaries who also are creating their own time refuse to accept. And they refuse to accept it for a very simple reason and that is that they do not have to accept it for any reason. They themselves that is everybody in their entering the modern composition and they do enter it, if they do not enter it they are not so to speak in it they are out of it and so they do enter it; but in as you may say the non-competitive efforts where if you are not in it nothing is lost except nothing at all except what it not had, there are naturally all the refusals, and the things refused are only important if unexpectedly somebody happens to need them. In the case of the arts it is very definite. Those who are creating the modern composition authentically are naturally only of importance when they are dead because by that time the modern composition having become past is classified and the description of it is classical. That is the reason why the creator of the new composition in the arts is an outlaw until he is a classic, there is hardly a moment in between and it is really too bad very much too bad naturally for the creator but also very much too bad for the enjoyer, they all really would enjoy the created so much better just after it has been made than when it is already a classic, but it is perfectly simple that there is no reason why the contemporary should see, because it would not make any difference as they lead their lives in the new composition anyway, and as every one is naturally indolent why naturally they don't see. For this reason as in quoting Lord Grey it is quite certain that nations not actively threatened are at least several generations behind themselves militarily so aesthetically they are more than several generations behind themselves and it is very much too bad, it is so very much more exciting and satisfactory for everybody if one can have contemporaries, if all one's contemporaries could be one's contemporaries.

There is almost not an interval.

For a very long time everybody refuses and then almost without a pause almost everybody accepts. In the history of the refused in the arts and literature the rapidity of the change is always startling. Now the only difficulty with the *volte-face* concerning the arts is this. When the acceptance comes, by that acceptance the thing created becomes a classic. It is a natural phenomena a rather extraordinary natural phenomena that a thing accepted becomes a classic. And what is the characteristic quality of a classic. The characteristic quality of a classic is that it is beautiful. Now of course it is perfectly true that a more or less first rate work of art is beautiful but the trouble is that when that first rate work of art becomes a classic because it is accepted the only thing that is important from then on to the majority of the acceptors the enormous majority, the most intelligent majority of the acceptors is that it is so wonderfully beautiful. Of course it is wonderfully beautiful, only when it is still a thing irritating annoying stimulating then all quality of beauty is denied to it.

Of course it is beautiful but first all beauty in it is denied and then all the beauty of it is accepted. If every one were not so indolent they would realize that beauty is beauty even when it is irritating and stimulating not only when it is accepted and classic. Of course it is extremely difficult nothing more so than to remember back to its not being beautiful once it has become beautiful. This makes it so much more difficult to realize its beauty when the work is being refused and prevents every one from realizing that they were convinced that beauty was denied, once the work is accepted. Automatically with the acceptance of the time sense comes the recognition of the beauty and once the beauty is accepted the beauty never fails any one.

Beginning again and again is a natural thing even when there is a series.

Beginning again and again and again explaining composition and time is a natural thing.

It is understood by this time that everything is the same except composition and time, composition and the time of the composition and the time in the composition.

Everything is the same except composition and as the composition is different and always going to be different everything is not the same. Everything is not the same as the time when of the composition and the time in the composition is different. The composition is different, that is certain.

The composition is the thing seen by every one living in the living that they are doing, they are the composing of the composition that at the time they are living is the composition of the time in which they are living. It is that that makes living a thing they are doing. Nothing else is different, of that almost any one can be certain. The time when and the time of and the time in that composition is the natural phenomena of that composition and of that perhaps every one can be certain.

No one thinks these things when they are making when they are creating what is the composition, naturally no one thinks, that is no one formulates until what is to be formulated has been made.

Composition is not there, it is going to be there and we are here. This is some time ago for us naturally.

The only thing that is different from one time to another is what is seen and what is seen depends upon how everybody is doing everything. This makes the thing we are looking at very different and this makes what those who describe it make of it, it makes a composition, it confuses, it shows, it is, it looks, it likes it as it is, and this makes what is seen as it is seen. Nothing changes from generation to generation except the thing seen and that makes a composition.

Now the few who make writing as it is made and it is to be remarked that the most decided of them are those that are prepared by preparing, are prepared just as the world around them is prepared and is preparing to do it in this way and so if you do not mind I will again tell you how it happens. Naturally one does not know how it happened until it is well over beginning happening.

Each period of living differs from any other period of living not in the way life is but in the way life is conducted and that authentically speaking is composition. After life has been conducted in a certain way everybody knows it but nobody knows it, little by little, nobody knows it as long as nobody knows it. Any one creating the composition in the arts does not know it either, they are conducting life and that makes their composition what it is, it makes their work compose as it does.

Their influence and their influences are the same as that of all of their contemporaries only it must always be remembered that the analogy is not obvious until as I say the composition of a time has become so pronounced that it is past and the artistic composition of it is a classic.

[. . .]

So far then the progress of my conceptions was the natural progress entirely in accordance with my epoch as I am sure is to be quite easily realized if you think over the scene that was before us all from year to year.

As I said in the beginning, there is the long history of how every one ever acted or has felt and that nothing inside in them in all of them makes it connectedly different. By this I mean all this.

The only thing that is different from one time to another is what is seen and what is seen depends upon how everybody is doing every thing.

It is understood by this time that everything is the same except composition and time, composition and the time of the composition and the time in the composition.

Everything is the same except composition and as the composition is different and always going to be different everything is not the same. So then I as a contemporary creating the composition in the beginning was groping toward a continuous present, a using everything a beginning again and again and then everything being alike then everything very simply everything was naturally simply different and so I as a contemporary was creating everything being alike was creating everything naturally being naturally simply different, everything being alike. This then was the period that brings me to the period of the beginning of 1914. Everything being alike everything naturally would be simply different and war came and everything being alike and everything being simply different brings everything being simply different brings it to romanticism.

Romanticism is then when everything being alike everything is naturally simply different, and romanticism.

Then for four years this was more and more different even though this was, was everything alike. Everything alike naturally everything was simply different and this is and was romanticism and this is and was war. Everything being alike everything naturally everything is different simply different naturally simply different.

And so there was the natural phenomena that was war, which had been, before war came, several generations behind the contemporary composition, because it became war and so completely needed to be contemporary became completely contemporary and so created the completed recognition of the contemporary composition. Every one but one may say every one became consciously became aware of the existence of the authenticity of the modern composition. This then the contemporary recognition, because of the academic thing known as war having been forced to become contemporary made every one not only contemporary in act not only contemporary in thought but contemporary in self-consciousness made every one contemporary with the modern composition. And so the art creation of the contemporary composition which would have been outlawed normally outlawed several generations more behind even than war, war having been brought so to speak up to date art so to speak was allowed not completely to be up to date, but nearly up to date, in other words we who created the expression of the modern composition were to be recognized before we were dead some of us even quite a long time before we were dead. And so war may be said to have advanced a general recognition of the expression of the contemporary composition by almost thirty years.

And now after that there is no more of that in other words there is peace and something comes then and it follows coming then.

[. . .]

28
HUGH MACDIARMID (CHRISTOPHER MURRAY GRIEVE) (1892–1978)
FROM 'ENGLISH ASCENDANCY IN BRITISH LITERATURE' 1931

Scottish poet and literary critic. Born in Langholm in the Scottish borders he trained as a teacher in Edinburgh before becoming a journalist in 1912. After serving in the First World War he returned to journalism and published his first book Annals of Five Senses *in 1923 under his own name. After that he published as Hugh MacDiarmid and became a central figure in the twentieth-century Scottish Rennaissance. Politically controversial, he was ejected from both the Communist Party and the Scottish National Party during the 1930s but rejoined the Communist Party in 1956. In 1931 he met his second wife Valda Trevlyn and during 1933–42 they lived in self-imposed 'exile' in Whalsay in the Shetlands. This was a troubled but productive period. In 1951 he finally settled at Brownsbank, near Biggar and from the early 1960s enjoyed ever-increasing recognition and popularity both in Britain and abroad. His experimentations lie chiefly in his attempts to fuse Modernist formal techniques with the potential offered by the use of the Scots language. MacDiarmid's revived or synthetic Scots drew on dictionaries, dialect, glossaries, literary diction and contemporary speech. His main works in this style include* The Sangschaw *(1925),* Penny Weep *(1926) and* A Drunk Man Looks at the Thistle *(1926). In the 1930s he experimented with what he called 'synthetic English'. This mode is exemplified in 'On a Raised Beach' (1934), and in two of his major works,* In Memoriam James Joyce *(1954) and* The Kind of Poetry I Want *(1961). A prolific writer, he was a notable translator of Gaelic and modern European poetry, and edited several literary journals and anthologies. His two-volume* Complete Poems *(1920–76), edited by Michael Grieve and W. K. Aitken, appeared after his death in 1978. The following extract is taken from an essay published in* The Criterion, *July 1931.*

The Consultative Committee of the Board of Education has just published a report on 'The Primary School' in which there is a passage stressing the need to realize that there are many varieties of English; that it is not the function of schools to decry any special or local peculiarities of speech; and that a racy native turn of speech is better than any stilted phraseology, especially for literary purposes.

This is excellently said and represents a departure or suggested departure in Departmental attitude which, it is to be hoped, may be speedily followed up in the schools themselves, relieving the children of to-morrow from a subtle but far-reaching psychological outrage which has been inflicted on many generations of pupils and seriously affected the quality and direction of those of them who had literary inclinations. The passage may be commended in particular to the attention of the B.B.C. and to such typical spokesmen of the contrary spirit as Sir John Squire, who thinks that Burns might just as well have written in English, and Mr. St. John Ervine, who declares that 'we are resolved to use language for its purpose, the understanding of each other, and not the preservation of quaintnesses or the indulgence of literary idiosyncrasies'.

The essence of Mr. Ervine's arguments (and practically the whole case for 'correct English') is given away when he exclaims: 'What would be the use of writing Ulster plays full of dialect expressions if nobody outside Ulster could understand them and there were not enough playgoers in Ulster to enable a dramatist to earn a living? Tennyson wrote in the dialect of Lincolnshire. He also wrote in the language of England. Which Tennyson is known, the first or the second?' That is certainly one question, but it begs many far more important ones, and a Scottish writer may be allowed to give it a Scottish answer by asking another question: 'Which was the better dramatist, Mr. St. John Ervine when he was struggling to get plays with Ulster dialect elements a London presentation (with a non-success which accounts for the intolerance of his 'English ascendancy' attitude now) and producing such comparatively excellent works as 'John Ferguson', or Mr. St. John Ervine, resolved on the flesh-pots of Egypt, and winning the London success, and international vogue of a kind, denied to his earlier and better work with such a production as 'The First Mrs. Fraser'?' Burns knew what he was doing when he reverted from eighteenth century English to a species of synthetic Scots and was abundantly justified in the result. He was not contributing to English literature, but to a clearly defined and quite independent tradition of Scottish poetry hailing from the days of Dunbar and the other great fifteenth-century 'makars' – the golden age of Scottish poetry when the English impulse seemed to have gone sterile and Scotland, not England, was apparently destined to produce the great poetry of the United Kingdom. To ask why this promise was not redeemed and why English, a far less concentrated and expressive language, became the medium of such an incomparably greater succession of poets, involves deep questions of the relationship of literature to economic, political and other considerations and both the causal and the casual in history; but at the moment it is more germane to ask if the potentialities of the Scottish literary tradition can yet be realized? There are signs that they may be. The problem of the British Isles is the problem of English Ascendancy. Ireland, after a protracted struggle, has won a considerable measure of autonomy; Scotland and Wales may succeed in doing the same; but what is of importance to my point in the meantime is that, in breaking free (or fairly free) politically, Ireland not only experienced the Literary Revival associated with the names of Yeats, 'A.E.', Synge and the others, but has during the past half century recovered almost entirely her ancient Gaelic literature.

[. . .]

Literature, so far from manifesting any trend towards uniformity or standardization, is evolving in the most disparate ways; and there are few literatures in which dialect elements, and even such extreme employments of – and plays upon – them as render them permanently untranslatable and unintelligible to all but a handful of readers in their own countries, are not peculiarly and significantly active. On this account (as isolating it from general contemporary tendency which must have some deep-seated relation to the needs of modern, and prospective, consciousness) it is a pity that English literature is maintaining a narrow ascendancy tradition instead of broad-basing itself on all the diverse cultural elements and the splendid variety of languages and dialects, in the British Isles. (I do not refer here to the Empire, and the United States of America, though the evolution of genuine independent literatures in all of these is a matter of no little consequence and, already clearly appreciated in America, is being increasingly so realized in most of the Dominions, which is perhaps the cultural significance of the anti-English and other tendencies in most of them which are making for those changes in the Imperial organization which will deprive England of the hegemony it has maintained too long). To recognize and utilize these, instead of excluding them, could only make for its enrichment. It is absurd that intelligent readers of English, who would be ashamed not to know something (if only the leading names, and roughly, what they stand for) of most Continental literatures, are content to ignore Scottish, Irish, and Welsh Gaelic literatures, and Scots Vernacular literature.

Surely the latter are nearer to them than the former, and the language difficulty no greater. These Gaelic, and Scots dialect poets were products of substantially the same environment, and concerned for the most part with the same political, psychological, and practical issues, the same traditions and tendencies, the same landscapes, as poets in English to whom, properly regarded, they are not only valuably complementary, but (in view of their linguistic, technical, and other divergencies) corrective. Confinement to the English central stream is like refusing to hear all but one side of a complicated case – and in view of the extent to which the English language is definitely adscripted in certain important moral and psychological directions, and incapable of dealing with certain types of experience which form no inconsiderable part of certain other European literatures, and may well be of far greater consequence to the future of humanity as a whole than the more 'normal matters' with which it is qualified to deal, becomes a sort of self-infliction of an extensive spiritual and psychological blindness.

[. . .]

Since the Renaissance there have been, strictly speaking, no self-contained national cultures in Europe. The antithesis of Renaissance art in this regard is national art. To some it may seem as if the Renaissance has justified itself in thus introducing a common strain into the are-consciousness of all European countries. That common strain was certainly brilliant, shapely, worldly-wise, strong, if not indeed gigantic, over-bounding in energy, in life. Yet all the time there was a latent weakness in it, a strain, a sham strength, an uneasy energy, a death in life. It always protested too much. Dissembling always, it was never single-hearted enough to speak plainly, and, so, intensely. It therefore dazzles us rather that moves us. If it has justified itself, then should we swap Rheims cathedral for St. Peter's and Rouen for St. Paul' s! 'One would, however, swap Dante for Shakespeare?' – Yes, but what did Shakespeare's native wood-notes wild know of the Unities? Happy England! – so naïvely ignorant of the Renaissance at the close of the sixteenth century. Unhappy France! – where even before Shakespeare was born they had ceased to develop their native Christian literary modes, had indeed begun to fling them aside for those of Euripides and Seneca . . . The Renaissance may have justified itself, but not, we feel, either on the plane of genuine Christian art or genuine pagan art. It is not as intense or as tender as the one, nor so calm, majestic, and wise as the other. A Romantic movement is not usually thought of as a violent effort to rediscover the secret power that lay behind Greek art; yet in essence that is what every Romantic movement has been.'

And that most romantic of all movements, the search for a new classicism to-day, is not a quest for any mere neo-classical formalism, but an effort to get down to *Ur-motives* – to get back behind the Renaissance!

As to the second point – 'The Defence of the West', or the Conservation of European Civilization – the old balance or conflict between the North and the South has been violently disrupted by the emergence of Russia and the Soviet concept of things. That constitutes a third side; where is the fourth to come from – not from England; but whence else if not from Gaelic culture – the fourth side upon which European civilization can re-establish itself, just as, to switch the argument into other terms, the old duality of Man versus Nature having been disrupted by the emergence of the Third Factor – the Machine – balance can only be re-secured by a fourth factor, the effective emergence of 'disinterestedness'.

29
MARIANNE MOORE (1887–1972)
'NEW POETRY SINCE 1912' 1926

American poet. Born in Missouri, she graduated from Bryn Maur in 1909. Moore studied business science in Pennsylvania and headed the Commercial department of the Carlisle Indian School (1911–15), after which she became a professional writer. She worked for the New York Public Library from 1921–25. Her earliest poetry appeared in 1915 in Poetry: A Magazine of Verse. *Her* Observations *(1924) won her* The Dial *Award and appointment on the staff of the* Dial *where she worked until 1929. Her* Selected Poems *(1935) earned her wider recognition followed by the Pulitzer Prize for her* Collected Poems *(1935). The essay, from which extracts are reproduced below, was first published in William Stanley Braithwaite ed.,* Anthology of Magazine Verse for 1926, *Boston, 1926.*

In America what is often referred to as modern poetry received marked impetus in 1912. Converted from the manner of *A Dome of Many Colored Glass* (1912) to the apparent newness of Imagisme (1913), Amy Lowell became 'the recognized spokesman of the Imagist group'. Inaugurally arresting, however – that is to say really inaugural – Ezra Pound invented the term Imagisme; and 'A Few Dont's by an Imagist' presented by him in 1913 in the March issue of *Poetry, A Magazine of Verse*, advocated composing 'in sequence of the musical phrase, not in sequence of a metronome; direct treatment of the thing, whether subjective or objective; the use of absolutely no word that does not contribute to the presentation'; and in 1914 with work of his own, appeared poems by Richard Aldington, F. S. Flint, H. D., Amy Lowell, Skipwith Cannell, William Carlos Williams, James Joyce, John Cournos, F. M. 'Hueffer,' and Alan Upward.

Mr. Braithwaite felt in Imagisme, 'an intensifying quality of mood', Richard Aldington felt it 'an accurate mystery', and in answer to the objection that Imagist poetry was 'petty poetry, minutely small and intended to be so', Miss May Sinclair observed that the critic 'is not justified in counting lines'. Of image-making power as 'common to all poets', she remarked, 'When Dante saw the souls of the damned falling like leaves down the banks of Acheron, it is an image, it is also imagery. It makes no difference whether he says *are* leaves or only *like* leaves. The flying leaves are the perfect image of the damned souls. But when Sir John Suckling says his lady's feet peep in and out like mice he is only using imagery.' H. D.'s 'Pines', *i. e.*, 'Oread', which appeared first in Wyndham Lewis' *Blast* (1914), Richard Aldington's 'The Poplar', and Ezra Pound's 'The Garret' seem to one incontrovertibly illustrative of the Imagist doctrine.

In 1915 and 1916, under the direction of Richard Aldington, 'The Poets' Translation Series' was published by The Egoist Press, which was under the direction of Miss Harriet Shaw Weaver, and the starkness and purity of these translations is allied in one's mind with Imagism and Vorticism – Ezra Pound and certain of his Imagists being identical with certain of Wyndham Lewis' Vorticists.

The 'new' poetry seemed to justify itself as a more robust form of Japanese poetry – that is perhaps to say, of Chinese poetry – although a specific and more lasting interest in Chinese poetry came later. In 1913, coincident with the translating into English of 'Gitanjali', Rabindranath Tagore visited the United States, was termed by our press, 'The creator of a new age in literature,' and W. B. Yeats wrote in 'The Athenaeum', 'A whole people, a whole civilization, immeasurably strange to us, seems to have been taken up into this imagination; and yet we are not moved because of its strangeness, but because we have met our own image; as though we had walked in Rossetti's willow wood, or heard, perhaps for the first time in literature, our voice as in a dream.' Felt by public and poets alike to be important, *North of Boston* by Robert Frost, appeared in 1914, *A Boy's Will* having been published the previous year.

The Egoist, Poetry of Chicago, and *The Little Review* of Chicago, were hospitable to 'new' poetry, as was Alfred Kreymborg's *Others*. With a subsequently diverse and justifiable use of no rhyme, part rhyme, all rhyme, Alfred Kreymborg had to some, in his early practice of vers libre and his encouragement of the 'vers libertine' as Louis Untermeyer denominates the writer of free verse – the aspect of a Cambodian devil-dancer. One recalls the emphatic work of William Carlos Williams whose book, *The Tempers* had appeared in 1913; a sliced and cylindrical, complicated yet simple use of words by Mina Loy; an enigmatically axiomatic 'Progression of the Verb "To Be"' by Walter Arensberg, and a poem by him entitled 'Ing' which corroborated the precisely perplexing verbal exactness of Gertrude Stein's 'Tender Buttons' – a book which had already appeared.

Ing

Ing? Is it possible to mean ing?
Suppose
   for the termination in *g*
     a disoriented
     series
   of the simple fractures
     in sleep.
     Soporific
   has accordingly a value for soap
     so present to
     sew pieces.
     And *p* says: Peace is.
   And suppose the *i*
     to be big in ing
     as Beginning.
     Then Ing is to ing
   as aloud
     accompanied by times
   and the meaning is a possibility
     of ralsis.

In Ezra Pound one recognized that precise explicit 'positiveness' – felt in him by Wallace Stevens – and he was the 'new' poetry's perhaps best apologist as he reiterated in articles contributed to Miss Monroe's magazine, his feeling that 'there should be in America the *"gloire de cénacle."*' 'He is knowledge's lover,' as Glenway Wescott has said, 'speaking of it and to it an intimate idiom which is sometimes gibberish', and if his equivalents for that which is 'dead' or foreign seems to some not always perspicuous, his contagiously enjoyable enjoyment of and his unpedantic rendering of 'dead' language have done as much as have his own poems, one feels – to create an atmosphere in which poetry is likely to be written. Adelaide Crapsey's apartness and delicately differentiated footfalls, her pallor and color, were impressive. Wallace Stevens' sensory and technical virtuosity was perhaps the 'new' poetry's greatest ornament and the almost imperceptibly modern, silver-chiming resonance of 'Peter Quince at the Clavier' did much to ameliorate popular displeasure. One recalls in 'Primordia' an insisted upon starkness:

> The blunt ice flows down the Mississippi,
> At night

and a complexity of apprehension:

> Compilation of the effects
> Of magenta blooming in the Judas-tree
> And of purple blooming in the eucalyptus.

As Kenneth Jewett remarked (in *The Transatlantic Review*, April, 1924) 'his perfected, two-dimensional still lifes stand like rests or held chords in the progression of his complete harmony.' T. S. Eliot's scrutiny of words and of behavior was apparent in his 'Portrait of a Lady'. Mr. Eliot 'has not confined himself to genre nor to society portraiture,' says Ezra Pound. 'His

> lonely men in shirt sleeves leaning out of windows

are as real as his ladies who

> come and go
> Talking of Michelangelo.

Writers of free verse were, for the most part, regarded as having been influenced by Laforgue, Rimbaud, and other French poets. Alfred Kreymborg, Maxwell Bodenheim, Carl Sandburg, Marsden Hartley, Muna Lee, Wallace Gould, Man Ray, Adolf Wolff, Helen Hoyt, Orrick Johns, Conrad Aiken, Amy Lowell, Evelyn Scott, Lola Ridge, Marjorie Allen Seiffert, Donald Evans, Emanuel Carnevali, Arthur Davison Ficke, and Witter Bynner, contributed to making respectable as poetry, verse which was not rhymed. In 1916, certain of these, under the names of Emanuel Morgan, Anne Elijah Hay, purporting to be a new school termed themselves Spectrists. Vachel Lindsay's declamatory and in some respects unaesthetic pictorialism (1915–16), pleased, displeased, and pleased the public – his originality 'trading rhymes for bread' having earlier made a good impression. Resisted and advertised, Edgar Lee Masters' *Spoon River Anthology* (1915) seemed a technical pronunciamento.

One associates with 1921 rather than with 1913, 1915, 1916, or 1917 the morosely imaginative and graphic work of D. H. Lawrence and his introversive but in mood none the less emancipated poem, 'Snake'.

> He drank enough
> And lifted his head, dreamily as one who has drunken,
> And flickered his tongue like a forked night on the air, so black,
> Seeming to lick his lips,
> And looked around like a god, unseeing into the air.

In 1920 and 1921, readers of new poetry noted the work of E. E. Cummings – its sleights of motion and emotion. A great deal has been made of the small 'i' as used by Mr. Cummings and of certain subsidiary characteristically intentional typographic revivals and innovations on his part. While 'extreme', he is, however, 'only superficially modern', as has been pointed out by Dr. W. C. Blum, and truly major aspects of his work are 'feeling for American speech', 'rapid unfailing lyrical invention', to convey the sense of speed, 'of change of position', 'the sensations of effective effort'.

Various child poets received, in 1920, the respectful attention public. American Indian poetry has also, at intervals, been introduced to us, as has the Negro spiritual. Leon Srabian Herald, though as yet without full command of technique, Glenway Wescott, and Yvor Winters – the one somewhat delicately Persian, the other somewhat constricted – R. Ellsworth Larsson, Harold Monro, Peter Quennell, Edith Sitwell, Osbert and Sacheverell Sitwell, have produced work which is, if not purely modern, properly within the new movement. Catholic in using either rhyme or no rhyme, certain others, not modern, yet by no means old-fashioned, manifest vigor which predominates it would seem, over newness. In Joseph Auslander, for example, we find a centaur-like and entrenched individuality of this non-conforming variety.

One recognizes in Ralph Cheever Dunning's depth and sobriety of treatment, a phase of contemporary watchfulness against ineptness. Although not especially recent, Mr. Dunning evinces, as Ezra Pound has observed, 'clarity of impact', 'surely', 'exact termination of expression', 'originality' in being superior to current fashions in verse.

Categorically 'formal', as are George Dillon and Archibald MacLeish, Scofield Thayer is a new Victorian – reflective, bi-visioned, and rather will-fully unconventional. We have a mixture, apparently, of reading and of asserted detachment from reading, emotion being expressed through literal use of detail:

> I agitate the gracile crescent
> Which calls itself a fern:

and through what seems a specific reviving of incident. Tension affords strength, as is felt in certain verbally opposed natural junctures of the unexpected – 'a gentle keenness', 'gradual flames', 'concision of a flame gone stone' – the mechanics being that of resistance.

It is perhaps beside the point to examine novel aspects of successive phases of poetic expression, inherited poetry having been at one time new, and new poetry even in its eccentricities seeming to have its counterpart in the poetry of the past – in Hebrew poetry, Greek poetry, Chinese poetry. That which is weak is soon gone; that which has value does, by some strange perpetuity, live as part of the serious continuation of literature.

30
ROBERT GRAVES (1895–1985) AND LAURA (RIDING) JACKSON (1901–91) FROM *MODERNIST POETRY* 1926

English poet, novelist and critic. Having been declared dead by The Times *in 1916, Graves went on to produce more than a hundred books of poetry, criticism and fiction, including the historical novel* I, Claudius *(1934) and the controversial bestselling autobiography* Goodbye to All That *(1929) in which he caricatured, and finally took his leave of, 'godawful' post-war England. His association with the American poet and writer Laura Riding in the 1920s resulted in* Modernist Poetry *(1926), a highly critical study of current poetic trends, including a detailed and programmatic formulation of modernism. Graves's own critical output includes studies of the relationship between dream psychology and the poetic imagination.* The White Goddess *(1948) is a study of poetic inspiration in archaeological, anthropological and mythological terms. That aspect of his writing is heavily influenced by Laura Riding's early concerns with the 'archaeology' of gender and its linguistic and literary manifestations – she later claimed, in fact, that Graves had simply reformulated, misconstruing in the process, her work. The following extracts from Graves's and Riding's study are taken from the 1949 edition of Graves's collected essays on poetry,* The Common Asphodel. *[See IIIb 7]*

[. . .]

Modernist poetry, if nothing else, is an ironic criticism of false literary survivals. [. . .]

An important distinction must be drawn between peculiarities in the work of modern poets resulting from a deliberate attempt to improve the status of poetry by jazzing up its programme and those resulting from a concentration on the poetic process itself. The first sort constitutes a commercial advertising of poetry; the second, while equally caused by the cloud under which poetry has fallen, is concentrated on curing its sickness, even if that means making it temporarily more unpopular than ever. The plain reader has an exaggerated antagonism towards peculiarities of this second sort: he seems to be presented with clinical observations rather than with the benefits resulting from the cure. He is more likely to be seduced by the first sort, which are expressive of a dead movement in literature.

[. . .]

Imagism is one of the earliest and the most typical of these twentieth-century dead movements. It had the look of a movement of pure experimentalism and reformation in poetry. But the issuing of a public manifesto of Imagism, the organization of the Imagists as a literary party with a defined political programme, the war they carried on with reviewers, the annual appearance of their Imagist anthology – all this showed that poetic results to them meant a popular demand for their work, not the discovery of new values in poetry with an indifference to its recognition by the public. The Imagists had decided what kind of poetry was needed by the time: a poetry to match certain up-to-date movements in music and art. They wanted to be *new* rather than to be poets; which meant that they could go only so far as to say, in a slightly different style, what had already been often said. 'Imagism refers to the manner of presentation, not to the subject.' Authentic 'advanced' poetry of the present day differs from such programmes for poetry in its concern with a reorganization of the matter (not in the sense of subject-matter, but of poetic thought as distinguished from other kinds of thought) rather than the manner of poetry. This is why the plain reader feels so balked by it: he must enter into that matter without expecting to be given a cipher-code to the meaning. The ideal modernist poem is identical with its own clearest, fullest and most accurate meaning. Therefore since his poem does not give a rendering of a poetical picture or of an idea existing outside itself, the modernist poet does not need to talk about the use of images 'to render particulars exactly', but presents the very substance of poetry. His poem has the character of an independent creature. In Imagism, on the other hand, and all other similar dead movements, it is taken for granted that poetry is a translation of certain poetic subjects into the language which will bring the reader emotionally closest to them. It is assumed that a natural separation between the reader and the subject can be bridged by the manner in which it is presented.

[. . .]

All dead movements are focused on the problem of style. Style may be defined as that old-fashioned element of sympathy with the reader which allows a poem to be used as an illustration to the text of the reader's experience; and much modernist poetry may be said to be literally without style. The modernist poet does not need to issue a programme declaring his intentions towards the reader, or an announcement of tactics. He does not need to call himself an individualist (as the Imagist poet did) or a mystic (as the poet of the Anglo-Irish dead movement did) or a nature-lover (as the poet of the Georgian dead movement did). He does not have to describe or docket himself for the reader, because now the importance of poetry does not lie in its style, namely the personality of the poet as expressed by a poem, but in the personality of the poem itself, namely its independence of both reader and poet once the poet has separated it from his personality by making it complete – a new and self-explanatory creature.

The most striking characteristic of modernist poetry is that it declares the independence of the poem. This implies a new sense of the poem's rights comparable with the new sense in modern times of the independence of the child, and a new respect for the originality of the poem as for the originality of the child. It is no longer considered proper to keep a child in its place by repressing its personality or laughing down its strange questions until it turns into a rather dull and ineffectual edition of the parent; the modernist poet is similarly freeing the poem of repressive nursery rules and, instead of telling it exactly what to do, encouraging it to do things, even queer things, by itself. He pledges himself to take them seriously on the principle that the poem, being a new and mysterious form of life, has more to teach him than he it. It is a popular superstition that the poet is the child; really the child is the poem and the most that the poet can be is a wise, experimenting parent.

Experiment, however, may be interpreted in two ways. In the first and better sense it is a delicate alertness directed towards the discovery of something to which some slight clue has been given; and system in such experiment means only the constant shifting and adjustment of the experimenter to the unknown creature as it becomes more and more known – the constant readiness to change system. The important element is the initial clue or, in old-fashioned language, the inspiration. The true scientist should have power equal to the poet's, with the difference that the scientist is inspired to discover things which exist already (his results are facts), while the poet is inspired to discover things which are created by his discovery of them (his results are not statements about things already known to exist, or knowledge, but truths which existed before only as potential truths). Experiment in the second and worse sense is the use of a system for system's sake and brings about, whether in science or poetry, only limited results. As the scientific genius is alone capable of using experiment in the first of these senses, and since the personnel of science is necessarily far more numerous than that of poetry, experiment in the second sense is the general method of the systematic, as opposed to the inventive, side of science; perhaps properly so.

Poets, then, who need the support of a system – routine labourers pretending to be inventors, since poetry, unlike science, has no place or use for routine – are obliged to adopt not only the workshop method of science, but its whole philosophical attitude, which directly contradicts that of poetry. For in science no personality is granted to the things discovered, which are looked upon as soulless integers of a soulless aggregate, with no independent rights of their own. Such poets, therefore, produce poems which are at best only well-ordered statements about chosen subjects, not new, independent living organisms; facts, not truths; examples of literature, not distinct poetic personalities. Poetry of this sort (and there has been little poetry of any other sort, because there have been few real poets) is thus the science of poem-coercion rather than the art of poem-appreciation. The real poet is proved by his creative vision of the poem, as the real parent is proved by his creative vision of the child: authorship is not a matter of the right use of the will but of an enlightened withdrawal of the will to make room for a new one.

It is this watchful withdrawal of the author's will at the right moments which gives the poem, or the child, an independent spirit – though several poets, anxious to be modernists, have misunderstood the principle and forced their poems by violent training to behave independently when they have no natural independence.

If the poem is left to shift entirely for itself and its independence is only a sign of the irresponsibility of the poet, poetry becomes a form of automatic writing, which inevitably leads to the over-emphasis of the dream element in its writing. Granted, dreams seem to exercise the same kind of control over the mind as the poem over the poet. But in dreams uncreative thought runs itself out to a solution in sheer inertia, unrefreshed by any volitional criticism; a solution which is like the negative image of the one that creative volitional thought would reach. The automatic poem is a very poor substitute for the poem resulting from the deliberate adjustment of the creative will to a solution which seems to come nearer and nearer as this will grows more and more discreet.

[. . .]

Modernism is used as a term of condemnation by the stolid critics for whom poetry is centred in the past; but as a boast by the energetic young intellectuals who hold that it should keep pace with new developments in painting, music and philosophy, and with civilization in general. Between the two parties poetry becomes a matter of temperamental politics, and in the ensuing battle of words both lose sight of the main issue: may a poet write as a poet or must he write as a period? Genuine modernism is not part of a 'modernist' programme of contemporary mannerisms but a natural personal manner and attitude in the poet to his work; he accepts the term 'modernist' because he believes that there is now a new spirit struggling at great odds to free poems of the cramping traditional habits which have prevented them from realizing their full capacities. If this spirit is kept in mind, more excuse can be found for applying the term 'modernist' to poems than to the poet. Yet no matter how restrained and impersonal a literary attitude modernist poets may adopt it is difficult for them to resist the temptation of making converts, especially when they are defamed. Literary loose-ends are always anxious to acquire character and reputation by attaching themselves to a cause, and liberal-minded readers who regard civilization as a steady human progress which does not exclude the idea of a modernist, historically advanced, poetry offer themselves as ripe for conversion. It is difficult when clarifying some aspects of genuine poetic modernism to avoid appealing to this progressive population – that is to say, presenting poetry as an instrument of historical progress – or to avoid the appearance of condoning that false modernism which disguises feebleness with eccentricity. It is at first difficult, in fact, to distinguish false modernism, or faith in history, from genuine modernism, or faith in the immediate performances of poems as not necessarily derived from history. Modernist poetry need mean no more than poetry sprung from honest invention rather than from conscientious attendance on the time-spirit.

[. . .]

A strong distinction must be drawn between poetry as something developing through civilization and as something developing organically by itself. Civilization develops only in the sense that one thing follows another, not in the sense that things become progressively better or more harmonious because they follow on one another's heels. Poetry does develop in the sense that it is contemporaneous with civilization; but it has to protect itself from contemporaneous influences rather than woo them, since there is no merit in believing in modernism for modernism's sake. One must always therefore keep this distinction in mind: between what is historically new in poetry because the poet is acting as a barker for civilization, and what is intrinsically new in poetry because the poet is an original interpreter of the fortunes of mankind. [. . .]

Many contemporary poets not only snap their fingers at civilization; they elaborate their superior attitude by casually proving that they can not only keep up with civilization but outstrip it. [. . .]

Exploitation of modern musical theory appears in the poetry of W. J. Turner, of modern painting theory in that of Edith and Sacheverell Sitwell, of psychological theory in that of Herbert Read and Archibald Macleish, of modern sex-engrossment in that of D. H. Lawrence, of philosophical theory in that of Conrad Aiken, of encyclopediac learning in that of Marianne Moore and T. S. Eliot – and so on and so on. This reaction inspires not only an emulative display of modernist learning, but also cultivation of fine writing to prove that this generation can beat the most cunning Elizabethan, Romantic Revivalist or Victorian at his own game. [. . .]

Literary internationalism – the incorporation of foreign tongues and atmospheres – is another method of civilizing and enlarging poetry. French is the most common language introduced to this end, with Italian and Spanish closely following. Mr. Eliot not only makes free use of French side by side with English: he has written poems entirely in French. An even greater enlargement is made by a cultivation of the more remote classics. Some poets are able to maintain a sense of balance and dignity in this, if only because they are good scholars; but not so Mr. Ezra Pound. In a single volume of his, *Lustra*, occur literary references to Greek, Latin, Spanish, Italian, Provençal and Chinese literature – several of these incorrectly quoted. Mr. Eliot, a more serious scholar, refers in *The Waste Land* to Greek, Latin, Spanish, Italian, French, German and Sanskrit literature. [. . .]

Among the few unexploited elegances left to poetry, as opposed to drama, is an affectation of the vocabulary of low life. Wordsworth's use of the language of simple men was, in a conservative way, a similar counter-elegance; but modernist poets outdo Wordsworth in literary slumming.

[. . .]

Of some contemporary poets 'modernist' is used merely to describe a certain independence of mind, without definitely associating them with modernism as a literary cause: though content to stay in the main stream of poetry, they make judicious splashes to show that they are aware of the date. This has been the tactical position adopted both by those whose modernism consists in a studied aloofness from literary politics and by those who have had neither the courage nor the capacity to go the whole way with modernism and yet do not wish to be left behind. To the first class belong such poets as Mr. Siegfried Sassoon, and Mr. Robert Frost whose nature-poems are, with the exception of two or three of Mr. Frank Prewett's, perhaps the only unaffected ones of our period. [. . .]

To the second class belong poets like Mr. Yeats who, observing that his old poetical robes had worn rather shabby, recently acquired a new outfit. But confirmed literary habits are not so easily discarded: even when he writes of 'Lois Fuller's Chinese Dancers' – a high-brow Vaudeville turn – instead of Eire and the ancient ways, And the Red Rose upon the Rood of Time.

Such are the shifts to which poets are driven in trying to cope with civilization and in rejecting or keeping up with the social requirements which seem to be laid upon poetry. In the confusion which results it is clear at least that modernist verse, however much it has been weakened or perverted by its race with civilization, embodies the best and most enduring contemporary poetry. 'Modernist' should describe a quality in poetry which has nothing to do with the date or with reacting to the demands of civilization, though the poets in whose works this quality is most evident are not so stupid or unhumorous as to ignore their contemporaneous universe. Evidences of time naturally occur in their writing; but its modernism always lies in its independence, in its not relying on any of the traditional devices of poetry-making nor on any of the effects artificially achieved by using the atmosphere of contemporary life and knowledge to startle or to convey reality; the most intelligent attitude towards history is not to take one's own date too seriously. If a topical institution, person or object happens to be mentioned by these poets, this is only because it supplies an image more accurately suited to the particular requirements of a poem than another less recent one. Their work is especially characterized by a lack of strain by an intelligent ease.

[. . .]

Many common symbols of civilization are, in any case, naturally absorbed by poetry, although to begin with they cannot be used without self-consciousness. The naturalness with which some new invention or scientific discovery may be mentioned in poetry depends on its newness. There is even an assessable time-limit before any such novelty becomes a common object and until the completion of which one cannot write of it in poetry without a certain affectation. This time-limit varies with the nature of the novelty. During the period of acclimatization its name gradually loses the initial capital or the italics with which it was originally printed, and comes to be pronounced without any sense of strangess or second-thought. [. . .]

But it is necessary for the poet to come to the point, after slowly acclimatizing his verse to what were once considered unpoetical subjects, where he can, with Miss Moore, bring himself to insert in his poem fourteen unrevised and consecutive words straight from a newspaper advertisement, and put them into quotation marks as well? Though a feat of poetic self-martyrdom and perhaps the logical conclusion of giving civilization what it wants – verse actually interpretative of what is called 'the poetry of modern business' – it is bad for both poetry and business: the quotation would have been much more effective if left in the original setting to compose the daily synthetic advertisement-poem of the morning paper.

True modernist poetry can appear equally at all stages of historical development from Wordsworth to Miss Moore. And it does appear when the poet forgets what is the correct literary conduct demanded of him in relation to contemporary institutions (by civilization speaking through the literary critic) and can write a poem which has the power of survival in spite of its disregarding these demands; a poem of a certain old-fashionedness, if only because the policy of the popular newspapers has long been to shrink the current vocabulary to a few thousand words and because popular novelists have followed suit. If the poet is to allow his poem to achieve its full meaning he must often use words which are practically obsolete. English has never been so rich and flexible, so capable of conveying nice shades of meaning, as it was in Ben Jonson's day. Yet it would be absurd for a poet to disregard all that has since happened to the language. Poems which deserve to endure are at once old-fashioned and modernist. [. . .]

When modernist poetry or what not so long ago passed for modernist poetry, can reach the stage where the following piece by Mr. Ezra Pound:

PAPYRUS
Spring . . .
Too long . . .
Gongula . . .

is seriously offered as a poem, there is some justification for the plain reader and orthodox critic who shrinks from anything that may be labelled 'modernist' either in terms of condemnation or approbation. Who or what is Gongula? Is it the name of a person? Of a town? Of a musical instrument? Or is it the obsolete botanical word meaning 'spores'? Or is it a mistake for Gongora, the Spanish poet from whose name the word 'gongorism' is formed, meaning 'an affected elegance of style'? And why 'Papyrus'? Is the poem a fragment from a real papyrus? Or from an imaginary one? Or are these Mr. Pound's thoughts about either a real or imaginary fragment? Or about Spring seeming too long because of the gongula of the papyrus-reeds? Rather than answer any of these questions and be driven to the shamefaced bluff of making much out of little, the reader retires to safer ground. Better, he thinks, that ten authentic poets should be left for posterity to discover than that one charlatan should be allowed to steal into the Temple of Fame.

[. . .]

31
F. (FRANCIS) SCOTT FITZGERALD (1896–1940)
FROM 'ECHOES OF THE JAZZ AGE' 1931

American novelist and short-story writer. Fitzgerald studied at Princeton where he met his lifelong friends Edmund Wilson and John Peale Bishop. In 1917 he left to join the army. While stationed in Montgomery, Alabama he met Zelda Sayre whom he married after the publication of his first novel, This Side of Paradise *(1920). Fame and wealth followed with the Fitzgeralds living an extravagant and public life. After* The Beautiful and Damned *(1922) they moved to the Riviera to live among a group of American expatriates. In 1925 Fitzgerald completed* The Great Gatsby, *followed the next year by a collection of stories,* All the Sad Young Men. *The next decade was marked by Zelda's severe mental illness and Fitzgerald's alcoholism.* Tender Is the Night, *his last completed novel, was published in 1934. The unfinished* The Last Tycoon *was printed posthumously in 1941. The following extracts are from* The Crack-Up *(1945), a collection of Fitzgerald's confessional essays compiled by Edmund Wilson.*

It is too soon to write about the Jazz Age with perspective, and without being suspected of premature arteriosclerosis. Many people still succumb to violent retching when they happen upon any of its characteristic words – words which have since yielded in vividness to the coinages of the underworld. It is as dead as were the Yellow Nineties in 1902. Yet the present writer already looks back to it with nostalgia. It bore him up, flattered him and gave him more money than he had dreamed of, simply for telling people that he felt as they did, that something had to be done with all the nervous energy stored up and unexpended in the War.

The ten-year period that, as if reluctant to die outmoded in its bed, leaped to a spectacular death in October, 1929, began about the time of the May Day riots in 1919. When the police rode down the demobilized country boys gaping at the orators in Madison Square, it was the sort of measure bound to alienate the more intelligent young men from the prevailing order. [. . .] But, because we were tired of Great Causes, there was no more than a short outbreak of moral indignation, typified by Dos Passos' *Three Soldiers*. Presently we began to have slices of the national cake and our idealism only flared up when the newspapers made melodrama out of such stories as Harding and the Ohio Gang or Sacco and Vanzetti. The events of 1919 left us cynical rather than revolutionary, in spite of the fact that now we are all rummaging around in our trunks wondering where in hell we left the liberty cap – 'I know I *had* it' – and the moujik blouse. It was characteristic of the Jazz Age that it had no interest in politics at all.

It was an age of miracles, it was an age of art, it was an age of excess, and it was an age of satire. A Stuffed Shirt squirming to blackmail in a lifelike way, sat upon the throne of the United States; a stylish young man hurried over to represent to us the throne of England. A world of girls yearned for the young Englishman; the old American groaned in his sleep as he waited to be poisoned by his wife, upon the advice of the female Rasputin who then made the ultimate decision in our national affairs. But such matters apart, we had things our way at last. With Americans ordering suits by the gross in London, the Bond Street tailors perforce agreed to moderate their cut to the American long-waisted figure and loose-fitting taste, something subtle passed to America, the style of man. During the Renaissance, Francis the First looked to Florence to trim his leg. Seventeenth-century England aped the court of France, and fifty years ago the German Guards officer bought his civilian clothes in London. Gentlemen's clothes – symbol of 'the power that man must hold and that passes from race to race'.

We were the most powerful nation. Who could tell us any longer what was fashionable and what was fun? Isolated during the European War, we had begun combing the unknown South and West for folkways and pastimes, and there were more ready to hand.

The first social revelation created a sensation out of all proportion to its novelty. As far back as 1915 the unchaperoned young people of the smaller cities had discovered the mobile privacy of that automobile given to young Bill at sixteen to make him 'self-reliant'. At first petting was a desperate adventure even under such favorable conditions, but presently confidences were exchanged and the old commandment broke down.

[. . .]

But petting in its more audacious manifestations was confined to the wealthier classes – among other young people the old standard prevailed until after the War, and a kiss meant that a proposal was expected, as young officers in strange cities sometimes discovered to their dismay. Only in 1920 did the veil finally fall – the Jazz Age was in flower.

Scarcely had the staider citizens of the republic caught their breaths when the wildest of all generations, the generation which had been adolescent during the confusion of the War, brusquely shouldered my contemporaries out of the way and danced into the limelight. This was the generation whose girls dramatized themselves as flappers, the generation that corrupted its elders and eventually overreached itself less through lack of morals than through lack of taste. May one offer in exhibit the year 1922! That was the peak of the younger generation, for though the Jazz Age continued, it became less and less an affair of youth.

The sequel was like a children's party taken over by the elders, leaving the children puzzled and rather neglected and rather taken aback. By 1923 their elders, tired of watching the carnival with ill-concealed envy, had discovered that young liquor will take the place of young blood, and with a whoop the orgy began. The younger generation was starred no longer.

A whole race going hedonistic, deciding on pleasure. The precocious intimacies of the younger generation would have come about with or without prohibition – they were implicit in the attempt to adapt English customs to American conditions. [. . .] But the general decision to be amused that began with the cocktail parties of 1921 had more complicated origins.

The word jazz in its progress toward respectability has meant first sex, then dancing, then music. It is associated with a state of nervous stimulation, not unlike that of big cities behind the lines of a war. To many English the War still goes on because all the forces that menace them are still active – Wherefore eat, drink and be merry, for to-morrow we die. But different causes had now brought about a corresponding state in America – though there were entire classes (people over fifty, for example) who spent a whole decade denying its existence even when its puckish face peered into the family circle. [. . .] Meanwhile their granddaughters pass the well-thumbed copy of *Lady Chatterley's Lover* around the boarding-school and, if they get about at all, know the taste of gin or corn at sixteen. But the generation who reached maturity between 1875 and 1895 continue to believe what they want to believe.

Even the intervening generations were incredulous. In 1920 Heywood Broun announced that all this hubbub was nonsense, that young men didn't kiss but told anyhow. But very shortly people over twenty-five came in for an intensive education. Let me trace some of the revelations vouch-safed them by reference to a dozen works written for various types of mentality during the decade. We begin with the suggestion that Don Juan leads an interesting life (*Jurgen*, 1919; then we learn that there's a lot of sex around if we only knew it (*Winesburg, Ohio*, 1920), that adolescents lead very amorous lives (*This Side of Paradise*, 1920), that there are a lot of neglected Anglo-Saxon words (*Ulysses*, 1921), that older people don't always resist sudden temptations (*Cytherea*, 1922), that girls are sometimes seduced without being ruined (*Flaming Youth*, 1922), that even rape often turns out well (*The Sheik*, 1922), that glamorous English ladies are often promiscuous (*The Green Hat*, 1924), that in fact they devote most of their time to it (*The Vortex*, 1926), that it's a damn good thing too (*Lady Chatterley's Lover*, 1928), and finally that there are abnormal variations (*The Well of Loneliness*, 1928, and *Sodom and Gomorrah*, 1929).

[. . .]

Contrary to popular opinion, the movies of the Jazz Age had no effect upon its morals. The social attitude of the producers was timid, behind the times and banal – for example, no picture mirrored even faintly the younger generation until 1923, when magazines had already been started to celebrate it and it had long ceased to be news. There were a few feeble splutters and then Clara Bow in *Flaming Youth*; promptly the Hollywood hacks ran the theme into its cinematographic grave. Throughout the Jazz Age the movies got no farther than Mrs. Jiggs, keeping up with its most blatant superficialities. This was no doubt due to the censorship as well as to innate conditions in the industry. In any case, the Jazz Age now raced along under its own power, served by great filling stations full of money.

The people over thirty, the people all the way up to fifty, had joined the dance. [. . .] Society, even in small cities, now dined in separate chambers, and the sober table learned about the gay table only from hearsay. There were very few people left at the sober table. One of its former glories, the less sought-after girls who had become resigned to sublimating a probable celibacy, came across Freud and Jung in seeking their intellectual recompense and came tearing back into the fray.

By 1926 the universal preoccupation with sex had become a nuisance. (I remember a perfectly mated, contented young mother asking my wife's advice about 'having an affair right away', though she had no one especially in mind, 'because don't you think it's sort of undignified when you get much over thirty?') For a while bootleg Negro records with their phallic euphemisms made everything suggestive, and simultaneously came a wave of erotic plays – young girls from finishing-schools packed the galleries to hear about the romance of being a Lesbian and George Jean Nathan protested.

[. . .]

By 1927 a wide-spread neurosis began to be evident, faintly signalled, like a nervous beating of the feet, by the popularity of cross-word puzzles. I remember a fellow expatriate opening a letter from a mutual friend of ours, urging him to come home and be revitalized by the hardy, bracing qualities of the native soil. It was a strong letter and it affected us both deeply, until we noticed that it was headed from a nerve sanitarium in Pennsylvania.

[. . .]

Nevertheless, Americans were wandering ever more widely – friends seemed eternally bound for Russia, Persia, Abyssinia and Central Africa. And by 1928 Paris had grown suffocating. With each new shipment of Americans spewed up by the boom the quality fell off, until toward the end there was something sinister about the crazy boatloads. They were no longer the simple pa and ma and son and daughter, infinitely superior in their qualities of kindness and curiosity to the corresponding class in Europe, but fantastic neanderthals who believed something, something vague, that you remembered from a very cheap novel. I remember an Italian on a steamer who promenaded the deck in an American Reserve Officer's uniform picking quarrels in broken English with Americans who criticised their own institutions in the bar. I remember a fat Jewess, inlaid with diamonds, who sat behind us at the Russian ballet and said as the curtain rose, 'Thad's luffly, dey ought to baint a bicture of it.' This was low comedy, but it was evident that money and power were falling into the hands of people in comparison with whom the leader of a village Soviet would be a gold-mine of judgment and culture. There were citizens travelling in luxury in 1928 and 1929 who, in the distortion of their new condition, had the human value of Pekinese, bivalves, cretins, goats. I remember the judge from some New York district who had taken his daughter to see the Bayeux Tapestries and made a scene in the papers advocating their segregation because one scene was immoral. But in those days life was like the race in *Alice in Wonderland*, there was a prize for every one.

[. . .]

It ended two years ago, because the utter confidence which was its essential prop received an enormous jolt, and it didn't take long for the flimsy structure to settle earthward. And after two years the Jazz Age seems as far away as the days before the War. It was borrowed time anyhow – the whole upper tenth of a nation living with the insouciance of grand ducs and the casualness of chorus girls. But moralizing is easy now and it was pleasant to be in one's twenties in such a certain and unworried time. Even when you were broke you didn't worry about money, because it was in such profusion around you. Toward the end one had a struggle to pay one's share; it was almost a favor to accept hospitality that required any travelling. Charm, notoriety, mere good manners, weighed more than money as a social asset. This was rather splendid, but things were getting thinner and thinner as the eternal necessary human values tried to spread over all that expansion. Writers were geniuses on the strength of one respectable book or play; just as during the War officers of four months' experience commanded hundreds of men, so there were now many little fish lording it over great big bowls.

[. . .]

Now once more the belt is tight and we summon the proper expression of horror as we look back at our wasted youth. Sometimes, though, there is a ghostly rumble among the drums, an asthmatic whisper in the trombones that swings me back into the early twenties when we drank wood alcohol and every day in every way grew better and better, and there was a first abortive shortening of the skirts, and girls all looked alike in sweater dresses, and people you didn't want to know said 'Yes, we have no bananas', and it seemed only a question of a few years before the older people would step aside and let the world be run by those who saw things as they were – and it all seems rosy and romantic to us who were young then, because we will never feel quite so intensely about our surroundings any more.

32
ROBERT MCALMON (1896–1956)
FROM *BEING GENIUSES TOGETHER 1920–1930* 1938

American writer, publisher, critic and bon viveur, friend of Joyce, Pound, and many other writers. With William Carlos Williams, McAlmon founded the little magazine Contact. *Married to Winifred Bryher, her father's financial support enabled him to set up Contact Publishing Company in Paris in 1923. His account of his life between 1920 and 1934,* Being Geniuses Together, *written in 1934 and published 1938, is 'the most candid and knowledgeable record of the literary argiebargies of that time', according to Kay Boyle who revised the book in 1968, adding alternate chapters of her own. In the following extracts, McAlmon reminisces about Paris in the early 1920s and encounters with T. S. Eliot, James Joyce, Wyndham Lewis, Ezra Pound and Djuna Barnes.*

[. . .]

I decided to get in touch with T. S. Eliot, although his cautious articles on criticism did not impress me, nor did his erudition, scholarship, or his lack of a sense of either life or literature. His mouldy poetry struck me as the perfect expression of a clerkly and liverish man's apprehension of life, and to me he *was* Prufrock. I prefer his then main influence, Laforgue. (Eliot never had Ezra Pound's health and vitality.) Laforgue's outlook at least has a fever and an alive wit, without the perverse intent on being a 'hollow man'. Much of Eliot's poetry had been written before the war, so that I knew his 'spirit' had not been created by war events.

At this time the Egoist Press published a book of my poetry, *Explorations*, but as nobody paid it any attention I need not apologize, and can dare to say that much worse had been done before and is being done yet by others. In it was a poem which was rather harsh on Eliot, and in America I had written an article which caused me to think he might not receive me with pleasure.

I telephoned Eliot so that if he wished he could quickly dismiss me. It was for me a method of escaping Audley Street and that awful service flat, and to placate the family, I had promised to stay in London for at least three months. When Eliot was at the other end of the line and caught my name there was a pause, and he agreed to an appointment, but not today and not tomorrow, but would I 'phone again? I thought if he wished for an appointment he could drop me a note. He did. I was surprised to find him very likeable indeed, with a quality – to save sparring for words – of charm that few people possess. He looked tired and overworked, which was understandable as he was then employed in a bank. Present that first evening was J. W. N. Sullivan, who at the time was religious and worshipful about Dostoevsky, mainly *The Brothers Karamazov*. We drank a quantity of whisky and the evening was amiable and entertaining. Eliot and I indulged in a bit of legpulling with Sullivan, trying to convince him that Dostoevsky was too much a soul-searcher to be an artist, but Sullivan brought in higher mathematics and a wealth of earnestness. We none of us proved a thing, but we did have a sociable time.

During the course of the evening at Eliot's I had evidently regretted my comments on him in a New York paper. At any rate he wrote me: 'As for your criticism, it was so intelligent that you need not worry about my opinion of it. I like your mind and that is all that matters.'

While in Paris I heard from him again and his letter made me feel that distinctly never would he and I agree on what makes literature or life. He said of Paris that the right way to take it is as a place and a tradition, rather than as a congeries of people who are mostly futile and time-wasting, except when you want to pass an evening agreeably in a café. When he was living there years ago he had only the genuine stimulus of the place, for he had not known any of the writers or painters as companions – knew them rather as spectacles, listened to, on rare occasions, but never spoken to. Joyce he admired as a person who seemed to be independent of outside stimulus (had he read Joyce's *Ulysses*?).

[. . .]

There was your snob-governess attitude. Possibly the lives of the Elizabethans and Greeks would indicate that Eliot's attitude was wrong, and it is hard to understand what gives validity to a tradition if it is not the lives and conventions of living people. Is Eliot afraid of the interchange of relationships, with their attractions and antagonisms and experiences? Derain, Brancusi, Proust, Picasso, Satie, and quantities of others of various nationalities and races were in Paris at this period, and many of them spent much time in cafés and bistros, drinking considerably upon occasion.

Eliot appeals to the adolescent emotions of despair and defeat. His cerebral tearfulness, his liverish and stomach-achey wail, dominated his poetry during his college days, long before the war, at the time he was writing 'Prufrock', and with artifice having people come and go talking of Michelangelo, while the long-haired Pole plays Chopin. He became then quite a butler to the arts, the 'classes', and later to the Church. If Ezra Pound spoke of tradition and discipline it could be worth listening to, because Pound has interiorly disciplined his craft (when he is not scolding, but is being the poet he can be). He has at least not subjected himself to the sterile cant of a vested interest or religion, and when reading, for example, the compact impressions of Marianne Moore, does appear to understand what is being said, and that Miss Moore is as definitely modelling or sculpturing as, let us say cautiously, Benvenuto Cellini. However, others have detected that Eliot, in his essays, seems unable to realize the clearly stated meaning of certain sentences, so that perhaps overcaution and gentility are inherent in him and stultify his 'intelligence'.

In Paris I had a note from Harriet Weaver, publisher of the Egoist Press, to present to James Joyce. His *Dubliners* I much liked. The Stephen Dedalus of his *Portrait of the Artist as a Young Man* struck me as precious, full of noble attitudinizings, and not very admirable in its soulful protestations. He seemed to enjoy his agonies with a self-righteousness which would not let the reader in on his actual ascetic ecstasies. Nevertheless, the short stories made me feel that Joyce would be approachable, as indeed did passages of *Ulysses* which had already appeared in the *Little Review*.

At his place on the Boulevard Raspail I was greeted by Mrs. Joyce, and although there was a legend that Joyce's eyes were weak, it was evident that he had used eyesight in choosing his wife. She was very pretty, with a great deal of simple dignity and a reassuring manner. Joyce finally appeared, having just got up from bed. Within a few minutes it was obvious that he and I would get on. Neither of us knew anybody much in Paris, and both of us like companionship. As I was leaving he suggested that we have dinner together that night, and we met at eight for an apéritif and later went to dine.

At that time Joyce was by no means a worldly man, or the man who could later write to the Irish Academy that, living in Paris as he did, it was difficult to realize the importance of their academy. He had come but recently from Zürich, and before that Trieste, in both of which cities he had taught languages at the Berlitz school in order to support his family. He was still a Dublin-Irish provincial, as well as a Jesuit-Catholic provincial, although in revolt. He refused to understand that questions of theology did not disturb or interest me, and never had. When I assured him that instead of the usual 'religious crises' in one's adolescent life I had studied logic and metaphysics and remained agnostic, he did not listen. He would talk about the fine points of religion and ethics as he had been taught by the Jesuits. His favourite authors were Cardinal Newman and St. Thomas Aquinas, and I had read neither. He told me some tale of how St. Thomas once cracked a woman – possibly a prostitute – over the head with a chair, and explained that the Jesuits were clever at logic. They could justify anything if it suited their purposes.

He was working on *Ulysses* at the time and often would make appointments to read rather lengthy extracts of what he had most recently written. Probably he read to me about a third of the book. It was impressive to observe how everything was grist to his mill. He was constantly leaping upon phrases and bits of slang which came naturally from my American lips, and one night, when he was slightly spiffed, he wept a bit while explaining his love or infatuation for words, mere words. Long before this explanation I had recognized that malady in him, as probably every writer has had that disease at some time or other, generally in his younger years. Joyce never recovered. He loved particularly words like 'ineluctable', 'metempsychosis' – grey, clear, abstract, fine-sounding words that are 'ineluctable' a bit themselves.

[. . .]

I don't think I ever did get around to telling Joyce that the high-minded struttings and the word prettifications and the Greek beauty part of his writings palled on me, as did Stephen Dedalus when he grew too noble and forbearing. Stephen's agonies about carnal sin seemed melodramatic, but perhaps they were not so. Several years later a son of Augustus John, Henry, who was studying to be a priest, wrote essays and letters equally intent upon carnal desire and the searing sin of weakening. Mercifully I was not brought up by the Jesuits.

[. . .]

At the time Valery Larbaud, the French author-critic, was keen about Joyce's work and had written his article noting *Ulysses* as the first Irish book to belong to world literature. He dined with us at times and we generally went later to the Gypsy Bar off the Boul' Mich'. Wyndham Lewis arrived for a stay in Paris and he was a different man from the Lewis of London. He was free and easy and debonair. Indeed, too many Englishmen will do on the Continent what it does not do to do in London. Lewis was intent upon going to the Picasso exhibition; he must meet Picasso and Braque and Derain, although these painters of Paris were cagy and suspicious about English painters of talent. Picasso at the time was doing his pneumatic nudes, which always made me want to stick a pin in them to see if they would deflate.

Lewis was most gracious and jovial and instructed me with a constant flow of theories on abstraction and plastic values. It would not have done to let him know that I had heard most of what he was saying before, in New York, when Marsden Hartley, Alfred Stieglitz, and art critics held forth in speech or newspaper articles. Somehow there was no wonder in Lewis' discovery that the engineering demand of structures often gives them an aesthetic value. The Egyptians, Greeks, and Mayans seemed to have known that before Lewis.

It was spring, however, and for a time Lewis, Joyce, and I met nightly, and upon occasions would stay out till nearly dawn. The Gypsy Bar was usually our late night hangout. The *patron* and the 'girls' knew us well, and knew that we would drink freely and surely stay till four or five in the morning. The girls of the place collected at our table and indulged in their Burgundian and Rabelaisian humours. Jeannette, a big draught horse of a girl from Dijon, pranced about like a mare in heat and restrained no remark or impulse which came to her. Alys, sweet and pretty-blonde, looked fragile and delicate, but led Jeannette to bawdier and altogether earthy vulgarities of speech and action. Joyce, watching, would be amused, but inevitably there came a time when drink so moved his spirit that he began quoting from his own work or reciting long passages of Dante in rolling sonorous Italian. I believed that Joyce might have been a priest upon hearing him recite Dante as though saying mass. Lewis sometimes came through with recitations of Verlaine, but he did not get the owl eyes and mesmerizing expression upon his face which was automatically Joyce's. Amid the clink of glasses, jazz music badly played by a French orchestra, the chatter and laughter of the whores, Joyce went on reciting Dante.

[. . .]

Ezra Pound was in town also, and I dropped him a note. He had been a boyhood friend of William Carlos Williams and of Hilda Doolittle (H.D.), and I wrote to him as a friend of theirs and not as to an older poet. He had not written any of his cantos at the time (to my knowledge), and while I mildly liked a poem or so of his, I disliked his critical work generally. Emanuel Carnevali had, in *Poetry* of Chicago, written a review of Ezra's work, declaring the main impulse behind it was irritation. I agreed, but Bill Williams and Hilda both assured me he was – *he was* – Ezra. I could understand that he was a bit of a character and perhaps difficult, but I'm not easy myself.

[. . .]

In any case, while I still don't care for the irritated portion in his work, I thoroughly admire his poetry and much of his criticism, and would hand *How to Read* to every youngster with ordinary brightness by the time he is twelve years old. Ezra may be a bit too much the poet poetizing, but no one touches him for craft and the power of evocation when he succeeds. Where Eliot is mouldy and sogs and is everlastingly the adolescent who will perversely be an old man blubbering, Ezra is hard, and his images flash at you and awaken clear and stimulating response. Where Joyce goes Irish-twilighty and uses a word or words for their isolated beauty, without attaining much more than the beauty of the word alone as it stands in the dictionary, Ezra gives entire passages, which evoke historic and legendary memories, and satirizes coolly. His cantos don't carry on throughout. They're jumpy, often axe-grinding, pedantic, scolding, but there are other passages which compensate, and no poem of such length carries on throughout the whole. Homer's *Iliad* and *Odyssey* are narrative and epic novels; but *The Divine Comedy* of Dante and Milton's *Paradise Lost* are insufferably boring through long passages – and to me particularly because they possess the medieval or Catholic mind.

[. . .]

The influx of people who came to be called 'expatriates' had begun before this, but now they hung out in Montparnasse at the Dôme and the Rotonde. At the time

I was doing Lipps, the Deux Magots, various bistros, all around St. Germain or the Boulevard St. Michel. I was hardly aware of Montparnasse, even as a legend, and Sylvia Beach informed me it was ghastly, a hangout for pederasts. In the daytime I was busy writing the short stories which went into *A Hasty Bunch*, a title which Joyce suggested because he found my American use of language racy. I was at that six weeks, and just as it was finished a flock of 'expatriates' descended upon the Rue Jacob, Sts. Pères, St. Germain section. They were Kate Buss, critic for some Boston paper, Djuna Barnes, the *Broom* outfit – Alfred Kreymborg, Harold Loeb, Frances Midner, late of the Washington Square Bookshop, and Kreymborg's wife, Dorothy.

[. . .]

I had known Djuna only slightly in New York, because Djuna was a very haughty lady, quick on the uptake, and with a wise-cracking tongue that I was far too discreet to try and rival. Once I had written a letter to the *Little Review*, asking how came it that Miss Barnes was both so Russian and so Synge-Irish, a comment Jane Heap apparently used frequently to cow Djuna. Jane kept assuring her that McAlmon was not taken in by her cape-throwing gestures but understood her for the sentimentalist she was. In the end, Djuna had gathered the idea that I disliked her, and that I was a very sarcastic individual. She was wrong about the first idea at least, for Djuna is far too good-looking and fundamentally likeable for anything but fond admiration, if not a great deal more, even when she is rather overdoing the *grande dame* manner and talking soul and ideals. In conversation she is often great with her comedy, but in writing she appears to believe she must inject her work metaphysics, mysticism, and her own strange version of a 'literary' quality. In her *Nightwood* she has a well-known character floundering in the torments of soul-probing and fake philosophies, and he just shouldn't. The actual person doubtlessly suffered enough without having added to his character this unbelievable dipping into the deeper meanings. Drawn as a wildly ribald and often broadly funny comic, he would have emerged more impressively.

[. . .]

33
VLADIMIR DIXON (1900–29)
A LITTER TO MR. JAMES JOYCE 1929

The author of the following letter to 'Mr. Germs Choice' (included in Our Examination Round His Factification for Incamination of Work in Progress, *the collective response to Joyce's* Work in Progress, *first published in Paris by Shakespeare & Co. in 1929) was until recently believed to have been James Joyce himself. It is now clear, however, that Vladimir Dixon did exist. Son of a naturalised American-English father and a Russian mother, Vladimir joined the Singer Company's European headquarters in Paris as auditor in 1923. A polyglot, polymath and keen follower of avant-garde activities, Dixon became fascinated with Joyce's work and, as his 'Litter' suggests, a successful mimic of the Joycean style.*

Dear Mister Germ's Choice,
in gutter dispear I am taking my pen toilet you know that, being Leyde up in bad with

the prewailent distemper (I opened the window and in flew Enza), I have been reeding one half ter one other the numboars of 'transition' in witch are printed the severeall instorments of your 'Work in Progress'.

You must not stink I am attempting to ridicule (de sac!) you or to be smart, but I am so disturd by my inhumility to onthorstand most of the impslocations constrained in your work that (although I am by nominals dump and in fact I consider myself not brilliantly ejewcatered but still of above Averroëge men's tality and having maid the most of the oporto unities I kismet) I am writing you, dear mysterre Shame's Voice, to let you no how bed I feeloxerab out it all.

I am überzeugt that the labour involved in the composition of your work must be almost supper humane and that so much travail from a man of your intellacked must ryeseult in somethink very signicophant. I would only like to know have I been so strichnine by my illnest white wresting under my warm Coverlyette that I am as they say in my neightive land 'out of the mind gone out' and unable to combprehen that which is clear or is there really in your work some ass pecked which is Uncle Lear?

Please froggive my t'Emeritus and any inconvince that may have been caused by this litter.

Yours veri tass
Vladimir Dixon

34
SAMUEL BECKETT (1906–89)
FROM 'DANTE . . . BRUNO . VICO . . JOYCE' 1929; FROM *PROUST* 1931

Irish author, playwright and critic. After graduating from Trinity College, Dublin, in 1927, Beckett taught English in Paris where he met James Joyce. He settled in the French capital in 1937 and was involved with the Resistance for a time during the war. His pre-war publications include essays on Proust and Joyce, volumes of poetry, a collection of stories entitled More Pricks than Kicks *(1934) and the novel* Murphy *(1938). After the war he enjoyed a prolific few years during which he produced prose narratives in French,* Molloy *(1951),* Malone meurt *(1951: Malone Dies) and* L'Innommable *(1953: The Unnamable), and* Watt *(1953) in English. His major plays began with* Waiting for Godot *(French 1953, English 1955) and include* Endgame *(French 1957, English 1958),* Happy Days *(1961) and* Krapp's Last Tape *(1958). He was awarded the Nobel Prize for Literature in 1969. The following extracts are from his essay, 'Dante . . . Bruno . Vico . . Joyce', published in* Our Exagmination Round his Factification for Incamination of Work in Progress *by Samuel Beckett and others (1929), and from his 1931 study of Proust. [See Ib 18]*

The danger is in the neatness of identifications. The conception of Philosophy and Philology as a pair of nigger minstrels out of the Teatro dei Piccoli is soothing, like the contemplation of a carefully folded ham-sandwich. Giambattista Vico himself could not resist the attractiveness of such coincidence of gesture. He insisted on complete identification between the philosophical abstraction and the empirical illustration, thereby annulling the absolutism of each conception – hoisting the real unjustifiably clear of its dimensional limits, temporalizing that which is extratemporal. And now here am I, with my handful of abstractions, among which notably: a mountain, the coincidence of contraries, the inevitability of cyclic evolution, a system of Poetics, and the prospect of self-extension in the world of Mr Joyce's *Work in Progress*. There is the temptation to treat every concept like 'a bass dropt neck fust in till a bung crate', and make a really tidy job of it. Unfortunately such an exactitude of application would imply distortion in one of two directions. Must we wring the neck of a certain system in order to stuff it into a contemporary pigeon-hole, or modify the dimensions of that pigeon-hole for the satisfaction of the analogymongers? Literary criticism is not book-keeping.

[. . .]

Apart from this emphasis on the tangible conveniences common to Humanity, we find frequent expressions of Vico's insistence on the inevitable character of every progression – or retrogression: 'The Vico road goes round to meet where terms begin. Still onappealed to by the cycles and onappalled by the recoursers, we feel all serene, never you fret, as regards our dutyful cask . . . before there was a man at all in Ireland there was a lord at Lucan. We only wish everyone was as sure of anything in this watery world as we are of everything in the newlywet fellow that's bound to follow . . .' 'The efferfresh-painted livy in beautific repose upon the silence of the dead from Pharoph the next first down to ramescheckles the last bust thing.' 'In fact, under the close eyes of the inspectors the traits featuring the chiaroscuro coalesce, their contrarieties eliminated, in one stable somebody similarly as by the providential warring of heartshaker with housebreaker and of dramdrinker against freethinker our social something bowls along bumpily, experiencing a jolting series of prearranged disappointments, down the long lane of (it's as semper as oxhousehumper) generations, more generations and still more generations' – this last a case of Mr Joyce's rare subjectivism. In a word, here is all humanity circling with fatal monotony about the Providential fulcrum – the 'convoy wheeling encirculing abound the gigantig's lifetree'. [. . .]

On turning to the *Work in Progress* we find that the mirror is not so convex. Here is direct expression – pages and pages of it. And if you don't understand it, Ladies and Gentlemen, it is because you are too decadent to receive it. You are not satisfied unless form is so strictly divorced from content that you can comprehend the one almost without bothering to read the other. The rapid skimming and absorption of the scant cream of sense is made possible by what I may call a continuous process of copious intellectual salivation. The form that is an arbitrary and independent phenomenon can fulfil no higher function than that of stimulus for a tertiary or quartary conditioned reflex of dribbling comprehension. When Miss Rebecca West clears her decks for a sorrowful deprecation of the Narcisstic element in Mr Joyce by the purchase of 3 hats, one feels that she might very well wear her bib at all her intellectual banquets, or alternatively, assert a more noteworthy control over her salivary glands than is possible for Monsieur Pavlov's unfortunate dogs. The title of this book is a good example of a form carrying a strict inner determination. It should be proof against the usual volley of cerebral sniggers: and it may suggest to some a dozen incredulous Joshuas prowling around the Queen's Hall, springing their tuning-forks lightly against finger-nails that have not yet been refined out of existence. Mr Joyce has a word to say to you on the subject: 'Yet to concentrate solely on the literal sense or even the psychological content of any document to the sore neglect of the enveloping facts themselves circumstantiating it is just as harmful; etc.' And another: 'Who in his heart doubts either that the facts of feminine clothiering are there all the time or that the feminine fiction, stranger than the facts, is there also at the same time, only a little to the rere? Or that one may be separated from the other? Or that both may be contemplated simultaneously? Or that each may be taken up in turn and considered apart from the other?'

Here form *is* content, content *is* form. You complain that this stuff is not written in English. It is not written at all. It is not to be read – or rather it is not only to be read. It is to be looked at and listened to. His writing is not *about* something; *it is that something itself.* (A fact that has been grasped by an eminent English novelist and historian whose work is in complete opposition to Mr Joyce's.) When the sense is sleep, the words go to sleep. (See the end of *Anna Livia.*) When the sense is dancing, the words dance. Take the passage at the end of Shaun's pastoral: 'To stirr up love's young fizz I tilt with this bridle's cup champagne, dimming douce from her peepair of hide-seeks tight squeezed on my snowybreasted and while my pearlics in their sparkling wisdom are nippling her bubblets I swear (and let you swear) by the bumper round of my poor old snaggletooth's solidbowel I ne'er will prove I'm untrue to (thearc!) you liking so long as my hole looks. Down.' The language is drunk. The very words are tilted and effervescent. How can we qualify this general esthetic vigilance without which we cannot hope to snare the sense which is for ever rising to the surface of the form and becoming the form itself? St Augustine puts us on the track of a word with his '*intendere*', Dante has: '*Donne ch'avette intelletto d'amore*', and *Voi che, intendendo, il terzo ciel movette*', but his '*intendere*' suggests a strictly intellectual operation. When an Italian says to-day '*Ho inteso*', he means something between '*Ho udito*' and '*Ho capito*', a sensuous untidy art of intellection. Perhaps 'apprehension' is the most satisfactory English word. Stephen says to Lynch: 'Temporal or spatial, the esthetic image is first luminously apprehended as selfbounded and selfcontained upon the immeasurable background of space or time which is not it . . . You apprehend its wholeness'. There is one point to make clear: the Beauty of *Work in Progress* is not presented in space alone, since its adequate apprehension depends as much on its visibility as on its audibility. There is a temporal as well as a spatial unity to be apprehended. Substitute 'and' for 'or' in the quotation, and it becomes obvious why it is as inadequate to speak of 'reading' *Work in Progress* as it would be extravagant to speak of 'apprehending' the work of the late Mr Nat Gould. Mr Joyce has desophisticated language. [. . .]

Proust

[. . .] Proust's creatures, then, are victims of this predominating condition and circumstance – Time; victims as lower organisms, conscious only of two dimensions and suddenly confronted with the mystery of height, are victims: victims and prisoners. There is no escape from the hours and the days. Neither from tomorrow nor from yesterday. There is no escape from yesterday because yesterday has deformed us, or been deformed by us. The mood is of no importance. Deformation has taken place.

Yesterday is not a milestone that has been passed, but a daystone on the beaten track of the years, and irremediably part of us, within us, heavy and dangerous. We are not merely more weary because of yesterday, we are other, no longer what we were before the calamity of yesterday. A calamitous day, but calamitous not necessarily in content. The good or evil disposition of the object has neither reality nor significance. The immediate joys and sorrows of the body and the intelligence are so many superfoetations. Such as it was, it has been assimilated to the only world that has reality and significance, the world of our own latent consciousness, and its cosmography has suffered a dislocation. So that we are rather in the position of Tantalus, with this difference, that we allow ourselves to be tantalised. And possibly the perpetuum mobile of our disillusions is subject to more variety. The aspirations of yesterday were valid for yesterday's ego, not for to-day's. We are disappointed at the nullity of what we are pleased to call attainment. But what is attainment? The identification of the subject with the object of his desire. The subject has died – and perhaps many times – on the way. For subject B to be disappointed by the banality of an object chosen by subject A is as illogical as to expect one's hunger to be dissipated by the spectacle of Uncle eating his dinner. Even suppose that by one of those rare miracles of coincidence, when the calendar of facts runs parallel to the calendar of feelings, realization takes place, that the object of desire (in the strictest sense of that malady) is achieved by the subject, then the congruence is so perfect, the time-state of attainment eliminates so accurately the time-state of aspiration, that the actual seems the inevitable, and, all conscious intellectual effort to reconstitute the invisible and unthinkable as a reality being fruitless, we are incapable of appreciating our joy by comparing it with our sorrow. Voluntary memory (Proust repeats it ad nauseam) is of no value as an instrument of evocation, and provides an image as far removed from the real as the myth of our imagination or the caricature furnished by direct perception. There is only one real impression and one adequate mode of evocation. Over neither have we the least control.

[. . .]

The laws of memory are subject to the more general laws of habit. Habit is a compromise effected between the individual and his environment, or between the individual and his own organic eccentricities, the guarantee of a dull inviolability, the lightning-conductor of his existence. Habit is the ballast that chains the dog to his vomit. Breathing is habit. Life is habit. Or rather life is a succession of habits, since the individual is a succession of individuals; the world being a projection of the individual's consciousness (an objectivation of the individual's will, Schopenhauer would say), the pact must be continually renewed, the letter of safe-conduct brought up to date. The creation of the world did not take place once and for all time, but takes place every day. Habit then is the generic term for the countless treaties concluded between the countless subjects that constitute the individual and their countless correlative objects. The periods of transition that separate consecutive adaptations (because by no expedient of macabre transubstantiation can the grave-sheets serve as swaddling-clothes) represent the perilous zones in the life the individual, dangerous, precarious, painful, mysterious and fertile, when for a moment the boredom of living is replaced by the suffering of being. [. . .]

The suffering of being: that is, the free play of every faculty. Because the pernicious devotion of habit paralyses our attention, drugs those handmaidens of perception whose co-operation is not absolutely essential. [. . .]

'If Habit,' writes Proust, 'is a second nature, it keeps us in ignorance of the first, and is free of its cruelties and its enchantments.' Our first nature, therefore, corresponding, as we shall see later, to a deeper instinct than the mere animal instinct of self-preservation, is laid bare during these periods of abandonment. And its cruelties and enchantments are the cruelties and enchantments of reality. 'Enchantments of reality' has the air of a paradox. But when the object is perceived as particular and unique and not merely the member of a family, when it appears independent of any general notion and detached from the sanity of a cause, isolated and inexplicable in the light of ignorance, then and then only may it be a source of enchantment.

[. . .]

The respite is brief. 'Of all human plants,' writes Proust, 'Habit requires the least fostering, and is the first to appear on the seeming desolation of the most barren rock.' Brief, and dangerously painful. The fundamental duty of Habit, about which it describes the futile and stupefying arabesques of its supererogations, consists in a perpetual adjustment and readjustment of our organic sensibility to the conditions of its worlds. Suffering represents the omission of that duty, whether through negligence or inefficiency, and boredom its adequate performance. The pendulum oscillates between these two terms: Suffering – that opens a window on the real and is the main condition of the artistic experience, and Boredom – with its host of top-hatted and hygienic ministers, Boredom that must be considered as the most tolerable because the most durable of human evils. Considered as a progression, this endless series of renovations leaves us as indifferent as the heterogeneity of any one of its terms, and the inconsequence of any given me disturbs us as little as the comedy of substitution. Indeed, we take as little cognisance of one as of the other, unless, vaguely, after the event, or clearly, when, as in the case of Proust, two birds in the bush are of infinitely greater value than one in the hand, and because – if I may add this nux vomica to an apéritif of metaphors – the heart of the cauliflower or the ideal core of the onion would represent a more appropriate tribute to the labours of poetical excavation than the crown of bay. I draw the conclusion of this matter from Proust's treasury of nutshell phrases: 'If there were no such thing as Habit, Life would of necessity appear delicious to all those whom Death would threaten at every moment, that is to say, to all Mankind.'

[. . .]

There is no right and wrong in Proust nor in his world. (Except possibly in those passages dealing with the war, when for a space he ceases to be an artist and raises his voice with the plebs, mob, rabble, canaille.) Tragedy is not concerned with human justice. Tragedy is the statement of an expiation, but not the miserable expiation of a codified breach of a local arrangement, organised by the knaves for the fools. The tragic figure represents the expiation of original sin, of the original and eternal sin of him and all his 'socii malorum', the sin of having been born.

[. . .]

The point of departure of the Proustian exposition is not the crystalline agglomeration but its kernel – the crystallised. The most trivial experience – he says in effect – is encrusted with elements that logically are not related to it and have consequently been rejected by our intelligence: it is imprisoned in a vase filled with a certain perfume and a certain colour and raised to a certain temperature. These vases are suspended along the height of our years, and, not being accessible to our intelligent memory, are in a sense immune, the purity of their climatic content is guaranteed by forgetfulness, each one is kept at its distance, at its date. So that when the imprisoned microcosm is besieged in the manner described, we are flooded by a new air and a new perfume (new precisely because already experienced), and we breathe the true air of Paradise, of the only Paradise that is not the dream of a madman, the Paradise that has been lost.

The identification of immediate with past experience, the recurrence of past action or reaction in the present, amounts to a participation between the ideal and the real, imagination and direct apprehension, symbol and substance. Such participation frees the essential reality that is denied to the contemplative as to the active life. What is common to present and past is more essential than either taken separately. Reality, whether approached imaginatively or empirically, remains a surface, hermetic. Imagination, applied – a priori – to what is absent, is exercised in vacuo and cannot tolerate the limits of the real. Nor is any direct and purely experimental contact possible between subject and object, because they are automatically separated by the subject's consciousness of perception, and the object loses its purity and becomes a mere intellectual pretext or motive. But, thanks to this reduplication, the experience is at once imaginative and empirical, at once an evocation and a direct perception, real without being merely actual, ideal without being merely abstract, the ideal real, the essential, the extratemporal. But if this mystical experience communicates an extratemporal essence, it follows that the communicant is for the moment an extratemporal being. Consequently the Proustian solution consists, in so far as it has been examined, in the negation of Time and Death, the negation of Death because the negation of Time. Death is dead because Time is dead.

[. . .]

IIIb

The 1930s: Modernist regroupings

1
SIEGFRIED KRACAUER (1889–1966)
FROM 'THE MASS ORNAMENT' 1927

German architect and philosopher, Kracauer was a key cultural commentator in Weimar Germany, also associated with the Frankfurt Institute for Social Research. His writing often focused on marginal or 'superficial' aspects of modern life and aimed to throw an indirect critical light on modernity itself. His work in that respect parallels that of Theodor Adorno and Walter Benjamin. After the rise of the Nazis, Kracauer went into exile, first in Paris and then the USA. Reproduced below are extracts from an essay originally published in 1927. It is translated by Barbara Correll and Jack Zipes from Critical Theory and Society: A Reader, *ed. Stephen Eric Bronner and Douglas MacKay Kellner, 1989. [See Ia 20]*

An analysis of the simple surface manifestations of an epoch can contribute more to determining its place in the historical process than judgments of the epoch about itself. As expressions of the tendencies of a given time, these judgments cannot be considered valid testimonies about its overall situation. On the other hand, the very unconscious nature of surface manifestations allows for direct access to the underlying meaning of existing conditions. Conversely, the interpretation of such manifestations is tied to an understanding of these conditions. The underlying meaning of an epoch and its less obvious pulsations illuminate one another reciprocally.

A change in taste has been taking place quietly in the field of physical culture, always a popular subject in illustrated newspapers. It began with the Tiller Girls. These products of American 'distraction factories' are no longer individual girls, but indissoluble female units whose movements are mathematical demonstrations. Even as they crystallize into patterns in the revues of Berlin, performances of the same geometrical exactitude are occurring in similarly packed stadiums in Australia and India, not to mention America. Through weekly newsreels in movie houses they have managed to reach even the tiniest villages. One glance at the screen reveals that the ornaments consist of thousands of bodies, sexless bodies in bathing suits. The regularity of their patterns is acclaimed by the masses, who themselves are arranged in row upon ordered row.

These spectacular pageants, which are brought into existence not only by the girls and the spectators at the stadium, have long since taken on an established form. They have achieved an *international* stature and have attracted aesthetic interest.

The bearers of the ornaments are the *masses*. This is not the same as the people, for whenever the people form patterns, these patterns do not hover in mid-air but emerge from community. A current of organic life flows from these communal groups, whose shared destiny connects them with their ornaments. These ornaments appear as a magic force so laden with meaning that they cannot be reduced to a purely linear structure. Even those who have left the community and who are conscious of themselves as individual personalities with unique souls, cannot partake in the forming of new patterns. Should they be included in such a performance, these individuals do not get incorporated into the ornament. For the result would be a colorful composition which could not be worked out to its logical conclusion, since – like prongs of a rake – its points would sink into the remaining vestiges of the spiritual middle layers, weighing it down with its residue. The patterns seen in the stadiums and cabarets reveal nothing of such origins. They are composed of elements which are mere building blocks, nothing more. The construction of an edifice depends on the size of the stones and their number. It is the mass which makes the impact. Only as parts of a mass, not as individuals who believe themselves to be formed from within, are human beings components of a pattern.

The ornament is an *end in itself*. In its early stages the ballet also yielded ornaments which moved kaleidoscopically. But even after they had discarded their ritual meaning, they remained still the plastic formation of the erotic life which gave rise to them and determined their traits. In contrast, the synchronized movement of the girls is devoid of any such connections; it is a linear system which no longer has erotic meaning but at best points to the place where the erotic resides. Nor do the living constellations in the stadiums have the meaning of military demonstrations. No matter how orderly the latter appeared, that order was considered a means to an end; the parade march evolved out of patriotic feelings and in turn aroused them in soldiers and loyal subjects. The constellations of girls, however, have no meaning outside of themselves, and the masses are not a moral unit like a company of soldiers. The patterns cannot even be described as ornamental accessories for gymnastic discipline. The training of the units of girls is intended instead to produce an immense number of parallel lines, and the desired effect is to train the greatest number of people in order to create a pattern of unimaginable dimensions. In the end there is the closed ornament, whose life components have been drained of their substance.

[. . .]

The structure of the mass ornament reflects that of the general contemporary situation. Since the principle of the *capitalist production process* does not stem purely from nature, it must destroy the natural organisms which it regards either as a means or as a force of resistance. Personality and national community [*Volksgemeinschaft*] perish when calculability is demanded; only as a tiny particle of the mass can the individual human being effortlessly clamber up charts and service machines. A system which is indifferent to variations of form leads necessarily to the obliteration of national characteristics and to the fabrication of masses of workers who can be employed and used uniformly throughout the world.

– Like the mass ornament, the capitalist production process is an end in itself. The commodities which it creates are not actually produced to be possessed but to make unlimited profits. Its growth is bound up with that of the factory. The producer does not work for private gains of which he can only make limited use – the surplus profits in America are transferred to cultural accumulation centers such as libraries, universities, etc., in which intellectuals are groomed who through their later activity reimburse with interest the capital advanced to them. The producer works for the expansion of the business; values are not produced for values' sake. Though such work may once have concerned itself with the production and consumption of values, these have now become side effects which serve the production process. The activities which have been invested in the process have divested themselves of their substantial meaning.

– The production process runs its course publicly in secret. Everyone goes through the necessary motions at the conveyor belt, performs a partial function without knowing the entirety. Similar to the pattern in the stadium, the organization hovers above the masses as a monstrous figure whose originator withdraws it from the eyes of its bearers, and who himself hardly reflects upon it.

– It is conceived according to rational principles which the Taylor system only takes to its final conclusion. The hands in the factory correspond to the legs of the Tiller Girls. Psycho-technical aptitude tests seek to compute emotional dispositions above and beyond manual abilities. The mass ornament is the aesthetic reflex of the rationality aspired to by the prevailing economic system.

[. .]

The process of history is a battle between weak and distant reason and the *forces of nature*, which in myth ruled over heaven and earth. After the twilight of the gods, the gods did not abdicate; the old nature within and outside of human beings continues to assert itself. The great cultures of humanity have arisen from it, and they must die just like all creatures of nature. The superstructures of *mythological* thinking grow from this source, affirming nature in its omnipotence. With all the differences in its structure, which undergoes transformations from epoch to epoch, mythological thinking stays within the limits which nature has drawn, it acknowledges the organism as the basic model; it adapts itself to existing forms of being [*Gestalthaftigkeit des Seienden*]; it bows to the rule of fate. It reflects the premises of nature in all spheres without rebelling against their existence. Organic sociology, which projects the natural organism as a model for social organization, is no less mythological than is nationalism, which knows no higher unity than that of the nation.

Reason does not move in the circle of natural life. It is concerned with bringing truth into the world. Its realm has already been dreamed of in genuine *folktales* [*Märchen*], which are not stories about miracles but statements about the miraculous arrival of justice. There is a deep historical meaning in the fact that the tales of the Arabian Nights found their way to France during the Enlightenment, and that reason in the eighteenth century recognized the reason of the folktales as its own. In the early periods of history, pure nature was already superseded [*aufgehoben*] by the triumph of truth in the fairy tale. Natural power is defeated by the impotence of good; fidelity triumphs over the art of magic.

In serving the breakthrough of truth, the historical process becomes a *process of demythologizing* and effects a radical dismantling of those positions continually occupied anew by the natural process. The French Enlightenment is a great example of the struggle between reason and the mythological delusions which have encroached upon religious and political areas. This struggle continues, and in the course of historical development nature, increasingly divested of its magic, may become more penetrable by reason.

The *capitalist epoch* is a stage in the process of demystification [*Entzauberung*]. The kind of thinking which is associated with the present economic system has made possible a domination and use of self-contained nature which was not granted to any earlier epoch. The fact that this thinking makes the exploitation of nature possible is not decisive here.

– If human beings were merely exploiters of nature, then nature would have triumphed over nature.

– But what is decisive here is that this process allows for greater independence from natural conditions and in this way makes room for the interjection of reason. We owe the bourgeois revolutions of the last hundred and fifty years precisely to this kind of *rationality* (which emanates partly, though not totally, from the reason of folktales). These revolutions settled scores with the natural powers: the Church, which itself was entangled in worldly affairs, monarchy, and feudalism. The inevitable decomposition of these powers and other mythological ties is the good fortune of reason, since it is only in those places where natural unities collapse that the folktale comes into being.

However, the rationale of the capitalist economic system is not reason itself but obscured reason. From a certain point, it abandons the truth in which it has a stake. *It does not encompass human beings.* The operation of the production process is not set up to take them into consideration, nor is the formation of the socioeconomic organization based on them. There is not one single instance where the system is based on human essences: the question is not whether capitalist thinking should cultivate humanity as a historically nurtured formation, or whether it must let human beings go unchallenged as personalities and satisfy their natural demands. The representatives of this point of view accuse the rationalism of the capitalist system of violating human beings, and in so doing long for the resurrection of a community which will harbor the alleged humanistic element in a way that capitalism cannot. The regressive effect of such involutions aside, they fail to hit upon the central defect of the system. Capitalism does not rationalize too much but *too little*. The thinking it promulgates resists the fulfillment of the reason that is deeply rooted in human nature.

[. . .]

Viewed from the perspective of reason, the mass ornament stands revealed as *mythological cult* wrapped in abstractness. The weight granted to reason in the ornament is therefore an illusion which the ornament assumes in contrast to physical presentations of concrete immediacy. In reality, it is the crass manifestation of inferior nature. The more decisively capitalist rationale is cut off from reason and bypasses humanity vanishing into the emptiness of the abstract, the more this primitive nature can make itself felt. The natural in its impenetrability rises up in the mass pattern, despite the rationality of this pattern. Certainly, people as organic beings have disappeared from the ornaments, but that does not bring basic human nature to the fore; rather, the remaining mass particle isolates itself from this essence just as any formal general concept does. Certainly, the legs of the Tiller Girls and not the natural units of their bodies swing in unison with one another; and certainly the thousands in the stadium are also one single star. But this star does not shine, and the legs of the Tiller Girls are the abstract signs of their bodies. Wherever reason breaks down the organic unity and rips open the cultivated natural surface, it speaks out; there it dissects the human form so that undistorted truth itself can model humanity anew. But reason has not permeated the mass ornament, whose patterns are *mute*. [. . .] In the mass ornament we see the *rational, empty form* of the cult stripped of any express meaning. As such, it proves itself to be a regression to mythology (a greater regression is scarcely imaginable) – a regression which once again reveals the intransigence of the capitalist rationale to reason. [. . .] There are numerous attempts being made, which for the sake of reaching a higher sphere, are about to give up the rationality and level of reality reached by the mass ornament. The exertions of physical culture in the field of *rhythmical gymnastics* have set a goal beyond that of personal hygiene – namely, the expression of appealing emotional contents, to which in turn the teachers of physical culture often add worldviews. Even disregarding their aesthetic impossibility, these events seek to recapture precisely what the mass ornament has happily left behind: the organic connection of nature with something that is regarded by overly modest people as soul or spirit. [. . .] This is just one example typical of many other hopeless attempts to reach the higher life from mass existence.

[. . .]

Undertakings which attempt to reconstruct a form of state, a community, an artistic formulation, without considering our historical place – having as bearers human beings already affected by contemporary thinking, but beings who by all rights no longer exist – cannot hold their own against the baseness of the mass ornament. Turning to them is not an elevation above its empty and external insipidity, but a flight from its reality. The process leads directly through the mass ornament, not away from it. It can move forward only when thinking sets limits to nature and produces human beings in a way reason would produce them. Then society will change. Then, too, the mass ornament will vanish and human life itself will assume the traits of that ornament which expresses itself in the folktales, face to face with truth.

2
MAX HORKHEIMER (1895–1971)
FROM 'THE STATE OF CONTEMPORARY SOCIAL PHILOSOPHY AND THE TASKS OF AN INSTITUTE FOR SOCIAL RESEARCH' 1931

A philosopher by training, Horkheimer became the second director of the Frankfurt Institute for Social Research in 1931 after the retirement of Carl Grünberg. It was under Horkheimer's leadership that the Institute undertook the task of developing a radical and comprehensive social theory based on an interdisciplinary approach. Reproduced below is an extract from Horkheimer's inaugural lecture of 1931 (translated by Peter Wagner from Critical Theory and Society: A Reader, *ed. Stephen Eric Bronner and Douglas MacKay Kellner, 1989). Members of the Institute included some of the central figures of the Marxist Weimar intelligentsia; Theodor Adorno, Leo Lowenthal, Herbert Marcuse, Frederick Pollock, Erich Fromm and their writings for the Institute journal* Zeitschrift für Sozialforschung *formed an immensely influential body of cultural and social criticism. Forced into exile by the Nazis, the Institute members established new headquarters at Columbia University in New York, from where more important works of critical theory and 'ideology critique' were produced. Horkheimer, in particular, collaborated with Adorno on* Dialectic of Enlightenment *(1944; 1972), a critical project which set out to investigate the origins of Fascism, the cultural phenomena of modern capitalism and the contradictions at the heart of modern rationality.*

Although social philosophy is the focus of general philosophical concern, it is in no better shape today than most philosophical, indeed most fundamentally intellectual, efforts. One is unable to find a substantive conception of social philosophy that could be considered everywhere as binding. Given the present situation in the sciences, in which the traditional boundaries between disciplines are in question and we do not yet know where they might be drawn in the future, the attempt to give ultimate definitions for academic domains seems rather untimely. Nevertheless, one can reduce the general views of social philosophy to one brief idea. According to it, the final goal of social philosophy is the philosophical interpretation of human fate – insofar as humans are not mere individuals but members of a community. Social philosophy must therefore primarily concern itself with those phenomena that can be interpreted only in the context of the social existence of humans, such as the state, law, economy, religion: in short, with all of the material and spiritual culture of humanity as such.

[. . .]

Social philosophy today, as we have seen, has taken a generally polemical stand against positivism. Positivism, it is charged, sees only the particular and in the realm of society thus sees only the individual and the relations between individuals; all is exhausted by facts. That there are facts that can be ascertained by means of analytical science, philosophy does not dispute. But philosophy posits against these facts more or less constructively, more or less in its own philosophizing, ideas, essences, totalities, independent spheres of objective spirit, units of meaning, spirit of peoples that it considers to be 'more original' or even 'genuine' elements of being. The discovery of certain unprovable metaphysical presuppositions within positivism is taken by philosophy as constituting lawful ground for raising the metaphysical stakes. So it happens that against the school of Vilfredo Pareto, for example – a school that, because of its positivist understanding of reality, has to deny the existence of class, nation, humanity – various standpoints, from which these entities are posited, are offered as a 'different world view', a 'different metaphysics', or a 'different consciousness', without ever making a binding commitment possible. There are, one might say, different conceptions of reality, which make it possible to investigate what kind of genesis they had, to which sensibility of life and to which social group they belong, without providing an objectively grounded priority.

It is precisely in this dilemma of social philosophy, which speaks of its subject, the cultural life of humanity, in terms of professions of faith, and which sees the differences between the social theories of Auguste Comte, Karl Marx, Max Weber, and Max Scheler as different acts of faith, rather than distinguishing them in terms of true/false or, as of now, problematic theories – precisely in this dilemma do we perceive the deficiency that has to be overcome. To be sure, the simultaneous existence and validity of varying conceptions of reality signify the contemporary intellectual situation at large, but this variety addresses a plethora of scientific areas and spheres of life; it does not concern one and the same concentual field. The constitutive categories of philology and those of physics might thus diverge so far that it seems difficult to harmonize them; but within physics, indeed within the sciences of inorganic sciences in general, there is no such tendency to construct noncompatible concepts of reality: the opposite is rather the case. Here, the concrete scientific investigation of the empirical subject matter proves to be a corrective.

At this point one might interject the view that social philosophy is not a scientific discipline, that it is materialist sociology whose subject matter involves distinct forms of socialization. As a discipline it investigates, the various concrete ways in which people live together, all forms of associations: from the family to economic groups, and from political associations to the state and to humanity. In it, one might find objective determinations on the same level as in political economy. But sociology has nothing to say either about the degree of reality or about the value of those phenomena. All that is the province of social philosophy; and for these essential questions as it deals with them there are final pronouncements, but no universally binding, true statements which are an integrate part of large-scale investigations.

This view presupposes a conception of philosophy that is no longer tenable. However one might want to draw the boundaries between the particular disciplines of sociology and social philosophy, which, I believe, would necessitate a high degree of arbitrariness, one thing is certain: If socio-philosophical thought about the relationship of the individual to society, the meaning of culture, the formation of communities, or the overall status of social life – in short, about the great, principal questions – should be left behind as the sediment in the reservoir of social scientific problems after those problems that can be advanced in concrete investigations have been drained off, then social philosophy can still perform a social function (e.g., that of transfiguration), but its intellectual fruitfulness would be destroyed. The relationship between the philosophical and the empirical disciplines should not be conceptualized as if it were philosophy that treated the essential problems, constructing theories that cannot be attacked by the empirical sciences, its own conceptions of reality and systems embracing the totality, while in contrast empirical science comes out of its long, boring studies fragmented into a thousand individual questions, in order only to end up in the chaos of specialization. This view, according to which the empirical scientist has to regard philosophy as a beautiful yet scientifically fruitless enterprise, and the philosopher in contrast emancipates himself from the empirical scientist because the former assumes that he cannot wait for the latter in his far-reaching quest, is presently being superseded by the thought of an ongoing dialectical permeation and evolution of philosophical theory and empirical-scientific praxis. In this regard the relations between the philosophy of nature and the natural sciences present us with good examples. Chaotic specialization is not being superseded by bad syntheses of specialized research results, nor is the impartiality of empirical research secured through the attempt to eliminate the theoretical elements with it. Rather, chaotic specialization is overcome by the fact that philosophy is able to inject spiritual impulses into empirical research through its own theoretical intention towards the whole, the essential, while being open enough to be itself influenced and transformed by the developments in concrete research.

The correction of the deficiency in the situation of social philosophy hinted at above seems to us to lie neither in a profession of faith of a more or less constructive interpretation of cultural life, nor in positing a new meaning for society, state, law, and what have you. Today, on the contrary, and I am surely not alone in this opinion, all depends on organizing research around current philosophical problematics which, in turn, philosophers, sociologists, political economists, historians, and psychologists engage by joining enduring research groups in order to do together what in other areas one is able to do alone in the laboratory and what all true scientists have always done: namely, to pursue their philosophical questions directed at the big picture with the finest scientific methods, to transform and to make more precise these questions as the work progresses, to find new methods, and yet never lose sight of the whole. In this way, no positive or negative answers to philosophical questions can be given. Instead, the philosophical questions themselves are dialectically integrated into the empirical scientific process; that is to say, their answers are to be found in the progress of substantive knowledge which also effects the form. This approach to the science of society cannot be mastered by one person alone – given the vast subject matter as well as the variety of indispensable scientific methods whose assistance is called for.

[. . .]

There is little time left to give a necessarily summary and insufficient overview of the most important paths that the full members of the Institute will have to follow in close-knit fashion to initially gather the empirical material with which the relations in question can be studied. At the top of the list is obviously the interpretation of the published statistics, reports of organizations and political associations, the material of public corporations, and so on. This can happen only in connection with the ongoing analysis of the overall economic situation. Furthermore, it is necessary to investigate sociologically and psychologically the press and literature for the value of their pronouncements on the situation of the groups in question, but also because of literature's categorical structure, which enables it to influence the members of these groups. Especially important is then the development of a variety of survey methods. Questionnaires, amongst others, can be integrated into our research in manifold ways and can be of good service, if one always keeps in mind that inductive conclusions derived through them alone are always prematurely drawn. The essential purpose of questionnaires in our case is twofold: first, they should stimulate the research and keep it in touch with reality; second, they can be used to check knowledge gained by other means and thereby pre-empt errors. For the design of these questionnaires American social research has done important preliminary work which we will assimilate and advance for our own purposes. Also, we will have to use expert opinions on a grander scale. Where it is possible to advance particular aspects of problems by as yet unrecorded experiences of competent evaluators, one should try to include them wherever one might find them. Most times that will mean using the experience of practitioners for the sciences. A special task, moreover, is the collection and interpretation of documents that cannot be found in books. To that end, namely to employ scientifically the extremely rich sociological archives of the International Labor Bureau in Geneva, we will create a branch of the Institute there. Mr. Albert Thomas, the director of the International Labor Organization, has welcomed our plan and assured us, in a most pleasant manner, of his support. One has to add to all these paths, naturally, the methodological study of all published and forthcoming scientific treatises on the subject.

Each of these methods alone is completely insufficient, but perhaps all together, through years of patient and extended research, they might bear fruit for the general problematic. This can only be the case, in turn, if the members of the Institute constantly refer to the material and form their opinions not according to their own preferences, but according to the demands of the subject; if they refrain from all terms of transfiguration – and, finally, if we can preserve the unified intention to oppose both dogmatic ossification and descent into the technical-empirical.

I conclude. It has only been possible for me to delineate from all the tasks of the Institute the collective research work whose implementation will be the focus of the years to come. Besides that, the independent research of the individual members in the areas of theoretical economics, economic history, and the history of the labor movement should equally be borne in mind. [. . .]

I could only hint at all these special tasks. On the other hand, it seems to me as if even this short report about the specifics has weakened our ability to remember the fundamentals. Indeed, this lecture has become almost a symbol for the strange difficulty of social philosophy that the universal and the particular, the theoretical conceptualization and individual experience, penetrate each other. I am convinced that my explication in this regard has been insufficient. Allowing myself to hope that you have followed this lecture with forbearance, I ask for your good wishes and trust for the work itself. Carl Grünberg talked at the opening of the Institute about the fact that everyone is led in his/her scientific work by the impulse of a worldview. May the guiding impulse of this Institute be the unchangeable will to unflinchingly serve the truth!

3
BERTOLT BRECHT (1898–1956)
FROM 'THE MODERN THEATRE IS THE EPIC THEATRE' 1930

German playwright, poet and director who lived mostly in Germany. When the Nazis came to power in 1933 he lived in exile in Denmark, Sweden, Finland and mostly the USA where he attempted to work in Hollywood. He returned to East Berlin in 1948 where he and his wife the actress Helen Weigel set up the Berliner Ensemble. Brecht's work from the 1920s onwards was concerned with creating an aesthetics of dialectical materialism. His formulations on epic theatre bring together and further the experiments of Erwin Piscator and Vsevolod Meyerhold. For Brecht, as for his friend and collaborator Benjamin, epic theatre was an example of socialist aesthetics which combined theory and practice. This formal experimentation, combined with popular themes and forms (parables, story-

telling, etc.) sought to engage actors and audiences alike, establishing a new relationship between performance and its reception. Brecht's Modernist realism was in sharp contrast to socialist realism and helped fuel one of the most important debates on form and content in political art. Reproduced here are extracts from the 1930 essay 'Modern Theatre Is the Epic Theatre', from Brecht on Theatre: The Development of an Aesthetics *(ed. and trans. John Willett, 1990). [See IIa 23, 24]*

With innovations!

Opera had to be brought up to the technical level of the modern theatre. The modern theatre is the epic theatre. The following table shows certain changes of emphasis as between the dramatic and the epic theatre:

DRAMATIC THEATRE	EPIC THEATRE
plot	narrative
implicates the spectator in a stage situation	turns the spectator into an observer, but
wears down his capacity for action	arouses his capacity for action
provides him with sensations	forces him to take decisions
experience	picture of the world
the spectator is involved in something	he is made to face something
suggestion	argument
instinctive feelings are preserved	brought to the point of recognition
the spectator is in the thick of it, shares the experience	the spectator stands outside, studies
the human being is taken for granted	the human being is the object of the inquiry
he is unalterable	he is alterable and able to alter
eyes on the finish	eyes on the course
one scene makes another	each scene for itself
growth	montage
linear development	in curves
evolutionary determinism	jumps
man as a fixed point	man as a process
thought determines being	social being determines thought
feeling	reason

When the epic theatre's methods begin to penetrate the opera the first result is a radical *separation of the elements*. The great struggle for supremacy between words, music and production – which always brings up the question 'which is the pretext for what?': is the music the pretext for the events on the stage, or are these the pretext for the music? etc. – can simply be bypassed by radically separating the elements. So long as the expression 'Gesamtkunstwerk' (or 'integrated work of art') means that the integration is a muddle, so long as the arts are supposed to be 'fused' together, the various elements will all be equally degraded, and each will act as a mere 'feed' to the rest. The process of fusion extends to the spectator, who gets thrown into the melting pot too and becomes a passive (suffering) part of the total work of art. Witchcraft of this sort must of course be fought against. Whatever is intended to produce hypnosis, is likely to induce sordid intoxication, or creates fog, has got to be given up.

Words, music and setting must become more independent of one another.

Queen

(a) Music

For the music, the change of emphasis proved to be as follows:

DRAMATIC OPERA	EPIC OPERA
The music dishes up	The music communicates
music which heightens the text	music which sets forth the text
music which proclaims the text	music which takes the text for granted
music which illustrates	which takes up a position
music which paints the psychological situation	which gives the attitude

Music plays the chief part in our thesis

(b) Text

We had to make something straightforward and instructive of our fun, if it was not to be irrational and nothing more. The form employed was that of the moral tableau. The tableau is performed by the characters in the play. The text had to be neither moralizing nor sentimental, but to put morals and sentimentality on view. Equally important was the spoken word and the written word (of the titles). Reading seems to encourage the audience to adopt the most natural attitude towards the work.

(c) Setting

Showing independent works of art as part of a theatrical performance is a new departure. Neher's projections adopt an attitude towards the events on the stage; as when the real glutton sits in front of the glutton whom Neher has drawn. In the same way the stage unreels the events that are fixed on the screen. These projections of Neher's are quite as much an independent component of the opera as are Weill's music and the text. They provide its visual aids.

Of course such innovations also demand a new attitude on the part of the audiences who frequent opera houses.

Effect of the innovations: a threat to opera?

It is true that the audience had certain desires which were easily satisfied by the old opera but are no longer taken into account by the new. What is the audience's attitude during an opera; and is there any chance that it will change?

Bursting out of the underground stations, eager to become as wax in the magicians' hands, grown-up men, their resolution proved in the struggle for existence, rush to the box office. They hand in their hat at the cloakroom, and with it they hand their normal behaviour: the attitudes of 'everyday life'. Once out of the cloakroom they take their seats with the bearing of kings. How can we blame them? You may think a grocer's bearing better than a king's and still find this ridiculous. For the attitude that these people adopt in the opera is unworthy of them. Is there any possibility that they may change it? Can we persuade them to get out their cigars?

Once the content becomes, technically speaking, an independent component, to which text, music and setting 'adopt attitudes'; once illusion is sacrificed to free discussion, and once the spectator, instead of being enabled to have an experience, is forced as it were to cast his vote; then a change has been launched which goes far beyond formal matters and begins for the first time to affect the theatre's social function.

In the old operas all discussion of the content is rigidly excluded. If a member of the audience had happened to see a particular set of circumstances portrayed and had taken up a position *vis-à-vis* them, then the old opera would have lost its battle: the 'spell would have been broken'. Of course there were elements in the old opera which were not purely culinary; one has to distinguish between the period of its development and that of its decline. *The Magic Flute, Fidelio, Figaro* all included elements that were philosophical, dynamic. And yet the element of philosophy, almost of daring, in these operas was so subordinated to the culinary principle that their *sense* was in effect tottering and was soon absorbed in sensual satisfaction. Once its original 'sense' had died away the opera was by no means left bereft of sense, but had simply acquired another one – a sense *qua* opera. The content had been smothered in the opera. Our Wagnerites are now pleased to remember that the original Wagnerites posited a sense of which they were presumably aware. Those composers who stem from Wagner still insist on posing as philosophers. A philosophy which is of no use to man or beast, and can only be disposed of as a means of sensual satisfaction (*Elektra, Jonny spielt auf*). We still maintain the whole highly-developed technique which made this pose possible: the vulgarian strikes a philosophical attitude from which to conduct his hackneyed ruminations. It is only from this point, from the death of the sense (and it is understood that this sense *could* die), that we can start to understand the further innovations which are now plaguing opera: to see them as desperate attempts to supply this art with a posthumous sense, a 'new' sense, by which the sense comes ultimately to lie in the music itself, so that the sequence of musical forms acquires a sense simply *qua* sequence, and certain proportions, changes, etc. from being a means are promoted to become an end. Progress which has neither roots nor result; which does not spring from new requirements but satisfies the old ones with new titillations, thus furthering a purely conservative aim. New material is absorbed which is unfamiliar 'in this context', because at the time when 'this context' was evolved it was not known in any context at all. (Railway engines, factories, aeroplanes, bathrooms, etc. act as a diversion. Better composers choose instead to deny all content by performing – or rather smothering – it in the Latin tongue.) This sort of progress only indicates that something has been left behind. It is achieved without the overall function being changed; or rather, with a view to stopping any such change from taking place. And what about *Gebrauchsmusik*?

At the very moment when neo-classicism, in other words stark Art for Art's sake, took the field (it came as a reaction against the emotional element in musical impressionism) the idea of utilitarian music, or Gebrauchsmusik, emerged like Venus from the waves: music was to make use of the amateur. The amateur was used as a woman is 'used'. Innovation upon innovation. The punch-drunk listener suddenly wants to play. The struggle against idle listening turned into a struggle for keen listening, then for keen playing. The cellist in the orchestra, father of a numerous family, now began to play not from philosophical conviction but for pleasure. The culinary principle was saved.

What is the point, we wonder, of chasing one's own tail like this? Why this obstinate clinging to the pleasure element? This addiction to drugs? Why so little concern with one's own interests as soon as one steps outside one's own home? Why this refusal to discuss? Answer: nothing can come of discussion. To discuss the present form of our society, or even of one of its least important parts, would lead inevitably and at once to an outright threat to our society's form as such.

We have seen that opera is sold as evening entertainment, and that this puts definite bounds to all attempts to transform it. We see that this entertainment has to be devoted to illusion, and must be of a ceremonial kind. Why?

In our present society the old opera cannot be just 'wished away'. Its illusions have an important social function. The drug is irreplaceable; it cannot be done without.

Only in the opera does the human being have a chance to be human. His entire mental capacities have long since been ground down to a timid mistrustfulness, an envy of others, a selfish calculation. The old opera survives not just because it is old, but chiefly because the situation which it is able to meet is still the old one. This is not wholly so. And here lies the hope for the new opera. Today we can begin to ask whether opera hasn't come to such a pass that further innovations, instead of leading to the renovation of this whole form, will bring about its destruction.

Perhaps *Mahagonny* is as culinary as ever – just as culinary as an opera ought to be – but one of its functions is to change society; it brings the culinary principle under discussion, it attacks the society that needs operas of such a sort; it still perches happily on the old bough, perhaps, but at least it has started (out of absent-mindedness or bad conscience) to saw it through. . . . And here you have the effect of the innovations and the song they sing.

Real innovations attack the roots.

FOR INNOVATIONS – AGAINST RENOVATION!

The opera *Mahagonny* was written three years ago, in 1927. In subsequent works attempts were made to emphasize the didactic more and more at the expense of the culinary element. And so to develop the means of pleasure into an object of instruction, and to convert certain institutions from places of entertainment into organs of mass communication.

4
ANTONIN ARTAUD (1896–1948)
'THEATRE AND CRUELTY' 1933

French actor, director, writer and poet; also acted in films of Abel Gance and Carl Dreyer. The high-priest of Modernist theatre, Artaud stands as Brecht's counterpart in proposing the mythopoeic and 'cosmic' as opposed to the political and historical in constructing a theory of performance and a relationship to the audience. As a founding member of the Surrealist group in 1924, he worked for the journal The Surrealist Revolution, *produced plays with his newly-formed Alfred Jarry Theatre in 1925, but was ejected from the group the following year, when Breton and Aragon joined the Communist party. Artaud's formulations on 'The Theatre of Cruelty' appeared in his book* The Theatre and Its Double *(1938). In his search for a ritualistic and sacrificial theatre Artaud was greatly influenced by the Balinese theatre, an example of which he first encountered in the Colonial Exhibition of 1931 in the outskirts of Paris. For ten years he was committed to a mental institution and was only released after the mediation of the playwright Adamov and his friends. Although he left no concrete theory of acting or theatre, he has been hugely influential on later generations of theatre experimenters like the Polish director Jerzy Grotowski and the American Living Theatre. 'Theatre and Cruelty' (reproduced below in Victor Corti's translation) was written in May 1933. [See Ib 14, IIb 13]*

We have lost the idea of theatre. And in as much as theatre restricts itself to probing the intimacy of a few puppets, thereby transforming the audience into Peeping Toms, one understands why the elite have turned away from it or why the masses go to the cinema, music-hall and circus to find violent gratification whose intention does not disappoint them.

Our sensibility has reached the point where we surely need theatre that wakes us up heart and nerves.

The damage wrought by psychological theatre, derived from Racine, has rendered us unaccustomed to the direct, violent action theatre must have. Cinema in its turn, murders us with reflected, filtered and projected images that no longer *connect* with our sensibility, and for ten years has maintained us and all our faculties in an intellectual stupor.

In the anguished, catastrophic times we live in, we feel an urgent need for theatre that is not overshadowed by events, but arouses deep echoes within us and predominates over our unsettled period.

Our longstanding habit of seeking diversions has made us forget the slightest idea of serious theatre which upsets all our preconceptions, inspiring us with fiery, magnetic imagery and finally reacting on us after the manner of unforgettable soul therapy.

Everything that acts is cruelty. Theatre must rebuild itself on a concept of this drastic action pushed to the limit.

Infused with the idea that the masses think with their senses first and foremost and that it is ridiculous to appeal primarily to our understanding as we do in everyday psychological theatre, the Theatre of Cruelty proposes to resort to mass theatre, thereby rediscovering a little of the poetry in the ferment of great, agitated crowds hurled against one another, sensations only too rare nowadays, when masses of holiday crowds throng the streets.

If theatre wants to find itself needed once more, it must present everything in love, crime, war and madness.

Everyday love, personal ambition and daily worries are worthless except in relation to the kind of awful lyricism that exists in those Myths to which the great mass of men have consented.

This is why we will try to centre our show around famous personalities, horrible crimes and superhuman self-sacrifices, demonstrating that it can draw out the powers struggling within them, without resorting to the dead imagery of ancient Myths.

In a word, we believe there are living powers in what is called poetry, and that the picture of a crime presented in the right stage conditions is something infinitely more dangerous to the mind than if the same crime were committed in life.

We want to make theatre a believable reality inflicting this kind of tangible lac- eration, contained in all true feeling, on the heart and senses. In the same way as our dreams react on us and reality reacts on our dreams, so we believe ourselves able to associate mental pictures with dreams, effective in so far as they are projected with the required violence. And the audience will believe in the illusion of theatre on condition they really take it for a dream, not for a servile imitation of reality. On condition it releases the magic freedom of daydreams, only recognisable when imprinted with terror and cruelty.

Hence this full scale invocation of cruelty and terror, its scope testing our entire vitality, confronting us with all our potential.

And in order to affect every facet of the spectator's sensibility, we advocate a revolving show, which instead of making stage and auditorium into two closed worlds without any possible communication between them, will extend its visual and oral outbursts over the whole mass of spectators.

Furthermore, leaving the field of analysable emotional feelings aside, we intend using the actor's lyricism to reveal external powers, and by this means to bring the whole of nature into the kind of theatre we would like to evoke.

However extensive a programme of this kind may be, it does not overreach theatre itself, which all in all seems to us to be associated with ancient magic powers.

Practically speaking, we want to bring back the idea of total theatre, where theatre will recapture from cinema, music-hall, the circus and life itself, those things that always belonged to it. This division between analytical theatre and a world of move- ment seems stupid to us. One cannot separate body and mind, nor the senses from the intellect, particularly in a field where the unendingly repeated jading of our organs calls for sudden shocks to revive our understanding.

Thus on the one hand we have the magnitude and scale of a show aimed at the whole anatomy, and on the other an intensive mustering of objects, gestures and signs used in a new spirit. The reduced role given to understanding leads to drastic curtailment of the script, while the active role given to dark poetic feeling necessitates tangible signs. Words mean little to the mind; expanded areas and objects speak out. New imagery speaks, even if composed in words. But spatial, thundering images replete with sound also speak, if we become versed in arranging a sufficient interjection of spatial areas furnished with silence and stillness.

We expect to stage a show based on these principles, where these direct active means are wholly used. Therefore such a show, unafraid of exploring the limits of our nervous sensibility, uses rhythm, sound, words, resounding with song, whose nature and startling combinations are part of an unrevealed technique.

Moreover, to speak clearly, the imagery in some paintings by Grünewald or Hieronymus Bosch gives us a good enough idea of what a show can be, where things in outside nature appear as temptations just as they would in a Saint's mind.

Theatre must rediscover its true meaning in this spectacle of a temptation, where life stands to lose everything and the mind to gain everything.

Besides we have put forward a programme which permits pure production methods discovered on the spot to be organised around historic or cosmic themes familiar to all.

And we insist that the first Theatre of Cruelty show will hinge on these mass concerns, more urgent and disturbing than any personal ones.

We must find out whether sufficient production means, financial or otherwise, can be found in Paris, before the cataclysm occurs, to allow such theatre (which must remain because it is the future) to come to life. Or whether real blood is needed right now to reveal this cruelty.

5

SIGMUND FREUD (1856–1939)
FROM 'THE DISSECTION OF THE PSYCHICAL PERSONALITY' 1933

The following extract is taken from a lecture delivered by Freud in Vienna in 1932 and first published in German in 1933. It appears here in James Strachey's translation for The Standard Edition of the Complete Psychological Works of Sigmund Freud *(1953–74), from the volume* New Introductory Lectures on Psychoanalysis. *Here Freud is concerned with those features of the psychical personality which were first outlined in his earlier study* The Ego and the Id *(1923).* [See Ia 14]

[. . .]

But let us return to the super-ego. We have allotted it the functions of self-observation, of conscience and of [maintaining] the ideal. It follows from what we have said about its origin that it presupposes an immensely important biological fact and a fateful psychological one: namely, the human child's long dependence on its parents and the Oedipus complex, both of which, again, are intimately interconnected. The super-ego is the representative for us of every moral restriction, the advocate of a striving towards perfection – it is, in short, as much as we have been able to grasp psychologically of what is described as the higher side of human life. Since it itself goes back to the influence of parents, educators and so on, we learn still more of its significance if we turn to those who are its sources. As a rule parents and authorities analogous to them follow the precepts of their own super-egos in educating children. Whatever understanding their ego may have come to with their super-ego, they are severe and exacting in educating children. They have forgotten the difficulties of their own childhood and they are glad to be able now to identify themselves fully with their own parents who in the past laid such severe restrictions upon them. Thus a child's super-ego is in fact constructed on the model not of its parents but of its parents' super-ego; the contents which fill it are the same and it becomes the vehicle of tradition and of all the time-resisting judgements of value which have propagated themselves in this manner from generation to generation. You may easily guess what important assistance taking the super-ego into account will give us in our understanding of the social behaviour of mankind – in the problem of delinquency, for instance – and perhaps even what practical hints on education. It seems likely that what are known as materialistic views of history sin in under-estimating this factor. They brush it aside with the remark that human 'ideologies' are nothing other than the product and superstructure of their contemporary economic conditions. That is true, but very probably not the whole truth. Mankind never lives entirely in the present. The past, the tradition of the race and of the people, lives on in the ideologies of the super-ego, and yields only slowly to the influences of the present and to new changes; and so long as it operates through the super-ego it plays a powerful part in human life, independently of economic conditions.

[. . .]

I return now to our topic. In face of the doubt whether the ego and super-ego are themselves unconscious or merely produce unconscious effects, we have, for good reasons, decided in favour of the former possibility. And it is indeed the case that large portions of the ego and super-ego can remain unconscious and are normally unconscious. That is to say, the individual knows nothing of their contents and it requires an expenditure of effort to make them conscious. It is a fact that ego and conscious, repressed and unconscious do not coincide. We feel a need to make a fundamental revision of our attitude to the problem of conscious-unconscious. At first we are inclined greatly to reduce the value of the criterion of being conscious since it has shown itself so untrustworthy. But we should be doing it an injustice. As may be said of our life, it is not worth much, but it is all we have. Without the illumination thrown by the quality of consciousness, we should be lost in the obscurity of depth-psychology; but we must attempt to find our bearings afresh.

There is no need to discuss what is to be called conscious: it is removed from all doubt. The oldest and best meaning of the word 'unconscious' is the descriptive one; we call a psychical process unconscious whose existence we are obliged to assume – for some such reason as that we infer it from its effects –, but of which we know nothing. In that case we have the same relation to it as we have to a psychical process in another person, except that it is in fact one of our own. If we want to be still more correct, we shall modify our assertion by saying that we call a process unconscious if we are obliged to assume that it is being activated *at the moment*, though *at the moment* we know nothing about it. This qualification makes us reflect that the majority of conscious processes are conscious only for a short time; very soon they become *latent*, but can easily become conscious again. We might also say that they had become unconscious, if it were at all certain that in the condition of latency they are still something psychical. So far we should have learnt nothing new; nor should we have acquired the right to introduce the concept of an unconscious into psychology. But then comes the new observation that we were already able to make in parapraxes. In order to explain a slip of the tongue, for instance, we find ourselves obliged to assume that the intention to make a particular remark was present in the subject. We infer it with certainty from the interference with his remark which has occurred; but the intention did not put itself through and was thus unconscious. If, when we subsequently put it before the speaker, he recognizes it as one familiar to him, then it was only temporarily unconscious to him; but if he repudiates it as something foreign to him, then it was permanently unconscious. From this experience we retrospectively obtain the right also to pronounce as something unconscious what had been described as latent. A consideration of these dynamic relations permits us now to distinguish two kinds of unconscious – one which is easily, under frequently occurring circumstances, transformed into something conscious, and another with which this transformation is difficult and takes place only subject to a considerable expenditure of effort or possibly never at all. In order to escape the ambiguity as to whether we mean the one or the other unconscious, whether we are using the word in the descriptive or in the dynamic sense, we make use of a permissible and simple way out. We call the unconscious which is only latent, and thus easily becomes conscious, the 'preconscious' and retain the term 'unconscious' for the other. We now have three terms, 'conscious', 'preconscious' and 'unconscious', with which we can get along in our description of mental phenomena. Once again: the preconscious is also unconscious in the purely descriptive sense, but we do not give it that name, except in talking loosely or when we have to make a defence of the existence in mental life of unconscious processes in general.

You will admit, I hope, that so far that is not too bad and allows of convenient handling. Yes, but unluckily the work of psychoanalysis has found itself compelled to use the word 'unconscious' in yet another, third, sense, and this may, to be sure, have led to confusion. Under the new and powerful impression of there being an extensive and important field of mental life which is normally withdrawn from the ego's knowledge so that the processes occurring in it have to be regarded as unconscious in the truly dynamic sense, we have come to understand the term 'unconscious' in a topographical or systematic sense as well; we have come to speak of a 'system' of the preconscious and a 'system' of the unconscious, of a conflict between the ego and the system $Ucs.$, and have used the word more and more to denote a mental province rather than a quality of what is mental. The discovery, actually an inconvenient one, that portions of the ego and super-ego as well are unconscious in the dynamic sense, operates at this point as a relief – it makes possible the removal of a complication. We perceive that we have no right to name the mental region that is foreign to the ego 'the system $Ucs.$', since the characteristic of being unconscious is not restricted to it. Very well; we will no longer use the term 'unconscious' in the systematic sense and we will give what we have hitherto so described a better name and one no longer open to misunderstanding. Following a verbal usage of Nietzsche's and taking up a suggestion by Georg Groddeck [1923], we will in future call it the 'id'. This impersonal pronoun seems particularly well suited for expressing the main characteristic of this province of the mind – the fact of its being alien to the ego. The super-ego, the ego and the id – these, then, are the three realms, regions, provinces, into which we divide an individual's mental apparatus, and with the mutual relations of which we shall be concerned in what follows.

[. . .]

You will not expect me to have much to tell you that is new about the id apart from its new name. It is the dark, inaccessible part of our personality; what little we know of it we have learnt from our study of the dream-work and of the construction of neurotic symptoms, and most of that is of a negative character and can be described only as a contrast to the ego. We approach the id with analogies: we call it a chaos, a cauldron full of seething excitations. We picture it as being open at its end to somatic influences, and as there taking up into itself instinctual needs which find their psychical expression in it, but we cannot say in what substratum. It is filled with energy reaching it from the instincts, but it has no organization, produces no collective will, but only a striving to bring about the satisfaction of the instinctual needs subject to the observance of the pleasure principle. The logical laws of thought do not apply in the id, and this is true above all of the law of contradiction. Contrary impulses exist side by side, without cancelling each other out or diminishing each other: at the most they may converge to form compromises under the dominating economic pressure towards the discharge of energy. There is nothing in the id that could be compared with negation; and we perceive with surprise an exception to the philosophical theorem that space and time are necessary forms of our mental acts. There is nothing in the id that corresponds to the idea of time; there is no recognition of the passage of time, and – a thing that is most remarkable and awaits consideration in philosophical thought – no alteration in its mental processes is produced by the passage of time. Wishful impulses which have never passed beyond the id, but impressions, too, which have been sunk into the id by repression, are virtually immortal; after the passage of decades they behave as though they had just occurred. They can only be recognized as belonging to the past, can only lose their importance and be deprived of their cathexis of energy, when they have been made conscious by the work of analysis, and it is on this that the therapeutic effect of analytic treatment rests to no small extent.

[. . .]

The relation to time, which is so hard to describe, is also introduced into the ego by the perceptual system; it can scarcely be doubted that the mode of operation of that system is what provides the origin of the idea of time. But what distinguishes the ego from the id quite especially is a tendency to synthesis in its contents, to a combination and unification in its mental processes which are totally lacking in the id. When presently we come to deal with the instincts in mental life we shall, I hope, succeed in tracing this essential characteristic of the ego back to its source. It alone produces the high degree of organization which the ego needs for its best achievements. The ego develops from perceiving the instincts to controlling them; but this last is only achieved by the [psychical] representative of the instinct being allotted its proper place in a considerable assemblage, by its being taken up into a coherent context. To adopt a popular mode of speaking, we might say that the ego stands for reason and good sense while the id stands for the untamed passions.

So far we have allowed ourselves to be impressed by the merits and capabilities of the ego; it is now time to consider the other side as well. The ego is after all only a portion of the id, a portion that has been expediently modified by the proximity of the external world with its threat of danger. From a dynamic point of view it is weak, it has borrowed its energies from the id, and we are not entirely without insight into the methods – we might call them dodges – by which it extracts further amounts of energy from the id. One such method, for instance, is by identifying itself with actual or abandoned objects. The object-cathexes spring from the instinctual demands of the id. The ego has in the first instance to take note of them. But by identifying itself with the object it recommends itself to the id in place of the object and seeks to divert the id's libido on to itself. We have already seen that in the course of its life the ego takes into itself a large number of precipitates like this of former object-cathexes. The ego must on the whole carry out the id's intentions, it fulfils its task by finding out the circumstances in which those intentions can best be achieved. The ego's relation to the id might be compared with that of a rider to his horse. The horse supplies the locomotive energy, while the rider has the privilege of deciding on the goal and of guiding the powerful animal's movement. But only too often there arises between the ego and the id the not precisely ideal situation of the rider being obliged to guide the horse along the path by which it itself wants to go.

[. . .]

We are warned by a proverb against serving two masters at the same time. The poor ego has things even worse: it serves three severe masters and does what it can to bring their claims and demands into harmony with one another. These claims are always divergent and often seem incompatible. No wonder that the ego so often fails in its task. Its three tyrannical masters are the external world, the super-ego and the id. When we follow the ego's efforts to satisfy them simultaneously – or rather, to obey them simultaneously – we cannot feel any regret at having personified this ego and having set it up as a separate organism. It feels hemmed in on three sides, threatened by three kinds of danger, to which, if it is hard pressed, it reacts by generating anxiety. Owing to its origin from the experiences of the perceptual system, it is earmarked for representing the demands of the external world, but it strives too to be a loyal servant of the id, to remain on good terms with it, to recommend itself to it as an object and to attract its libido to itself. In its attempts to mediate between the id and reality, it is often obliged to cloak the *Ucs.* commands of the id with its own *Pcs.* rationalizations, to conceal the id's conflicts with reality, to profess, with diplomatic disingenuousness, to be taking notice of reality even when the id has remained rigid and unyielding. On the other hand it is observed at every step it takes by the strict super-ego, which lays down definite standards for its conduct, without taking any account of its difficulties from the direction of the id and the external world, and which, if those standards are not obeyed, punishes it with tense feelings of inferiority and of guilt. Thus the ego, driven by the id, confined by the super-ego, repulsed by reality, struggles to master its economic task of bringing about harmony among the forces and influences working in and upon it; and we can understand how it is that so often we cannot suppress a cry: 'Life is not easy!' If the ego is obliged to admit its weakness, it breaks out in anxiety – realistic anxiety regarding the external world, moral anxiety regarding the super-ego and neurotic anxiety regarding the strength of the passions in the id.

[. . .]

And here is another warning, to conclude these remarks, which have certainly been exacting and not, perhaps, very illuminating. In thinking of this division of the personality into an ego, a super-ego and an id, you will not, of course, have pictured sharp frontiers like the artificial ones drawn in political geography. We cannot do justice to the characteristics of the mind by linear outlines like those in a drawing or in primitive painting, but rather by areas of colour melting into one another as they are presented by modern artists After making the separation we must allow what we have separated to merge together once more. You must not judge too harshly a first attempt at giving a pictorial representation of something so intangible as psychical processes. It is highly probable that the development of these divisions is subject to great variations in different individuals; it is possible that in the course of actual functioning they may change and go through a temporary phase of involution. Particularly in the case of what is phylogenetically the last and most delicate of these divisions – the differentiation between the ego and the super-ego – something of the sort seems to be true. There is no question but that the same thing results from psychical illness. It is easy to imagine, too, that certain mystical practices may succeed in upsetting the normal relations between the different regions of the mind, so that, for instance, perception may be able to grasp happenings in the depths of the ego and in the id which were otherwise inaccessible to it. It may safely be doubted, however, whether this road will lead us to the ultimate truths from which salvation is to be expected. Nevertheless it may be admitted that the therapeutic efforts of psychoanalysis have chosen a similar line of approach. Its intention is, indeed, to strengthen the ego, to make it more independent of the super-ego, to widen its field of perception and enlarge its organization, so that it can appropriate fresh portions of the id. Where id was, there ego shall be. It is a work of culture – not unlike the draining of the Zuider Zee.

6
NATHANAEL WEST (1903–40)
'SOME NOTES ON VIOLENCE' 1932; 'SOME NOTES ON MISS L.' 1933

Jewish American writer, born Nathan Weinstein in New York. West was educated at Brown University where he met his friend (and later brother-in-law), S. J. Perelman, and published in the college magazine under the name Nathaniel von Wallenstein Weinstein. In the 1920s he went to Paris where he met and mixed with the Dada/Surrealist group, Max Ernst, Louis Aragon and Philippe Soupault, and where he began his first novel, The Dream Life of Balso Snell *(1931). In 1932 he worked as co-editor of* Contact *magazine with his friend William Carlos Williams, and contributed to George Grosz's* Americana. *In 1933 he helped edit the Hollywood issue of* Americana. *Extracts from West's second satiric novel,* Miss Lonelyhearts *(1933), were published in* Contempo *magazine (edited by Kay Boyle and Ezra Pound). His anti-Fascist satire,* A Cool

Million, *was published in 1934 and for the remaining years of his life he worked as a film writer in Hollywood. Not a member of the Communist Party, he attended meetings of the John Reed Club and the League of American Writers whose revolutionary manifesto he signed in 1935. He spoke on 'Makers of Mass Neuroses' at the Western Writers' Congress of 1936; and in 1937–38 worked for the Spanish Refugee Relief Campaign. In 1939 he was a sponsor for the Hollywood fund-raising exhibition of Picasso's* Guernica. *His last novel,* The Day of the Locust, *a satire on Hollywood, was published the same year. West and his wife, Eileen, the famous model for Ruth McKenney's novel (and later play),* My Sister Eileen, *died in a car crash in 1940. Reproduced below are 'Some Notes on Violence' and 'Some Notes on Miss L.', from 1932 and 1933 respectively.*

Some Notes on Violence

Is there any meaning in the fact that almost every manuscript we receive has violence for its core? They come to us from every state in the Union, from every type of environment, yet their highest common denominator is violence. It does not necessarily follow that such stories are the easiest to write or that they are the first subjects that young writers attempt. Did not sweetness and light fill the manuscripts rejected, as well as accepted, by the magazines before the war, and Art those immediately after it? We did not start with the ideas of printing tales of violence. We now believe that we would be doing violence by suppressing them.

In America violence is idiomatic. Read our newspapers. To make the front page a murderer has to use his imagination, he also has to use a particularly hideous instrument. Take this morning's paper: FATHER CUTS SON'S THROAT IN BASEBALL ARGUMENT. It appears on an inside page. To make the first page, he should have killed three sons and with a baseball bat instead of a knife. Only liberality and symmetry could have made this daily occurence interesting.

And how must the American writer handle violence? In the July 'Criterion', H. S. D. says of a story in our first number that ' . . . the thing is incredible, as an event, in spite of its careful detail, simply because such things cannot happen without arousing the strongest emotions in the spectator. (Does not H. S. D. mean, 'in the *breast* of the spectator'?) Accordingly (the reviewer continues), only an emotional description of the scene will be credible . . .' Credible to an Englishman, yes, perhaps, or to a European, but not to an American. In America violence is daily. If an 'emotional description' in the European sense is given an act of violence, the American should say, 'What's all the excitement about,' or, 'By God, that's a mighty fine piece of writing, that's art.'

What is melodramatic in European writing is not necessarily so in American writing. For a European writer to make violence real, he has to do a great deal of careful psychology and sociology. He often needs three hundred pages to motivate one little murder. But not so the American writer. His audience has been prepared and is neither surprised nor shocked if he omits artistic excuses for familiar events. When he reads a little book with eight or ten murders in it, he does not necessarily condemn the book as melodramatic. He is far from the ancient Greeks, and still further from those people who need the naturalism of Zola or the realism of Flaubert to make writing seem 'artistically true'.

Some Notes on Miss L.

I can't do a review of *Miss Lonelyhearts*, but here, at random, are some of the things I thought when writing it:

As subtitle: 'A novel in the form of a comic strip.' The chapters to be squares in which many things happen through one action. The speeches contained in the conventional balloons. I abandoned this idea, but retained some of the comic strip technique: Each chapter instead of going forward in time, also goes backward, forward, up and down in space like a picture. Violent images are used to illustrate commonplace events. Violent acts are left almost bald.

Lyric novels can be written according to Poe's definition of a lyric poem. The short novel is a distinct form especially fitted for use in this country. France, Spain, Italy have a literature as well as the Scandinavian countries. For a hasty people we are too patient with the Bucks, Dreisers and Lewises. Thank God we are not all Scandinavians.

Forget the epic, the master work. In America fortunes do not accumulate, the soil does not grow, families have no history. Leave slow growth to the book reviewers, you only have time to explode. Remember William Carlos Williams' description of the pioneer women who shot their children against the wilderness like cannonballs. Do the same with your novels.

Psychology has nothing to do with reality nor should it be used as motivation. The novelist is no longer a psychologist. Psychology can become something much more important. The great body of case histories can be used in the way the ancient writers used their myths. Freud is your Bulfinch; you can not learn from him.

With this last idea in mind, Miss Lonelyhearts became the portrait of a priest of our time who has a religious experience. His case is classical and is built on all the cases in James' *Varieties of Religious Experience* and Starbuck's *Psychology of Religion.* The psychology is theirs not mine. The imagery is mine. Chapt. I – maladjustment. Chapt. III – the need for taking symbols literally is described through a dream in which a symbol is actually fleshed. Chapt. IV – deadness and disorder; see Lives of Bunyan and Tolstoy. Chapt. VI – self-torture by conscious sinning: see life of any saint. And so on.

> I was serious therefore I could not be obscene.
> I was honest therefore I could not be sordid.
> A novelist can afford to be everything but dull.

7
LAURA (RIDING) JACKSON (1901–91)
FROM *THE WORD 'WOMAN'* 1934–35

American poet, critic and short-story writer. Born Laura Reichenthal, she legally adopted the name Riding after coming to England from New York in 1925. Although her first book of poems (The Close Chaplet) was published in England by the Hogarth Press in 1926, she had already enjoyed early success with her poetry in the USA, where she was briefly associated with (and awarded a prize by) the 'Fugitives' group which included John Crowe Ransom, Allen Tate and Robert Penn Warren. She co-founded and co-operated, with Robert Graves, the Seizin Press (1928–38) and together they wrote A Survey of Modernist Poetry *(1927) and* A Pamphlet Against Anthologies *(1928). Along with her collection of essays,* Contemporaries and Snobs *(1928), she published several volumes of poetry, short stories and the novel* A Trojan Ending *(1937) and was the originator and editor of the critical series* Epilogue, A Critical Summary *(1935–38). Riding married Schuyler B. Jackson in 1941 and together they undertook the monumental study* Rational Meaning: A New Foundation for the Definition of Words *(1997). She stopped writing poetry in 1939, but her concern with language and truth urged a constant and consistent experimentation with words. In 1991, she was awarded the Bollingen Prize for her lifelong services to poetry. Her examination of 'the woman factor in the nature of human beings',* The Word 'Woman', *was composed in 1934–35 but was left unfinished, as she and Robert Graves fled Spain in August 1936. [See IIIa 30]*

Woman is the major incident in man's life. She is man's most different experience – the most unselflike material of perception that confronts his consciousness. The uses to which man puts this experience, and the standing he assigns to it, will be the subjects of later chapters. In this chapter we shall consider what it is to *be* this experience – what it feels like to be a woman. The uses to which she is put, and the standing assigned to her, do not describe the nature of woman: woman does not become what man variously 'makes' of her. So when a certain imaginative interpretation is put upon the moon's movements and prevails as a convention by which conveniently to describe the moon, the moon and its movements do not adapt itself to the interpretation; a new lunar manifestation would change the interpretation, but no new idea about the moon changes the moon.

Woman, in the drama 'life' (man's life), plays a part. The part is assigned to her: she does not say, 'I shall be this,' or 'I shall be that.' But, on the other hand, the part assigned must suit her nature – at least externally; man cannot assign her a part which she does not 'look'. Man may construe the part as he pleases; and she is affected by the part to the extent of seeming the character of the part. But the actions which the playing of the part involves cannot differ essentially from what she herself characteristically does. Whatever she may be doing from man's point of view in playing the part he assigns her, she is all the time internally being a woman.

To assume the separate man-made rôle requires no effort of self-falsification in woman. It is her function to register and to measure the effect of man's separate existence, a separate entity, in a totality in which she, though the source of man, is herself, technically, a separate existence herself. There is no self-falsification required because she puts no construction of positive separateness on herself contradicted by her man-made rôle; she merely lets man determine his own separateness and, fixed in her own unchangeableness, marks the result: herself *and* man, as a whole. So, if we were to make a drama 'The World and Man' and reduce the world to a character in the drama playing 'opposite' man, the nature of the world, as something in which man was contained, would condition the lines we made it speak; and if the world itself played the part it would not be falsifying its nature but registering and measuring the relations between man and itself – reincluding man in itself in more precise proportion than before, though, throughout the drama, man was continually disentangling himself as an independency.

But however unaffected woman may be by the uses to which man puts her and the standing he assigns to her, the appearance for the time being is an invidious one: she is put to certain uses, she is assigned various standings according to the standing it pleases man himself to occupy at the moment. She accepts the human appearance she has for the time being in order to advance the drama toward its end. Her life with man is a life of insult; she must inculcate in herself a capacity to endure insult. Woman's capacity to endure insult is not 'a sense of humour'; or a morbid delight in passivity; or an equally morbid belief in her inevitable unfortunateness in all contact with man. Woman does not regard any particular unfortunateness of use or standing as permanent – or, for that matter, any merely living contact with man as representative of her final relations with man. Her prevailing mood in her life with man, which includes her capacity to endure insult or any other purely human misfortune, is an impersonal biding of time.

The temporal life of woman with man has necessarily been a life of insult: however flattering it may seem in some aspects, it has been a life governed at every point by the behaviour of man. But woman does not 'mind'. It could not have been otherwise, since her object in living with man has been to discover what, precisely, man's intentions were; and her policy, to countenance these intentions as they might be consistent with an ultimate unity of being. Any authority invites insult because, in being accessible at all, it is exposing itself to the improper as well as the proper proposal; and woman is an authority, man a mass of contradictory elements under observation. It is the fate of any authority to know the worst, as it is its privilege to choose the best. Woman, in her impersonal time-biding, is knowing the worst: this is her life, her experience, as an authority. Her positive action as an authority is in the judgement she finally delivers; but before she delivers her judgement she must educate herself in man. Self-education in the subject *man* constitutes being a woman; and in so far as she is merely the student, not yet the judge, of her subject, woman must endure insult – all the improper proposals with which man tempts her indulgence.

The insult has been softened in different ways, according to man's opinion of the kind of behaviour that did him credit – according to his own notions of creditable behaviour; but never according to a standard of courtesy sought in woman herself. Man does not willingly accept judgement from woman: his greatest fear is that of provoking premature judgement. In woman he has a judge who lets him experiment with himself until he is incapable of further experiment: a judge who lets him ward off judgement by playing – insultingly – the judge of himself.

The most constant activity of woman in her time-biding complaisance has been motherhood. In mothering man woman is allowing him a likeness to herself as the enduring person of reality: she is recognizing his will to continue, to be also – bestowing on him the continuity his will deserves. In becoming the mother she is letting man be. But in accepting the mother-rôle she has had also to accept the insult that she is the original enemy of man, the enemy who has been overcome by his will to continue – and all the incidental insults attendant on the status of enemy. And although the fact that man still is is the result of his being endowed with continuity by woman, to him his continuance is the result of his own achievement – an act of conquest; and many of the courtesies extended to woman are the courtesies of the conqueror to the conquered.

'Woman' thus comes to represent, as a word, man's power over his own fortuitousness; woman is the symbol for the conquered, or conquerable, enemy. He resists understanding woman in any other sense because he fears to go beyond the momentary reality: that he lives. And woman, on her side, in seeming to accept the status not merely of enemy, but that of conquered enemy, is agreeing with him in a point of fact: that he lives, and by her consent. The other implications she is willing to let go by because she is in as little a hurry for conclusion and reckoning as man is; man needs time to adapt his ambitions to his inadequacies, she to know her subject thoroughly. And meanwhile man's life is a war, and his secure daily world a temporal victory which he sentimentally envisages as final: the spirit of conquest precedes him into finality. The final reconciliation of all incompatibilities he sees as a reconciliation with himself – of his ambitions with his inadequacies. He cannot see it as an ultimate explicit relation between himself and woman because his immediate consciousness of woman, his sense of difference, has little validity with him except as an irritant. When the irritation disappears, it seems to do so by his own power – by the yielding rather than the active consent of woman. Woman disappears from his consciousness in his momentary sensations of victory, and still more effectively, therefore, in his vision of final transfigurement: not merely the immediate fact, but the very word 'woman' disappears. In Heaven men are rid of their mortal oppositeness to woman, and so of woman; they are equal unto the angels – children of God.

Woman as the mother serves, from man's point of view, his purpose of continuity. Apart from this cardinal use there are secondary domestic uses associated with her humanity – the humanity of woman consists of the uses to which man finds he can put her. Her standing, as distinct from her uses, is a more intangible matter; it is difficult to endow her, precisely, with the human status, however human the uses to which she is put. Man is conscious that she is something different; and as such she is an irritant. But having succeeded in surviving, by silencing, as he imagines, the opposition to his being which woman represents to him, he ceases, as he imagines, to be conscious of her. The irritation has disappeared, woman has disappeared: she is the gratuitous stranger in his midst, the reason for whose presence he has forgotten. He is obliged continually to make use of her as a mother, but once he has renewed himself in her he is immediately off to his thoughts again. And the further he removes himself from the irritating memory of his dependence on her consent, the more complete the translation of this consent into terms of complaisance, and of complaisance into terms of his own will and power; and the dimmer woman herself seems as a distinct personality.

Woman thus becomes for man his own past put behind – his humiliating childhood, in which he was conditioned by his preoccupation with her. And man becomes for himself his own future; his preoccupation is with himself. As the mother woman is continually put behind. As the being whom man must continually reconquer she is repeatedly and uninterruptedly alive to him in his anomalous present. Only the future can he safely call his own. But the future is an abstraction. It is, true, the completely private region of his thoughts; woman is absent from it. But it is unreal in its very privacy. It satisfies man better than his 'life' because woman is absent from it, and so all difference; but her absence from it makes it, somehow, a problematical plane of being. Again and again he returns to what he calls deprecatingly 'reality' – not to remember woman but himself; for his own identity is infuriatingly bound up with hers. Woman, in this spiritual rise and fall, seems merely a concrete necessity to be satisfied and dismissed. She exists for man in the lower plane of his consciousness; her spiritual connotations are refuted by her physical connotations. Man does not consider his spiritual activities refuted by his own physicality, since he does not demand of them mere 'reality'. Woman is excluded from them, indeed, because she is too 'real'; that is, he is able to exclude her from them because they are unreal.

It has been easy for a woman to accept the insult of being confined to the lower plane of man's consciousness; for she is interested only in knowing man as he actually is, and the higher plane of man's consciousness has been given up for the most part to pretensions or illusions of freedom from actuality. Man's intellectual consciousness became a means of escape from his emotional consciousness, his mind a place to which to escape from his body and from woman. And so long as he denies woman presence in his thoughts, so long as he gives to the still unconquered difference that confronts him, even in his thoughts, compatible philosophic names, or the most comprehensively compatible name 'God', so long does woman prefer the plane where difference is stated in crude, undeniable, sexual terms. Difference can only be reconciled; it cannot be eliminated. Man's intellectualizations are false in so far as they mean the elimination of the fact of femaleness from his consciousness. And so woman as a whole has preferred the sexual insult, by which she is recognized as an enemy but nevertheless recognized, to the intellectual insult, by which she is admitted into the higher plane of man's consciousness only if she renounces her distinct identity as woman – if she allows herself, the different one, to become the negation of difference.

Woman has two works to perform: a work of differentiation, of man from herself, and a work of unification, of man with herself. In the first work she has at least the however ungracious co-operation of man, in his self-interested will to be. In the second work, the more purely co-operative, mere self-interest cannot pass for co-operative interest. And the second work follows automatically on the first work: when man has been completely differentiated, there remains for him destruction, or salvation – the rejoining of himself to that from which he has been differentiated, from which he has differentiated himself. Final unity is an act of rejoining. When man tries to achieve unity by himself, his notion of unity is a futurism. It derives from a state of imperfect distinctness in the present, an arbitrary suppression of the sense of difference, which enables him to 'create' unity out of himself.

[. . .]

When man rejects the egoistic ecstacies to be achieved on a higher, solitary, plane of consciousness and tries to create, somewhere between the lower and the higher planes, a rational plane of being, free from the lower brutalities and the higher ecstacies, woman then ceases to have strong sexual significance. She is elevated to the uses and standing of a 'companion'; her difference is erased in the magic word 'equality'. And she accepts equality as she accepted, in the past, the seemingly more invidious standing of being different. For though as an equal she must suffer the insult of being not merely included in the generalization 'man' but of being, particularly, the equivalent of man, she has, by her persistent time-biding, brought man down from his futuristic flights; for in treating her as an equal he is, at least, treating her as an ever-immediate presence.

It is, in fact, man himself who invented feminism, not woman; for woman is not embarrassed by her difference. The notion of woman's equality results from man's relaxation from the strain of artificial solitariness. It is an assertion, the first crude assertion, of a sense of necessitous togetherness with woman. For a time, in the assertion, the sense of difference is naturally obscured – more obscured perhaps than in traditional male thought. But woman herself lets it be obscured, because the assertion marks the transition from her first work to her second work. We, woman, are now entering upon our second work. Our difference, our not-manness, is here the basic principle of relation, as in the first work it was the basic principle of distinction. Having got from man an assertion of necessitous togetherness, we ourself must assume the responsibility of restating our difference even in togetherness – even as we are now beginning to dress once more like the traditional woman, after our neither-this-nor-that dress of the equality-period.

In that period there was attached to our rôle the last and most paradoxical insult: that we were as men. We were indifferent to the insult, as we had been to other insults, because from our side the rôle corresponded with our natural action: in this rôle woman, like or unlike man, was co-operating in the assertion of her ever-immediate validity, unbroken by reversion to the dim mother-status of the past or by romantic disappearances in the negations on which male spirituality rests. In assuming this rôle we ceased to be the mother and, equally, the fantastic beloved. In assigning us the rôle man was asserting his desire to be himself 'real' – like us. For the moment our identity hung suspended. Indeed, for the moment there was no drama at all – man did not live at all. This atmosphere of deliberate simplicity – in which everyone was equal to everyone else (not merely women to men) and every view which could be called 'intelligent' was as right as every other 'intelligent' view – marked the breakdown of fanatic beliefs into mild opinions, mere pacifism, mere fairness; as against righteousness, mere feminism.

Unlike nineteenth-century materialistic views, which were as violent in their way as earlier idealistic views, these opinions were all compromise views. The War occurred during the period of opinions, but it marked, really, the death of personalistic extremism. Modernism was man's renunciation of the special, arbitrary value; a quieting down of all the egoistic hysterias. And while modernism at first expressed itself hysterically, this was the hysteria of reaction against the strain of sustaining the artificial values by which man had raised himself beyond himself. Modernism was the death of futurism; its real spirit was the spirit of intellectual mildness and emotional simplicity. In modernism the mind of man came to a halt, seeking, self-protectively, the safe thought. And in that halt, the end of history, man for the moment ceased to live; he was waiting for the next turn of his story, resolved that he would not try to make it himself. He knew from his own exhaustion, in fact, that he was incapable of making it.

Imperceptibly – so imperceptibly that man has not yet himself noticed it – the story has begun to turn. Out of the 'modern' togetherness of man and woman, woman emerges as the unifier, leaving behind the now dead historical woman – the played out historical rôle. Imperceptibly the word 'woman' itself becomes another word, other words: the word for unity, the word for that difference which is yet the standard of unity – the diverse, all-consistent word which is truth. Imperceptibly history, the story of man, of woman's living with man, changes into truth, the story of man and woman, of man's unity with woman. To be a woman historically was to play the rôle, woman. To be a woman finally is to be truth, to make unity, to be about the second work.

[. . .]

Yet woman, in her first work, has always had a secret consciousness that in it no end was reached. It is this conviction of the purely temporary significance of human existence that has permitted woman to let herself be so dangerously absorbed in it. It has not mattered to her what became of her, what use was made of her, what standing assigned to her: no insult has mattered, because she knew internally that it was not the end. Woman has always lived with man in anticipation of a unity not possible in the violent world of time. And meanwhile man has interpreted woman's living with him as a confirmation of his spiritual predominance – adapting the apparent acquiescence of woman in his spiritual designs to his illusions of independence, disregarding her as a spiritual presence. Independence from woman has been the object of all the so-called 'creative' activity of man: the very notion of 'creation' implies the disappearance of the separate phenomenon 'woman' in male activity. The whole of D. H. Lawrence's creative activity may be described as a complaint against the resistance of woman to absorption in male identity. He did not, like the conventional male visionary, content himself with a picture of triumphant maleness. He knew that such pictures were finally false without the consent of woman to final self-annihilation in man. And because his maleness was more outrageous and self-conscious than conventional maleness, his visionary picture was of woman voluntarily annihilating herself: he did not shirk the responsibility of stating what, as man, he really wanted. His very outrageousness gave him an acute sense of what was lacking to make the conventional visionary picture real. He knew that for all her apparent acquiescence woman perpetually made one absolute reservation: herself. And indeed, while woman does not reserve her energy, her interest, her attachment, her sympathy, she reserves, finally, her identity; for it is the ground of her second work.

[. . .]

8
DOROTHY M. RICHARDSON (1873–1957)
FOREWORD TO *PILGRIMAGE* 1938

English novelist. Dorothy Richardson left formal education when she was sixteen and worked variously as a teacher, clerk and journalist. She married the artist Alan Odle in 1917. From 1914 she was engaged in the composition of her Proustian Künstlerroman, Pilgrimage, *an ambitious sequence of twelve novels (or 'chapters' as Richardson preferred), beginning with* Pointed Roofs, *published in 1915, and concluding with* Dimple Hill *(1938).* Pilgrimage *follows the life and development into a writer of Miriam Henderson, through a sustained (and early) use of the stream of consciousness technique. In her 1923 review of* Revolving Lights *(volume seven of* Pilgrimage*) for* The Times Literary Supplement, *Virginia Woolf famously claimed that Richardson had created 'a sentence which we might call the psychological sentence of the feminine gender. It is of a more elastic fibre than the old, capable of stretching to the extreme, of suspending the frailest particles, of enveloping the vaguest shapes'. Richardson wrote the following 'Foreword' in 1938. [See IIIa 9]*

Although the translation of the impulse behind his youthful plan for a tremendous essay on *Les Forces humaines* makes for the population of his great cluster of novels with types rather than with individuals, the power of a sympathetic imagination, uniting him with each character in turn, gives to every portrait the quality of a faithful self-portrait, and his treatment of backgrounds, contemplated with an equally passionate interest and themselves, indeed, individual and unique, would alone qualify Balzac to be called the father of realism.

Less deeply concerned with the interplay of human forces, his first English follower portrays with complete fidelity the lives and adventures of inconspicuous people, and for a while, when in the English literary world it began its career as a useful label, realism was synonymous with Arnold Bennett.

But whereas both Balzac and Bennett, while representing, the one in regard to a relatively concrete and coherent social system, the other in regard to a society already showing signs of disintegration, the turning of the human spirit upon itself, may be called realists by nature and unawares, their immediate successors possess an articulate creed. They believe themselves to be substituting, for the telescopes of the writers of romance whose lenses they condemn as both rose-coloured and distorting, mirrors of plain glass.

By 1911, though not yet quite a direct supply of documentary material for the dossiers of the cause célèbre, Man versus conditions impeached as the authors of his discontent, realist novels are largely explicit satire and protest, and every form of conventionalized human association is being arraigned by biographical and autobiographical novelists.

Since all these novelists happened to be men, the present writer, proposing at this moment to write a novel and looking round for a contemporary pattern, was faced with the choice between following one of her regiments and attempting to produce a feminine equivalent of the current masculine realism. Choosing the latter alternative, she presently set aside, at the bidding of a dissatisfaction that revealed its nature without supplying any suggestion as to the removal of its cause, a considerable mass of manuscript. Aware, as she wrote, of the gradual falling away of the preoccupations that for a while had dictated the briskly moving script, and of the substitution, for these inspiring preoccupations, of a stranger in the form of contemplated reality having for the first time in her experience its own say, and apparently justifying those who acclaim writing as the surest means of discovering the truth about one's own thoughts and beliefs, she had been at the same time increasingly tormented, not only by the failure, of this now so independently assertive reality, adequately to appear within the text, but by its revelation, whencesoever focused, of a hundred faces, any one of which, the moment it was entrapped within the close mesh of direct statement, summoned its fellows to disqualify it.

In 1913, the opening pages of the attempted chronicle became the first chapter of 'Pilgrimage,' written to the accompaniment of a sense of being upon a fresh pathway, an adventure so searching and, sometimes, so joyous as to produce a longing for participation; not quite the same as a longing for publication, whose possibility, indeed, as the book grew, receded to vanishing point.

To a publisher, nevertheless, at the bidding of Mr. J. D. Beresford, the book was ultimately sent. By the time it returned, the second chapter was partly written and the condemned volume, put away and forgotten, would have remained in seclusion but for the persistence of the same kind friend, who acquired and sent it to Edward Garnett, then reading for Messrs Duckworth. In 1915, the covering title being at the moment in use elsewhere, it was published as 'Pointed Roofs'.

The lonely track, meanwhile, had turned out to be a populous highway. Amongst those who had simultaneously entered it, two figures stood out. One a woman mounted upon a magnificently caprisoned charger, the other a man walking, with eyes devoutly closed, weaving as he went a rich garment of new words wherewith to clothe the antique dark material of his engrossment.

News came from France of one Marcel Proust, said to be producing an unprecedently profound and opulent reconstruction of experience focused from within the mind of a single individual, and, since Proust's first volume had been published and several others written by 1913, the France of Balzac now appeared to have produced the earliest adventurer.

Finally, however, the role of pathfinder was declared to have been played by a venerable gentleman, a charmed and charming high priest of nearly all the orthodoxics, inhabiting a softly enclosure he mistook, until 1914, for the universe, and celebrated by evolving, for the accommodation of his vast tracts of urbane commentary, a prose style demanding, upon the first reading perfection of sustained concentration akin to that which brought it forth, and bestowing, again upon the first reading, the recreative delights peculiar to this form of spiritual exercise.

And while, indeed, it is possible to claim for Henry James keeping the reader incessantly watching the conflict of human forces through the eye of a single observer, rather than taking him, before the drama begins, upon a tour amongst the properties or breaking in with descriptive introductions of the players as one by one they enter his enclosed resounding chamber where no plant grows and no mystery pours in from the unheeded stars, a far from inconsiderable technical influence, it was nevertheless not without a sense of relief that the present writer recently discovered, in 'Wilhelm Meister', the following manifesto:

> In the novel, reflections and incidents should be featured; in drama character and action. The novel must proceed slowly, and the thought-processes of the principal figure must, by one device or another, hold up the development of the

whole. . . . The hero of the novel must be acted upon, or, at any rate, not himself the principal operator. . . . Grandison, Clarissa, Pamela, the Vicar of Wakefield, and Tom Jones himself, even where they are not acted upon, are still retarding personalities and all the incidents are, in a certain measure, modelled according to their thoughts.

Phrases began to appear, formulae devised to meet the exigencies of literary criticism. 'The Stream of Consciousness' lyrically led the way, to be gladly welcomed by all who could persuade themselves of the possibility of comparing consciousness to a stream. Its transatlantic successors, 'Interior Monologue' and 'Slow-motion Photography', may each be granted a certain technical applicability leaving them, to this extent, unhampered by the defects of their qualities.

Lives in plenty have been devoted to the critic's exacting art and a lifetime might be spent in engrossed contemplation of the movements of its continuous ballet. When the dancers tread living boards, the boards will sometimes be heard to groan. The present writer groans, gently and resignedly, beneath the reiterated tap-tap accusing her of feminism, of failure to perceive the value of the distinctively masculine intelligence, of pre-War sentimentality, of post-War Freudianity. But when her work is danced upon for being unpunctuated and therefore unreadable, she is moved to cry aloud. For here is truth.

Feminine prose, as Charles Dickens and James Joyce have delightfully shown themselves to be aware, should properly be unpunctuated, moving from point to point without formal obstructions. And the author of 'Pilgrimage' must confess to an early habit of ignoring, while writing, the less of the stereotyped system of signs, and, further, when finally sprinkling in what appeared to be necessary, to a small unconscious departure from current usage. While meeting approval, first from the friend who discovered and pointed it out to her, then from an editor who welcomed the article she wrote to elucidate and justify it, and, recently, by the inclusion of this article in a text-book for students of journalism and its translation into French, the small innovation, in further complicating the already otherwise sufficiently complicated task of the official reader, helped to produce the chaos for which she is justly reproached.

For the opportunity, afforded by the present publishers, of eliminating this source of a reputation for creating avoidable difficulties, and of assembling the scattered chapters of 'Pilgrimage' in their proper relationship, the author desires here to express her gratitude and, further, to offer to all those readers who have persisted in spite of every obstacle, a heart-felt apology.

9
CECIL DAY LEWIS (1904–72)
FROM *A HOPE FOR POETRY* 1934

Irish poet, critic and (as Nicholas Blake) writer of detective fiction. While studying at Oxford he met W. H. Auden and entourage. In 1935 he left teaching to become a freelance writer. He was a member of the Communist Party 1935–38. His volumes of poetry include Transitional Poem *(1929),*

From Feathers to Iron (1931), The Magnetic Mountain (1933), A Time to Dance (1935), and Overtures to a Death (1938). A Hope for Poetry was published in 1934. The following extract is taken from chapter five of that book, from its eighth edition in 1947.

Poetry was born from magic: it grew up with religion: it lived through the age of reason: is it to die in the century of propaganda? Not death, perhaps, but a self-defensive cataleptic trance. For what hope has it of making itself heard in such a pandemonium of slogans, national anthems, headlines, tips from the horse's mouth, straight talks, loud speakers, manifestos, monkey business, madhouse gossip and high-explosive ideals? Poetry is based on the principle of free individual interpretation; you must create the meaning of each poem out of your private experience. But life for the average child of the twentieth century becomes an endless series of extension-lectures on everything under the sun; every item of his experience is explained to him – and worse, he is told exactly what his reaction to it should be. Who is he, then, to claim an individual interpretation of anything, let alone poetry? Bread, that once contained a deity, is an affair of calories now: you could put your own interpretation on the deity, but you cannot make calories mean anything but calories – they can neither receive life from your private experience nor add life to it.

[· · ·]

But it is too late. We know better. Man is an anatomy. The X ray has defeated the intuition of kinship and the inspiration of solitude. There has never been complete freedom of interpretation for anyone at any time: the more vital a religion has been, the more plainly it has told man what he must believe in one direction – and the more freedom of choice and interpretation it has given him in all other directions. There is a lost world between "This is the Catholick Faith: which except a man believe faithfully, he cannot be saved', and 'Drink Guinness: it is good for you'. Poetry has its roots in incantation; its effect has always been to create a state of mind: but it may well despair of competing with the incantation of Big Business, Bigger Navies, Brighter Churches, and all the other gang-yells of Hell's Angels. Poetry was born from magic, and science is the great enemy of magic: for magic is the personal interpretation of the universe; science, the impersonal rationalisation. So it would seem that in a 'scientific' age the flower of poetry must wither. Yet it need not be so. As a magician can prevail against a rival witch-doctor by getting possession of some hair from his head or a few of his toe-nails, vehicles by which the rival influence may pass into the control of his own spirit, so it is possible for poetry to steal the thunder of science, to absorb these trivial business incantations and turn them to its own uses.

It is a truism that a sound society makes for sound individuals, and sound individuals instance a sound society. For the post-war poet, living in a society undeniably sick, that truism has turned into a dilemma. We have seen him on the one hand rendered more acutely conscious of individuality by the acceptance of current psychological doctrines; and on the other hand, rendered both by poetic intuition and ordinary observation acutely conscious of the present isolation of the individual and the necessity for a social organism which may restore communion. He looks to one side and he sees D. H. Lawrence, the extreme point of individualism in this century's literature, its zenith or its nadir: he admits the force of Lawrence's appeal, but he has watched him driven from continent to continent, driven ill and mad, a failure unable to recreate a satisfactory social group from the nucleus of his own individuality. He looks to the other side and he sees Communism, proclaiming – though with a different meaning from Lawrence's – 'revolution for life's sake', the most whole-hearted attempt ever made to raise the individual to his highest power by a conditioning of his environment: yet here too he notices the bully and the spy, and wonders if any system can expel and survive that poison.

So there arises in him a conflict; between the old which his heart approves and the new which fructifies his imagination; between the idea of a change of heart that should change society and the idea of a new society making a new man; between individual education and mass economic conditionment. At which end should one begin? The poet, you will say, has no business to be trespassing: if he will wander into other people's fields, he must take the consequences. But it is not as simple as that. The poet, besides being a poet, is also a man, 'fed with the same food, hurt with the same weapons' as other men. Where there is hope in the air, he will hear it; where there is agony about, he will feel it. He must feel as a man what he reveals as a poet. It is as absurd to tell him that he must only feel strongly about natural scenery as it is to call every 'nature-poet' an escapist. Nor is it right for us to say that the poet should be concerned only with eternal facts, with summer and winter, birth, marriage and death. These are the mountain-peaks, the final and everlasting limits of his known world, but they are always the background against which stand out and are measured temporal things – the rise and fall of cities, the year's harvest, the moment's pain. To-day the foreground is a number of fluid, confused and contradictory patterns. Standing at the end of an epoch, the poet's arms are stretched out to opposite poles, the old life and the new; that is his power and his crucifixion.

[. . .]

Standing as a man between two worlds, he stands as a poet between two fires. On the one hand the Communist tells him that he is no better than a dope-peddler unless he 'joins the revolution', that he is unhappy and ineffective because he is trying to live in two worlds at once, and that (although the achievements of 'bourgeois' art are undeniable and to be respected) the function of artists at the present crisis is to help lead men out of the bourgeois position towards the proletarian, to be propagandists for the new world. On the other hand, the bourgeois critic rebukes him for allowing a sympathy with Communism to drive him into a kind of writing that at any rate sounds very like propaganda, asserting that an ideology is only useful to the poet in so far as it is felt and that ideas, whether revolutionary or reactionary, must never be more to the poet than the raw material out of which his poetry is formed.

They are both right up to a point. Yet the bourgeois critic must remember that there is no reason why poetry should not also be propaganda; the effect of invocation, of poetry, and of propaganda is to create a state of mind; and it is not enough to say that poetry must do unconsciously what propaganda does consciously, for that would be to dismiss all didactic poetry from that of the Bible downwards. All one can say is that propaganda verse is to be condemned when the didactic is achieved at the expense of the poetic: poetry, in fact, whatever else it may or may not be, must be poetry – a sound, if obvious, conclusion.

[. . .]

The poet is a sensitive instrument, not a leader. Ideas are not material for the poetic mind until they have become commonplaces for the 'practical' mind. On the other hand, when the Communist tells the poet that he must 'join the revolution', he is right in the sense that there can be no divorce for the Marxist between theory and practice, and that only revolutionary activity can make a revolutionary poet. Nothing, however, is to be gained by accusing the poet of employing each poem as a solution of his own difficulties, of drugging himself and thus unfitting himself through his poetry to be a happy class warrior. The poet is made like that, he has to protest; and while it is true, in a sense, that each poem solves its own conflict, it is only a temporary solution; his agonies of mind are drugged, perhaps, but not ended.

[. . .]

We shall probably find in the near future a cleavage in this poetical movement. Communist ideology and symbolism will be very much less obtrusive in poetry: for those who, as men, made Communism the nearest port in a storm, and as poets assumed it as the fashionable dress of the moment, will have departed elsewhere; while others, having made up their minds and taken it to heart, will be producing work of which Communism is the foundation and the integral framework, not the decoration and façade. Such poetry will, of course, not be communist, proletarian poetry: we could not expect that till a classless society existed in fact. To the orthodox criticism that the poet should never associate himself with any system, political or economic, except to the extent that its ideas provide stimulus and material for his poetry, I should answer by stressing the distinction made above between the poet as a man and the poet as a poet. It is a question not so much of æsthetic theory as of fact. A man, by developing the poetic faculty in himself, does not automatically secede from his common humanity. It is true that some artists have cultivated the former successfully to the almost complete exclusion of the latter, and some but by no means all great poets have been – in Keats's phrase – men that 'have not any individuality, any determined character'. But this kind of passive, plastic nature, where the whole man is metamorphosed into an impersonal poetic instrument, is, I believe, rare. In most poets there is an intermittent conflict between the poetic self and the rest of the man; and it is by reconciling the two, not by eliminating the one, that they can reach their full stature. I can agree with Eliot's statement that 'the more perfect the artist, the more completely separate in him will be the man who suffers and the mind which creates', but it must be realized that 'separate' means 'distinct', and not 'unconnected'. It is this conflict more than anything else which drives artists to drugs, dissipation, madness or death, and the conflict is bound to be particularly acute in a state of society that is inimical to the well-being of humanity as a whole and therefore both obstructs and challenges the artist's own humanity. So we may say that, while the poetic function of the man cannot be directly concerned with political ideas, his humanity may be concerned with them; in which case, they will inevitably come into communication with his poetical function and to some extent affect his poetry.

We may go further and say that, if a poet is going to be receptive of political ideas, it is essential for him as a man to feel strongly about them. For this strong 'human' emotion, working upon ideas, makes them a more tractable material for poetry; the poetic faculty will, in fact, have to deal – not with an abstract idea, but with an idea suffused and moulded by emotion; and that is a common subject for poetry. What is really undesirable is that the poet should have dealings with political ideas as a poet without first having feelings about them as a man: for direct contact between the poetic function and abstract ideas can give birth only to rhetoric. The man must pass the idea through the medium of his emotion before the poet can get to work upon it.

'We make out of the quarrel with others rhetoric,' Yeats has said, 'but of the quarrel with ourselves, poetry.' This conception of the quarrel with ourselves has, I believe, a twofold significance. It conveys first the idea of spiritual doubt as a poetic agent (we have seen this conflict at work in Gerard Manley Hopkins). And secondly it expresses the opposition between the divided selves of the poet, his poetic self and his 'human' self, a conflict of which Yeats has always been acutely aware. Yeats's own magnificent political poems – 'Easter 1916', for instance, or 'Sixteen Dead Men' – are sufficient proof that a deep feeling about political ideas and events is not necessarily synonymous with that 'quarrel with others' which produces only rhetoric. Unsuccessful propaganda verse *is* an example of this kind of rhetoric: it is the result of the poet trying to convince others without having experienced either uncertainty or conviction himself; or else, of his not being a poet: the 'quarrel with others' must, for the poet, be expressed in terms of the quarrel with himself. And failure to do this accounts for the failure of much so-called revolutionary verse.

It accounts, also, to a certain extent, for its frequent vagueness. It is not asked that poetry should offer naked argument and skeleton plans. But English revolutionary verse of to-day is too often neither poetry nor effective propaganda for the cause it is intended to support. Its vague *cris-de-cœur* for a new world, its undirected and undisciplined attack upon the whole world-broad front of the status quo, are apt to produce work which makes the neutral reader wonder whether it is aimed to win him for the communist or the fascist state. Here again the influence of D. H. Lawrence assists to confuse the issue. We find, for instance, in Auden's preoccupation with the search for 'the truly strong man', Lawrence's evangel of spiritual submission to the great individual: 'All men say they want a leader. Then let them in their souls submit to some greater soul than theirs.' And though this does not necessarily contradict communist theory, it is likely in practice to give a fascist rather than a communist tone to poetry.

There are, however, poems recently written which show that the writer has emotionally experienced a political situation and assimilated it through his specific function into the substance of poetry. It is of this kind of poetry that Wilfred Owen is the real ancestor. It is animated by the same unsentimental pity and sacred indignation. It does not wish to make poetic capital out of the suffering of others. As Spender says in a poem about the unemployed:

> . . . No, I shall weave no tracery of pen-ornament
> To make them birds upon my singing tree.

It is simple and emphatic. It gets probably as near to communist poetry as bourgeois writers under a bourgeois régime can hope to get. And it suggests the lines on which such writers must work for the present.

[. . .]

10
T. S. (THOMAS STEARNS) ELIOT (1888–1965)
FROM *THE USE OF POETRY AND THE USE OF CRITICISM* 1933

The extracts below are taken from Eliot's influential piece of cultural and literary criticism, first published in 1933. [See IIIa 14]

[. . .]

From time to time, every hundred years or so, it is desirable that some critic shall appear to review the past of our literature, and set the poets and the poems in a new order. This task is not one of revolution but of readjustment. What we observe is partly the same scene, but in a different and more distant perspective; there are new and strange objects in the foreground, to be drawn accurately in proportion to the more familiar ones which now approach the horizon, where all but the most eminent become invisible to the naked eye. The exhaustive critic, armed with a powerful glass, will be able to sweep the distance and gain an acquaintance with minute objects in the landscape with which to compare minute objects close at hand; he will be able to gauge nicely the position and proportion of the objects surrounding us, in the whole of the vast panorama.

And it is not merely the passage of time and accumulation of new artistic experience, nor the ineradicable tendency of the great majority of men to repeat the opinions of those few who have taken the trouble to think, nor the tendency of a nimble but myopic minority to progenerate heterodoxies, that makes new assessments necessary. It is that no generation is interested in Art in quite the same way as any other; each generation, like each individual, brings to the contemplation of art its own categories of appreciation, makes its own demands upon art, and has its own uses for art. ('Pure' artistic appreciation is to my thinking only an ideal, when not merely a figment, and must be, so long as the appreciation of art is an affair of limited and transient human beings existing in space and time. Both artist and audience are limited). There is for each time, for each artist, a kind of alloy required to make the metal workable into art; and each generation prefers its own alloy to any other.

[. . .]

The extreme of theorising about the nature of poetry, the essence of poetry if there is any, belongs to the study of aesthetics and is no concern of the poet or of a critic with my limited qualifications. Whether the self-consciousness involved in aesthetics and in psychology does not risk violating the frontier of consciousness, is a question which I need not raise here; it is perhaps only my private eccentricity to believe that such researches are perilous if not guided by sound theology. The poet is much more vitally concerned with the social 'uses' of poetry, and with his own place in society; and this problem is now perhaps more importunately pressed upon his conscious attention than at any previous time. The uses of poetry certainly vary as society alters, as the public to be addressed changes. In this context something should be said about the vexed question of obscurity and unintelligibility. The difficulty of poetry (and modern poetry is supposed to be difficult) may be due to one of several reasons. First, there may be personal causes which make it impossible for a poet to express himself in any but an obscure way; while this may be regrettable, we should be glad, I think, that the man has been able to express himself at all. Or difficulty may be due just to novelty: we know the ridicule accorded in turn to Wordsworth, Shelley and Keats, Tennyson and Browning – but must remark that Browning was the first to be *called* difficult; hostile critics of the earlier poets found them difficult, but called them silly. Or difficulty may be caused by the reader's having been told, or having suggested to himself, that the poem is going to prove difficult. The ordinary reader, when warned against the obscurity of a poem, is apt to be thrown into a state of consternation very unfavourable to poetic receptivity. Instead of beginning, as he should, in a state of sensitivity, he obfuscates his senses by the desire to be clever and to look very hard for something, he doesn't know what – or else by the desire not to be taken in. There is such a thing as stage fright, but what such readers have is pit or gallery fright. The more seasoned reader, he who has reached, in these matters, a state of greater *purity*, does not bother about understanding; not, at least, at first. I know that some of the poetry to which I am most devoted is poetry which I did not understand at first reading; some is poetry which I am not sure I understand yet: for instance, Shakespeare's. And finally, there is the difficulty caused by the author's having left out something which the reader is used to finding; so that the reader, bewildered, gropes about for what is absent, and puzzles his head for a kind of 'meaning' which is not there, and is not meant to be there.

The chief use of the 'meaning' of a poem, in the ordinary sense, may be (for here again I am speaking of some kinds of poetry and not all) to satisfy one habit of the reader, to keep his mind diverted and quiet, while the poem does its work upon him: much as the imaginary burglar is always provided with a bit of nice meat for the house-dog. This is a normal situation of which I approve. But the minds of all poets do not work that way; some of them, assuming that there are other minds like their own, become impatient of this 'meaning' which seems superfluous, and perceive possibilities of intensity through its elimination. I am not asserting that this situation is ideal; only that we must write our poetry as we can, and take it as we find it. It may be that for some periods of society a more relaxed form of writing is right, and for others a more concentrated. I believe that there must be many people who feel, as I do, that the effect of some of the greater nineteenth-century poets is diminished by their bulk. Who now, for the pure pleasure of it, reads Wordsworth, Shelley and Keats even, certainly Browning and Swinburne and most of the French poets of the century – entire? I by no means believe that the 'long poem' is a thing of the past; but at least there must be more in it for the length than our grandparents seemed to demand; and for us, anything that can be said as well in prose can be said better in prose. And a great deal, in the way of meaning, belongs to prose rather than to poetry. The doctrine of 'art for art's sake', a mistaken one, and more advertised than practised, contained this true impulse behind it, that it is a recognition of the error of the poet's trying to do other people's work. But poetry has as much to learn from prose as from other poetry; and I think that an interaction between prose and verse, like the interaction between language and language, is a condition of vitality in literature.

To return to the question of obscurity: when all exceptions have been made, and after admitting the possible existence of minor 'difficult' poets whose public must always be small, I believe that the poet naturally prefers to write for as large and miscellaneous an audience as possible, and that it is the half-educated and ill-educated, rather than the uneducated, who stand in his way: I myself should like an audience which could neither read nor write. The most useful poetry, socially, would be one which could cut across all the present stratifications of public taste – stratifications which are perhaps a sign of social disintegration. The ideal medium for poetry, to my mind, and the most direct means of social 'usefulness' for poetry, is the theatre. In a play of Shakespeare you get several levels of significance. For the simplest auditors there is the plot, for the more thoughtful the character and conflict of character, for the more literary the words and phrasing, for the more musically sensitive the rhythm, and for auditors of greater sensitiveness and understanding a meaning which reveals itself gradually. And I do not believe that the classification of audience is so clear-cut as this; but rather that the sensitiveness of every auditor is acted upon by all these elements at once, though in different degrees of consciousness. At none of these levels is the auditor bothered by the presence of that which he does not understand, or by the presence of that in which he is not interested.

[. . .]

Every poet would like, I fancy, to be able to think that he had some direct social utility. By this, as I hope I have already made clear, I do not mean that he should meddle with the tasks of the theologian, the preacher, the economist, the sociologist or anybody else; that he should do anything but write poetry, poetry not defined in terms of something else. He would like to be something of a popular entertainer, and be able to think his own thoughts behind a tragic or a comic mask. He would like to convey the pleasures of poetry, not only to a larger audience, but to larger groups of people collectively; and the theatre is the best place in which to do it. There might, one fancies, be some fulfilment in exciting this communal pleasure, to give an immediate compensation for the pains of turning blood into ink. As things are, and as fundamentally they must always be, poetry is not a career, but a mug's game. No honest poet can ever feel quite sure of the permanent value of what he has written: he may have wasted his time and messed up his life for nothing. All the better, then, if he could have at least the satisfaction of having a part to play in society as worthy as that of the music-hall comedian. Furthermore, the theatre, by the technical exactions which it makes and limitations which it imposes upon the author, by the obligation to keep for a definite length of time the sustained interest of a large and unprepared and not wholly perceptive group of people, by its problems which have constantly to be solved, has enough to keep the poet's *conscious* mind fully occupied, as the painter's by the manipulation of his tools. If, beyond keeping the interest of a crowd of people for that length of time, the author can make a play which is real poetry, so much the better.

I have not attempted any definition of poetry, because I can think of none which does not assume that the reader already knows what it is, or which does not falsify by leaving out much more than it can include. Poetry begins, I dare say, with a savage beating a drum in a jungle, and it retains that essential of percussion and rhythm; hyperbolically one might say that the poet is *older* than other human beings – but I do not want to be tempted to ending on this sort of flourish. I have insisted rather on the variety of poetry, variety so great that all the kinds seem to have nothing in common except the rhythm of verse instead of the rhythm of prose: and that does not tell you much about all poetry. Poetry is of course not to be defined by its uses. If it commemorates a public occasion, or celebrates a festival, or decorates a religious rite, or amuses a crowd, so much the better. It may effect revolutions in sensibility such as are periodically needed; may help to break up the conventional modes of perception and valuation which are perpetually forming, and make people see the world afresh, or some new part of it. It may make us from time to time a little more aware of the deeper, unnamed feelings which form the substratum of our being, to which we rarely penetrate; for our lives are mostly a constant evasion of ourselves, and an evasion of the visible and sensible world. But to say all this is only to say what you know already, if you have felt poetry and thought about your feelings. And I fear that I have already, throughout these lectures, trespassed beyond the bounds which a little self-knowledge tells me are my proper frontier. If, as James Thomson observed, 'lips only sing when they cannot kiss', it may also be that poets only talk when they cannot sing. I am content to leave my theorising about poetry at this point. The sad ghost of Coleridge beckons to me from the shadows.

11
EZRA POUND (1885–1972)
FROM *'PREFATIO AUT CIMICIUM TUMULUS'* 1933

The following is an extract from Ezra Pound's introduction to Active Anthology *from 1933. [See IIIa 15]*

Mr. F. V. Morley, with a misplaced sense of humour, has suggested that I write a fifty page preface to two hundred pages of contemporary poesy. This to me, who have for a quarter of a century contended that critics should know more and write less. No two hundred pages of contemporary poetry would sustain the demands I could make in half such a preface. I am moreover confining my selection to poems Britain has not accepted and in the main that the British literary bureaucracy does not want to have printed in England.

I shall therefore write a preface mainly about something else.

Mr. Eliot and I are in agreement, or 'belong to the same school of critics', in so far as we both believe that existing works form a complete order which is changed by the introduction of the 'really new' work.

His contempt for his readers has always been much greater than mine, by which I would indicate that I quite often write as if I expected my reader to use his intelligence, and count on its being fairly strong, whereas Mr. Eliot after enduring decennial fogs in Britain practically always writes as if for very very feeble and brittle mentalities, from whom he can expect neither resilience nor any faculty for seeing the import instead of the details or surfaces.

When he talks of 'commentation and elucidation' and of the 'correction of taste', I go into opposition, or rather, having been there first, I note that if I was in any sense the revolution I have been followed by the counter-revolution. Damn your taste, I would like if possible to sharpen your perceptions, after which your taste can take care of itself.

'Commentation' be damned. 'Elucidation' can stand if it means 'turn a searchlight on' something or preferably some work or author lying in shadow.

Mr. Eliot's flattering obeisance to 'exponents of criticism', wherein he says that he supposes they have not assumed that criticism is an 'autotelic activity', seems to me so much apple-sauce. In so far as the bureaucracy of letters has considered their writing as anything more than a short cut to the feeding trough or a means of puffing up their personal importances, they have done little else for the past thirty years than boost the production of writing about writing, not only as autotelic, but as something which ought to receive more attention from the reading victim than the great books themselves.

Granted that nobody ought to be such a presumptuous imbecile as to hold up the autotelic false horizon, Mr. Eliot describes a terrestrial paradise and not the *de facto* world, in which more immediate locus we observe a perpetual exchange of civilities between pulex, cimex, vermiformis, etc., each holding up his candle before the shrines of his similars.

A process having no conceivable final limit and illustratable by my present activity: I mean on this very page, engaging your attention while I talk about Mr. Eliot's essay about other essayists' essays. In the course of his eminently professorial volume he must have mentioned at least forty-five essayists whom tomorrow's readers will be most happy not to hear mentioned, but mention of whom must have contributed enormously to Mr. Eliot's rise to his deserved position as arbiter of British opinion.

Krino

'Existing monuments form an ideal order among themselves.' It would be healthier to use a zoological term rather than the word monument. It is much easier to think of the *Odyssey* or *Le Testament* or Catullus' *Epithalamium* as something living than as a series of cenotaphs. After all, Homer, Villon, Propertius, speak of the world as I know it, whereas Mr. Tennyson and Dr. Bridges did not. Even Dante and Guido with their so highly specialised culture speak of a part of life as I know it. ATHANATOS.

However, accepting for the moment Mr. Eliot's monumental or architectural simile: the krino, 'to pick out for oneself, choose, prefer' (page 381 my edition of Liddell and Scott) which seems to me the major job, is to determine, first, the main form and main proportions of that order of extant letters, to locate, first the greater pyramids and then, possibly, and with a decently proportioned emphasis, to consider the exact measurements of the stone-courses, layers, etc.

Dryden gives T. S. E. a good club wherewith to smack Milton. But with a modicum of familiarity or even a passing acquaintance with Dante, the club would hardly be needed.

A volume of quite sound statistical essays on poesy may quite easily drive a man to the movies, it may express nothing save the most perfect judgements and the utmost refinements of descriptivity and whet, nevertheless, no appetite for the unknown best, or for the best still unread by the neophyte.

A book 66 per cent concerned with manipulating and with rehandling the errors of seventy contemporary pestilential describers and rehashers of opinion, and only 34 per cent concerned with focusing the reader's attention on the *virtu* of books worth reading is, at least to the present victim, more an annoyance than a source of jocundity.

And if I am to put myself vicariously in the place of the younger reader or if I am to exercise parental protectiveness over some imagined offspring, I can find myself too angry for those mincing politenesses demanded by secondary editorial orders.

My opinion of critics is that:

The best are those who actually cause an amelioration in the art which they criticise.

The next best are those who most focus attention on the best that is written (or painted or composed or cut in stone).

And the pestilential vermin are those who distract attention *from* the best, either to the second rate, or to hokum, or to their own critical writings.

Mr. Eliot probably ranks very high in the first of these three groups, and deserves badly of us for his entrance into the last.

[. . .]

Mr. Eliot's grief

Mr. Eliot's misfortune was to find himself surrounded by a horrible and micro-cephalous bureaucracy which disliked poetry, it might be too much to say 'loathed' it. But the emotion was as strong as any in the bureaucratic bosom. Bureaucracy has no loves and is composed mainly of varied minor dislikes. The members of this bureaucracy, sick with inferiority complex, had just enough wits to perceive that Eliot was their superior, but no means of detecting his limits or measuring him from the outside, and no experience that would enable them to know the poisons wherewith he had been injected. For that diagnosis perhaps only a fellow American is qualified, one having suffered an American University. The American University is or was aware of the existence of both German and English institutions, being younger and in a barbarous country, *its* inferiority complex impelled it to comparison and to a wish to equal and surpass, but gave it no immunity from the academical bacilli, inferiority complex directed against creative activity in the arts.

That there is a percentage of bunk in the *Selected Essays* Mr. Eliot will possibly be the last to deny, but that he had performed a self-analysis is still doubtful.

This kind of essay assumes the existence of a culture that no longer subsists and does nothing to prepare a better culture that must or ought to come into being. I say 'better', for the new paideuma will at least be a live paideuma not a dead one.

Such essays are prepared not for editors who care about a living literature or a live tradition, or who even want the best of Eliot's perception applied to an author of second or third or fourth category (per ex. Seneca), they want to maintain a system wherein it is possible to receive fifteen guincas for an article of approximately 3,000–4,000 words, in a series to which Mr. Eliot's sensitivity and patience will give lustre and wherein his occasional eminence will shed respectability on a great mass of inferior writing.

[. . .]

In happier era

The study of Latin authors was alive a century and a quarter, perhaps hardly more than a century ago.

Young men are now lured into colleges and universities largely on false pretences.

We live in a vile age when it is impossible to get reprints of the few dozen books that are practically essential to a competent knowledge of poetry.

[. . .]

In the matter of education, if the young are not to profit by our sweats, if they are not to pluck the fruits of our experience in the form of better curricula, it might be well to give it up altogether. At any rate the critic not aiming at a better curriculum for the serious study of literature is a critic half baked, swinging in a vacuum. It would be hypocrisy to pretend that Eliot's essays are not aimed at professors and students.

The student is best aided by being able to read and to own conveniently the best that has been created.

Yeats, who has always been against the gang and the bureaucracy, now muddled, now profound, now merely Celtic or erroneously believing that a free Ireland, or at least a more Oirish Ireland, would help the matter, long ago prayed for a new sacred book.

Every age has tried to compound such a volume. Every great culture has had such a major anthology. Pisistratus, Li Po, the Japanese Emperor who reduced the number of Noh dramas to about 450; the hackneyed Hebrew example; in less degree the Middle Ages, with the matter of Britain, of France, and of Rome le Grant.

[. . .]

There is gongorism in critical writing as well as in bad poetry. You might say that discussion of books ceases to be critical writing and becomes just the functioning of bureaucracy when the main end (telos) is forgotten.

As we cannot educate our grandfathers, one supposes that critical writing is committed for the purpose of educating our offspring, our contemporaries, or ourselves, and that the least a critic can do is to be aware of the present even if he be too swinish to consider the future.

The critic is either a parasite or he is concerned with the growth of the next paideuma.

Marinetti is thoroughly *simpatico*. Writing and orating *ut moveat*, he has made demands that no one considers in their strict literal sense, but which have, and have had, a definite scope.

'An early play of no merit whatever', 'the brain of a fourth-rate playwright' as matters of an highly specialised clinic may conceivably have something to do with critical standards. The impression is that their importance must be limited to some very minor philological field. Their import for tomorrow's paideuma is probably slight.

[. . .]

In the present decomposition and under the yoke of the present bureaucracy it would probably be too much to demand that before discussing an author a reviewer answer the following questions:

1. Have you read the original text of the author under discussion? or how much of it have you read?
2. Is it worth reading? or how much of it is worth reading? and by whom?

As for Elizabeth dramedy, Lamb and Hazlitt are supposed to have set the fad, but Lamb at any rate did pick out a volume of selections; showing what he thought might be the basis of an interest.

The proportion between discussion and the exhibits the discusser dares show his reader is possibly a good, and probably a necessary, test of his purpose. In a matter of degree, I am for say 80 per cent exhibit and 20 per cent yatter.

Mr. Eliot and Miss Moore are definitely fighting against an impoverishment of culture, against a paucity of reading programme. Neither they nor anyone else is likely to claim that they have as much interest in life as I have, or that I have their patience in reading.

That does not make it any less necessary to distinguish between Eliot registering his belief *re* a value, and Eliot ceding to the bad, not to say putrid habits of the bureaucracy which has surrounded him.

As alarmist, as capricious perverse, etc., I repeat that you cannot get the whole cargo of a sinking paideuma on to the lifeboat. If you propose to have any live literature of the past kept in circulation, available (flat materialism) in print at prices the eager reader can pay, there has got to be more attention to the best and to the basic. Once that is established you can divagate into marginalia, but the challenge will be more incisive and the criteria will be more rigorous.

[. . .]

I believe that Britain, in rejecting certain facts (facts, not opinions) in 1912–15 entered a sterile decade.

Willingness to experiment is not enough, but unwillingness to experiment is mere death.

If ten pages out of its two hundred and fifty go into a Corpus Poetarum of a.d. 2033, the present volume will amply be justified. (Yes, I know I have split the future of that verb. Var. will. and amply.)

I have not attempted to represent all the new poets, I am leaving the youngest, possibly some of the brightest, to someone else or to future effort, not so much from malice or objection to perfect justice, as from inability to do everything all at once.

[. . .]

The assertion implicit in this volume is that after ten or twenty years of serious effort you can consider a writer uninteresting, but the charges of flightiness and dilettantism are less likely to be valid. In fact they are unlikely to be valid if a consistent direction can be discovered

Other things being equal, the results of processes, even of secondary processes, application, patience, etc., are more pertinent from living writers than from dead ones, or are more pertinent when demonstrably in relation with the living present than with the classified past.

Classic in current publishers' advertisements seems to have attained its meaning via classé, rangé.

The history of literature as taught in many institutions (? all) is nothing more (hardly more) than a stratified record of snobisms in which chronology sometimes counts for more than the causal relation and is also often wholly ignored, I mean ignored usually when it conflicts with prejudice and when chronological fact destroys a supposed causal relation.

[. . .]

As for experiment: the claim is that without constant experiment literature dies. Experiment is one of the elements necessary to its life. Experiment aims at writing that will have a relation to the present analogous to the relation which past masterwork had to the life of its time.

[. . .]

'Active Anthology'
(Retrospect twenty months later)

A dislike of Bunting's poetry and Zukofsky's is possibly due to haste. Their verse is more thoughtful than toffee-lickers require. At intervals, months apart, I remember a passage, or I re-open my volume of excerpts and find something solid. It did not incinerate any Hudson river. Neither did Marianne Moore's when it first (20 years since) came to London. You have to read such verse slowly.

Apart from Bunting and Zukofsky, Miss Moore's is the solidest stuff in the Anthology. Williams' is simple by comparison – not so thoughtful. It has a larger audience because of its apparent simplicity. It is the lyric of an aptitude. Aptitude, not attitude. Anschauung, that Dr. Williams has stuck in and to for half a century. The workmanship is not so much cared for. And yet Williams has become the first prose writer in America, the best prose writer who now gets into print, McAlmon having disappeared from circulation, and being a different case altogether, panoramic Velasquez, where Williams is just solid.

What goes into his case note is there. If there is any more solid solidity outside Papa Gustave, I don't know where to find it.

Joyce was not more substantial in the *Portrait of the Artist*. I am not sure that the cutting hasn't lightened his block.

In his verse Williams' integrity passes for simplicity. Unadulterated non-elaboration in the phrase, a 'simple substance', simple has an analogous meaning; whereas Zukofsky, Bunting and Miss Moore are all thoughtful, much more so than the public desires.

'Man is not an end product', is much too condensed a phrase to tickle the gobbler.

The case of Cumming's 'eimi' and the bearing of Cocteau's sensibility on this discussion will have to wait further, and more thorough, treatment than I have given them. Mr. Wyndham Lewis' *Apes* looms somewhere in the domain of Gulliver and Tristram Shandy.

12
F. R. (FRANK RAYMOND) LEAVIS (1895–1978)
FROM *NEW BEARINGS IN ENGLISH POETRY.*
A *STUDY OF THE CONTEMPORARY SITUATION* 1932

Cambridge literary critic and founding editor of the quarterly Scrutiny *(1932–53). Along with I. A. Richards, William Empson, and T. S. Eliot, he was responsible for shaping the foundations of the modern academic discipline (methodology and canon formation) of English Literature. His most influential works include* The Great Tradition: George Eliot, James and Conrad *(1948), and* New Bearings in English Poetry *(1932) from which the following piece is extracted.*

Poetry matters little to the modern world. That is, very little of contemporary intelligence concerns itself with poetry. It is true that a very great deal of verse has come from the press in the last twenty years, and the uninterested might take this as proving the existence both of a great deal of interest in poetry and of a great deal of talent. Indeed, anthologists do. They make, modestly, the most extravagant claims on behalf of the age.

[. . .]

Such claims are symptoms of the very weakness that they deny: they could have been made only in an age in which there were no serious standards current, no live tradition of poetry, and no public capable of informed and serious interest. No one *could* be seriously interested in the great bulk of the verse that is culled and offered to us as the fine flower of modern poetry. For the most part it is not so much bad as dead – it was never alive. The words that lie there arranged on the page have no roots: the writer himself can never have been more than superficially interested in them. Even such genuine poetry as the anthologies of modern verse do contain is apt, by its kind and quality, to suggest that the present age does not favour the growth of poets. A

study of the latter end of *The Oxford Book of Victorian Verse* leads to the conclusion that
something has been wrong for forty or fifty years at the least.

For it seems unlikely that the number of potential poets born varies as much from
age to age as literary history might lead one to suppose. What varies is the use made
of talent. And the use each age makes of its crop of talent is determined largely by
the preconceptions of 'the poetical' that are current, and the corresponding habits,
conventions, and techniques. There are, of course, other very important conditions,
social, economic, philosophical, and so on; but my province is that of literary criticism,
and I am confining myself as far as possible to those conditions which it rests with
the poet and the critic to modify – those which are their immediate concern.

Every age, then, has its preconceptions and assumptions regarding poetry: these
are the essentially poetical subjects, these the poetical materials, these the poetical
modes. The most influential are apt to be those of which we are least aware. The
preconceptions coming down to us from the last century were established in the period
of the great Romantics, Wordsworth, Coleridge, Byron, Shelley, and Keats. To attempt
to define them is to risk misrepresenting them, for it is largely in their being vague and
undefined that their power has lain.

[. . .]

Poetry tends in every age to confine itself by ideas of the essentially poetical which,
when the conditions which gave rise to them have changed, bar the poet from his
most valuable material, the material that is most significant to sensitive and adequate
minds in his own day; or else sensitive and adequate minds are barred out of poetry.
Poetry matters because of the kind of poet who is more alive than other people, more
alive in his own age. He is, as it were, at the most conscious point of the race in his
time. [. . .] The potentialities of human experience in any age are realized only by a tiny
minority, and the important poet is important because he belongs to this (and has also,
of course, the power of communication). Indeed, his capacity for experiencing and
his power of communicating are indistinguishable; not merely because we should not
know of the one without the other, but because his power of making words express
what he feels is indistinguishable from his awareness of what he feels. He is unusually
sensitive, unusually aware, more sincere and more himself than the ordinary man can
be. He knows what he feels and knows what he is interested in. He is a poet because
his interest in his experience is not separable from his interest in words; because, that
is, of his habit of seeking by the evocative use of words to sharpen his awareness of
his ways of feeling, so making these communicable. And poetry can communicate the
actual quality of experience with a subtlety and precision unapproachable by any other
means. But if the poetry and the intelligence of the age lose touch with each other,
poetry will cease to matter much, and the age will be lacking in finer awareness. What
this last prognostication means it is perhaps impossible to bring home to anyone who
is not already convinced of the importance of poetry. So that it is indeed deplorable
that poetry should so widely have ceased to interest the intelligent.

[. . .]

To make a fresh start in poetry under such conditions is a desperate matter. It is easy
enough to say that poetry must be adequate to modern life, and it has often been said.

But nothing has been done until such generalities have been realized in particulars, that is, in the invention of new techniques, and this, in an age when the current conventions will not serve even to provide a start, is something beyond any but a very unusually powerful and original talent. The established habits form a kind of atmosphere from which it is supremely difficult to escape.

[. . .] The only technique that matters is that which compels words to express an intensely personal way of feeling, so that the reader responds, not in a general way that he knows beforehand to be 'poetical', but in a precise, particular way that no frequenting of *The Oxford Book* could have made familiar to him. To invent techniques that shall be adequate to the ways of feeling, or modes of experience, of adult, sensitive moderns is difficult in the extreme. Until it has been once done it is so difficult as to seem impossible. One success makes others more probable because less difficult.

That is the peculiar importance of Mr T. S. Eliot. For, though there is, inevitably, a great deal of snobbism in the cult he suffers from, mere snobbism will not account for his prestige among the young. Having a mind unquestionably of rare distinction he has solved his own problem as a poet, and so has done more than solve the problem for himself. His influence has been the more effective in that he is a critic as well as a poet, and his criticism and his poetry reinforce each other. It is mainly due to him that no serious poet or critic today can fail to realize that English poetry in the future must develop (if at all) along some other line than that running from the Romantics through Tennyson, Swinburne, *A Shropshire Lad*, and Rupert Brooke. He has made a new start, and established new bearings.

[. . .]

13
W. H. (WYSTAN HUGH) AUDEN (1907–73)
REVIEW OF LEAVIS ET AL. 1933;
FROM INTRODUCTION TO *THE POET'S TONGUE* 1935

English poet and essayist. Born in York, he was educated at Christ Church, Oxford. In the 1930s he wrote passionately on social problems as a Marxist and went to Spain as a civilian in support of the Republican cause. His report on the Civil War, Spain *(1937), was followed by a verse commentary on the Sino-Japanese war in* Journey to a War *(1939) which also included prose reports by Christopher Isherwood, his friend and collaborator. He also worked closely with Louis MacNeice, as well as with Benjamin Britten and wrote the libretto for the latter's* Ballad of Heroes *(1939). Auden emigrated to New York in 1939 and taught at Michigan University, before being appointed Professor of Poetry at Oxford in 1956. His later period is marked by his conversion to Anglicanism, as well as by significant and influential critical collections, most notably* The Dyer's Hand *(1963). Reproduced below is Auden's review of* Culture and Environment *(by F. R. Leavis and Denys Thompson),* How to Teach Reading *(by F. R. Leavis) and* How Many Children Had Lady Macbeth? *(by L. C. Knights), for* The Twentieth Century, May 1933. *It is followed by extracts from his introduction to the 1935 anthology* The Poet's Tongue *(co-edited with John Garrett).*

What is a highbrow? Someone who is not passive to his experience but who tries to organise, explain and alter it, someone in fact, who tries to influence his history: a man struggling for life in the water is for the time being a highbrow. The decisive factor is a conflict between the person and his environment; most of the people who are usually called highbrows had either an unhappy childhood and adolescence or suffer from physical defects. Mr. Leavis, Mr. Thompson, Mr. Knights, Mr. Pound, the author and the reader of this review, are highbrows, and these books are a plea for the creation of more.

I think rightly. We live in an age in which the collapse of all previous standards coincides with the perfection in technique for the centralised distribution of ideas; some kind of revolution is inevitable, and will as inevitably be imposed from above by a minority; in consequence, if the result is not to depend on the loudest voice, if the majority is to have the slightest say in its future, it must be more critical than it is necessary for it to be in an epoch of straightforward development.

All these three books are concerned with school education. *How Many Children Had Lady Macbeth?* is an attack on the bunk in most teaching of Shakespeare, with its concentration on the characters and plot, and its omission of the poetry. *How to Teach Reading* is a demand for training in the technique of critical reading. *Culture and Environment* is a practical text book for assisting children to defeat propaganda of all kinds by making them aware of which buttons are being pressed.

All three books are good and will, I hope, be read seriously by all school teachers. *Culture and Environment* is particularly excellent because it sets the examination papers; teachers are usually hard-worked, and, while agreeing with the importance of this kind of instruction, are either too busy or too tired to prepare it themselves.

Also I am inclined to think that advertising is a better field than literature for such work, the aim of which, like that of psycho-analysis, is primarily destructive, to dissipate a reaction by becoming conscious of it. Advertising and machines are part of the environment of which literature is a reaction; those who are critically aware of their environment and of themselves will be critical of what they read, and not otherwise. I think it extremely doubtful whether any direct training of literary sensibility is possible.

Our education is far too bookish. To give children masterpieces to read, the reaction of exceptional adult minds to vast experiences, is fantastic. A boy in school remains divorced from the means of production, from livelihood; it is impossible to do much, but I believe that for the time being the most satisfactory method of teaching English to children is through their environment and their actions in it; e.g., if they are going to read or write about sawing wood, they should saw some themselves first: they should have plenty of acting, if possible, and under their English teacher movement classes as well, and very, very little talk.

These books all imply the more general question 'What is to be done?' though, perhaps intentionally, they all avoid specifically stating or answering it. Mass production, advertising, the divorce between mental and manual labour, magazine stories, the abuse of leisure, all these are symptoms of an invalid society, and can only be finally cured by attending to the cause. You can suppress one symptom but only to create another, just as you can turn a burglar into an epileptic. Opinions differ both on cause and cure, but it is the duty of an investigator to state his own, and if possible the more important conflicting ones. Consciousness always appears to be uncontaminated by its

object, and the danger of the methods advocated in these books is of making the invalid fascinated by his disease, of enabling the responsible minority to derive such intellectual satisfaction from contemplating the process of decay, from which by the nature
of consciousness itself they feel insulated, that they lose the will and power to arrest it.

From 'Introduction to the Poet's Tongue'

Of the many definitions of poetry, the simplest is still the best: 'memorable speech'.
That is to say, it must move our emotions, or excite our intellect, for only that which
is moving or exciting is memorable, and the stimulus is the audible spoken word and
cadence, to which in all its power of suggestion and incantation we must surrender,
as we do when talking to an intimate friend. We must, in fact, make exactly the
opposite kind of mental effort to that we make in grasping other verbal uses, for in
the case of the latter the aura of suggestion round every word through which, like
the atom radiating lines of force through the whole of space and time, it becomes
ultimately a sign for the sum of all possible meanings, must be rigorously suppressed
and its meaning confined to a single dictionary one. For this reason the exposition of
a scientific theory is easier to read than to hear. No poetry, on the other hand, which
when mastered is not better heard than read is good poetry.

All speech has rhythm, which is the result of the combination of the alternating
periods of effort and rest necessary to all living things, and the laying of emphasis on
what we consider important; and in all poetry there is a tension between the rhythms
due to the poet's personal values, and those due to the experiences of generations
crystallised into habits of language such as the English tendency to alternate weak
and accented syllables, and conventional verse forms like the hexameter, the heroic
pentameter, or the French Alexandrine. Similes, metaphors of image or idea, and
auditory metaphors such as rhyme, assonance, and alliteration help further to clarify
and strengthen the pattern and internal relations of the experience described.

Poetry, in fact, bears the same kind of relation to Prose, using prose simply in the
sense of all those uses of words that are not poetry, that algebra bears to arithmetic.
The poet writes of personal or fictitious experiences, but these are not important in
themselves until the reader has realised them in his own consciousness.

> Soldier from the war returning,/ Spoiler of the taken town.

It is quite unimportant, though it is the kind of question not infrequently asked, who
the soldier is, what regiment he belongs to, what war he had been fighting in, etc. The
soldier is you or me, or the man next door. Only when it throws light on our own experience, when these lines occur to us as we see, say, the unhappy face of a stockbroker
in the suburban train, does poetry convince us of its significance. The test of a poet
is the frequency and diversity of the occasions on which we remember his poetry.

Memorable speech then. About what? Birth, death, the Beatific Vision, the abysses
of hatred and fear, the awards and miseries of desire, the unjust walking the earth
and the just scratching miserably for food like hens, triumphs, earthquakes, deserts of
boredom and featureless anxiety, the Golden Age promised or irrevocably past, the
gratifications and terrors of childhood, the impact of nature on the adolescent, the

despairs and wisdoms of the mature, the sacrificial victim, the descent into Hell, the devouring and the benign mother? Yes, all of these, but not these only. Everything that we remember no matter how trivial: the mark on the wall, the joke at luncheon, word games, these, like the dance of a stoat or the raven's gamble, are equally the subject of poetry.   [. . .]

A great many people dislike the idea of poetry as they dislike over-earnest people, because they imagine it is always worrying about the eternal verities.

Those, in Mr. Spender's words, who try to put poetry on a pedestal only succeed in putting it on the shelf. Poetry is no better and no worse than human nature; it is profound and shallow, sophisticated and naïve, dull and witty, bawdy and chaste in turn.

In spite of the spread of education and the accessibility of printed matter, there is a gap between what is commonly called 'highbrow' and 'lowbrow' taste, wider perhaps than it has ever been.

The industrial revolution broke up the agricultural communities, with their local conservative cultures, and divided the growing population into two classes: those whether employers or employees who worked and had little leisure, and a small class of shareholders who did no work, had leisure but no responsibilities or roots, and were therefore preoccupied with themselves. Literature has tended therefore to divide into two streams, one providing the first with a compensation and escape, the other the second with a religion and a drug. The Art for Art's sake of the London drawing-rooms of the '90's, and towns like Burnley and Rochdale, are complementary.

[. . .]

Artistic creations may be produced by individuals, and because their work is only appreciated by a few it does not necessarily follow that it is not good; but a universal art can only be the product of a community united in sympathy, sense of worth, and aspiration; and it is improbable that the artist can do his best except in such a society.

Something of this lies behind the suspicion of and attack upon the intellectual which is becoming more and more vocal. It is hardly possible to open a number of *Punch* without seeing him spectacled, round-shouldered, rabbit-toothed, a foil to a landscape of beautifully unconscious cows, or a whipping-boy for a drawing room of dashing young sahibs and elegant daughters of the chase. Cross the channel and this dislike, in more countries than one, has taken a practical form, to which the occasional ducking of an Oxford æsthete seems a nursery tiff.

If we are still of the opinion that poetry is worth writing and reading, we must be able to answer such objections satisfactorily at least to ourselves.

The 'average' man says: 'When I get home I want to spend my time with my wife or in the nursery; I want to get out on to the links or go for a spin in the car, not to read poetry. Why should I? I'm quite happy without it.' We must be able to point out to him that whenever, for example, he makes a good joke he is creating poetry, that one of the motives behind poetry is curiosity, the wish to know what we feel and think, and how, as E. M. Forster says, can I know what I think till I see what I say, and that curiosity is the only human passion that can be indulged in for twenty-four hours a day without satiety.

The psychologist maintains that poetry is a neurotic symptom, an attempt to compensate by phantasy for a failure to meet reality. We must tell him that phantasy is only the beginning of writing; that, on the contrary, like psychology, poetry is a struggle to reconcile the unwilling subject and object; in fact, that since psychological truth depends so largely on context, poetry, the parabolic approach, is the only adequate medium for psychology.

The propagandist whether moral or political, complains that the writer should use his powers over words to persuade people to a particular course of action, instead of fiddling while Rome burns. But poetry is not concerned with telling people what to do, but with extending our knowledge of good and evil, perhaps making the necessity for action more urgent and its nature more clear, but only leading us to the point where it is possible for us to make a rational and moral choice.

In compiling an anthology such considerations must be borne in mind. First, one must overcome the prejudice that poetry is uplift and show that poetry can appeal to every level of consciousness. We do not want to read 'great' poetry all the time, and a good anthology should contain poems for every mood. Secondly, one must disabuse people of the idea that poetry is primarily an escape from reality. We all need escape at times, just as we need food and sleep, and some escape poetry there must always be. One must not let people think either that poetry never enjoys itself, or that it ignores the grimmer aspects of existence. Lastly, one must show those who come to poetry for a message, for calendar thoughts, that they have come to the wrong door, that poetry may illuminate but it will not dictate.

As regards arrangement we have, after some thought, adopted an alphabetical, anonymous order. It seems best to us, if the idea of poetry as something dead and suitable for a tourist-ridden museum – a cultural tradition to be preserved and imitated rather than a spontaneous living product – is to be avoided, that the first approach should be with an open mind, free from the bias of great names and literary influences, the first impression that of a human activity, independent of period and unconfined in subject.

14
W. B. (WILLIAM BUTLER) YEATS (1865–1939)
FROM INTRODUCTION TO
THE OXFORD BOOK OF MODERN VERSE 1892–1935 1936

Reproduced below are extracts from Yeats's introduction to this important anthology from 1936. It is followed by the first entry of the collection, Walter Pater's famous 'Mona Lisa' passage from The Renaissance *(1873), laid out by Yeats in verse form. [See Ib 17, IIIa 6]*

To the generation which began to think and read in the late eighties of the last century the four poets whose work begins this book were unknown, or, if known, of an earlier generation that did not stir its sympathy. Gerard Hopkins remained unpublished for thirty years. Fifty-odd years ago I met him in my father's studio on different occasions, but remember almost nothing. A boy of seventeen, Walt Whitman in his pocket, had little interest in a querulous, sensitive scholar. Thomas Hardy's poems were unwritten or unpublished. Robert Bridges seemed a small Victorian poet whose poetry, published in expensive hand-printed books, one could find behind glass doors in the houses of wealthy friends. I will consider the genius of these three when the development of schools gives them great influence.

All these writers were, in the eye of the new generation, in so far as they were known, Victorian, and the new generation was in revolt. But one writer, almost unknown to the general public – I remember somebody saying at his death 'no newspaper has given him an obituary notice' – had its entire uncritical admiration, Walter Pater. That is why I begin this book with the famous passage from his essay on Leonardo da Vinci. Only by printing it in *vers libre* can one show its revolutionary importance. Pater was accustomed to give each sentence a separate page of manuscript, isolating and analysing its rhythm.

[. . .]

The revolt against Victorianism meant to the young poet a revolt against irrelevant descriptions of nature, the scientific and moral discursiveness of *In Memoriam* – 'When he should have been broken-hearted,' said Verlaine, 'he had many reminiscences' – the political eloquence of Swinburne, the psychological curiosity of Browning, and the poetical diction of everybody. Poets said to one another over their black coffee – a recently imported fashion – 'We must purify poetry of all that is not poetry', and by poetry they meant poetry as it had been written by Catullus, a great name at that time, by the Jacobean writers, by Verlaine, by Baudelaire. Poetry was a tradition like religion and liable to corruption, and it seemed that they could best restore it by writing lyrics technically perfect, their emotion pitched high, and as Pater offered instead of moral earnestness life lived as 'a pure gem-like flame' all accepted him for master.

[. . .]

Occasionally at some evening party some young woman asked a poet what he thought of strikes, or declared that to paint pictures or write poetry at such a moment was to resemble the fiddler Nero, for great meetings of revolutionary Socialists were disturbing Trafalgar Square on Sunday afternoons; a young man known to most of us told some such party that he had stood before a desk in an office not far from Southampton Row resolved to protect it with his life because it contained documents that would hang William Morris, and wound up by promising a revolution in six months. Shelley must have had some such immediate circle when he wrote to friends urging them to withdraw their money from the Funds. We poets continued to write verse and read it out at 'The Cheshire Cheese', convinced that to take part in such movements would be only less disgraceful than to write for the newspapers.

III.

Then in 1900 everybody got down off his stilts; henceforth nobody drank absinthe with his black coffee; nobody went mad; nobody committed suicide; nobody joined the Catholic church; or if they did I have forgotten.

[. . .]

Conflict bequeathed its bias. Folk-song, unknown to the Victorians as their attempts to imitate it show, must, because never declamatory or eloquent, fill the scene. If anybody will turn these pages attending to poets born in the 'fifties, 'sixties, and 'seventies, he will find how successful are their folk-songs and their imitations. In Ireland, where still lives almost undisturbed the last folk tradition of western Europe, the songs of Campbell and Colum draw from that tradition their themes, return to it, and are sung to Irish airs by boys and girls who have never heard the names of the authors; but the reaction from rhetoric, from all that was prepense and artificial, has forced upon these writers now and again, as upon my own early work, a facile charm, a too soft simplicity. In England came like temptations. *The Shropshire Lad* is worthy of its fame, but a mile further and all had been marsh. Thomas Hardy, though his work lacked technical accomplishment, made the necessary correction through his mastery of the impersonal objective scene. John Synge brought back masculinity to Irish verse with his harsh disillusionment, and later, when the folk movement seemed to support vague political mass excitement, certain poets began to create passionate masterful personality.

[. . .]

Eliot has produced his great effect upon his generation because he has described men and women that get out of bed or into it from mere habit; in describing this life that has lost heart his own art seems grey, cold, dry. He is an Alexander Pope, working without apparent imagination, producing his effects by a rejection of all rhythms and metaphors used by the more popular romantics rather than by the discovery of his own, this rejection giving his work an unexaggerated plainness that has the effect of novelty. He has the rhythmical flatness of *The Essay on Man* – despite Miss Sitwell's advocacy I see Pope as Blake and Keats saw him – later, in *The Waste Land*, amid much that is moving in symbol and imagery there is much monotony of accent:

> When lovely woman stoops to folly and
> Paces about her room again, alone,
> She smooths her hair with automatic hand,
> And puts a record on the gramophone.

I was affected, as I am by these lines, when I saw for the first time a painting by Manet. I longed for the vivid colour and light of Rousseau and Courbet, I could not endure the grey middle-tint – and even to-day Manet gives me an incomplete pleasure; he had left the procession. Nor can I put the Eliot of these poems among those that descend from Shakespeare and the translators of the Bible. I think of him as satirist rather than poet.

[. . .]

Not until *The Hollow Men* and *Ash-Wednesday*, where he is helped by the short lines, and in the dramatic poems where his remarkable sense of actor, chanter, scene, sweeps him away, is there rhythmical animation. Two or three of my friends attribute the change to an emotional enrichment from religion, but his religion compared to that of John Gray, Francis Thompson, Lionel Johnson in *The Dark Angel*, lacks all strong emotion; a New England Protestant by descent, there is little self-surrender in his personal relation to God and the soul.

[. . .]

Ezra Pound has made flux his theme; plot, characterization, logical discourse, seem to him abstractions unsuitable to a man of his generation. He is mid-way in an immense poem in *vers libre* called for the moment *The Cantos*, where the metamorphosis of Dionysus, the descent of Odysseus into Hades, repeat themselves in various disguises, always in association with some third that is not repeated. Hades may become the hell where whatever modern men he most disapproves of suffer damnation, the metamorphosis petty frauds practised by Jews at Gibraltar. The relation of all the elements to one another, repeated or unrepeated, is to become apparent when the whole is finished. There is no transmission through time, we pass without comment from ancient Greece to modern England, from modern England to medieval China; the symphony, the pattern, is timeless, flux eternal and therefore without movement. Like other readers I discover at present merely exquisite or grotesque fragments. He hopes to give the impression that all is living, that there are no edges, no convexities, nothing to check the flow; but can such a poem have a mathematical structure? Can impressions that are in part visual, in part metrical, be related like the notes of a symphony; has the author been carried beyond reason by a theoretical conception? His belief in his own conception is so great that since the appearance of the first Canto I have tried to suspend judgement.

When I consider his work as a whole I find more style than form; at moments more style, more deliberate nobility and the means to convey it than in any contemporary poet known to me, but it is constantly interrupted, broken, twisted into nothing by its direct opposite, nervous obsession, nightmare, stammering confusion; he is an economist, poet, politician, raging at malignants with inexplicable characters and motives, grotesque figures out of a child's book of beasts. This loss of self-control, common among uneducated revolutionists, is rare – Shelley had it in some degree – among men of Ezra Pound's culture and erudition. Style and its opposite can alternate, but form must be full, sphere-like, single. Even where there is no interruption he is often content, if certain verses and lines have style, to leave unbridged transitions, unexplained ejaculations, that make his meaning unintelligible. He has great influence, more perhaps than any contemporary except Eliot, is probably the source of that lack of form and consequent obscurity which is the main defect of Auden, Day Lewis, and their school, a school which, as will presently be seen, I greatly admire. Even where the style is sustained throughout one gets an impression, especially when he is writing in *vers libre*, that he has not got all the wine into the bowl, that he is a brilliant improvisator translating at sight from an unknown Greek masterpiece.

[. . .]

I recall Pater's description of the Mona Lisa; had the individual soul of da Vinci's sitter gone down with the pearl divers or trafficked for strange webs? or did Pater foreshadow a poetry, a philosophy, where the individual is nothing, the flux of *The*

Cantos of Ezra Pound, objects without contour as in *Le Chef-d'œuvre Inconnu*, human experience no longer shut into brief lives, cut off into this place and that place, the flux of Turner's poetry that within our minds enriches itself, re-dreams itself, yet only in seeming – for time cannot be divided? Yet one theme perplexes Turner, whether in comedy, dialogue, poem. Somewhere in the middle of it all da Vinci's sitter had private reality like that of the Dark Lady among the women Shakespeare had imagined, but because that private soul is always behind our knowledge, though always hidden it must be the sole source of pain, stupefaction, evil. A musician, he imagines Heaven as a musical composition, a mathematician, as a relation of curves, a poet, as a dark, inhuman sea.

[. . .]

I have a distaste for certain poems written in the midst of the great war; they are in all anthologies, but I have substituted Herbert Read's *End of a War* written long after. The writers of these poems were invariably officers of exceptional courage and capacity, one a man constantly selected for dangerous work, all, I think, had the Military Cross; their letters are vivid and humorous, they were not without joy – for all skill is joyful – but felt bound, in the words of the best known, to plead the suffering of their men. In poems that had for a time considerable fame, written in the first person, they made that suffering their own. I have rejected these poems for the same reason that made Arnold withdraw his *Empedocles on Etna* from circulation; passive suffering is not a theme for poetry. In all the great tragedies, tragedy is a joy to the man who dies; in Greece the tragic chorus danced.

[. . .]

If war is necessary, or necessary in our time and place, it is best to forget its suffering as we do the discomfort of fever, remembering our comfort at midnight when our temperature fell, or as we forget the worst moments of more painful disease.

[. . .]

Ten years after the war certain poets combined the modern vocabulary, the accurate record of the relevant facts learnt from Eliot, with the sense of suffering of the war poets, that sense of suffering no longer passive, no longer an obsession of the nerves; philosophy had made it part of all the mind.

[. . .]

Much of the war poetry was pacificist, revolutionary; it was easier to look at suffering if you had somebody to blame for it, or some remedy in mind. Many of these poets have called themselves communists, though I find in their work no trace of the recognized communist philosophy and the practising communist rejects them. The Russian government in 1930 silenced its Mechanists, put Spinoza on his head and claimed him for grandfather; but the men who created the communism of the masses had Stendhal's mirror for a contemporary, believed that religion, art, philosophy, expressed economic change, that the shell secreted the fish. Perhaps all that the masses accept is obsolete – the Orangeman beats his drum every Twelfth of July – perhaps fringes, wigs, furbelows, hoops, patches, stocks, Wellington boots, start up as armed men; but were a poet sensitive to the best thought of his time to accept that belief, when time is restoring the soul's autonomy, it would be as though he had swallowed a stone and kept it in his bowels. None of these men have accepted it, communism is their *Deus ex Machina*, their Santa Claus, their happy ending, but speaking as a poet I prefer tragedy to tragi-comedy. No matter how great a reformer's energy a still greater is required to face, all activities expended in vain, the unreformed. 'God,' said an old country-woman, 'smiles alike when regarding the good and condemning the lost.' MacNeice, the anti-communist, expecting some descent of barbarism next turn of the wheel, contemplates the modern world with even greater horror than the communist Day Lewis, although with less lyrical beauty. More often I cannot tell whether the poet is communist or anti-communist. On what side is Madge? Indeed I know of no school where the poets so closely resemble each other. Spender has said that the poetry of belief must supersede that of personality, and it is perhaps a belief shared that has created their intensity, their resemblance; but this belief is not political. If I understand aright this difficult art the contemplation of suffering has compelled them to seek beyond the flux something unchanging, inviolate, that country where no ghost haunts, no beloved lures because it has neither past nor future.

[. . .]

Mona Lisa

She is older than the rocks among which she sits;
Like the Vampire,
She has been dead many times,
And learned the secrets of the grave;
And has been a diver in deep seas,
And keeps their fallen day about her;
And trafficked for strange webs with Eastern merchants;
And, as Leda,
Was the mother of Helen of Troy,
And, as St. Anne,
Was the mother of Mary;
And all this has been to her but as the sound of lyres and flutes,
And lives
Only in the delicacy
With which it has moulded the changing lineaments,
And tinged the eyelids and the hands.

15
MICHAEL ROBERTS (1902–48)
FROM INTRODUCTION TO *THE FABER BOOK OF MODERN VERSE* 1936

English poet, critic and anthologist. Roberts worked variously as a teacher and wartime propagandist after leaving Cambridge. He published three volumes of his own poetry in the 1930s, beginning with These Our Matins *(1930). As an anthologist, he produced a set of very important and influential collections, such as* New Signatures *(1932) and* New Country *(1933) which featured the work of W. H. Auden, Cecil Day Lewis and William Empson. His selections for* The Faber Book of Modern Verse *(1936), extracts from the introduction to which are reproduced below, included poetry by Dylan Thomas and George Barker, while omitting established Georgian poets, such as Walter de la Mare and John Masefield.*

Roughly speaking, [. . .] the poets in this book may be divided into two classes: those whose poetry is primarily a defence and vindication of existing cultural values, and those who, using the poetic qualities of the English language, try to build up poetry out of the realities implicit in the language, and which they find in their own minds rather than base it upon humanistic learning and memories of other poetry. The poets of the first kind possess what might be called a 'European' sensibility: they are aware of Baudelaire, Corbière, Rimbaud, Laforgue and the later Symbolists (it is notable that German poetry has had little influence upon them), they turn to Dante or Cavalcanti more readily than to Milton, they are more likely to be interested in a Parisian movement in poetry, such as Surrealism, than in the corresponding tendency in *Alice Through the Looking Glass* or Young's *Night Thoughts*. Most of them are Americans by birth, but their appeal is as much to the English as to the American reader. Among their English predecessors they might number Donne, Crashaw and Pope.

Poets in whose work the 'English' element predominates take the language as they find it, developing the implications of its idioms, metaphors and symbols. They are 'first order' poets: that is to say, it is not necessary to have a wide acquaintance with European literature, or even with English literature, to appreciate their work. They may be given an ancestry in Langland, Skelton, Doughty, on the one hand, and Blake, Shelley and perhaps Edward Lear, on the other, but their work does not depend upon a knowledge of literary history: it is an intensification of qualities inherent in the English language itself, and for this reason it is less easy to translate than that of the 'European' poets, in whose poems the specific properties of the language they are using is a more casual element.

These classes are not exclusive: they represent two moods of poetry rather than two kinds of poet. The poetry of W. B. Yeats, for example, must be considered under both headings: but the work of Ezra Pound and T. S. Eliot is clearly 'European' in cast. Robert Graves for a time hesitated between the two, then identified himself with that view of poetry which Laura Riding has increasingly emphasized – poetry as the final residue of significance in language, freed from extrinsic decoration, superficial contemporaneity, and didactic bias.

The 'European' poet is acutely aware of the social world in which he lives, he criticizes it, but in a satirical rather than in an indignant manner, he adjusts himself to it, he is interested in its accumulated store of music, painting, sculpture, and even in its bric-à-brac. There is something of the dandy, something of the dilettante, in his make-up, but he is aware of the futility and evanescence of all this, and of the irresponsibility of big business, conventional politics and mass education. He is witty, and acutely self-conscious. His attitude is the outcome of a genuine care for much that is valuable in the past, and it gains its strength from a desire to preserve these things: to preserve them, not by violence, but by exercise, for they are not 'things' at all, but certain attitudes and activities.

Every vital age, perhaps, sees its own time as crucial and full of perils, but the problems and difficulties of our own age necessarily appear more urgent to us than those of any other, and the need for an evaluating, clarifying poetry has never been greater than it appears to be today. Industrial changes have broken up the old culture, based on an agricultural community in which poor and wealthy were alike concerned, and on a Church which bore a vital relation to the State. Parallel with this, and related to it, there has been a decay of the old moral and religious order, and a change in the basis of education, which has become more and more strictly scientific. Religion and classical learning, which once provided myths and legends symbolizing the purposes of society and the role of the individual, have declined, and the disorder weighs heavily upon the serious poet, whether in England or America.

[. . .]

If the poet is in the 'European' tradition, he describes the elements of civilization wherever he finds them: in Rome, in Greece, in Confucius, or in the Church of the Middle Ages; and against these he contrasts the violence and disorder of contemporary life. It is inevitable that poetry concerned with such issues should have political implications; but the poet is not arguing for one party against another: he is remodelling the basis upon which political creeds are founded, though sometimes immediate implications may appear in his poems.

Younger poets than Mr. Eliot and Mr. Pound may feel more acutely the interrelation of culture and politics, but nevertheless they would agree with Mr. Auden that 'poetry is not concerned with telling people what to do, but with extending our knowledge of good and evil, perhaps making the necessity for action more urgent and its nature more clear, but only leading us to the point where it is possible for us to make a rational and moral choice'.

[. . .]

Between 1920 and 1926, many poets were trying to write long poems which would present a unified view of the social crisis as they saw it, and imply their criticism of it. Conrad Aiken, who had been for a brief time influenced by the ideals of the Imagists, began to work for something which would lead to more profound and more highly organized poems, and turned to music. The predominant pattern of his poems is musical, whereas the more important pattern of some poems, as St. J. Perse's *Anabase* (translated by T. S. Eliot), is one of vivid visual and tactile images.

Conrad Aiken's *Senlin* (1918), T. S. Eliot's *The Waste Land* (1922), Richard Aldington's *Fool i' the Forest* (1925), and Archibald MacLeish's *Hamlet of A. MacLeish* (1928), were all poems of this kind. *The Waste Land* is the most concise, the most evocative, the widest in scope, and the most highly organized of these poems. It possesses 'imaginative order', by which I mean, that to some minds it is cogent even before its narrative and argumentative continuity is grasped. This 'imaginative order' is not something arbitrary, specific and inexplicable. If the images which are used to denote complex situations were replaced by abstractions much of the apparent incoherence of the poem would vanish. It would become a prose description of the condition of the world, a restatement of a myth and a defence of the tragic view of life. But being a poem it does more than this; a poem expresses not merely the idea of a social or scientific fact, but also the sensation of thinking or knowing, and it does not merely defend the tragic view, it may communicate it.

The images and rhythms of *The Waste Land* are not conventionally poetical: their aura of suggestion radiates from a definite meaning relating to the ordinary world, and their full significance is not seen until the essentially tragic attitude of the poem is grasped. The omission of explanatory connecting matter when contrasting a 'modern' situation with an old or the life of one class with that of another may be puzzling at first, but given a general understanding of the poem it becomes clear. Thus one situation may be described in the terms and rhythms appropriate to another, so that both the similarities and the differences are illuminated.

[. . .]

To myths, rather than to dreams, many poets still turn for the content of their poems, and the researches of Sir James Frazer and other anthropologists have provided the *motif* of a few good poems and many bad ones. Myths are more than fumbling attempts to explain historical and scientific facts: they control and organize the feeling, thought and action of a people: their function is symbolic as well as significant. But often the stories have become the conventional material of second-rate poetry, and have become perverted so that the symbolism has been lost, and we are left with the mere husk of a story, a story easily discredited by scientific and historical research. When Mr. Yeats turned to the myth as a means of giving shape and significance to his vision of the world, he was returning to the essential purpose of the myth and setting an example which Mr. Eliot, among others, has followed. But the modern reader cannot be expected to be influenced by a myth whose plain narrative sense is counter to his everyday beliefs. Either the poet must break away from any such direct narrative, or he must attempt, as I think Mr. Day Lewis has attempted in his *Flight* poem, to present a story credible in the ordinary everyday sense. If the poet turns to an existing myth or legend, however shop-soiled, and sees in it a profound significance, he will see the legend itself exemplified and symbolized in the world about him.

'So,' says Hart Crane, in an unpublished manuscript, 'I found "Helen" sitting in a street car; the Dionysian revels of her court and her seduction were transferred to a Metropolitan roof garden with a jazz orchestra: and the *katharsis* of the fall of Troy I saw approximated in the recent world war.'

[. . .]

If a poet is to give new life to a legend, if indeed he is to write good poetry at all, he must charge each word to its maximum poetic value. It must appeal concurrently to all the various levels of evocation and interpretation: experiments in new rhythms and new images, if they are not used in this specifically poetic way, are of no more than technical interest. In discussing new technical devices a distinction must be drawn between those which produce an effect upon the reader even before he has noticed them, and those which, like some of the devices of Mr. Cummings, attract the reader's attention and lead him to infer, by ordinary reasoning, what effect the poet intended to produce. There are, I think, many examples of the first kind in this book, and of the many auditory devices of this kind, none, perhaps, are more effective, or have had greater effect upon later poets, than those of Wilfred Owen.

[. . .]

When in pre-war days a few poets began to write, not in regular metres, but in cadences, as Whitman and the translators of the Bible had done, it was objected that this practice would destroy the art of verse entirely. It is true that a more delicate sensibility and a more careful training are necessary if we are to appreciate cadenced verse, and it is true that the existence of cadenced verse blurs the distinction between prose and poetry; but the critical vocabulary must be revised to fit the facts: to deny the facts and close your ears to the rhythms is to behave like the Inquisitor who refused to look through Galileo's telescope. Every discovery creates disorder: it is not the duty of the critic to prevent discovery or to deny it, but to create new order to replace the older. Today, the quarrel over cadenced verse has died down, and it is very hard to draw a sharp line, or to see any purpose in trying to draw a sharp line, between 'free' verse and *varied* regular verse. One or two points may be noted, however. There is verse which is intended to be 'free': that is to say, whose rhythm is composed to please the ear alone; there is verse which is quantitative, depending on a recurrent pattern of long and short syllables, there is verse which is accentual, depending on a recurrent pattern of accented and unaccented syllables; and there is syllabic verse. In the latter (some of the poems of Marianne Moore and Herbert Read are examples) the lines are evaluated by the number of syllables they contain, and the pattern will be something like this – 11:11:11:6. It is not very difficult to train the ear to recognize and enjoy syllabic patterns, and if it is objected that this training is 'unnatural' it must be pointed out that all training is 'unnatural' and yet inevitable. Even the writer of 'free' verse has been trained to enjoy and detect certain patterns, and his 'free' verse often shows the skeleton of a 'regular' pattern underneath.

[. . .]

New poetry is never popular unless it accepts the prejudices of the immediate past, and, giving an aura of heroism to actions which are already inevitable, stifles those misgivings out of which the real decisions of the present are to grow. Often in reading poems for this anthology, I have come upon one which, though its beginning seemed to show an apprehension beyond the commonplace, lapsed at the end into a false simplicity: a statement in familiar terms which had been given no new significance and depth. I have found Mr. Aldington's poems, in spite of their innovations, disappointing in that way; the earlier poems of Mr. Monro, and many of the poems of Mr. Cummings affect me similarly. The poet has seen something, and almost seen it clearly; and then at the end, unable to say it, he has been content to say some lesser thing, and the true poem remains unwritten.

For a time, the false poem may be more popular than the true one could have been. 'The poet,' Johnson said, 'must divest himself of the prejudice of his age and country; he must consider right and wrong in their abstracted and invariable state; he must disregard present laws and opinions, and rise to general and transcendental truths, which will always be the same. He must, therefore, content himself with the slow progress of his name, contemn the praise of his own time, and commit his claims to the justice of posterity.'

Sometimes it is argued that readers, too, must leave the judgment of contemporary literature to posterity; but the judgment of posterity is only another name for the accumulated judgments of those who read most carefully and with least prejudice and preconception. To read merely to concur in the judgments of our ancestors is to inhibit all spontaneous response and to miss the pleasure of that reading which moulds the opinions, tastes and actions of our time.

[. . .]

16
WALLACE STEVENS (1879–1955)
FROM 'THE IRRATIONAL ELEMENT IN POETRY' 1936

American poet. Stevens was educated at Harvard Law School and was admitted to the Bar in 1904. In 1916 he became associated with the Hartford Accident and Indemnity Company of which he became vice-president in 1934 and continued in its service until his retirement. From 1910 his poetry appeared in various little magazines, especially Poetry: A Magazine of Verse. *His first volume of poetry,* Harmonium, *was published in 1923. Other volumes include* Ideas of Order *(1935) and the acclaimed* The Man with the Blue Guitar *(1937), inspired by a Picasso painting. Unlike many other American Modernists, Stevens did not make a pilgrimage to Europe where his poetry was nevertheless highly influential. Reproduced below are extracts from a lecture delivered by Stevens at Harvard University on 8 December 1936.*

[. . .]

III.

There is, of course, a history of the irrational element in poetry, which is after all, merely a chapter of the history of the irrational in the arts generally. With the irrational in a pathological sense we are not concerned. Fuseli used to eat raw beef at night before going to bed in order that his dreams might attain a beefy violence otherwise lacking. Nor are we concerned with that sort of thing; nor with any irrationality provoked by prayer, whiskey, fasting, opium, or the hope of publicity. The Gothic novels of eighteenth-century England are no longer irrational. They are merely boring. What interests us is a particular process in the rational mind which we recognize as irrational in the sense that it takes place unaccountably. Or, rather, I should say that what interests us is not so much the Hegelian process as what comes of it. We should probably be much more intelligently interested if from the history of the irrational there had developed a tradition. It is easy to brush aside the irrational with the statement that we are rational beings, Aristotelians and not brutes. But it is becoming easier every day to say that we are irrational beings; that all irrationality is not of a piece and that the only reason why it does not yet have a tradition that its tradition is in progress. When I was here at Harvard, a long time ago, it was a commonplace to say that all the poetry had been written and all the paintings painted. It may be something of that sort that first interested us in the irrational. One of the great figures in the world since then has been Freud. While he is responsible for very little in poetry, as compared, for example, with his effect elsewhere, he has given the irrational a legitimacy that it never had before. More portentous influences have been Mallarmé and Rimbaud.

IV.

It may be that my subject expressed with greater nicety is irrational manifestations of the irrational element in poetry; for if the irrational element is merely poetic energy, it is to be found wherever poetry is to be found. One such manifestation is the disclosure of the individuality of the poet. It is unlikely that this disclosure is ever visible as plainly to anyone as the poet himself. In the first of the poems that I shall read to you in a moment or two the subject that I had in mind was the effect of the depression on the interest in art. I wanted a confronting of the world as it had been imagined in art and as it was then in fact. If I dropped into a gallery I found that I had no interest in what I saw. The air was charged with anxieties and tensions. To look at pictures there was the same thing as to play the piano in Madrid this afternoon. I was as capable of making observations and of jotting them down as anyone else; and if that is what I had wished to do, I could have done it. I wanted to deal with exactly such a subject and I chose that as a bit of reality, actuality, the contemporaneous. But I wanted the result to be poetry so far as I was able to write poetry. To be specific, I wanted to apply my own sensibility to something perfectly matter-of-fact. The result would be a disclosure of my own sensibility or individuality, as I called it a moment ago, certainly to myself. The poem is called 'The Old Woman and the Statue'. The old woman is a symbol of those who suffered during the depression and the statue is a symbol of art, although in several poems of which *Owl's Clover*, the book from which I shall read, consists, the statue is a variable symbol. While there is nothing automatic about the poem, nevertheless it has an automatic aspect in the sense that it is what I wanted it to be without knowing before it was written what I wanted it to be, even though I knew before it was written what I wanted to do. If each of us is a biological mechanism, each poet is a poetic mechanism. To the extent that what he produces is mechanical; that is to say, beyond his power to change, it is irrational. Perhaps I do not mean wholly beyond his power to change, for he might, by an effort of the will, change it. With that in mind, I mean beyond likelihood of change so long as he is being himself. This happens in the case of every poet.

V.

I think, too, that the choice of subject-matter is a completely irrational thing, provided a poet leaves himself any freedom of choice. If you are an imagist, you make a choice of subjects that is obviously limited. The same thing is true if you are anything else in particular and profess rigidly. But if you elect to remain free and to go about in the world experiencing whatever you happen to experience, as most people do, even when they insist that they do not, either your choice of subjects is fortuitous or the identity of the circumstances under which the choice is made is imperceptible. Lyric poets are bothered by spring and romantic poets by autumn. As a man becomes familiar with his own poetry, it becomes as obsolete for himself as for anyone else. From this it follows that one of the motives in writing is renewal. This undoubtedly affects the choice of subjects as definitely as it affects changes in rhythm, diction and manner. It is elementary that we vary rhythms instincively. We say that we perfect diction. We simply grow tired. Manner is something that has not yet been disengaged adequately. It does not mean style; it means the attitude of the writer, his bearing rather than his point of view. His bearing toward what? Not toward anything in particular, simply his pose. He hears the cat on the snow. The running feet set the rhythm. There is no subject beyond the cat running on the snow in the moonlight. He grows completely tired of the thing, wants a subject, thought, feeling, his whole manner changes. All these things enter into the choice of subject. The man who has been brought up in an artificial school becomes intemperately real. The Mallarmiste becomes the proletarian novelist. All this is irrational. If the choice of subject was predictable it would be rational. Now, just as the choice of subject is unpredictable at the outset, so its development, after it has been chosen, is unpredictable. One is always writing about two things at the same time in poetry and it is this that produces the tension characteristic of poetry. One is the true subject and the other is the poetry of the subject. The difficulty of sticking to the true subject, when it is the poetry of the subject that is paramount in one's mind, need only be mentioned to be understood. In a poet who makes the true subject paramount and who merely embellishes it, the subject is constant and the development orderly. If the poetry of the subject is paramount the true subject is not constant nor its development orderly. This is the case of Proust and Joyce, for example, in modern prose.

[. . .]

VII.

The pressure of the contemporaneous from the time of the beginning the World War to the present time has been constant and extreme. No one can have lived apart in a happy oblivion. For a long time before the war nothing was more common. In those days the sea was full of yachts and the yachts were full of millionaires. It was a time when only maniacs had disturbing things to say. The period was like a stage-setting that since then has been taken down and trucked away. It had been taken down by the end of the war, even though it took ten years of struggle with the consequences of the peace to bring about a realization of that fact. People said that if the war continued it would end civilization, just as they say now that another such war will end civilization. It is one thing to talk about the end of civilization and another to feel that the thing is not merely possible but measurably probable. If you are not a communist, has not civilization ended in Russia? If you are not a Nazi, has it not ended in Germany? We no sooner say that it never can happen here than we recognize that we say it without any illusions. We are preoccupied with events, even when we do not observe them closely. We have a sense of upheaval. We feel threatened. We look from an uncertain present toward a more uncertain future. One feels the desire to collect oneself against all this in poetry as well as in politics. If politics is nearer to each of us because of the pressure of the contemporaneous, poetry, in its way, is no less so and for the same reason. Does anyone suppose that the vast mass of people in this country was moved at the last election by rational considerations? Giving reason as much credit as the radio, there still remains the certainty that so great a movement was emotional and, if emotional, irrational. The trouble is that the greater the pressure of the contemporaneous, the greater the resistance. Resistance is the opposite of escape. The poet who wishes to contemplate the good in the midst of confusion is like the mystic who wishes to contemplate God in the midst of evil. There can be no thought of escape. Both the poet and the mystic may establish themselves on herrings and apples. The painter may establish himself on a guitar, a copy of *Figaro* and a dish of melons. These are fortifyings, although irrational ones. The only possible resistance to the pressure of the contemporaneous is a matter of herrings and apples or, to be less definite, the contemporaneous itself. In poetry, to that extent, the subject is not the contemporaneous, because that is only the nominal subject, but the poetry of the contemporaneous. Resistance to the pressure of ominous and destructive circumstance consists of its conversion, so far as possible, into a different, an explicable, an amenable circumstance.

VIII.

M. Charles Mauron says that a man may be characterized by his obsessions. We are obsessed by the irrational. This is because we expect the irrational to liberate us from the rational. In a note on Picasso with the tell-tale title of 'Social Fact and Cosmic Vision,' Christian Zervos says:

> The explosion of his spirit has destroyed the barriers which art . . . impressed on the imagination. Poetry has come forward with all that it has of the acute, the enigmatical, the strange sense which sees in life not only an image of reality but which conceives of life as a mystery that wraps us round everywhere.

To take Picasso as the modern one happens to think of, it may be said of him that his spirit is the spirit of any artist that seeks to be free. A superior obsession of all such spirits is the obsession of freedom. There is, however, no longer much excuse for explosions for, as in painting, so in poetry, you can do as you please. You can compose poetry in whatever form you like. If it seems a seventeenth-century habit to begin lines with capital letters, you can go in for the liquid transitions of greater simplicity; and so on. It is not that nobody cares. It matters immensely. The slightest sound matters. The most momentary rhythm matters. You can do as you please, yet everything matters. You are free, but your freedom must be consonant with the freedom of others. To insist for a moment on the point of sound. We no longer like Poe's tintinnabulations. You are free to tintinnabulate if you like. But others are equally free to put their hands over their ears. Life may not be a cosmic mystery that wraps us round everywhere. You have somehow to know the sound that is the exact sound; and you do in fact know, without knowing how. Your knowledge is irrational. In that sense life is mysterious; and if it is mysterious at all, I suppose that it is cosmically mysterious. I hope we agree that it is at least mysterious. What is true of sounds is true of everything: the feeling for words, without regard to their sound, for example. There is, in short, an unwritten rhetoric that is always changing and to which the poet must always be turning. That is the book in which he learns the desire for literature is the desire for life. The incessant desire for freedom in literature or in any of the arts is a desire for freedom in life. The desire is irrational. The result is the irrational searching the irrational, a conspicuous happy state of affairs, if you are so inclined.

Those who are so inclined and without reserve say: The least fastidiousness in the pursuit of the irrational is to be repudiated as an abomination. Rational beings are canaille. Instead of seeing, we should make excavations in the eye; instead of hearing, we should juxtapose sounds in an emotional clitter-clatter.

This seems to be freedom for freedom's sake. If we say that we desire freedom when we are already free, it seems clear that we have in mind a freedom not previously experienced. Yet is not this an attitude toward life resembling the poet's attitude toward reality? In spite of the cynicisms that occur to us as we hear of such things, a freedom not previously experienced, a poetry not previously conceived of, may occur with the suddenness inherent in poetic metamorphosis. For poets, that possibility is the ultimate obsession. They purge themselves before reality, in the meantime, in what they intend to be saintly exercises.

You will remember the letter written by Rimbaud to M. Delahaye, which he said:

> It is necessary to be a seer, to make oneself a seer. The poet makes himself a seer by a long, immense and reasoned unruliness of the senses. . . . He attains the unknown.

IX.

Let me say a final word about the irrational as part of the dynamic poetry. The irrational bears the same relation to the rational that the unknown bears to the known. In an age as harsh as it is intelligent, phrases about the unknown are quickly dismissed. I do not for a moment mean to indulge in mystical rhetoric, since for my part, I have no patience with that sort of thing. That the unknown as the source of knowledge, as the object of thought, is part of the dynamics of the known does not permit of denial. It is the unknown that excites the ardor of scholars, who, in the known alone, would shrivel up with boredom. We accept the unknown even when we are most skeptical. We may resent the consideration of it by any except the most lucid minds; but when so considered, it has seductions more powerful and more profound than those of the known.

Just so, there are those who, having never yet been convinced that the rational has quite made us divine, are willing to assume the efficacy of the irrational in that respect. The rational mind, dealing with the known, expects to find it glistening in a familiar ether. What it really finds is the unknown always behind and beyond the known, giving it the appearance, at best, of chiaroscuro. There are, naturally, charlatans of the irrational. That, however, does not require us to identify the irrational with the charlatans. I should not want to be misunderstood as having the poets of surrealism in mind. They concentrate their prowess in a technique which seems singularly limited but which, for all that, exhibits the dynamic influence of the irrational. They are extraordinarily alive and that they make it possible for us to read poetry that seems filled with gaiety and youth, just when we were beginning to despair of gaiety and youth, is immensely to the good. One test of their dynamic quality and, therefore, of their dynamic effect, is that they make other forms seem obsolete. They, in time, will be absorbed, with the result that what is now so concentrated, so inconsequential in the restrictions of a technique, so provincial, will give and take and become part of the process of give and take of which the growth of poetry consists.

Those who seek for the freshness and strangeness of poetry in fresh and strange places do so because of an intense need. The need of the poet for poetry is a dynamic cause of the poetry that he writes. By the aid of the irrational he finds joy in the irrational. When we speak of fluctuations of taste, we are speaking of evidences of the operation of the irrational. Such changes are irrational. They reflect the effects of poetic energy; for where there are no fluctuations, poetic energy is absent. Clearly, I use the word irrational more or less indifferently, as between its several senses. It will be time enough to adopt a more systematic usage, when the critique of the irrational comes to be written, by whomever it may be that this potent subject ultimately engages. We must expect in the future incessant activity by the irrational and in the field of the irrational. The advances thus to be made would be all the greater if the character of the poet was not so casual and intermittent a character. The poet cannot profess the irrational as the priest professes the unknown. The poet's role is broader, because he must be possessed, along with everything else, by the earch and by men in their earthy implications. For the poet, the irrational is elemental; but neither poetry nor life is commonly at its dynamic utmost. We know Sweeney as he is and, for the most part, prefer him that way and without too much effulgence and, no doubt, always shall.

17
GEORGE DANGERFIELD (1904–86)
FROM *THE STRANGE DEATH OF LIBERAL ENGLAND* 1935

British writer, historian and lecturer. He studied classics and English Literature at Oxford. He taught English in Prague and Hamburg before emigrating to New York in 1930 where he joined the editorial staff of Vanity Fair *magazine and was literary editor from 1933–35. He became an American citizen in 1943 and served in the US Army during the Second World War. He was a writer and lecturer for most of his working life, and lectured in Anglo-American history at the University of California 1968–72. Dangerfield's first popular history book,* Bengal Mutiny: The Story of the Sepoy Rebellion *(1932), was the result of an assignment for* Vanity Fair. *His next book was a very successful account of English political history before the First World War:* The Strange Death of Liberal England *(1935). His study of nineteenth-century American political history,* The Era of Good Feelings *(1952) won a Pulitzer Prize.*

And the Parliament Bill was now a Parliament Act; the Constitution, still un-materialized in its mighty progress, had planted one more large footstep in the sands of history. Its appearance was an ominous one. It meant the death of aristocracy and it meant the resignation of Mr. Balfour: above all, it meant the triumph of everything that Parnell had suffered for. When Lord Rosebery, four bishops and ten unimportant peers signed their names to a protest in the little-used House of Lords Protest Book, the casual reader must have seen little more there than the lamentations of fifteen gentlemen concerning the curtailment of an obviously unfair veto. But those were more prophetic subscriptions and, like hieroglyphics, they were beyond the common reading. They set forth three years of undignified bickering, a gun-running, a mutiny, a threat of civil war; and, beyond these, more indistinct and more awful, the barricades of Easter Week and the long, blood-stained wastes of the Troubles.

For the moment, however, there was peace. The King 'has gone off happy' – said his secretary, Lord Knollys – 'and please God we shall have no more crises.' But Providence, as most men feared, was not to be so merciful: it may temper the wind to the shorn lamb, but not to the dying sheep.

(*Dying!* In the streets of London, the last horse-bus clattered towards extinction. The aeroplane, that incongruous object, earth-bound and wavering, still called forth exclamations of rapture and alarm. Country roads, with blind corners and precipitous inclines, took a last revenge upon the loud invading automobile. There was talk of wild young people in London, more wild and less witty than you would ever guess from the novels of Saki; of night clubs; of negroid dances. People gazed in horror at the paintings of Gauguin, and listened with delighted alarm to the barbaric measures of Stravinsky. The old order, the old bland world, was dying fast: and the Parliament Act was its not too premature obituary. . . .)

If rumours of earthly actions ever reach the dead, one wonders what Mr. Gladstone's subtle and pompous soul made of this great Liberal victory: or how the Duke of Devonshire received the news in that place where his slow-moving conscience was now doubtless reconciling itself to eternal bliss. In their day, would the House of Lords ever have dared to reject a Budget? And if it had, would Mr. Gladstone have advanced to revenge himself with the dubious but necessary support of eight score Irish patriots? Was not this triumph, after all, only the last uphill charge of a weak and almost leaderless army?

18
ANDREI ZHDANOV (1896–1948)
FROM SPEECH AT THE FIRST ALL-UNION CONGRESS OF SOVIET WRITERS 1934

The first Congress of Soviet Writers held in Moscow in 1934 was the event which determined future Soviet policy by approving the doctrine of Socialist Realism. Reproduced below is an extract from the keynote address by Andrei Zhdanov, Secretary of the Communist Party and Stalin's cultural commissar (from Russian Art of the Avant-Garde, *ed. John E. Bowlt, 1988).*

Comrades, in the name of the Central Committee of the All-Union Communist Party of Bolsheviks and the Soviet of People's Commissars of the Union of Soviet Socialist Republics, allow me to present our warmest greetings to the first congress of Soviet writers and thereby to all the writers of our Soviet Union – headed by the great proletarian writer Aleksei Maksimovich Gorky [*Loud applause*].

Comrades, your congress is meeting at a time when the basic difficulties confronting us on the path of Socialist construction have already been overcome, when our country has laid the foundation of a Socialist economy – something that is bound closely to the victorious policy of industrialization and the construction of state and collective farms.

Your congress is meeting at a time when the Socialist way of life has gained final and complete victory in our country – under the leadership of the Communist Party and under our leader of genius, Comrade Stalin [*Loud applause*]. Consequently, advancing from milestone to milestone, from victory to victory, from the time of the Civil War to the reconstruction period, and from the reconstruction period to the Socialist reconstruction of the entire national economy, our Party has led the country to victory over capitalist elements, ousting them from all spheres of the national economy. . . .

In our hands we hold a sure weapon, thanks to which we can overcome all the difficulties besetting our path. This weapon is the great and invincible doctrine of Marx-Engels-Lenin-Stalin, a doctrine that has been put into practice by our Party and by our soviets.

The great banner of Marx-Engels-Lenin-Stalin is victorious. It is thanks precisely to this victorious banner that the first congress of Soviet writers has met together here. If there had been no such victory, then there would have been no congress. Only we Bolsheviks, no one else, could have convoked such a congress as this. . . .

Comrade Stalin has called our writers 'engineers of human souls.' What does this mean? What obligations does this title impose on us?

First of all, it means that we must know life so as to depict it truthfully in our works of art – and not to depict it scholastically, lifelessly, or merely as 'objective reality'; we must depict reality in its revolutionary development.

In this respect, truth and historical concreteness of the artistic depiction must be combined with the task of the ideological transformation and education of the working people in the spirit of Socialism. This method of artistic literature and literary criticism is what we call socialist realism. . . .

To be an engineer of human souls means to stand with both feet on the ground of real life. And this, in turn, denotes a break with the old-style romanticism that depicted a nonexistent life with nonexistent heroes and that spirited the reader away from the contradictions and oppression of life to an unreal world, to a world of utopias. Romanticism cannot be alien to our literature, which stands with both feet on the firm basis of materialism; but it must be a romanticism of a new kind, a revolutionary romanticism. We say that socialist realism is the basic method of Soviet artistic literature and literary criticism, and this presupposes that revolutionary romanticism must enter literary creativity as an integral part, because the whole life of our Party, of our working class and its struggle consists of a combination of the most severe, most sober practical work with supreme heroism and grand prospects. Our Party has always derived its strength from the fact that it united – and continues to unite – particular activity and practicality with grand prospects, with a ceaseless aspiration onward, with the struggle for the construction of a Communist society. *Soviet literature must be able to show our heroes, must be able to catch a glimpse of our tomorrow. This will not be a utopia, because our tomorrow is being prepared today by our systematic and conscious work. . . .*

Create works with a high level of craftsmanship, with high ideological and artistic content!

Be as active as you can in organizing the transformation of the human consciousness in the spirit of Socialism!

Be in the vanguard of the fighters for a classless Socialist society! [Loud applause].

19
HERBERT READ (1893–1968)
FROM 'WHAT IS REVOLUTIONARY ART?' 1935

English art historian, critic and poet. Read was assistant keeper at the Victoria and Albert Museum in London (1922–31) and Professor of Fine Art at Edinburgh University (1931–33). As an art critic he revived interest in the Romantic movement and championed modern art movements in Britain. He had a special interest in industrial design and his Art and Industry *of 1936 was crucial for the development of this new discipline. He was a prolific writer of poetry, art and literary criticism, as well as an exponent and supporter of the European avant-garde and of left-wing cultural theories. The following extracts are taken from the essay 'What Is Revolutionary Art?', included in his edition of 5 on Revolutionary Art, 1935.*

[. . .]

Revolutionary art should be revolutionary. That surely is a simple statement from which we can begin the discussion. We can at once dismiss the feeble interpretation of such a statement as an injunction to paint pictures of red flags, hammers and sickles, factories and machines, or revolutionary subjects in general (if I take examples from the plastic arts, I do so only for convenience, and what I say I would apply equally to music and poetry and all the arts we are concerned with). But such a feeble interpretation does actually persist among Communists, and was in fact responsible for the failure of the first exhibition organised by the Artists' International. It is responsible for the partisan adulation of a competent but essentially second-rate artist like Diego Rivera.

We can best approach the question from the angle of an abstract art like architecture. (That this particular art is undergoing some queer transformations in Russia is beside the point; there are explanations of the anomaly, but they have little to do with æsthetics.) Architecture is a necessary art, and it is intimately bound up with the social reconstruction which must take place under a Communist régime. How do we, as Englishmen, conceive a Communist architecture? As a reversion to Tudor rusticity, or Georgian stateliness, or the bourgeois pomp of the neo-classical style? Surely none of these styles can for a moment be considered in relation to the city of the future. Must we not rather confidently look forward to a development of the new architecture of which Walter Gropius is the foremost exponent; of that architecture which, in his own words, 'bodies itself forth, not in stylistic imitation or ornamental frippery, but in those simple and sharply modelled designs in which every part merges naturally into the comprehensive volume of the whole.' Only in this manner, by following the path clearly indicated by Gropius in his work and writings, can we find 'a concrete expression of the life of our epoch.'

That surely must be admitted. If we then pass from architecture and ask ourselves what is the parallel to this new style in the arts of painting and sculpture, can we for a moment be satisfied with a Rivera or a Tsalpine? Is there not rather an essential contradiction between such anecdotal and 'literary' art and the vitality and intellectual strength of the new architecture?

But corresponding to the new architecture, to a large extent arising from the same fertile ground of the Bauhaus experiment founded and directed by Gropius, is the art generally known as 'abstract'. The name is admittedly a makeshift, and between an abstract artist like Mondrian or Ben Nicholson at one end of the scale, and an equally so-called 'abstract' artist like Miró or Henry Moore, there is only a remote connection. But for the moment these differences do not matter. Such names represent the modern school in painting and sculpture in its widest and most typical aspect, and these artists, I wish to claim, are the true revolutionary artists, whom every Communist should learn to respect and encourage.

Such an opinion will be met by a formidable opposition, precisely among Communists who are interested in art. Communist artists from Germany will tell you that they have 'been through all that'; that abstract art is dead, and that in any case it is incomprehensible to the proletariat and of no use to the revolutionary movement. Like the simple bourgeois of another generation, they ask for something they can understand, a 'realistic' art above all, something they can use as propaganda.

Actually, I believe that such artists are confessing their failure – as artists. The abstract movement in art is not dead, and not likely to be for many years to come. That it will gradually be transformed not only the dialectical conception of history, but the slightest acquaintance with the history of art, compels us to admit. But how it will be transformed is more than we can tell. The facts we have to recognise are: that all the artists of any intellectual force belong to this movement; that this movement is contemporary and revolutionary; and that only the apparent independence and isolation of the abstract artist – his refusal to toe the line and become an emotional propagandist – only this fact hinders the Communist from accepting the abstract movement in art as the contemporary revolutionary movement in art.

[. . .]

Let us return to the actualities of modern art. Excluding the great mass of academic bourgeois art, and within the general category of revolutionary art, we have two distinct movements, both professing to be modern, both *intentionally* revolutionary.

The first of these has no very descriptive label, but it is essentially formalist, in the sense already mentioned. It is sometimes called abstract, sometimes non-figurative, sometimes constructivist, sometimes geometric. It is most typically represented by painters like Mondrian, Hélion, Ben Nicholson, Moholy-Nagy; and by sculptors like Brancusi, Gabo and Barbara Hepworth.

The second movement has a distinctive name – Surréalisme or Superrealism, and is represented by painters like Max Ernst, Salvador Dalí, Miró, Tanguy, and by a sculptor like Arp.

The first movement is plastic, objective and ostensibly non-political.

The second group is literary (even in paint), subjective, and actively Communist.

Those distinctions are obvious, on the surface. But I want to suggest that we cannot be satisfied with such superficial distinctions. We cannot accept the surréalistes at their own valuation, and welcome them as the only true revolutionary artists. Nevertheless, they are performing a very important revolutionary function, and it must be said on their behalf that they realise the importance of their function with far more clarity than the official Marxians, who have shown them no favour. For official Marxians, concentrating on their economic problems, do not see the relevance of the cultural problem, more particularly the artistic problem. The mind of the artist, they complacently assume, that too will, in Trotsky's phrase, limp after the reality they are creating.

But everywhere the greatest obstacle to the creation of this new social reality is the existence of the cultural heritage of the past – the religion, the philosophy, the literature and the art which makes up the whole complex ideology of the bourgeois mind. The logic of the facts – the economic facts: war, poverty amidst plenty, social injustice – that logic cannot be denied. But so long as the bourgeois mind has its bourgeois ideology, it will deny the facts; it will construct an elaborate rationalisation which effectively ignores them.

The superrealists, who possess very forceful expositors of their point of view – writers like André Breton – realise this very clearly, and the object of their movement is therefore to discredit the bourgeois ideology in art, to destroy the academic conception of art. Their whole tendency is negative and destructive. The particular method they adopt, in so far as they have a common method, consists in breaking down the barriers between the conscious reality of life and the unconscious reality of the dream-word – to so mingle fact and fancy that the normal concept of reality no longer has existence. It is a similar tendency which Carl Einstein found in the later work of Braque, and to some extent Braque may be considered as a surréaliste – Picasso too. Surréalistes like Ernst and Dalí complete the disintegration of the academic concept of reality begun by Picasso and Braque.

We can see, therefore, the place of surréalisme in the revolutionary movement. What of this other kind of modern art – the art of pure form immured in its Ivory Tower?

That art too, I wish to contend, has its revolutionary function, and in the end it is the most important function of all. Superrealism is a negative art, as I have said, a destructive art; it follows that it has only a temporary rôle; it is the art of a transitional period. It may lead to a new romanticism, especially in literature, but that lies beyond its immediate function.

But abstract art has a positive function. It keeps inviolate, until such time as society will once more be ready to make use of them, the universal qualities of art – those elements which survive all changes and revolutions. It may be said that as such it is merely art in pickle – an activity divorced from reality, of no immediate interest to the revolutionary. But that, I maintain, is a very short view of the situation. And actually such art is not so much in pickle as might be supposed. For in one sphere, in architecture and to some extent in industrial arts, it is already in social action. There we find the essential link between the abstract movement in modern painting and the most advanced movement in modern architecture – the architecture of Gropius, Markelius, Le Corbusier. . . . It is not merely a similarity of form and intention, but an actual and intimate association of personalities.

This single link points the way to the art of the future – the art of the new classless society. It is impossible to predict all the forms of this art, and it will be many years before it reaches its maturity. But you cannot build a new society – and you must *build* such a society, with bricks and mortar, steel and glass – you cannot build such a society without artists.

[. . .]

20
Eric Gill (1882–1940)
'All Art is Propaganda' 1935

British engraver, letter-cutter, sculptor, typographer and writer. Educated Chichester Art School. In 1913 he became a Roman Catholic. He designed the lettering known as Gill Sans-serif and other distinctive alphabets. He carved the Stations of the Cross at Westminster Cathedral (1913–18). His books include The Necessity of Belief *(1936) and* Autobiography *(1940). The following piece comes from 5 on Revolutionary Art (1935, ed. Herbert Read).*

In the confusion of our time few things are more uncertain than the relations between art and life. On the one hand we have the high and lifted-up exponents of 'pure' art (industrialism has released the artist from the necessity of making anything useful). On the other we have people who say: all things made are works of art; all art is commercial art (for commerce is the business of exchanging things and no painter can eat a picture so he must exchange it for bread); machine-made things are works of art (for someone had to design them and superintend their making, and to use a machine, however elaborate, is simply to use an elaborate kind of tool – the machine-minders being simply parts of the machinery; all art is politically significant (for nothing can be made which does not contribute, in small ways or big, to the order or disorder of society); and so, of course, all art is propaganda because, whether the artist is conscious of it or not, there is nothing he can do but must have propaganda value, that is to say value for or against one cause or another.

The paintings and sculptures and architectural designs exhibited at the Royal Academy every year express the 'values' of the dominant class. Therefore, they are propaganda for the successful bourgeois.

Of course the painter doesn't say to himself: now I'm going to do a spot of propaganda for the idle rich. He'd be ashamed to. So he has to wrap himself in art jargon instead, and talk about another kind of values – 'tone values', 'formal relations', the 'relations of masses', and so his work becomes propaganda for *studio* values.

Confronted by innumerable contradictory religions and philosophies, none of which compels his assent or claims his service, the artist is thrown back on to the specialities of the studio; aided and abetted by art critics and connoisseurs, he ends by thinking that they alone are art, and so art, having no connection with meaning, seems to have no connection with propaganda. Art and propaganda are held to be mutually exclusive terms and to say such and such is propaganda is to say it is a bad work of art.

The fact remains. All art is propaganda, for it is in fact impossible to do anything, to make anything which is not expressive of 'value'. The artist may say he does not care who likes his work or dislikes it, whether it effects anything or not, but directly he shows his work to anyone, and more so if he shows it in a public place, he becomes a responsible propagandist for the 'values', the ethos expressed in his work and therefore promoted by it.

There is no escape from this. The artist cannot escape being a man. He cannot escape responsibility, he cannot escape being a propagandist.

But there is not generally any need to talk about it.

It is only necessary to recognize the fact, and it is specially necessary to-day because both the art critics, at one end of the pole, and the complacent bourgeoisie, at the other, are united in trying to make art meaningless, to keep the artist in the studio, to regard him simply as an entertainer.

Am I saying that a Catholic novelist has got to have his creed sticking out on every page of his book so that people can use it instead of the Penny Catechism? Of course I am not. But I am saying that to be a really good novel from a Christian point of view it has got to be such that no one but a Catholic could have written it. (Must I point out that by 'Catholic' here I do not mean only those who are explicitly practising members of the Church? 'He that is not against me is for me.')

Am I saying that painters must only paint pictures of starved Welsh miners? Of course I am not. But I am saying that no painter can paint a picture without being in effect a propagandist for something, and that, therefore, no decent Catholic painter could paint a picture whose effect was to add another buttress to the bourgeois (bourgeois: i.e. buyers and sellers, the founders of the modern world, in which all things are merchandise, money is the ruling power and all things are made for the profit of investors).

Of course it's a pity to be too conscious of being a propagandist. It's a pity even in a preacher in the pulpit. But the world's in a rotten mess and we are the Church Militant (or aren't we?), so we can't help being a bit more conscious of a mission than if we were living in a heavenly Jerusalem.

21
CHRISTINA STEAD (1902–83)
FROM 'THE WRITERS TAKE SIDES' 1935

Australian novelist. Stead's first published work was a collection of stories, The Salzburg Tales *(1934). Her debut novel,* Seven Poor Men of Sydney, *was published the same year and concerns a group of young revolutionaries on Sydney's waterfront. Her best-known novel is* The Man Who Loved Children *(1940), a portrayal of marriage as a state of savage and implacable conflict. In the 1940s Stead worked as a screenwriter in Hollywood before settling in London. She returned to*

Australia in 1974. The following extracts are from her report on the first International Congress of Writers for the defence of culture, held in the Salle de la Mutualité, Paris, June 21–25, 1935. It was published in Left Review *the same year.*

The burning of books, the persecution, exile and proscription of writers and teachers, the rigorous censorship of press, radio, and even mail, and the more frequent brutal expressions of class conflicts every day have hammered it home to every writer that the armies of reaction are trampling into the very heart of his own country: like the most ignorant peasant, he rises to defend what has come to him from his father, is his and makes him one of a community. He defends the soil he has to till and from which he gets his living, the language, thoughts and theories of his people, the freedom to use these, the freedom to use his tools and earn his living. In all countries but one, the pauperization of the middle-class, militarization and barbarism of the upper class and rationalization, enfeebling and unemployment of the lower classes have withdrawn from the writer his ready public. Since his spiritual and economic needs call for a public, his chief concern now becomes the attainment of that public together with an understanding of the embroiled world he lives in, so that he can transmit it recognizably to the people who live in it with him. The only people with money left, the masters, are exigent: gone the time for trifling, for the pampering of snarling, elegant, whimsical Pekingese. Writers must, now, for them, be watchdogs and catch burglars and rats. Third, the disruption of the bourgeois world, its disorders and anomalies, the frightful insistence of economic questions leaves the writer, whatever his origin, quite at sea. He is reduced to consultation with his brotherwriters, young or old, for their experience, intuition or natural seamanship. Many books of these writers in the present day remind one of the cub reporter sent to report a rail smash in a country town. His paper waited with presses ready and editors fuming for twenty-four hours and, hearing nothing, finally wired him, 'Report at once!' The honest young one wired back, 'Nothing to report; all is confusion here.' We are all in the position of the young reporter; all is confusion here. The problems of most serious liberal-minded writers outside the USSR are real. If they are not persecuted nor in exile, they pant for a public. The giant circulations of the USSR suggest a way out. But they have to switch from the macadam of bourgeois culture which is leading them obviously into a morass, to a new clay road, hardly rollered. They are floundering, their feet are getting sticky, the sweat is pouring down their faces, they are figures of fun to their more conservative contemporaries. They seem to have missed their way and, with the hallucinations of hunger and thirst, to see meat and suck among the unlettered shepherds of some vast desolate Plynlimmon. They are loved neither by those they seek nor those they leave: they disgust themselves. Their works, when they try to change, show all the marks of indecision and partial enlightenment, of neophytism, haste, fear. They have at once to earn their livings, satisfy their publishers, keep on writing, change their minds and study politics. These dilemmas brought to the Paris Congress many different types.

Apart from the Russian writers, who do not face our problems, there were roughly two classes of writers present, the writer whose career was established before the war and who is usually of bourgeois origin: the young writer whose career began to be established after the war. The first appear more liberal, balanced, humane, witty, scrupulous and sensitive; on the whole, they suppress in a manly way their regret that they have to study politics and know something about unemployment. The younger writers are tougher, more fiery, humourless and discontented than has been seen since 1830–1849. The first sacrifice the repose their success brought them, easy sales and the soft pedals of critics. Their courageous, exemplary behaviour in taking their place, not as generals, but as privates alongside the young and inexperienced, should be honoured. The younger writers, trembling and eloquent with their will to survive and create, have to give up their poetic solitudes and soft self-probings to study worldly subjects, enter the political arena, take lessons from workmen and use their pen as a scalpel for lifting up the living tissues, cutting through the morbid tissues, of the social anatomy. The best of both parties seem aware that they have no future, that the true 'great writers' will come after them, that they are breaking ground. It is evidence of a tremendous social pressure that they leave the fostered hopes and vanities of men of talent. It is a sure sign of the rising influence of yet another class – more powerful, eventually richer and offering more opportunities to the writer. Those attracted to this congress were those who expect their work to survive them, and the young who need a public and can still wait for one. Can this powerful, eventually rich class be the working class? Artists are sensitized plates, bathed and kept out of the glare of day, to be, when exposed, indicators and interpreters. Every man's economic interest primes his intelligence. Then one of the most significant events of the time is this international congress of writers, this class-split which has at last affected even the denizens of the ivory tower.

The decadence of the bourgeoisie has been a long time on the way; 'We live on the shadow of a shade, on the perfume of an empty flask; on what will they live who come after us?' says Renan. The whole romantic movement of the nineteenth century was the coronach of the bourgeoisie, that ugly duckling. Or we hear the last swish of the last vertebra of the dinosaur's tail as he breathes his vegetarian last in the antediluvian grass. We are prehistoric men, but a breed that will survive, and the saurian will dwindle to some lizard sunning himself on a pumpkin. That is the belief of the revolting young bourgeois of to-day. That is why they can still forge ahead with such a will and still sacrifice their talents and sensibility. Rimbaud was the first of their breed. Each one has now his Season in Hell. But instead of remaining silent they are pouring forth their fervid words, pounding them in the mortar of midnight trials, bringing them out whole in the daylight of criticism. 'One must be absolutely modern. No canticles: hold the step gained. . . . The spiritual combat is as brutal as the combat of men', is the word of Rimbaud. Why has the conflict come now? It has increased with the speed of the machine, the precipitation of the conveyor-belt. The war of 1914–1918, that great incentive to mechanical improvement and the instruments of class-struggle, smashed the bourgeois machine; since, the nations have fallen helter-skelter into all the last corruptions of capitalist decay.

This speed of development is perhaps a secret hope of the writers who gathered at the Paris Congress. They may live to grasp the truth, they may live to translate their environment, reach the people, make their name. It is no dishonour to wish to be honoured: creation of something out of nothing is the most primitive of human passions and the most optimistic. There is no question but that all but a few of those present at the Paris Congress felt these two desires: no question but that the audience of 2,500 workmen, students and writers, took a vivid interest in them. The hall was not full of half-feminine masculine revolutionaries and half-masculine feminine rebels. They were neat, had no postures and poses. The air was clean and pure intellectually (although decidedly stuffy, and oppressive climatically).

There was more than this abnegation, there was also a new unexpressed hope in all the artists gathered there. There was in their emphatic voices the accent of the peasant who loves the earth because it is the wheat he eats. The bourgeoisie have starved art too far and abstracted it too far, with themselves, into their magic, mythic world of coupon-clipping and commodity-markets at two removes. There was the breath of a new crop, fresh shower, hot summer in the young men and women who spoke – Tikhonov, Malraux, Anna Seghers, Gold. To quote Proudhon, 'It is by possession that man puts himself in communion with nature, while by property he separates himself from it: in the same way that man and woman are in communion by domestic habitude, while voluptuousness holds them apart.' These writers decidedly believed they were cohabiting with the future. The great spirit of revolutionary France, of red France, returned to her true tradition, was with us and breathed in the hall with the hot breath of those oppressive summer days. It was incarnated on the platform in the speakers, the French, Americans, Russians, Germans, those from the French Antilles, from Portugal and Tadjikistan. That same fire did not appear in the genial, gentle speeches of the Englishmen. As Mark Twain says, 'The English are mentioned in the Bible, where it is said, "The meek shall inherit the earth."' Mr. Forster now hopes that the English who 'do not cut much ice on the Continent' will begin to do so by reducing this revolutionary fury, but it is ice which melts in the flame and not, usually, the flame which is extinguished by a little drop of frost. Mr. Forster himself was carried away by something of that flame and made a statement which did him credit. It is not by ice, but by fire, rather by sharp blades that we can hope to blaze a trail to the new masses that are arising: these blades should be of steel tempered in fire, not of savage blades smoothed in the ice-flow.

The subjects of the speeches and discussions were divided into nine chapters: The Cultural Heritage (Mr. Forster spoke here), the Rôle of the Writer in Society (Mr. Huxley and Mr. Strachey spoke), the Individual, Humanism, the Nation and Culture (Mrs. Williams-Ellis spoke), the Problems of Creation and the Dignity of Thought, Questions of Organization, the Defence of Culture. The persons presiding varied with the subjects. The opening discourse was made by André Gide, dean of French letters, whose reverberating conversion to communism in 1933 consolidated a position gained in thirty-five years of writing.

[. . .]

This speech introduced the first session of the Congress, which was devoted to the Cultural Heritage. The first speaker was Mr. E. M. Forster, whose long, cordial and characteristic speech on liberty of expression and on the safeguarding of the cultural tradition, expressed the ideas of many English people. He expressed a desire for greater liberty of speech in England and mentioned some particular and general attacks on the liberty of the subject. He said that love of liberty is an old English tradition, but this English liberty is but a class and race liberty, the liberty of the privileged British citizen and not of the colonial, or the man out of a job. Great Britain is not threatened by a brutal fascism, in his opinion, but by a much more insidious danger – the progressive restriction of liberties in all departments of public life.

[. . .]

Mr. Forster desires, particularly, a much greater liberty for the writer, whether he be critic or creator. For example, the sexual question which is practically forbidden in England, can be treated as well seriously as in comedy. 'The last treatment is usually ignored by the advocates of the cause.' 'Finally, I desire the maintenance of non-official culture. How would I attain these ends? In trying in my own country to use the existing machinery and in extending to all races and classes these liberties, the privilege now of some few rich white men. . . . My colleagues are probably of my mind on the situation in our country but they may dissent from my old-fashioned attitude and feel that we lose time talking about liberty and tradition when the economic substructure of society is at fault. They will say, perhaps, that if a new war breaks out, writers of the liberal and individualist type, like Mr. Aldous Huxley and myself will be simply swept aside. I am sure that we will be swept aside, and I consider as very possible a new war. It seems to me that if the nations continue to gorge themselves with armaments, they will no more escape elimination finally, than an animal which stuffs endlessly can escape excretion. This said, my rôle and the rôle of those with the same sentiments as myself, is a temporary rôle. We must continue to potter about with our old tools until the moment when everything falls about our ears. When everything crashes, nothing will serve any more. After – if there is an after – the task of civilization will be taken up by men whose spiritual training will have been different from mine. I am more often pursued by the idea of war than by that of my own death: and nevertheless, the line to adopt towards these two vexations is the same. One must act as if one were immortal and as if civilization were eternal . . . Whatever are the necessary divergences between the remedies proposed for our ills, we all believe in courage. . . . And the courage I will find among so many men come here from so many countries can only strengthen mine.' Mr. Forster was particularly applauded for the courageous self-abnegation, modesty and desire for truth in his statement, and, by the youth of the audience, for the remark, 'You have guessed that I am not a Communist: perhaps I should be one if I were younger and braver, because in Communism I see hope. I know that its intentions are good, although I think bad many of the acts resulting from these intentions. You have guessed that I am not a fascist – fascism does evil that evil may come of it.' The great virtue of this liberal and radical congress, which will never close its gates in the name of sectarian vanity, is that it can secure the adherence of men of the talent, standing and influence of Mr. E. M. Forster: this could not be achieved by a purely partisan grouping. [. . .] Writers are not properly propagandists, as Mr. Huxley justly remarked, but their influence is immense: it is essential to creation that the writer should think himself, as a writer, individual. This belief gives power, pungency, joy to his writings. We cannot therefore expect writers to take a purely political view and it certainly seems that the form the new association takes will assure to us much wider support than we could get by any other means.

[. . .]

The International Association

The Congress, before closing, set up the *International Association of Writers for the defence of culture*. The French section of the Association is even now is session. At the moment of closing the Congress the following declaration was made:

1. The writers, representatives of thirty-eight countries, who have taken part in the first International Congress of Writers for the defence of culture, think the work of the Congress should be extended. They found, therefore, an International Association of Writers for the defence of culture. This Association is directed by a permanent International Bureau whose mission is to maintain and develop those contracts that the Congress made possible.

2. The International Bureau will stimulate translations between the different countries, will control the quality of those submitted to its judgment and will endeavour in every way to have them published.

3. The Bureau charges itself, as one of its chief duties, with the translation and publication of works of distinction, both books and manuscripts, which are interdicted in their own countries and will obtain for such works the support and authority of its most qualified members.

4. The Bureau will endeavour to make it easy for its writers to travel and sojourn in the various countries, on a basis of mutual hospitality.

5. It will draw up, periodically, lists of works of distinction, published in all countries, which it thinks should have a widespread circulation.

6. It will examine the different methods of advancing the most eminent productions of contemporary literature, notably by the foundation of a world prize in letters.

7. It will prepare in due course a second international congress of writers.

8. This Bureau, made up of writers of diverse philosphic, literary and political tendencies, will be ready to fight on its own ground, which is culture, against war, fascism, and generally speaking, against everything that menaces civilization.

The International Association of Writers for the defence of culture is directed by a bureau of 112 members. The Bureau has, at its head, a central committee including André Gide, Henri Barbusse, Romain Rolland, Heinrich Mann, Thomas Mann, Maxim Gorki, E. M. Forster and Aldous Huxley.

The Central Committee is assisted by national secretariats, which, united, constitute the secretariat of the international organization.

The national secretariats consist of members of local committees, whose number varies according to the country.

The chief office of the organization is in Paris.

The international Bureau will hold at least one plenary session yearly, each meeting to be in a different country.

Details of the membership and plans of the National Committees in this and other countries will be announced in the next issue of Left Review.

The English delegation to the Congress consisted of E. M. Forster, Aldous Huxley, John Strachey, with Amabel Williams-Ellis and Ralph Fox, organizers of a group which included Pearl Binder, John Fisher (Australian), James Hanley, Nettie Palmer (Australian), Herbert Read, Montagu Slater, Christina Stead, Shelley Wang. To the statement made by Mrs. Williams-Ellis, the following appended their names, Walter Greenwood, James Hanley, Winifred Holtby, Storm Jameson and Naomi Mitchison.

22
LEWIS GRASSIC GIBBON (JAMES LESLIE MITCHELL) (1901–35)
'NOTE', A SCOTS QUAIR 1932–34

Scottish writer, born in Aberdeenshire. He worked as a journalist in Glasgow, and became a member of the Communist Party in 1919. He served in the Royal Army Service Corps in Persia, India and Egypt, and then as a clerk in the Royal Air Force (1923–29). He then lived in London for his remaining years. Lewis Grassic Gibbon is the name he used for his specifically Scottish projects of which the best known is the trilogy A Scots Quair *(1932–34). He also collaborated with Hugh MacDiarmid on* Scottish Scene: or, The Intelligent Man's Guide to Albyn *(1934), an important document of the Scottish Renaissance. As James Leslie Mitchell he published historical novels – for example,* Spartacus *(1933) – and works of history, archaeology and anthropology, informed by his version of Diffusionist theory.*

If the great Dutch language disappeared from literary usage and a Dutchman wrote in German a story of the Lekside peasants, one may hazard he would ask and receive a certain latitude and forbearance in his usage of German. He might import into his pages some score or so untranslatable words and idioms – untranslatable except in their context and setting; he might mould in some fashion his German to the rhythms and cadence of the kindred speech that his peasants speak. Beyond that, in fairness to his hosts, he hardly could go – to seek effect by a spray of apostrophes would be both impertinence and mistranslation.

The courtesy that the hypothetical Dutchman might receive from German a Scot may invoke from the great English tongue.

23
JAMES BARKE (1905–58)
FROM 'LEWIS GRASSIC GIBBON' 1935–36

Scottish novelist who retired from his position as accountant to a shipbuilding firm to devote himself to writing. His novels include The World His Pillow *(1933) and* The Land of the Leal *(1939). His devoted research on the life of Robert Burns resulted in a five-volume cycle of novels (1946–54) and an edition of Burns's poems and songs (1955). The following extracts are taken from an article celebrating Lewis Grassic Gibbon's work which appeared in* Left Review *(Vol. 2, 1935–36).*

It is doubtful if there are more than four Scottish novelists worthy of serious critical consideration. Of the four, Mr. Neil M. Gunn is, perhaps, the greatest, and Lewis Grassic Gibbon the most important, literary artist. This comparison will not seriously be questioned by the student of Scottish literature. Nevertheless an analysis and explanation may help to clarify the present writer's standpoint and prepare the reader for what follows.

Gunn is a Gaelic culture revivalist: and it follows that, philosophically, he is an Idealist. He distils from the Gaelic past something of the quality which he believes to be the dominant racial quality of the Gael: an aristocratic, individualist quality. The survival of this quality is all-important to Gunn. Hence his Scottish Nationalist alignment. For Scottish Nationalism is largely inspired by the superior race-theory of the Gael and the 'currency' demagogy of Major Douglas. The identity of Gunn's Nationalist ideology with that of the Aryan theoreticians of Hitler Fascism is not so fortuitous as its superficial form and expression might indicate.

Gibbon on the other hand is an internationalist: he looks forward, he is consumed with the vision of Cosmopolis. Philosophically he is a materialist. True, his view of history is distorted by a discredited and unscientific 'Diffusionism'. But, in the main, he is a materialist. He sees clearly enough that 'the mode of production in material life determines the general character of the social, political and spiritual processes of life.'

The fundamental difference of approach between Gunn and Gibbon is of first importance. Gunn is no more a 'pure' idealist than Gibbon is a 'pure' materialist. Gunn, having a smaller field of vision than Gibbon, is able to concentrate more intensely on it. The result is that his literary art is on a higher level than Gibbon's. Gunn is, in fact, one of the greatest literary artists writing in the English tongue. Gibbon, having a much wider field of vision and working at much higher pressure than Gunn, is not such a great artist. But because of the breadth of his vision (and since he deals with decisive and fundamental issues) he is a much more important artist than Gunn.

Gibbon's most important work is *A Scots Quair*. *Sunset Song*, the first part, deals with the pre-War Scottish countryside: depicts the life of a small farming community and shows the effect of the Great War on rural life. The second part, *Cloud Howe*, shows a small Scottish town in the grip of the first post-War depression. The third part, *Grey Granite*, sketches a Scottish industrial city in the grip of the general economic crisis.

Such is the bare synopsis of *A Scots Quair*. It is the synopsis of an important work; as important as could have been chosen by a contemporary artist.

How did Gibbon work out this synopsis? Had he the necessary equipment and ability? For *Sunset Song* there can be no question that he had. He was familiar with the small farming life of the Mearns. This was the background to his early life. It influenced and moulded his life more than he knew. The scene lay to his heart as much as his mind. No writer ever fails to write well of his youth even though he has cause to hate his youth. Clearly Gibbon hated much in the rural life of the Mearns: its meanness, drudgery, dirt, ignorance and poverty. But there was much in it that he loved. A coarse, robust vitality; an independence; and a quality of individualism obtaining only in the countryside.

Alternately loathing and loving this countryside and the people in his youth, Gibbon wrote of them; depicted their background and environment.

It has been suggested that the medium he chose for this is only ostensibly prose: that it has a deliberate rhythm; that it scans; that it is anapaestic. But Gibbon justified this by pointing out that his characters spoke with a rhythm and cadence from which he distilled the quintessence; that this rhythm and cadence he tried to infuse into his prose. For this he has been condemned and praised; his style has been ridiculed as 'God-awful'; it has been compared to the Ballads. But comparisons apart, the style is perfectly suited to the content. Nearly all peasants speak with a cadence, a slow moving cadence, since their labour and their days are slow moving.

The prose style of *Sunset Song* is magnificently adequate to its subject matter. None but a literary pedant could read a page and fail to be thrilled by its freshness, aptness and perfect harmony. It is indeed the most beautifully vital prose created by a Scottish writer.

[. . .]

To the reader unsympathetic or unconcerned with the struggle of the working class, to the critic who does not recognize the class war (far less the class nature of society) and who concerns himself with 'art' and 'literature' (deprecating, scorning 'propaganda') this insistence of the essential class content of *A Scots Quair* may appear irrelevant or even distorted. But there is no irrelevance or distortion. Even a superficial understanding of the content of *A Scots Quair* should reveal its true purpose, nature and significance. All art is propaganda. Gibbon had no illusions about this elementary truth. ('All my books are explicit or implicit propaganda.' Left Review, February, 1935.) Nor had he any doubt as to the nature of his propaganda. ('I am a revolutionary writer.' *Ibid.*).

*   *   *   *

There remains the task of evaluating *A Scots Quair* with relation to the literature, not only of Scotland, but of Great Britain.

Born and brought up in the Mearns country, Gibbon, early in his life, passed over to the English: that is he became ('like the overwhelming majority of British Islanders') a British citizen. That he loved the country of his birth did not mean that he was a perverted, illogical and reactionary Nationalist. He realized that Scotland and England had become, since the Union (and before it), inseparably welded together in economic and cultural interest: that there was no essential difference between the Scots and the English. He was certainly 'much more at home' in London than he would have been in Glasgow, Edinburgh or Aberdeen. Nevertheless there is a Scottish literature: that is, a literature dealing with Scottish Life and Character. *A Scots Quair* is probably the greatest Scots novel in Scottish literature. Certainly it is in the first three. (It is possible to place it so accurately: Scottish fiction is not so rich that such a 'placing' is unwise or valueless.)

There is an increasing body of commercial fictionists who can (rather arbitrarily no doubt) be labelled Scots. A few of them have been choices or recommendations of various clubs or societies whose function it is to choose fictional soporifics for their members. These fictionists do their job almost as well as their English contemporaries: supply a commercial want; and are no more to be sneered at than other commercial people *as such*. But though the corpus of genuine Scottish literature is almost negligible in quantity, its quality is indisputably high. In the quality of his art, Neil Gunn has little to learn from his English, Welsh or Irish contemporaries. He can stand four square with the best of modern bourgeois art. But Gibbon on the other hand, though he had not shed all his acquired bourgeois characteristics, was, in the main, a revolutionary writer.

The importance and significance of *A Scots Quair* has compelled recognition from many of the bourgeois critics: they have been forced to recognize Gibbon as a literary artist of the highest standing. But if Gibbon stands high in the estimation of the more honest bourgeois critic he stands higher than they know or can know. For *A Scots Quair* is a worthy forerunner of the novel that will dominate the coming literary scene: the novel that will be written by workers for workers, expressing the hopes, ideals and aspirations of workers. And in that day when 'proletarian humanism' (to use Gorky's phrase) is victorious, *A Scots Quair* will still be read and Lewis Grassic Gibbon remembered for a magnificent and heroic pioneer achievement.

24
NEIL M. (MILLER) GUNN (1891–1973)
'SCOTLAND A NATION' 1935–36

Scottish novelist, born in Caithness, the setting of some his best-known novels, including Morning Tide *(1930),* Butcher's Broom *(1934),* Highland River *(1937), and* Silver Darlings *(1941). Having worked as a civil servant in London, he returned to Scotland in 1909 and entered Customs and Excise in 1911, working for various distilleries. A friend of Hugh MacDiarmid and Naomi Mitchison, he was active as a socialist and a nationalist. The following piece was published in* Left Review *(Vol. 2, 1935–36) and is a response to James Barke's article in the same journal on Lewis Grassic Gibbon which is reproduced above.*

In the Left Review for last February, Mr. James Barke has an article that is by far the most searching piece of criticism on the late Lewis Grassic Gibbon that I have seen. In the beginning of that article, where he has occasion to contrast my work with Gibbon's, he writes, 'The identity of Gunn's Nationalist ideology with that of the Aryan theoreticians of Hitler Fascism is not so fortuitous as its superficial form and expression might indicate.' This was an aspect of the matter that had not occurred to me, possibly for the reason that my knowledge of the work of the Aryan theoreticians is even less than my knowledge of the intricacies of Marxian controversy. Perhaps, therefore, some sense of ironic humour should stop me from going on; yet as my interest in Scottish Nationalism is shared in varied form by a great body of the Scottish people, it is possible that my particular attitude may have for your more confirmed readers at least a curiosity value.

My first difficulty with the proletarian as with the racial theoretician is his penchant for absolute categories. Because I may have been concerned with Scotland and the Gaelic form of civilisation Mr. Barke classifies me as 'idealist', and because Gibbon was 'consumed with the vision of Cosmopolis', Mr. Barke sees him as a 'materialist'. Now it seems to me that anyone who is concerned with a vision of a new social order must logically be concerned with ideal speculation, whereas one dealing with a given nation and its known social or cultural factors must in exposition be essentially realist or materialist. It may be held that the whole special doctrine of dialectical materialism was telescoped into the word 'materialist'. Even so, that would not fundamentally alter my contrast, while it would endanger the use of language as a medium for the communication of individual thought.

Now the basic idea in the Scottish Nationalist movement is that Scotland is a nation, precisely as England or Germany or Russia is a nation, but that by the Union with England she lost control of her nationhood, became governed by the English parliamentary and financial system, and so has been rendered incapable not only of helping herself, but of taking a direct part in any world movement. I am aware of how the word nationalism may offend the nostrils of whole-hearted proletarians of how the word nationhood may be as out-moded as last season's favourite slang word in Mayfair. But I may not allow such emotional reactions here to cloud the fact that in the world to-day the nation is still the instrument of social experiment. Recently the French nation went Left and immediately set about making and enforcing such laws as suited its ideology. If Scotland went Left to-morrow (even now in Parliamentary votes she is majority Socialist), she could do nothing about it. At Westminster she would be outvoted by eight to one. And if she decided on revolution – though she has no national mechanism even to permit of such a decision – she would be immediately and automatically overpowered.

That a violin may be made to produce the most excruciating noises, that strychnine may be used for murder, explosives for war, are hardly in themselves sufficient cause for the abolition of music, medicine, and mining engineering. That a nation may be used by capitalism, Fascism, or Socialism, hardly implies the need for abolishing the nation. If the nation is the actual instrument by which the proletarian theory is being put into practice in the world to-day (as it is – and the only one), then to deny the instrument out of some vague zeal for its international manifestation would seem to me an act of desertion and cowardice in the proletarian struggle. Scottish Nationalism explicitly has nothing to do with Communism any more than it has anything to do with Fascism. Its fundamental aim is to reintegrate the people of Scotland into a nation so that they may then, according to their lights, work out their own destiny and assist in working out the destiny of the world. For them not to do this is to abdicate in the human struggle, and represents incidentally an acquiescence in national self-destruction without parallel in the history of the world.

All that may seem very obvious. But its pith, for my purpose here, lies in this, that it compels Scottish Communists into the category of theorists, makes them lookers-on or hangers-on in the proletarian struggle, their destiny to conceive of themselves as educational or intellectual apostles to the English. Bernard Shaw said that the first thing to be noticed about Stalin is that he is a nationalist statesman. And it would seem reasonable to suggest that if Stalin succeeds in the Russian experiment, the fact of that success will be a thousand times more powerful in its effect on the workers of the world than all the theorisings and plottings of the Communist intelligentsias in all the capitals of Europe. For Stalin to endanger his experiment, or to lengthen the time of its fruition, by wasting his force in extra-national intrigue, now that he is *in the process* of turning theory into practice, and with sufficient elbow-room and resources to do it, would arguably be a tactical mistake of the worst kind, both to his immediate purpose and to the realisation of the full Marxist doctrine.

From recent happenings in Russia, it would appear that Stalin is aware of this, aware of how some purely psychological factor like the 'will to power' may act on those divorced from a specific job of work. Yet though I see him thus clearly concentrating on his national effort, it would not occur to me to align his 'national ideology' with 'Hitler Fascism.' And Lenin, however he may now be held by the orthodox to differ from Stalin on the vexed question of the primacy of national or international action, did in fact not only use Russia the nation for his purposes, but inside Russia herself encouraged the re-birth of old nationalisms with a practical and cultural success that recently drew high tribute from Ernst Toller.

So much for the nation as an instrument.

Now, apart from the satisfaction it gives the normal man to work within his own nation, it presents him with a 'closed area' where theory may most readily be translated into practice. I am aware that many readers of this Review may expect me to show that Scotland is still a nation of sufficient worth to the world to wind up and set going again. For the world can use its past only in so far as it is of value to the present and future.

But this is an impossible task in a short essay, though, given a little space, it might be a fascinating one. It would not only begin by showing that Scotland is one of the oldest nations in Europe, and, I believe, the only one that was never conquered, but would, for the earliest times, have to delineate a society that functioned on a communal basis. But not a primitive society as that phrase is usually understood. It had, for example, a highly developed literature – an art-poetry as well as a folk-poetry. It had different orders of poets. When this Gaelic polity was converted to Christianity, it sent its scholars over Europe. (All this would throw a revealing commentary on some recent Marxian impatience with anthropology.) Out of it came a social consciousness that can be traced in all distinctively Scottish institutions to this day. For instance, in this Gaelic commonwealth the land was communally held and responsibility of rulers and officials was downwards to the people: in direct contrast to the feudal system where responsibility of the rulers was upwards to the king. The feudal system came in with English influence and vitiated the native system; yet the native system was so inbred that as late as 1886 the crofters, fighting on the old idea that the land belonged to the men of the clan, by a remarkable agitation forced the Westminster government to pass an Act conceding security of tenue and the fixing of an economic rent by an impartial tribunal. In religious government the same tendency may be traced. Scotland still has her own legal system. And so on.

But this ancient belief in the importance of the folk went deeper than a natural tendency to form democratic institutions, for in its social manifestations we come across all sorts of interesting communal expressions, such as the folk music that accompanied folk labour. In other words, this Gaelic society from which we in Scotland have emerged is the only one which imbues for me the superficially vague expression 'proletarian humanism' with a deep significance.

Mr. Barke talks of 'a Gaelic culture revivalist' distilling 'from the Gaelic past something of the quality which he believes to be the dominant racial quality of the Gael: an aristocratic, individualist quality'. And he may be right. What he may not quite have understood is that the 'aristocratic, individualist quality' is not inconsistent with an extreme belief in the folk, but in fact may be implicit in it. If Communism isn't going to abolish the haunting fear of economic want, and so free the individual to indulge his powers of aristocratic discrimination on any plane he likes, then it doesn't seem to me worth discussing.

Accordingly, what I fail to understand is how Scottish intellectuals of any persuasion, and particularly the proletarian, are not prepared to accept this historic past subsumed in this country of their own and attempt therein to make a concrete contribution to social reconstruction in the interests of the folk. Their historic background and educational facilities – if there is anything in the idea of dialectical materialism – equip them for the task in a way undreamt of by the Russian mass, and should enable them to short-circuit the more obvious crudities of dictatorship and bloody violence. Anyway, it is a job of work. But they fly from it and cover their desertion by calling the Scot who would like to attempt the job a Fascist. Marx knew the primary value of practice. He also strove to make it clear that in his theories he envisaged living working men, not economic abstractions. But when we avoid the concrete job in front of us in order to go theorising internationally, no wonder we become 'consumed with the vision of Cosmopolis' – that typical bourgeois vision that Wells has made all his own, and is not merely the negation of the 'aristocratic, individualist quality,' but surely a conception of a beehive tyranny unspeakably repugnant to the free-thinking developing mind.

25
WILLIAM PHILLIPS (b. 1907) AND PHILIP RAHV (1908–73)
FROM 'RECENT PROBLEMS OF REVOLUTIONARY LITERATURE' 1935

PHILIP RAHV

Russian-born Jewish American literary and cultural critic, editor and academic. Rahv was fourteen when his family emigrated to the USA after the Russian Revolution. He was educated in Rhode Island then moved west to work in advertising, returning to New York in 1932. He became active in the John Reed Club and in 1932 became secretary to the monthly magazine Prolit Folio, *which was published by the Revolutionary Writers Federation, and wrote for* The New Masses. *He is best known as the co-founder (1934) and co-editor of* Partisan Review *(with William Phillips). He also founded and edited the periodical* Modern Occasions. *In 1935 Rahv contributed editorial work and a manifesto for young writers to the radical journal* Rebel Poet. *From 1957–1973 he was Professor of English and American Literature at Brandeis University. Among his students one summer was Anne Sexton who later credited Rahv as a powerful inspiration in her career as a poet.*

WILLIAM PHILLIPS

American academic, editor and author who used the pen name Wallace Phelps until 1935. Founding editor of Partisan Review *(which he still edits) with Philip Rahv. In the 1930s he was active in the New York John Reed Club and wrote reviews for* The Communist *(1933) and contributed to* The Dynamo *(1934). He later became Professor of English at Rutgers (1963–78) and Boston Universities (1978–). The following extract is from the groundbreaking anthology,* Proletarian Literature in the United States, *edited by Granville Hicks, Michael Gold et al. (1935).*

The last year (1933–34) has seen a quickening in the growth of revolutionary literature in America. The maturing of labor struggles and the steady increase of Communist influence have given the impetus and created a receptive atmosphere for this literature. As was to be expected, the novel – which is the major literary form of today – has taken the lead. Cantwell, Rollins, Conroy, and Armstrong have steered fiction into proletarian patterns of struggle. In the theatre, *Peace on Earth, Stevedore,* and *They Shall Not Die* show a parallel growth. The emergence of a number of little revolutionary magazines, together with the phenomenal success of the weekly *New Masses,* has provided an outlet for the briefer forms of writing. *The Great Tradition,* by Granville Hicks, has launched us on a revaluation of American literary history.

This new literature is unified not only by its themes but also by its perspectives. Even a casual reading of it will impress one with the conviction that here is a new way of looking at life – the bone and flesh of a revolutionary sensibility taking on literary form. The proletarian writer, in sharing the moods and expectations of his audience, gains that creative confidence and harmonious functioning within his class which gives him a sense of responsibility and discipline totally unknown in the preceding decade. Lacking this solidarity with his readers, the writer, as has been the case with the aesthetes of the twenties and those who desperately carry on their traditions today, ultimately becomes skeptical of the meaning of literature as a whole, sinking into the Nirvana of peaceful cohabitation with the Universe. Indeed, it is largely this intimate relationship between reader and writer that gives revolutionary literature an activism and purposefulness long since unattainable by the writers of other classes.

However, despite the unity of outlook of revolutionary literature, it contains a number of trends embodying contradictory aims and assumptions. It would be strange indeed, if the class struggle did not operate *within* revolutionary literature, though it is most clearly defined in the fight against bourgeois literature. The varying backgrounds of revolutionary writers and the diverse ways through which they come to Marxism set the frame for this inner struggle. Moreover, since forms and methods of writing do not drop like the gentle rain of heaven, but are slowly evolved in creative practice conditioned by the developing social relations, it is only natural that sharp differences of opinion should arise. To a Marxist such differences are not personal and formal, but actually reflect the stress of class conflict. Thus, the development of revolutionary literature is not unilinear; its progress is a process unfolding through a series of contradictions, through the struggle of opposed tendencies, and it is the business of criticism to help writers resolve these contradictions. Unless criticism fulfills this task, the progress of revolutionary literature is retarded and certain writers may even be shunted off their revolutionary rails.

Thus far Marxian criticism in this country has not faced the problem squarely, nor has it stated the diverse tendencies. The illusion has been allowed to spread that revolutionary writers constitute one happy family, united in irreconcilable struggle against capitalism. To a considerable extent, therefore, an atmosphere of empiricism has resulted, where writers clutch at the nearest method at hand without conscious selection, unfortified by criticism with the Marxian equipment necessary for coping with the problems of creative method. [. . .]

Neither have critics given writers adequate guidance in their quest of realistic revolutionary themes. Many young writers have declared themselves for Communism, and have joined the John Reed Clubs, but with few exceptions, they have not shown as yet a sufficient understanding of the meaning of such declarations in practice. What does the present paucity of authentic revolutionary short stories prove? Most of our writers have not grasped the fact that workers' struggles cannot be written about on the basis of inventiveness or a tourist's visit. The profile of the Bolshevik is emerging in America, heroic class battles are developing, new human types and relations are budding in and around the Communist Party; obviously, therefore, revolutionary fiction cannot be produced by applying abstract Communist ideology to old familiar surroundings. The assimilation of this new material requires direct participation instead of external observation; and the critic's task is to point out the dangers inherent in the *spectator's* attitude. [. . .]

The question of creative method is primarily a question of the imaginative assimilation of political content. We believe that the sensibility is the medium of assimilation: political content should not be isolated from the rest of experience but must be merged into the creation of complete personalities and the perception of human relations in their physical and sensual immediacy. The class struggle must serve as a premise, not as a discovery. This the 'leftist' does not do on the grounds that such a method dilutes the political directness that he aims at; actually, however, he defeats his purpose, inasmuch as he dissolves action and being in political abstractions. To a Marxist the bourgeois claims of universality are an empty concept; those elements in art that have been called universal are merely those that have recurred so far. The problem of the revolutionist is not to seek universals but usables, for his task is to create a synthesis and not merely an innovation. Ultimately, of course, the question of usables involves, first, the retaining of the cultural acquisitions of humanity as a *background of values*, and secondly, a selection of specific contributions by individual bourgeois writers.

Unless we are acutely aware of the body of literature as a whole, no standards of merit are possible. The measure of a revolutionary writer's success lies not only in his sensitiveness to proletarian material, but also in his ability to create new landmarks in the perception of reality; that is, his success cannot be gauged by immediate agitational significance, but by his recreation of social forces in their entirety. This becomes specific literary criticism when applied to choice of theme, character, and incident. And here it is necessary to stress what many writers tend to forget: literature is a medium steeped in sensory experience, and does not lend itself to the conceptual forms that the social-political content of the class struggle takes most easily. Hence the translation of this content into images of *physical life* determines – in the aesthetic sense – the extent of the writer's achievement.

26
JOHN DOS PASSOS (1896–1970)
'THE WRITER AS TECHNICIAN' 1935

The piece reproduced below was written by Dos Passos for The American Writers' Congress, a convention of radical writers which took place on 26–27 April 1935 in New York. Dos Passos did not attend the convention, but 'The Writer as Technician' was included in the publication of its proceedings, American Writers' Congress *(ed. Henry Hart, 1935). [See IIIa 5]*

[The American Writers' Congress, a convention of radical writers, took place on 26–27 April 1935 in New York. Although Dos Passos did not attend the convention, he contributed 'The Writer As Technician' to the volume devoted to addresses delivered at the convention.]

Anybody who can put the words down on paper is a writer in one sense, but being able to write no more makes a man a professional writer than the fact that he can scratch up the ground and plant seeds in it makes him a farmer, or that he can trail a handline overboard makes him a fisherman. That is fairly obvious. The difficulty begins when you try to work out what really distinguishes professional writing from the average man's letters to his family and friends.

In a time of confusion and rapid change like the present, when terms are continually turning inside out and the names of things hardly keep their meaning from day to day, it's not possible to write two honest paragraphs without stopping to take crossbearings on every one of the abstractions that were so well ranged in ornate marble niches in the minds of our fathers. The whole question of what writing is has become particularly tangled in these years during which the industry of the printed word has reached its high point in profusion and wealth, and, to a certain extent, in power.

Three words that still have meaning, that I think we can apply to all professional writing, are discovery, originality, invention. The professional writer discovers some aspect of the world and invents out of the speech of his time some particularly apt and original way of putting it down on paper. If the product is compelling, and important enough, it molds and influences ways of thinking to the point of changing and rebuilding the language, which is the mind of the group. The process is not very different from that of scientific discovery and invention. The importance of a writer, as of a scientist, depends upon his ability to influence subsequent thought. In his relation to society a professional writer is a technician just as much as an electrical engineer is.

As in industrialized science, we have in writing all the steps between the complete belt conveyor factory system of production and one man handicraft. Newspapers, advertising offices, moving picture studios, political propaganda agencies, produce the collective type of writing where individual work is indistinguishable in the industrial effort. Historical and scientific works are mostly turned out by the laboratory method by various coworkers under one man's supervision. Songs and ballads are often the result of the spontaneous feelings of a group working together. At present stories and poems are the commonest output of the isolated technician.

Any writer who has ever worked in any of these collective undertakings knows the difficulties of bucking the routine and the office-worker control that seems to be an inseparable part of large industrial enterprises, whether their aims are to make money or to improve human society. It is a commonplace that business aims, which are to buy cheap and sell dear, are often opposed to the aims of the technician, which are, insofar as he is a technician and not a timeserver, the development of his material and of the technical possibilities of his work. The main problem in the life of every technician is to secure enough freedom from interference from the managers of the society in which he lives to be able to do his work. As the era of free competition gives way to that of monopoly, with the corresponding growth of office-worker control, inner office intrigue and other stifling diseases of bureaucracy, it becomes increasingly hard for the technician to get that freedom. Even in a country that is organizing to build for socialism, instead of for the growth of the wealth and power of a few bosses, the need for functional hierarchies on an enormous scale and the difficulty of keeping the hierarchies alive through popular control, makes the position of the technician extremely difficult, because, by his very function, he has to give his time to his work instead of to 'organizational problems'. When you add the fact that the men behind the desks in the offices control the police power, indirectly in this country, but directly in many others, which can at the whim of some group of officials, put a man in jail or deprive him of his life and everything that makes life worth living, you can see that the technician, although the mechanical means in his power are growing every day, is in a position of increasing danger and uncertainty.

The only name you can give a situation in which a technician can do his best work, and be free to give rein to those doubts and unclassified impulses of curiosity that are at the root of invention and discovery and original thinking, is liberty. Liberty in the abstract is meaningless outside of philosophical chessgames. Then too the word has taken on various misleading political colorations. In America it means liberty for the exploiter to cut wages and throw his workers out on the street if they don't like it; in most of the newspapers of the world it means something connected with the privileges of the commercial classes. But, underneath, it still has a meaning that we all know, just as we know that a nickel is a nickel even if the Indian and the buffalo have been rubbed off. A writer, a technician, must never, I feel, no matter how much he is carried away by even the noblest political partisanship in the fight for social justice, allow himself to forget that his real political aim, for himself and his fellows, is liberty.

A man can't discover anything, originate anything, invent anything unless he's at least morally free, without fear or preoccupation insofar as his work goes. Maintaining that position in the face of the conflicting pulls of organized life demands a certain amount of nerve. You can see a miniature of the whole thing whenever a man performs even the smallest technical task, such as cleaning a carburetor, or taking a bead on a target with a rifle. His state of mind is entirely different from that of the owner of the car who wants to get somewhere, or of the man himself a second before he put his eye to the sight, all of a fluster to win the match or in a panic of fear lest his enemy shoot him first. This state of mind, in which a man is ready to do good work, is a state of selfless relaxation, with no worries or urges except those of the work at hand. There is a kind of happiness about it. It is much nearer the way an ordinary day-laborer feels than it is the way a preacher, propagandist or swivelchair organizer feels. Anybody who has seen war knows the astonishing difference between the attitude of the men at the front, who are killing and dying, and that of the atrocity-haunted citizenry in the rear.

At this particular moment in history, when machinery and institutions have so outgrown the ability of the mind to dominate them, we need bold and original thought more than ever. It is the business of writers to supply that thought, and not to make of themselves figureheads in political conflicts. I don't mean that a writer hasn't an obligation, like any other citizen, to take part if he can in the struggle against oppression, but that his function as a citizen and his function as a technician are different, although the eventual end aimed at may in both cases be the same.

To fight oppression, and to work as best we can for a sane organization of society, we do not have to abandon the state of mind of freedom. If we do that we are letting the same thuggery in by the back door that we are fighting off in front of the house. I don't see how it is possible to organize effectively for liberty and the humane values of life without protecting and demanding during every minute of the fight the liberties of investigation, speech and discussion that are the greatest part of the ends of the struggle. In any organization a man gives up his liberty of action. That is necessary discipline. But if men give up their freedom of thought what follows is boss rule thuggery and administrative stagnation. It is easy to be carried away by the temporary effectiveness of boss rule, but it has always ended, in small things and in great, in leaving its victims stranded bloodless and rotten, with all the problems of a living society of free men unsolved. The dilemma that faces honest technicians all over the world to-day is how to combat the imperial and bureaucratic tendencies of the groups whose aims they believe in, without giving aid and comfort to the enemy. By the nature of his function as a technician, the writer finds himself in the dangerous and uncomfortable front line of this struggle.

In such a position a man is exposed to crossfire and is as likely to be mowed down by his friends as his enemies. The writer has to face that. His only safety lies in the fact that the work of an able technician cannot be replaced. It is of use and pleasure to mankind. If it weren't for that fact, reluctantly recognized, but everywhere and always recognized, the whole tribe of doubters, inventors and discoverers would have been so often wiped out that the race would have ceased to produce types with those peculiar traits.

It's an old saying, but a very apt one, that a writer writes not to be saved but to be damned.

I feel that American writers who want to do the most valuable kind of work will find themselves trying to discover the deep currents of historical change under the surface of opinions, orthodoxies, heresies, gossip and the journalistic garbage of the day. They will find that they have to keep their attention fixed on the simple real needs of men and women. A writer can be a propagandist in the most limited sense of the word, or use his abilities for partisan invective or personal vituperation, but the living material out of which his work is built must be what used to be known as the humanities: the need for clean truth and sharply whittled exactitudes, men's instincts and compulsions and hungers and thirsts. Even if he's to be killed the next minute a man has to be cool and dispassionate while he's aiming his gun.

There is no escaping the fact that if you are a writer you are dealing with the humanities, with the language of all the men of your speech of your generation, with their traditions of the past and their feelings and perceptions. No matter from how narrow a set of convictions you start, you will find yourself in your effort to probe deeper and deeper into men and events as you find them, less and less able to work with the minute prescriptions of doctrine; and you will find more and more that you are on the side of the men, women and children alive right now against all the contraptions and organizations, however magnificent their aims may be, that bedevil them; and that you are on the side, not with phrases or opinions, but really and truly, of liberty, fraternity, and humanity. The words are old and dusty and hung with the dirty bunting of a thousand crooked orations, but underneath they are still sound. What men once meant by these words needs defenders to-day. And if those who have, in all kinds of direct and devious ways, stood up for them throughout history do not come out for them now to defend them against the thuggery of the bosses and the zeal of the administrators, the world will be an even worse place for men, women and children to live in than it is at present.

27
JOHN CORNFORD (1915–36)
FROM 'LEFT?' 1933–34

British poet and writer on politics. Educated at Trinity College, Cambridge, Cornford was a brilliant history scholar. He resigned a Research Scholarship in August 1936 and subsequently became the first Englishman to go to Spain to fight against Franco. He was killed at the Cordoba Front. Joint-leader of the Cambridge University Communist Party (which he joined in 1933), and later joint-secretary of the Socialist Club, Cornford published numerous essays and articles on politics. The following extracts are from the memorial volume, John Cornford: A Memoir, *edited by Pat Sloan (1938), the royalties from which went to the International Brigade Wounded and Dependent's Aid Committee.* Understand the Weapon, Understand the Wound: Selected Writings of John Cornford, *edited by Jonathan Galassi, was published in 1976.*

Finally, as the class struggle nears its decisive stage, disintegration of the ruling class and the old order of society becomes so active, so acute, that a small part of the ruling class breaks away to make common cause with the revolutionary class, the class which holds the future in its hands. Just as in former days, part of the nobility went over to the bourgeoisie, so now part of the bourgeoisie goes over to the proletariat. Especially does this happen in the case of some of the bourgeois ideologists, who have achieved theoretical understanding of the historical movement as a whole. – *The Communist Manifesto, 1848.*

In England in the literary field this tendency has expressed itself chiefly in the revolutionary fermentation in the work of the younger poets – W. H. Auden, Charles Madge, Stephen Spender, C. Day Lewis, Richard Goodman, H. V. Kemp. As the crisis deepens, the situation more and more urgently demands a choice between revolution and reaction. The collapse into subjectivity of Eliot, Joyce, or Pound shows more and more clearly the fate of those who refuse to admit the necessity of choice. The traditional artist's 'impartiality' is unmasked as a denial of the class struggle – as a powerful instrument in the hands of the possessing class who would prefer to keep in their hands the means of production without a struggle. And the bankruptcy of the older writers – for the most part comfortably assured of a parasitic position under the present system – becomes clearer and clearer to the younger writers, faced with unemployment, with no prospect of living as writers, and for the first time beginning to consider objectively the causes and the way out of the position with which they and we are faced.

Thus there are the beginnings of a politically-conscious revolutionary literature for the first time in the history of English culture. At the same time there exists side by side with it a very dangerous attempt to deck out the old class literature in new revolutionary-utopian trappings, to exploit the leftward movement among the younger students and intellectuals in order to serve up the old dope in a 'revolutionary' form, to make a literary fashion of 'revolution' among bourgeois intellectuals whilst denying the possibility of the growth of a genuinely revolutionary literature with a new class-basis. The fashionable reactionary critics confuse the two tendencies; it is in their interests to do so. And it is not easy to make a clear demarcation between them. Often they exist side by side in the work of a single writer. But as the crisis matures the division becomes clearer. And the differentiation is essential to the growth of a revolutionary literature. It is essential that this second tendency should be ruthlessly exposed, or otherwise the movement will be poisoned at its source. It is the task of this essay to provide a basis for this demarcation.

The fundamental antagonism of these two tendencies was exposed most clearly in a recent controversy between Stephen Spender and Charles Madge on the question of Poetry and Revolution. The question disputed was the fundamental question of the objective participation of the writer in the class-struggle. Spender's article is so significant as to be worth quoting in detail.

> Of human activities, writing poetry is one of the least revolutionary. The states of being a rentier, a merchant, a capitalist, contribute their bits to revolution, they actively crumble (!) But the writing of a poem in itself solves the poem's problem. If a poem is not complete in itself, if its content spills over into our world of confused emotions, then it is a bad poem. . . .

This is very interesting, because it is in seemingly complete contradiction to the revolutionary-utopian expressions of some of his poetry. It shows quite clearly that

Spender adheres to the doctrine that has become fundamental to the bourgeois writers of our epoch – the contradiction between art and life, between the life of the artist and the life of society. The world of the artist is considered as a metaphysical abstraction unrelated to the world in which he lives, which produced him and his art. In so far as he is related to it, it is as the 'impartial' observer.

And here is a fundamental confusion – a confusion between the 'impartiality' of the bourgeois writer and the objectivity of the revolutionary writer. Bourgeois 'impartiality' is a denial of the objective fact of the class struggle, a deliberate self-protection from the conclusion to which an objective study of the world to-day will lead. But there is no middle position between revolution and reaction. Not to take sides is to support the *status quo*, to prefer to leave things as they are rather than risk losing one's own position, and thus to remain indirectly an instrument of reaction. But an objective study of the world as it is to-day, an objective contrast between the capitalist world and the Soviet Union, between the conditions of bourgeoisie and proletariat in this country, can lead to only one conclusion – a revolutionary conclusion, which bourgeois 'impartiality' strives to mask.

And so the objective writer cannot remain a 'detached' observer of society. He must actively participate in the revolutionary struggles of society if he is not going to collapse into the super-subjectivity of the older writers. He must emphatically deny the contradiction between art and life.

In his reply to Stephen Spender, Charles Madge showed himself more or less clearly aware of this. He realises that there is no ideal poets' world unrelated to the reality.

> The problem which the poem solves is not the poem's but the poet's problem. As a consequence of the poem it is the poet, or his reader, who moves. There is no world but the world and that world is the poem's world.

And yet his reply is inadequate. He does nothing to clarify the subjective confusions and contradictions, into which Spender has fallen, by reducing them to an objective terminology. Against Spender's counter-revolutionary dogmas he offsets his own revolutionary dogmas. This is not due to an accidental lack of clarity of exposition. It is due to a contradiction in the work even of the genuinely revolutionary and leftward moving poets.

This is not hard to explain. It is because, although politically they have rejected their class, they are still writing mainly for it. Their training as writers has been a direct barrier to the writing of straightforward revolutionary poetry which can only be overcome by direct participation in revolutionary struggles. C. Day Lewis makes great play of the fact that Lawrence, who came from the working class, is not read by the working class. But this is true precisely because he cut himself off from his class, because he became so isolated from it that he ceased to represent it. In a passage in *The Rainbow* he gives an extraordinarily clear and moving description of class-oppression. But, as he himself was divorced from industry and never participated in a single struggle of his class, he never conceived of it acting as a unit to emancipate itself. Thus, instead of struggling against class oppression and exploitation, he railed against 'industrialism', and ran half round the world looking for an escape into some more primitive non-industrial form of life. The working-class is not in a position to run round the world looking for an escape from 'industrialism'. That is why it does not read Lawrence. It may seem contradictory to believe that these young intellectual writers can more directly write for the workers than could the miner's son, Lawrence. But who represented the interests of the workers, the ex-railwayman, Jimmy Thomas, or Lenin, who was by his class-origin cut off from industry?

This contradiction is as transient a phenomenon as the disintegration of the bourgeoisie. It can no more become the basis of a lasting literary movement than the section of left-moving intellectuals can become a permanent class differentiated from bourgeoisie and proletariat. The lesson of Germany shows perfectly clearly that as the crisis matures, choice between one side or the other is demanded by the conditions of existence. Only a particular and temporary set of historical circumstances can allow this section to appear for a time as an independent class which is not compelled to throw in its full weight with bourgeoisie or proletariat. As the struggle develops, they must follow the process they have started to its logical conclusion – active participation in the class struggle. For within the framework of dying capitalism they can only continue their existence as official apologies for the *status quo* – all other forms of expression, however non-political, are banned as dangerous in the 'totalitarian' state, and the drive towards Fascism in the 'democratic' countries is rapidly imposing similar restrictions on freedom of expression.

[. . .]

There can be no doubt that the future is with the revolutionary participator and not the 'impartial' observer, nor the romantic-utopian idealist. And just as out of the rise to power of the bourgeoisie, out of the violent shattering of the feudal remnants, out of the violent expropriation of the independent producers, was born the tremendous revolutionary movement of the Elizabethan drama, so out of the violent struggle for power between bourgeoisie and proletariat, as the Communist Party in this country develops from its sectarian beginnings to a mass revolutionary party, there will arise a revolutionary literature stronger and more various than any which preceded it.

28
SERGEI EISENSTEIN (1898–1948)
FROM 'A DIALECTIC APPROACH TO FILM FORM' 1929

Russian film director and theoretician. He trained initially under Vsevolod Meyerhold, whose Constructivist theories influenced Eisenstein's use of character-types and cinematic framing. His theories on montage parallel those of Brecht's on epic theatre (see IIIb 3). Like Brecht, and always in the context of Marxist aesthetics, his project consisted of making film a popular political medium. The films Strike *(1925),* Battleship Potemkin *(1927) and* October *(1928) are landmarks in the political use of montage. The Stalinist purges of the 1930s forced Eisenstein to leave the Soviet Union and seek work in the* USA. *While working for Hollywood he made* Que Viva Mexico! *which brought him into conflict with the major studios. During the war he returned to the Soviet Union and made* Ivan the Terrible, Part I *(1944) and its sequel the following year,* The Boyars Plot, *which was banned and never released in Eisenstein's lifetime. Reproduced below is an extract from*

'A Dialectic Approach to Film Form', written in 1929 (appearing here in Jay Leyda's translation from Film Form, *1949). [See IIa 23]*

   According to Marx and Engels the dialectic system is only the conscious reproduction of the dialectic course (substance) of the external events of the world.
Thus:

> The projection of the dialectic system of things
> into the brain
> *into creating abstractly*
> *into the process of thinking*
> yields: dialectic methods of thinking;

dialectic materialism – PHILOSOPHY
And also:

> The projection of the same system of things
> *while creating concretely*
> *while giving form*
> yields: ART

The foundation for this philosophy is a *dynamic* concept of things:
Being – as a constant evolution from the interaction of two contradictory opposites.
Synthesis – arising from the opposition between thesis and antithesis.
A dynamic comprehension of things is also basic to the same degree, for a correct understanding of art and of all art-forms. In the realm of art this dialectic principle of dynamics is embodied in

conflict

as the fundamental principle for the existence of every artwork and every art-form.

For art is always conflict

(1) according to its social mission,
(2) according to its nature,
(3) according to its methodology.

   According to its social mission *because:* It is art's task to make manifest the contradictions of Being. To form equitable views by stirring up contradictions within the spectator's mind, and to forge accurate intellectual concepts from the dynamic clash of opposing passions.
   According to its nature *because:* Its nature is a conflict between natural existence and creative tendency. Between organic inertia and purposeful initiative. Hypertrophy of the purposive initiative – the principles of rational logic – ossifies art into mathematical technicalism. (A painted landscape becomes a topographical map, a painted Saint Sebastian becomes an anatomical chart.) Hypertrophy of organic naturalness – of

organic logic – dilutes art into formlessness. (A Malevich becomes a Kaulbach, an Archipenko becomes a wax-works side-show.)

Because the limit of organic form (the passive principle of being) is *Nature*. The limit of rational form (the active principle of production) is *Industry*. At the intersection of Nature and Industry stands *Art*.

The logic of organic form *vs.* the logic of rational form yields, in collision,

the dialectic of the art-form

The interaction of the two produces and determines Dynamism. (Not only in the sense of a space-time continuum, but also in the field of absolute thinking. I also regard the inception of new concepts and viewpoints in the conflict between customary conception and particular representation as dynamic – as a dynamization of the inertia of perception – as a dynamization of the 'traditional view' into a new one.)

The quantity of interval determines the pressure of the tension. (See in music, for example, the concept of intervals. There can be cases where the distance of separation is so wide that it leads to a break – to a collapse of the homogeneous concept of art. For instance, the 'inaudibility' of certain intervals.)

> *The spatial form of this dynamism is expression.*
> *The phrases of its tension: rhythm.*

This is true for every art-form, and, indeed, for every kind of expression.

Similarly, human expression is a conflict between conditioned and unconditioned reflexes. (In this I cannot agree with Klages, who, *a*) does not consider human expression dynamically as a process, but statically as a result, and who, *b*) attributes everything in motion to the field of the 'soul', and only the hindering element to 'reason'. ['Reason' and 'Soul' of the idealistic concept here correspond remotely with the ideas of conditioned and unconditioned reflexes.])

This is true in every field that can be understood as an art. For example, logical thought, considered as an art, shows the same dynamic mechanism:

> . . . the intellectual lives of Plato or Dante or Spinoza or Newton were largely guided and sustained by their delight in the sheer beauty of the rhythmic relation between law and instance, species and individual, or cause and effect.

This holds in other fields, as well, e.g., in speech, where all its sap, vitality, and dynamism arise from the irregularity of the part in relation to the laws of the system as a whole.

In contrast we can observe the sterility of expression in such artificial, totally regulated languages as Esperanto.

It is from this principle that the whole charm of poetry derives. Its rhythm arises as a conflict between the metric measure employed and the distribution of accents, over-riding this measure.

The concept of a formally static phenomenon as a dynamic function is dialectically imaged in the wise words of Goethe:

Die Baukunst ist eine ertarrte Musik.
(Architecture is frozen music.)

Just as in the case of a homogeneous ideology (a monistic viewpoint), the whole, as well as the least detail, must be penetrated by a sole principle. So, ranged alongside the conflict of *social conditionality*, and the conflict of *existing nature*, the *methodology* of an art reveals this same principle of conflict. As the basic principle of the rhythm to be created and the inception of the art-form.

Art is always conflict, according to its methodology.

Here we shall consider the general problem of art in the specific example of its highest form – film.

Shot and montage are the basic elements of cinema.

Montage

has been established by the Soviet film as the nerve of cinema.

To determine the nature of montage is to solve the specific problem of cinema. The earliest conscious film-makers, and our first film theoreticians, regarded montage as a means of description by placing single shots one after the other like building-blocks. The movement within these building-block shots, and the consequent length of the component pieces, was then considered as rhythm.

A completely false concept!

This would mean the defining of a given object solely in relation to the nature of its external course. The mechanical process of splicing would be made a principle. We cannot describe such a relationship of lengths as rhythm. From this comes metric rather than rhythmic relationships, as opposed to one another as the mechanical-metric system of Mensendieck is to the organic-rhythmic school of Bode in matters of body exercise.

According to this definition, shared even by Pudovkin as a theoretician, montage is the means of *unrolling* an idea with the help of single shots: the 'epic' principle.

In my opinion, however, montage is an idea that arises from the collision of independent shots – shots even opposite to one another: the 'dramatic' principle.

A sophism? Certainly not. For we are seeking a definition of the whole nature, the principal style and spirit of cinema from its technical (optical) basis.

We know that the phenomenon of movement in film resides in the fact that two motionless images of a moving body, following one another, blend into an appearance of motion by showing them sequentially at a required speed.

This popularized description of what happens as a *blending* has its share of responsibility for the popular miscomprehension of the nature of montage that we have quoted above.

Let us examine more exactly the course of the phenomenon we are discussing –

how it really occurs – and draw our conclusion from this. Placed next to each other, two photographed immobile images result in the appearance of movement. Is this accurate? Pictorially – and phraseologically, yes.

But mechanically, it is not. For, in fact, each sequential element is perceived not *next* to the other, but on *top* of the other. For the idea (or sensation) of movement arises from the process of superimposing on the retained impression of the object's first position, a newly visible further position of the object. This is, by the way, the reason for the phenomenon of spatial depth, in the optical superimposition of two planes in stereoscopy. From the superimposition of two elements of the same dimension always arises a new, higher dimension. In the case of stereoscopy the superimposition of two nonidentical two-dimensionalities results in stereoscopic three-dimensionality.

In another field; a concrete word (a denotation) set beside a concrete word yields an abstract concept – as in the Chinese and Japanese languages, where a material ideogram can indicate a transcendental (conceptual) result.

The incongruence in contour of the first picture – already impressed on the mind – with the subsequently perceived second picture engenders, in conflict, the feeling of motion. Degree of incongruence determines intensity of impression, and determines that tension which becomes the real element of authentic rhythm.

Here we have, temporally, what we see arising spatially on a graphic or painted plane.

What comprises the dynamic effect of a painting? The eye follows the direction of an element in the painting. It retains a visual impression, which then collides with the impression derived from following the direction of a second element. The conflict of these directions forms the dynamic effect in apprehending the whole.

I. It may be purely linear: Fernand Léger, or Suprematism.

II. It may be 'anecdotal'. The secret of the marvelous mobility of Daumier's and Lautrec's figures dwells in the fact that the various anatomical parts of a body are represented in spatial circumstances (positions) that are temporally various, disjunctive. For example, in Toulouse-Lautrec's lithograph of Miss Cissy Loftus, if one logically develops position A of the foot, one builds a body in position A corresponding to it. But the body is represented from knee up already in position A + a. The cinematic effect of joined motionless pictures is already established here! From hips to shoulders we can see A + a + a. The figure comes alive and kicking!

III. Between I and II lies primitive Italian futurism – such as in Balla's 'Man with Six Legs in Six Positions' – for II obtains its effect by retaining natural unity and anatomical correctness, while I, on the other hand, does this with purely elementary elements. III, although destroying naturalness, has not yet pressed forward to abstraction.

IV. The conflict of directions may also be of an ideographic kind. It was in this way that we have gained the pregnant characterizations of a Sharaku, for example. The secret of his extremely perfected strength of expression lies in the anatomical and *spatial disproportion* of the parts – in comparison with which, our I might be termed *temporal disproportion*.

[. . .]

Step by step, by a process of comparing each new image with the common denotation, power is accumulated behind a process that can be formally identified with that of logical deduction. The decision to release these ideas, as well as the method used, is already *intellectually* conceived.

The conventional *descriptive* form for film leads to the formal possibility of a kind of filmic reasoning. While the conventional film directs the *emotions*, this suggests an opportunity to encourage and direct the whole *thought process*, as well.

These two particular sequences of experiment were very much opposed by the majority of critics. Because they were understood as purely political. I would not attempt to deny that *this form is most suitable for the expression of ideologically pointed theses*, but it is a pity that the critics completely overlooked the purely filmic potentialities of this approach.

In these two experiments we have taken the first embryonic step towards a totally new form of film expression. Towards a purely intellectual film, freed from traditional limitations, achieving direct forms for ideas, systems, and concepts, without any need for transitions and paraphrases. We may yet have a

synthesis of art and science.

This would be the proper name for our new epoch in the field of art. This would be the final justification for Lenin's words, that 'the cinema is the most important of all the arts.'

29
STORM JAMESON (1891–1986)
FROM 'DOCUMENTS' 1937

Published in Fact *magazine (July 1937), the piece from which extracts are reproduced below represents Storm Jameson's commitment to continued experimentation with modern forms in the context of political and social awareness. [See IIIa 1]*

I believe we should do well to give up talking about proletarian literature and talk about socialist literature instead – and mean by it writing concerned with the lives of men and women in a world which is changing and being changed. A socialist must be intimately concerned with this change; he must be struggling continually to understand it. His writing must reflect his experience of it and his understanding of his experience. And since the change is worldwide, and is taking place on innumerable levels at once and all the time, the difficulty of attempting to write anything on the scale of *War and Peace* is so great as to make it unlikely that it will be written – yet. The difficulty excuses none of us for retreating into a world made artificially static by excluding from it all the factors of change and the rumour of the real world.

Literature concerned with change and the changing world is concerned with revolution, and with all the stages of revolutionary action.

[. . .]

The use of the term 'proletarian novel' suggests, quite falsely, that socialist literature ought to concern itself only or mainly with working-class life. In fact, a novel about

Lord Invernairn, written from full insight into what this man actually is doing, a novel which exposed him, laid him open, need not bring on to the stage a single one of the people who do not exist for him as human beings. It would still be socialist literature. The process of change, of decay, of growth, is taking place everywhere all the time: it does not matter where you open up the social body if you know what you are looking for.

This misconception is not the worst of it. The worst is a dreadful self-consciousness which seizes the middle-class writer who hears the command to sell all he has and write a proletarian novel. He discovers that he does not even know what the wife of a man earning two pounds a week wears, where she buys her food, what her kitchen looks like to her when she comes into it at six or seven in the morning. It has never happened to him to stand with his hands in greasy water at the sink, with a nagging pain in his back, and his clothes sticking to him. He (or she) actually has to take a look into the kitchen to know what it smells and looks like: at that he does not know as much as the woman's forefinger knows when it scrapes the black out of a crack in the table or the corner of a shelf.

The impulse that made him want to know is decent and defensible. If he happens to have been born and brought up in Kensington the chances are that he has never lifted the blind of his own kitchen at six in the morning, with thoughts in his mind of tumbled bed-clothes, dirty grates, and the ring of rust on the stove. But there is something very wrong when he has to contort himself into knots in order to get to know a worker, man or woman. What is wrong is in him, and he cannot blame on to his upbringing what is really a failure of his own will; it is still clenched on his idea of himself, given to him by that upbringing but now to be cast off as the first condition of growth. Too much of his energy runs away in an intense interest in and curiosity about his feelings. 'What things I am seeing for the first time! What smells I am enduring! There is the woman raking ashes with her hands and here I am watching her!' This self-centred habit is not peculiar to the middle-class writer (see R. M. Fox's *Smoky Crusade*), but it is natural to him. If, as a child, he had escaped from the nursery and been found in some Hoxton backyard he would have been bathed and disinfected and made conscious of having run an awful danger, much as though he had been visiting savages. The mental attitude persists. Breeding will out!

The first thing a socialist writer has to realize is that there is no value in the emotions, the spiritual writhings, started in him by the sight, smell, and touch of poverty. The emotions are no doubt unavoidable. There is no need to record them. Let him go and pour them down the drain.

[. . .]

He must not, he ought not to indulge himself in self-analysis, since that is to nail himself inside his own small ego at a moment when what is individual to each man is less real, less actual, than that which he shares with every other man – insecurity, the need to become a rebel for the sake of human dignity. What then should he do?

A task of the greatest value, urgent and not easy, is waiting to be done. George Orwell has begun on it in the first half of *The Road to Wigan Pier*. The instinct which drives a writer to go and see for himself may be sound. If a writer does not know, if his senses and imagination have not told him, what poverty smells like, he had better find out. Even if in the end he prefers to write about Invernairn or Krupp. But if he goes for his own sake, for some fancied spiritual advantage to be got from the experience, he had better stay at home: his presence in Wigan or Hoxton is either irrelevant or impudent. He must go for the sake of *the fact*, as a medical student carries out a dissection, and to equip himself, not to satisfy his conscience or to see what effect it has on him. His mind must remain cool; he must be able to give an objective report, neither superficial nor slickly dramatic. And, for pity's sake, don't let us have any 'slices of life' in the manner of the Naturalists of the 'eighties. In their determination to show life up they became as sentimental, as emotionally dishonest, as Miss So-and-so 'embosoming freely' with her readers in the fiction columns of the woman's magazines. For their own purposes they fictionalized reality as obtusely as she does.

The conditions for the growth of a socialist literature scarcely exist. We have to create them. We need documents, not, as the Naturalists needed them, to make their drab tuppeny-ha'penny dramas, but as charts, as timber for the fire some writer will light to-morrow morning. The detailed and accurate presentment, rather than the representation, of this moment, and this society. A new *Comédie Humaine* – offered to us without the unnecessary and distorting gloss of the writer's emotions and self-questionings. Writers should be willing to go and live for a long enough time at one of the points of departure of the new society. To go, if you like, into exile. Without feeling heroic, or even adventurous, or curious about their own spiritual reactions. Willing to sink themselves for the time, so that they become conduits for a feeling which is not personal, nor static.

[. . .]

The number of documents to be got is infinite. How are they to be presented? This is the crux. A journalist can observe and report. No writer is satisfied to write journalism, nor is this what is wanted – visits to the distressed areas in a motor-car. Nor must the experience, the knowledge waited for and lived through, be fictionalized, in the sense of making up a story or a novel on the basis of facts collected (e.g., *The Stars Look Down*, by Cronin). Perhaps the nearest equivalent of what is wanted exists already in another form in the documentary film. As the photographer does, so must the writer keep himself out of the picture while working ceaselessly to present the *fact* from a striking (poignant, ironic, penetrating, significant) angle. The narrative must be sharp, compressed, concrete. Dialogue must be short – a seizing of the significant, the revealing word. The emotion should spring directly from the fact. It must not be squeezed from it by the writer, running forward with a, 'When I saw this, I felt, I suffered, I rejoiced . . .' His job is not to tell us what he felt, but to be coldly and industriously presenting, arranging, selecting, discarding from the mass of his material to get the significant detail, which leaves no more to be said, and implies everything.

And for goodness' sake let us get some fun out of it. Nothing is less to our taste, and less realist, than the inspissated gloom of Naturalism. A novel by Ignazio Silone, *Fontamara*, offers itself as a model – this tragic, bitter story of a village is extremely funny, and sticks faster in the memory by it. Let us write decent straight English, too; not American telegraphese. Social documents are familiar in our literature. The sermons of preaching friars are still alive wherever the preacher threw in a scene that was under his eyes as he walked about – often a savage indictment of poverty created by greedy merchants and landlords.

For the sake of compression – the field to be covered is, after all, enormous – and for the sake of sharpness, much must be left out that a writer will be tempted to put in. 'Atmosphere', for one thing. It has been overdone, too – all those novels in which infinite pains have gone to the evocation of rain and moonlight, novels 'set' in Cumberland, in Sussex, in Paris and Patagonia. For another thing, the static analysis of feeling, and thought. No more peeling of the onion to strew the page with layer after layer. No stream of consciousness – that famous stream which we pretend to see flowing, as in the theatre we agree to pretend that the stream on the backcloth flows. No commentary – the document is a comment. No æsthetic, moral, or philosophic enquiry – that is, none which is not implicit.

[. . .]

Writers write to be read. If they are not read, by as many people as will do to keep them vigorously alive, they have failed *as writers*. People will listen even to what is disagreeable to them if the speaker's tone takes them by the ear. The Naturalists flung tear-sodden lumps of raw life in the public's face and complained because the public went home to amuse itself in its own way. There is a technical job to be done. It can't be done until the instruments have been made and improved, as astronomy had to wait on a lens. How to make people listen to what they don't want to hear. How not to bore the people who do want to hear. If they want to hear, you say, they'll take anything. But why the devil should they? Why should they be bored by what is nothing more or less than incompetence or amateurishness? It is not a question of setting out to be a best-seller – if that is what you want there are shorter and easier ways – but of learning a craft. Again the relevant comparison is with the documentary film. It takes a sharpened and disciplined mind to handle a mass of material in such a way that only the significant details emerge. We're confronted by the extreme difficulty of finding phrases which are at once compressed and highly suggestive. It's hardly a job for an amateur unless he happens to be a genius. When a genius arrives he can and will look after himself.

The isolation of writers from each other is almost as deadly as their isolation from the life of farmers, labourers, miners and the other men on whom the life of the nation depends. If something of this unnatural apartness can be broken down, by writers working together, by their coming into relation with their fellow-men and women, they may, between them, provide the conditions, the warmth, for a new literature. We have been attending the death-bed of an old one for some time; a birth is about due. It may actually be the birth of a great writer, and the documents we have collected, the activity we have stirred up, will form the conditions into which he is born. They will shape him and he will use them. A great writer has more than one father and mother, as well as more than one nurse.

One technical difficulty remains to be solved. The solution may turn up any day, in the course of the experiments going on all the time. This is the frightful difficulty of expressing, in such a way that they are at once seen to be intimately connected, the relations between things (men, acts) widely separated in space or in the social complex.

It has been done in poetry. At certain levels of the mind we see and feel connections which we know rationally in another way. In dreams things apparently distinct are seen to be related (but Surrealism is not the solution). We may stumble on the solution in the effort of trying to create the literary equivalent of the documentary film.

30
ADOLF HITLER (1889–1945)
FROM SPEECH INAUGURATING THE
'GREAT EXHIBITION OF MODERN ART', MUNICH 1937

The exhibition of 'Degenerate Art' was held in Munich in 1937 and featured works of the avant-garde as examples of corruption, insanity, degeneration and cultural bolshevism. The following extracts from Hitler's inaugural speech are taken from Ilse Falk's translation from Theories of Modern Art *(Herschel B. Chipp ed., 1968).*

[. . .]

Germany's collapse and general decline had been – as we know – not only economic or political, but probably even to a much greater extent, cultural. Moreover, this process could not be explained exclusively on the grounds of the lost war. Such catastrophes have very often afflicted peoples and states, only to provide an impetus to their purification and give rise to an inner elevation.

However, that flood of slime and ordure which the year 1918 belched forth into our lives was not a product of the lost war, but was only freed in its rush to the surface by that calamity. Through the defeat, an already thoroughly diseased body experienced the total impact of its inner decomposition. Now, after the collapse of the social, economic, and cultural patterns which continued to function in appearance only, the baseness already underlying them for a long time, triumphed, and indeed this was so in all strata of our life.

It is obvious that, due to its nature, the economic decline was felt most strongly, since the masses always become most urgently conscious of these conditions. In comparison to this economic decline, the political collapse was either flatly denied or at least not recognized by a great number of Germans, while the cultural collapse was neither seen nor understood by the vast majority of our people. [. . .]

To begin with:

1. The circle of those who are consciously occupied with cultural matters is by nature not nearly as large as the number of those who have to deal with economic matters.
2. On these cultural grounds, more than on any others, Judaism had taken possession of those means and institutions of communication which form, and thus finally rule over public opinion. Judaism was very clever indeed, especially in employing its position in the press with the help of so-called art criticism and succeeding not only in confusing the natural concepts about the nature and scope of art as well as its goals, but above all in undermining and destroying the general wholesome feeling in this domain. [. . .]

Art, on the one hand, was defined as nothing but an international communal experience, thus killing altogether any understanding of its integral relationship with an ethnic group. On the other hand its relationship to time was stressed, that is: There was no longer any art of peoples or even of races, but only an art of the times. According to this theory, therefore, Greek art was not formed by the Greeks, but by a certain period which formed it as their expression. The same, naturally, was true of Roman art, which, for the same reasons, coincided only by accident with the rise of the Roman empire. Again in the same way the more recent art epochs of humanity have not been created by the Arabs, Germans, Italians, French, etc., but are only appearances conditioned by time. Therefore today no German or French or Japanese or Chinese art exists, but plainly and simply only a 'modern art'. Consequently, art as such is not only completely isolated from its ethnic origins, but it is the expression of a certain vintage which is characterized today by the word 'modern', and thus, of course, will be un-modern tomorrow, since it will be outdated.

According to such a theory, as a matter of fact, art and art activities are lumped together with the handiwork of our modern tailor shops and fashion industries. And to be sure, following the maxim: Every year something new. One day Impressionism, then Futurism, Cubism, maybe even Dadaism, etc. A further result is that even for the most insane and inane monstrosities thousands of catchwords to label them will have to be found, and have indeed been found. If it weren't so sad in one sense, it would almost be a lot of fun to list all the slogans and clichés with which the so-called 'art initiates' have described and explained their wretched products in recent years. [. . .]

Until the moment when National-Socialism took power, there existed in Germany a so called 'modern art', that is, to be sure, almost every year another one, as the very meaning of this word indicates. National-Socialist Germany, however, wants again a 'German Art', and this art shall and will be of eternal value, as are all truly creative values of a people. Should this art, however, again lack this eternal value for our people, then indeed it will mean that it also has no higher value today. [. . .]

Art can in no way be a fashion. As little as the character and the blood of our people will change, so much will art have to lose its mortal character and replace it with worthy images expressing the life-course of our people steadily unfolding growth of its creations. Cubism, Dadaism, Futurism, Impressionism, etc., have nothing to do with our German people. For these concepts are neither old nor modern, but are only the artifactitious stammerings of men to whom God has denied the grace of a truly artistic talent, and in its place has awarded them the gift of jabbering or deception. I will therefore confess now, in this very hour, that I have come to the final inalterable decision to clean house, just as I have done in the domain of political confusion, and from now on rid the German art life of its phrase-mongering.

'Works of art' which cannot be understood in themselves but, for the justification of their existence, need those bombastic instructions for their use, finally reaching that intimidated soul, who is patiently willing to accept such stupid or impertinent nonsense – these works of art from now on will no find their way to the German people.

All those catchwords: 'inner experience', 'strong state of mind', 'forceful will', 'emotions pregnant with the future', 'heroic attitude', 'meaningful empathy', 'experienced order of the times', 'original primitivism', etc. – all these dumb, mendacious excuses, this claptrap or jabbering will no longer be accepted as excuses or even recommendations for worthless, integrally unskilled products. *Whether or not anybody has a strong will or an inner experience, he will have to prove through his work, and not through gibberish. And anyhow, we are all much more interested in quality than in the so-called will.* [. . .]

I have observed among the pictures submitted here, quite a few paintings which make one actually come to the conclusion that the eye shows things differently to certain human beings than the way they really are, that is, that there really are men who see the present population of our nation only as rotten cretins; who, on principle, see meadows blue, skies green, clouds sulphur yellow, and so on, or, as they say, experience them as such. I do not want to enter into an argument here about the question of whether the persons concerned really do or do not see or feel in such a way; but, in the name of the German people, I want to forbid these pitiful misfortunates who quite obviously suffer from an eye disease, to try vehemently to foist these products of their misinterpretation upon the age we live in, or even to wish to present them as 'Art'.

No, here there are only two possibilities: Either these so-called 'artists' really see things this way and therefore believe in what they depict; then we would have to examine their eyesight-deformation to see if it is the product of a mechanical failure or of inheritance. In the first case, these unfortunates can only be pitied; in the second case, they would be the object of great interest to the Ministry of Interior of the Reich which would then have to take up the question of whether further inheritance of such gruesome malfunctioning of the eyes cannot at least be checked. If, on the other hand, they themselves do not believe in the reality of such impressions but try to harass the nation with this humbug for other reasons, then such an attempt falls within the jurisdiction of the penal law. [. . .]

For the artist does not create for the artist, but just like every one else he creates for the people.

And we will see to it that from now on the people will once again be called upon to be the judges of their own art. . . .

I do not want anybody to have false illusions: National-Socialism has made it its primary task to rid the German Reich, and thus, the German people and its life of all those influences which are fatal and ruinous to its existence. And although this purge cannot be accomplished in one day, I do not want to leave the shadow of a doubt as to the fact that sooner or later the hour of liquidation will strike for those phenomena which have participated in this corruption.

But with the opening of this exhibition the end of German art foolishness and the end of the destruction of its culture will have begun.

From now on we will wage an unrelenting war of purification against the last elements of putrefaction in our culture. However, should there be someone among those elements who still believes that he is destined to higher ranks, then he has had ample time in these four years to prove it. For us, in any case, these four years are long enough to reach a final judgment. From now on – I assure you – all those cliques of babblers, dilettantes and art crooks which lend support to each other and are therefore able to survive, will be eliminated and abolished. For our sake those prehistoric stone-age culture-vultures and art stammerers may just as well retreat to the caves of their ancestors to adorn them with their primitive international scribblings.

But the House for German Art in Munich has been built by the German people for their own German art. [. . .]

Many of our young artists will now recognize in what is being offered them which road they should take; but perhaps they will also gain a new impetus from the greatness of the times in which we all live, and from which we take courage and, above all, retain the courage to produce a really diligent and, thus, in the final run, competent work.

AND WHEN ONCE AGAIN IN THIS REALM OF ART THE HOLY CONSCIENTIOUSNESS WILL HAVE REGAINED ITS FULL RIGHTS, THEN, I HAVE NO DOUBT, THE ALMIGHTY WILL ELEVATE A FEW FROM THIS MULTITUDE OF DECENT CREATORS OF ART INTO THE STARRY SKIES OF THE IMMORTAL, DIVINELY INSPIRED ARTISTS OF THE GREAT PAST. FOR WE DO NOT BELIEVE THAT WITH THE GREAT MEN OF THE CENTURIES GONE BY, THE TIME FOR THE CREATIVE POWER OF A FEW BLESSED MEN HAS COME TO AN END, NOR THAT THE CREATIVE POWER OF A COLLECTIVE BROAD MASS WILL TAKE ITS PLACE IN FUTURE. NO! WE BELIEVE THAT ESPECIALLY TODAY, WHEN IN SO MANY REALMS THE HIGHEST ACHIEVEMENTS ARE BEING ACCOMPLISHED, THAT ALSO IN THE REALM OF ART THE HIGHEST VALUE OF A PERSONALITY AS AN INDIVIDUAL WILL MAKE A TRIUMPHANT REAPPEARANCE.

I CAN THEREFORE EXPRESS NO OTHER WISH AT THIS MOMENT THAN THE NEW HOUSE BE PRIVILEGED TO REVEAL AGAIN TO THE GERMAN PEOPLE A NUMBER OF WORKS BY GREAT ARTISTS IN THESE HALLS DURING THE COMING CENTURIES, AND THUS CONTRIBUTE NOT ONLY TO THE GLORY OF THIS TRUE CITY OF ART, BUT ALSO TO THE HONOR AND PRESTIGE OF THE ENTIRE GERMAN NATION.

I HEREWITH DECLARE THE GREAT EXHIBITION OF GERMAN ART 1937 IN MUNICH OPENED!

31
WALTER BENJAMIN (1892–1940)
FROM 'SURREALISM:
THE LAST SNAPSHOT OF THE EUROPEAN INTELLIGENTSIA' 1929;
FROM 'THE WORK OF ART IN THE AGE OF MECHANICAL REPRODUCTION' 1936

German writer, theorist and critic who lived mostly in Germany and, after 1933, in France. Benjamin occupies a special position in the Marxist tradition of critical writing, combining a materialist position with a mystical/theological one, heavily influenced by Judaism. His writing is concerned with theories of language, literature and culture, as well as the tasks of historical materialism. Never an official member of the Communist Party, or an established academic, he always remained a perceptive 'outsider'. A close friend and collaborator of some of the central figures of the German Marxist intelligentsia, including Gershom Scholem, Theodor Adorno, Ernst Bloch and Bertolt Brecht, Benjamin was actively involved in theoretical debates on the relationship between Marxism and the avant-garde, while forging his own, and in some cases, contradictory, path of cultural critique. His early study of German Baroque theatre, The Origin of German Tragic Drama *(1928; 1977) is now considered a landmark in the development of a modern theory of allegory, while his essays on various aspects of modern culture and art are insightful and indispensable guides to an era in modern European thought which could still draw hope from the experience of Modernism. His ambitious* Arcades Project, *a case study of*

Paris in the nineteenth century, left unfinished at the time of his suicide in 1940 when fleeing from
the Nazis in Spain, was meant as the synthesis of his critical (and historical materialist) concerns.
Three pieces from that study have been collected under the title Charles Baudelaire: A Lyric Poet
in the Era of High Capitalism *(1973). Reproduced below are extracts from the 1929 essay on*
Surrealism (translated by Edmund Jephcott and Kingsley Shorter for the collection One-Way Street
and Other Writings, *1978). They are followed by extracts from an influential essay originally*
published in 1936 (translated by Harry Zohn for the collection Illuminations, *edited by Hannah*
Arendt, 1968). [See Ib5, IIb 13]

Intellectual currents can generate a sufficient head of water for the critic to install his
power station on them. The necessary gradient, in the case of Surrealism, is produced
by the difference in intellectual level between France and Germany. What sprang up
in 1919 in France in a small circle of literati – we shall give the most important names
at once: André Breton, Louis Aragon, Philippe Soupault, Robert Desnos, Paul Eluard
– may have been a meagre stream, fed on the damp boredom of post-war Europe and
the last trickle of French decadence. The know-alls who even today have not advanced
beyond the 'authentic origins' of the movement, and even now have nothing to say
about it except that yet another clique of literati is here mystifying the honourable
public, are a little like a gathering of experts at a spring who, after lengthy deliberation,
arrive at the conviction that this paltry stream will never drive turbines.

The German observer is not standing at the head of the stream. That is his opportunity. He is in the valley. He can gauge the energies of the movement. As a German
he is long acquainted with the crisis of the intelligentsia, or, more precisely, with that
of the humanistic concept of freedom; and he knows how frantic is the determination
that has awakened in the movement to go beyond the stage of eternal discussion and,
at any price, to reach a decision; he has had direct experience of its highly exposed
position between an anarchistic *fronde* and a revolutionary discipline, and so has no
excuse for taking the movement for the 'artistic', 'poetic' one it superficially appears. If
it was such at the outset, it was, however, precisely at the outset that Breton declared his
intention of breaking with a praxis that presents the public with the literary precipitate
of a certain form of existence while withholding that existence itself. Stated more
briefly and dialectically, this means that the sphere of poetry was here explored from
within by a closely knit circle of people pushing the 'poetic life' to the utmost limits of
possibility. And they can be taken at their word when they assert that Rimbaud's *Saison*
en enfer no longer had any secrets for them. For this book is indeed the first document
of the movement (in recent times; earlier precursors will be discussed later). Can the
point at issue be more definitively and incisively presented than by Rimbaud himself
in his personal copy of the book? In the margin, beside the passage 'on the silk of the
seas and the arctic flowers', he later wrote, 'There's no such thing.'

In just how inconspicuous and peripheral a substance the dialectical kernel that later
grew into Surrealism was originally embedded, was shown by Aragon in 1924 – at a
time when its development could not yet be foreseen – in his *Vague de rêves*. Today it
can be foreseen. For there is no doubt that the heroic phase, whose catalogue of heroes
Aragon left us in that work, is over. There is always, in such movements, a moment

when the original tension of the secret society must either explode in a matter-of-fact, profane struggle for power and domination, or decay as a public demonstration and be transformed. Surrealism is in this phase of transformation at present. But at the time when it broke over its founders as an inspiring dream wave, it seemed the most integral, conclusive, absolute of movements. Everything with which it came into contact was integrated. Life only seemed worth living where the threshold between waking and sleeping was worn away in everyone as by the steps of multitudinous images flooding back and forth, language only seemed itself where sound and image, image and sound interpenetrated with automatic precision and such felicity that no chink was left for the penny-in-the-slot called 'meaning'. Image and language take precedence.

[. . .]

Not only before meaning. Also before the self. In the world's structure dream loosens individuality like a bad tooth. This loosening of the self by intoxication is, at the same time, precisely the fruitful, living experience that allowed these people to step outside the domain of intoxication. This is not the place to give an exact definition of Surrealist experience. But anyone who has perceived that the writings of this circle are not literature but something else – demonstrations, watchwords, documents, bluffs, forgeries if you will, but at any rate not literature – will also know, for the same reason, that the writings are concerned literally with experiences, not with theories and still less with phantasms. And these experiences are by no means limited to dreams, hours of hashish eating, or opium smoking.

[. . .]

But the true, creative overcoming of religious illumination certainly does not lie in narcotics. It resides in a *profane illumination*, a materialistic, anthropological inspiration, to which hashish, opium, or whatever else can give an introductory lesson. (But a dangerous one; and the religious lesson is stricter.) This profane illumination did not always find the Surrealists equal to it, or to themselves, and the very writings that proclaim it most powerfully, Aragon's incomparable *Paysan de Paris* and Breton's *Nadja*, show very disturbing symptoms of deficiency.

[. . .]

In other respects Breton's book illustrates well a number of the basic characteristics of this 'profane illumination'. He calls *Nadja* 'a book with a banging door'. (In Moscow I lived in a hotel in which almost all the rooms were occupied by Tibetan lamas who had come to Moscow for a congress of Buddhist churches. I was struck by the number of doors in the corridors that were always left ajar. What had at first seemed accidental began to be disturbing. I found out that in these rooms lived members of a sect who had sworn never to occupy closed rooms. The shock I had then must be felt by the reader of *Nadja*.) To live in a glass house is a revolutionary virtue par excellence. It is also an intoxication, a moral exhibitionism, that we badly need.

[. . .]

The lady, in esoteric love, matters least. So, too, for Breton. He is closer to the things that Nadja is close to than to her. What are these things? Nothing could reveal more about Surrealism than their canon. Where shall I begin? He can boast an extraordinary discovery. He was the first to perceive the revolutionary energies that appear in the 'outmoded', in the first iron constructions, the first factory buildings, the earliest photos, the objects that have begun to be extinct, grand pianos, the dresses of five years ago, fashionable restaurants when the vogue has begun to ebb from them. The relation of these things to revolution – no one can have a more exact concept of it than these authors. No one before these visionaries and augurs perceived how destitution – not only social but architectonic, the poverty of interiors, enslaved and enslaving objects – can be suddenly transformed into revolutionary nihilism.

[. . .]

The Surrealists' Paris, too, is a 'little universe'. That is to say, in the larger one, the cosmos, things look no different. There, too, are crossroads where ghostly signals flash from the traffic, and inconceivable analogies and connections between events are the order of the day. It is the region from which the lyric poetry of Surrealism reports. And this must be noted if only to counter the obligatory misunderstanding of *l'art pour l'art*. For art's sake was scarcely ever to be taken literally; it was almost always a flag under which sailed a cargo that could not be declared because it still lacked a name. This is the moment to embark on a work that would illuminate as has no other the crisis of the arts that we are witnessing: a history of esoteric poetry.

[. . .]

The last page would have to show an X-ray picture of Surrealism. Breton indicates in his *Introduction au discours sur le peu de réalité* how the philosophical realism of the Middle Ages was the basis of poetic experience. This realism, however – that is, the belief in a real, separate existence of concepts whether outside or inside things – has always very quickly crossed over from the logical realm of ideas to the magical realm of words. And it is as magical experiments with words, not as artistic dabbling, that we must understand the passionate phonetic and graphical transformational games that have run through the whole literature of the avant-garde for the past fifteen years, whether it is called Futurism, Dadaism, or Surrealism. How slogans, magic formulas, and concepts are here intermingled is shown by the following words of Apollinaire's from his last manifesto, *L'esprit nouveau et les poètes*. He says, in 1918: 'For the speed and simplicity with which we have all become used to referring by a single word to such complex entities as a crowd, a nation, the universe, there is no modern equivalent in literature. But today's writers fill this gap; their synthetic works create new realities the plastic manifestations of which are just as complex as those referred to by the words standing for collectives.'

[. . .]

'The thought of all human activity makes me laugh.' This utterance of Aragon's shows very clearly the path Surrealism had to follow from its origins to its po-liticization. In his excellent essay '*La révolution et les intellectuels*', Pierre Naville, who originally belonged to this group, rightly called this development dialectical. In the transformation of a highly contemplative attitude into revolutionary opposition, the hostility of the bourgeoisie toward every manifestation of radical intellectual freedom played a leading part. This hostility pushed Surrealism to the left.

[. . .]

Characteristic of this whole left-wing bourgeois position is its irremediable coupling of idealistic morality with political practice. Only in contrast to the helpless compromises of 'sentiment' are certain central features of Surrealism, indeed of the Surrealist tradition, to be understood. Little has happened so far to promote this understanding. The seduction was too great to regard the Satanism of a Rimbaud and a Lautréamont as a pendant to art for art's sake in an inventory of snobbery. If, however, one resolves to open up this romantic dummy, one finds something usable inside. One finds the cult of evil as a political device, however romantic, to disinfect and isolate against all moralizing dilettantism. Convinced of this, and coming across the scenario of a horror play by Breton that centres about a violation of children, one might perhaps go back a few decades. Between 1865 and 1875 a number of great anarchists, without knowing of one another, worked on their infernal machines. And the astonishing thing is that independently of one another they set its clock at exactly the same hour, and forty years later in Western Europe the writings of Dostoyevsky, Rimbaud, and Lautréamont exploded at the same time. One might, to be more exact, select from Dostoyevsky's entire work the one episode that was actually not published until about 1915, 'Stavrogin's Confession' from *The Possessed*. This chapter, which touches very closely on the third canto of the *Chants de Maldoror*, contains a justification of evil in which certain motifs of Surrealism are more powerfully expressed than by any of its present spokesmen. For Stavrogin is a Surrealist *avant la lettre*. No one else understood, as he did, how naïve is the view of the Philistines that goodness, for all the manly virtue of those who practise it, is God-inspired; whereas evil stems entirely from our spontaneity, and in it we are independent and self-sufficient beings.

[. . .]

The pitch of tension that enabled the poets under discussion to achieve at a distance their astonishing effects is documented quite scurrilously in the letter Isidore Ducasse addressed to his publisher on October 23, 1869, in an attempt to make his poetry look acceptable. He places himself in the line of descent from Mickiewicz, Milton, Southey, Alfred de Musset, Baudelaire, and says: 'Of course, I somewhat swelled the note to bring something new into this literature that, after all, only sings of despair in order to depress the reader and thus make him long all the more intensely for goodness as a remedy. So that in the end one really sings only of goodness, only the method is more philosophical and less naïve than that of the old school, of which only Victor Hugo and a few others are still alive.'

[. . .]

On the other hand, and happily, a similar attempt in the case of Rimbaud was successful, and it is the achievement of Marcel Coulon to have defended the poet's true image against the Catholic usurpation by Claudel and Berrichon. Rimbaud is indeed a Catholic, but he is one, by his own account, in the most wretched part of himself, which he does not tire of denouncing and consigning to his own and everyone's hatred, his own and everyone's contempt: the part that forces him to confess that he does not understand revolt. But that is the concession of a communard dissatisfied with his own contribution who, by the time he turned his back on poetry, had long since – in his earliest work – taken leave of religion. 'Hatred, to you I have entrusted my treasure', he writes in the *Saison en enfer*. This is another dictum around which a poetics of Surrealism might grow like a climbing plant, to sink its roots deeper than the theory of 'surprised' creation originated by Apollinaire, to the depth of the insights of Poe.

Since Bakunin, Europe has lacked a radical concept of freedom. The Surrealists have one. They are the first to liquidate the sclerotic liberal-moral-humanistic ideal of freedom, because they are convinced that 'freedom, which on this earth can only be bought with a thousand of the hardest sacrifices, must be enjoyed unrestrictedly in its fullness without any kind of pragmatic calculation, as long as it lasts.' And this proves to them that 'mankind's struggle for liberation in its simplest revolutionary form (which, however, is liberation in every respect), remains the only cause worth serving.' But are they successful in welding this experience of freedom to the other revolutionary experience that we have to acknowledge because it has been ours, the constructive, dictatorial side of revolution? In short, have they bound revolt to revolution?

[. . .]

To win the energies of intoxication for the revolution – this is the project about which Surrealism circles in all its books and enterprises. This it may call its most particular task. For them it is not enough that, as we know, an ecstatic component lives in every revolutionary act. This component is identical with the anarchic. But to place the accent exclusively on it would be to subordinate the methodical and disciplinary preparation for revolution entirely to a praxis oscillating between fitness exercises and celebration in advance. Added to this is an inadequate, undialectical conception of the nature of intoxication. The aesthetic of the painter, the poet, *en état de surprise*, of art as the reaction of one surprised, is enmeshed in a number of pernicious romantic prejudices. Any serious exploration of occult, surrealistic, phantasmagoric gifts and phenomena presupposes a dialectical intertwinement to which a romantic turn of mind is impervious. For histrionic or fanatical stress on the mysterious side of the mysterious takes us no further; we penetrate the mystery only to the degree that we recognize it in the everyday world, by virtue of a dialectical optic that perceives the everyday as impenetrable, the impenetrable as everyday.

[. . .]

The reader, the thinker, the loiterer, the *flâneur*, are types of illuminati just as much as the opium eater, the dreamer, the ecstatic. And more profane. Not to mention that most terrible drug – ourselves – which we take in solitude.

'To win the energies of intoxication for the revolution' – in other words, poetic politics? 'We have tried that beverage. Anything, rather than that!' Well, it will interest you all the more how much an excursion into poetry clarifies things. For what is the programme of the bourgeois parties? A bad poem on springtime, filled to bursting with metaphors. The socialist sees that 'finer future of our children and grandchildren' in a condition in which all act 'as if they were angels', and everyone has as much 'as if he were rich', and everyone lives 'as if he were free'. Of angels, wealth, freedom, not a trace. These are mere images. And the stock imagery of these poets of the social-democratic associations? Their *gradus ad parnassum*? Optimism.

[. . .]

Surrealism has come ever closer to the Communist answer. And that means pessimism all along the line. Absolutely. Mistrust in the fate of literature, mistrust in the fate of freedom, mistrust in the fate of European humanity, but three times mistrust in all reconciliation: between classes, between nations, between individuals.

[. . .]

For to organize pessimism means nothing other than to expel moral metaphor from politics and to discover in political action a sphere reserved one hundred percent for images. This image sphere, however, can no longer be measured out by contemplation. If it is the double task of the revolutionary intelligentsia to overthrow the intellectual predominance of the bourgeoisie and to make contact with the proletarian masses, the intelligentsia has failed almost entirely in the second part of this task because it can no longer be performed contemplatively. And yet this has hindered hardly anybody from approaching it again and again as if it could, and calling for proletarian poets, thinkers, and artists. To counter this, Trotsky had to point out – as early as *Literature and Revolution* – that such artists would only emerge from a victorious revolution. In reality it is far less a matter of making the artist of bourgeois origin into a master of 'proletarian art' than of deploying him, even at the expense of his artistic activity, at important points in this sphere of imagery. Indeed, might not perhaps the interruption of his 'artistic career' be an essential part of his new function?

The jokes he tells are the better for it. And he tells them better. For in the joke, too, in invective, in misunderstanding, in all cases where an action puts forth its own image and exists, absorbing and consuming it, where nearness looks with its own eyes, the long-sought image sphere is opened, the world of universal and integral actualities, where the 'best room' is missing the sphere, in a word, in which political materialism and physical nature share the inner man, the psyche, the individual, or whatever else we wish to throw to them, with dialectical justice, so that no limb remains unrent. Nevertheless – indeed, precisely after such dialectical annihilation – this will still be a sphere of images and, more concretely, of bodies. For it must in the end be admitted: metaphysical materialism, of the brand of Vogt and Bukharin, as is attested by the experience of the Surrealists, and earlier of Hegel, Georg Büchner, Nietzsche, and Rimbaud, cannot lead without rupture to anthropological materialism. There is a residue. The collective is a body, too. And the *physis* that is being organized for it in technology can, through all its political and factual reality, only be produced in that image sphere to which profane illumination initiates us. Only when in technology body and image so interpenetrate that all revolutionary tension becomes bodily collective innervation, and all the bodily innervations of the collective become revolutionary discharge, has reality transcended itself to the extent demanded by the *Communist Manifesto*. For the moment, only the Surrealists have understood its present commands. They exchange, to a man, the play of human features for the face of an alarm clock that in each minute rings for sixty seconds.

The Work of Art in the Age of Mechanical Reproduction

I.

[. . .] In principle a work of art has always been reproducible. Man-made artifacts could always be imitated by men. Replicas were made by pupils in practice of their craft, by masters for diffusing their works, and, finally, by third parties in the pursuit of gain. Mechanical reproduction of a work of art, however, represents something new. Historically, it advanced intermittently and in leaps at long intervals, but with accelerated intensity. The Greeks knew only two procedures of technically reproducing works of art: founding and stamping. Bronzes, terra cottas, and coins were the only art works which they could produce in quantity. All others were unique and could not be mechanically reproduced. With the woodcut graphic art became mechanically reproducible for the first time, long before script became reproducible by print. The enormous changes which printing, the mechanical reproduction of writing, has brought about in literature are a familiar story. However, within the phenomenon which we are here examining from the perspective of world history, print is merely a special, though particularly important, case. During the Middle Ages engraving and etching were added to the woodcut; at the beginning of the nineteenth century lithography made its appearance.

With lithography the technique of reproduction reached an essentially new stage. This much more direct process was distinguished by the tracing of the design on a stone rather than its incision on a block of wood or its etching on a copperplate and permitted graphic art for the first time to put its products on the market, not only in large numbers as hitherto, but also in daily changing forms. Lithography enabled graphic art to illustrate everyday life, and it began to keep pace with printing. But only a few decades after its invention, lithography was surpassed by photography. For the first time in the process of pictorial reproduction, photography freed the hand of the most important artistic functions which henceforth devolved only upon the eye looking into a lens. Since the eye perceives more swiftly than the hand can draw, the process of pictorial reproduction was accelerated so enormously that it could keep pace with speech. A film operator shooting a scene in the studio captures the images at the speed of an actor's speech. Just as lithography virtually implied the illustrated newspaper, so did photography foreshadow the sound film. The technical reproduction of sound was tackled at the end of the last century. These convergent endeavours made predictable a situation which Paul Valéry pointed up in this sentence: 'Just as water, gas, and electricity are brought into our houses from far off to satisfy our needs in response to a minimal effort, so we shall be supplied with visual or auditory images, which will appear and disappear at a simple movement of the hand, hardly more than a sign'. Around 1900 technical reproduction had reached a standard that not only permitted it to reproduce all transmitted works of art and thus to cause the most profound change in their impact upon the public; it also had captured a place of its own among the artistic processes. For the study of this standard nothing is more revealing than the nature of the repercussions that these two different manifestations – the reproduction of works of art and the art of the film – have had on art in its traditional form.

II.

Even the most perfect reproduction of a work of art is lacking in one element: its presence in time and space, its unique existence at the place where it happens to be. This unique existence of the work of art determined the history to which it was subject throughout the time of its existence. This includes the changes which it may have suffered in physical condition over the years as well as the various changes in its ownership. The traces of the first can be revealed only by chemical or physical analyses which it is impossible to perform on a reproduction; changes of ownership are subject to a tradition which must be traced from the situation of the original.

The presence of the original is the prerequisite to the concept of authenticity. Chemical analyses of the patina of a bronze can help to establish this, as does the proof that a given manuscript of the Middle Ages stems from an archive of the fifteenth century. The whole sphere of authenticity is outside technical – and, of course, not only technical – reproducibility. Confronted with its manual reproduction, which was usually branded as a forgery, the original preserved all its authority; not so *vis à vis* technical reproduction. The reason is twofold. First, process reproduction is more independent of the original than manual reproduction. For example, in photography, process reproduction can bring out those aspects of the original that are unattainable to the naked eye yet accessible to the lens, which is adjustable and chooses its angle at will. And photographic reproduction, with the aid of certain processes, such as enlargement or slow motion, can capture images which escape natural vision. Secondly, technical reproduction can put the copy of the original into situations which would be out of reach for the original itself. Above all, it enables the original to meet the beholder halfway, be it in the form of a photograph or a phonograph record. The cathedral leaves its locale to be received in the studio of a lover of art; the choral production, performed in an auditorium or in the open air, resounds in the drawing room.

The situations into which the product of mechanical reproduction can be brought may not touch the actual work of art, yet the quality of its presence is always depreciated. This holds not only for the art work but also, for instance, for a landscape which passes in review before the spectator in a movie. In the case of the art object, a most sensitive nucleus – namely, its authenticity – is interfered with whereas no natural object is vulnerable on that score. The authenticity of a thing is the essence of all that is transmissible from its beginning, ranging from its substantive duration to its testimony to the history which it has experienced. Since the historical testimony rests on the authenticity, the former, too, is jeopardized by reproduction when substantive duration ceases to matter. And what is really jeopardized when the historical testimony is affected is the authority of the object.

One might subsume the eliminated element in the term 'aura' and go on to say: that which withers in the age of mechanical reproduction is the aura of the work of art. This is a symptomatic process whose significance points beyond the realm of art. One might generalize by saying: the technique of reproduction detaches the reproduced object from the domain of tradition. By making many reproductions it substitutes a plurality of copies for a unique existence. And in permitting the reproduction to meet the beholder or listener in his own particular situation, it reactivates the object reproduced. These two processes lead to a tremendous shattering of tradition which is the obverse of the contemporary crisis and renewal of mankind. Both processes are intimately connected with the contemporary mass movements. Their most powerful agent is the film. Its social significance, particularly in its most positive form, is inconceivable without its destructive, cathartic aspect, that is, the liquidation of the traditional value of the cultural heritage. This phenomenon is most palpable in the great historical films. It extends to ever new positions.

[. . .]

IV.

The uniqueness of a work of art is inseparable from its being imbedded in the fabric of tradition. This tradition itself is thoroughly alive and extremely changeable. An ancient statue of Venus, for example, stood in a different traditional context with the Greeks, who made it an object of veneration, than with the clerics of the Middle Ages, who viewed it as an ominous idol. Both of them, however, were equally confronted with its uniqueness, that is, its aura. Originally the contextual integration of art in tradition found its expression in the cult. We know that the earliest art works originated in the service of a ritual – first the magical, then the religious kind. It is significant that the existence of the work of art with reference to its aura is never entirely separated from its ritual function. In other words, the unique value of the 'authentic' work of art has its basis in ritual, the location of its original use value. This ritualistic basis, however remote, is still recognizable as secularized ritual even in the most profane forms of the cult of beauty. The secular cult of beauty, developed during the Renaissance and prevailing for three centuries, clearly showed that ritualistic basis in its decline and the first deep crisis which befell it. With the advent of the first truly revolutionary means of reproduction, photography, simultaneously with the rise of socialism, art sensed the approaching crisis which has become evident a century later. At the time, art reacted with the doctrine of *l'art pour l'art*, that is, with a theology of art. This gave rise to what might be called a negative theology in the form of the idea of 'pure' art, which not only denied any social function of art but also any categorizing by subject matter. (In poetry, Mallarmé was the first to take this position.)

An analysis of art in the age of mechanical reproduction must do justice to these relationships, for they lead us to an all-important insight: for the first time in world history, mechanical reproduction emancipates the work of art from its parasitical dependence on ritual. To an ever greater degree the work of art reproduced becomes the work of art designed for reproducibility. From a photographic negative, for example, one can make any number of prints; to ask for the 'authentic' print makes no sense. But the instant the criterion of authenticity ceases to be applicable to artistic production, the total function of art is reversed. Instead of being based on ritual, it begins to be based on another practice – politics.

V.

Works of art are received and valued on different planes. Two polar types stand out: with one, the accent is on the cult value; with the other, on the exhibition value of the work. Artistic production begins with ceremonial objects destined to serve in a cult. One may assume that what mattered was their existence, not their being on view. The elk portrayed by the man of the Stone Age on the walls of his cave was an instrument of magic.

[. . .]

With the different methods of technical reproduction of a work of art, its fitness for exhibition increased to such an extent that the quantitative shift between its two poles turned into a qualitative transformation of its nature. This is comparable to the situation of the work of art in prehistoric times when, by the absolute emphasis on its cult value, it was, first and foremost, an instrument of magic. Only later did it come to be recognized as a work of art. In the same way today, by the absolute emphasis on its exhibition value the work of art becomes a creation with entirely new functions, among which the one we are conscious of, the artistic function, later may be recognized as incidental. This much is certain: today photography and the film are the most serviceable exemplifications of this new function.

VI.

In photography, exhibition value begins to displace cult value all along the line. But cult value does not give way without resistance. It retires into an ultimate retrenchment: the human countenance. It is no accident that the portrait was the focal point of early photography. The cult of remembrance of loved ones, absent or dead, offers a last refuge for the cult value of the picture. For the last time the aura emanates from the early photographs in the fleeting expression of a human face. This is what constitutes their melancholy, incomparable beauty. But as man withdraws from the photographic image, the exhibition value for the first time shows its superiority to the ritual value. To have pinpointed this new stage constitutes the incomparable significance of Atget, who, around 1900, took photographs of deserted Paris streets.

[. . .]

XII.

Mechanical reproduction of art changes the reaction of the masses toward art. The reactionary attitude toward a Picasso painting changes into the progressive reaction toward a Chaplin movie. The progressive reaction is characterized by the direct, intimate fusion of visual and emotional enjoyment with the orientation of the expert. Such fusion is of great social significance. The greater the decrease in the social significance of an art form, the sharper the distinction between criticism and enjoyment by the public. The conventional is uncritically enjoyed, and the truly new is criticized with aversion. With regard to the screen, the critical and the receptive attitudes of the public coincide. The decisive reason for this is that individual reactions are predetermined by the mass audience response they are about to produce, and this is nowhere more pronounced than in the film. The moment these responses become manifest they control each other. Again, the comparison with painting is fruitful. A painting has always had an excellent chance to be viewed by one person or by a few. The simultaneous contemplation of paintings by a large public, such as developed in the nineteenth century, is an early symptom of the crisis of painting, a crisis which was by no means occasioned exclusively by photography but rather in a relatively independent manner by the appeal of art works to the masses.

Painting simply is in no position to present an object for simultaneous collective experience, as it was possible for architecture at all times, for the epic poem in the past, and for the movie today. Although this circumstance in itself should not lead one to conclusions about the social role of painting, it does constitute a serious threat as soon as painting, under special conditions and, as it were, against its nature, is confronted directly by the masses. In the churches and monasteries of the Middle Ages and at the princely courts up to the end of the eighteenth century, a collective reception of paintings did not occur simultaneously, but by graduated and hierarchized mediation. The change that has come about is an expression of the particular conflict in which painting was implicated by the mechanical reproducibility of paintings. Although paintings began to be publicly exhibited in galleries and salons, there was no way for the masses to organize and control themselves in their reception. Thus the same public which responds in a progressive manner toward a grotesque film is bound to respond in a reactionary manner to surrealism.

[. . .]

XV.

The mass is a matrix from which all traditional behaviour toward works of art issues today in a new form. Quantity has been transmuted into quality. The greatly increased mass of participants has produced a change in the mode of participation. The fact that the new mode of participation first appeared in a disreputable form must not confuse the spectator. Yet some people have launched spirited attacks against precisely this superficial aspect. Among these, Duhamel has expressed himself in the most radical manner. What he objects to most is the kind of participation which the movie elicits from the masses. Duhamel calls the movie 'a pastime for helots, a diversion for uneducated, wretched, worn-out creatures who are consumed by their worries . . . , a spectacle which requires no concentration and presupposes no intelligence . . . , which kindles no light in the heart and awakens no hope other than the ridiculous one of someday becoming a "star" in Los Angeles.' Clearly, this is at bottom the same ancient lament that the masses seek distraction whereas art demands concentration from the spectator. That is a commonplace. The question remains whether it provides a platform for the analysis of the film. A closer look is needed here. Distraction and concentration form polar opposites which may be stated as follows: A man who concentrates before a work of art is absorbed by it. He enters into this work of art the way legend tells of the Chinese painter when he viewed his finished painting. In contrast, the distracted mass absorbs the work of art. This is most obvious with regard to buildings. Architecture has always represented the prototype of a work of art the reception of which is consummated by a collectivity in a state of distraction. The laws of its reception are most instructive.

Buildings have been man's companions since primeval times. Many art forms have developed and perished. Tragedy begins with the Greeks, is extinguished with them, and after centuries its 'rules' only are revived. The epic poem, which had its origin in the youth of nations, expires in Europe at the end of the Renaissance. Panel painting is a creation of the Middle Ages, and nothing guarantees its uninterrupted existence. But the human need for shelter is lasting. Architecture has never been idle. Its history is more ancient than that of any other art, and its claim to being a living force has significance in every attempt to comprehend the relationship of the masses to art. Buildings are appropriated in a twofold manner: by use and by perception – or rather, by touch and sight. Such appropriation cannot be understood in terms of the attentive concentration of a tourist before a famous building. On the tactile side there is no counterpart to contemplation on the optical side. Tactile appropriation is accomplished not so much by attention as by habit. As regards architecture, habit determines to a large extent even optical reception. The latter, too, occurs much less through rapt attention than by noticing the object in incidental fashion. This mode of appropriation, developed with reference to architecture, in certain circumstances acquires canonical value. For the tasks which face the human apparatus of perception at the turning points of history cannot be solved by optical means, that is, by contemplation, alone. They are mastered gradually by habit, under the guidance of tactile appropriation.

The distracted person, too, can form habits. More, the ability to master certain tasks in a state of distraction proves that their solution has become a matter of habit. Distraction as provided by art presents a covert control of the extent to which new tasks have become soluble by apperception. Since, moreover, individuals are tempted to avoid such tasks, art will tackle the most difficult and most important ones where it is able to mobilize the masses. Today it does so in the film. Reception in a state of distraction, which is increasing noticeably in all fields of art and is symptomatic of profound changes in apperception, finds in the film its true means of exercise. The film with its shock effect meets this mode of reception halfway. The film makes the cult value recede into the background not only by putting the public in the position of the critic, but also by the fact that at the movies this position requires no attention. The public is an examiner, but an absent-minded one.

Epilogue

The growing proletarianization of modern man and the increasing formation of masses are two aspects of the same process. Fascism attempts to organize the newly created proletarian masses without affecting the property structure which the masses strive to eliminate. Fascism sees its salvation in giving these masses not their right, but instead a chance to express themselves. The masses have a right to change property relations; Fascism seeks to give them an expression while preserving property. The logical result of Fascism is the introduction of aesthetics into political life. The violation of the masses, whom Fascism, with its *Führer* cult, forces to their knees, has its counterpart in the violation of an apparatus which is pressed into the production of ritual values.

All efforts to render politics aesthetic culminate in one thing: war. War and war only can set a goal for mass movements on the largest scale while respecting the traditional property system. This is the political formula for the situation. The technological formula may be stated as follows: Only war makes it possible to mobilize all of today's technical resources while maintaining the property system. It goes without saying that the Fascist apotheosis of war does not employ such arguments. Still, Marinetti says in his manifesto on the Ethiopian colonial war: 'For twenty-seven years we Futurists have rebelled against the branding of war as antiaesthetic . . . Accordingly we state: . . . War is beautiful because it establishes man's dominion over the subjugated machinery by means of gas masks, terrifying megaphones, flame throwers, and small tanks. War is beautiful because it initiates the dreamt-of metallization of the human body. War is beautiful because it enriches a flowering meadow with the fiery orchids of machine guns. War is beautiful because it combines the gunfire, the cannonades, the cease-fire, the scents, and the stench of putrefaction into a symphony. War is beautiful because it creates new architecture, like that of the big tanks, the geometrical formation flights, the smoke spirals from burning villages, and many others . . . Poets and artists of Futurism! . . . remember these principles of an aesthetics of war so that your struggle for a new literature and a new graphic art . . . may be illumined by them!'

This manifesto has the virtue of clarity. Its formulations deserve to be accepted by dialecticians. To the latter, the aesthetics of today's war appears as follows: If the natural utilization of productive forces is impeded by the property system, the increase in technical devices, in speed, and in the sources of energy will press for an unnatural utilization, and this is found in war. The destructiveness of war furnishes proof that society has not been mature enough to incorporate technology as its organ, that technology has not been sufficiently developed to cope with the elemental forces of society. The horrible features of imperialistic warfare are attributable to the discrepancy between the tremendous means of production and their inadequate utilization in the process of production – in other words, to unemployment and the lack of markets. Imperialistic war is a rebellion of technology which collects, in the form of 'human material', the claims to which society has denied its natural material. Instead of draining rivers, society directs a human stream into a bed of trenches; instead of dropping seeds from airplanes, it drops incendiary bombs over cities; and through gas warfare the aura is abolished in a new way.

'*Fiat ars – pereat mundus*,' says Fascism, and, as Marinetti admits, expects war to supply the artistic gratification of a sense perception that has been changed by technology. This is evidently the consummation of '*l'art pour l'art*.' Mankind, which in Homer's time was an object of contemplation for the Olympian gods, now is one for itself. Its self-alienation has reached such a degree that it can experience its own destruction as an aesthetic pleasure of the first order. This is the situation of politics which Fascism is rendering aesthetic. Communism responds by politicizing art.

THEODOR ADORNO (1903–69)
FROM LETTER TO WALTER BENJAMIN, 18 MARCH 1936;
FROM 'ON THE FETISH CHARACTER IN MUSIC AND THE
REGRESSION OF LISTENING' 1938

German philosopher and cultural theorist. His major works include Dialectic of Enlightenment, *written with his close collaborator Max Horkheimer (1944; 1972),* Minima Moralia *(1951; 1974),* Negative Dialectics *(1966; 1973) and the seminal exploration of modern aesthetics in* Aesthetic Theory *(1970; 1984). An accomplished musician he also wrote extensively on music (*Philosophy of Modern Music, *1948; 1973). His work is often caricatured as defending high art (or 'élitism') against mass culture. In fact, Adorno's conception of the 'culture industry' (both the term and the phenomenon were scrutinised by Adorno and Horkheimer in* Dialectic of Enlightenment*) saw the split between manual and intellectual labour and between art and mass culture as an aspect of the phenomenon of commodity fetishism in modern capitalist societies. An example of this type of critique may be found in the 1938 essay 'On the Fetish Character in Music', extracts from which we reproduce below (from* The Essential Frankfurt School Reader, *ed. Andrew Arato and Eike Gebhardt, 1982). Also reproduced below is an extract from Adorno's letter to his friend Walter Benjamin containing Adorno's response to and criticism of the latter's argument expounded in 'The Work of Art in the Age of Mechanical Reproduction' (extracts from which are reproduced in the same section). It appears in Harry Zohn's translation from* Aesthetics and Politics *(ed. Ronald Taylor, 1977).*

London, 18 March 1936

Derr Herr Benjamin:

If today I prepare to convey to you some notes on your extraordinary study ['The Work of Art in the Age of Mechanical Reproduction'], I certainly have no intention of offering you criticism or even an adequate response.

[. . .]

Let me therefore confine myself to one main theme. My ardent interest and my complete approval attach to that aspect of your study which appears to me to carry out your original intention – the dialectical construction of the relationship between myth and history – within the intellectual field of the materialistic dialectic: namely, the dialectical self-dissolution of myth, which is here viewed as the disenchantment of art.

[. . .]

In your earlier writings, of which your present essay is a continuation, you differentiated the idea of the work of art as a structure from the symbol of theology and from the taboo of magic. I now find it disquieting – and here I see a sublimated remnant of certain Brechtian motifs – that you now casually transfer the concept of magical aura to the 'autonomous work of art' and flatly assign to the latter a counter-revolutionary function. I need not assure you that I am fully aware of the magical element in the bourgeois work of art (particularly since I constantly attempt to expose the bourgeois philosophy of idealism, which is associated with the concept of aesthetic autonomy, as mythical in the fullest sense). However, it seems to me that the centre of the autonomous work of art does not itself belong on the side of myth – excuse my topic parlance – but is inherently dialectical; within itself it juxtaposes the magical and the mark of freedom. If I remember correctly, you once said something similar in connection with Mallarmé, and I cannot express to you my feeling about your entire essay more clearly than by telling you that I constantly found myself wishing for a study of Mallarmé as a counterpoint to your essay, a study which, in my estimation, you owe us as an important contribution to our knowledge. Dialectical though your essay may be, it is not so in the case of the autonomous work of art itself; it disregards an elementary experience which becomes more evident to me every day in my own musical experience – that precisely the uttermost consistency in the pursuit of the technical laws of autonomous art changes this art and instead of rendering it into a taboo or fetish, brings it close to the state of freedom, of something that can be consciously produced and made. I know of no better materialistic programme than that statement by Mallarmé in which he defines works of literature as something not inspired but made out of words; and the greatest figures of reaction, such as Valéry and Borchardt (the latter with his essay about villas which, despite an unspeakable comment about workers, could be taken over in a materialistic sense in its entirety), have this explosive power in their innermost cells. If you defend the *kitsch* film against the 'quality' film, no one can be more in agreement with you than I am; but *l'art pour l'art* is just as much in need of a defence, and the united front which exists against it and which to my knowledge extends from Brecht to the Youth Movement, would be encouragement enough to undertake a rescue.

[. . .]

Understand me correctly. I would not want to claim the autonomy of the work of art as a prerogative, and I agree with you that the aural element of the work of art is declining – not only because of its technical reproducibility, incidentally, but above all because of the fulfilment of its own 'autonomous' formal laws (this is the subject of the theory of musical reproduction which Kolisch and I have been planning for years). But the autonomy of the work of art, and therefore its material form, is not identical with the magical element in it. The reification of a great work of art is not just loss, any more than the reification of the cinema is all loss. It would be bourgeois reaction to negate the reification of the cinema in the name of the ego, and it would border on anarchism to revoke the reification of a great work of art in the spirit of immediate use-values.

[. . .]

Both bear the stigmata of capitalism, both contain elements of change (but never, of course, the middle-term between Schönberg and the American film). Both are torn halves of an integral freedom, to which however they do not add up. It would be romantic to sacrifice one to the other, either as the bourgeois romanticism of the conservation of personality and all that stuff, or as the anarchistic romanticism of blind confidence in the spontaneous power of the proletariat in the historical process – a proletariat which is itself a product of bourgeois society.

To a certain extent I must accuse your essay of this second romanticism. You have swept art out of the corners of its taboos – but it is as though you feared a consequent inrush of barbarism (who could share your fear more than I?) and protected yourself by raising what you fear to a kind of inverse taboo. The laughter of the audience at a cinema – I discussed this with Max, and he has probably told you about it already – is anything but good and revolutionary; instead, it is full of the worst bourgeois sadism. I very much doubt the expertise of the newspaper boys who discuss sports; and despite its shock-like seduction I do not find your theory of distraction convincing – if only for the simple reason that in a communist society work will be organized in such a way that people will no longer be so tired and so stultified that they need distraction. On the other hand, certain concepts of capitalist practice, like that of the test, seem to me almost ontologically congealed and taboo-like in function – whereas if anything does have an aural character, it is surely the film which possesses it to an extreme and highly suspect degree. To select only one more small item: the idea that a reactionary is turned into a member of the avant-garde by expert knowledge of Chaplin's films strikes me as out-and-out romanticization. For I cannot count Kracauer's favourite director, even after *Modern Times*, as an avant-garde artist (the reason will be perfectly clear from my article on jazz), nor do I believe that any of the decent elements in this work will attract attention. One need only have heard the laughter of the audience at the film to know what is actually happening.

[. . .]

Accordingly, what I would postulate is *more* dialectics. On the one hand, dialectical penetration of the 'autonomous' work of art which is transcended by its own technology into a planned work; on the other, an even stronger dialecticization of utilitarian art in its negativity, which you certainly do not fail to note but which you designate by relatively abstract categories like 'film capital', without tracking it down to its ultimate lair as immanent irrationality. When I spent a day in the studios of Neubabelsberg two years ago, what impressed me most was how *little* montage and all the advanced techniques that you emphasize are actually used; rather, reality is everywhere *constructed* with an infantile mimetism and then 'photographed'. You under-estimate the technicality of autonomous art and over-estimate that of dependent art; this, in plain terms, would be my main objection. But this objection could only be given effect as a dialectic between extremes which you tear apart. In my estimation, this would involve nothing less than the complete liquidation of the Brechtian motifs which have already undergone an extensive transformation in your study – above all, the liquidation of any appeal to the immediacy of interconnected aesthetic effects, however fashioned, and to the actual consciousness of actual workers who have absolutely no advantage over the bourgeois except their interest in the revolution, but otherwise bear all the marks of mutilation of the typical bourgeois character. This prescribes our function for us clearly enough – which I certainly do not mean in the sense of an activist conception of 'intellectuals'. But it cannot mean either that we may only escape the old taboos by entering into new ones – 'tests', so to speak. The goal of the revolution is the abolition of fear. Therefore we need have no fear of it, nor need we ontologize our fear. It is not bourgeois idealism if, in full knowledge and without mental prohibitions, we maintain our solidarity with the proletariat instead of making of our own necessity a virtue of the proletariat, as we are always tempted to do – the proletariat which itself experiences the same necessity and needs us for knowledge as much as we need the proletariat to make the revolution. I am convinced that the further development of the aesthetic debate which you have so magnificently inaugurated, depends essentially on a true accounting of the relationship of the intellectuals to the working-class.

[. . .]

'On the Fetish Character in Music and the Regression of Listening'

[. . .]

The concept of musical fetishism cannot be psychologically derived. That 'values' are consumed and draw feelings to themselves, without their specific qualities being reached by the consciousness of the consumer, is a later expression of their commodity character. For all contemporary musical life is dominated by the commodity form; the last pre-capitalist residues have been eliminated. Music, with all the attributes of the ethereal and sublime which are generously accorded it, serves in America today as an advertisement for commodities which one must acquire in order to be able to hear music. If the advertising function is carefully dimmed in the case of serious music, it always breaks through in the case of light music. The whole jazz business, with its free distribution of scores to bands, has abandoned the idea that actual performance promotes the sale of piano scores and phonograph records. Countless hit song texts praise the hit songs themselves, repeating their titles in capital letters. What makes its appearance, like an idol, out of such masses of type is the exchange-value in which the quantum of possible enjoyment has disappeared. Marx defines the fetish character of the commodity as the veneration of the thing made by oneself which, as exchange-value, simultaneously alienates itself from producer to consumer – 'human beings.' 'A commodity is therefore a mysterious thing, simply because in it the social character of men's labor appears to them as an objective character stamped upon the product of that labor; because the relation of the producers to the sum total of their own labor is presented to them as a social relation, existing not between themselves, but between the products of their labor.' This is the real secret of success. It is the mere reflection of what one pays in the market for the product. The consumer is really worshipping the money that he himself has paid for the ticket to the Toscanini concert. He has literally 'made' the success which he reifies and accepts as an objective criterion, without recognizing himself in it. But he has not 'made' it by liking the concert, but rather by buying the ticket. To be sure, exchange-value exerts its power in a special way in the realm of cultural goods. For in the world of commodities this realm appears to be exempted from the power of exchange, to be in an immediate relationship with the goods, and it is this appearance in turn which alone gives cultural goods their exchange-value. But they nevertheless simultaneously fall completely into the world of commodities, are produced for the market, and are aimed at the market. The appearance of immediacy is as strong as the compulsion of exchange-value is inexorable. The social compact harmonizes the contradiction. The appearance of immediacy takes possession of the mediated, exchange-value itself. If the commodity in general combines exchange-value and use-value, then the pure use-value, whose illusion the cultural goods must preserve in completely capitalist society, must be replaced by pure exchange-value, which precisely in its capacity as exchange-value deceptively takes over the function of use-value. The specific fetish character of music lies in this *quid pro quo*. The feelings which go to the exchange value create the appearance of immediacy at the same time as the absence of a relation to the object belies it. It has its basis in the abstract character of exchange-value. Every 'psychological' aspect, every *ersatz* satisfaction, depends on such social substitution.

The change in the function of music involves the basic conditions of the relation between art and society. The more inexorably the principle of exchange-value destroys use-values for human beings, the more deeply does exchange-value disguise itself as the object of enjoyment. It has been asked what the cement is which still holds the world of commodities together. The answer is that this transfer of the use-value of consumption goods to their exchange-value contributes to a general order in which eventually every pleasure which emancipates itself from exchange-value takes on subversive features. The appearance of exchange-value in commodities has taken on a specific cohesive function. The woman who has money with which to buy is intoxicated by the act of buying. In American conventional speech, having a good time means being present at the enjoyment of others, which in its turn has as its only content being present. The auto religion makes all men brothers in the sacramental moment with the words: 'That is a Rolls Royce', and in moments of intimacy, women attach greater importance to the hairdressers and cosmeticians than to the situation for the sake of which the hairdressers and cosmeticians are employed. The relation to the irrelevant dutifully manifests its social essence. The couple out driving who spend their time identifying every passing car and being happy if they recognize the trademarks speeding by, the girl whose satisfaction consists solely in the fact that she and her boyfriend 'look good', the expertise of the jazz enthusiast who legitimizes himself by having knowledge about what is in any case inescapable, all this operates according to the same command. Before the theological caprices of commodities, the consumers become temple slaves. Those who sacrifice themselves nowhere else can do so here, and here they are fully betrayed.

In the commodity fetishists of the new model, in the 'sadomasochistic character', in those receptive to today's mass art, the same thing shows itself in many ways. The masochistic mass culture is the necessary manifestation of almighty production itself. When the feelings seize on exchange-value it is no mystical transubstantiation. It corresponds to the behavior of the prisoner who loves his cell because he has been left nothing else to love. The sacrifice of individuality, which accommodates itself to the regularity of the successful, the doing of what everybody does, follows from the basic fact that in broad areas the same thing is offered to everybody by the standardized production of consumption goods. But the commercial necessity of concealing this identity leads to the manipulation of taste and the official culture's pretense of individualism, which necessarily increases in proportion to the liquidation of the individual. Even in the realm of the superstructure, the appearance is not merely the concealment of the essence, but proceeds of necessity from the essence itself. The identical character of the goods which everyone must buy hides itself behind the rigor of the universally compulsory style. The fiction of the relation between supply and demand survives in the fictitiously individual nuances.

[. . .]

The counterpart to the fetishism of music is a regression of listening. This does not mean a relapse of the individual listener into an earlier phase of his own development, nor a decline in the collective general level, since the millions who are reached musically for the first time by today's mass communications cannot be compared with the audience of the past. Rather, it is contemporary listening which has regressed, arrested at the infantile stage. Not only do the listening subjects lose, along with freedom of choice and responsibility, the capacity for conscious perception of music, which was from time immemorial confined to a narrow group, but they stubbornly reject the possibility of such perception. They fluctuate between comprehensive forgetting and sudden dives into recognition. They listen atomistically and dissociate what they hear, but precisely in this dissociation they develop certain capacities which accord less with the concepts of traditional esthetics than with those of football and motoring. They are not childlike, as might be expected on the basis of an interpretation of the new type of listener in terms of the introduction to musical life of groups previously unacquainted with music. But they are childish; their primitivism is not that of the undeveloped, but that of the forcibly retarded. Whenever they have a chance, they display the pinched hatred of those who really sense the other but exclude it in order to live in peace, and who therefore would like best to root out the nagging possibility. The regression is really from this existent possibility, or more concretely, from the possibility of a different and oppositional music. Regressive, too, is the role which contemporary mass music plays in the psychological household of its victims. They are not merely turned away from more important music, but they are confirmed in their neurotic stupidity, quite irrespective of how their musical capacities are related to the specific musical culture of earlier social phases. The assent to hit songs and debased cultural goods belongs to the same complex of symptoms as do those faces of which one no longer knows whether the film has alienated them from reality or reality has alienated them from the film, as they wrench open a great formless mouth with shining teeth in a voracious smile, while the tired eyes are wretched and lost above. Together with sport and film, mass music and the new listening help to make escape from the whole infantile milieu impossible.

[. . .]

Deconcentration is the perceptual activity which prepares the way for the forgetting and sudden recognition of mass music. If the standardized products, hopelessly like one another except for conspicuous bits such as hit lines, do not permit concentrated listening without becoming unbearable to the listeners, the latter are in any case no longer capable of concentrated listening. They cannot stand the strain of concentrated listening and surrender themselves resignedly to what befalls them, with which they can come to terms only if they do not listen to it too closely. Benjamin's reference to the apperception of the cinema in a condition of distraction is just as valid for light music. The usual commercial jazz can only carry out its function because it is not attended to except during conversation and, above all, as an accompaniment to dancing. Again and again one encounters the judgment that it is fine for dancing but dreadful for listening. But if the film as a whole seems to be apprehended in a distracted manner, deconcentrated listening makes the perception of a whole impossible.

[. . .]

The reactions to isolated charms are ambivalent. A sensory pleasure turns into disgust as soon as it is seen how it only still serves to betray the consumer. The betrayal here consists in always offering the same thing. Even the most insensitive hit song enthusiast cannot always escape the feeling that the child with a sweet tooth comes to know in the candy store. If the charms wear off and turn into their opposite – the short life of most hit songs belongs in the same range of experience – then the cultural ideology which clothes the upper-level musical business finishes things off by causing the lower to be heard with a bad conscience. Nobody believes so completely in prescribed pleasure. But the listening nevertheless remains regressive in assenting to this situation despite all distrust and all ambivalence. As a result of the displacement of feelings into exchange-value, no demands are really advanced in music anymore. Substitutes satisfy their purpose as well, because the demand to which they adjust themselves has itself already been substituted. But ears which are still only able to hear what one demands of them in what is offered, and which register the abstract charm instead of synthesizing the moments of charm, are bad ears. Even in the 'isolated' phenomenon, key aspects will escape them; that is, those which transcend its own isolation. There is actually a neurotic mechanism of stupidity in listening, too; the arrogantly ignorant rejection of everything unfamiliar is its sure sign. Regressive listeners behave like children. Again and again and with stubborn malice, they demand the one dish they have once been served.

[. . .]

Regressive listening is always ready to degenerate into rage. If one knows that he is basically marking time, the rage is directed primarily against everything which could disavow the modernity of being with-it and up-to-date and reveal how little has in fact changed. From photographs and movies, one knows the effect produced by the modern grown old, an effect originally used by the surrealists to shock and subsequently degraded to the cheap amusement of those whose fetishism fastens on the abstract present. For the regressive listener, this effect is fantastically foreshortened. They would like to ridicule and destroy what yesterday they were intoxicated with, as if in retrospect to revenge themselves for the fact that the ecstasy was not actually such.

[. . .]

This furnishes a criticism of the 'new possibilities' in regressive listening. One might be tempted to rescue it if it were something in which the 'auratic' characteristics of the work of art, its illusory elements, gave way to the playful ones. However it may be with films, today's mass music shows little of such progress in disenchantment.

[. . .]

Not popular music but artistic music has furnished a model for this possibility.

[. . .]

Such music really crystallizes the whole, into which it has incorporated the vulgarized fragments, into something new, yet it takes its material from regressive listening.

[. . .]

The terror which Schönberg and Webern spread, today as in the past, comes not from their incomprehensibility but from the fact that they are all too correctly understood. Their music gives form to that anxiety, that terror, that insight into the catastrophic situation which others merely evade by regressing. They are called individualists, and yet their work is nothing but a single dialogue with the powers which destroy individuality – powers whose 'formless shadows' fall gigantically on their music. In music, too, collective powers are liquidating an individuality past saving, but against them only individuals are capable of consciously representing the aims of collectivity.

33
GEORG LUKÁCS (1885–1971)
FROM 'REALISM IN THE BALANCE' 1938

The following extracts are taken from Lukács's contribution to the late-1930s animated debate on the progressive or reactionary nature of artistic and literary experimentation. 'Realism in the Balance' was his attack on Expressionism (championed at the time by the fellow-Marxist Ernst Bloch) and his attempt to outline the features and radical nature of the great works of European Realism. The exchange between Bloch and Benjamin took place in the magazine Das Wort *in 1938. Reproduced below is Rodney Livingstone's translation from the collection* Aesthetics and Politics *(ed. Ronald Taylor, 1977). [See IIa 18]*

The development of literature, particularly in capitalist society, and particularly at capitalism's moment of crisis, is extraordinarily complex. Nevertheless, to offer a crude over-simplification, we may still distinguish three main currents in the literature of our age; these currents are not of course entirely distinct but often overlap in the development of individual writers:

1) Openly anti-realist or pseudo-realist literature which is concerned to provide an apologia for, and a defence of, the existing system. Of this group we shall say nothing here.

2) So-called avant-garde literature (we shall come to authentic modern literature in due course) from Naturalism to Surrealism. What is its general thrust? We may briefly anticipate our findings here by saying that its main trend is its growing distance from, and progressive dissolution of, realism.

3) The literature of the major realists of the day. For the most part these writers do not belong to any literary set; they are swimming against the mainstream of literary development, in fact, against the two currents noted above. As a general pointer to the complexion of this contemporary form of realism, we need only mention the names of Gorky, Thomas and Heinrich Mann and Romain Rolland.

In the articles which leap so passionately to the defence of the rights of modern art against the presumptuous claims of the so-called neo-classicists, these leading figures of contemporary literature are not even mentioned. They simply do not exist in the eyes of modernist literature and its chroniclers.

[...]

Views such as these turn the entire discussion on its head. It is high time to put it back on its feet and take up cudgels on behalf of the best modern literature, against its ignorant detractors. So the terms of the debate are not classics versus modernists; discussion must focus instead on the question: which are the progressive trends in the literature of today? It is the fate of realism that hangs in the balance.

[. . .]

The literary practice of every true realist demonstrates the importance of the overall objective social context and the 'insistence on all-round knowledge' required to do it justice. The profundity of the great realist, the extent and the endurance of his success, depends in great measure on how clearly he perceives – as a creative writer – the true significance of whatever phenomenon he depicts. This will not prevent him from recognizing, as Bloch imagines, that the surface of social reality may exhibit 'subversive tendencies', which are correspondingly reflected in the minds of men.

[. . .]

However, what is at issue here above all is not the mere recognition that such a factor actually exists in the context of the totality. It is even more important to see it as a factor in this totality, and not magnify it into the sole emotional and intellectual reality. So the crux of the matter is to understand the correct dialectical unity of appearance and essence. What matters is that the slice of life shaped and depicted by the artist and re-experienced by the reader should reveal the relations between appearance and essence without the need for any external commentary. We emphasize the importance of shaping [gestalten] this relation, because, unlike Bloch, we do not regard the practice of left-wing Surrealists as an acceptable solution to the problem. We reject their method of 'inserting' [Einmontierung] theses into scraps of reality with which they have no organic connection.

By way of illustration, just compare the 'bourgeois refinement' of Thomas Mann with the Surrealism of Joyce. In the minds of the heroes of both writers we find a vivid evocation of the disintegration, the discontinuities, the ruptures and the 'crevices' which Bloch very rightly thinks typical of the state of mind of many people living in the age of imperialism. Bloch's mistake lies merely in the fact that he identifies this state of mind directly and unreservedly with reality itself. He equates the highly distorted image created in this state of mind with the thing itself, instead of objectively unravelling the essence, the origins and the mediations of the distortion by comparing it with reality.

[. . .]

4

The modern literary schools of the imperialist era, from Naturalism to Surrealism, which have followed each other in such swift succession, all have one feature in common. They all take reality exactly as it manifests itself to the writer and the characters he creates. The form of this immediate manifestation changes as society changes. These changes, moreover, are both subjective and objective, depending on modifications in the reality of capitalism and also on the ways in which class struggle and changes in class structure produce different reflections on the surface of that reality. It is these changes above all that bring about the swift succession of literary schools together with the embittered internecine quarrels that flare up between them.

But both emotionally and intellectually they all remain frozen in their own immediacy; they fail to pierce the surface to discover the underlying essence, i.e. the real factors that relate their experiences to the hidden social forces that produce them. On the contrary, they all develop their own artistic style – more or less consciously – as a spontaneous expression of their immediate experience.

The hostility of all modern schools towards the very meagre vestiges of the older traditions of literature and literary history at this time, culminates in a passionate protest against the arrogance of critics who would like to forbid writers, so it is alleged, to write as and how they wish. In so doing, the advocates of such movements overlook the fact that authentic freedom, i.e. freedom from the reactionary prejudices of the imperialist era (not merely in the sphere of art), cannot possibly be attained through mere spontaneity or by persons unable to break through the confines of their own immediate experience. For as capitalism develops, the continuous production and reproduction of these reactionary prejudices is intensified and accelerated, not to say consciously promoted by the imperialist bourgeoisie. So if we are ever going to be able to understand the way in which reactionary ideas infiltrate our minds, and if we are ever going to achieve a critical distance from such prejudices, this can only be accomplished by hard work, by abandoning and transcending the limits of immediacy, by scrutinizing all subjective experiences and measuring them against social reality. In short it can only be achieved by a deeper probing of the real world.

[. . .]

It goes without saying that without abstraction there can be no art for otherwise how could anything in art have representative value? But like every movement, abstraction must have a direction, and it is on this that everything depends. Every major realist fashions the material given in his own experience, and in so doing makes use of techniques of abstraction, among others. But his goal is to penetrate the laws governing objective reality and to uncover the deeper, hidden, mediated, not immediately perceptible network of relationships that go to make up society. Since these relationships do not lie on the surface, since the underlying laws only make themselves felt in very complex ways and are realized only unevenly, as trends, the labour of the realist is extraordinarily arduous, since it has both an artistic and an intellectual dimension. Firstly, he has to discover these relationships intellectually and give them artistic shape. Secondly, although in practice the two processes are indivisible, he must artistically conceal the relationships he has just discovered through the process of abstraction – i.e. he has to transcend the process of abstraction. This twofold labour creates a new immediacy, one that is artistically mediated; in it, even though the surface of life is sufficiently transparent to allow the underlying essence to shine through (something which is not true of immediate experience in real life), it nevertheless manifests itself as immediacy, as life as it actually appears. Moreover, in the works of such writers we observe the whole surface of life in all its essential determinants, and not just a subjectively perceived moment isolated from the totality in an abstract and over-intense manner.

This, then, is the artistic dialectic of appearance and essence. The richer, the more diverse, complex and 'cunning' (Lenin) this dialectic is, the more firmly it graps hold of the living contradictions of life and society, then the greater and the more profound the realism will be.

In contrast to this, what does it mean to talk of an abstraction away from reality? When the surface of life is only experienced immediately, it remains opaque, fragmentary, chaotic and uncomprehended. Since the objective mediations are more or less consciously ignored or passed over, what lies on the surface is frozen and any attempt to see it from a higher intellectual vantage-point has to be abandoned.

There is no state of inertia in reality. Intellectual and artistic activity must move either towards reality or away from it. It might seem paradoxical to claim that Naturalism has already provided us with an instance of the latter. The milieu theory, a view of inherited characteristics fetishized to the point of mythology, a mode of expression which abstractly pinpointed the immediate externals of life, along with a number of other factors, all those things thwarted any real artistic breakthrough to a living dialectic of appearance and essence. Or, more precisely, it was the absence of such a breakthrough that led to the Naturalist style. The two things were functions of each other.

This is why the photographically and phonographically exact imitations of life which we find in Naturalism could never come alive; this is why they remained static and devoid of inner tension. This is why the plays and novels of Naturalism seem to be almost interchangeable – for all their apparent diversity in externals.

[...]

In contrast to the Naturalist, the artistic 'refinement' introduced by Impressionism 'purifies' art even more completely of the complex mediations, the tortuous paths of objective reality, and the objective dialectics of Being and Consciousness. The symbolist movement is clearly and consciously one dimensional from the outset, for the gulf between the sensuous incarnation of a symbol and its symbolic meaning arises from the narrow, single-tracked process of subjective association which yokes them together.

Montage represents the pinnacle of this movement and for this reason we are grateful to Bloch for his decision to set it so firmly in the centre of modernist literature and thought. In its original form, as photomontage, it is capable of striking effects, and on occasion it can even become a powerful political weapon. Such effects arise from its technique of juxtaposing heterogeneous, unrelated pieces of reality torn from their context. A good photomontage has the same sort of effect as a good joke. However, as soon as this one-dimensional technique – however legitimate and successful it may be in a joke – claims to give shape to reality (even when this reality is viewed as unreal), to a world of relationships (even when these relationships are held to be specious), or of totality (even when this totality is regarded as chaos), then the final effect must be one of profound monotony. The details may be dazzlingly colourful in their diversity, but the whole will never be more than an unrelieved grey on grey. After all, a puddle can never be more than dirty water, even though it may contain rainbow tints.

This monotony proceeds inexorably from the decision to abandon any attempt to mirror objective reality, to give up the artistic struggle to shape the highly complex mediations in all their unity and diversity and to synthesize them as characters in a work of literature. For this approach permits no creative composition, no rise and fall, no growth from within to emerge from the true nature of the subject-matter.

[. . .]

The ideological struggle against war was one of the principal themes of the best expressionists. But what did they do or say to anticipate the new imperialist war raging all around us and threatening to engulf the whole civilized world? I hardly imagine that anyone today will deny that these works are completely obsolete and irrelevant to the problems of the present. On the other hand the realist writer Arnold Zweig anticipated a whole series of essential features of the new war in his novels *Sergeant Grischa* and *Education before Verdun*. What he did there was to depict the relationship between the war at the front and what went on behind the lines, and to show how the war represented the individual and social continuation and intensification of 'normal' capitalist barbarity.

There is nothing mysterious or paradoxical about any of this – it is the very essence of all authentic realism of any importance. Since such realism must be concerned with the creation of types (this has always been the case, from *Don Quixote* down to *Oblomov* and the realists of our own time), the realist must seek out the lasting features in people, in their relations with each other and in the situations in which they have to act; he must focus on those elements which endure over long periods and which constitute the objective human tendencies of society and indeed of mankind as a whole.

Such writers form the authentic ideological avant-garde since they depict the vital, but not immediately obvious forces at work in objective reality. They do so with such profundity and truth that the products of their imagination receive confirmation from subsequent events – not merely in the simple sense in which a successful photograph mirrors the original, but because they express the wealth and diversity of reality, reflecting forces as yet submerged beneath the surface, which only blossom forth visibly to all at a later stage. Great realism, therefore, does not portray an immediately obvious aspect of reality but one which is permanent and objectively more significant, namely man in the whole range of his relations to the real world, above all those which outlast mere fashion. Over and above that, it captures tendencies of development that only exist incipiently and so have not yet had the opportunity to unfold their entire human and social potential. To discern and give shape to such underground trends is the great historical mission of the true literary avant-garde. Whether a writer really belongs to the ranks of the avant-garde is something that only history can reveal, for only after the passage of time will it become apparent whether he has perceived significant qualities, trends, and the social functions of individual human types, and has given them effective and lasting form. After what has been said already, I hope that no further argument is required to prove that only the major realists are capable of forming a genuine avant-garde.

So what really matters is not the subjective belief, however sincere, that one belongs to the avant-garde and is eager to march in the forefront of literary developments. Nor is it essential to have been the first to discover some technical innovation, however dazzling. What counts is the social and human content of the avant-garde, the breadth, the profundity and the truth of the ideas that have been 'prophetically' anticipated.

[. . .]

7

Is our discussion purely literary? I think not. I do not believe that any conflict between literary trends and their theoretical justification would have had such reverberations or provoked such discussion were it not for the fact that, in its ultimate consequences, it was felt to involve a political problem that concerns us all and influences us all in equal measure: the problem of the Popular Front.

Bernhard Ziegler raised the issue of popular art in a very pointed manner. The excitement generated by this question is evident on all sides and such a vigorous interest is surely to be welcomed. Bloch, too, is concerned to salvage the popular element in Expressionism. He says: 'It is untrue that Expressionists were estranged from ordinary people by their overweening arrogance. Again, the opposite is the case. The *Blue Rider* imitated the stained glass at Murnau, and in fact was the first to open people's eyes to this moving and uncanny folk art. In the same way, it focused attention on the drawings of children and prisoners, on the disturbing works of the mentally sick, and on primitive art.' Such a view of popular art succeeds in confusing all the issues. Popular art does not imply an ideologically indiscriminate, 'arty' appreciation of 'primitive' products by connoisseurs. Truly popular art has nothing in common with any of that. For if it did, any swank who collects stained glass or negro sculpture, any snob who celebrates insanity as the emancipation of mankind from the fetters of the mechanistic mind, could claim to be a champion of popular art.

Today, of course, it is no easy matter to form a proper conception of popular art. The older ways of life of the people have been eroded economically by capitalism, and this has introduced a feeling of uncertainty into the world-view, the cultural aspirations, the taste and moral judgement of the people; it has created a situation in which people are exposed to the perversions of demagogy. Thus it is by no means always progressive simply to collect old folk products indiscriminately. Nor does such a rescue operation necessarily imply an appeal to the vital instincts of the people, which do remain progressive against all obstacles. Similarly, the fact that a literary work or a literary trend is greatly in vogue does not in itself guarantee that it is genuinely popular. Retrograde traditionalisms, such as regional art [*Heimatkunst*], and bad modern works, such as thrillers, have achieved mass circulation without being popular in any true sense of the word.

[. . .]

In the first place, there is the question of the cultural heritage. Wherever the cultural heritage has a living relationship to the real life of the people it is characterized by a dynamic, progressive movement in which the active creative forces of popular tradition, of the sufferings and joys of the people, of revolutionary legacies, are buoyed up, preserved, transcended and further developed. For a writer to possess a living relationship to the cultural heritage means being a son of the people, borne along by the current of the people's development. In this sense Maxim Gorky is a son of the Russian people, Romain Rolland a son of the French and Thomas Mann a son of the German people. For all their individuality and originality, for all their remoteness from an artiness which artificially collects and aestheticizes about the primitive, the tone and content of their writings grow out of the life and history of their people, they are an organic product of the development of their nation. That is why it is possible for them to create art of the highest quality while at the same time striking a chord which can and does evoke a response in the broad masses of the people.

The attitude of the modernists to the cultural heritage stands in sharp contrast to this. They regard the history of the people as a great jumble sale. If one leafs through the writings of Bloch, one will find him mentioning the topic only in expressions like 'useful legacies', 'plunder', and so on. Bloch is much too conscious a thinker and stylist for these to be mere slips of the pen. On the contrary, they are an index of his general attitude towards the cultural heritage. In his eyes it is a heap of lifeless objects in which one can rummage around at will, picking out whatever one happens to need at the moment. It is something to be taken apart and stuck together again in accordance with the exigencies of the moment.

[. . .]

Objectively, however, the life of the people is a continuum. A theory like that of the modernists which sees revolutions only as ruptures and catastrophes that destroy all that is past and shatter all connection with the great and glorious past, is akin to the ideas of Cuvier, not those of Marx and Lenin. It forms an anarchistic pendant to the evolutionary theories of reformism. The latter sees nothing but continuity, the former sees nothing but ruptures, fissures and catastrophes. History, however, is the living dialectical unity of continuity and discontinuity, of evolution and revolution.

[. . .]

A vital relationship to the life of the people, a progressive development of the masses' own experiences – this is the great social mission of literature.

[. . .]

The Popular Front means a struggle for a genuine popular culture, a manifold relationship to every aspect of the life of one's own people as it has developed in its own individual way in the course of history. It means finding the guidelines and slogans which can emerge out of this life of the people and rouse progressive forces to new, politically effective activity. To understand the historical identity of the people does not of course, imply an uncritical attitude towards one's own history – on the contrary, such criticism is the necessary consequence of real insight into one's own history. For no people, and the Germans least of all, has succeeded in establishing progressive democratic forces in a perfect form and without any setbacks. Criticism must be based, however, on an accurate and profound understanding of the realities of history. Since it was the age of imperialism which created the most serious obstacles to progress and democracy in the spheres of both politics and culture, a trenchant analysis of the decadent manifestations of this period – political, cultural and artistic – is an essential prerequisite for any breakthrough to a genuinely popular culture. A campaign against realism, whether conscious or not, and a resultant impoverishment and isolation of literature and art is one of the crucial manifestations of decadence in the realm of art.

[. . .]

34

ERNST BLOCH (1885–1977)

FROM *THE PRINCIPLE OF HOPE* 1938–47

German philosopher, critic and socialist. After studying philosophy in Munich and Würzburg, Bloch moved to Berlin where he was befriended by Georg Simmel and, later, Georg Lukács. From 1911 he began work on his own philosophical project, developing his concept of the Not-Yet-Conscious which he had formulated in 1907. In 1918 he published The Spirit of Utopia, *his first major work, written in a mystical, prophetic and Expressionist style. In the 1920s Bloch's friendship with Lukács was strained by disagreements over their respective views of Marxism and Bloch became closer to Theodor Adorno and Walter Benjamin. Bloch's interest in literature and the theatre also brought him close to Bertolt Brecht, whose work he admired and on which he based his critical views. In 1930 he published a collection of prose pieces,* Spuren *('Traces') which prefigure aspects of the style of* The Principle of Hope. *This last 'magnum opus', published in three volumes, attempts a critical history of the utopian vision – a true encyclopaedia of hope. It was written between 1938 and 1947 in the United States, where Bloch had fled from the Nazis. It was revised in the 1950s after Bloch's return to Germany to take up the chair of philosophy at the University of Leipzig. The extracts reproduced below are from the first volume of* The Principle of Hope *(translated by Neville Plaice, Stephen Plaice and Paul Knight, 1986). [See Ia 15, IIb 5]*

The unconscious in Freud is therefore one into which something can only be pushed back. Or which at best, as id, surrounds consciousness as if this were a closed ring: a phylogenetic inheritance all around conscious man. 'With the help of the super-ego, the ego draws, in a way that is still obscure to us, on the experiences of prehistory stored up in the id.' The unconscious of psychoanalysis is therefore, as we can see, never a *Not-Yet-Conscious*, an element of progressions; it consists rather of regressions. Accordingly, even the process of making this unconscious conscious only clarifies What Has Been; i.e. *there is nothing new in the Freudian unconscious.* This became even clearer when C. G. Jung, the psychoanalytic fascist, reduced the libido and its unconscious contents entirely to the primeval. According to him, exclusively phylogenetic primeval memories or primeval fantasies exist in the unconscious, falsely designated 'archetypes'; and all wishful images also go back into this night, only suggest prehistory. Jung even considers the night to be so colourful that consciousness pales beside it; as a spurner of the light, he devalues consciousness. In contrast, Freud does of course uphold illuminating consciousness, but one which is itself surrounded by the ring of the id, by the fixed unconsciousness of a fixed libido. Even highly productive artistic creations do not lead out of this Fixum; they are simply *sublimations* of the self-enclosed libido: imagination is a substitute for the fulfilment of drives. 'The problem to be solved then', says Freud, 'is to displace the drive-goals, in such a way that they cannot be affected by the failure of the external world.' The sex-drive can be refined into caritas, into devotion to the well-being of one's neighbour, ultimately of humanity. More highly sublimated libido constitutes the pleasure the artist derives from his creation, but also the enjoyment and the (vicarious) satisfaction the non-artist derives from a work of art. The latter does after all provide pure wish-fulfilment of a shaped yet uninhibited kind: women, wedding, heroes and even the beautiful tragic corpse. It provides the man in the stalls with what he lacks in life, provides cloth of gold like a beautiful dream in the night does. The viewer or the spectator works off his wishes in this way so that they no longer cause him pain. But every 'catharsis' of this kind remains temporary, in fact illusory: art, according to Freud, works exclusively with the illusions with which the unsatisfied libido allows itself to be fooled.

In Freud, however, there remain only sexual libido, its conflict with the ego-drives, and the cellar of consciousness as a whole, from which the illusions then rise.

Power-drive, frenzy-drive, collective unconscious

No matter how dully grasped the body is, the sexual drive does not live in it all the time, nor alone. After he had taken this road, Freud, as we know, was therefore contradicted by several of his pupils. These pupils were quick either to distinguish a quite different driving force or to bronze the libido. Alfred Adler, the originator of so-called individual psychology, attempted to do the first, C. G. Jung the second (with a mythical patina). Thus 'the problem of sexuality which weighs upon us all' was 'eliminated at a stroke', for which Freud criticizes them both. At any rate, it seemed it could be eliminated. In systems based on different motivating forces, it is not the complete be all and end all. On a bi-sexual foundation, Adler posits, in supreme capitalist fashion, the will to power as the basic human drive: primarily man wants to rule and overpower. He wants to get from the bottom to the top, wants to lie on top, to pass from the female line in him to the male, feel himself individually confirmed as the victor. Vanity, ambition, 'male protest' are accordingly the emotions in which this basic drive appears most visibly. Wounded vanity, failed ambition are the source of most neuroses. Sexuality is itself only a means to the final goal, the attainment of power.

[. . .]

But as skin hardens over a wound, as a protective measure, as it were, against future damage, and as the failure of one kidney strengthens the functioning of the other, mental inferiorities are likewise overcompensated by the ego. Partly through masks and fictions: will to power then becomes will to appearance; partly also, however, through higher achievements: will to power then recoups its losses, possibly in a beautiful fantasy world. Though we do not see where it takes its material from here; for the will to power, in itself necessarily bare, cannot of course be sublimated as regards content. Nevertheless, goal-setting remains essential in this will, precisely in accordance with the desire to be out in front; it takes the place of mere innate drivenness from below, i.e. from the Freudian sexual libido. The individual person builds himself up by means of a guiding image or even just by means of play-acting and fiction: 'The insecurity which is felt to be embarrassing is reduced to its smallest proportions and then reversed into its extreme opposite, into its contradiction which as a fictional goal is made into the guiding point of all wishes, fantasies and endeavours.' In this way the person forms – nothing other than the individual person appears in this individual psychology – his character: 'So as not to miss the path to the summit, to make it perfectly safe, he draws constantly effective guidelines in the form of character traits in the broad chaotic fields of his soul.' Fundamentally, everything personal is thus made and cultivated from the outset in Adler through a largely unconscious but no longer in any way naive purposive will. Thus, fundamentally, the causa finalis rules, the biological factor is subjugated to the capitalistically interested goal which is geared to the safeguarding of the personality, to raising the feeling of personality. Because Adler therefore drives sex out of the libido and inserts individual power, his definition of drives takes the ever steeper capitalist path from Schopenhauer to Nietzsche and reflects this path ideologically and psychoanalytically. Freud's concept of libido bordered on the 'will to life' in Schopenhauer's philosophy; Schopenhauer in fact described the sexual organs as 'the focal points of the will'. Adler's 'will to power' conversely coincides verbally, and partly also in terms of content with Nietzsche's definition of the basic drive from his last period; in this respect Nietzsche has triumphed over Schopenhauer here, that is to say, the imperialist elbow has triumphed over the gentlemanly pleasure-displeasure body in psychoanalysis. The competitive struggle which hardly leaves any time for sexual worries stresses industriousness rather than randiness; the hectic day of the businessman thus eclipses the hectic night of the rake and his libido.

But even that did not last, for fewer and fewer people were attracted by the day which had become inhospitable. The petit bourgeois' wish grew ever stronger to allow himself to lapse back into irresponsible, but also more or less wild obscurity. Above all the path to the so-called heights lost some of its interest and prospects, in exact proportion to the decline of free enterprise, as a result of monopoly capitalism. The path became more attractive which led into the so-called depths, in which the eyes roll instead of aiming at a goal. C. G. Jung, the fascistically frothing psychoanalyst, consequently posited the frenzy-drive in place of the power-drive. Just as sexuality is only part of this Dionysian general libido, so also is the will to power, in fact the latter is completely transformed into battle-frenzy, into a stupor which in no way strives towards individual goals. In Jung, libido thus becomes an archaically undivided primeval unity of all drives, or 'Eros' per se: consequently it extends from eating to the Last Supper, from coitus to unio mystica, from the frothing mouth of the shaman, even the berserker, to the rapture of Fra Angelico. Even here, therefore, Nietzsche triumphs over Schopenhauer, but he triumphs as the affirmation of a mescalin Dionysus over the negation of the will to life. As a result, the unconscious aspect of this mystified libido is also not contested and there is no attempt to resolve it into current consciousness, as in Freud. Rather the neurosis, particularly that of modern, all too civilized and conscious man, derives according to Jung precisely from the fact that men have emerged too far out of what is unconsciously growing, outside the world of 'elemental feel-thinking'. Here Jung borders not only on the fascist version of Dionysus, but also partly on the vitalistic philosophy of Bergson. Bergson had already, though still in a secessionist-liberal way, played off intuition against reason, creative unrest against closed order and rigid geometry. But far more so than with Bergson's 'élan vital', the fascist Jung borders on the Romantic reactionary distortions which Bergson's vitalism underwent; as in sentimental penis-poets like D. H. Lawrence, in complete Tarzan philosophers like Ludwig Klages. Bergson's élan vital was still directed forwards; it corresponded to the 'Art Nouveau' or 'Secessionism' of the

Nineties, it contained watchwords of freedom, none of regressive enslavement. D. H. Lawrence, on the other hand, and Jung along with him, sings the wildernesses of the elemental age of love, which to his misfortune man has emerged from; he seeks the nocturnal moon in the flesh, the unconscious sun in the blood. And Klages blows in a more abstract way on the same bull-horn; he does not only hark back like the earlier Romantics to the Middle Ages, but to the diluvium, to precisely where Jung's impersonal, pandemonic libido lives. There are of course egos and individuals, Jung teaches, but they do not go deep in the soul; the personality itself is only a mask or a socially played role. What works in the personality and as such is instead supposed to be vital pressure, from much deeper, much older layers, from the magical collective layers of the race, for example.

[. . .]

Accordingly, primal memories are supposed to be active from the time of our animal forefathers, i.e. a long way behind the diluvium; Jung appropriates the concept of the 'engram' for this, which Semon introduced into biology, the concept of a memory of the whole of organic matter and its memory traces. They are incorporated in libido as a primal animal plan, but they also keep the unconscious per se in the archaic primal dimension of What Has Been. Thus psychosynthesis does not disperse into day and into external pieces, but 'reflects' and takes the neurotically or otherwise given symbol back into its ancestral night: 'Just as analysis (the causal reductive process) divides the symbol into its components, the synthetic process condenses the symbol into a general and comprehensible expression.' Freud's unconscious, despite phylogenetic archaic elements which he no doubt believed he saw and which in his school have been 'excavated' down to the primal memories of the first land animals – Freud's unconscious was therefore largely individual, that is, filled with individually acquired repressions and with repressions from the recent past of a modern individual. Jung's unconscious on the other hand is entirely general, primeval and collective, it purports to be 'the five-hundred-thousand-year-old shaft beneath the few thousand years of civilization', particularly beneath the few years of individual life. In this basic ground there is not only nothing new, but what it contains is decidedly primeval; everything new is ipso facto without value, in fact hostile to value; according to Jung and Klages, the only thing that is new today is the destruction of instinct, the undermining of the ancient basic ground of the imagination by the intellect. Even neurotic conflict is the suffering caused by intellect to this basic ground of the drives and of the imagination; or as Lawrence said: men have lost the moon in their flesh, the sun in their blood. Thus the neurotic must not be completely removed from the unconscious material which he still has, rather what is necessary is guidance back to the collective unconscious to the 'age-old forces of life'. Psychosynthesis – fleeing the present, hating the future, searching for primeval time – thus becomes the same as 'religion in the etymological sense of the word: namely re-ligio, connecting back.

Then the most rampant superstition ranks more than ever above enlightenment; since, of course, Jung's collective unconscious flows thicker in witch-crazes than in pure reason.

[. . .]

But the most important expectant emotion, the most authentic emotion of longing and thus of self, always remains in all of this – hope. For the negative expectant emotions of anxiety and fear are still completely suffering, oppressed, unfree, no matter how strongly they reject. Indeed, something of the extinction of self announces itself in them, and something of the nothingness into which ultimately the merely passive passion streams. Hope, this expectant counter-emotion against anxiety and fear, *is therefore the most human of all mental feelings and only accessible to men and it also refers to the furthest and brightest horizon.* It suits that appetite in the mind which the subject not only has, but of which, as unfulfilled subject, it still essentially consists.

[. . .]

Even stammering nonsense of the night in the attempt to travel, on the basis of such dissolutions of the former day connections, to a new land, to better shores, even to rationally ordered shores. An object-lesson in these transitions was given by James Joyce in *'Ulysses'*; highly post-Romantic, highly un-Romantic. The cellar of the unconscious discharges itself in Joyce into a transitory Now, provides a mixture of prehistoric stammering, smut and church music; the author does not interrupt with a single comma the decoction that surges over the levelled threshold of consciousness for eighty pages. But in the midst of the monkey-chatter (from one day and a thousand subconscious human reactions strictly mixed up) there appears something clearly viewed, applied montage shows quite rational cross-connections or *analogiae entis*; Lot's wife and The Old Ireland Tavern near the salt water down by the docks, cutting straight through time and space, celebrate their meeting, their everyday beyond space and time. 'So that', says Stephen Dedalus, 'so that gesture, not music, not odours, would be a universal language, the gift of tongues rendering visible not the lay sense but the first entelechy, the structural rhythm' (Ulysses, Part II (Circe)). Primeval caves, with babbling and speaking in tongues inside them, are thus conjured up in day-fantasies and these are then lowered down again; a continual merging of grotesque night-faces and outlines develops. And in Surrealism, i.e. corresponding to the very time of collapse to which Surrealism belongs, as always in the sudden combination of incompatibles, there is no lack of humour; a contemptible humour sometimes, one which then unmasks the design merely to épater le bourgeois, or even a humour of pettily contrived jokes, and after that things become quite cosy in the dream-house at the sign of the Double Strangeness. But more essential in Surrealism remains the fundamental coupling of Hecate and Minerva, remains the visionary face, a montage of mere shreds and collapses.

[. . .]

35
DAVID ALFARO SIQUEIROS (1896–1974)
FROM 'LETTER FROM THE FRONT LINE IN SPAIN' 1938

Mexican mural painter and revolutionary. He took part in the Mexican Revolution of 1910–11 and remained an active trade unionist and revolutionary activist throughout his life. He was expelled from the USA in 1932 after founding the Experimental Workshop in New York City and during the

1930s he worked in South America. In 1944 he founded the Centre of Realist Art in Mexico. The
following extract is taken from Siqueiros's letter to the Mexican writer Maria Teresa Leon de Alberti,
April 27th, 1938, while fighting with the Republicans in Spain (from Art and Revolution,
translated by Sylvia Calles, 1975).

Dear Maria Teresa,

I was so happy to get your letter. I had already lost hope of ever hearing from you two again.

[. . .]

I am working very hard. I was in command of Group No. 2 in the Sierra Herrera operation. Recently, in the Sordo operation, I was liaison officer for Colonel Burillo, commander of the Extremadura army. Then I was given the job of forming the 29th Division. As commander of my old brigade, I have been in charge of the Puente del Arzobispo sector, in Sierra Altamira, and it is possible that within the next few days my command will be extended to include Guadalupe. I am quite pleased about this, as it provides me with more problems and as you know there is nothing better in life than a problem. The harder and more complicated the better.

Well, war is like modern art (hardly as envisaged in my obsessive solitary attempts) – it is mechanics and physics, chemistry and geometry, geography and cadence, it is equilibrium and synthesis. War, like art, can express in one go both the positive and negative of human nature. So there is nothing surprising in my returning to my original profession, the one I practised in my already somewhat distant youth. I rather feel I have gained something by it, perhaps war suits my hasty, impatient nature.

Curiously enough, as you will see, in both war and art I spend my time fighting against the academicians. I will give you a short example.

The academic soldier considers defence to be rigid containment of the enemy offensive. His only aim and purpose is that the enemy shall not pass. But I, a functionalist in both war and art, conceive defence as an offensive, because it is really a counter-offensive; it implies infinite mobility. The academic defends and fortifies a line; we functionalists defend and fortify a zone and fill it with traps. They work on a linear plane while we work in spatial depth. The academic only sees one facet, the functionalist has a multi-faceted view of the problem. (It is the same thing with painting – the academician paints flat pictures within the limits of a frame, whereas the muralist is functional.) We functionalists conceive our fortifications in topographical terms; they must be the living expression of the forms to be found in local topography. You might say that the basic functionalist concept of fortification is mimicry, because the fundamental object is that the fortification should be resistant, but also that it should be both objectively and subjectively camouflaged; the scenography is important. (You write to me of stage design, and as you can see I am doing some military scenography myself). However, the academic conception of fortification is totally isolated from the surroundings. He feels that there are good plans for fortifications, trenches and refuges. He talks in formulae, like a tree with no roots in the ground. The old academic builds linear trenches and the new academic builds square trenches. The functionalist conceives of fortifications as active, changing and varied as nature itself, with its mountains, plains and so on. He feels that fortifications should be in accordance with the nature of the terrain.

And here's another thing.

The academician says: the enemy must not pass; he must not breach the line anywhere, he must not overrun the line. The functionalist says: he must not occupy the zone, he must not overrun the zone. For the academician the advance posts (what he calls the front line) are fragile, i.e. if too much pressure is brought to bear on them they may break. But the advance posts of the functionalists are elastic; if they are pressed too hard, they stretch as the enemy expends his offensive and then snap back, when the time comes, with all the strength of a coiled spring. In academic defence, when the line is broken, there is inevitably a withdrawal (or drastic retreat) to a second line of defence and so on. It is obvious that in war as in art, the academician conceives of spatial depth as a series of curtains situated one behind the other at more or less equal intervals. Here is the number one defence line; here is the number two defence line, etc., etc. The functionalist has a more integral concept of defence, which covers the whole area, both flanks and rearguard, in fact every yard of the defensive zone. There are no neutral spaces between one line and another; there are no stages. He does not conceive of defence like a game of chess with a rigid and inevitable pattern of movements; his defensive moves cover and whole area and the whole problem in every possible direction.

What do you think? Isn't there a great similarity between *camouflage* and the spatial organization of your stage design? In war as in other things, there is a violent struggle between formalism, rhetoric and dialectics. This is why anyone who really wants to and has an active rather than a passive, isolated view of his problems, can do good work anywhere. I shall try and send you some of my articles on military instruction, mobile troop transport, etc., so that you can see in rather more detail what I am doing at the present time.

I could carry on writing, with my habitual spate of words, which used to afford us amusement when we were together in Mexico and Paris ... but the fact is that my unit is about to change its position and the orderlies are making such a racket that my beloved assistant, the big little lieutenant Belmar, who is typing this letter for me, can hardly hear me dictate.

[. . .]

36
André Breton (1896–1966), Leon Trotsky (1879–1940) and Diego Rivera (1886–1957)
'Manifesto: Towards a Free Revolutionary Art' 1938

While on a lecture tour of Mexico in 1938, Breton was introduced to the exiled Leon Trotsky by the Mexican painter Diego Rivera. The product of this meeting of kindred spirits was a declaration of resistance against Stalinist and Fascist repression, reproduced here in Dwight MacDonald's translation (first published in Partisan Review, *IV, no. 1, Fall 1938). The authors of the piece were Breton and Trotsky, but the latter thought it safer that Rivera's name replaced his own – a precaution which only postponed his eventual assassination by a Stalinist agent two years later. [See IIa 19, IIb 13]*

[handwritten margin notes: "full of paradoxes", "free writing + writer is ideologue", "art is political"]

We can say without exaggeration that never has civilization been menaced so seriously as today. The Vandals, with instruments which were barbarous, and so comparatively ineffective, blotted out the culture of antiquity in one corner of Europe. But today we see world civilization, united in its historic destiny, reeling under the blows of reactionary forces armed with the entire arsenal of modern technology. We are by no means thinking only of the world war that draws near. Even in times of 'peace', the position of art and science has become absolutely intolerable.

Insofar as it originates with an individual, insofar as it brings into play subjective talents to create something which brings about an objective enriching of culture, any philosophical, sociological, scientific, or artistic discovery seems to be the fruit of a precious *chance*, that is to say, the manifestation, more or less spontaneous, of necessity. Such creations cannot be slighted, whether from the standpoint of general knowledge (which interprets the existing world), or of revolutionary knowledge (which, the better to change the world, requires an exact analysis of the laws which govern its movement). Specifically, we cannot remain indifferent to the intellectual conditions under which creative activity take place, nor should we fail to pay all respect to those particular laws which govern intellectual creation.

In the contemporary world we must recognize the ever more widespread destruction of those conditions under which intellectual creation is possible. From this follows of necessity an increasingly manifest degradation not only of the work of art but also of the specifically 'artistic' personality. The regime of Hitler, now that it has rid Germany of all those artists whose work expressed the slightest sympathy for liberty, however superficial, has reduced those who still consent to take up pen or brush to the status of domestic servants of the regime, whose task it is to glorify it on order, according to the worst possible aesthetic conventions. If reports may be believed, it is the same in the Soviet Union, where Thermidorean reaction is now reaching its climax.

It goes without saying that we do not identify ourselves with the currently fashionable catchword: 'Neither fascism nor communism!' a shibboleth which suits the temperament of the Philistine, conservative and frightened, clinging to the tattered remnants of the 'democratic' past. True art, which is not content to play variations on ready-made models but rather insists on expressing the inner needs of man and of mankind in its time – true art is unable *not* to be revolutionary, *not* to aspire to a complete and radical reconstruction of society. This it must do, were it only to deliver intellectual creation from the chains which bind it, and to allow all mankind to raise itself to those heights which only isolated geniuses have achieved in the past. We recognize that only the social revolution can sweep clear the path for a new culture. If, however, we reject all solidarity with the bureaucracy now in control of the Soviet Union, it is precisely because, in our eyes, it represents not communism but its most treacherous and dangerous enemy.

The totalitarian regime of the USSR, working through the so-called 'cultural' organizations it controls in other countries, has spread over the entire world a deep twilight hostile to every sort of spiritual value. A twilight of filth and blood in which, disguised as intellectuals and artists, those men steep themselves who have made of servility a career, of lying for pay a custom, and of the palliation of crime a source of pleasure.

The official art of Stalinism mirrors with a blatancy unexampled in history their efforts to put a good face on their mercenary profession.

The repugnance which this shameful negation of the principles of art inspires in the artistic world – a negation which even slave states have never dared carry so far – should give rise to an active, uncomprising condemnation. The *opposition* of writers and artists is one of the forces which can usefully contribute to the discrediting and overthrow of regimes which are destroying, along with the right of the proletariat to aspire to a better world, every sentiment of nobility and even of human dignity.

The communist revolution is not afraid of art. It realizes that the role of the artist in a decadent capitalist society is determined by the conflict between the individual and various social forms which are hostile to him. This fact alone, insofar as he is conscious of it, makes the artist the natural ally of revolution. The process of *sublimation*, which here comes into play, and which psychoanalysis has analyzed, tries to restore the broken equilibrium between the integral 'ego' and the outside elements it rejects. This restoration works to the advantage of the 'ideal of self', which marshals against the unbearable present reality all those powers of the interior world, of the 'self', which are *common to all men* and which are constantly flowering and developing. The need for emancipation felt by the individual spirit has only to follow its natural course to be led to mingle its stream with this primeval necessity: the need for the emancipation of man.

The conception of the writer's function which the young Marx worked out is worth recalling. 'The writer,' he declared, 'naturally must make money in order to live and write, but he should not under any circumstances live and write in order to make money. The writer by no means looks at his work as a means. It is *an end in itself* and so little a means in the eyes of himself and of other that if necessary he sacrifices his existence to the existence of his work. . . . *The first condition of the freedom of the press is that it is not a business activity.*' It is more than ever fitting to use this statement against those who would regiment intellectual activity in the direction of ends foreign to itself, and prescribe, in the guise of so-called 'reasons of State', the themes of art. The free choice of these themes and the absence of all restrictions on the range of his explorations – these are possession which the artist has a right to claim as inalienable. In the realm of artistic creation, the imagination must escape from all constraint and must, under no pretext, allow itself to be placed under bonds. To those who would urge us, whether for today or for tomorrow, to consent that art should submit to a discipline which we hold to be radically incompatible with its nature, we give a flat refusal, and we repeat our deliberate intention of standing by the formula: *complete freedom for art.*

We recognize, of course, that the revolutionary State has the right to defend itself against the counterattack of the bourgeoisie, even when this drapes itself in the flag of science or art. But there is an abyss between these enforced and temporary measures of revolutionary self-defense and the pretension to lay commands on intellectual creation. If, for the better development of the forces of material production, the revolution must build a *socialist* regime with centralized control, to develop intellectual creation an *anarchist* regime of individual liberty should from the first be established. No authority, no dictation, not the least trade of orders from above! Only on a base

Lenin – mean free when we stand that we must obey the higher authority.

paradox ↓

pre-existing platform

of friendly cooperation, without the constraint from outside, will it be possible for scholars and artists to carry out their tasks, which will be more far-reaching than ever before in history.

It should be clear by now that in defending freedom of thought we have no intention of justifying political indifference, and that it is far from our wish to revive a so-called 'pure' art which generally serves the extremely impure ends of reaction. No, our conception of the role of art is too high to refuse it an influence on the fate of society. We believe that the supreme task of art in our epoch is to take part actively and consciously in the preparation of the revolution. But the artist cannot serve the struggle for freedom unless he subjectively assimilates it social content, unless he feels in his very nerves its meaning and drama and freely seeks to give his own inner world incarnation in his art.

In the present period of the death agony of capitalism, democratic as well as fascist, the artist sees himself threatened with the loss of his right to live and continue working. He sees all avenues of communication choked with the debris of capitalist collapse. Only naturally, he turns to the Stalinist organizations, which hold out the possibility of escaping from his isolation. But if he is to avoid complete demoralization, he cannot remain there, because of the impossibility of delivering his own message and the degrading servility which these organizations exact from him in exchange for certain material advantages. He must understand that his place is elsewhere, not among those who betray the cause of the revolution and of mankind, but among those who with unshaken fidelity bear witness to this revolution, among those who, for this reason, are alone able to bring it to fruition, and along with it the ultimate free expression of all forms of human genius.

The aim of this appeal is to find a common ground on which may be reunited all revolutionary writers and artists, the better to serve the revolution by their art and to defend the liberty of that art itself against the usurpers of the revolution. We believe that aesthetic, philosophical, and political tendencies of the most varied sort can find here a common ground. Marxists can march here hand in hand with anarchists, provided both parties uncompromisingly reject the reactionary police-patrol spirit represented by Joseph Stalin and by his henchman, Garcia Oliver.

We know very well that thousands on thousands of isolated thinkers and artists are today scattered throughout the world, their voices drowned out by the loud choruses of well-disciplined liars. Hundreds of small local magazines are trying to gather youthful forces about them, seeking new paths and not subsidies. Every progressive tendency in art is destroyed by fascism as 'degenerate'. Every free creation is called 'fascist' by the Stalinists. Independent revolutionary art must now gather its forces for the struggle against reactionary persecution. It must proclaim aloud its right to exist. Such a union of forces is the aim of the *International Federation of Independent Revolutionary Art* which we believe it is now necessary to form.

We by no means insist on every idea put forth in this manifesto, which we ourselves consider only a first step in the new direction. We urge every friend and defender of art, who cannot but realize the necessity for this appeal, to make himself heard at once.

We address the same appeal to all those publications of the left-wing which are ready to participate in the creation of the International Federation and to consider its task and its methods of action.

When a preliminary international contact has been established through the press and by correspondence, we will proceed to the organization of local and national congresses on a modest scale. The final step will be the assembling of a world congress which will officially mark the foundation of the International Federation.

Our aims:

The independence of art – for the revolution;

The revolution – for the complete liberation of art!

What do you think an artist is? An imbecile who has only his eyes if he's a painter, or ears if he's a musician, or a lyre at every level of his heart if he's a poet, or even, if he's a boxer, just his muscles? On the contrary, he's at the same time a political being, constantly alive to heartrending, fiery, or happy events, to which he responds in every way. How would it be possible to feel no interest in other people and by virtue of an ivory indifference to detach yourself from the life which they so copiously bring you? No, painting is not done to decorate apartments. It is an instrument of war for attack and defense against the enemy.

37
EUGENE JOLAS ET AL.
FROM 'INQUIRY INTO THE SPIRIT AND LANGUAGE OF THE NIGHT' 1938

Reproduced below are some of the responses to one of the questionnaires featuring in transition. *The 'Inquiry into the Spirit and Language of the Night' appeared in Issue 27 of the journal, published in 1938. [See IIb 14]*

Inquiry Into The Spirit And Language of Night

I have asked a number of writers to answer the following questions:

1. *What was your most recent characteristic dream (or day-dream, waking-sleeping hallucination phantasma)?*
2. *Have you observed any ancestral myths or symbols in your collective unconscious?*
3. *Have you ever felt the need for a new language express the experiences of your night mind?*

EUGENE JOLAS

Sherwood Anderson:

(1) It seems to me that my night and days cum together, the night almost invariably carrying on the thoughts of the day. There is some matter of health, in work, concerned in this – a flow sought for and often active and perhaps in sleep. There is often a phantasy – face of people, old and young, appearing, one at a time, sometimes slowly, sometimes rapidly. They seem to me to be accusing, and I have thought of them as people hungering to have their stories told.

2nd. I know of none.

3. No. There seems to me to be infinite opportunity, as yet untouched by me, in the language as it is.

Kenneth Burke:

Here's betting you get a lot of wise-cracking answers to your questionnaire, as our bad boys over here are very irreverent on such subject. They gotta be, or they'd be scared – and they're scared of being scared. There's no place for it, in the all-modern-convenience Weltanschauung.

One's dreams, if one is a writer, tend to be gross caricatures of the work on which one is engaged. Hence, cash in on them as they are. Or one may use them for admonitory purposes. Every once in a while, there may be a dream that sets one's mood for days. Does it really set the mood or did we have the mood already, and did the dream simply crystallize it? No savvy. In any case, I won't tell mine, since I'd provide too good a cue for adverse presentation of my concerns. If the enemy wants to find a caricature of my work, let him dig it up for himself.

That is my avoidance of question one. As for question two: I don't believe there are 'ancestral myths and symbols'. Symbols recur because, in each man's life, the same *situations* recur. I.e., one may dream of things like fire or running or mountains, in the way that people thousands of years ago did, because he has the same kind of body as they did, and so gets into the same patterns of experience. Thus, the situations are 'ancestral', and the symbols that fit them keep rising anew. Thus similarly, one has no 'collective unconscious.' One has a 'collective conscious'. (One's mind is made up largely of forensic, or *public* materials, as grounded in language and in the patterns of social cooperation out of which language arises.) In one's dreams, one privately draws upon this public material, reshaping it grotesquely, breaking it down and reassembling it in new ways, to get 'perspectives by incongruity'.

And that gets us to point three, the only one on which I feel able to give something like a direct answer. I see no reason why we should not have terms to express the night-life of the mind. Particularly when there are somnambulists all about us, and our knowledge of dreams may, through the extreme, over-simplified, caricature-like quality of dreams, give us valuable cues as to the ways in which people are hypnotized when awake. A certain kind of issue to be met, may also be found to call forth its 'automatic response', as though one were merely one of Pavlov's dogs. Knowledge of such processes may help one to guard against them in practical situations where they would, unless guarded against, induce the wrong response. One may be bellicose, for instance, not because bellicosity would produce the desired result, but because the situation happens to be the kind that hypnotizes him into bellicosity. An accurate critique, as provided by 'new language', might conceivably serve to make such processes accessible to consciousness, hence assisting to greater rationality of conduct.

However:

Such a vocabulary must be fitted into the *whole* of our social situation. It must not specialize in introspection. A few may martyrize themselves, make themselves into cases for the good of mankind, if they want. Joyce is apparently doing so – and I can imagine that, when our psychological instruments become more acute, we may find that he made himself uncomfortable for our greater comfort. We may be able to use him, for admonitory purposes. But though a genius is a special case, for the general run of the mine the problem must be different. The general run of the mine must be concerned with the ways of fitting this specialization into a wider texture.

Hence, I should hold that a vocabulary for the night-life of the mind must be widened in ways that the researchers of your group have been too little concerned with. We are not merely embryos autistically dreaming as we are automatically fed in the womb. We are that plus. You have to integrate your dream-vocabulary with this forensic, public plus. In doing so, you get beyond mere reverie, into the problems of social cooperation. The 'purity' of surrealisme becomes submerged beneath the quali- fications and modifications of realism. As Thomas Mann might say your vocabulary is not complete until Hölderlin has read Marx.

Malcolm Cowley:

I wish you had found a different wording for your questionnaire. You are trying to get at something important, but the questions aren't likely to bring forth the right sort of answers. I particularly boggle at the second question, with its *ancestral* myths and *collective* unconscious. What is a collective unconscious, anyhow?

As for my own dreams, their sexual symbolism is of such a primer-book quality that I should blush to repeat them.

[. . .]

T. S. Eliot:

I am afraid I cannot be of much use to you with your questionnaire. Questions number 1 and 2 are really matters I prefer to keep to myself. The answer to number 3 is defi- nitely *no*. I am not, as a matter of fact, particularly interested in my 'night-mind'. This is not a general assertion about night-minds, nor does it carry any suggestion about other people's interest in their night-minds. It is only that I find my own quite uninteresting.

[. . .]

Michael Gold:

1. Ever since my war experiences my most persistent night-mare has been that of being pursued by a gang of monsters of one sort or another. Used to be a hellish dream, this fashist fantasy, but in the last 3 or 4 years I know I have matured, because even in the dream they no longer frighten me and I use my head and manage to bump off a few and fight back. But it's not pleasant at any time!
2nd. As a Jew, the figure of Moses haunts me, I guess – tying up with today – the people's leader taking them from slavery thru the wilderness – Lenin, Marx, Lincoln, Paris Commune, Communism – the people today, myself one of the million Moses rank and filers, maybe.

3rd. Every writer needs to be able to give a full picture of man and the night mind is part of the picture. – But the day mind seems to me the only important mind to understand today. Reason, objective truth alone can lead us out of this night-hell of a world of fascism and war.

Light, more light! is the need! The night-mind is closest to the dark, bloody fog of the Fascists; the sun-mind is Communism!

Ernest Hemingway:

Answering your first question – I usually dream about whatever am doing at the time or what I have read in the paper; i.e., run into grizzly with wrong caliber shells for rifle; trigger spring sometimes broken, etc. when shooting; sometimes shoot very large animal of some kind I've never seen; or very detailed fighting around Madrid, house to house fighting, etc., after the paper; or even find myself in bed with Mrs. S . . . (not too good). Have had lovely experiences with Miss Dietrich, Miss Garbo and others in dreams too, they always being awfully nice (in dreams).

2. Second question, don't know much about.

3. I haven't ever felt this as would like to be able to handle day and night with same tools and believe can be done but respect anyone approaching any problem of writing with sincerity and wish them luck.

[. . .]

Archibald MacLeish:

Did you notice the marvelous story that Dr. Jung told, of the medecine man in Africa who complained that the tribe had no dreams any more now the British were in the country – the trouble was that the district commissioner knew everything. It seems to me a lovely and pertinent tale.

[. . .]

Eugene Jolas:

The replies to the inquiry I addressed to British and American writers about the night-mind in relation to creative expression, speak for themselves. Perhaps I may be permitted to once more summarize briefly my view-point about this problem.

All my life I have been haunted by the idea of Night. All my life I have dreamed and day-dreamed. In the little border-town of Lorraine, where French and German civilizations sought and fled each other in a ceaseless tension, I spent my childhood before the World-War dreaming escape from the millenary struggle of languages and races. There I dreamed my boyhood away in the phantasma of an utopian America, where I was born and which my immigrant parents had abandoned for the ancestral loam, when I was two years old. I dreamed my days away, when I worked as an immigrant in my native-land – paradoxically my native-land – and wrestled with the Columbian reality, with the English language, with the ambience of a continent passing through an industrial revolution. I dreamed my days away as a vagabond newspaperman, gipsying through the North-American cities, seeking to solve my inter-continental problem as a human being, as a linguist, as a poet.

Ever the question followed me: Is it I who am dreaming or am I being dreamed? Am I the stage on which some mystic or cosmic forces are playing their apparently irrational dramas? Were the romantics right in assuming that in the dream we see a game of polarity between the powers of the earth, the daemonic powers, and those of an invisible, celestial, world? Did my dreams reveal the angelic and lucifernian perspectives which my indigenous Catholicism had instilled in me? How can this be expressed?

From a study of my dreams over a period of many years I am inclined to believe that this vertical principle is definitely at work in my unconscious.

Modern psychology and the discoveries of J. W. Dunne (*An Experiment with Time*) opened new vistas in this exploratory process. The romantic conception of the night-mind found its prolongation and elaboration in Freud and Jung. Jung's idea of the 'collective unconscious' – the demonstration that we continue to carry in our night-mind the ancestral mass inheritance – has been definitely established in my own experience. What Jung calls the 'archaic man' is still part of our psyche. Dunne, the engineer, studied his own dreams for many years and established to his satisfaction the existence of a multi-dimensional world which, he claims, our three-dimensional being is as yet unable to grasp – and I might add, to express.

In my most personal dreams I have often seen an analogy with the secular myths of mankind.

[. . .]

In attempting to express this world of the 'night mind', I instinctively used my native German language at first, since it continued to be the language of my unconscious. I discovered a de-rationalized grammar in which the word and syntax followed the organic laws of metamorphosis contained in the psyche. Gradually I came to try this new grammar in English and French as well, and sometimes attempted an inter-linguistic alloyage which seemed to be the exact replica of my tri-lingual conscious experiences. The images translated themselves into German sounds first and then into new amalgamations which led me to a dream-language of irrationalist nuances. I am still engaged in a search for this *language of night*.

38
GEORGE ORWELL (ERIC ARTHUR BLAIR) (1903–50)
FROM 'INSIDE THE WHALE'

English novelist, essayist and critic. Orwell was born Eric Arthur Blair in Bengal, the son of a minor British official. The family returned to England in 1911 where Orwell was educated, winning a scholarship to Eton. He did not go to university but instead joined the Indian Imperial Police in Burma. His experiences there convinced him of the wrongs of imperialism, reflected in the essays 'Shooting an Elephant' and 'A Hanging', as well as in Burmese Days *(1935). Back in Europe, Orwell immersed himself in the life of the destitute of Paris and London, working in low-grade employment and living rough. These years are recounted in* Down and Out in Paris and London

(1933). In the 1930s he became interested in socialism. His experiences in the Spanish Civil War, however, triggered a lifelong dread of communism, expressed in his political fable Animal Farm *(1944). After the Second World War, he worked for the* BBC *and edited the journal* Tribune. Nineteen Eighty-Four, *his dystopian vision of the consequences of totalitarian rule (and a study of the power of language as propaganda tool), was published in 1949. 'Inside the Whale' was published in the book* Inside the Whale *in 1940.*

When Henry Miller's novel, *Tropic of Cancer*, appeared in 1935, it was greeted with rather cautious praise, obviously conditioned in some cases by a fear of seeming to enjoy pornography. Among the people who praised it were T. S. Eliot, Herbert Read, Aldous Huxley, John dos Passos, Ezra Pound – on the whole, not the writers who are in fashion at this moment. And in fact the subject matter of the book, and to a certain extent its mental atmosphere, belong to the twenties rather than to the thirties.

[. . .]

The mental connexion between pessimism and a reactionary outlook is not doubt obvious enough. What is perhaps less obvious is just *why* the leading writers of the twenties were predominantly pessimistic. Why always the sense of decadence, the skulls and cactuses, the yearning after lost faith and impossible civilizations? Was it not, after all, *because* these people were writing in an exceptionally comfortable epoch? It is just in such times that 'cosmic despair' can flourish. People with empty bellies never despair of the universe, nor even think about the universe, for that matter. The whole period 1910–30 was a prosperous one, and even the war years were physically tolerable if one happened to be a non-combatant in one of the Allied countries. As for the twenties, they were the golden age of the *rentier*-intellectual, a period of irresponsibility such as the world had never before seen. The war was over, the new totalitarian states had not arisen, moral and religious tabus of all descriptions had vanished, and the cash was rolling in. 'Disillusionment' was all the fashion. Everyone with a safe £500 a year turned highbrow and began training himself in *taedium vitae*. It was an age of eagles and of crumpets, facile despairs, backyard Hamlets, cheap return tickets to the end of the night. In some of the minor characteristic novels of the period, books like *Told by an Idiot*, the despair-of-life reaches a Turkish-bath atmosphere of self-pity. And even the best writers of the time can be convicted of a too Olympian attitude, a too great readiness to wash their hands of the immediate practical problem. They see life very comprehensively, much more so than those who come immediately before or after them, but they see it through the wrong end of the telescope. Not that that invalidates their books, as books. The first test of any work of art is survival, and it is a fact that a great deal that was written in the period 1910–30 has survived and looks like continuing to survive. One has only to think of *Ulysses, Of Human Bondage*, most of Lawrence's early work, especially his short stories, and virtually the whole of Eliot's poems up to about 1930, to wonder what is now being written that will wear so well.

But quite suddenly, in the years 1930–5, something happens. The literary climate changes. A new group of writers, Auden and Spender and the rest of them, has made its appearance, and although technically these writers owe something to their predecessors, their 'tendency' is entirely different. Suddenly we have got out of the twilight of the gods into a sort of Boy Scout atmosphere of bare knees and community singing. The typical literary man ceases to be a cultured expatriate with a leaning towards the Church, and becomes an eager-minded schoolboy with a leaning towards Communism. If the keynote of the writers of the twenties is 'tragic sense of life', the keynote of the new writers is 'serious purpose'.

[. . .]

But at the same time, by being Marxized literature has moved no nearer to the masses. Even allowing for the time-lag, Auden and Spender are somewhat farther from being popular writers than Joyce and Eliot, let alone Lawrence. As before, there are many contemporary writers who are outside the current, but there is not much doubt about what *is* the current. For the middle and late thirties, Auden, Spender & Co. *are* 'the movement', just as Joyce, Eliot & Co. were for the twenties. And the movement is in the direction of some rather ill-defined thing called Communism. As early as 1934 or 1935 it was considered eccentric in literary circles not to be more or less 'left'. Between 1935 and 1939 the Communist Party had an almost irresistible fascination for any writer under forty. It became as normal to hear that so-and-so had 'joined' as it had been a few years earlier, when Roman Catholicism was fashionable, to hear that so-and-so had 'been received'. For about three years, in fact, the central stream of English literature was more or less directly under Communist control.

[. . .]

By 1937 the whole of the intelligentsia was mentally at war. Left-wing thought had narrowed down to 'anti-Fascism', i.e. to a negative, and a torrent of hate-literature directed against Germany and the politicians supposedly friendly to Germany was pouring from the Press. The thing that, to me, was truly frightening about the war in Spain was not such violence as I witnessed, nor even the party feuds behind the lines, but the immediate reappearance in left-wing circles of the mental atmosphere of the Great War. The very people who for twenty years had sniggered over their own superiority to war hysteria were the ones who rushed straight back into the mental slum of 1915. All the familiar wartime idiocies, spy-hunting, orthodoxy-sniffing (Sniff, sniff. Are you a good anti-Fascist?), the retailing of atrocity stories, came back into vogue as though the intervening years had never happened. Before the end of the Spanish war, and even before Munich, some of the better of the left-wing writers were beginning to squirm. Neither Auden nor, on the whole, Spender wrote about the Spanish war in quite the vein that was expected of them. Since then there has been a change of feeling and much dismay and confusion, because the actual course of events has made nonsense of the left-wing orthodoxy of the last few years. But then it did not need very great acuteness to see that much of it was nonsense from the start. There is no certainty, therefore, that the next orthodoxy to emerge will be any better than the last.

On the whole the literary history of the thirties seems to justify the opinion that a writer does well to keep out of politics. For any writer who accepts or partially accepts the discipline of a political party is sooner of later faced with the alternative: toe the line, or shut up. It is, of course, possible to toe the line and go on writing – after a fashion. Any Marxist can demonstrate with the greatest of ease that 'bourgeois' liberty of thought is an illusion. But when he has finished his demonstration there remains the psychological *fact* that without this 'bourgeois' liberty the creative powers wither away. In the future a totalitarian literature may arise, but it will be quite different from anything we can now imagine. Literature as we know it is an individual thing, demanding mental honesty and a minimum of censorship. And this is even truer of prose than of verse. It is probably not a coincidence that the best writers of the thirties have been poets. The atmosphere of orthodoxy is always damaging to prose, and above all it is completely ruinous to the novel, the most anarchical of all forms of literature. How many Roman Catholics have been good novelists? Even the handful one could name have usually been bad Catholics. The novel is practically a Protestant form of art; it is a product of the free mind, of the autonomous individual. No decade in the past hundred-and-fifty years has been so barren of imaginative prose as the nineteen-thirties. There have been good poems, good sociological works, brilliant pamphlets, but practically no fiction of any value at all. From 1933 onwards the mental climate was increasingly against it. Anyone sensitive enough to be touched by the *zeitgeist* was also involved in politics. Not everyone, of course, was definitely *in* the political racket, but practically everyone was on its periphery and more or less mixed up in propaganda campaigns and squalid controversies. Communists and near-Communists had a disproportionately large influence in the literary reviews. It was a time of labels, slogans, and evasions. At the worst moments you were expected to lock yourself up in a constipating little cage of lies; at the best a sort of voluntary censorship ('Ought I to say this? Is it pro-Fascist?') was at work in nearly everyone's mind. It is almost inconceivable that good novels should be written in such an atmosphere. Good novels are not written by orthodoxy-sniffers, nor by people who are conscience-stricken about their own unorthodoxy. Good novels are written by people who are *not frightened*.

[. . .]

It is perhaps worth noticing that everyone, at least every English-speaking person, invariably speaks of Jonah and the *whale*. Of course the creature that swallowed Jonah was a fish, and was so described in the Bible (Jonah i, 17), but children naturally confuse it with a whale, and this fragment of baby-talk is habitually carried into later life – a sign, perhaps, of the hold that the Jonah myth has upon our imaginations. For the fact is that being inside a whale is a very comfortable, cosy, homelike thought. The historical Jonah, if he can be so called, was glad enough to escape, but in imagination, in day-dream, countless people have envied him. It is, of course, quite obvious why. The whale's belly is simply a womb big enough for an adult. There you are, in the dark, cushioned space that exactly fits you, with yards of blubber between yourself and reality, able to keep up an attitude of the completest indifference, no matter *what* happens. A storm that would sink all the battleships in the world would hardly reach you as an echo. Even the whale's own movements would probably be imperceptible to you. He might be wallowing among the surface waves or shooting down in the blackness of the middle seas (a mile deep, according to Herman Melville), but you would never notice the difference. Short of being dead, it is the final, unsurpassable stage of irresponsibilty. And however it may be with Anais Nin, there is no question that Miller himself is inside the whale. All his best and most characteristic passages are written from the angle of Jonah, a willing Jonah. Not that he is especially introverted

– quite the contrary. In his case the whale happens to be transparent. Only he feels no impulse to alter or control the process that he is undergoing. He has performed the essential Jonah act of allowing himself to be swallowed, remaining passive, *accepting*.

It will be seen what this amounts to. It is a species of quietism, implying either complete unbelief or else a degree of belief amounting to mysticism. The attitude is '*Je m'en fous*' or 'Though He slay me, yet will I trust in Him', whichever way you like to look at it; for practical purposes both are identical, the moral in either case being 'Sit on your bum'. But in a time like ours, is this a defensible attitude? Notice that it is almost impossible to refrain from asking this question. At the moment of writing we are still in a period in which it is taken for granted that books ought always to be positive, serious, and 'constructive'. A dozen years ago this idea would have been greeted with titters. ('My dear aunt, one doesn't write *about* anything, one just *writes*.') Then the pendulum swung away from the frivolous notion that art is merely technique, but it swung a very long distance, to the point of asserting that a book can only be 'good' if it is founded on a 'true' vision of life. Naturally the people who believe this also believe that they are in possession of the truth themselves. Catholic critics, for instance, tend to claim that books are only 'good' when they are of Catholic tendency. Marxist critics make the same claim more boldly for Marxist books.

[. . .]

While I have been writing this essay another European war has broken out. It will either last several years and tear Western civilization to pieces, or it will end inconclusively and prepare the way for yet another war which will do the job once and for all. But war is only 'peace intensified'. What is quite obviously happening, war or no war, is the break-up of *laissez-faire* capitalism and of the liberal-Christian culture. Until recently the full implications of this were not foreseen, because it was generally imagined that socialism could preserve and even enlarge the atmosphere of liberalism. It is now beginning to be realized how false this idea was. Almost certainly we are moving into an age of totalitarian dictatorships – an age in which freedom of thought will be at first a deadly sin and later on a meaningless abstraction. The autonomous individual is going to be stamped out of existence. But this means that literature, in the form in which we know it, must suffer at least a temporary death. The literature of liberalism is coming to an end and the literature of totalitarianism has not yet appeared and is barely imaginable. As for the writer, he is sitting on a melting iceberg; he is merely an anachronism, a hangover from the bourgeois age, as surely doomed as the hippopotamus. [. . .] But from now onwards the all-important fact for the creative writer is going to be that this is not a writer's world. That does not mean that he cannot help to bring the new society into being, but he can take no part in the process *as a writer*. For *as a writer* he is a liberal, and what is happening is the destruction of liberalism. [. . .] The passive attitude will come back, and it will be more consciously passive than before. Progress and reaction have both turned out to be swindles. Seemingly there is nothing left but quietism – robbing reality of its terrors by simply submitting to it. Get inside the whale – or rather, admit you are inside the whale (for you *are*, of course). Give yourself over to the world-process, stop fighting against it or pretending that you control it; simply accept it, endure it, record it. That seems to be the formula that any sensitive novelist is now likely to adopt. A novel on more positive, 'constructive' lines, and not emotionally spurious, is at present very difficult to imagine.

[. . .]

39
VIRGINIA WOOLF (1882–1941)
FROM 'THE LEANING TOWER' 1940

Reproduced below are extracts from a paper read by Woolf (see also section IIIa) to the Workers' Educational Association, Brighton, in 1940. It was subsequently published in Folios of New Writing, *Autumn 1940. Woolf touches here on familiar concerns – access to education and to the material spaces for writing and engaging with literature. [See IIIa 19]*

If we want to risk a theory then, we can say that peace and prosperity were influences that gave the nineteenth-century writers a family likeness. They had leisure; they had security; life was not going to change; they themselves were not going to change. They could look; and look away. They could forget; and then – in their books – remember. Those then are some of the conditions that brought about a certain family likeness, in spite of the great individual differences, among the nineteenth-century writers. The nineteenth century ended; but the same conditions went on. They lasted, roughly speaking, till the year 1914. Even in 1914 we can still see the writer sitting as he sat all through the nineteenth century looking at human life; and that human life is still divided into classes; he still looks most intently at the class from which he himself springs; the classes are still so settled that he has almost forgotten that there are classes; and he is still so secure himself that he is almost unconscious of his own position and of its security. He believes that he is looking at the whole of life; and will always so look at it. That is not altogether a fancy picture. Many of those writers are still alive. Sometimes they describe their own position as young men, beginning to write, just before August 1914. How did you learn your art? one can ask them. At College they say – by reading; by listening; by talking.

[. . .]

They wrote too – but they were in no hurry to publish. They travelled; – some of them went far afield – to India, to the South Seas. But for the most part they rambled happily in the long summer holidays through England, through France, through Italy. And now and then they published books – books like Rupert Brooke's poems; novels like E. M. Forster's *Room with a View*; essays like G. K. Chesterton's essays, and reviews. It seemed to them that they were to go on living like that, and writing like that for ever and ever. Then suddenly, like a chasm in a smooth road, the war came.

But before we go on with the story of what happened after 1914, let us look more closely for a moment, not at the writer himself, nor at his model; but at his chair. A chair is a very important part of a writer's outfit. It is the chair that gives him his attitude towards his model; that decides what he sees of human life; that profoundly affects his power of telling us what he sees. By his chair we mean his upbringing, his education. It is a fact, not a theory, that all writers from Chaucer to the present day, with so few exceptions that one hand can count them, have sat upon the same kind of chair – a raised chair. They have all come from the middle class; they have had good, at least expensive, educations. They have all been raised above the mass of people upon a tower of stucco – that is their middle-class birth; and of gold – that is their expensive education. That was true of all the nineteenth-century writers, save D. H. Lawrence. Let us run through what are called 'representative names': G. K. Chesterton; T. S. Eliot; Belloc; Lytton Strachey; Somerset Maugham; Hugh Walpole; Wilfred Owen; Rupert Brooke; J. E. Flecker; E. M. Forster; Aldous Huxley; G. M. Trevelyan; O. and S. Sitwell; Middleton Murry. Those are some of them; and all, with the exception of D. H. Lawrence, came of the middle class, and were educated at public schools and universities. There is another fact, equally indisputable: the books they wrote were among the best books written between 1910 and 1925. Now let us ask, is there any connection between those facts? Is there a connection between the excellence of their work and the fact that they came of families rich enough to send them to public schools and universities?

Must we not decide, greatly though those writers differ, and shallow as we admit our knowledge of influences to be, that there must be a connection between their education and their work? It cannot be a mere chance that this minute class of educated people has produced so much that is good as writing; and that the vast mass of people without education has produced so little that is good. It is a fact, however. Take away all that the working class has given to English literature and that literature would scarcely suffer; take away all that the educated class has given, and English literature would scarcely exist. Education must then play a very important part in a writer's work.

That seems so obvious, that it is astonishing how little stress has been laid upon the writer's education. Perhaps it is because a writer's education is so much less definite than other educations. Reading, listening, talking, travel, leisure – many different things it seems are mixed together. Life and books must be shaken and taken in the right proportions. A boy brought up alone in a library turns into a book worm; brought up alone in the fields he turns into an earth worm. To breed the kind of butterfly a writer is you must let him sun himself for three or four years at Oxford or Cambridge – so it seems. However it is done, it is there that it is done – there that he is taught his art. And he has to be taught his art. Again, is that strange? Nobody thinks it strange if you say that a painter has to be taught his art; or a musician; or an architect. Equally a writer has to be taught. For the art of writing is at least as difficult as the other arts. And though, perhaps because the education is indefinite, people ignore this education, if you look closely you will see that almost every writer who has practised his art successfully had been taught it. He had been taught it by about eleven years of education – at private schools, public schools and universities. He sits upon a tower raised above the rest of us; a tower built first on his parents' station, then on his parents' gold. It is a tower of the utmost importance; it decides his angle of vision; it affects his power of communication.

All through the nineteenth century, down to August 1914, that tower was a steady tower. The writer was scarcely conscious either of his high station, or of his limited vision. Many of them had sympathy, great sympathy, with other classes; they wished to help the working class to enjoy the advantages of the tower class; but they did not wish to destroy the tower, or to descend from it – rather to make it accessible to all. Nor had the model, human life changed essentially since Trollope looked at it, since Hardy looked at it: and Henry James, in 1914, was still looking at it. Also, the tower itself held firm beneath the writer during all the most impressionable years, when he was learning his art, and receiving all those complex influences and instructions that are summed up by the word education. These were conditions that influenced their work profoundly. For when the crash came in 1914 all those young men who were to be the representative writers of their time, had their past, their education, safe behind them, safe within them. They had known security; they had the memory of a peaceful boyhood, the knowledge of a settled civilization. Even though the war cut into their lives, and ended some of them, they wrote, and still write, as if the tower were firm beneath them. In one word, they are aristocrats; the unconscious inheritors of a great tradition.

[. . .]

From that group let us pass to the next – to the group which began to write about 1925 and, it may be, came to an end as a group in 1939. If you read current literary journalism you will be able to rattle off a string of names – Day Lewis, Auden, Spender, Isherwood, Louis MacNeice and so on. They adhere much more closely than the names of their predecessors. But at first sight there seems little difference, in station, in education. Mr. Auden in a poem written to Mr. Isherwood says: Behind us we have stucco suburbs and expensive educations. They are tower dwellers like their predecessors, the sons of well-to-do parents, who could afford to send them to public schools and universities. But what a difference in the tower itself, in what they saw from the tower! When they looked at human life what did they see? Everywhere change; everywhere revolution. In Germany, in Russia, in Italy, in Spain, all the old hedges were being rooted up; all the old towers were being thrown to the ground. Other hedges were being planted; other towers were being raised. There was communism in one country; in another fascism. The whole of civilization, of society, was changing. There was, it is true, neither war nor revolution in England itself. All those writers had time to write many books before 1939. But even in England towers that were built of gold and stucco were no longer steady towers. They were leaning towers. The books were written under the influence of change, under the threat of war. That perhaps is why the names adhere so closely; there was one influence that affected them all and made them, more than their predecessors, into groups. And that influence, let us remember, may well have excluded from that string of names the poets whom posterity will value most highly, either because they could not fall into step, as leaders or as followers, or because the influence was adverse to poetry, and until that influence relaxed, they could not write. But the tendency that makes it possible for us to group the names of these writers together, and gives their work a common likeness, was the tendency of the tower they sat on – the tower of middle-class birth and expensive education – to lean.

Let us imagine, to bring this home to us, that we are actually upon a leaning tower and note our sensations. Let us see whether they correspond to the tendencies we observe in those poems, plays and novels. Directly we feel that a tower leans we become acutely conscious that we are upon a tower. All those writers too are acutely tower conscious; conscious of their middle-class birth; of their expensive educations. Then when we come to the top of the tower how strange the view looks – not altogether upside down, but slanting, sidelong. That too is characteristic of the leaning-tower writers; they do not look any class straight in the face; they look either up, or down, or sidelong. There is no class so settled that they can explore it unconsciously. That perhaps is why they create no characters. Then what do we feel next, raised in imagination on top of the tower? First discomfort; next self-pity for that discomfort; which pity soon turns to anger – to anger against the builder, against society, for making us uncomfortable. Those too seem to be tendencies of the leaning-tower writers. Discomfort; pity for themselves; anger against society. And yet – here is another tendency – how can you altogether abuse a society that is giving you after all a very fine view and some sort of security? You cannot abuse that society wholeheartedly while you continue to profit by that society. And so very naturally you abuse society in the person of some retired admiral or spinster or armament manufacturer; and by abusing them hope to escape whipping yourself. The bleat of the scapegoat sounds loud in their work, and the whimper of the schoolboy crying 'Please Sir it was the other fellow, not me.' Anger; pity; scapegoat bleating; excuse finding – these are all very natural tendencies; if we were in their position we should tend to do the same. But we are not in their position; we have not had eleven years of expensive education. We have only been climbing an imaginary tower. We can cease to imagine. We can come down.

But they cannot. They cannot throw away their education; they cannot throw away their upbringing. Eleven years at school and college have been stamped upon them indelibly. And then, to their credit but to their confusion, the leaning tower not only leant in the thirties, but it leant more and more to the left.

[. . .]

In 1930 young men at college were forced to be aware of what was happening in Russia; in Germany; in Italy; in Spain. They could not go on discussing aesthetic emotions and personal relations. They could not confine their reading to the poets; they had to read the politicians. They read Marx. They became communists; they became anti-fascists. The tower they realized was founded upon injustice and tyranny; it was wrong for a small class to possess an education that other people paid for; wrong to stand upon the gold that a bourgeois father had made from his bourgeois profession. It was wrong; yet how could they make it right? Their education could not be thrown away; as for their capital – did Dickens, did Tolstoy ever throw away their capital? Did D. H. Lawrence, a miner's son, continue to live like a miner? No; for it is death for a writer to throw away his capital; to be forced to earn his living in a mine or a factory. And, thus trapped by their education, pinned down by their capital they remained on top of their leaning tower, and their state of mind as we see it reflected in their poems and plays and novels is full of discord and bitterness, full of confusion and of compromise.

[. . .]

If politics were 'real', the ivory tower was an escape from 'reality'. That explains the curious bastard language in which so much of this leaning over the prose and poetry is written. It is not the rich speech of the aristocrat: it is not the racy speech of the peasant. It is betwixt and between. The poet is a dweller in two worlds, one dying, the other struggling to be born. And so we come to what is perhaps the most marked tendency of leaning-tower literature – the desire to be whole; to be human. 'All that I would like to be is human' – that cry rings through their books – the longing to be closer to their kind, to write the common speech of their kind, to share the emotions of their kind, no longer to be isolated and exalted in solitary state upon their tower, but to be down on the ground with the mass of human kind.

These then, briefly and from a certain angle, are some of the tendencies of the modern writer who is seated upon a leaning tower. No other generation has been exposed to them. It may be that none has had such an appallingly difficult task. Who can wonder if they have been incapable of giving us great poems, great plays, great novels? They had nothing settled to look at; nothing peaceful to remember; nothing certain to come. During all the most impressionable years of their lives they were stung into consciousness – into self-consciousness, into class-consciousness, into the consciousness of things changing, of things falling, of death perhaps about to come. There was no tranquillity in which they could recollect. The inner mind was paralysed, because the surface mind was always hard at work.

Yet if they have lacked the creative power of the poet and the novelist, the power – does it come from a fusion of the two minds, the upper and the under? – that creates characters that live, poems that we all remember, they have had a power which, if literature continues, may prove to be of great value in the future. They have been great egotists. That too was forced upon them by their circumstances. When everything is rocking round one, the only person who remains comparatively stable is oneself. When all faces are changing and obscured, the only face one can see clearly is one's own. So they wrote about themselves – in their plays, in their poems, in their novels. No other ten years can have produced so much autobiography as the ten years between 1930 and 1940. No one, whatever his class or his obscurity, seems to have reached the age of thirty without writing his autobiography.

[. . .]

He has had the courage to tell the truth, the unpleasant truth, about himself. That is the first step towards telling the truth about other people. By analysing themselves honestly, with help from Dr. Freud, these writers have done a great deal to free us from nineteenth-century suppressions. The writers of the next generation may inherit from them a whole state of mind, a mind no longer crippled, evasive, divided. They may inherit that unconsciousness which as we guessed – it is only a guess – at the beginning of this paper is necessary if writers are to get beneath the surface, and to write something that people remember when they are alone. For that great gift of unconsciousness the next generation will have to thank the creative and honest egotism of the leaning-tower group.

The next generation – there will be a next generation, in spite of this war and whatever it brings. Have we time then for a rapid glance, for a hurried guess at the next generation? The next generation will be, when peace comes, a post-war generation too. Must it too be a leaning-tower generation – an oblique, sidelong self-centred, self-conscious generation – with a foot in two worlds? Or will there be no more towers and no more classes and shall we stand, without hedges between us, on the common ground?

There are two reasons which lead us to think, perhaps to hope, that the world after the war will be a world without classes or towers. Every politician who has made a speech since September 1939 has ended with a peroration in which he has said that we are not fighting this war for conquest; but to bring about a new order in Europe. In that order, they tell us, we are all to have equal opportunities, equal chances of developing whatever gifts we may possess. That is one reason why, if they mean what they say, and can effect it, classes and towers will disappear. The other reason is given by the income tax. The income tax is already doing in its own way what the politicians are hoping to do in theirs. The income tax is saying to middle-class parents: You cannot afford to send your sons to public schools any longer; you must send them to the elementary schools.

[. . .]

If the pressure of the income tax continues, classes will disappear. There will be no more upper classes; middle classes; lower classes. All classes will be merged in one class. How will that change affect the writer who sits at his desk looking at human life? It will not be divided by hedges any more. Very likely that will be the end of the novel, as we know it. Literature, as we know it, is always ending, and beginning again. Remove the hedges from Jane Austen's world, from Trollope's world, and how much of their comedy and tragedy would remain? We shall regret our Jane Austens and our Trollopes; they gave us comedy, tragedy and beauty. But much of that old-class literature was very petty; very false; very dull. Much is already unreadable. The novel of a classless and towerless world should be a better novel than the old novel. The novelist will have more interesting people to describe – people who have had a chance to develop their humour, their gifts, their tastes; real people, not people cramped and squashed into featureless masses by hedges. The poet's gain is less obvious; for he has been less under the dominion of hedges. But he should gain words; when we have pooled all the different dialects, the clipped and cabined vocabulary which is all that he uses now should be enriched. Further, there might then be a common belief which he could accept, and thus shift from his shoulders the burden of didacticism, of propaganda. These then are a few reasons, hastily snatched, why we can look forward hopefully to a stronger, a more varied literature in the classless and towerless society of the future.

But it is in the future; and there is a deep gulf to be bridged between the dying world, and the world that is struggling to be born. For there are still two worlds, two separate worlds.

[. . .]

It is easy to see that gulf; it is easy to lay the blame for it upon England. England has crammed a small aristocratic class with Latin and Greek and logic and metaphysics and mathematics until they cry out like the young men on the leaning tower, 'All that I would like to be is human'. She has left the other class, the immense class to which almost all of us must belong, to pick up what we can in village schools; in factories; in workshops; behind counters; and at home. When one thinks of that criminal injustice one is tempted to say England deserves to have no literature. She deserves to have nothing but detective stories, patriotic songs and leading articles for generals, admirals and business men to read themselves to sleep with when they are tired of winning battles and making money. But let us not be unfair; let us avoid if we can joining the embittered and futile tribe of scapegoat hunters. For some years now England has been making an effort – at last – to bridge the gulf between the two worlds. Here is one proof of that effort – this book. This book was not bought; it was not hired. It was borrowed from a public library. England lent it to a common reader, saying 'It is time that even you, whom I have shut out from all my universities for centuries, should learn to read your mother tongue. I will help you.' If England is going to help us, we must help her. But how? Look at what is written in the book she has lent us. 'Readers are requested to point out any defects that they may observe to the local librarian.' That is England's way of saying: 'If I lend you books, I expect you to make yourselves critics.'

We can help England very greatly to bridge the gulf between the two worlds if we borrow the books she lends us and if we read them critically. We have got to teach ourselves to understand literature. Money is no longer going to do our thinking for us. Wealth will no longer decide who shall be taught and who not. In future it is we who shall decide whom to send to public schools and universities; how they shall be taught; and whether what they write justifies their exemption from other work. In order to do that we must teach ourselves to distinguish – which is the book that is going to pay dividends of pleasure for ever; which is the book that will pay not a penny in two years' time? Try it for yourselves on new books as they come out; decide which are the lasting, which are the perishing. That is very difficult. Also we must become critics because in future we are not going to leave writing to be done for us by a small class of well-to-do young men who have only a pinch, a thimbleful of experience to give us. We are going to add our own experience, to make our own contribution. That is even more difficult. For that too we need to be critics. A writer, more than any other artist, needs to be a critic because words are so common, so familiar, that he must sieve them and sift them if they are to become enduring. Write daily; write freely; but let us always compare what we have written with what the great writers have written. It is humiliating, but it is essential. If we are going to preserve and to create, that is the only way. And we are going to do both. We need not wait till the end of the war. We can begin now. We can begin, practically and prosaically, by borrowing books from public libraries; by reading omnivorously, simultaneously, poems, plays, novels, histories, biographies, the old and the new. We must sample before we can select. It never does to be a nice feeder; each of us has an appetite that must find for itself the food that nourishes it. Nor let us shy away from the kings because we are commoners. That is a fatal crime in the eyes of Aeschylus, Shakespeare, Virgil and Dante, who, if they could speak – and after all they can – would say, 'Don't leave me to the wigged and gowned. Read me, read me for yourselves.' They do not mind if we get our accents wrong, or have to read with a crib in front of us. Of course – are we not commoners, outsiders? – we shall trample many flowers and bruise much ancient grass. But let us bear in mind a piece of advice that an eminent Victorian who was also an eminent pedestrian once gave to walkers: 'Whenever you see a board up with "Trespassers will be prosecuted", trespass at once.'

Let us trespass at once. Literature is no one's private ground; literature is common ground. It is not cut up into nations; there are no wars there. Let us trespass freely and fearlessly and find our own way for ourselves. It is thus that English literature will survive this war and cross the gulf – if commoners and outsiders like ourselves make that country our own country, if we teach ourselves how to read and write, how to preserve and how to create.

40
RICHARD WRIGHT (1908–60)
FROM 'HOW "BIGGER" WAS BORN' 1940

African-American writer, born in Mississippi. His acclaimed autobiography Black Boy: A Record of Childhood and Youth *(1945) recounts the story of his poverty-stricken childhood. After living in Memphis and Chicago, Wright moved to New York City in 1937. His first published book was the collection of short stories,* Uncle Tom's Children *(1938). He was a member of the Communist Party (1932–44), and worked for the Federal Writers' Project and the Federal Negro Theater Project (1937). He was Harlem editor for the* Daily Worker, New York. *In 1939 he was awarded a Guggenheim fellowship. Wright's most famous novel,* Native Son *(1940), his introduction to which is extracted below, is a cautionary tale for whites of black violence. His documentary history,* 12 Million Black Voices: A Folk History of the Negro in the United States *(1941), is written in poetic prose using a collective first-person narrative. In 1940 Wright moved to Mexico and then in 1946 to Paris where he lived for the rest of his life.*

[. . .]

Always, as I wrote, I was both reader and writer, both the conceiver of the action and the appreciator of it. I tried to write so that, in the same instant of time, the objective and subjective aspects of Bigger's life would be caught in a focus of prose. And always I tried to *render, depict*, not merely to tell the story. If a thing was cold, I tried to make the reader *feel* cold, and not just tell about it. In writing in this fashion, sometimes I'd find it necessary to use a stream of consciousness technique, then rise to an interior monologue, descend to a direct rendering of a dream state, then to a matter-of-fact depiction of what Bigger was saying, doing, and feeling. Then I'd find it impossible to say what I wanted to say without stepping in and speaking outright on my own; but when doing this I always made an effort to retain the mood of the story, explaining everything only in terms of Bigger's life and, if possible, in the rhythms of Bigger's thought (even though the words would be mine). Again, at other times, in the guise of the lawyer's speech and the newspaper items, or in terms of what Bigger would overhear or see from afar, I'd give what others were saying and thinking of him. But always, from the start to the finish, it was Bigger's story, Bigger's fear, Bigger's flight, and Bigger's fate that I tried to depict. I wrote with the conviction in mind (I don't know if this is right or wrong; I only know that I'm temperamentally inclined to feel this way) that the main burden of all serious fiction consists almost wholly of character-destiny and the items, social, political, and personal, of that character-destiny.

As I wrote I followed, almost unconsciously, many principles of the novel which my reading of the novels of other writers had made me feel were necessary for the building of a well-constructed book. For the most part of the novel is rendered in the present; I wanted the reader to feel that Bigger's story was happening *now*, like a play upon the stage or a movie unfolding upon the screen. Action follows action, as in a prize fight. Wherever possible, I told of Bigger's life in close-up, slow-motion, giving the feel of the grain in the passing of time. I had long had the feeling that this was the best way to 'enclose' the reader's mind in a new world, to blot out all reality except that which I was giving him.

[. . .]

I don't know if *Native Son* is a good book or a bad book. And I don't know if the book I'm working on now will be a good book or a bad book. And I really don't care. The mere writing of it will be more fun and a deeper satisfaction than any praise or blame from anybody.

I feel that I'm lucky to be alive to write novels today, when the whole world is caught in the pangs of war and change. Early American writers, Henry James and Nathaniel Hawthorne, complained bitterly about the bleakness and flatness of the American scene. But I think that if they were alive, they'd feel at home in modern America. True, we have no great church in America; our national traditions are still of such a sort that we are not wont to brag of them; and we have no army that's above the level of mercenary fighters; we have no group acceptable to the whole of our country upholding certain humane values; we have no rich symbols, no colorful rituals. We have only a money-grubbing, industrial civilization. But we do have in the Negro the embodiment of a past tragic enough to appease the spiritual hunger of even a James; and we have in the oppression of the Negro a shadow athwart our national life dense and heavy enough to satisfy even the gloomy broodings of a Hawthorne. And if Poe were alive, he would not have to invent horror; horror would invent him.

Copyright acknowledgements

His Paintings' from *D. H. Lawrence: Selected Essays* (Penguin & Heinemann, 1950). Peter Owen Publishers, London and David Higham Associates Limited: Gertrude Stein, 'Composition as Explanation' from *Gertrude Stein: Writing and Lectures 1911–1945*, edited by Patricia Meyerowitz, published by Peter Owen Publishers, London, 1967. Carcanet Press Limited: Hugh MacDiarmid, 'English Ascendency in British Literature' from *Selected Prose*, edited by Alan Riach, published by Carcanet Press Ltd, 1992. The Samuel Beckett Estate, the Calder Educational Trust, London and Grove/Atlantic, Inc, for permission to quote from *Proust and Three Dialogues with Georges Duthuit* published by John Calder (Publishers) Ltd, London. Copyright © *Proust* Samuel Beckett 1931, 1987 and copyright © *Three Dialogues with Georges Duthuit* 1949, 1987. Random House UK Ltd on behalf of the Estate of Walter Benjamin: Walter Benjamin, 'The Work of Art in the Age of Mechanical Reproduction' from *Illuminations*, edited by Hannah Arendt, translated by Harry Zohn, published by Jonathan Cape, 1973. Random House U.K. Ltd on behalf of Pat Sloan, for permission to quote from John Cornford, *John Cornford: A Memoir*, edited by Pat Sloan and published by Jonathan Cape. David Higham Associates Limited: Herbert Read, from 'Myth, Dream and Poem' from *transition*, No. 27, April–May 1938, Tenth Anniversary Issue. David Higham Associates Limited: James Barke, from 'Lewis Grassic Gibbon' from *Left Review*, Vol. 2, 1935–36. The Antonin Artaud Estate and The Calder Educational Trust, London, for permission to quote from 'The Theatre of Cruelty' from *The Theatre and Its Double* by Antonin Artaud, translated by Victor Corti, published by Calder Publications Ltd, London. Copyright © Editions Gallimard and copyright © this translation Calder Publications 1993 and John Calder (Publishers) Ltd, 1970, 1974, 1977, 1981, 1985, 1989. C. Day Lewis, from *A Hope for Poetry*, reprinted by permission of the Peters, Fraser & Dunlop Group Ltd on behalf of: *The Estate of C. Day Lewis*. Rosalind Erangey: Eric Gill, 'All Art Is Propaganda' from *5 on Revolutionary Art*, edited by Herbert Read and published by Wishart Books Ltd, 1935. David Higham Associates Limited: Herbert Read, from 'What Is Revolutionary Art?' from *5 on Revolutionary Art*, edited by Herbert Read and published by Wishart Books Ltd, 1935. Lawrence and Wishart Limited: William Philips and Philip Rahv, from 'Recent Problems of Revolutionary Literature' from *Proletarian Literature in the United States: An Anthology*, edited by Granville Hicks, Michael Gold, Isidor Scheider, Joseph North, Paul Peters, Alan Calmer and published by Lawrence and Wishart, 1935. Margaret Harris, literary trustee for the estate of the late Christina Stead: Christina Stead, 'The Writers Take Sides'. Excerpts from 'On the Fetish Character in Music and the Regression of Listening' by Theodor Adorno from *The Essential Frankfurt School Reader* edited by Andrew Arato and Eike Gebhardt. Copyright © 1982 by The Continuum Publishing Company. Reprinted with the permission of The Continuum Publishing Company. Faber and Faber: Ezra Pound, from 'A Retrospect' from *Literary Essays of Ezra Pound* edited by T. S. Eliot; from 'Preface' to Pound's translation of Remy de Gourmont's *The Natural Philosophy of Love*, 1926; 'Prefatio Aut Cimicium Tumulus' from *Selected Prose 1909–1965*. Marianne Moore, 'New Poetry since 1912' from *The Complete Prose of Marianne Moore* edited by Patricia C. Willis. T. S. Eliot, from *The Use of Poetry and the Use of Criticism*, 1933. Eric Satie, 'The Musician's Day'; 'Some Notes on Modern Music' from *The Writings of Eric Satie*, 1980, translated by Nigel Wilkins. Michael Roberts, from 'Introduction' to *The Faber Book of Modern Verse*, 1936. T. S. Eliot, from 'Tradition and the Individual Talent' and from '*Ulysses*, Order and Myth' from *Selected Prose of T. S. Eliot*. W. H. Auden, from 'Introduction' to *The Poet's Tongue* from *The English Auden: Poems, Essays and Dramatic Writings 1927–1939*, edited by Edward Mendelson. Edwin Muir, from 'What is Modern?' from *We Moderns: Enigmas and Guesses*, 1918. Wallace Stevens, 'The Irrational Element in Poetry' from *Opus Posthumous*. Used with permission. The University of Michigan Press: André Breton, from the *Manifesto of Surrealism*. Translated by Richard Seaver and Helen R. Lane, 1969. Alexandra Kollontai, 'Make Way for the Winged Eros' from *Bolshevik Visions: First Phase of the Cultural Revolution in Soviet Russia, Part I*, edited by William G. Rosenberg, 1990. Excerpts from *The Interpretation of Dreams* by Sigmund Freud. Translated from German and edited by James Strachey. Published in the United States by Basic Books Inc., 1956 by arrangement with George Allen & Unwin, Ltd. and the Hogarth Press Ltd. Reprinted by permission of Basic Books, a division of HarperCollins Publishers, Inc. Macmillan: Henri Bergson, from *Creative Evolution*, translated by Arthur Mitchell. Thames and Hudson Ltd: Adolf Loos, from 'Ornament and Crime' from Ludwig Minz and Gustav Kuenstler, *Pioneer of Modern Architecture*. Reed Consumer Books: Erwin Piscator, from 'Basic Principles of Sociological Drama' from *Twentieth-Century Theatre: A Sourcebook* edited by Richard Drain, 1995. Routledge: Johan Jakob Bachofen, from *Myth, Religion, and Mother Right: Selected Writings of*

J. J. Bachofen, translated by Ralph Manheim, 1967. Desmond MacCarthy, 'The Post-Impressionists', from J. B. Bullen, *Post-Impressionists in England*, 1988. Vsevolod Meyerhold, from 'The Reconstruction of the Theatre' from *Twentieth-Century Theatre: A Sourcebook*, edited by Richard Drain, 1995. Siegfried Kracauer, from 'The Mass Ornament' translated by Barbara Correll and Jack Zipes, from *Critical Theory and Society: A Reader*, edited by Stephen Eric Bronner and Douglas MacKay Kellner, 1989. Max Horkheimer, from 'The State of Contemporary Social Philosophy and the Tasks of an Institute for Social Research' translated by Peter Wagner, from *Critical Theory and Society: A Reader*. Johnson Reprint Company: Charlotte Perkins Gilman, from *The Man-Made World or Our Androcentric Culture*, 1911. The Merlin Press: Georg Lukács, from *The Theory of the Novel*, translated by Anna Bostock, 1971. PAJ Publications: F. T. Marinetti, 'The Variety Theatre', translated by W. Flint, from *Futurist Performance*, edited by Michael Kirby and Victoria Nes Kirby, 1986. George Wittenborn, Inc: Guillaume Apolinaire, from *The Cubist Painters: Aesthetic Meditations* translated by Lionel Abel, 1970. Prentice Hall: Wassily Kandinsky, from 'The Problem of Form' from *Voices of German Expressionism*, translated and edited by Victor H. Miesel, 1970. New Directions Publishing Corporation: F. S. Fitzgerald, from 'Echoes of the Jazz Age' from *The Crack-Up*, 1945. Chatto & Windus: Sigmund Freud, from 'The Dissection of the Psychical Personality', translated by James Strachey, from *The Standard Edition of the Complete Psychological Works of Sigmund Freud*, 1953–74. Extracts from chapters IV and V of *The Word "Woman" and other related writings* by Laura (Riding) Jackson. Copyright © 1993. Reprinted by permission of Persea Books, New York, Carcanet Press, Manchester, and the author's Board of Literary Management. Virago Press: Dorothy M. Richardson, 'Foreword' to *Pilgrimage*. Diarmid Gunn: Neil M. Gunn, 'Scotland a Nation', 1935–36. New Left Books: Walter Benjamin, from 'Surrealism: The Last Snapshot of the European Intelligentsia' translated by Edmund Jephcott and Kingsley Shorter, from *One-Way Street and Other Writings*, 1978. New Left Books, Verso: Theodor Adorno, from Letter to Walter Benjamin, translated by Harry Zohn, from *Aesthetics and Politics*, edited by Ronald Taylor, 1977. Georg Lukács, from 'Realism in the Balance', translated by Rodney Livingstone, from *Aesthetics and Politics*. Basil Blackwell Publishers: Ernst Bloch, from *The Principle of Hope*, translated by Neville Plaice, Stephen Plaice and Paul Knight, 1986. Penguin UK: Charles Baudelaire, from 'The Painter of Modern Life' from *Selected Writings on Art and Artists*, translated by P. E. Charvet, 1972. © by Charvet. George Orwell, from 'Inside the Whale', 1940. Harcourt Brace and The Hogarth Press: Virginia Woolf, 'The Moment: Summer's Night' from *The Moment and Other Essays*. The Society of Authors as the Literary Representative of the Estate of Virginia Woolf: Virginia Woolf, from 'Mr Bennett and Mrs Brown'; from 'The Leaning Tower' in: *Folios of New Writing*, 1940. The Society of Authors on behalf of the Bernard Shaw Estate: Bernard Shaw, from *The Sanity of Art; An Exposure of Some Current Nonsense about Artists Being Degenerate*, 1908. Used by permission. Harcourt Brace: Sergei Eisenstein, 'A Dialectic Approach to Film Form', from *Film Form*, translated by Jay Leyda, 1949. Allan Wingate: Marcel Proust, from 'Days of Reading: I' from *Marcel Proust: A Selection from His Miscellaneous Writings* translated by Gerard Hopkins, 1948. Reprinted by permission of Farrar, Straus & Giroux Inc: 'Feminist Manifesto; from *The Lost Lunar Baedeker: Poems* by Mina Loy. Edition copyright © 1996 by Roger L. Conover. Mrs. Ellen Craig: Edward Gordon Craig, from 'The Actor and the *Über-marionette*' from *The Mask*, 1909. Haskell House: Émile Zola, from 'Naturalism on the Stage' translated by Belle M. Sherman, from *The Experimental Novel and Other Essays*, 1964. Hermann Hesse from 'Recent German Poetry' from *Criterion*, 1922; reprinted by permission of Suhrkamp Verlag, Frankfurt a.M.

INDEX

Note: Page ranges in bold denote the authorship of an article.